Culinary Fundamentals

Culinary Fundamentals

Fifth Edition

Educational Task Force

JOHNSON & WALES UNIVERSITY College of Culinary Arts *Volume* I

Photography: YUM and Others
Photographer: Ronald Manville, YUM
Food Stylist: James E. Griffin

ISBN: 0-7872-7666-9

Printed in the United States of America
10 9 8 7 6 5 4 3 2

Contents

Foreword by Louis Szathmary.................................xix
Preface by Educational Task Force.......................xxi
Acknowledgments by Thomas L. Wright,
    Vice President, Culinary Education...................xxiii

Cooking: A Journey Through Time **1**

The Stone Age...3
    Neolithic Revolution 3
    Ancient Egypt..4
Greek and Roman Civilizations 4
Middle Ages 5
Modern Cooking 6
Nouvelle Cuisine 10
American Cookery 11

Nutrition **2**

Nutrients 17
    Energy-Yielding Nutrients.....................................17
    Cholesterol 19
    Vitamins...20
    Minerals...20
    Water 20
    Recommended Daily Allowances...........................20
Diet for a Healthy Lifestyle 20
    United States Department of Agriculture Dietary
    Guidelines 20
    The Food Guide Pyramid....................................21
    Vegetarianism 21
    Recipe Modification 21
Nutrition in the Foodservice Industry 24
    Current Nutritional Trends 24
    Guidelines for Meeting Nutritional Principles 24
    Managing Nutrients in Food Preparation..............25

Sanitation **3**

Bacteria 31
    Environmental Elements 31
    Pathogenic Microorganisms.................................31

Controlling Food-borne and Water-borne
Diseases...31
Hazard Analysis Critical Control Point System......33
Kitchen Control Points...34
Receiving 34
Food Storage..35
Preparation and Food Handling...........................36
Cooking 36
Holding 36
Reheating 36
Cooling 36
Cleaning and Sanitizing.....................................36
Safety 37

Costing and Converting Recipes **4**
Costing 42
Assigning the Task of Recipe Costing 42
Explanation of Each Part of the Recipe-Costing
Example in Figure 4–2 42
Recipe Conversion 46
Charts for Measurement in Food Preparation..........46
Metric System 47
Temperature Conversion 47

Purchasing and Product Identification **5**
Purchasing 53
Buying versus Purchasing 53
Pricing...53
Types of Products Purchased..............................54
Specifications...54
Quantity Purchasing...54
Vendor Relationships..55
Common Methods of Purchasing 55
Receiving 55
Storage...56
Product Identification...56
Fruits and Vegetables 56
Dairy Products 69
Nonperishables and Dry Goods 72
Fats and Oils..76
Pasta and Noodles 78
Convenience-Food Products 78
Sweeteners 81

Food Enhancers..85
   Herbs and Spices..85
   Flavorings, Seasonings, and Condiments 89

Seafood and Fish **6**

History 95
Regulations..95
Nutritional Benefits...95
Fish..96
Shellfish 96
   Crustaceans..96
   Mollusks 97
Manufactured Products......................................98
Market Forms of Seafood...................................98
   Fin Fish...98
Purchasing Fresh versus Frozen Fish...................100
Purchasing 101
   Quality Assurance.......................................101
   Factors Affecting Quality 101
Determining the Freshness of Seafood.................102
   Fresh Fish...102
   Live Shellfish 103
   Frozen Seafood..103
Storage..103
   Fresh Fish...103
   Frozen Fish 104
   Live Lobsters 104
   Live Mollusks 105
   Miscellaneous Seafood Products 105
Fabrication 105
   Fin Fish..105
   Shrimp...110
   Lobster...111
   Bivalves 112
   Clams..112
   Oysters..112
Cooking 113
   Fin Fish..113
   Shrimp...113
   Lobster...114
   Bivalves 114
   Raw Fish...114

Meat Products 7

Meat Composition 117
Meat Structure 117
Inspection 117
Grading 118
   Federal and Private 118
Aging 118
Handling and Storage 119
Meat Cuts 119
   Variety Meats 121
Poultry 121
   Inspection and Grading 121
   Handling and Storage 122
   Poultry Market Forms 122
Game 123
   Hanging Game 123

Equipment and Smallwares 8

The Cooking Line 127
   Grills, Broilers, and Salamanders 127
   Ranges 128
   Deep-Fat Fryers 129
   Steam Table 130
   Ovens 131
   Steam Pressure Cooker 134
   Convection or Tabletop Low-Pressure Steamers 135
   Pressureless Steamer 135
   Tilting Skillet 135
   Steam-Jacketed Kettle 136
   Trunion Kettles 136
Kitchen Machinery 136
   Mixer (Universal Kitchen Machine) 136
   Vertical Cutter Mixer 137
   Food Processor 138
   Food Chopper 138
   Food Slicer 138
   Automatic Potato Peeler 139
   Meat Grinder 139
Smallwares 139
Metals in the Kitchen 143
   Heat Efficiency of Metals 143

Sensory Perception **9**

What Is Sensory Perception?................................147
The Senses 147
   Color and Appearance 147
   Flavor 148
   Texture 149
Sensory Evaluation of Food 150
   Product Factors Affecting Flavor Perception......150
   Factors Affecting the Ability to Taste...............152
   Plate Composition 153
   The Special Flavor Challenges of Fat-Free
   Foods 155

Culinary Skills, Cooking Techniques, **10**
and Preparation

Knife Skills 159
   Safety...159
   Sharpening Stone 159
   Rules for Sharpening a Knife 159
Types of Knives 160
   Knife Alloys 160
Steel 160
Various Cuts 162
Cooking 162
   Cooking Techniques..162
Applications and Reactions 182
   Texture 182
   Color 182
   Aroma and Nutritive Value...............................182
Guidelines for Cooking Various Food Products 183
   Vegetables..183
   Rice...183
   Grains..184
   Pasta...184

Stocks, Sauces, Emulsions, and Soups **11**

Fonds/Stocks 187
   Composition of a Stock 187
   Classification of Stocks...................................188
   Production of Stocks 188
Glace/Glaze..189
   Preparation of a Glaze 189
   Uses of Glazes...189
Fumet 190
   Uses of Fumets..190

Essences (Extracts) 190
  Uses of Essences..190
Sauces..190
  Mother, or Leading, Sauces 190
Methods of Thickening Liquids..........................191
  Liaison..191
  Applying Liaisons..191
  Liaison Finale 193
  Quality of a Sauce 193
Compound Sauces...194
  Classifications 194
  Cold Emulsion Sauces 194
  Independent, Nonderivative Sauces 194
Compound Butters...194
  Simple Compound Butters 194
  Complex Compound Butters...........................197
Soups 197
  Classification of Soups 197
  General Methods for Making Soups 198

Garde-Manger **12**

Duties of the Chef Garde-Manger 203
Kitchen Equipment Needed by the
Chef Garde-Manger 203
Tools Commonly Used by the Chef
Garde-Manger 203
Garde-Manger Brigade..203
Menu Planning for Parties and Garde-Manger
Functions 204
  Gastronomic Aspects.....................................204
  Economic Aspects..204
  Practical Aspects 204
  Language...204
Salads..205
  Components of Salads....................................205
  Types of Salads 205
  Salad as a Variety of Courses 206
  Salad Dressings 206
Hors d'Oeuvre..206
  A Single Food..206
  Hors d'Oeuvre Varies 207
  A Finger Food 207
  Hot Hors d'Oeuvre...207
  Cold Hors d'Oeuvre 209

Forcemeats 212
   Elements of Forcemeats 212
   Types of Basic Forcemeats 213
   Forcemeat Derivatives 213
   Guidelines 215
   Assembling Forcemeats 215
   Panadas 215
Food Preservation 216
   Preserving Techniques 217
Smoking 218
   Four Types of Smoking 219
Buffets and Buffet Catering 220
   Different Types of Buffets 220
   Creating and Planning the Buffet.................221
   Preparation Schedule of Food-Related
   Buffet Elements 222
Aspic 227
   Reasons for Using Aspic 228
   Various Methods of Applying Aspic 228
   Steps for Using Aspic 228
Chaud-Froid Sauce 229
   Types of Chaud-Froid 229
   Reasons for Using Chaud-Froid...................229
   Points to Remember When Using Chaud-Froid ...229
   Mayonnaise Collée....................................231
Preparation of Buffet the Day of the Event............231

Introduction to Baking **13**

The History of Bread and Baking..........................235
   History in America 236
Basic Ingredients in Bread Making.......................237
   Wheat Flour...238
   Water 244
   Yeast 244
   Salt 246
   Dough Improvers 247
Common Ingredients Used in Baking 247
   Sweeteners...247
   Eggs 251
   Milk 255
   Cream 258
   Fats and Oils...258
   Leavening Actions 260
   Thickening Agents 262

Gelling Agents 263
Herbs and Spices 264
Nuts 268

Yeast-Raised Doughs **14** The Temperature of the Dough 275
    Calculating the DDT...................................275
The Ten Steps of Bread Making 276
    Step 1. Scale Ingredients...........................276
    Step 2. Mixing Yeast-Raised Dough..................277
    Step 3. Bulk, or Flour, Fermentation 277
    Step 4. Dividing the Dough and Punchdown 278
    Step 5. Rounding or Folding Over.....................278
    Step 6. Bench Rest or Intermediate Proof.........278
    Step 7. Shaping 278
    Step 8. Panning 279
    Step 9. Final Proof 279
    Step 10. Baking 280
Staling and Storage 280
Young Dough versus Old Dough...........................281
Types of Doughs...281
    Lean Dough 281
    Soft-Roll Dough 283
    Rich Dough and Sweet Dough 284
Whole-Wheat Breads...285
Rye Breads..286
    Rye Flours 286
    Sourdough Rye...286
    Sourdough Wheat.......................................288
Appendix 14A: Bake-Shop Conversion for
Straight Doughs..289
Appendix 14B: Conversions for Sponge Doughs ...290

Laminated Doughs **15** Puff-Pastry Dough 295
    Ingredients of Puff Pastry.............................295
    Roll-In Methods...296
    Guidelines for Puff Pastry.............................297
    Oven Temperatures 297
    Storage of Puff Pastry 298
    Scraps..298
    Items Made from Puff Pastry.........................298
Laminated Yeast Doughs 298

Guidelines for Laminated Yeast Doughs 299
Croissants..300
Danish Pastry...301

Quick Breads, Tea Cakes, and Coffee Cakes 16 Mixing Methods...307
Creaming Method 307
Blending Method...307
Rubbing, or Biscuit, Method 307
Tips 308
Do Not Overmix 308
Do Not Overflavor 308
Do Not Overbake..308
Classic Quick Breads, Tea Cakes, and
Coffee Cakes..308

Cookies 17 Cookie Textures 311
Crisp-Textured Cookies 311
Chewy-Textured Cookies 311
Cake-Textured Cookies....................................311
Ingredients 311
Sugar 311
Fat 312
Eggs 312
Flour...312
Leaveners 312
Forming Cookies...312
Deposit Cookies 312
Rolled/Refrigerator Cookies 312
Baking Cookies...312
Decorating Cookies...313
Types of Cookies 313
Creamed Cookies..313
Shaped, or Formed, Cookies.............................313
Twice-Baked Cookies 314
Brownies...314
Petits Fours 314
Petits Fours Glacés 315
Petits Fours Sec..315
Petits Fours Demi-Sec......................................315
Petits Fours Variés 316
Tips for Cookie Production 316

Pies and Tarts 18

Pie Dough 319
Ingredients in Pie Dough 319
Making a Pie Dough 320
Types of Pies 321
Procedures for Pie Fillings 321
Purchase Forms of Fruit 322
Procedures for Pie Fillings Continued 324
Tarts 326
Glazes 327
Examples of Tarts 327

Layer Cakes and Buttercreams 19

Layer Cakes 331
Ingredients in Cake Making 331
Mixing Methods 332
Baking Cakes 335
Storage of Cakes 335
Classic Cakes and Tortes 335
Buttercreams and Icings 337
Buttercream 337
Fudge Icing 338
Boiled Icing 338
Royal Icing 338
Fondant 338
Methods of Building Tortes 338
Appendix 19A: Bake Shop Conversion for
Cake Formulas 343
Appendix 19B: Chocolate/Cocoa Substitutions 345

Slow Baking 20

Wet Slow Baking 349
Custards 349
Soufflés 350
Cheesecakes 351
Dry Slow Baking 351
Types of Meringues 352
Baking Meringues 352
Storage of Meringues 353
Items Made from Meringues 353

Basic Desserts **21**

Creams and Mousses 357
   Pastry Cream 357
   Chantilly Cream 357
   Crème Diplomat 358
   Crème Chiboust 358
   Bavarian Cream 358
   Ganache 359
   Mousses 360
Crêpes 360
Fruit-Based Desserts 361
   Poached Fruit 361
   Compotes 362
   Salads and Salsas 362
   Fruit Chutneys 362
   Fritters 363
   Flambéed Fruits/Tableside Desserts 363
Pâte à Choux 363
   Ingredients 364
   Cooking 364
   Baking 364
   Storing 365
   Items Made from a Pâte à Choux 365
Spoon Desserts 365
   Trifle 366
   Zuppa Inglese 366
   Gratin 366
   Clafoutis 366
   Banana Pudding 367
Stretched Doughs 367
   Phyllo Dough 367
   Baklava 367
   Strudel 368
   Cannoli 368

Ice Creams and Frozen Desserts **22**

Types of Ice Cream 371
Qualities of Ice Cream 371
Freezing and Overrun 372
Ingredients in Ice Cream 373
   Milk and Cream 373
   Eggs 373
   Sweeteners 374
   Total Solids 374
   Flavoring 374

Ice-Cream Products 374
    Coupes or Sundaes 375
    Parfait Glace and Soufflé Glace 375
    Ice-Cream Bombes 375
    Semifreddo 376
Classic Ice-Cream Presentations 376
    Pears Belle Hélène 376
    Peach Melba 376
    Baked Alaska 376
Sorbets and Other Ices 376
    Special Problems with Sorbets, Sherbets,
    and Spooms 377
    Stabilizers 378
    Sugar Content 378
    Granita 378
    Frozen Yogurt 378

Chocolate **23**

The Making of Chocolate 382
The Cocoa Bean 382
Producing Chocolate 382
Cleaning and Roasting 382
Ingredients 383
Conching 383
Cocoa Butter and Cocoa Powder 383
Couverture 384
Tempering 384
    Table Method 385
    Vaccination Method No. 1 385
    Vaccination Method No. 2 385
    Resting Method 385
    Microwave Method 385
    Machine Method 385
    Cold-Water Bath Method 385
Chocolate Compound (Compound Chocolate) 386
Enemies of Chocolate 386
    Moisture 386
    Excessive Heat 386
Storage 387
Texture Changes in Melted Chocolate 387
    Cold 387
    Overheating 387
    Air 387

Moisture 387
Overuse 387
Buying Chocolate 388
Pralines 388
Types of Fillings 388
Items Not Used for Fillings 391
Dipping Conditions for Pralines 391
Storage for Pralines 392
Molded Chocolates 392
Molded Pralines Used in Production 393

Dessert Presentations 24

The Four Components of a Plated Dessert 398
Types of Plating 398
Banquet Style 398
À la Minute 398
Plating Contrasts 398
Texture 398
Temperature 399
Shape 399
Flavor 399
Color 399
Tips for Plating 399
Sauces 399
Buffets and Buffet Catering 400
Planning Buffets 400
Different Types of Buffets 401
Breakfast Buffets 401
Full Buffets 401
Fork Buffets 401
Finger Buffets 401
Zones 402
Food Presentation on Buffet Platters 402
Color 402
Texture 402
Shape 402
Height 402
Contrast 402

Appendix A: The Chef's Uniform 403
Appendix B: Vitamin and Mineral Charts and
RDA Chart 407

Appendix C: Chart for Converting Units of Measurement from Weight to Volume Table for Identifying the Serving Utensils Required for a Specified Portion Size 411
Appendix D: Classical Garnishes for Consommés..421
Bibliography 429
Glossary...433
Index...453

Foreword

Culinary: Fundamentals could well be one of the most important books of your professional life in the foodservice and hospitality industry, regardless of your ultimate goal: chief executive officer of a hotel chain; general manager of a resort; executive chef of a large food corporation; chef-owner of a renowned restaurant; or food processing plant official.

The knowledge of food in this three-volume work, the curriculum of Johnson & Wales University, is as important to you as the knowledge of your language, whether you aspire to be playwright, journalist, lawyer, scientist, or any other role that requires expressing your thoughts in words, sentences, and paragraphs.

If you were to become a musician composing grand operas or advertising jingles, writing film music or the scores for Broadway musicals, creating classical symphonies or rap, you would have to start your studies with the basic scale, just as you would have to start with elementary mathematics whether aiming to be a stockbroker, computer scientist, medical researcher, astronaut, or bookkeeper.

The authors of this work, all well-versed in the daily duties of the working chef and the professional educator, did their utmost to give you, the student, a potential leader of our industry in the 21st century, the very best tools for success.

Don't expect to succeed throughout your professional life solely on the basis of this book. But don't believe you can succeed without it. A professional curriculum cannot give you all the detailed knowledge and applied specific skills you will need in your career. We can, however, promise to make it smoother, easier, and quicker for you to approach, analyze, work with, and solve the problems facing you if you absorb what is offered here.

It is gratifying for us to participate in this project and pass along the knowledge of the authors and participants of this work, founded on what they learned from their masters in their years as apprentices, kitchen workers, chefs, and executives around the world.

An ancient proverb explains why children can see farther than their parents; after all, children sit on their parents' shoulders.

We offer you our knowledge, assembled in these three volumes, for two main purposes—to benefit you and to enable you to continue where we leave off. It's up to you to keep the vision of *Culinary: Fundamentals* alive for future generations.

Louis Szathmary
Chef Laureate
Johnson & Wales University

Preface

The Johnson & Wales University, College of Culinary Arts, Volume I—*Culinary: Fundamentals,* Volume II—*Culinary: Service,* and Volume III—*Culinary: Recipes* represent the University's commitment to excellence in education. This new edition will enable the college to be on the cutting edge as a trendsetter, introducing new ideas, procedures, and technologies to our students and to the foodservice industry.

Each volume will be used as a reference tool from which faculty and students can learn. These textbooks will emphasize theory and practical applications in nutrition, sanitation, cost control, and marketing.

Volume I, *Culinary: Fundamentals,* teaches students the theoretical principles of food, such as history, nutrition, and purchasing. The student is taught practical applications by learning how to apply the fundamental principles of sanitation, cooking techniques, sauces, and garde-manger. In the baking chapters, the student learns the importance of understanding the chemical interaction of ingredients within baked products. The student is introduced to folded doughs, cakes, and frozen desserts.

Educational Task Force

Acknowledgments

The three volumes of Culinary—I: Fundamentals; II: Service; *and* III: Recipes—*have been written by people who truly love culinary arts. I wish to thank all the faculty, administration, and friends of the University for their support and participation in this tremendous undertaking. Their collective work represents their dedication to educating students who will keep the flame of culinary inspiration alive for future generations.*

Thomas L. Wright

Vice President
Culinary Education

Special thanks to the following individuals for their tireless efforts and dedication in producing these textbooks:

Pauline Allsworth	James Griffin	Paul J. McVety	Christine Stamm
Linda Beaulieu	Karl Guggenmos	Robert Nograd	Michel Vienne
Dr. Barbara Bennett	Edward Korry	Pamela Peters	Bradley Ware
Lynn Dieterich	Victoria A. McCrae	Jacquelyn B. Scott	

Educational Task Force

Carolyn Buster	Jean-Jacques Dietrich	Edward Korry	Christine Stamm
Martha Crawford	Meridith Ford	Robert Nograd	Frank Terranova
Elaine Cwynar	Karl Guggenmos	Pamela Peters	William Travis
Mary Ann DeAngelis	Frederick Haddad	Patrick Reed	Bradley Ware
John Dion	Lars Johannson	Janet Rouslin	

Providence Administration, Faculty and Support Staff

Thomas L. Wright, M.S., Vice President of Culinary Education

Jean-Michel Vienne, C.C.P., C.E.P., C.A.P., Dean, College of Culinary Arts

Dorothy Jeanne Allen, M.S., Associate Professor; A.S., B.S., M.S., Johnson & Wales University

Pauline Allsworth, Office Manager

Frank Andreozzi, B.S., Assistant Professor; B.S., Providence College

Charles Armstrong, A.O.S., Instructor; A.O.S., Culinary Institute of America

Soren Arnoldi, Danish Master Chef, Associate Instructor; Falke Hotel, Tivoli Gardens Wivex, Palace Hotel, Copenhagen, Apprenticeship

John Aukstolis, A.S., Instructor; A.S., Johnson & Wales University

Adrian Barber, A.O.S., Associate Instructor; A.O.S., Culinary Institute of America

Claudia Berube, A.S., Instructor; A.S., Johnson & Wales University

Steven Browchuk, M.A., Certified T.I.P.S. Trainer, Associate Professor; B.A., Roger Williams College; M.A., University of Sorbonne; M.A., Middlebury College

Victor Calise, Associate Instructor

Carl Calvert, B.S., Instructor; A.O.S., B.S., Johnson & Wales University

Gerianne Chapman, M.B.A., Associate Professor; A.O.S., B.S., Johnson & Wales University; B.A., George Washington University; M.B.A., University of Rhode Island

John S. Chiaro, M.S., C.E.C., C.C.E., Associate Professor; B.A., Rhode Island College; M.S., Johnson & Wales University

Cynthia Coston, A.S., Instructor; A.S., Schoolcraft College

Laurie Coughlin, Administrative Assistant

Martha Crawford, B.S., C.W.P.C., Instructor; A.O.S., Culinary Institute of America; B.S., University of Michigan

Elaine R. Cwynar, B.A., Associate Instructor; A.S., Johnson & Wales University; B.A., University of Connecticut

William J. Day, M.S., C.F.E., Associate Professor and Director of Continuing Education; B.S., Bryant College; M.S., Johnson & Wales University

Mary Ann DeAngelis, M.S., Assistant Professor; B.S., M.S., University of Rhode Island

Richard DeMaria, B.S., Instructor; B.S., University of Rhode Island

Jean-Luc Derron, Associate Instructor; Hotel Schwanen Switzerland; steinli Trade School, Switzerland, Apprenticeship; Certification, Department of Labor and Trade, Switzerland; Confiserie Bachmann, Switzerland, Apprenticeship

Lynn Dieterich, Coordinator Faculty Support Services

Jean Jacques Dietrich, M.A., Senior Instructor; A.S., New York City Technological College; B.A., Hunter College; M.A., Johnson & Wales University

John R. Dion, B.S,., C.E.C., C.C.E., Associate Instructor; A.O.S., Culinary Institute of America; B.S., Johnson & Wales University

Rene R. Dionne, Director of Corporate Relations/ Purchasing

Reginald B. Dow, A.O.S., Storeroom Manager; A.O.S., Culinary Institute of America

Kevin Duffy, B.S., Instructor; B.S., Johnson & Wales University

Thomas Dunn, B.S., Instructor; A.O.S., B.S., Johnson & Wales University

Roger Dwyer, B.A., Instructor; B.A., George Washington University

Neil Fernandes, B.S., Storeroom Office Manager; B.S. Johnson & Wales University

Paula Figoni, M.B.A., Instructor; B.S., University of Massachusetts; M.S., University of California; M.B.A., Simmons College Graduate School of Management

Ernest Fleury, M.S., Associate Professor, A.O.S., Johnson & Wales University; A.S., Community College of Rhode Island; B.S., M.S., Johnson & Wales University

Meridith Ford, B.S., Instructor; A.O.S., B.S., Johnson & Wales University

James Fuchs, A.O.S., Instructor; A.O.S., Johnson & Wales University

Nancy Garnett-Thomas, M.S., R.D., L.D.N., Associate Professor; A.O.S., Culinary Institute of America; B.A., Colby College; M.S., University of Rhode Island

William Gormley, B.S., Instructor; A.O.S., B.S., Johnson & Wales University

James Griffin, M.S., C.W.C., C.C.E., Associate Dean & Associate Professor; A.O.S., B.S., M.S., Johnson & Wales University

Frederick Haddad, A.O.S., C.E.C., C.C.E., Associate Instructor; A.O.S., Culinary Institute of America

Rainer Hienerwadel, B.S., Instructor; A.O.S., B.S., Johnson & Wales University

J. Jeffrey Howard, B.A., Instructor; B.A., University of Massachusetts

Lars E. Johansson, C.P.C., C.C.E., Director, International Baking & Pastry Institute

Steven Kalble, A.S., Instructor; A.S., Johnson & Wales University

Linda Kender, B.S., Associate Instructor; A.S., B.S., Johnson & Wales University

Edward Korry, M.A., Assistant Professor; B.A., University of Chicago; M.A., University of Cairo

C. Arthur Lander, B.S.; Instructor; B.S., Johnson & Wales University

Kelly Lawton, Administrative Assistant

Hector Lipa, B.S., C.E.C., C.C.E., Associate Instructor; B.S., University of St. Augustine, the Philippines

Laird Livingston, A.O.S., C.E.C., C.C.E., Associate Instructor; A.O.S., Culinary Institute of America

Michael D. Marra, M.Ed., Associate Professor; B.A., M.Ed., Providence College

Susan Desmond-Marshall, M.S., Associate Professor; B.S., University of Maine; M.S., Johnson & Wales University

Victoria A. McCrae, Assistant to the Vice President

Diane McGarvey, B.S., Instructor; A.O.S., B.S., Johnson & Wales University

Jack McKenna, B.S., C.E.C., C.C.E., C.C.P., Director of Special Projects

Paul J. McVety, M.Ed., Assistant Dean and Associate Professor; A.S., B.S., Johnson & Wales University; M.Ed., Providence College

Michael Moskwa, M.Ed., Assistant Professor; B.A., University of Rhode Island; M.Ed., Northeastern University

Sean O'Hara, M.S., Certified T.I.P.S. Trainer, Instructor; A.O.S., B.S., M.S., Johnson & Wales University

George O'Palenick, M.S., C.E.C., C.C.E., Associate Professor; A.O.S., Culinary Institute of America; A.S., Jamestown Community College; B.S., M.S., Johnson & Wales University

Robert Pekar, B.S., Associate Instructor; A.O.S., Culinary Institute of America; A.S., Manchester Community College; B.S., Johnson & Wales University

Pamela Peters, A.O.S.,C.E.C., C.C.E., Director of Culinary Education; A.O.S., Culinary Institute of America

David Petrone, B.S., Associate Instructor; A.O.S., B.S., Johnson & Wales University

Felicia Pritchett, M.S., Associate Professor; A.O.S., B.S., M.S., Johnson & Wales University

Thomas J. Provost, Instructor

Ronda Robotham, B.S., Instructor; B.S., Johnson & Wales University

Robert Ross, B.S., Associate Instructor; A.S., B.S., Johnson & Wales University

Janet Rouslin, B.S., Instructor; B.S., University of Maine

Cynthia Salvato, A.S., C.E.P.C., Instructor; A.S., Johnson & Wales University

Stephen Scaife, B.S., C.E.C., C.C.E., Associate Instructor; A.O.S., Culinary Institute of America, B.S., Johnson & Wales University

Gerhard Schmid, Associate Instructor; European Apprenticeship, Germany

Louis Serra, B.S., C.E.C., Instructor; A.O.S., B.S, Johnson & Wales University

Christine Stamm, M.S., C.W.C., Associate Professor; A.O.S., B.S., M.S., Johnson & Wales University

Laura Schwenk, Administrative Assistant

Adela Tancayo-Sannella, Certified T.I.P.S. Trainer, Associate Instructor

Mary Ellen Tanzi, B.A., Instructor; B.A., Rhode Island College

Frank Terranova, B.S., C.E.C., C.C.E., Associate Instructor; B.S., Johnson & Wales University

Segundo Torres, B.S., Associate Instructor; B.S., Johnson & Wales University

Helene Houde-Trzcinski, M.S., Instructor; B.S., M.S., Johnson & Wales University

Peter Vaillancourt, B.S., Instructor; B.S., Roger Williams College

Paul VanLandingham, Ed.D, C.E.C., IMP, CFBE, C.C.E., Professor; A.O.S, Culinary Institute of America; B.S., Roger Williams College; M.A., Anna Maria College; Ed.D., Nova University

Suzanne Vieira, M.S., R.D., L.D.N., Department Chair, Foodservice Academic Studies; Associate Professor; B.S., Framingham State College; M.S., University of Rhode Island

Bradley Ware, M.Ed., C.C.C., C.C.E., Associate

Professor; A.S., Johnson & Wales University; B.S., Michigan State University; M.Ed., Providence College; C.A.G.S., Salve Regina University

Gary Welling, A.O.S., Instructor; A.O.S., Johnson & Wales University

Robin Wheeler, Receptionist

Ed Wilroy, B.A., Continuing Education Coordinator; A.O.S., Johnson Wales University; B.A., Auburn University

Kenneth Wollenberg, B.S., Associate Instructor; A.O.S., B.S., Johnson & Wales University

Robert Zielinski, A.S., Instructor; A.S., Johnson & Wales University

Branch Campuses Administration and Faculty

CHARLESTON

Karl Guggenmos, B.S., C.E.C., G.C.M.C., Director of Culinary Education

Diane Aghapour, B.S., Instructor

Patricia Agnew, M.E., Assistant Professor

Donna Blanchard, B.A., Instructor

Robert Bradham, Instructor

Matthew Broussard, C.W.C., Instructor

Jan Holly Callaway, Instructor

Wanda Crooper, B.S., C.C.E., C.W.P.C., Associate Instructor

James Dom, M.S., Associate Professor

Armin Gronert, G.C.M.P.C., Associate Instructor

Kathy Hawkins, Instructor

David Hendrieksen, B.S., C.C.E., C.C.C., Associate Instructor

Andrew Hoxie, M.A., Assistant Professor

John Kacaia, C.E.C., Instructor

Michael Koons, A.O.S., C.E.C., C.C.E., Associate Instructor

Audrey McKnight, A.O.S., Instructor

Mary McLellan, M.S., Adjunct

Marcel Massenet, C.E.P.C., Associate Instructor

Stephen Nogle, A.A.S., C.E.C., C.C.E., Associate Instructor

Daniel Polasek, Instructor

Frances Ponsford, B.S., Instructor

Lloyd Regier, Ph.D., Adjunct

Victor Smurro, B.S., C.C.C., Associate Instructor

Susan Wigley M.Ed., C.C.E., C.W.C., Associate Professor

NORFOLK

Robert Nograd, Acting Director

Fran Adams, M.S., Instructor; B.S., M.S., Old Dominion University

Guy Allstock, III, M.S., Storeroom Instructor; B.S., M.S., Johnson & Wales University

Christian Barney, B.A., Associate Instructor; B.A., Old Dominion University

Ed Batten, A.O.S., Instructor; A.O.S., Johnson & Wales University

Susan Batten, C.E.C., C.C.E., Culinary Technology Degree, Associate Instructor; Culinary Technology Degree, Asheville Buncombe Technical Institute

Bettina Blank, M.S., Instructor; B.S., Grand Valley State University; M.S., Boston University

Dedra Butts, B.S., Instructor; B.S., Johnson & Wales University

Tim Cameron, M.A., C.E.C., Associate Professor; B.A., Milligan College; M.A., Old Dominion

Donna Curtis, B.A., Instructor; B.A., Northern Michigan University; Reading Specialist Degree, Memphis State University.

Art M. Elvins, A.A.S., C.E.C., Associate Instructor; A.A.S., Johnson & Wales University

Kristen Fletcher, R.D., M.S., Instructor; B.S., M.S., Virginia Polytechnic Institute

Scarlett Holmes-Paul, M.A., Instructor; B.S. Western Michigan University; M.A. Eastern Michigan University

Joan Hysell, M.Ed., Instructor; B.P.S., SUNY Institute of Technology at Utica/Rome; M.Ed., Ohio University

John Keating, M.S., Oenology Instructor; B.S., Georgetown University; M.S., George Washington University

Lisa Kendall, M.A., Instructor; B.A., State University of New York; M.A., Old Dominion University

Greg Kopanski, M.S., Instructor; B.S., New York University; M.S., Old Dominion University.

Jerry Lanuzza, B.S., Instructor; B.S., Johnson & Wales University

Peter Lehmuller, B.A., Instructor; A.O.S., Culinary Institute of America; B.A., State University of New York, Albany

Alex Leuzzi, M.S., Associate Instructor; B.S., Pikesville College; M.S., Fairleigh Dickinson University

Melanie Loney, M.S., Associate Instructor; B.S., M.S., Old Dominion University

Mary Matthews, M.S., Instructor; B.S., M.S., Old Dominion University

Carrie Moranha, A.A.S., Dining Room /Beverage Instructor; A.A.S. Johnson & Wales University

Maureen Nixon, M.A., Instructor; B.A., North Carolina State University; M.A., Norfolk State University.

Shelly Owens, B.A., Baking & Pastry Instructor; B.A., Townson State University

Patrick Reed, A.O.S, C.C.C., C.C.E., Associate Instructor; A.O.S., Culinary Institute of America

Gregory Retz, B.S., Instructor; A.A.S., Johnson & Wales University; B.S., Virginia Polytechnic

Steven Sadowski, C.E.C., A.O.S., Associate Instructor; A.O.S., Johnson & Wales University

Bonita Startt, M.S ., Instructor; B.S., M. S., Old Dominion University

Fred Tiess, A.A.S., Instructor; A.A.S., State University of New York, Poughkeepsie; A.O.S., Culinary Institute of America

NORTH MIAMI

Donato Becce, Instructor; Diploma di Qualifica, Instituto Professionale, Alberghiero di Stato, Italy

Kenneth Beyer, B.B.A., Instructor; A.B.A., Nichols College; B.B.A., University of Miami

Drue Brandenburg, B.S., C.C.E., C.E.C., Instructor; A.O.S., Culinary Institute of America; B.S., Oklahoma State University

Dennis Daugherty, M.Ed., Instructor; B.S., University of Maryland; M.Ed., Pennsylvania State University

Melvin Davis, B.A., Instructor; B.A. University of Maryland

Alberto Diaz, English Master Pastry Chef, Instructor

Claus Esrstling, C.E.C., Instructor

John Goldfarb, B.S., Instructor; A.O.S., Culinary Institute of America; B.S., Florida International University

John Harrison, B.S., Instructor; A.O.S., Culinary Institute of America; B.S., University of New Haven

James Hensley, Instructor

Giles Hezard, Instructor; Certification of Professional Aptitide - College D'Enseignement Technique Masculin, Audincourt, France

Alan Lazar, B.A., Instructor; B.A. Monmouth College

Lucille Ligas, M.Ed., Assistant Professor, Indiana University of Pennsylvania; B.S. Ed. Indiana University of Pennsylvania

Charles Miltenberger, C.E.P.C., Instructor

Betty Murphy, M.S.Ed. Instructor; B.S.Ed. Eastern Illinois University; M.S.Ed., University of Guam

Larry Rice, M.S., Instructor; A.S., Johnson & Wales University; B.S., Florida International University; M.S., Florida International University

Mark Testa, Ph.D., Associate Professor; A.A.S., State University of New York at Farmingdale; B.P.S., New York Institute of Technology; M.A.L.S. State University of New York at Stony Brook; Ph.D., Barry University

Todd Tonova, M. S., Instructor; A.O.S., Culinary Institute of America; B.S., Florida International University; M.S., Florida International University

Karen Woolley, B.S., Instructor; A.O.S., Culinary Institute of America; B.S., Florida State University

VAIL

Todd M. Rymer, M.S., Director; B.A., New College; M.S., Florida International University

Paul Ferzacca, A.O.S., Instructor; A.O.S. Kendall College

David Hite, A.S., Instructor; A.S. Johnson & Wales University

Robert Kuster, Instructor; Diploma, Swiss Hotel School, Lucerne; Diploma, Trade School, Cook's Apprenticeship, Lucerne; Diploma, Institute Stavia, Estavater Le-Lac

Katie Mazzia; B.S. R.D., Instructor; R.D., Saint Joseph's Health Center; B.S., Ohio State

Paul Reeves, B.S., Instructor; B.S., Saint Cloud State University

David B. Sanchez, A.O.S., Instructor; A.O.S., Johnson & Wales University

Culinary Advisory Council

Scott Armendinger, Editor, Journal Publications, Rockland, ME

Michael P. Berry, Vice President of Food Operations and Concept Development, Walt Disney World, Orlando, FL

Edward Bracebridge, Chef Instructor, Blackstone Valley Tech, Upton, MA

Gerry Fernandez, Technical Service Specialist, General Mills, Inc., Minneapolis, MN

John D. Folse, C.E.C., A.A.C., Owner, Executive Chef, Chef John Folse & Company, Donaldsonville, LA

Ira L. Kaplan, President, Servolift/Eastern Corp., Boston, MA

Gustav Mauler, VP, Food & Beverage, Treasure Island Hotel, Las Vegas, NV

Franz Meier, President, MW Associates, Columbia, SC

Roland Mesnier, Executive Pastry Chef, The White House, Washington, DC

Stanley Nicas, Chef/Owner, Castle Restaurant, Leicester, MA

Robert J. Nyman, President, The Nyman Group, Livingston, NJ

Johnny Rivers, Food & Beverage Manager/Executive Chef, Thyme & Associates,

Joseph Schmidt, Owner, Joseph Schmidt Confections, San Francisco, CA

Martin Yan, President, Yan Can Cook, Inc., Foster City, CA

Johnson & Wales University *Distinguished Visiting Chefs 1979–1997*

1 Dr. Jean Joaquin	8 Bernard S. Urban	16 Dr. Pierre Franey 🍴	24 Hans K. Roth
2 Garry Reich 🍴	9 Marcel Paniel 🍴	17 Jean-Jacques Dietrich	25 Gerhard Daniel
3 Dr. Hans J. Bueschkens	10 Lutz Olkiewicz	18 Uri Guttmann	26 Jacques Noe
4 Michael Bourdin	11 Dr. Joel Robuchon	19 William Spry 🍴	27 Andre Rene
5 Christian Inden	12 Ray Marshall 🍴	20 Dr. Stanley Nicas	28 Dr. Anton Mosimann
6 Casey Sinkeldam	13 Francis Hinault	21 Dr. Paul Elbling	29 Dr. Roger Verge
7 John Kempf	14 Wally Uhl	22 Angelo Paracucchi	30 Gerhard Schmid
	15 Gunther Heiland	23 Albert Kellner	31 Karl Ronaszeki

32 Jacques Pepin
33 Klauss Friedenreich
34 Arno Schmidt
35 Lucien Vannier 🏛
36 Dr. Wolfgang Bierer
37 Dr. John L. Bandera
38 Albert Marty
39 Dr. Siegfried Schaber
40 Dr. Michael Minor
41 Raimund Hofmeister
42 Henry Haller
43 Dr. Noel Cullen
44 Dr. Carolyn Buster
45 Dr. Madeleine Kamman
46 Udo Nechutnys
47 Andrea Hellrigl 🏛
48 George Karousos
49 Warren LeRuth
50 Rene Mettler
51 Dr. Johnny Rivers

52 Milos Cihelka
53 Dr. Louis Szathmary 🏛
54 Philippe Laurier
55 Dr. Hans J. Schadler
56 Franz Klampfer
57 Jean-Pierre Dubray
58 Neil Connolly
59 Joachim Caula
60 Dr. Emeril LaGasse†
61 Dr. Roland Mesnier
62 Bernard Dance
63 Hartmut Handke
64 James Hughes†
65 Paul Bocuse
66 Dr. Martin Yan
67 Marcel Desaulniers
68 Heinz H. Veith
69 Benno Eigenmann
70 Johanne Killeen & George Germon
71 Dr. John D. Folse

72 Dr. Christian Rassinoux
73 Dr. Gustav E. Mauler
74 Dr. Keith Keogh
75 Clayton Folkners
76 Kenneth Wade
77 Dr. Roland E. Schaeffer
78 Dr. William Gallagher
79 Van P. Atkins
80 Hiroshi Noguchi
81 Jasper White
82 Albert Kumin
83 Alfonso Contrisciani†
84 Dr. Victor Gielisse
85 Reimund D. Pitz
86 Daniel Bruce†
87 Antoine Schaefers
88 Michael Ty
89 Phil Learned
90 Joseph Schmidt
91 John Halligan

92 Willy O. Rossel
93 John J. Vyhnanek
94 Roberto Gerometta
95 Robert A. Trainor†
96 Ewald & Susan Notter
97 Joseph Amendola
98 David Paul Johnson
99 Thomas Pedersen
100 André Soltner
101 Christian Clayton†
102 Konstantinos Exarchos
103 Christian Chemin
104 Lars Johansson
105 Paul O'Connell†

SPECIAL FRIENDS
John J. Bowen
Joseph P. Delaney
Socrates Inonog
Franz K. Lemoine

† Alumni
🏛 Deceased

Partial List of Companies Associated with Johnson & Wales University

Adam's Mark Hotels and Resorts
Allied Domecq Retailing
American General Hospitality, Inc.
AmeriClean Systems, Inc.
Angelica Uniform Group
Antigua Hotel Association
Aramark Services, Inc.
Automatic Sales, Inc.
AVTECH Industries
Bacardi & Company, Ltd.

Bacon Construction Company
Balfour Foundation
Banfi Vintners
Basic American Frozen Foods
Bertoill, USA, Inc.
Boston Chicken, Inc.
Boston Park Plaza Hotel
Braman Motors
Brinker International
Bristol Hotel Company

Bugaboo Creek Steakhouse
Bushiri Hotel Aruba
Campbell Food Service Company
Carlson Companies, Inc.
Carnival Cruise Lines
Cartier, Inc.
Celebrity Cruise Lines
Choice Hotels
Citizens Financial Group
Cleveland Range, Inc.

Club Corporation International
Comstock-Castle Stove Company
Concord Hospitality
Cookshack
Cookson America, Inc.
Coors Brewing Company
Crabtree McGrath Associates
Daka Restaurants, Inc.
Darden Restaurants
Deer Valley Resort

Denny's Restaurants
Dial Corporation
Digital Equipment
   Corporation
DiLeonardo International
Doral Arrowwood
E.A. Tosi & Sons Company,
   Inc.
E-H Enterprises
Ecolab, Inc.
Edison Electric Institute
Edwards Super Food Store
EGR International
Electric Cooking Council
Eurest Dining Service
F. Dick
Felchlin, Inc.
Feinstein Foundation
Flik International
   Corporation
Forbes
Friendly Ice Cream
   Corporation
Frymaster
G.S. Distributors
Garland Commercial
   Industries
Gavin Sales Company
General Mills
Godfather's Pizza, Inc.
The Golden Corral
   Corporation
Grand Western Brands,
   Inc.
Grisanti, Inc.
Groen, a Dover Industries
   Co.
Hallsmith-Sysco Food
   Services
Harman Management
   Corporation
Harris-Teeter, Inc.
Harvard University

Hasbro, Inc.
Hatch-Jennings, Inc.
HERO
Hiram Walker & Sons, Inc.
Hilton Hotels
Hobart Corporation
Houlihan's Restaurant
   Group
Houston's Restaurants
Hyatt Hotels Corporation
Ice-O-Matic
Ikon
Intercontinental Hotels
International Metro
   Industries
Interstate Hotels
Keating of Chicago, Inc.
Kiawah Island Resorts
Kraft Foods, Inc.
Lackman Food Service
Le Meridien Hotel Boston
L.J. Minor Corporation
Legal Sea Foods, Inc.
Loews Hotels
Longhorn Steaks, Inc.
Lyford Cay Foundation,
   Inc.
Manor Care Health
   Services
Market Forge Company
Marriott International, Inc.
Max Felchlin, Inc.
Massachusetts Electric
   Company
McCormick & Company,
   Inc.
Moet & Chandon
Morris Nathanson Design
Motel 6
MTS Seating
Nabisco Brands, Inc.
Narragansett Electric
   Company

National Votech Educators
National Banner Company,
   Inc.
National Prepared Foods
   Assoc.
National Student
   Organization
Nestle USA, Inc.
New England Electric
   System
New World Development
   Company
Norwegian Seafood
   Council
Opryland Hotel
Paramount Restaurant
   Supply
PepsiCo, Inc.
Pillsbury Corp.
The Proctor & Gamble Co.
Providence Beverage
Prudential Insurance
   Company
Quadlux
The Quaker Oats
   Company
Radisson Hospitality
   Worldwide
Ralph Calise Fruit &
   Produce
Red Lion Hotels
Renaissance Hotels &
   Resorts
Restaurant Data Concepts
Rhode Island Distributing
   Company
Rhode Island Foundation
Rich Products Corporation
The Ritz-Carlton Hotel
Robert Mondavi Winery
Robot Coupe
Ruth's Chris Steak House
Saunders Hotel Group

Joseph Schmidt
   Confections
Schott Corporation
Select Restaurants, Inc.
Servolift/Eastern Corp.
Sharp Electronic
   Corporation
Somat Corporation
Southern Foods
State of Rhode Island,
   Department of
   Education
Stonehard
Sun International
Sunrise Assisted Living
Swiss American Imports,
   Ltd.
Swiss Chalet Fine Foods
Sysco Corporation
TACO, Inc.
Taco Bell
Tasca Ford Sales, Inc.
Tekmatex, Inc.
The Delfield Company
The Waldorf-Astoria
Thermodyne Foodservice
   Products
Toastmaster
Tufts University
Tyson Foods, Inc.
U.S.D.A./Bell Associates
United States Army
United States Navy
University of Connecticut
Vail Associates
Vulcan Hart Corporation
Walt Disney World
Wells Manufacturing
   Company
Wyatt Corporation
Wyndham Hotels &
   Resorts

1

Cooking: A Journey Through Time

1

Cooking: A Journey Through Time

Cooking has a rich history; as humans evolved, so too did cooking and dining. The foundation of modern cookery lies in developments over the past 400 years. Historical research and a review of the literature have revealed the accomplishments of history's greatest chefs. This chapter provides only a taste of the breadth and depth of information available regarding culinary history.

Students new to cooking should pursue an active reading schedule to increase their knowledge of the history and techniques of cooking. A modern chef should possess tenacity and depth of knowledge to survive in the increasingly competitive foodservice industry.

The Stone Age

The Stone Age, so named because during that prehistoric time the primary weapons and tools used by humans were made of stone, is divided into three periods: *Paleolithic*, or Old Stone Age (750,000 years ago), *Mesolithic*, Middle Stone Age (15,000 years ago), and *Neolithic*, New Stone Age (10,000 years ago).

Glacial activity in Europe and Asia during the old and middle Stone Ages destroyed most traces of human civilization. What little remains of this period includes stone implements found in European caves, although some of the oldest known tools have been found in Kenya, Africa, and date back to 600,000 B.C. Pictures depicting the lives and activities of the prehistoric people exist on some of the walls of the caves. During the Stone Age, life centered around the gathering and preparation of food. Humans' fascination with eating was evident.

So little data are available that any attempt to describe cooking during the Stone Age must be based on archeological evidence, from which logical deductions can be drawn. Archeological discoveries indicate that Peking man, living around 450,000 B.C., may have practiced cannibalism, although evidence is not conclusive. Cave drawings from the Mesolithic age reveal an understanding of the eating habits of humankind. Some of the drawings show scenes of hunting and food gathering. The fact that the drawings exist suggests that food was probably plentiful, allowing for activities other than hunting. Artifacts found at Vestonice, Czechoslovakia, show that people ate mammoth, reindeer, horse, fox, wolf, and tortoise. Other evidence from this period indicates that fish, fowl, and water lilies were additional sources of food. It is estimated that about 10 million people were living on earth between 15,000 and 10,000 B.C.

Neolithic Revolution

The Neolithic revolution occurred around 7800 B.C. and is characterized by some of the most significant changes in human behavior. Humans began to grow food rather than gather it. Discoveries at Jericho in Palestine, where a town was unearthed, suggest a settled life and a sedentary existence. The domestication of animals and plants, which were necessary to support this progressive lifestyle, was evident. At Catal Hüyük, Turkey, a town was excavated that was twice the size of Jericho. Pottery, baskets, food particles such as wheat and barley, and woven woolen textiles were discovered. The diet of the people who lived there included apples, lentils, peas, almonds, acorns, and honey (their main sweetener). These discoveries are clear examples of early food preparation and cooking skills.

From 5000 to 3000 B.C., some civilizations, notably Mesopotamian and Egyptian, flourished. Elements integral to today's society, such as architecture, art, class systems, the division of labor, politics, trade, and writing were developed. Farming practices advanced with the invention of the plow in approximately 3550 B.C. Food production increased, which in turn gave birth to granaries, silos, and selected cattle breeding.

During this time, cooking was done over an open flame or glowing hot coals and included broiling and roasting. Food was placed inside clay cylinders, which were laid on top of hot ashes. With the advent of the Bronze Age, pots were fabricated, and cooking techniques using liquid became widespread. More tools and utensils became available, making daily life easier. In Mesopotamia, the diet probably consisted of beef, lamb, pork, deer, fowl (but no chicken), fish, turtles, grains, vegetables, and fruits. Soups were made by cooking food in water, and beer was served for all festive occasions in Babylon. Egyptians followed traditions similar to those of the Mesopotamians. Some Egyptian tombs read, "Give to me bread when I am hungry.

Give to me beer when I am thirsty," indicating the heavy use of grain in their diet.

Ancient Egypt

No formal manuscripts or cookbooks exist from ancient Egypt. However, tomb paintings and hieroglyphics depict the preparation of foods. Based on this evidence, we know that food was essential to various Egyptian cultural and religious ceremonies. Unearthed ancient tombs have yielded remnants of foods such as figs and bread, which were typical funerary offerings. Barley, wheat, preserved meats, beer, and wine have been found in various Egyptian states in tombs dating back as far as 2613 to 2181 B.C. Open-hearth baking of unleavened bread and salt preservation of meats and fish are examples of food-preparation techniques from ancient Egypt that are still used today.

The fertile soil of the Nile Valley was essential to the barley and wheat production used to prepare the beer and bread diet that sustained most Egyptians. Paired with the domestication of livestock and the farming of various plants and grains, a complex agricultural system evolved. Evidence suggests that Egyptian agriculture was so successful that excess grains and preserved meats were exported to Greece and Rome.

The cooking techniques of the Egyptians and Mesopotamians slowly improved after the decline of the Egyptian empire (713–332 B.C.). Scientifically based, learned cuisine that set food-preparation standards and ritualized

Figure 1–1 Egyptian print

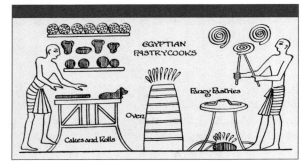

cooking procedures was their legacy. Some of the additional preserving techniques used were drying, smoking, and storing fruits in honey and fish in oil.

Greek and Roman Civilizations

Although no complete documentation of early Greek cuisine has been found, there are quotes and references from such Greek writers as Archestrates (fourth century B.C.), Athenaeus (third century B.C.), and Plato (427–347 B.C.). The Greek cooks practiced culinary arts with considerable thought and refinement. Cheese making, bread baking, and wine production developed in Greece along with the use of seasonings and spices. Archeological evidence suggests that the Greeks prepared food for ceremony and enjoyment. Grilling became popular again, while boiling lost its attraction. Certain foods and cooking styles enjoyed popularity for a time and then went out of fashion. Rabbit was the most sought-after meat. Oil and cheese were used in sauces, and cultivated olives were prized for their flavor.

Historians theorize that the Grecian diet paralleled Greek medicine; food items that were consumed for medicinal purposes were consumed for nutritional purposes as well. This would later have an impact on Middle Eastern and Western European cuisines. Roman civilization, from the Etruscans of 400 B.C. to the demise of Rome around A.D. 400, influenced European history until modern times.

Greek and Roman societies introduced the tradition of lavish dinner parties for the upper class. Greek dinner parties customarily included five guests; nine guests were usually seated at a Roman dinner party. A full dinner required 12 cooks for preparation, and each was responsible for a specific function.

In a typical Roman kitchen, the master cook supervised the food preparation from a platform at the rear of the room, which served as a classroom. Square hearth fires were in the middle of the room. Pots were small cooking vessels made of bronze, brass, clay, or silver. Ovens were made of stone and fired with wood.

A meal started with appetizers and was followed by two to seven courses, depending on the occasion. Many sweets and fruits were offered. Wines were served throughout the meal and were fortified with spices or honey. Some cooks became wealthy by selling leftovers from extravagant meals. Takeout shops developed as a direct result of this practice of selling leftovers.

Most knowledge of Roman cooking comes from Marcus Apicius's (400 B.C.) recipes, which are some of the earliest written works on food. In his writings, Apicius created a list of characteristics regarding Roman cuisine:

- A mortar and pestle were used to grind meats.
- Food was roasted on a spit.
- There was heavy use of saffron.
- Pungent seasonings were used.
- There was high regard for rabbit.
- Honey and *garum*, a fermented liquid made from fish viscera, were used in almost every sauce.

Formal dining developed during the Roman empire. The most common Roman banquet consisted of three courses: the appetizer (eggs, salads, oysters), the main course, and a final course of fruit. Historical research suggests that various forms of etiquette were observed during these formal meals. Guests were greeted at the door and provided with a change of robes and sandals. Once inside the host's home, the guests were allowed to wash their hands and feet and were adorned with a garland of flowers, which was believed to repel the ill effects of alcohol consumption.

Middle Ages

During the Middle Ages, the Roman tradition persisted in cooking and dining practices. Culinary staples included leeks, carrots, and turnips. The meat supply was limited to game, some cattle, and an abundance of fish. The cauldron, an iron vessel hanging from a metal arm over hot coals, was the main cooking pot. Garum was widely used as a seasoning over mashed boiled meats and fish.

Kitchens were typically constructed apart from the main house to reduce the risk of fire. The ceiling was vented to allow the release of smoke and heat from the roasting spits and simmering iron kettles. Ovens were set into stone walls fronted by iron doors. Foods were kept cold in cellars or along the floor of the kitchen. Kitchen equipment included iron pots, pans, various hooks, spoons, and knives (Figure 1–2).

By the end of the Middle Ages (A.D. 1200–1400), as a result of the Crusades, spices, sugar, tropical fruits, and nuts were brought to Europe and were considered novelties. Agricultural expansion took place, leading to the formation of food markets and trade routes with the rest of the known world.

One of the first cookbooks in modern Europe, *Le Viander de Taillevent* (1375), was written by Guillaume Tirel, cook

Figure 1–2 A Middle Ages kitchen scene

to Charles VI (1346–1422). The book included recipes for soups, stews, and sauces. Guillaume's illustrious career began in 1326 when he served—under the name *Taillevent*—as an adolescent apprentice to Queen Jeanne of France.

Taillevent is widely recognized as the first master chef and *Le Viander* documented his style of cooking in such a way as to mark the beginning of modern cooking. From the time of Taillevent, a succession of cookbooks and records on eating and dining followed. By 1346, Taillevent had risen to head cook to King Phillip VI and soon after he was granted the title of squire and traveled from household to household within King Phillip's court producing extravagant meals. During this period, the tablecloth became part of the ceremonial dinner.

The Roman cooking techniques of chopping, mashing, and heavy seasoning of foods continued through the 14th and 15th centuries. Seasonings and sauces were added to mask the poor quality of the meat. The octagonal shape of the traditional Roman kitchen was crowded, noisy, hot, and smoky. The chimney hearth accommodated three cauldrons. The cauldron on the left side of the hearth was used for roasting, and the other cauldrons were used for boiling. Generally, an oven was placed on the side of the chimney where breads and pies were baked.

In 1474, the recipes of the Italian cook Martino were published in *De Honesta Voluptate et Valetndine*. *De Honesta Voluptate* was the work of the Roman philosopher and humanist Platina (1421–1481). Platina included five chapters of Martino's recipes at the end of his book. Martino's recipes provided the cook with numerous suggestions on food preparation. For example, Martino suggested covering simmering soup with a damp cloth to keep the smoke from the hearth from overpowering the flavor of the soup. In addition, a recipe for macaroni also provided instruction that included wrapping the dough around a stick to form tubes before drying.

The age of discovery reached its zenith when Christopher Columbus landed in America in 1492. Columbus came to shore in the Caribbean as he searched for an eastern passage to the Spice Islands of Indonesia. One of Columbus's most significant accomplishments was the discovery of new ingredients and methods of food preparation. Native

Americans shared their precious metals and foods with Columbus and other explorers. These explorers returned to Europe with their culinary treasures. Tomatoes, chili peppers, potatoes, avocados, and corn eventually found their way from the Native American to the European table.

Another notable explorer, Hernando Cortés, conquered Aztec Mexico and returned to Spain with the vanilla bean and cacao, the staple ingredient to chocolate. Pastry and dessert preparation in Europe was forever changed with the introduction of chocolate and vanilla.

Italy continued to influence the development of culinary arts and gastronomy throughout the 16th century, which is sometimes referred to as the Renaissance, or Elizabethan era, in reference to the reign of England's Queen Elizabeth I (1558–1603). The Italian master chef Bartolomeo Scappi published his cookbook *Opera* in 1570, complete with illustrations and step-by-step descriptions of cooking processes and recipes. Scappi was the first to name his various kitchen knives and equipment and also standardized the measurement of ingredients to a 12-ounce pound. (The same troy measurement system is still used today for gold and precious metals.) Some of the culinary art used in Italian noble households was introduced to French nobility at this time (see Figure 1–3).

The Renaissance period provided Europe with a revival of the arts and letters and the development of culinary arts. Fresh fruit and vegetable markets increased in number, and fish became important in the daily diet. Also during this time, masking the flavor and appearance of food with sauces became less acceptable.

Modern Cooking

The 17th century marked the beginning of modern cooking. François Pierre de la Varenne, the founder of French classical cooking, published *Le Cuisinier François* in 1651 and forever changed culinary arts. *Le Cuisinier François* was the first book since *Le Viander*, which was published 300 years earlier. *Le Cuisinier François* fully documented French cooking and the Italian influence on French cuisine. Princess Catherine de Medici (1519–1589) of Italy married

Figure 1–3 Scappi's print of knives

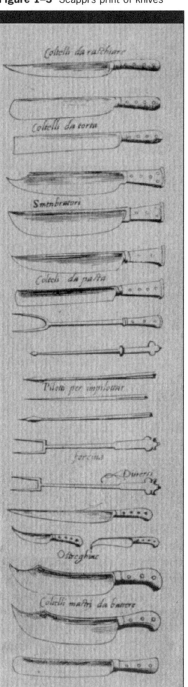

Henry II during the mid-1500s, and, in 1600, Italian Marie de Medici married Henri IV. Catherine de Medici is often credited with the introduction of Italian cooking to the French court. Historians speculate on the true impact of both Medici marriages but agree that at the very least they symbolized the open dialogue between the two countries during the Renaissance period.

Chefs during the time of François Pierre de la Varenne were interested in detail, balance, and harmony regarding cooking and ingredients. La Varenne detailed how to reduce cooking juices to concentrate their flavor, much as we do today. The use of nuts, truffles, and mushrooms is also present in *Le Cuisinier François*. La Varenne wrote the first published reference to the use of *roux* as a thickening agent for bouillon. The classical system of naming various dishes after French nobility began during the time of La Varenne and continued to the era of Escoffier. For example, béchamel sauce was named after the Marquis de Béchamel, steward of King Louis XIV. La Varenne was also master chef to the Marquis d'Uxelles, for whom he named the mixture of sautéed mushrooms, shallots, and seasonings, referred to today as *duxelles*.

One of the most important aspects of modern cooking that la Varenne catalyzed was the shift from using many spices and herbs to using few. During this time, emphasis was placed on the natural taste of food. Roux slowly replaced toasted bread as a thickening agent in sauces. Butter became the preferred fat in place of lard for cooking. Kitchens were designed smaller, with specific rooms assigned to various functions. For example, separate rooms were assigned for bread making and appetizers.

During the 18th century, cookbooks similar to la Varenne's 30-volume masterpiece were written for the aristocracy. However, the first popular cookbook written for the middle class, Hannah Glass's *The Art of Cookery Made Plain and Easy*, was published in 1758. Simple recipes using ingredients other than meat were included in Glass's book because meat was not always available or within the budget of the working class. Use of the pungent sauces of Roman times slowly diminished. Roux and butter greatly improved the sauces, and béchamel, espagnole, and tomato were developed.

By the end of the 18th century, a definitive break occurred between the cooking of the old world and the contemporary cooking of the time. Pastry arts also broke free as its own branch of cooking and has remained so. The number of professional cookery books and the popularity of cooking and dining surged during the 1700s. The great French chef Menon authored *La Cuisiniere Bourgeoise* for the female cook of modest wealth. However, Menon continued to invent dishes that he named after the nobility. Du-Barry, Richelieu, and Soubise were names associated with food during the era of Menon.

During the 19th century, chefs were displaced from houses of nobility to public houses. As a result of the French Revolution, noble families disbanded, leaving the chefs without livelihood. To survive, chefs turned to public houses. They prepared food and sold it to whomever could pay, thus establishing the first modern restaurants. *Restaurant,* first used in 1765, means "to restore" and originated in Paris during the time of the French Revolution in reference to the new public dining establishments.

Dishes were invented bearing the names of chefs instead of the names of their noble employers. Cookbooks were written using new ingredients and sauces. One of the great-est writers of the time was Marie Antoine Carême (1784–1835), who systemized French cooking using basic or mother sauces, compound sauces, standard garnitures, and standard terminology for recipes (see Figure 1–4). Carême was born to a poor family and became the chef of kings by his own accord. He is considered the father of classical French cooking, and his style is called *haute cuisine* in reference to the cooking for which he was known. In 1814, Carême published *L'Art du Cuisinier,* which documented his style of grand cuisine. Although he did not invent all the basic sauces and compounds, Carême finalized an already well-developed system. Carême served as a true role model to modern cooks because he achieved greatness through sheer determination and hard work.

Alexis Benoit Soyer (1809–1858) was a contemporary of Carême (see Figure 1–5). At 22 years old, Soyer became the chef of the Duke of Cambridge, where he designed a kitchen with a well-established work station and invented the Soyer oven, which is still used by the British military today. Soyer is most famous for his years as chef at the Reform Club in London, where he designed the kitchens and created classical dishes such as lamb

Figure 1–4 The life of Marie Antoine Carême

1784	Born June 8th
1800	Employed by Bailly, the famous French pastry chef
1801	Promoted to chief pastry cook by Bailly
1801–1814	Worked *en extra* (as an extra person) at the House of Talleyrand M. Gendron in the pastry shops M. Richaut at the House of Conde At the Elysée Bourbon under Laguipiere
1814	Chef de Cuisine to the emperor Alexander I of Russia in Paris
1815–1816	Worked at the Royal Pavilion, Brighton, for the Prince Regent
1819	Went to Russia to study the methods of the Russian Court
1819–1822	Wrote five books on cookery
1823	Engaged by Prince Esterhazy in Paris as Chief Cook
1835	Died in Paris

Figure 1-5 The life of Alexis Benoit Soyer

1809	Born October 14th
1821	Started at Chez Grignon with his brother, Philippe
1825	Engaged by Maison Douix, Boulevard des Italiennes, Paris, as second chef
1826	Made head chef at Maison Douix
1831	Traveled to England and worked for the Duke of Cambridge, Marquis of Waterford, Duke of Sutherland
1833	Engaged by Mr. Lloyd of Aston Hall at Oswestry
1837	Engaged by the Marquis Ailsa in London, appointed Chef de Cuisine at the Reform Club
1845	Published *Delassements Culinaires*
1846	Published *Gastronomic Regenerator*
1847	Went to Dublin to help relieve the famine
1850	Left Reform Club, wrote *Modern Housewife*
1851	Opened the Symposium of All Nations at the Great Exhibition, wrote *Shilling Cookery*
1855	Joined British forces in the Crimea
1857	Published *Soyer's Culinary Campaign*
1858	Died in London

reform. During the great famine in Ireland in 1847, Soyer, who was known as a compassionate, considerate man, traveled to Dublin to volunteer his services in feeding the hungry. Soyer wrote many books, including *The Gastronomic Regenerator* (1846), his most famous. *The Gastronomic Regenerator* was written while Soyer was the chef at the Reform Club and it sold over 2,000 copies within eight weeks of its release. Soyer is also credited with creating the *brigade system,* which was later refined by Georges Auguste Escoffier at the end of the 19th century at the Ritz Hotel in Paris. In 1847, Soyer used his own money to open the first soup kitchen for the poor. He was also a great culinary inventor whose products included tools, stoves, and dishes.

The gap from the 19th to the 20th century was easily bridged by one of the greatest masters of classical French cooking, Georges Auguste Escoffier (1846–1935) (see Figure 1–6 on page 10). Following in the footsteps of Carême and using his foundations, Escoffier wrote *Le Guide Culinaire*. *Le Guide Culinaire* was originally written to be used by Escoffier's staff when he was the chef of the Ritz hotels. A majority of the recipes were simplifications of Carême's recipes. Escoffier's forte was the standardization of mother sauces (espagnole, béchamel, velouté, and tomato) and their compounds. Escoffier is most recognized for his long association with the great Swiss-born hotelier and restaurateur Cesar Ritz (1850–1918). In 1889, Ritz hired Escoffier for the head chef position at the Savoy Hotel in London. The grand cuisine created by Escoffier—the speed, innovation, and quality food, as well as his style of organizing recipes and work stations—paired with the service and atmosphere maintained by Ritz attracted the wealth and nobility of Europe. Escoffier quickly became recognized as one of Europe's premier chefs. *Le Guide*

Figure 1–6 The life of Georges Auguste Escoffier

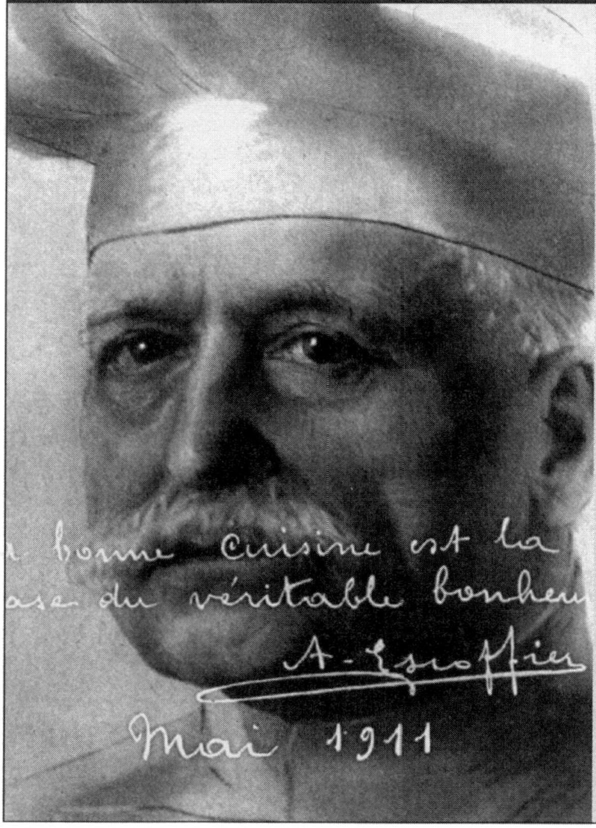

1846	Born October 28
1859	Began work at the Restaurant Français at Nice
1865	Commis Rotisseur at Petit Moulin Rouge, Paris
1870	Promoted to Chef Saucier at Moulin Rouge Head chef, Rhine Army Headquarters, Metz
1871	Head chef 17th Regiment, Colonel Comte de Waldner
1871-1872	Hotel de Luxembourg, Nice, for the winter as head chef
1872-1878	Head chef at Petit Moulin Rouge
1878	Maison Maire, Maison Chevet, both in Palais Royal, Paris
1879	Le Faisan D'Ore, Côte d'Azur. Divided time between there and Paris
1883-1884	Winter season at the Grand Hotel, Monte Carlo Summer season at the Grand National, Lucerne
1889	Savoy, London
1896	Ritz, Paris
1899	Carlton House, London
1904	Advised Hamburg America Line
1919	Awarded Legion of Honor
1924	Made Officer of the Legion of Honor
1935	Died in Monaco

Culinaire contains dozens of recipes that reflect the names of many of Escoffier's greatest patrons and is still the standard for basic culinary training today.

Nouvelle Cuisine

Fernand B. Point (1897–1955) is considered the epitome of the modern chef (see Figure 1–7). He not only used the classical techniques but also adapted and adjusted regional French cooking, merging both to produce what is known as nouvelle cuisine ("new cooking"). Nouvelle cuisine moved away from the classical French style of preparing rich sauces, foods, and tortes. It is a lighter and fresher cuisine served in smaller portions. Point's apprentices, Paul Bocuse and Roger Verge, became the culinary leaders of Europe during the 1960s and 1970s, and in turn influenced today's best chefs.

Point encouraged his apprentices to work for the great chefs of their time as part of their initial training. Today's chefs have modeled their training after this lineage-based system created by Escoffier and Point; and it is not unusual for modern cooks to list the important chefs for whom they have worked. In The United States, it is common

Figure 1–7 Fernand B. Point

for young chefs and culinary school graduates to seek employment with the most talented chefs in industry as a vehicle for career development.

American Cookery

The key influences on American cuisine, as with any other, are culture, geography, climate, economy, and technology. Early settlers brought culture and cooking methods from the Old World and combined them with native culinary techniques and ingredients. As a result, American cuisine is often viewed as a mosaic of ingredients that are combined using techniques from a variety of cultures. For this reason, defining the multifaceted characteristics of American cuisine is difficult.

America has truly undergone a renaissance in cooking over the past 25 years; however, many of today's developments originated during colonial times. The first book to promote the use of American ingredients, *American Cookery*, was published in Hartford, Connecticut, in 1796 by Amelia Simmon (see Figure 1–8). Simmon's book contains 130 recipes written for the experienced cook. The first references to using corncobs to smoke bacon and the preparation of cranberry sauce for service with roast turkey are contained in Simmon's book. *American Cookery* also contains the first recipes for johnnycakes and Indian

Figure 1–8 Amelia Simmon's book *American Cookery*

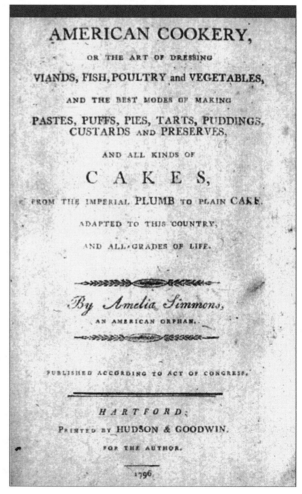

pudding, confirming Simmon's influence on the early development of American cuisine. Today, many American chefs emphasize the use of indigenous ingredients and continue to support the movement created by Simmons.

Female and minority chefs maintained their dominant influence in popular cooking in America during the 19th century. In 1827, the first cookbook by an African American appeared in Boston, *The House Servant's Directory* by Robert Roberts. Roberts, butler to the honorable Christopher Gore, governor of Massachusetts (1809), developed a manual that was similar in many aspects to the grand cookbooks of the royal households of Renaissance Europe. Of significance is Roberts's desire to produce a book that encouraged house servants to be caterers and managers rather than subservient workers.

In 1826, one year prior to the publication of Roberts's book on service, Ye Olde Union Oyster House opened for business in Boston, and shortly afterward, Durgin Park opened. Both are still in operation today near Boston's famed Faneuil Hall Marketplace. Fine-dining pioneer John Delmonico of Switzerland, along with his brother Peter and nephew Lorenzo, opened Delmonico's restaurant in New York City. The legacy of Delmonico's restaurant, established in 1834, lasted 103 years and included many innovations. Delmonico's was the first restaurant to offer a separate wine menu, to offer a hamburger on the menu, and to allow women into the main dining room. Charles Ranhofer, Delmonico's chef and employee for over 30 years, wrote *The Epicurean* in 1894, which included many of the famous dishes he created.

In 1879, Mrs. Sarah Hooper, chair of the Industrial Education Committee of the Women's Education Association, started the Boston Cooking School. In 1883, the Boston Cooking School became the first incorporated cooking school in America (see Figure 1–9).

Fannie Merritt Farmer (1857–1915) became the principal of the Boston Cooking School in 1891 and remained in that position until 1901 (see Figure 1–10). Farmer is widely known for *The Boston Cooking School Cookbook* (1896), which remained the most popular cookbook in

Figure 1–9 Early cooking school

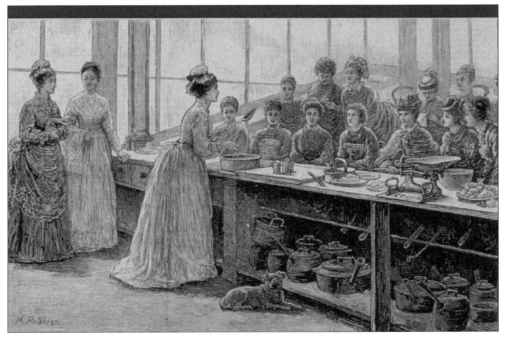

Figure 1–10 Fannie Merritt Farmer

America until 1931 when it was replaced by Irma Rombauer's *Joy of Cooking*.

From 1803, the year the icebox was invented, until 1906, when the Food and Drug Administration passed the Pure Food and Drug Act, American foodservice was influenced by many innovations. For example, the invention and mechanization of canning, pasteurization, electric ovens, and kitchen equipment, and the improvement of gas stoves and ranges helped to fuel the development of foodservice. Prior to the mid-19th century, most kitchens had no refrigeration, running water, electricity, or gas.

Many of the developments during the past 100 years have been a direct result of social change in America. The early 1900s brought an influx of immigrants from Eastern and Western Europe and China. As a result, ethnic communities spread across America. During the latter half of the 1950s,

more and more individuals began to eat at restaurants, and the food industry responded by creating fast and inexpensive meals that met the new demand. Along with the birth of the fast-food segment came restaurant franchising and systemized food purchasing and preparation.

Because of the importation and production of ethnic ingredients once unavailable in the United States, Asian, Italian, and Mexican foods became popular. During the 1960s, Julia Child appeared for the first time on public television and expounded the benefits and proper techniques of French cooking. In 1963, while assigned to the American Embassy in Paris, Child, a graduate of Smith College, fell in love with French cooking and enrolled in a six-month course at the Cordon Bleu cooking school. On completion of her classes, she trained privately with Chefs Max Bugnard, Claude Thilmond, and Pierre Mangelatte before returning to America. In 1961, Julia and her husband Paul returned to America and settled in Cambridge, Massachusetts, where she published *Mastering the Art of French Cooking*, cowritten with Simone Beck and Louisette Bertholle. Julia was invited to appear on a public television program to promote her new book, and, from there, her famous television series was launched. The marriage between mass media and cooking began.

By the 1970s, televised American chefs became celebrities. Many American chefs traveled to Europe in search of the best training. Educational institutions responded to the new interest in culinary arts and created programs for training professionals. In 1973, Johnson & Wales University enrolled its first class of culinary students in response to this new demand. In the same year, Dr. Louis Szathmary, now chef laureate of Johnson & Wales University, addressed the annual convention of the American Culinary Federation. He requested support to have the U.S. Department of Labor change the title of executive chef from a domestic category, as it was then listed, to the category of professional. Lt. General John McLaughlin, Dr. Lewis Minor, and Chef Szathmary (see Figure 1–11 on page 14) persevered, and, in 1977, the Department of Labor finally responded and changed the official job category for executive chefs to a professional, technical, and managerial occupation, thereby formally recognizing professional cooking in America.

Figure 1–11 Chef Louis Szathmary

During the 1980s, American chefs capitalized on mass media. Hundreds of cookbooks were written and published by professional chefs, documenting the many different movements that were occurring within the foodservice kitchens. Each book added to the mosaic of American cookery; some of the topics included American regional cuisine, the infusion of world cuisines, vegetarian cuisine, and comfort foods.

In the 1990s, technology continues to transform the foodservice industry. Sourcing food has depended on various modern farming practices such as aquaculture, hydroponics, and hybridization. Although not a new practice, organic farming has become increasingly important in providing safer and more healthful food. The use of irradiation, although still controversial, offers the consumer foods with a longer shelf life. Through the Internet, real-time information pertaining to the culinary arts is at the fingertips of every chef. The foodservice industry in America has yielded many developments that are used around the world. With the onslaught of technology, this trend will continue into the new millennium.

2

Nutrition

Nutrition

Nutrition is the process by which an animal takes in and uses food. *Food* is anything that animals (including people) eat or drink to sustain growth and to repair and maintain life. Numerous reports have identified nutrition as an important factor in maintaining good health.

According to a Gallup poll conducted by the National Restaurant Association in 1989, the public not only is aware of the relationship between nutrition and health but has begun to act on this awareness. The demand for food that is low in fat and high in complex carbohydrates has increased since 1972 (USDA Food Consumption Survey, 1988). The National Restaurant Association's Delphi Panel report (1988) predicted that this trend will continue well into the 21st century. The results of yet another survey, however, indicate that taste is still the primary criterion when ordering food in a restaurant (National Restaurant Association, 1990).

The chef must be able to respond to the demand for low-fat, high–complex-carbohydrate foods of excellent quality to be successful. Understanding the fundamentals of nutrition, as well as its relationship to health and the culinary arts, is vital.

As a leader in culinary education, Johnson & Wales University has developed a nutrition policy that reflects its commitment to the integration of nutrition throughout all aspects of student life and education. The goals are

- To stress nutrition programs within the university curriculum.
- To focus on nutrition in all methods of food preparation, reflecting the foodservice industry's commitment to the concept of healthy foods.
- To support the university's community programs that provide accurate nutrition information and cultivate a healthy lifestyle.

Nutrients

Food is made up of chemical compounds called **nutrients.** The body is also composed of nutrients. Nutrients in food perform one or more of the following functions in the body:

- Supply energy.
- Build and repair tissue.
- Regulate body processes.

There are six classes of nutrients:

1. Carbohydrates
2. Fats (lipids)
3. Minerals
4. Protein
5. Vitamins
6. Water

Carbohydrates, fats, protein, and vitamins are organic, which means they contain carbon.

Energy-Yielding Nutrients

Carbohydrates, protein, and fats provide the body with energy, which it uses to produce heat and to perform its various functions. Alcohol also provides energy, although it is not considered a nutrient because it is toxic. This energy is measured in kilocalories, commonly called **calories.** One calorie is equal to the unit of heat needed to increase the temperature of 1 liter of water 1° C (from 14.5° C to 15.5° C) under normal atmospheric pressure. If more energy is consumed than is needed, it can be stored in the form of fat or other compounds. The number of calories provided by 1 gram of each of these substances is listed in Table 2–1. Vitamins, minerals, and water do not supply energy.

Table 2–1 Caloric Content of Nutrients

Nutrient	Calories per gram
Carbohydrate	4
Protein	4
Fat	9

Carbohydrates

Carbohydrates are compounds made up of sugar units. They are classified as simple or complex. A **simple carbohydrate** is made up of single sugars (monosaccharides) and pairs of sugars linked together (disaccharides). **Complex carbohydrates** (polysaccharides) are made up of long chains of sugar units linked together. Simple carbohydrates include the sugars found in milk, honey, fruit, maple syrup, refined table sugar, and raw or unrefined sugar. Complex carbohydrates include starch, fiber, and glycogen. **Starch** is the form in which plants store carbohydrates. It is found in grains; pasta; and such vegetables as potatoes, corn, and legumes.

Glycogen is the form in which animals (including humans) store carbohydrates. It is found in limited amounts in long muscle tissue and in the liver.

Fiber is the part of plants the human body cannot digest. There are two types: insoluble and soluble. Both types are important. Insoluble fiber helps to maintain a healthy digestive tract, while soluble fiber may lower blood cholesterol levels and control blood sugar levels in diabetics. A combination of both may help to prevent certain forms of cancer. Because fiber is not digested, it does not supply energy. Fiber needs are best met by eating a variety of whole foods (such as whole grains, fruits, and vegetables), which also deliver other forms of carbohydrates and are often good sources of vitamins and minerals. Sources of soluble and insoluble fiber are listed in Table 2–2. When increasing fiber in the diet, it is important to remember to increase fiber gradually and to be sure to consume adequate amounts of fluids. Bowel problems could result if these precautions are not followed. The suggested amount of fiber is 25 to 30 grams, per day.

Proteins

Proteins are composed of nitrogenous substances called *amino acids*. Twenty amino acids make up the proteins in the human body and in food. While the body can supply most of these amino acids, those it cannot must be obtained through food sources, and are considered *essential*. In order for the body to be able to make all the proteins

Table 2-2 Sources of Fiber

Soluble	Insoluble
Fruits (pulp)	Fruits (skins)
Vegetables	Vegetables
Oats, rye, barley	Whole grains (such as wheat)
Seeds	Seeds
Legumes	Legumes
Gums	

it needs, ones diet must supply *all* of the essential amino acids.

Proteins that supply all of the essential amino acids are termed complete proteins. Animal proteins (meat, poultry, fish, eggs, milk, and milk products) are examples. On the other hand, plant proteins (usually from bread and cereal products, vegetables, legumes, and nuts) are low in or missing one or more of the essential amino acids and are referred to as *incomplete proteins*. These may be used, however, to create complete proteins through complementation, the process of combining (or complementing) two plant-sourced proteins. Table 2–3 shows food combinations that form complementary proteins.

The body is unable to store extra protein. Therefore, it is necessary that the diet supply adequate amounts of the essential amino acids daily. Most Americans eat more protein than is necessary. If more protein or amino acids are eaten than is needed, they are converted to fat (and, under certain circumstances, carbohydrates). Eating too much protein or amino acids on a regular basis stresses the kidneys and could cause a vitamin imbalance. Supplements of certain amino acids have been proven to be toxic.

The major functions of protein include the following:

- Grows and maintains body tissue
- Builds enzymes and hormones
- Forms part of a healthy immune system (fights infection)
- Regulates body fluids
- Helps maintain acid-base balance.

Protein can also be used for energy; however, this is not a primary function of protein.

Table 2–3 Complementary Protein Sources

Animal	Plant	Food Combinations to Obtain Complete Protein

Meats
Fish
Poultry
Eggs
Milk and milk products: cheese, yogurt, dry milk
	Grains: wheat, pasta, corn, rice, bulgur, oats, breads
	Legumes: dried beans, peas, lentils, soybeans, peanuts
	Nuts and seeds: sesame seeds, cashews, sunflower seeds, walnuts, all nuts
		Legumes and grain:
		  Peanut butter on bread
		  Rice and red beans
		  Refried beans and tortilla
		  Split pea soup and bread
		  Baked beans and brown bread
		  Noodles with peanut sauce
		  Pasta and beans
		Legumes and nuts or seeds:
		  Chick peas and sesame seeds
		  Salad, sunflower seeds, and beans

Fats and Lipids

Fats and oils belong to a class of chemical compounds called **lipids.** Fatty acids are the basic chemical units in fat. They may be saturated, monounsaturated, or polyunsaturated. Each of these fatty acids is found in certain foods:

Sources of Saturated fatty acids
- in largest proportions in fats of meat, poultry, and fish
- hydrogenated fat (for example, shortening)
- tropical oils (coconut and palm).

Sources of Monounsaturated fatty acids
- in largest proportions in olive oil, canola oil, and peanut oil
- in avocados and cashews.

Sources of Polyunsaturated fatty acids
- in safflower, sunflower, corn, soybean, and cottonseed oils, and in cold-water fish (ie., salmon, herring, mackerel).

All fats are composed of a mixture of the three kinds of fatty acids. The type of fatty acid in greatest proportion determines whether a fat is classified as saturated, monounsaturated, or polyunsaturated. It also determines some of the characteristics of the fat or oil and the effect it has on blood cholesterol levels. Saturated fats are usually solid at room temperature, while mono- and polyunsaturated fats are liquid at room temperature.

Dietary fats
- Concentrated dietary source of energy.
- Enhance food's aroma and flavor.
- Carry fat soluble vitamins.
- Provide essential fatty acids.
- Provide a feeling of fullness.

Cholesterol

Cholesterol is a fat-like substance found in the body cells of all animals. It is found only in foods of animal origin, such as meat, milk and milk products, eggs, and lard. Cholesterol is needed by humans to produce hormones, cell membranes, bile and vitamin D.

The human body makes all the cholesterol it needs. Dietary factors influence the amount of cholesterol the body produces. Saturated fats from any source tend to cause an increase in the amount of cholesterol in the blood.

Factors that increase the risk of having high blood cholesterol levels include:

- A diet high in total fat, particularly saturated fat
- A diet low in fiber
- Lack of exercise
- Obesity
- Smoking
- A significant family history of heart disease

Reducing total fat in the diet, increasing fiber, stopping smoking, losing weight, and exercising have been shown to lower serum cholesterol levels in many people.

Vitamins

Vitamins are essential nutrients needed by the body in very small amounts. Vitamins assist in regulating body functions. They do not supply energy, but some are needed to help the body use energy. Refer to Appendix B for descriptions of vitamins.

There are two classes of vitamins: fat soluble and water soluble. **Fat-soluble vitamins,** which include vitamins A, D, E, and K, are stored and carried in fat. Fat-soluble vitamins can be toxic if taken in large amounts over a period of time. **Water-soluble vitamins,** which include the B vitamins and vitamin C, dissolve in water. They cannot be stored by the body in significant amounts and must be replaced every day.

Balanced diets usually provide adequate amounts of vitamins for healthy people. It is not usually necessary to take vitamin supplements. Large doses of even water-soluble vitamins taken over long periods of time may be unhealthy.

Minerals

Minerals are essential elements needed by the body in very small amounts. They are classified as major minerals and trace minerals. **Major minerals** are those present in the body in amounts greater than 5 grams. Examples of major minerals are calcium and potassium. **Trace minerals** are those present in the body in amounts less than 5 grams. Examples of minor minerals are iron, zinc, and copper.

They function with other substances or with other minerals in various body processes or as part of the structure of the body. Mineral supplements should not be taken without consulting a doctor. Taking large amounts of certain minerals may cause an imbalance in other minerals. Minerals do not supply energy. Refer to Appendix B for descriptions of minerals.

Water

Water is essential to life. The human body is made up of about 60 percent water. Water is involved in chemical reactions, lubrication, and temperature regulation, as well as providing the medium for the transport of nutrients.

It is recommended that the healthy adult consume eight to ten 8-ounce cups of water each day. This can come from any substance that is mostly water and does not contain caffeine or significant amounts of alcohol (caffeine and alcohol cause the body to eliminate water through the kidneys). Juices, gelatin, milk, soups, and ices are good sources of water. They provide calories and are not 100-percent water. Water is calorie-free. Water requirements increase when the surrounding temperature is high, with strenuous physical activity for more than 30 minutes, and when a person urinates often (people taking water-elimination pills, for example).

Recommended Dietary Allowances

The RDAs, developed by the National Research Council of the Food and Nutrition Board of the National Academy of Sciences, are estimates of the amounts of several of the nutrients needed for good health. The RDAs are presented in Appendix B. The RDI (Reference Daily Intakes) found on food product labels is the highest RDA for the nutrient.

Diet for a Healthy Lifestyle

The word *diet* refers to the food and drink that a person usually consumes. Key principles for a diet for a healthy lifestyle are balance, moderation, and variety.

United States Department of Agriculture Dietary Guidelines

The Dietary Guidelines for Americans, produced by the United States Department of Agriculture (USDA) and the

United States Department of Health and Human Services, were developed to offer practical advice on how to eat to maintain good health. The following recommendations were made:

- Eat a variety of foods.
- Balance the food you eat with physical activity; maintain or improve your weight.
- Choose a diet with plenty of grain products, legumes, vegetables, and fruits.
- Choose a diet low in fat, saturated fat, and cholesterol.
- Choose a diet moderate in sugars.
- Choose a diet moderate in salt and sodium.
- If you drink alcoholic beverages, do so in moderation.

These guidelines reflect the recommendations of the American Cancer Society, the American Dietetic Association, and the American Heart Association. The guidelines recognize the role of the vegetarian diet, which can meet the RDAs of nutrients.

The Food Guide Pyramid

The Food Guide Pyramid, developed by the USDA, illustrates the importance of variety and moderation in the diet:

- The broad base of the pyramid conveys the message that grains should be abundant in the diet (6 to 11 servings per day).
- Fruits and vegetables are on the second level from the bottom, indicating that they are still important, but not as prominent in the diet (2 to 4 servings and 3 to 5 servings per day, respectively).
- Products from the milk and meat groups are on the third level, denoting that just a few servings will contribute the recommended amount of nutrients (2 to 3 servings per day for each group).
- Fats, oils, and sweets occupy the top of the pyramid, emphasizing that they should be consumed sparingly (see Figure 2–1 on page 22).

Vegetarianism

Knowledge in and preparation of vegetarian meals are a necessary component of the chef's culinary training because of their increasing popularity. People choose vegetarian diets for many reasons, including health benefits, ethics, cultural beliefs, religious beliefs, and economics.

Vegetarians are generally categorized not by their motivations, but by the foods they choose not to eat. The three current categories of vegetarians are

- *Vegan:* consumption of plant-origin food only
- *Lacto:* consumption of plant-origin foods plus dairy products
- *Lacto-Ovo:* consumption of plant-origin foods plus dairy and eggs

Vegetarian diets are usually high in fiber and complex carbohydrates, low in fat, and, with careful planning, adequate in protein. Vegan diets may be low in such nutrients as calcium, iron, zinc, vitamin D and vitamin B_{12}. For vegan diets to be adequate in protein, they must include selections and careful combinations of legumes, grains, and seeds throughout the day (see Figure 2–2 on page 22 for a sample vegan meal).

Recipe Modification

The ability to break down a recipe into its nutritional components is essential to understanding the fundamentals of recipe modification. The foodservice industry must be able to meet the demands of the increasingly health-conscious consumer. People consume food because it tastes good, not necessarily because it is healthfully prepared. The goal of future chefs should be to acquire and use the skills needed to make a meal healthful, palatable, and appealing to the senses.

Steps in the Recipe Modification Process

Step 1. Identify ingredient(s) that need adjustment. *Adjustment* can refer to increasing or decreasing the quantity of an ingredient used, or substituting another ingredient

Figure 2–1 The Food Guide Pyramid

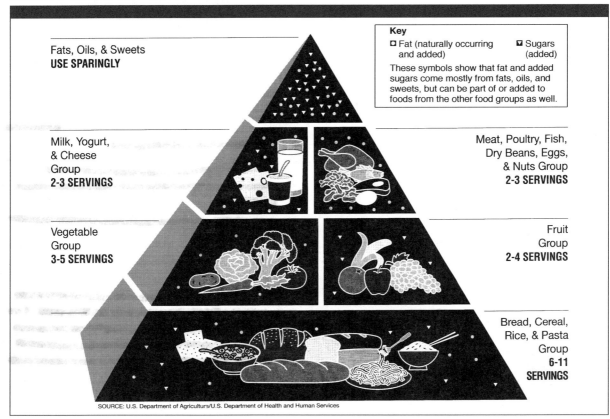

SOURCE: U.S. Department of Agriculture/U.S. Department of Health and Human Services

in its place. It does not necessarily mean that the ingredient has to be eliminated from the recipe; doing so often changes the characteristics of the final product so much that it loses sensory appeal and palatability. During the identification process, concentrate on increasing such ingredients as complex carbohydrates and dietary fiber, while reducing total fat, saturated fat, cholesterol, sodium, and protein.

Figure 2–2 A sample vegan meal

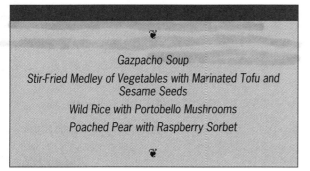

Gazpacho Soup

Stir-Fried Medley of Vegetables with Marinated Tofu and Sesame Seeds

Wild Rice with Portobello Mushrooms

Poached Pear with Raspberry Sorbet

Step 2. Determine the function or purpose of that ingredient in the recipe. Each ingredient in a recipe lends to the characteristics of the final product. It may add flavor, bind ingredients together, provide color, or tenderize the product. Whatever the purpose, identifying the function of the ingredient is imperative (see Table 2–4 for nutrients and their functions in food and recipes). Note that the same ingredient may have different functions in a different recipe, and that the ingredient may perform more than one function in the same recipe. All functions

Table 2–4 Functions of Nutrients in Food and Recipes

Fat	
Function	Example
Sensory	Butter
Tenderizer	Marbling in meat
Heat conductor	Oil in sautéing
Starch separation	Butter in roux
Sealing	Basting with fat
Lubrication	Coating pans with fat

Complex Carbohydrates	
Function	Example
Thickening	Flour in roux, water-soluble fiber, oat bran
Structure	Flour in cake and bread
Texture	Vegetables in recipes, water-insoluble fiber skins, seeds
Moisture retention	Applesauce in baking
Maillard browning	Toast

Simple Carbohydrates	
Function	Example
Sensory	Sugar in candy
Moisture retention	Quick breads
Caramelization	Butterscotch candy
Delays protein coagulation	Sugar in custard
Leavening	Creaming sugar and butter in cakes, food for yeast
Texture	Cake
Preservation	Dehydrates
Stabilizing egg foams	Meringues

Protein	
Function	Example
Thickening/gels	Egg protein in custard; raft in consommé
Moisture retention	Increases shelf life
Structure	Gluten in flour
Maillard browning	Browning meat
Leavening	Beaten egg white
Tenderizing	Enzymes

Salt	
Function	Example
Flavor enhancer	Tomato juice
Preservation	Bacon
Leavening	Bread
Lowers freezing point	Frozen desserts
Slows down protein coagulation	Custards

Eggs	
Function	Example
Binder	Meatballs
Thickener	Custard
Coating	Egg wash
Color	Yellow cake
Flavor	Egg noodles
Leavening	Egg foams
Emulsification	Hollandaise sauce

must be clearly identified before substitutions can be made.

Step 3. Substitute appropriate ingredients. There are three main ways a recipe can be modified:

- Increase or decrease the amount of a particular ingredient used in the recipe.
- Alter the original ingredients by substitution; the replacement must give similar results (function, sensory appeal) as the original ingredient.
- Evaluate the cooking method or method of preparation of the recipe.

Step 4. Evaluate the recipe for sensory desirability before production. Often, the original characteristic taste, texture, aroma, or mouth feel of a food is lost when a recipe is modified. Chefs need to keep in mind that customers choose to eat food that is flavorful, attractively presented, and nutritious. Some recipes may be better left alone, while, in others, major changes may be made without sacrificing sensory appeal. The use of fresh herbs, spices, wine, and lemon are just a few examples of how the sensory appeal of a food can be enhanced through seasoning without excessive amounts of fat, salt, or sodium. The chef plays an integral role alongside the nutrition expert, such as a Registered Dietitian, to produce a meal that is palatable, attractive, and nutritionally well-balanced.

Nutrition in the Foodservice Industry

Current Nutritional Trends

Current consumer trends in nutrition reflect the dietary guidelines. Surveys conducted by the National Restaurant Association show an increase in the number of consumers committed to health and nutrition and that the major concerns are reducing calories, total fats, saturated fats, and cholesterol. The population of the United States is aging. With age come concerns regarding high blood pressure, diabetes, and heart disease. The risks of developing each of these are associated with dietary habits and lifestyles. The consumption of red meats is down, while the consumption of poultry and seafood has risen.

The National Restaurant Association predicts that the trend toward reducing fat and calories will continue. Surveys also show, however, that people continue to order for taste more than any other factor. The challenge is to produce food that not only meets the dietary guidelines but also appeals to the senses.

The foodservice industry cannot force consumers to select healthful foods. It is the chef's responsibility to provide variety and healthful choices in a pleasing, appetizing way. It is the consumer's responsibility to select a balanced diet.

Guidelines for Meeting Nutritional Principles

The following list highlights practical ways food service professionals can meet nutritional principles.

1. **Plan the menu carefully.** Plan the menu to include nutritional items that complement the rest of the menu, the style of the restaurant, and the preferences of the patrons. Highlight these items in some way so interested patrons can find them easily. This allows the patron to select a variety of foods that meet his or her nutritional needs.

2. **Select nutritional recipes or modify recipes to make them more nutritious.** The following methods can help to reduce total fat, saturated fat, cholesterol, and calories:

   a. *Reduce the total fat used.* The amount of fat and oil specified in a recipe can generally be cut in half without changing the flavor.

      i. Experiment with the recipe by gradually reducing the amount of fat or oil used each time.

      ii. Stir-fry or sauté in a small amount of oil, replace oil with broth (which changes the cooking temperature and technique to a moist method), or use a well-seasoned pan and omit the oil.

   b. *Change the cooking method.* In some cases, fat can be eliminated by changing the cooking method. Roasting, baking, broiling without added fats, steaming, *en papillote,* poaching, simmering, blanching, and microwaving are examples of low-fat cooking methods.

   c. *Modify techniques to achieve nutritional goals.* Cook meat or poultry on a rack so the fat will drain off.

   d. *Reduce hidden fats in ingredients.*

      i. Chill meat or poultry broth until the fat becomes solid. Spoon off the fat before using the broth. Finish the removal of fat by floating paper towels on the surface of the broth.

      ii. Trim the fat from meat and remove the skin from poultry.

      iii. Use some of the substitutions listed in Table 2–5.

      iv. Replace high-fat sauces with *coulis*-based and reduced sauces.

   e. *Use alternative ingredients to season foods.*

      i. Use herbs, spices, or wine rather than sauces, butter, or margarine (see Chapter 5).

Table 2–5 Cooking Methods

High Fat	Low Fat
Frying	Broiling
Roasting while basting with fat	Baking or roasting
	Steaming
Cooking with fatty sauces and gravies	Grilling
	Microwaving
Sautéing with large amounts of fat	Braising
	Boiling
	Simmering
	Sautéing or stir-frying with small amount of oil

  ii. Use low-fat marinades to add flavor and moisture and to tenderize meats, poultry, and seafood.
 f. *Reduce saturated fats.*
  i. Replace part of the butter in a recipe with an oil.
  ii. Use flavorful oil such as olive oil or peanut oil. Because these are rich in flavor, less is needed.
  iii. Use margarine instead of butter (to at least eliminate the cholesterol). Reduced-calorie margarine contains water and may not be appropriate for all recipes (for example, sautéing).
 g. *Increase dietary fiber.* Use whole-grain flours to enhance the flavor of reduced-fat baked goods.
 h. *Alter egg products in recipes whenever possible.*
  i. Try substituting egg whites in recipes calling for whole eggs. However, egg whites do not contain emulsifiers, so they cannot be substituted when the whole egg is needed for that function.
  ii. Try using a commercial egg substitute in recipes not requiring emulsifiers, or eliminate only some of the yolks. Egg substitutes often contain more water than fresh whole eggs, so this may not be a viable substitution in certain baked goods, unless the recipe is adjusted accordingly.
 i. *Gradually introduce entrées containing less meat.*

  i. Take advantage of the popularity of ethnic foods to feature dishes that use rice, pasta, or other grains in place of or in combination with small portions of meats.
  ii. Offer low-fat meatless entrées such as grilled vegetables with couscous.
  iii. Offer entrées featuring fish more often.
 j. *Reduce portion size.*
  i. Most Americans are accustomed to large portions of meat, poultry, and seafood. Limit portion size to 3 to 4 ounces (cooked).
  ii. Replace the protein food with grains, pasta, vegetables, or legumes.
  iii. When reducing portion size, it may be necessary to select menus that camouflage the reduced amount, such as stir-fry beef with vegetables and oriental noodles, or shish kabob.
  iv. Purchase high-quality fresh produce and lower-fat meats. Refer to Table 2–6 on page 26.
  v. Use a variety of colors, textures, and shapes to enhance the eye appeal of the dish. The variety in texture also helps replace some of the high-fat ingredients and adds interest to the meal.

About 43 percent of American food dollars are spent on food prepared away from home. This places some of the responsibility for the nation's health on the foodservice industry. The foodservice industry is market driven, and that market is experiencing a greater demand for more healthful foods that not only are delicious but are presented with flair and art. Today's chef must meet this responsibility and these demands if he or she is to be successful. The chef must be able to provide appealing and healthful choices as well as traditional foods. It is toward this end that nutrition has been integrated throughout the chapters and recipes in this text.

Managing Nutrients in Food Preparation

In order to deliver the most nutritious product to the customer, it is critical, when preparing food, to maintain the

Table 2–6 Guidelines for Selecting Foods for Low–Total-Fat, Low–Saturated-Fat, and Low-Cholesterol Menu Items

Foods	Use Most Often	Use in Limited Amounts	Use Only Occasionally
Meats			
Beef	Lean cuts; select or choice grades; round	Lean ground; 10 percent or less fat; trimmed veal	Prime grades; regular ground, marbled, fatty cuts; hot dogs; luncheon meats; organ meats
Poultry	Without sauce; lean ground		Duck; goose
Lamb	Leg; loin; shoulder		
Pork	Tenderloin; leg; shoulder; picnic; Canadian bacon		Bacon; sausage; ribs
Fish and shellfish	Fish and shellfish		
Cheese	Low fat, with less than 3 grams of fat per ounce	Part-skim ricotta, mozzarella; reduced-fat cream cheese	Whole milk; cream cheese
Eggs	Whites; cholesterol-free egg substitutes		Yolks
Dairy			
Milk	Skim; 1 percent fat; low-fat buttermilk; evaporated skim milk	2 percent fat	Whole milk
Sour cream	Nonfat yogurt; nonfat sour cream	Low-fat yogurt; reduced-fat sour cream	Custard-style whole milk yogurt; sour cream; half & half; most nondairy creamers; whipped cream; nondairy toppings
Desserts	Nonfat frozen yogurt; nonfat ice milk	Sherbet; ice milk	Ice cream
Breads	Breads (especially whole grain); lean dough rolls; plain pasta; rice; low-fat crackers	Quick breads	Rich dough and sweet rolls; doughnuts; puff pastry; croissants; high-fat crackers; pasta made with egg yolks
Cereals	Most cereals; barley; quinoa; bulgur; pretzels; popcorn	Reduced-fat granola	Granola cereals made with saturated oils or coconut
Legumes	Dried peas; beans; soy; tofu		Legumes prepared with fat
Fruits and vegetables	Fresh, frozen, canned, or dried fruits and vegetables	Avocados	Coconut
Dessert items	Nonfat yogurt; nonfat ice milk; Jello; fat-free cakes; angel food cake; low-fat cookies such as ginger snaps, graham crackers, nonfat cookies; fruit ices; sorbet; poached or baked fruits	Ice milk; sherbet; frozen tofu; reduced-fat cakes, cookies, and pies; cobblers; low-fat fruit crisps; reduced-fat whipped toppings	Ice cream; frozen tofu; regular cakes, pies, fruit crisps, cookies
Fats and oils	Mono- and polyunsaturated vegetable oils; soft margarine made with unsaturated oil; reduced-fat spreads; nonfat salad dressings and mayonnaise	Olives; avocados; nuts; seeds; reduced-fat salad dressings	Butter; coconut palm, palm kernel oils; lard; beef tallow; bacon fat; hydrogenated oils; hard margarines; regular salad dressings and mayonnaise
Miscellaneous	Carob; cocoa powder		Chocolate; cocoa butter; carob chips

integrity of the nutrients in both the individual ingredients and final product. The following list highlights a variety of methods that may be employed to preserve this integrity.

- Purchase good-quality fresh products.
- Store foods under proper conditions for the shortest time possible.
- Serve fruits and vegetables in the fresh state whenever possible.
- Minimize cooking and holding time.
- Keep foods as whole as much as possible to minimize exposed surface area of foods. Retain the skin whenever possible.
- Use the least amount of water possible during cooking to minimize leaching of minerals and water-soluble vitamins.

- Reduce exposure to heat and water by cooking in small batches.
- Avoid using baking soda to enhance the color of vegetables, as it will destroy some B vitamins and change the product's texture.
- Control time, temperature, and exposure to ultraviolet light.
- Maximize recommended cooking methods naturally low in fat. *Dry:* Bake, roast (this adds flavor to vegetables), broil, or sauté in the minimum amount of fat using a well-seasoned pan or a small amount of broth. *Moist:* Steam or microwave. If poaching, braising, simmering, or stewing, reserve and use cooking liquids in sauces. Skim off any fat before use.

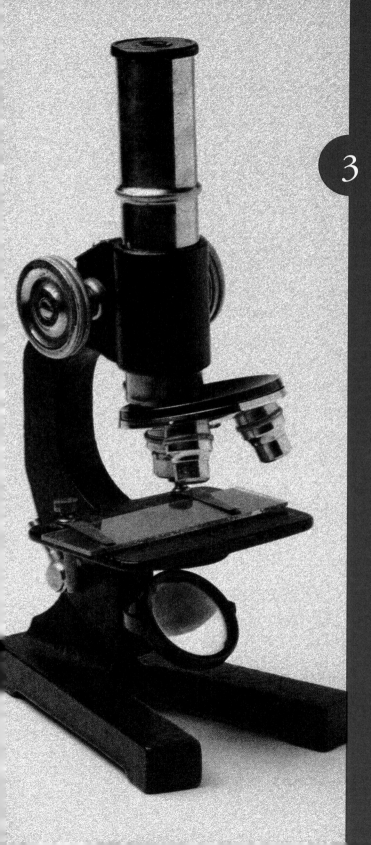

3

Sanitation

Sanitation

The word **sanitation** *is derived from the word* **sanus***, meaning sound and healthy or clean and whole. The modern interpretation of the term is broad, including knowledge of health and sanitary conditions as well as the full acceptance and effective application of sanitary measures. Today, more than ever, the chef has to prepare food in a safe and clean environment. State and local government regulations require foodservice management to employ a foodservice employee, whether the chef or manager, who has passed a state certification sanitation course.*

Bacteria

To understand the implications of good sanitation in the foodservice industry, one needs to become familiar with the study of microbiology. *Microbiology* is the study of small physical life such as bacteria, which is what causes food-borne illnesses. Bacteria have the following characteristics:

- They are single-cell plants.
- They are invisible to the naked eye.
- Some survive with oxygen (*aerobic*), some without oxygen (*anaerobic*), and others can survive with or without oxygen (*facultative*).
- They can survive in temperatures outside the temperature danger zone (*TDZ*, 40° to 140° F).
- They grow in number, not in physical size.
- They are classified as harmful (pathogenic) or beneficial.
- They need the correct amount of nutrients (food), moisture, time and temperature, and acidity/alkalinity (pH) level to survive.

Environmental Elements

Bacterial growth (reproduction) will increase in numbers sufficient to cause illness in the TDZ if it remains there for four hours or more. Although four hours is the allotted time, food should be prepared quickly. The increase in the number of bacteria during this time is what causes food-borne illness in humans. Temperature controls and time limits must be adhered to in order to prevent bacterial growth.

For most bacteria to grow in number, or multiply, the following elements are required:

- Moisture above 0.85 on the water activity (A_w) scale.
- Oxygen or no oxygen (facultative bacteria).
- Temperature range of 40° to 140°F (TDZ).

- A pH greater than 4.6 acidity to 9 alkalinity.
- Food for energy. Most of these foods—commonly referred to as *potentially hazardous foods*—are high usually in protein and moisture, and low in pH; for example, milk, meats, poultry, fish, and seafood. However, fruits and vegetables have also been implicated in food-borne illnesses.

To control the amount of bacteria in foods, the chef needs to eliminate at least one of the environmental elements.

Pathogenic Microorganisms

Harmful bacteria cause illness. Typical symptoms of food-borne illness caused by bacteria and viruses include:

- Nausea
- Abdominal pain
- Dizziness
- Chills
- Fever
- Dry mouth
- Vomiting
- Diarrhea
- Headache
- Prostration (occasionally)

Table 3–1 on page 32 lists some prevalent food-borne and water-borne diseases, the foods involved, and their control measures.

Controlling Food-borne and Water-borne Diseases

Some food-borne and water-borne illnesses can be caused by harmful bacteria and viruses spread by unsanitary food handlers. The first step in controlling harmful bacteria is to practice good personal hygiene in the foodservice establishment. The following is a personal-hygiene checklist:

Table 3–1 Food-borne and Water-borne Diseases

Disease	Foods Involved	Control Measures
Salmonellosis	Meat, poultry, eggs and their products; other incriminated foods include coconut, yeast, cottonseed protein, smoked fish, dry milk, and chocolate candy	Chill foods rapidly in small quantities. Cook foods thoroughly. Pasteurize egg products and milk. Avoid cross-contamination from raw to cooked foods. Wash hands after touching raw meat. Sanitize equipment. Heat-treat food and food ingredients. Process meat and poultry in a sanitary manner. Maintain poultry farm sanitation. Practice good personal hygiene.
Shigellosis (bacillary dysentery)	Moist, mixed food; potato, tuna, shrimp, turkey, and macaroni salads; milk, beans, apple cider, potato salad, and green salads.	Practice good personal hygiene. Dispose of sewage in a sanitary manner. Chill foods rapidly in small quantities. Prepare food in a sanitary manner; avoid touching foods that are not to be cooked. Cook foods thoroughly. Protect and treat water. Control flies.
Staphylococcal intoxication (staphyloentero-toxicosis, staphylococcus food poisoning)	Cooked ham, meat products; poultry and dressing; sauces and gravy; creamed potato, fish salad, milk, cheese, bread pudding; high-protein leftover food	Chill foods rapidly in small quantities. Prepare foods the day of serving whenever possible. If ill (diarrhea, colds, infected cuts), restrict from work. Sanitize equipment. Thorough cooking, reheating, or pasteurizing destroys the organism but not the toxin.
E. coli 1957:H7, enteritis	Raw or undercooked ground beef, unpasteurized milk, imported cheeses	Cook ground beef to an internal temperature of 155° F. Avoid cross-contamination. Practice good personal hygiene.
Clostridium perfringens	Cooked meat or poultry, gravy, stew, meat pies and leftovers	Chill food rapidly in small quantities. Prepare foods the day of serving whenever possible. Use clean pans for storage. Hold hot foods at 140° F or above. Practice good personal hygiene. Cure meats adequately. Dispose of sewage in a sanitary manner. Thorough cooking will destroy vegetative cells but not heat-resistant spores. Reheat leftover food to 165° F or above.
Norwalk virus, gastroenteritis (epidemic diarrhea, sewage poisoning, winter vomiting disease)	Oysters, cockles; any food contaminated with feces	Practice good personal hygiene. Dispose of sewage in a sanitary manner. Protect and treat water. Prepare food in a sanitary manner. Cook food thoroughly.
Hepatitis A, non-B hepatitis, infectious hepatitis	Any food contaminated with feces.	Prevent pollution of shellfish-growing areas. Dispose of sewage in a sanitary manner. Treat water by coagulation-settling-filtration-chlorination. Practice good personal hygiene. Cook foods thoroughly. Isolate cases for 7 to 10 days after jaundice.

1. Wear a clean uniform and apron.
2. Keep hair clean; wear hairnet or hat to keep hair off ears and collar.
3. Neatly trim mustaches; beards are not permissable.
4. Keep fingernails clean and short. Do not wear fingernail polish or false fingernails.
5. Wash hands before work and throughout the day; it is imperative to wash hands after
   a. Touching skin or hair.
   b. Coughing or sneezing.
   c. Using the toilet.
   d. Smoking.
   e. Using a handkerchief or tissue.
   f. Handling soiled dishes or tableware.
   g. Handling inventory.
6. Bathe daily.
7. Never serve food if you have an open cut or sore; cover cuts and sores with a bandage and gloves.
8. Do not report to work when ill with vomiting, diarrhea or respiratory infection.
9. Avoid smoking or chewing gum at the work station.

Hazard Analysis Critical Control Point System

The Hazard Analysis Critical Control Point (HACCP) System was established by the Pillsbury Company in 1971 for the National Aeronautics and Space Administration (NASA). The primary purpose of HACCP is to ensure that food served to the customer is safe.

All foods in a foodservice operation pass through a number of critical areas, including receiving, storage, preparation, cooking, holding, servicing, cooling, and reheating. At each step, contamination is possible. The foodservice operator must identify the critical control points as foods flow through the operation. The flow of the food is the path that foods travel in an establishment. The sequence includes the following:

- Choosing an item to include on the menu
- Developing the recipe
- Procuring ingredients

- Receiving the food order
- Storing the food order
- Preparing the food
- Holding (hot or cold) food
- Serving the food
- Cooling and storing
- Reheating

Each of the sections in Volume III includes a recipe flowchart that indicates how to apply the HACCP system in each particular food section.

The Seven Steps of HACCP

1. Assess hazards. The hazards most frequently found

- Contaminated raw foods.
- Cross-contamination.
- Improper cooking.
- Improper holding.
- Improper cooling.
- Improper reheating.
- Poor personal hygiene.
- Improper cleaning and sanitizing of equipment.

Any one of these hazards can lead to food-borne illness outbreak. Therefore, the foodservice manager and chef must have sanitation systems in place to prevent any outbreaks from occurring in their establishment.

2. Identify Critical Control Points (CCPs). Critical Control Points are points in the food-preparation process where contamination can occur. Two examples of CCPs are cooking and cooling; any other hazards listed in Step 1 could also be considered. Cooking is a CCP because cooking food thoroughly kills *vegetative bacteria*. Rapid cooling, on the other hand, prevents bacterial growth.

3. Establish standards and procedures for CCPs. *Standards* are developed based on research, food regulations, and past experience. All standards must be measurable and observable; for example, temperature and time control. See Table 3–2 for HACCP guidelines for

Table 3-2 HACCP Guidelines

Food	Internal Cooking Temperatures
Beef, roasts (rare)	140° F; temperature maintained for 12 minutes
Beef, roasts (rare)	130° F; temperature maintained for 121 minutes
Beef, ground	155° F
Veal	140° F
Poultry	165° F
Pork	145° F
Bacon	145° F
Sausage	145° F
Ham	145° F
Game (e.g., venison)	145° F
Lamb	140° F
Liver	140° F
All stuffed meats	165° F
Fish	145° F
Stuffed pasta and vegetables	165° F
Eggs	145° F
Leftovers	165° F

Cook milk- or cream-based soups (e.g., New England clam chowder, cream of broccoli) to a minimum temperature of 165° F.
Cook stews and seafood chowders to a minimum temperature of 165° F.
Ensure that the internal holding temperature for all foods is a minimum of 140° F.
Reheat all foods to a minimum temperature of 165° F.

internal cooking temperatures. *Procedures* are the steps taken to measure and observe the standards for each CCP. For example, all poultry should be cooked to a minimum internal temperature of 165° F. This procedure must be followed and documented in a log and is a standard that should be set up in every foodservice operation to prevent food-borne illness caused by salmonella.

4. Monitor CCPS. The chef or manager should implement the HACCP system in the foodservice establishment, creating checks and balances to ensure that the CCPs are being followed by employees and their immediate supervisors. For example, the temperature of a turkey breast should be monitored when received and the proper temperature of 40° F or below should be maintained throughout storage. Also, cross-contamination could conceivably

occur during this time. Raw turkey breast should be stored below previously cooked foods and any ready-to-eat foods such as salads. The chef or manager is directly responsible for making sure that each of these CCPs is monitored daily.

5. Take corrective action. When a CCP is not being followed, corrective action must be taken by the chef or manager. For example, a cook is found thawing a 3–5 pound chicken in water warmer than 70° F. The chef should bring corrective action by instructing the cook to thaw the chicken under refrigeration instead.

6. Develop a record-keeping system. Record-keeping systems can include flow charts, policy and procedure manuals, written logs, and spot-checks of temperatures. The record system should be easily implemented, simple to follow, and not time consuming. Logs should be completed at the end of each shift or meal period by the cook in charge.

7. Verify that the HACCP system is working. To determine that the standards and procedures are effective, the flow of food through the operation should be traced at the end of each shift by the chef or manager. For example, examine the logs of temperature and time, note errors, and any corrective action taken to evaluate the overall program. If necessary, take actions to revise the system.

Kitchen Control Points

Receiving

When receiving the food, the quality and condition of food products delivered should be carefully examined in the case of a large delivery, perishable products should be stored immediately. For example, fresh poultry should be stored before canned goods.

Food Storage

Storage of food must be done properly to prevent contamination, spoilage, and the growth of harmful bacteria. There types of storage: dry, refrigerated, and frozen. Temperature control is critical in all three areas. All perishable foods should be kept out of the TDZ as much as possible to prevent bacteria growth.

Dry Storage

Dry storage is designed for foods that do not require refrigeration and that have a relatively long shelf life. All food products in the dry storage area should be wrapped or covered, labeled, and dated. Store food products 6 inches off the floor and 6 inches away from the wall. The ideal temperature of dry storage is 50° F to 60° F with a 60 to 70 per cent relative humidity. The tmperature should be checked at least three times a day or after every shift.

Refrigerated Storage

All foods stored in the refrigerator should be labeled and dated. Most food products need to be kept at temperatures between 36° F and 40° F. Visible thermometers need to be checked at least four times a day.

Do not store food products near entrances to the cooling units, and open the doors for as short a time as possible. Shelving should be stainless steel and have open grates, which is easy to clean. The floors must be made of an approved material, such as quarry tile, and cleaned at least twice a day or as needed.

To prolong the shelf life of a product, use the First In, First Out (FIFO) inventory system. Chill foods by using an ice bath or by placing a product into a watertight plastic bag and then submerging the product into an ice bath. A 6-inch deep steam table pan of sliced beef and gravy at 140° F takes 23 hours to reach 45° F in a 38° F holding refrigerator, plenty of time for bacteria to multiply (see Table 3–3). All food needs to be wrapped or covered, labeled, and dated; for example: Ham, 20 lbs., received 9/6/97. Store food products 6 inches off the floor and 6 inches away from the wall. Store cooked foods and raw ingredients separately to prevent cross-contamination. Keep cooked foods above raw ingredients.

Freezer Storage

All frozen-food products should be kept at a maximum of 0° F. Visible thermometers must be checked four times a day. Store food products 6 inches off the floor and 6 inches away from the wall.

Carefully wrap and label leftovers to prevent freezer burn. Thawing foods from the freezer is safer and more efficient if the product is placed in the refrigerator, rather

Table 3-3 Cooling Times, in Hours

Food	Steam Table Pan Deep		
	2 Inches	4 Inches	6 Inches
Beef stew	12	16	22
Broccoli	7	9½	14
Broth	5	8	12
Chicken and turkey à la king	10	14	22
Cream of pea soup	10	13½	18
Gravy	11	14	21
Lasagna	11	17	21
Mashed potatoes	12	16	22
Peas	6	9	13
Sliced beef and gravy	10	13	23
Swiss steak with tomato sauce	13	17	20

than at room temperature. Thawing may take longer this way, but the food product is kept out of the TDZ and bacterial growth is minimized.

Preparation and Food Handling

During the preparation control point, there are two major concerns. First, food is normally in the TDZ for a period of time, which exposes the food product to rapid bacterial growth. Second, cross-contamination of food can occur in two ways: when the food product comes into contact with hands or with a contaminated piece of equipment such as cutting boards or knives, or when cooked foods come into contact with raw foods.

To avoid cross-contamination during preparation and food handling, use recommended utensils such as tongs, spatulas, deli paper or plastic gloves rather than hands, which may carry bacteria and viruses. Equipment, cutting boards, and table surfaces must be cleaned and sanitized.

Select all raw ingredients and wash fresh fruits and vegetables before preparing any recipe. Wash root vegetables and starches both before and after peeling.

Cooking

All foods should be cooked to the minimum appropriate internal temperature according to the HACCP Guidelines found in Table 3–2.

Holding

To maintain product quality during the holding stage, the holding temperature and time control must be monitored. Whenever possible, cook foods *a la minute* (just before needed) to avoid the holding stage. Thermometers for monitoring internal temperatures should be accurate and *calibrated.* Foods should be kept hot for service by using steam tables or other holding equipment that will keep all foods above 140° F. Personnel should replenish steam

tables every 15 to 30 minutes so product deterioration does not occur. If the food drops below 140° F the product needs to be reheated to 165° F.

Reheating

Reheat all foods to a minimum internal temperature of 165° F before serving. The steam table should not be used to heat cold foods for service within 2 hours.

Cooling

Cooling food is an important stage in controlling bacterial growth. HACCP guidelines require that all foods be cooled in a two-tiered cooling curve:

1. 140° F to 70° F within 2 hours **then**
2. 70° F to 41° F within 4 hours.

Most jurisdictions still accept a total of 4 hours of cooling time, providing the internal temperature drops from 140° F to 40° F in that period of time.

Cleaning and Sanitizing

Cleaning means the removal of soil or dirt that is out of place. Sanitizing destroys pathogens that remain on equipment and utensils even after cleaning.

Mechanical Dishwashing

There are numerous dishwashing machines on the market that are designed for the foodservice industry. Following is a general procedure that should be used when operating such equipment:

1. Scrape and rinse soiled dishes and presoak flatware.
2. Prerinse to remove all visible food and soil.
3. Rack dishes and flatware so the water will spray all surfaces.

4. Run machine for a full cycle.
   a. Machine wash water: 150° to 160° F
   b. Rinse water: 160° to 180° F
   c. Final rinse sanitizing: 180° to 195° F
   d. Air dry dishes and flatware
5. Do not touch dish surfaces that will come into contact with the food.
6. Store dishes and flatware in a clean, dry area.

Manual Dishwashing

The following procedure should be used when washing dishes by hand:

1. Scrape and prerinse.
2. Wash in warm water at 110° F.
3. Rinse using clear, potable hot water (120° F) to remove detergent; change water when needed.
4. Sanitize in hot (170° F) water (some states require 180° F) for a minimum of one (1) minute or in a chemical solution (using iodine, chlorine or QUATS) at a minimum of 75° F.
5. Drain.
6. Air dry and store.

Utensils

Use the same procedure for cleaning utensils as for manual dishwashing. Do not use steel wool or scouring pads. products may cause nicks or scratches allowing bacteria to remain. In addition, steel wool may remain on pots or pans and later appear in the food.

Kitchen Equipment

Unplug all equipment before cleaning or sanitizing. All equipment must be taken apart, then each piece cleaned individually and sanitized in the same manner as for kitchen utensils. All work surfaces that come into contact with food must be washed with a cleaning detergent and clean cloths. Sanitize the work surface regularly with clean cloths and the proper sanitizer. Air dry surfaces and reassemble equipment.

Safety

The safety of all personnel in the kitchen should be monitored by the chef or manager, but ultimately it is the responsibility of each employee. Accidents can occur because of lack of training, fatigue, or poor kitchen design or maintenance. Consider the following safety checklist when developing and implementing a safety training program. Ensure that

- Fire extinguishers are in working order and that the inspection tag is attached and up to date.
- Employees have been properly trained on all equipment, especially the deep-fat fryer; the steam equipment, such as steamer and kettles; the broiler, grill, and salamander; and the slicer, mandoline, grinder, food processor, and mixer.
- Safety devices are attached and in proper working order.
- Knife rack(s) are accessible, clean, and in use.
- Cutting boards are cleaned and sanitized after cutting meats, fish, or game, and before using for other food preparation.
- Glassware is handled with caution.
- Aisles and floors are clean and clear of debris.
- Spills are cleaned immediately.
- Hand sinks are properly supplied with hand soap and paper towels and nailbrushes.
- Employees wear proper uniform and shoes (with rubber, nonskid soles).
- Employees lift heavy objects properly (straight back, bent knees).
- First-aid kit or first-aid center (nurse's office) is adequately supplied and in an accessible location.
- Employees have been trained in cardiopulmonary resuscitation (CPR) and the Heimlich maneuver.
- Emergency telephone numbers are posted near all phones.
- Ongoing safety training program has been implemented.
- Employees take breaks to reduce fatigue.

4

Costing and Converting Recipes

4

Costing and Converting Recipes

The **food expense (cost)** *in a foodservice establishment is the total cost of food being purchased and sold.*

Food cost is just one of four major expenses that must be closely monitored to ensure profitability. Some foodservice operations include beverages in this category. The other expenses include the following:

1. *Labor expense* is the total cost of the labor employed in the foodservice establishment.
2. *Overhead expense* is broken down into two categories:
   a. *Controllable,* those expenses that do not fluctuate because of sales; for example, insurance, uniforms, equipment, water, electricity, and laundry.
   b. *Uncontrollable,* those expenses that do fluctuate with sales; for example, advertising and rent. Rent is an expense that could possibly exist in both categories of controllable *and* uncontrollable expenses. Rent would be considered controllable if each month the establishment paid a fixed amount of money for the use of the property. However, it is uncontrollable if the establishment must pay rent based on a percentage of sales each month.
3. *Profit expense* is an *accrual expense* before any cash flow or sales occur in the restaurant. As soon as a sales transaction has taken place, and all other expenses have been paid, profit no longer needs to be allocated to an expense but is considered an asset to the foodservice operation.

To control food costs, the establishment should develop and implement standards. Standards are criteria that are set up by the chef or manager and are followed so consistency is achieved in daily operations. In food production, this may involve standardizing recipes. A standardized recipe is one that is written out and has the following characteristics:

- *Quality:* specifications of quality of ingredients.
- *Quantity:* the measure of weight, count, or quantity. The quantity of each ingredient in the recipe should be specific and should be followed closely during preparation to ensure that costs determined for the recipe are accurate.
- *Portion size:* the amount of a food product that will be served to the guest. Portion size may be directly correlated with the concept of the restaurant. For instance, the portion size for menu items at a steak house may be comparatively larger than for those at a fine-dining establishment.
- *Yield:* the number of servings each recipe produces.

Standardizing a recipe helps to ensure that the product will be consistent every time it is made. It is important for cooks, bakers, and servers to understand that the customer expects the same product every time it is purchased. Standards of measurement have been established to guarantee consistency.

When a recipe has been standardized, it needs to be recorded in a format that is easy to use in costing out recipes (see Figures 4–1 on page 42 and 4–2 on page 43, for example). The form contains the following information:

A. Recipe name
B. Recipe identification number
C. Portion size
D. Yield, or number of portions
E. Ingredients
F. Waste percentage
G. Edible product
H. As purchased
I. Unit purchase price
J. Conversion measure
K. Ingredient cost
L. Subtotal recipe cost
M. Q factor, or 1 percent
N. Total recipe cost
O. Portion cost
P. Additional cost
Q. Desired overall food-cost percentage

Figure 4–1 Recipe-costing form

E. Ingredients	F. Waste %	G. Edible Product	H. As Purchased	I. Unit Purchase Price	J. Conversion Measure	K. Ingredient Cost
A. Recipe Name _____ B. Recipe I.D. No. _____						
C. Portion Size _____ D. Yield _____						

L. Subtotal   _____
M. Q Factor   _____
N. Total recipe cost   _____
O. Portion cost   _____
P. Additional cost   _____
Q. Desired overall food cost %   _____
R. Preliminary selling price   _____
S. Actual selling price   _____
T. Actual food cost %   _____

R. Preliminary selling price (based on food-cost percentage)
S. Actual selling price
T. Actual food-cost percentage

Costing

Assigning the Task of Recipe Costing

To accomplish recipe costing, the chef or manager needs to assign someone to be responsible for overseeing the entire process. In most establishments, it is actually the chef or manager who performs this function. The individu-al(s) is responsible for developing and maintaining the standardization and costing system.

Explanation of Each Part of the Recipe-Costing Example in Figure 4–2

A. Recipe name. The name listed here should read exactly as it does on the menu from which the guest will order.

B. Recipe identification number. The number as-signed to indicate the recipe's location in the filing system.

Figure 4–2 Recipe-costing example

A. Recipe Name Swiss Steak in Sour Cream					B. Recipe I.D. No. E-1	
C. Portion Size 8 oz.					D. Yield 10 servings	
E. Ingredients	F. Waste %	G. Edible Product	H. As Purchased	I. Unit Purchase Price	J. Conversion Measure	K. Ingredient Cost
Round steak	3	5.09 lb.	5.25 lb.	$2.25 lb.		$11.81
Salt			¾ tsp.	$0.34 lb.	$\frac{0.75 \text{ tsp.}}{96 \text{ tsp.}} = 0.008$	0.003
Pepper		Q factor	¼ tsp.			Q factor
Paprika			1¼ tsp.	$4.89 lb.	$\frac{1.25 \text{ tsp.}}{96 \text{ tsp.}} = 0.01$	0.05
Flour			¾ cup	$0.26 lb.	$\frac{0.75 \text{ C.}}{2 \text{ C.}} = 0.38$	0.10
Chopped onion	12	¾ cup	6.72 oz.	0.18 lb.	$\frac{6.72 \text{ oz.}}{16 \text{ oz.}} = 0.42$	0.08
Sour cream			¾ cup	1.10 pt.	$\frac{0.75 \text{ C.}}{2 \text{ C.}} = 0.38$	0.42
Boiling water		Q factor				Q factor
Chopped parsley			½ bu.	0.39 bu.	0.5	0.20

L.	Subtotal	$12.67
M.	Q Factor	$ 0.13
N.	Total recipe cost	$12.80
O.	Portion cost	$ 1.28
P.	Additional cost	$ 0.49
Q.	Plate cost	$ 1.77
R.	Desired overall food-cost percentage	$ .40
S.	Preliminary selling price	$ 4.43
T.	Actual selling price	$ 7.95
U.	Actual food-cost percentage	16% portion 56% plate

Each establishment may organize this system differently, and no one format is superior.

C. Portion size. The standard amount that each guest is served when the food item is ordered. Careful measuring is vital during service to ensure that the food-cost figures are accurate.

D. Yield, or number of portions. The number of servings that one preparation of the recipe yields. The yield will ultimately determine the portion cost because the total recipe cost *divided by* the total number of portions *equals* the portion cost. For example,

$$\frac{\$12.93}{10 \text{ servings}} = \$1.29 \text{ per serving}$$

E. Ingredients.   List the ingredients.

F. Waste percentage.   Most recipes call for ingredients that are 100 percent edible, having no waste. However, most fresh food products—poultry, fish, seafood, beef, fruits, and produce—contain a certain percentage of waste. For instance, with poultry, the bones, skin, trim, cartilage, and weight loss from cooking are potential elements of waste.

The chef must calculate the amount of waste a product has to be accurate in the amount of food product to be purchased. For example, if a recipe calls for 3 pounds of 100 percent edible round steak, the chef must take into account the fact that a piece of round steak usually will have excess fat that needs to be trimmed. If the chef does not take this into consideration before purchasing the meat, then he or she will end up with less than 3 pounds of meat, thus altering the yield of the recipe and leaving the cook with less than the six full portions that the recipe should yield.

To calculate the amount of round steak needed for this recipe to yield six portions, the chef must establish the amount of waste the round steak will produce. This is done by conducting a yield test on the round steak. A yield test will give the amount of edible product (EP) and the amount of waste product (WP).

G. Edible-product amount.   The EP amount of the ingredient in the recipe is the amount of a particular ingredient left after the waste product has been removed from the purchased amount. The as-purchased (AP) amount *minus* the waste *equals* the EP amount. For example,

$$5.25 - 0.16 \ (3\% \text{ of } 5.25 = 0.16) = 5.09$$

H. As-purchased amount.   The AP amount is the amount of product that needs to be purchased from the purveyor. When only the AP amount is given or needed in the recipe, it is not necessary to calculate the WP. An example is the salt amount; there is no waste product in salt. If the AP does need to be figured, however, the following formula is necessary:

If

$$AP = \frac{EP \times 100}{100\% - WP\%} =$$

Then

$$AP = \frac{5.09 \times 100}{0.97} = \frac{509}{0.97}$$

Therefore,

$$AP = 5.25 \text{ lb.}$$

To convert decimals into ounces, *multiply* the decimal portion from the EP *by* the ounces per pound, which *equals* the amount in ounces. Based on the example in Figure 4–2:

$$0.09 \times 16 = 1.44 \text{ or } 1.5 \text{ ounces}$$

Therefore, the EP for the Swiss steak equals 5 pounds, 1 1/2 ounces.

When the chef is cutting his or her own round steaks, cutting a 5-pound, 1 1/2-ounce piece is not a problem. Procuring 5 pounds, 1 1/2 ounces from the meat purveyor, however, may be a problem.

The chef should shop around for a meat purveyor who will accept the chef's meat specifications for the round steaks. There are purveyors who will cut meat to any specifications desired at an additional fee. The chef must determine which method is more profitable.

One way the chef can recover the extra cost is to use the waste of the round steak in another food product. The fat trimmed from the round steak can be rendered and used in sautéing other food products, thus reducing the amount of oil to be purchased for sautéing. The point is to recover the additional cost in any way possible to help maintain a lower food cost. Increasing menu prices should be considered only as a last resort.

I. Unit purchase price.   The unit purchase price is the price paid for a particular ingredient. Unit represents the unit of measurement in which the ingredient was purchased, (e.g., lb., box, oz., Each, cup, gallon, quart, etc.).

J. Conversion measure. The conversion-measure column is where the conversion formula and the converting factor are written. The AP unit amount will often be in ounces, while the AP unit will be expressed in pounds. When there are two different units of measure being used (e.g., ounces and pounds) one has to be converted into the same unit of measure as the other. The ingredient amount in the recipe *divided by* the number of ounces in a pound *equals* the conversion measure.

For example, to determine the conversion measure for the portion of chopped onions:

$$\frac{6.72}{16} = 0.42$$

6.72 ozs. is 42% of 16 ozs. Therefore, the cost of the onion is 42% of 0.18 or .42 × 0.18 = 0.08.

K: Ingredient cost. The ingredient-cost column is used to figure out the total cost of the ingredient being used in the recipe. Multiply the conversion measure (or AP) *by* the unit cost, which *equals* the total cost of the ingredient. For example,

Conversion Measure: Onion:

$$
\begin{array}{r}
0.42 \text{ (conversion measure)} \\
\times\ 0.18 \text{ (\textit{multiplied by} unit cost)} \\
\hline
\$\ 0.08 \text{ (\textit{equals} ingredient cost)}
\end{array}
$$

AP: Round steak:

$$
\begin{array}{r}
5.25 \text{ (AP)} \\
\times\ 2.25 \text{ (\textit{multiplied by} unit cost)} \\
\hline
\$11.81 \text{ (\textit{equals} ingredient cost)}
\end{array}
$$

L. Subtotal of the recipe cost. All the ingredient costs in Column K are added together to calculate a subtotal of $12.55.

M. Q factor (1 to 3 percent). The Q factor is the percentage that the chef or manager charges per recipe to recover the costs of all ingredients that are too small to calculate. For instance, when a recipe calls for a dash of an ingredient, this amount is too small to cost out. The Q-factor percentage can range from 1 to 3 percent, depending on the cost of the ingredients used in the recipe.

In the Swiss steak recipe, the only ingredient costs calculated with a Q factor were pepper and water; therefore, a low factor of 1 percent was used. The Q factor is calculated in the following way:

$$
\begin{array}{r}
\$12.67 \text{ (recipe subtotal)} \\
\times\ 0.01 \text{ (\textit{multiplied by} Q factor of 1 percent)} \\
\hline
\$\ 0.13 \text{ (\textit{equals} the monetary value of the Q)}
\end{array}
$$

N. Total recipe cost. The total cost of the recipe is calculated by adding the Q factor of 1 percent to the subtotal of the recipe. For example,

$$
\begin{array}{r}
\$\ 0.13 \text{ (the monetary value of Q factor)} \\
+\ 12.67 \text{ (\textit{plus} the subtotal amount)} \\
\hline
\$12.80 \text{ (\textit{equals} the total recipe cost)}
\end{array}
$$

O. Portion cost (PC). To calculate the portion cost (PC), *divide* the total recipe cost ($12.80) *by* the total number of portions that the recipe yields (10).

$$\frac{\$12.80}{10} = \$1.28$$

P. Additional cost. When food items are sold on a semi–à la carte menu, the portion cost of any additional items should be added to the original portion cost. For example, if the Swiss steak with sour cream was served with risotto and grilled vegetables, the chef or manager would calculate the portion cost of the risotto and grilled vegetables separately. The cost of the two accompaniments is then added to the cost of the Swiss steak to determine a complete plate cost. In the following example, the (prices for accompaniments are hypothetical.

$$
\begin{array}{r}
\$\ 1.28 \text{ (portion cost of Swiss steak with sour cream)} \\
+\ 0.29 \text{ (\textit{plus} portion cost of risotto)} \\
+\ 0.20 \text{ (\textit{plus} portion cost of grilled vegetables)} \\
\hline
\$\ 1.77 \text{ (\textit{equals} complete plate cost)}
\end{array}
$$

Q. Desired overall food-cost percentage. Desired overall food-cost percentage is established by determining what management would like its food cost to be at the end of the year.

R. Preliminary selling price. The preliminary selling price is established by *dividing* the portion cost ($1.77) *by* the desired overall food-cost percentage (0.04) as in the following example:

$$\frac{\$1.77}{0.40} = \$4.43$$

S. Actual selling price.   The actual selling price is the amount for which the product will be sold on the menu. The actual selling price is based on 3 criteria:

- Direct competition
- Labor intensity of preparing the product
- Demand (popularity) of the food product

T. Actual food-cost percentage.   When the actual selling price is determined, the actual daily food-cost percentage can be calculated. Because the actual selling price is usually higher than the amount of the preliminary selling price, the actual food-cost percentage will usually go down. To calculate the actual food-cost percentage, *divide* the portion cost ($1.28) *by* the actual selling price:

$$\frac{\$1.28}{7.95} = 0.1610 \text{ or } 16 \text{ perent}$$

Recipe Conversion

Recipes are designed and written to yield varying numbers of servings, and occasionally it is necessary to convert them to meet a different yield according to immediate production needs. Recipe conversion should be completed before any production occurs.

The process of converting recipes is relatively simple once the basic rules are understood.

Whether increasing or decreasing the number of servings of an original recipe, there is one basic guideline to follow:

Divide the number of portions you wish to prepare by the number or amount of portions the recipe calls for. The formula should look like this:

$$\frac{\text{the desired recipe amount}}{\text{the original recipe amount}}$$

For example, if the original recipe yield is 20 portions, but the yield needed for production has to be increased to 40 portions, the formula would look like this:

$$\frac{40}{20} = 2$$

The resulting division suggests that the original recipe amount of 20 needs to be doubled to provide the desired yield of 40 servings. The answer given by completing the math, the 2, is called the conversion factor. The quantity of each ingredient called for in the original recipe is then multiplied by this conversion factor. For example,

Ingredients	20 Servings	Conversion Factor	40 Servings
Green cabbage, grated	2 pounds	(× 2)	4 pounds
Red cabbage, grated	1 pound	(× 2)	2 pounds
Carrots, peeled, grated	2 cups	(× 2)	4 cups
Mayonnaise	2 1/4 cups	(× 2)	4 1/2 cups
Worcestershire sauce	1 1/2 Tbsp.	(× 2)	3 Tbsp.
White vinegar	1 Tbsp.	(× 2)	2 Tbsp.
Salt and pepper	as needed		as needed

The same rule applies to converting recipes when decreasing the yield. Suppose the original recipe calls for 20 portions, but the amount needed is only 2 servings. The formula would be set up in the same fashion:

$$\frac{2}{20} = 0.1$$

The result is a conversion factor of 0.1, or one-tenth. Just as you did in the above example, multiply the quantity of each ingredient called for in the original recipe by this factor of 0.1.

Charts for Measurement in Food Preparation

The standard measurements that cannot be scaled are measured by using graduated liquid measures or measuring spoons for ingredients used in small quantities (see Figure 4–3).

A portion scale may be used to portion items served by exact weights, such as sandwich-meat portions. Items can also be portioned by count or parts of a whole. For example, a pie that yields eight slices must be divided into eight equal slices.

Figure 4–3 Measuring abbreviations and equivalents

Liquid Measurement		
Name	**Abbreviation**	
Teaspoon	tsp. or t.	
Tablespoon	Tbsp. or T.	
Ounce	oz	
Cup	c.	
Pint	pt.	
Quart	qt.	
Gallon	gal. or G.	
Barrel	bbl.	
Dry Measurement		
Name	**Abbreviation**	
Ounce	oz.	
Pound	lb. or #	
Dozen	doz.	
Bunch	bch. or bu.	
Case	cs.	
Equivalent Measurements		
Name	**Abbreviation**	**Equivalent**
3 tsp.	= 1 T.	= ½ fluid oz.
2 T.	=	= 1 oz.
16 T.	= 1 c.	= 8 oz.
2 c.	= 1 pt.	= 16 oz.
2 pt.	= 1 qt.	= 32 oz.
4 qts.	= 1 gal.	= 128 oz.

Metric System

Metric is the most widely used system of measurement in the world. The units of measurement are the gram, liter, and meter. Each measures a different thing: *grams* measure weight, *liters* measure liquid and dry capacity, and *meters* measure linear measurement.

The metric system uses prefixes from two origins: Greek and Roman. A prefix is a letter, syllable, or word placed at the beginning of a word stem, root, or base to vary the significance. The prefixes of Greek origin are used to multiply the unit, and prefixes of Roman origin are used to divide the unit. See Figure 4–4.

Figure 4–5 on page 48 provides a summary of the metric system and a conversion chart for the measurement of ingredients in recipes.

Temperature Conversion

Various cookbooks may use either Fahrenheit or Celsius as the units of measure for temperature. Knowing how to convert one into the other may be helpful when a calculator with such a function is not available.

To convert temperature from Fahrenheit to Celsius,

$$(\text{Temperature } °F - 32) \times 5/9 = °C$$

The following example shows the conversion of the boiling point of water, 212° F.

Step 1. Insert numbers into formula:

$$(212° F. - 32) \times 5/9 = °C$$

Figure 4–4 Greek and Roman prefixes of the metric system

Greek Prefixes		Roman Prefixes		
Deka:	× 10	deci:	divided by 10	= 0.1
Hecto:	× 100	centi:	divided by 100	= 0.01
Kilo:	× 1,000	milli:	divided by 1,000	= 0.001
Myria:	× 10,000	micron:	divided by 1,000,000	= 0.000001
Mega:	× 10,000,000			

Figure 4–5 English and metric measurement equivalents

Weight	Extended Amount	Metric Conversion
0.035 ounce		= 1 gram
0.35 ounce		= 10 grams or 1 dekagram
1 ounce		= 28 grams
16 ounces	= 1 pound	= 0.45 kilogram
2.2 pounds		= 100 dekagrams or 1 kilogram
100 pounds	= 1 hundredweight	= 45.35 kilograms
2,000 pounds	= 1 short ton	= 1.01 megagrams
1.1 short tons		= 1,000 kilograms or 1 megagram
Liquid Capacity		
0.034 ounce		= 1 milliliter
1 ounce		= 29.5 milliliters
16 ounces	= 1 pint	= 0.47 liter
2 pints	= 1 quart	= 0.95 liter
1.06 quarts		= 1,000 milliliters or 1 liter
4 quarts	= 1 gallon	= 3.79 liters
31.5 gallons	= 1 barrel	= 119.24 liters
264.18 gallons	= 1,000 liters	= 1 kiloliter
Dry Capacity		
1 pint		= 0.55 liter
2 pints	= 1 quart	= 1.1 liters
8 quarts	= 1 peck	= 8.81 liters
4 pecks	= 1 bushel	= 35.24 liters
0.91 quart		= 1 liter
28.38 bushels		= 100 liters

Step 2. Calculate the math in the parentheses:

$$212 - 32 = 180$$

Step 3. Complete the second part of the formula, inserting 180:

$$180 \times 5 = 900$$

Step 4. Complete the third part of the formula, inserting 900:

$$900/9 = 100$$

The result of the formula simply means that the temperature at which water boils is 212° F or 100° C.

To convert temperature from Celsius to Fahrenheit,

$$(\text{Temperature } °C \times 9/5 + 32 = °F$$

The following example shows the conversion of a low oven temperature, 160° C.

Step 1. Insert the numbers into the formula:

$$160° C \times 9/5 + 32 = °F$$

Step 2. Calculate the math within the parentheses:

$$160 \times 9 = 1,440$$

Step 3. Insert 1,440 into the second part of the formula and calculate:

$$1,440/5 = 288$$

Step 4. Insert 288 into the third part of the formula and calculate:

$$288 + 32 = 320$$

The result of the formula simply means that a low oven temperature of 160° C is the same as the Fahrenheit temperature of 320°.

The freezing point of water is 32° F. To convert to Celsius,

Step 1. Insert numbers into the formula:

$$(32 - 32) \times 5/9 = °C$$

Step 2. Calculate the math in the parentheses:

$$32 - 32 = 0$$

Step 3. Insert 0 into the second part of the formula and calculate:

$$0 \times 5 = 0$$

Step 4. Insert 0 into the third part of the formula and calculate:

$$0/9 = 0$$

The result of the formula simply means that the freezing point of water is 32° F, or 0° C. In the metric system, anything below the freezing point is represented with a minus sign.

Purchasing and Product Identification

5

Purchasing and Product Identification

The primary objective of any purchasing system is to procure the correct product in terms of quality and quantity, at the proper time, for the lowest price available. Purchasing is considered one of the most important control points for controlling the cost of food and the development of menu diversity. The quality of the raw ingredients is vital and in direct proportion to the quality of the product served.

Purchasing

As soon as the chef has decided which ingredients will be used in the production of menu items, the purchasing agent arranges the purchase of the products from approved vendors. A *vendor* is anyone who supplies food or nonfood products to a foodservice operation. Vendors may be manufacturers or local producers. However, it is more common to purchase from wholesalers or distributors. *Wholesalers* or *distributors* are usually large companies who purchase from manufacturers and provide warehousing, delivery, and credit services to operations. The trend today is to develop large product lines so a distributor can become a one-stop shopping environment for restaurateurs. Usually, this is a less expensive and more practical way to do business, and savings can be passed along to the restaurateur.

Buying versus Purchasing

Compared to buying, purchasing is a complex process. Buying is simply the ordering of the product. Purchasing, however, requires the purchasing agent to carefully determine the quality and quantity of products to be purchased as well as to assess inventory stock levels. The purchasing agent must also establish how much of each item to buy based on the calculation of inventory on hand and projected production needs. Careful planning prevents delivery lags and excessive inventory. The purchasing agent is responsible for developing written specifications for all items purchased for the establishment. Once these functions have been performed, the chef, manager, or purchasing agent is ready to begin the purchasing process. The procedure for purchasing is as follows:

- Develop the order.
- Obtain price quotes from vendors.

- Select the vendor and place the order.
- Receive and store the order.
- Evaluate and follow up on mistakes within the order.
- Issue products to production.

Purchasing can be either *formal* or *informal*. The difference, primarily, revolves around bidding. The bidding system is part of the formal approach. It is typically used by large organizations or government agencies that are legally required to collect bids for goods or services.

Good purchasing procedure reflects the need to fulfill the following purchasing objectives:

- Maintain an adequate supply of products.
- Minimize the amount of investment.
- Maintain the quality of products.
- Procure a product at the best cost.
- Maintain the company's competitive position in the marketplace.

Pricing

The price structure for a product is complex. The cost to the wholesaler from the manufacturer, the wholesaler's profit margin, and the cost of the services that the wholesaler provides are all considered when determining price. Some of the services provided by the wholesaler may include sales services, timely deliveries, multiple sizes available, information services, credit services, bulk storage, and delivery on demand.

As purchased and edible food product are two prices with which restaurateurs must be concerned when purchasing products. The AP price is the price per unit paid to wholesalers. The EP price is the cost of a usable portion of the product. This incorporates loss from trimming, shrinkage, and packaging. The restaurateur must keep in mind the AP/EP relationship when purchasing and must buy at the best EP price.

Types of Products Purchased

In the foodservice industry, four types of products are purchased: perishable, semiperishable, nonperishable, and staple.

Perishable items are those food products that have a relatively short shelf life, typically fresh fruits and vegetables, and fresh meat, fish, and seafood. Perishable items are comparatively expensive and should be purchased in small enough quantities that they will be used during their shelf life.

Semiperishable products are food items with a longer shelf life than perishables. Examples of these products are frozen goods and such fresh products as winter squash.

Nonperishable food items are those with a long shelf life. The quality of these items—for example, canned foods—is unaffected when stored for up to one year.

Staple items are nonfood items such as cleaning materials, paper goods, and smallwares.

Specifications

In medium-to-large organizations, a more formalized approach is taken toward purchasing. Many of these operations use a written description of each product they wish to procure, commonly referred to as their *specification,* or *spec.* A spec is another tool for the operator to use in purchasing. It is a quality-control tool that tells vendors exactly what the foodservice establishment will or will not accept. It eliminates unnecessary communication because it is very specific.

The spec primarily tells the vendor what the restaurateur expects in each product. The spec may be very formal and lengthy or as short as a brand name and can size. Other information that may be included in the spec is

- Exact name, recognized by the industry
- Packer's brand name
- U.S. grade
- Size
- Yield
- Package size
- Preservation/processing method

- Form
- Point of origin
- Degree of ripeness
- Cost and quality limitations

Quantity Purchasing

There are several methods for establishing how much to purchase for a given restaurant. In general, the restaurateur must know how much of each product the chef expects to use in the production of menu items for the upcoming sales cycle (the period between deliveries). Many establishments create a policy concerning the amount of money that will be tied up in inventory.

The amount of storage space an establishment has available is another important consideration when purchasing. Appropriate storage space for costly perishable and semiperishable products is often at a premium and may determine the type of ordering method used. The two main ordering approaches used are the *periodic-ordering* method and the *perpetual-inventory* method.

If using the periodic method, the purchasing agent establishes how much product will be used for a given period of time. This method is more effective for semiperishables, but perishables can also be procured this way. The purchasing agent reviews what is on hand, what will be needed for the next sales-delivery cycle, and how much additional product the operator wants on hand in case of a sudden increase in sales (safety stock). By adding the safety stock and production needs together, then subtracting the amount on hand, the order amount is established. The equation for determining period ordering needs is as follows:

Safety stock + Production needs − Stock on hand = Order amount

The perpetual-inventory method is a more labor-intensive system that establishes *par* levels for products. Par levels require setting a reorder point based on delivery times and usage until the next delivery. The record keeping that is necessary for the perpetual system requires more time than does the periodic method because food products must be constantly inventoried and recorded. As a result, perpetual-inventory systems can be a time-consuming and expensive process.

Vendor Relationships

The relationship between the purchaser and the vendor should be based on mutual trust, honesty, and good business ethics. A purchasing agent should be able to assume that the prices charged by the vendor are not inflated and that they reflect market conditions. Unfortunately, this is not always the case and purchasing agents should be careful in soliciting their vendors.

Traditionally, prices in an open-market system are very competitive; thus, price is not the only criterion used to select vendors. For example, the success of a restaurant depends on the ability of a vendor to provide a constant supply of products according to specifications.

Common Methods of Purchasing

There are several methods of purchasing, including open-market or competitive buying and single-source buying.

Open-market, or *competitive buying,* is the most common method that operators use to procure products. This method is an informal but very cost-efficient and effective way to purchase. Open-market buying requires a restaurateur to secure price quotes for identical items from several different vendors. This method is used extensively to purchase perishable items.

Single-source buying is the linking of a foodservice establishment with one *purveyor* for most of the products that will be purchased. Distributors or wholesalers are large corporations (purveyors) involved in developing and supplying lines of products that will make them into single sources for foodservice establishments. They traditionally supply canned and frozen goods, but now also provide perishable products, smallwares, sundries, and equipment lines to make themselves more attractive. The more goods purchased from one source, the less expensive. Vendor delivery, inventory, and capital costs are all lowered, and this savings can be passed on to the foodservice establishment.

Receiving

The next function that takes place in a foodservice operation is receiving. The objectives of receiving are similar to purchasing.

To accomplish this function, management must develop formal receiving guidelines. The receiver should

- Be knowledgeable in the exact company specifications of quality products and be company approved as an employee experienced in receiving products according to formal receiving guidelines.
- Have the proper tools and equipment that facilitate receiving, which include
  - Heavy-duty gloves with no-slip fingertips.
  - Scales of proper size and calibrated regularly.
  - Calculator to spot-check the accuracy of the invoice.
  - Cutting apparatus for opening containers and boxes.
- Verify that the product was ordered. The purchasing agent's order sheet should match the invoice. The *invoice* is a listing of the products being delivered and includes
  - The quantity of each item ordered.
  - A description of each item.
  - Weight or count per package.
  - Unit price for each item.
  - Extension of all prices.
  - Total cost of the order (including taxes and transportation costs, if applicable).
  - Terms of payment.
- Verify that all items on the invoice are present, and are in the correct form, size, and quantity. Verification is accomplished at the time of inspecting each product.
- Physically inspect all perishable and nonperishable products. Depending on the product, the receiver should look for product tampering or mishandling, proper storage practices, and pest or rodent infestation.
- Look for excessive dents, leaks, or puffed cans in canned goods.

- Look for evidence of thawing or refreezing in frozen goods. Excess moisture that has refrozen into ice usually comes from the product; thus, it will be dehydrated and damaged when thawed.
- Weigh and record on the invoice products bought and priced by weight. Any discrepancies should be addressed immediately.
- Physically count the product if count is the criterion. Any discrepancies should be addressed immediately.
- Complete a credit voucher if there is a problem with the order. A *credit voucher* is used to report incorrect prices or weights, damaged goods, or product substitutions. Once completed, the credit voucher is retained by the receiver for company records, and a copy is given to the driver delivering the goods. The purchasing agent should follow up on the credit voucher with the vendor at a later point.
- Complete inventory-control procedures as soon as the order is received. Those procedures include the following:
  - Perishable products should be labeled, dated, and stored according to the FIFO method, which helps to ensure proper rotation and storage.
  - Some establishments may use a bar code and computer system to keep track of inventory. In this case, all products receive a bar-code sticker at the point of receiving.

Storage

After receiving and inventory-control procedures are complete, products are ready for storage. The steward or storeroom clerk is responsible for the storage, security, and issuing of the inventory once it has been transferred from receiving.

Goods must be properly stored in designated storage areas. FIFO is the preferred method of rotation for all food items, as it helps to control the loss of quality of all food products during storage. With all products, especially perishables, the product is in a constant state of deterioration. The longer the product is stored, the more its quality deteriorates because of moisture loss and spoilage.

The quality of the storage facilities is also of concern. Storerooms should be kept clean and orderly and should be inspected daily for insects and rodents. Food preparation should not occur in the storage area.

The removal of product from the storeroom is performed through an *issuing system.* This system requires the use of a written or printed *requisition,* which is an internal invoice that allows management to track the physical movement of inventory items and to calculate the cost of food produced daily. As with the invoices from vendors, close attention should be paid to completing the requisition. The exact cost of the inventory being removed from the storeroom must be recorded. The steward or storeroom clerk should be the only authorized personnel to fill orders submitted via the requisitioning system.

Product Identification

Chefs and managers need to be familiar with various food products that will be used in foodservice settings. These products are classified as fruits and vegetables; dairy products; nonperishable and dry goods; herbs and spices; flavorings, seasonings, and condiments; and seafood, fish, and meats.

Fruits and Vegetables

A system of description has been developed to familiarize the chef with the characteristics of fruits and vegetables (see Tables 5–1 on next page and 5–2 on page 64). An investigation of the following categories concerning these products is included in this system:

- Purchase specifications
- Receiving (pack and weight)
- Storage requirements
- Market forms available
- Peak seasons for fresh goods
- Appropriate U.S. grades

Table 5–1 Characteristics of Vegetables

Item Varieties	Purchasing Specifications	Receiving Pack and Weight	Storage	Market Form	Peak Season	Grade
Artichoke: globe	Properly trimmed, compact, and well formed; tightly fleshed leaf; scale of a green color.	Containers wax treated; by count and loose pack: 20 to 25 lb. (18, 24, 36, 48, or 60 count).	Short period of time at 38° F, 90–95 percent relative humidity.	Fresh and canned hearts and bottoms.	April–May; also available year-round.	U.S. No. 1, U.S. No. 2.
Asparagus: white and green	Fresh tip will be tightly closed; deep purple color; thin spear represents better quality; crisp.	½ carton: 15 lb. pyramid crates; loose pack: 30 lb.	35° to 40° F, 90 percent relative humidity.	Fresh, canned, and frozen.	April–May.	U.S. No. 1 Fresh, U.S. Fancy Canned and Standard Canned; Grade B Frozen.
Beans: green, snap, and white	Long, straight, well formed; bright green or yellow; should snap easily.	Bushel 22 lb; Florida: 22 lb; Texas and Georgia: 20 lb.	Short period of time at 45° to 50° F, 85 percent relative humidity.	Fresh, frozen, and canned.	May–September; peak season.	U.S. Fancy No. 1, Combination No. 2.
Beans: fava and lima	Canned: young and tender; 50 percent green, 50 percent light. Frozen: 60 to 65 percent green.	Bushel: 26–30 lb.	Short period of time at 45° to 50° F, 85 percent relative humidity.	Fresh, frozen, or canned.	May–September; peak season.	Canned: Grade B. Frozen: Grade B.
Bean sprouts: mung, alfalfa	Fresh looking; crisp; tips should not be dry; younger more tender.	Containers holding twelve 8-oz. cello bags: 6 lb. Lugs and crates, loose pack: 10 lb. Bag: 10 lb. Flat: 10 lb.	Refrigerate and wash well; 90 percent relative humidity.	Fresh.	Available year-round.	N/A*
Beets	Good globular shape; smooth, firm flesh; rich, deep red.	Bushel: 50 lb. Bunch: 1 to 1½ lb. Bag: 1 crate 25 to 50 lb.	35° to 45° F, 95 percent relative humidity.	Fresh or canned.	Available year-round.	U.S. No. 1, U.S. No. 2; buy Grade A canned.
Broccoli	Green-colored heads, leaves, and stems; stalks tender and firm; dark green color, purplish-green buds in the head.	½ containers wax treated. 18 bunches equals 23 lb.	35° to 45° F, 95 percent relative humidity; well iced.	Fresh or frozen.	Available year-round.	U.S. No. 1, U.S. No. 2; buy grade A frozen.

(continued)

Table 5–1 Characteristics of Vegetables *(continued)*

Item Varieties	Purchasing Specifications	Receiving Pack and Weight	Storage	Market Form	Peak Season	Grade
Brussels sprouts	Firm compact; fresh, bright appearance; good light green color.	Container wax treated. Loose pack: 25 lb. Trays: 9 lb. (12-count pint cello cups).	35° to 45° F, 95 percent relative humidity.	Fresh and frozen.	October–January.	Buy Grade B frozen.
Cabbage: green and red	Head should be firm and tightly formed, leaves brittle and crisp.	Bushel: 50 lb. Mesh sacks: 50 lb.	35° to 45° F, 90 percent relative humidity.	Fresh.	Available year-round.	U.S. No. 1 Commercial.
Cabbage: Chinese, bok choy, or nappa	Crisp, fresh, deep green leaves; crisp white stems.	Bushel: 70 lb.	35° to 45° F, 90 percent relative humidity.	Fresh.	Available year-round.	U.S. No. 1.
Cabbage: Savoy	Similar to green cabbage except for its yellowish, crimped leaves.	Bushel: 30 lb.	35° to 45° F, 90 percent relative humidity.	Fresh.	Available year-round.	U.S. No. 1 Commercial.
Carrots	Fresh appearance; firm, well formed, smooth; deep orange.	Comes in bunches if not topped; topped: 25, 50, or 100 lb. bags. Bushels 50 lb. Crate: 50 lb.	35° to 45° F, 90 percent relative humidity.	Fresh, frozen, and canned.	Available year-round.	U.S. Extra No. 1, No. 1, No. 1 Jumbo, No. 2; buy Grade A canned, Grade B frozen.
Cauliflower	The curd should be white or slightly creamy white; firm and compact; loose, open flower clusters indicate overmaturity.	Crate: 42 lb. holding 12 to 15 heads. ½ bushel: 20 lb. (12-count cello.)	35° to 45° F, 90 percent relative humidity.	Fresh and frozen.	October–December.	U.S. No. 1; buy Grade A frozen.
Celeriac (celery root)	Creamy white, solid center; tan or brown outside; firm, not wilted.	½ bushel: 20 lb.	35° to 45° F, relatively high humidity.	Fresh.	November–April.	U.S. No. 1.

(continued)

Table 5–1 Characteristics of Vegetables *(continued)*

Item Varieties	Purchasing Specifications	Receiving Pack and Weight	Storage	Market Form	Peak Season	Grade
Celery	Stalks should be straight, not stringy; outer branches or stalks light green.	Whole heads—carton: 50 to 56 lb. (18, 24, 30, 36, or 48 counts). Hearts—carton: 25 to 28 lb. (12, 18, 24 counts).	35° to 45° F, 90 to 95 percent relative humidity.	Fresh.	Available year-round.	U.S. Extra No. 1, No. 2.
Swiss chard	Leaves should be fresh, crisp; good green color.	Crate: 20 lb.	35° to 45° F, 90 percent relative humidity.	Fresh.	December–April.	No U.S. standard grade.
Collards	Crisp, clean, fresh; free from insects.	Bushel: 20 lb.	35° to 45° F, 90 percent relative humidity.	Fresh.	Fall-winter; available year-round.	U.S. No. 1.
Corn: sweet	Fresh-appearing husk green; silks brown, not green; kernels—bright, plump, and firm.	50-lb. bags holding 5 dozen ears. Crate: 48 count.	Refrigerate; use immediately for freshness; 40 percent relative humidity.	Fresh, frozen.	May–September; peak season.	U.S. Fancy, No. 1, No. 2; buy Grade B frozen and fresh.
Cucumber	Crispness; good shape; fresh appearance; medium sized; dark green appearance.	Carton: 25 to 28 lb. (24 count). Carton: 30 to 32 lb. (35 to 40 count). Bushel/Los Angeles Lug: 50 to 55 lb. (60, 70, 80, or 90 count).	Moderate cold, 45° to 50° F, 85 percent relative humidity.	Fresh.	August–October; peak season.	U.S. Fancy, Choice, Extra, No. 1, No. 1 small, No. 1 large, No. 2.
Eggplant	Dark purple color with a soft silky sheen; body plump and free of blemishes.	Bushel: 33 lb. Crates: 12 to 18, 24, or 30 each.	Briefly at 45° to 50° F, 85 percent relative humidity.	Fresh.	August–September.	U.S. Fancy, No. 1, No. 2.
Endive: Belgian	Crisp, firm; absence of blemishes; white.	Box: 10 lb. Bushel: 25 lb.	Hold briefly at 35° to 45° F, 90 percent humidity.	Fresh.	Available year-round.	No federal grades.

(continued)

Table 5–1 Characteristics of Vegetables *(continued)*

Item Varieties	Purchasing Specifications	Receiving Pack and Weight	Storage	Market Form	Peak Season	Grade
Endive: curly (chicory)	Crisp edge leaves that curl at the ends; center of head yellowish white.	California carton: 25 lb. (24 count). Florida carton: 18 lb. (12 to 18 count).	Hold briefly at 38° F, 90 percent relative humidity.	Fresh.	Available year-round.	U.S. No. 1.
Escarole (Batavian endive)	Broad green leaves do not curl at the ends and snap easily when broken.	California carton: 25 lb. (24 count). Florida carton: 18 lb. (12 to 18 count).	Hold briefly at 38° F, 90 percent relative humidity.	Fresh.	Available year-round.	U.S. No. 2.
Garlic	Well cured, compact; cloves fairly plump; free from mold.	Purchased by the pound. Crate: 25 or 30 lb.	Place cloves in a jar with a tight lid; store in a dark, dry area at 30° to 40° F.	Fresh.	Available year-round.	U.S. No. 1.
Kale	Clean crisp leaves; free from bruises and rot.	Bushel carton: 18 to 25 lb.	Cold and moist, 40° F, 90 percent relative humidity.	Fresh.	December—April.	U.S. No. 1 Commercial.
Leek	Fresh green tops and medium-sized necks; root and top tender and crisp; white color should appear 2 to 3 inches from root.	Bunch: 12 to 15. Bushel baskets or hampers: 24 to 30 lb. Carton: 12 count.	Keep refrigerated at 40° to 50° F.	Fresh.	September to November; available year-round.	U.S. No. 1.
Lettuce: butter-head, Boston and bibb	Soft, pliable, fresh crisp leaves; core should be small.	Carton: 15 lb. (24 count).	38° F, 85 to 90 percent relative humidity.	Fresh.	Available year-round.	U.S. Fancy, No. 1, No. 2 Commercial.
Lettuce: Iceberg and crisp head	Firm, semihard heads; free of rusty or burned tips; texture should be firm.	Case 45 to 48 lb. Salad-mix bags: 4 (5 lb.) or 2 (10 lb.).	38° F, 85 to 90 percent relative humidity.	Fresh.	Available year-round.	U.S. Fancy, No. 1, No. 2 Commercial.

(continued)

Table 5–1 Characteristics of Vegetables *(continued)*

Item Varieties	Purchasing Specifications	Receiving Pack and Weight	Storage	Market Form	Peak Season	Grade
Lettuce: Red or green leaf (bunching)	Leaves clustered, tender, crispy; green with a touch of red.	Carton: 30 lb. (24 bunches).	45° F, 85 to 90 percent relative humidity.	Fresh.	Available year-round.	U.S. Fancy, No. 1, No. 2 Commercial.
Lettuce: Romaine (cos)	Dark green outer leaves, golden yellow inner leaves.	Carton: 30 lb. (24 bunches).	45° F, 85 to 90 percent relative humidity.	Fresh.	Available year-round.	U.S. Fancy, U.S. 1, U.S. Commercial, U.S. No. 2.
Mushrooms (cultivated)	White or tan; no slime, dry; unblemished button mushrooms cap and stem should be fully intact.	Carton/basket: 1-, 3-, and 10-lb sizes: button, cup, and flat.	Refrigerate at 35° F, 85 to 90 percent relative humidity.	Fresh, canned, and dried.	Available year-round.	U.S. No. 1, No. 2; buy Grade B canned.
Wild mushrooms: Cèpe Chantrelle Morel Porcini Shiitake Truffles	Free of blemishes; somewhat clean; firm; good color and shape.	Carton: 3-, 5-, and 10-lb.	Refrigerate at 35° F, 85 to 90 percent relative humidity.	Fresh, canned, and dried.	Available year-round. Fall–winter. Early spring. Available year-round. Available year-round. Fall.	N/A
Okra	Small, pointed, deeply ridged green pods; young, small, firm, unblemished and unshriveled.	Carton: 10 lb. Bushel 25 lb.	Refrigerate at 35° to 40° F, 85 to 90 percent relative humidity.	Fresh and frozen.	April–July.	U.S. No. 1.
Onions (globe): Spanish, red, Bermuda, and white pearl	Solid, paper-lined skin; thin and crinkly; no stems, decay, or wetness.	Bag: 10, 25, and 50 lb.	Dark dry place, 50° to 60° F, no humidity.	Fresh.	Available year-round.	U.S. No. 1, Export, Commercial, No. 1, No. 2, Picklers, No. 2.

(continued)

Table 5–1 Characteristics of Vegetables *(continued)*

Item Varieties	Purchasing Specifications	Receiving Pack and Weight	Storage	Market Form	Peak Season	Grade
Onions (leaf): green, scallion, spring, and rareripes	Medium-sized necks; fresh tops; well-blanched for 2 or 3 inches from the root; wilted tops indicate unsatisfactory quality.	Carton: 15 to 25 lb. (48-bunch count). ½ carton: 7 to 12 lb. (24-bunch count).	Dark cool place, 40° to 50° F, 90 percent relative humidity.	Fresh.	Available year-round.	U.S. No. 1, No. 2.
Parsnip	Small to medium sized; well shaped and firm.	Bag: 12 to 20 oz. Bag: 25 lb. cello wrap: 12 (1-lb.) bags. Bushel: 28 to 30 lb.	38° F, 90 percent relative humidity.	Fresh.	October–May.	U.S. No. 1, No. 2.
Peas	Bright pods, bright green; well filled and snap easily.	Carton/tub: 25 lb. Lug: 10 lb.	38° F, 90 percent relative humidity.	Fresh, dried, canned, and frozen.	April–July.	U.S. No. 1 Fancy; Grade B canned or frozen.
Peppers (bell): green, red, yellow, and purple	Thick, firm, glossy skin; well shaped; no external bruises; (green stem) pepper was recently picked.	Bushel: 24 lb. Box: 11 lb.	40° F, 85 percent relative humidity.	Fresh.	Available year-round.	U.S. Fancy; buy Grade B canned or frozen.
Peppers (chili): Anaheim, jalapeño	Fresh: Firm, no external bruises. Dried: Will be wrinkled, no rot or moisture.	½ crate: 10 lb. Bushel/crate: 25 lb.	40° to 50° F, 85 percent relative humidity.	Fresh and dried.	Available year-round.	U.S. Fancy, U.S. No. 1, U.S. No. 2.
Potatoes: chef	Irregular size and shape; no wet spots; smooth; clean.	Carton: 50 lb. Sack: 50 or 100 lb.	Cool, dark, well-ventilated place at 45° F, no humidity.	Fresh.	Available year-round.	U.S. No. 1 Extra, No. 1 size B, No. 2.
Potatoes: new and red bliss	Usually 1½ inches in diameter; skin is thin.	Carton: 50 lb. (120 or more count).	Cool, dark, well-ventilated place at 45° to 50° F, no humidity.	Fresh.	Available year-round.	U.S. Fancy, U.S. No. 1.

(continued)

Table 5–1 Characteristics of Vegetables *(continued)*

Item Varieties	Purchasing Specifications	Receiving Pack and Weight	Storage	Market Form	Peak Season	Grade
Potatoes: Russet	Flat and oblong.	Carton: 50 lb. (70 to 80, 90, 100, 110, and 120 count).	Cool, dark, well-ventilated place at 45° to 50° F, no humidity.	Fresh and canned.	Available year-round.	U.S. No. 1 Extra, No. 1 size B, No. 2.
Potatoes: Sweet	Clean firm and free from blemishes; bright orange.	Carton: 40 to 50 lb. (count varies).	Cool, dark, well-ventilated place at 45° to 50° F, no humidity.	Fresh and canned.	Available year-round.	U.S. Extra No. 1, No. 1, Commercial No. 2.
Radicchio	Crisp, tender small heads; leaves with white ribs and veins.	Carton: 10 lb. (10 to 12 count).	Hold briefly at 40° to 50° F, 90 percent relative humidity.	Fresh.	Available year-round.	U.S. No. 1.
Radishes	Vary in size; root should be smooth, firm, and crisp, not spongy or soft.	Cello pack: 8 oz. Basket with tops: 2 dozen count. Basket without tops: 2 to 2½ dozen count.	40° to 50° F, very high humidity.	Fresh.	Available year-round.	U.S. No. 1, Commercial.
Shallots	Thin, papery skin; bronze in color, purple skin; avoid rot or browning.	Bag: 5 or 10 lb. Quarts.	Dark, dry place, 40° to 60° F, no humidity.	Fresh.	Available year-round.	U.S. No. 1.
Spinach	Fresh, clean, crisp; good green color leaves.	Carton/crate: 10 lb. (8-count 10-oz. cello bag).	37° F, 95 to 98 percent relative humidity.	Fresh, canned, and frozen.	March–May; available year-round.	U.S. No. 1, Commercial; buy Grade B canned or frozen.
Squash: summer and zucchini	Fresh; fair size; tender rind; no soft spots or blemishes.	Carton: 20 lb. Bushel/carton 50 lb.	35° to 40° F, 85 to 90 percent relative humidity.	Fresh and frozen.	July–November; available year-round.	U.S. No. 1, No. 2; buy Grade A frozen.
Squash (winter): acorn, butternut, hubbard, spaghetti, and others	Shell should be intact with no decay, cracks, blemishes, or soft spots.	Each. carton: 50 lb.	50° F, no humidity.	Fresh.	July–November; also available year-round.	U.S. No. 1, No. 2.

(continued)

Table 5–1 Characteristics of Vegetables *(continued)*

Item Varieties	Purchasing Specifications	Receiving Pack and Weight	Storage	Market Form	Peak Season	Grade
Tomatoes, beefsteak, cherry, and plum	Good color; firm, well shaped; no blemishes; smooth.	Flat: 10 lb. (40 count). Lug: 28 to 30 lb. (108, 126, or 147 count). Carton: 25 lb. Cherry-tray: 14 to 20 lb. (12-count, 1-pint trays).	Best-ripening temperatures: 65° to 70° F, 85 to 88 percent relative humidity; do not refrigerate until fully ripened; after ripening, refrigerate at 50° F.	Fresh.	Available year-round.	U.S. No. 1, Combination, No. 2, No. 3.
Turnips (purple top)	Firm; smooth; white at the tip; light purple near the top; free of blemishes.	½ bushel: 25 lb. Bag: 25 or 50 lb. Carton: 43 to 47 lb. (24 bushel count).	35° F.	Fresh and canned.	October–March; also available year-round.	U.S. No. 1, No. 2.
Rutabaga	Long; yellow; dense flesh; no blemishes.	Carton/bag: 50 lb.	35° F, no humidity.	Fresh.	October–March; and available year-round.	U.S. No. 1, No. 2.
Watercress	Bright, green; crisp.	Case: 12 or 24 count.	38° F, very high humidity.	Fresh.	Available year-round.	U.S. No. 1.

*Not available.

Table 5–2 Characteristics of Fruits

Item Varieties	Purchasing Specifications	Receiving Pack and Weight	Storage	Market Form	Peak Season	Grade
Apples: Greening, Rhode Island, red delicious, golden delicious, McIntosh, Granny Smith, Cortland, Rome beauty, and winesap	Good color; firm, not mealy; no spots or bruises; mature, not overripe; carefully hand-picked; clean.	Packed in 40-lb. bushel or box. Boxed: 88, 100, 113, 125, 138, 150, and 163. Canned: 46 oz. or #10.	Refrigerate at 40° F, 90 percent relative humidity; keep in carton to protect.	Fresh, canned, dehydrated, and juice.	Available year-round. California-controlled atmosphere. October–May; September–February; October–April; December–August.	U.S. Extra, Fancy, Fancy No. 1; buy Grade A canned.

(continued)

Table 5–2 Characteristics of Fruits *(continued)*

Item Varieties	Purchasing Specifications	Receiving Pack and Weight	Storage	Market Form	Peak Season	Grade
Apricots: moorpack, royal, and tilton	Golden yellow; plump and firm, not soft, wilted, or shriveled; no worms.	Lug: 24 to 28 lb. Flat: 12 lb. Dried: 5-lb. box.	Refrigerate at 40° to 45° F, 80 to 90 percent relative humidity.	Fresh, canned, dehydrated, and dried.	June–July.	U.S. No. 1, No. 2; buy Grade B canned, buy Grade A dehydrated and dried.
Avocado	California: Skin should be dark green to black. Florida: Not hard but firm, oblong, or round; rough or smooth.	½ carton: 15 lb. Carton: 24 to 25 lb. Case: 48 each. Pyramid: 30 lb. holding 12 bunches.	36° to 40° F.	Fresh.	California: January–April. Florida: July–January.	U.S. No. 1, Combination, No. 2, and No. 3.
Bananas: Gros michel, Cavendish, and plantain	Clean; bright; firm; well developed; free from damage, with no marks; good peel strength.	In bunches or clusters. Case: 40 lb. Box: 25 lb.	Store at about 50° to 60° F.	Fresh.	March–June; also available year-round.	U.S. No. 1, No. 2.
Berries: blackberries, boysenberries, loganberries, blueberries, elderberries, gooseberries, raspberries, and strawberries	Strawberry wears cap; firm, plump, and full-colored; no mold or wetness; no insect damage.	Quarts, pints, flats, 12½ pints or 12 pints per tray. Blue: 12 pints per tray. Strawberries: 24-quart crates. 5- or 10-lb. boxes.	Store at 40° F, 90 to 95 percent relative humidity.	Fresh, canned, and frozen.	May–September (varies with type). Available year-round.	U.S. No. 1; Strawberry: U.S. No. 1, Combination, No. 2; canned Grade B, frozen Grade A.
Cherries: bing and lambert	Firm; good size, dark color; well-matured juiciness; full flavored; no mold.	Lugs or baskets: 18 to 20 lb. Frozen: 30 lb.	40° to 50° F, 80 to 90 percent relative humidity.	Fresh, canned, and frozen.	Mid-June–July.	U.S. No. 1, Commercial; buy Grade A canned or frozen.
Cranberries	Glossy; firm; plump; red.	Carton: 25 to 50 lb. 24 1-lb. packages. Barrel: 100 lb. Frozen: 20 lb.	45° F.	Fresh and frozen.	Fresh: October–December. Frozen: Year-round.	U.S. No. 1, Commercial; buy Grade B frozen.

(continued)

Table 5–2 Characteristics of Fruits *(continued)*

Item Varieties	Purchasing Specifications	Receiving Pack and Weight	Storage	Market Form	Peak Season	Grade
Currants: red, black, and white	Firm; ripe; no grit, sand, or mold.	Case: 30 lb.	45° F.	Dried.	June–August.	Fancy, Choice, Substandard; Grade A dried.
Dates	Fully ripe; plump; shiny; not sticky; golden color; smooth skin; uniform size.	Bulk: 15 lb. Chopped: 30 lb.	Fresh: 50° to 60° F, 30 to 40 percent relative humidity.	Fresh and dry.	Available year-round.	None; Grade A dry.
Figs: mission and Smyrna	Firm, plump, well shaped; smooth skin; green, black, or purple.	1 (1-layer) flat: 5 to 6 lb. 2 (1-layer) flats: 10 to 15 lb.	38° F, 90 percent relative humidity.	Fresh, canned, and dried.	June–October.	U.S. No. 1; Grade B canned, dried.
Grapefruit; duncan, marsh, pinks and ruby red	Firm, plump, well shaped; skin is smooth.	Packed by count in ½ box: 18, 23, 32, 40, 48, and 56. Also packed in 8-lb. and 5-lb. bags. Segments: gallon.	40° to 45° F, 85 percent relative humidity.	Fresh and canned.	Florida: October–June. California and Arizona: March–August. Best: November–May.	U.S. Fancy, No. 1, No. 2, Combination No. 3; Grade B canned.
Grapes: Thompson, seedless, emperor, and cardinal	Well-formed, good looking; plump; juicy; stem green, not dry.	Lug or carton: 18 to 22 lb.	36° to 40° F, 90 percent relative humidity; handle carefully.	Fresh and juice.	California: June–November. Chile: December–May.	U.S. Fancy, U.S. No. 1.
Kiwi	Light-brown furry skin; 2½ to 3½ inches long; soft skin.	1-layer carton: New Zealand: 5 to 6 lb. California: 11 to 12 lb. (25, 27, 30, 33, 36, 39, 42, and 46 count).	40° F.	Fresh.	Available year-round.	U.S. Fancy, U.S. No. 1, No. 2.
Lemons: Lisbon and eureka	Fine-textured skin; heavy for size; uniform color.	Carton: 75, 95, 115, 140, 165, 200, and 235 count.	45° to 48° F, 89 to 91 percent relative humidity.	Fresh and juice.	Available year-round. June–September.	U.S. No. 1, Combination, No. 2.
Limes: Tahiti (Persian) and Mexican (Key)	Round or oval shape; smooth skin; fully ripe; heavy for size.	Carton: 10, 20, 38 lb. (27, 48, 54, and 63 count).	58° to 60° F, 90 percent relative humidity.	Fresh and juice.	Available year-round.	U.S. No. 1, Combination, No. 2.

(continued)

Table 5–2 Characteristics of Fruits *(continued)*

Item Varieties	Purchasing Specifications	Receiving Pack and Weight	Storage	Market Form	Peak Season	Grade
Mandarins, tangerines, and tangelos	Deep orange color; soft; short necked; pebbly skin; heavy for size; no mold.	4/5 bushel: 54, 66, 80, 100, 120, and 156 count.	38° to 40° F, 90 to 95 percent relative humidity.	Fresh and canned.	October–May.	U.S. Fancy, U.S. No. 1, No. 2, No. 3.
Mangos	Fresh, firm, plump; red-yellow color.	Flat: 10 to 12 lb. Lug: 24 lb. (16 count).	50° F, 85 percent relative humidity.	Fresh.	January–August.	None.
Melons:						
cantaloupe (muskmelon)	Heavy for size; firm, plump; skin by variety; melon aroma.	Crate: 12 to 15 lb. (18, 23, 27, 36, and 46 count).	Place in warm room away from sunlight if melon is hard.	Fresh and frozen balls.	July–October.	U.S. Fancy, U.S. No. 1; Grade A frozen.
Honeydew	Creamy white; weight: 5 to 7 lb.; no greenish exterior; thick green flesh.	4, 5, 6, 8, 9, and 12 count.	Same as above.	Fresh and frozen balls.	January–June.	U.S. No. 1; Grade A frozen.
Casaba	Soft white.	4 to 8 count.	Store at 40° F, 95 percent relative humidity.	Fresh. Fresh and frozen balls.	June–November.	U.S. No. 1.
Crenshaw	Yellow-red.	4 to 8 count.	Store at 40° F, 95 percent relative humidity.	Fresh. Fresh and frozen balls.	June–November.	U.S. No. 1.
Persian	Dark green, fine netting.	4 to 8 count.	Store at 40° F, 95 percent relative humidity.	Fresh. Fresh and frozen balls.	June–November.	U.S. No. 1.
Santa Claus	Green; light, broad netting.	8 to 10 count.	Ripen at 65° to 72° F, 95 percent humidity.	Fresh.	June–December.	U.S. No. 1, Commercial, No. 2.
Watermelon, Charleston gray, Carmon Ball	Mature, firm; symmetrical shape.	Watermelon: 8 to 15 count. Charleston gray: 8 to 15 count. Carmon Ball: 20 to 25 lb. is best.		Fresh.	April–November Best: June–August.	

(continued)

Table 5–2 Characteristics of Fruits *(continued)*

Item Varieties	Purchasing Specifications	Receiving Pack and Weight	Storage	Market Form	Peak Season	Grade
Nectarines	Fresh looking; plump; orange-yellow between red area; firm, not cracked skin.	Lug: 19 to 23 lb. (50 to 84 count).	Store at 40° F, 95 percent relative humidity; ripen at 65° to 72° F, 95 percent humidity.	Fresh.	May–September. Peak: June–August.	U.S. Fancy, Extra No. 1, No. 1, No. 2.
Oranges: Temple, Valencia, Ruby Red, Hamlin, and navel	Firm; heavy for size; free from blemishes; fine textured.	4/5 bushel. Case: 40 lb. California and Arizona: 48, 56, 72, 88, 113, 138, and 168 count. Florida: 100, 125, 163, 200, 252, and 324 count.	45° to 48° F, 90 percent relative humidity.	Fresh, canned and juice.	Available year-round.	U.S. Fancy, No. 1, Combination No. 2, No. 3.
Papayas: solo	Well colored, not green, ½ yellow; smooth, unbruised, unbroken.	Carton: 10 lb. (6 to 14 count).	Ripen, store at 38° F.	Fresh.	Late winter–early spring; also available year-round.	No federal grade; Hawaii: Fancy, No. 1, No. 2.
Peaches: Alberta, Hale, and Blake	Firm; red blush; best variety.	Los Angeles Lug: 22½ lb. (32 to 96 count). Bushel: 40 lb. (48 to 80 count).	Ripen 65° to 72° F, 95 percent relative humidity; store at 32° F, 90 percent relative humidity.	Fresh, canned, frozen, and dehydrated.	May–October; mid-July–August.	U.S. Fancy, Extra No. 1, No. 1, No. 2; Grade B canned and frozen, Grade A dehydrated.
Pears: Bartlett, D'anjou, and Bosc	Clean; bright, typical color for variety; no insect or worm injury.	Box: 20 to 245 count. Best: 110 to 135.	Ripen 3 to 5 days, 60° to 65° F; store at 40° F, 95 percent relative humidity.	Fresh and canned.	Summer: July–November; mid-August–mid-October. Winter: October–April.	U.S. No. 1, Combination, No. 2. Washington Extra Fancy.
Persimmons: Hachiya and Fuyu	Well shaped, plump; soft; good color.	Flats: 11 to 13 lb.	Cool, dark place.	Fresh.	October–January.	None.

(continued)

Table 5–2 Characteristics of Fruits *(continued)*

Item Varieties	Purchasing Specifications	Receiving Pack and Weight	Storage	Market Form	Peak Season	Grade
Pineapples	Heavy for size; green-yellow color; bright, firm eyes; clean surface; dry bottoms.	½ crates: 35 lb. (9 to 21 count). Best: 14 count. Gallon: chunks.	45° to 50° F, 85 to 90 percent relative humidity.	Fresh, canned, and juice.	April–May; also available year-round.	U.S. No. 1.
Plums: Purple, red, yellow, or green	Plump, firm, full colored; not bruised.	Lug: 25 lb.	Ripen 65° to 72° F, 95 percent relative humidity; store at 32° F, 90 percent relative humidity.	Fresh, canned, and frozen.	Available May–September. Peak: July–September.	U.S. Fancy, No. 1, Combination No. 2; Grade B canned, Grade A frozen.
Pomegranates: wonderful and red wonderful	Unbroken and heavy for size; fresh appearance; colored pink to bright red.	Los Angeles lug: 27 to 28 lb. Case: 48 lb.	Room temperature short period of time.	Fresh.	September to early December. Peak: October.	No U.S. standard.
Rhubarb	Fresh, firm; crisp; tender; good stalks; cherry red with pink.	Michigan: 5 lb. Washington: 20-lb. lug.	38° F, 90 percent humidity.	Fresh and frozen.	Hot house: January–mid-May. Field: April–Summer.	U.S. Fancy, No. 1, No. 2.

Dairy Products

The term *dairy products* is usually associated with products that are derived from milk. This category has been extended to include eggs and margarine as well. Dairy products in general are perishable goods and must be treated as such from the point of purchasing through consumption. All characteristics of these products must be familiar to the chef and manager.

Eggs

Eggs are the most versatile of raw products. They are traditionally considered to be a breakfast item. However, they are incorporated into many different dishes as binders, thickeners, or garnishes. Eggs are also used to add color or flavor, or as a leavening agent in different baked items. Eggs are comprised of five parts:

1. The *shell* is a thin, porous covering that protects the egg. It allows the egg to gain air and absorb odors. The shell color depends on the breed of chicken. White shells are softer than brown shells.
2. The *yolk* is high in both protein and fat. It contains many vitamins and may range in color from light to dark yellow.
3. The *white* is actually two parts, the thick white that surrounds the yolk and the thinner, more liquid white that surrounds the thick white. These are primarily protein. They are clear and watery when raw and coagulate to a solid white state when cooked.

4. The *Chalazae* are the white spiral bands that attach the yolk to the inner membrane of the lining.
5. The *air cell* is the space between the lining and the shell; it grows larger as the egg ages and dehydrates.

The availability of eggs in many forms allows for better handling and storage. Most foodservice uses call for *shell eggs* (eggs still in their shells). Eggs are graded by the USDA: Grades AA, A, and B. The difference in the quality is centered on factors that describe the egg's shell, air cell, yolk, and white.

For breakfast cookery, the freshest AA egg is best. The fresh egg has a thick white and yolk. The egg is more round when cracked than lower grades, and the yolk sets higher in the white when fried. Other grades are also suitable, but they give a different, flatter appearance when fried. If eggs are to be used for other purposes than fried eggs, any grade may be used.

Eggs also come in different sizes, based on the weight per dozen (see Table 5–3). Shell eggs are traditionally packed in cases of 30 dozen; one-half case lots of 15 dozen can also be found. The weight of the case at the time of receipt is usually indicative of the size of the eggs. Eggs lose moisture rather rapidly. Therefore, weights will decrease as the eggs age.

Processed eggs are shell eggs that have been frozen or dried. They are available as whole eggs, yolks, and whites. Processed eggs should be pasteurized at 145° F for three and one-half minutes to eliminate pathogens. For baking purposes, eggs are available frozen, packaged in 30-pound cans.

Eggs are available in the following forms:

- Whole
- Yolks
- Whites
- Salt whole eggs (2 percent salt or more)
- Fortified whole eggs
- Blends (include sugar and salt yolks)
- Egg substitutes (made primarily from egg whites, a cholesterol-free, low-fat egg product)

Eggs are also available dried, primarily for use in baking. Dried eggs come in the following forms:

- Whole (packaged in 13-ounce #10 cans or 25-pound packages)
- Yolks (packaged in 1- or 3-pound packages)
- Whites (packaged in 1- or 3-pound packages)

Milk and Cream

Milk is fresh fluid cow's milk with no impurities or objectionable odors and flavors (see Table 5–4). It should contain no less than 3.25 percent milk fat and 8.5 percent nonfat milk solids. By federal law, milk and milk products must be pasteurized. Milk can be **pasteurized** in numerous ways, including the *holder process,* and the *high-temperature short-time (HTST) method.* In the holder process, milk is processed at 145° F for 30 minutes. Using the HTST method, milk is processed at 161° F for 15 seconds. Both of these methods require rapid cooling below 40° F to kill bacteria. Milk and cream products should be stored in a refrigerator at a temperature of 35° to 40° F to maximize shelf life. The optimum shelf life is one week for fresh milk and cream.

Table 5–3 Egg Sizes

Size	Weight per Dozen (ounces)
Jumbo	30
Extra large	27
Large	24
Medium	21
Small	18
Peewee	15

Table 5–4 Milk and Cream Types

Product	Types	Package
Milk	Fluid, whole; low fat 2%, 1%; skim 0.1%	Norris 5 to 6 gallon, gallon, half gallon, quart, pint and half-pint
	Dried, nonfat	50 pounds, 24 oz.
	Evaporated and condensed	14.5 oz., 10 oz., and 6 oz.
Cream	Heavy, whipping, light; half & half	Quarts, pints, and half-pints

Other Milk Products

A number of other fluid milk products on the market have various uses in foodservice. These products include special milks, such as low-sodium milk, buttermilk, fortified milks (vitamin D added, acidophilus), lactose-free milk, eggnog, and flavored milks. Concentrated fluid milks such as evaporated and condensed contain less water. Sweetened condensed milk is 45 percent sugar and is used for baking.

Butter and Margarine

Butters are fatty foods that are prepared by *churning* cream until the milk fat gradually turns into lumps of butter that coalesce. Federal standards require butter to be a minimum of 80 percent milk fat, with the remaining composition made up of approximately 18 percent water and 2 percent milk solids. Butter is graded as U.S. Grade AA (93 score), Grade A (92 score), Grade B (90 score), and Grade C (89 score). The difference in the grades is based on the flavor, color, salt content, and body. These differences do not affect the wholesomeness of the butter. Unsalted butter is preferred in many recipes because it allows the cook to control salt content while offering improved flavor. It is generally used in baking pastries. Butter should be stored at 35° F.

Margarines or butter substitutes are fatty foods that were originally made from other animal fats, but today are made strictly from vegetable oils, which are usually hydrogenated. The oils are blended with other flavoring, coloring ingredients, cream, salt, vitamins A and D, and milk solids. The current trend is to use low-fat polyunsaturated fatty acids. Various kinds of margarine are available, including margarine from different oils and butter-margarine blends.

Cheeses

The main ingredient in all cheese is milk. The milk used may be cow's milk, but other milks, such as goat and sheep, are also used. The quality and type of the milk will determine the flavor and texture of the cheese. The federal grades for American-produced cheeses are U. S. Grades AA, A, B, and C. Foreign-produced cheeses are not graded by the USDA.

Cheeses are divided into several categories: hard, semisoft, and soft. The hardness of the cheese is affected by the degree of ripening and other factors, such as aging. Ripening is also a way of classifying cheese. Some cheeses are ripened by the addition of bacteria or mold. Other cheeses—for example, Roquefort and Swiss—are ripened from the inside out. Still others, such as Camembert, Brie, and Limburger, are ripened from the outside in. The outside-in varieties soften with the ripening. Classification of cheeses as shown in Tables 5–5, 5–6, and 5–7 on page 72 is based on hardness and bacteria or mold addition. Cream cheese, cottage cheese, farmer's cheese, and baker's cheese, however, are all examples of unripened cheeses.

Table 5–5 Classification of Hard Cheese (All Bacteria Ripened)

Ripened 2 to 3 Months	Ripened 3 to 12 Months	Ripened 12 to 16 Months
Appetitost	American	Cheshire
Nökkelost	Apple	Parmesan
Kuminost	Asiago	Reggiano
	Cheddar	Romano
	Edam	Sardo
	Gjetöst	
	Gruyère	
	Provolone	
	Sapsago	
	Sbrinz	
	Swiss	

Table 5–6 Classification of Semihard Cheese

Bacteria Ripened 1 to 8 Months	Mold Ripened 2 to 12 Months
Bel Paese	Bleu
Brick	Gorgonzola
Fontina	Roquefort
Gammelost	Stilton
Gouda or Edam	
Jack	
Münster	
Port au Salut	

Table 5–7 Classification of Soft Cheese

Bacteria Ripened 1 to 2 Months	Mold Ripened 2 to 5 Months	Unripened
Limburger	Brie	Cottage
	Camembert	Cream
	Livarot	Neufchâtel
	Pont l'Évêque	Primost
		Ricotta

Nonperishables and Dry Goods

Nonperishables and dry goods are categorized as

- Grains and flours.
- Dried legumes.
- Nuts and seeds.
- Fats, oils, and shortenings.
- Dried pastas and noodles.
- Convenience food products.
- Sweeteners, sugars, syrups, and sugar substitutes.

Grains and Flours

Product descriptions and purchasing information for grains and flours are presented in Table 5–8 in column form for easy reference and continuity of data.

Dried Legumes

The use of dried legumes is widespread, especially in ethnic dishes (see Table 5–9 on page 74). The USDA grades dried beans, lentils, and peas U.S. No. 1 and as U.S. Extra No. 1. There are also many ungraded products available. Traditionally, legumes are packaged in 1-pound cello or plastic bags, 24 bags to a case. There are canned varieties of some of these products available in #303 or #10 cans.

Nuts

Many baking formulas call for the use of a variety of nuts. Nuts have a wonderful way of adding color, texture, and flavor to baked products. Nuts may be divided into several groups: whole natural, whole blanched, sliced natural, roasted natural, roasted blanched slivered, sliced, sliced blanched, diced or granulated roasted, or ground blanched. Nuts are classified as follows:

- Almonds
- Brazils
- Cashews
- Chestnuts
- Coconuts
- Filberts
- Peanuts
- Pecans
- Pine nuts (pignoli)
- Pistachios
- Walnuts

Nuts should come from the current year's crop and be bought in small quantities because they may become rancid or infested with insects. Purchase broken pieces when available for products that require chopped nuts; the prices are usually much lower.

Almonds

Grown on the almond tree, the almond is covered with a medium-brown skin and is white inside. There are two kinds of almonds: sweet and bitter. Sweet almonds are eaten, and bitter almonds are used as a source of almond flavoring. In the United States, almonds are grown commercially in California. The best-known almond confection is marzipan. Almond extract is prepared from the oil of sweet or bitter almonds. To blanch almonds for removing the skin, cover with boiling water and let stand for three minutes.

Almonds may be purchased whole in the shell; whole shelled, skinned, sliced, in pieces; and as almond paste. They are graded by the USDA as U.S. Fancy, Extra No. 1, and No. 1. Broken pieces are graded U.S. Whole and Broken or U.S. No. 1 Pieces.

Brazils

Botanically speaking, Brazil nuts are not nuts at all. The fruit is globular, 4 to 6 inches in diameter, and hard-walled, and contain 8 to 24 seeds arranged like the sections of

Table 5–8 Product Descriptions and Purchasing Information for Grains and Flours

Item	Description	Packaging
Wheat		1-lb. boxes
Cracked	Coarsely ground; hull remains	
Bulgur	Hulled cracked wheat	
Semolina	Polished wheat kernels	
Farina	Polished wheat kernels	
Germ	Embryo of wheat kernel	
Wheat flours		100-lb., 50-lb., and 25-lb. bags
All-purpose	Mixture of hard and soft flours	
Whole wheat	Bran added, not separated	
Cake	Protein (gluten) 8 percent	
Durum	Used for pastas	
Graham	Contains wheat germ and bran	100-lb., 50-lb., and 25-lb. bags
Hard	Used for breads	
Self-rising	Soft wheat flour with leavening added	25-lb. bags
Barley		100-lb. and 25-lb. bags
Pearl	Bran removed	
Dot	Husk removed	
Scotch	Ground grain	
Rye	Ground to make rye meal; available in light, medium, and dark	100-lb. and 25-lb. bags
Rice		
Long grain	Polished grains	
Medium grain	Polished grains	
Short grain	Polished grains	
Pearl	Polished grains	
White	All bran removed	100-lb., 50-lb., and 25-lb. bags
Undermilled brown	Unpolished	100-lb., 10-lb., 5-lb., and 2-lb. bags
Converted	Steamed, dried, enriched	1-lb. boxes
Instant	Cooked, dried	1-lb. and 2-lb. boxes
Buckwheat	Seed ground into flour	1-lb. and 2-lb. boxes
Cornmeal	Ground yellow or white corn	100-lb., 50-lb., and 25-lb. bags
Grits	Bran and germ removed	1-lb. boxes, 25-lb. bags
Cornstarch	Starch made from corn	1-lb. boxes, 25-lb. bags
Potato starch	Starch made from potatoes	2-lb boxes
Oats	Endosperm (groats) for cereal and baking	100-lb., 50 lb., 25-lb. bags
Soy	Ground into meal or flour; used to enhance protein values	100-lb., 50-lb., 25-lb. bags

Table 5–9 Description and Use of Dried Legumes

Item	Description
Beans	
Black	Kidney shaped; used in soups and in Oriental and Mediterranean dishes
Garbanzo	Known as chickpeas; used in salads
Black-eyed peas	Oval shaped, cream white with a black spot on the side; these are truly beans
Fava	Flat, brown; used in many Mediterranean dishes
Great northern	Larger than peas but used similarly in soups and salads
Kidney	Large, red, kidney shaped; used in chili con carne; available dry or in cans
Lima	Broad, flat; used in vegetable dishes and casseroles
Navy	Broad term includes great northern and peas; small, flat, white bean
Pea	Small, oval, and white; pea beans hold their shape even when cooked tender; used for baked beans, soups, and casseroles
Pinto	Same species as kidney and red beans; beige and speckled; used mainly in salads and chili
Red and pink	Used in Mexican dishes; pink beans have a more delicate flavor than red
Soy	Round, black, or yellow; used in Oriental dishes
Lentil	
Chilean	Small, dark green, yellow, brown, orange; used in soups and stews
Peas	
Green dry	Distinct flavor; used in soups
Yellow dry	Less pronounced flavor than green; preferred in Canada, the Caribbean, and South America; used in soups and casseroles
Dry split	Skin is removed by machine; used for split pea soup
Dry whole	Used in making soups, casseroles, puddings, dips, and hors d'oeuvres

an orange. These seeds are what is known as Brazil nuts. The trees grow wild in the tropics, and attempts to cultivate them in the southern United States have failed because the climate is not warm enough.

To shell Brazil nuts, cover with cold water, bring to a boil, and boil for three minutes. Rinse with cold water, drain, and crack. Sliced Brazils may be used to decorate baked goods and desserts, and chopped Brazils may be added to cakes, cookies, and breads. Keep shelled Brazils tightly covered in a cool place. Brazils may be purchased either whole in the shell or shelled. Brazils are graded in the shell as U.S. No. 1.

Cashews

The cashew is the edible seed of a tropical evergreen tree, native to tropical America and found widely in India and Africa. Most of the cashews in the United States are imported from India. Cashews are available either raw or toasted and shelled. They have a high fat content. Most

cashews are salted and roasted. Keep cashews refrigerated in a closed container or frozen in a freezer container.

Chestnuts

The sweet chestnut has been grown for many centuries and used in soups, cereals, stews, and stuffings. They are the only nuts that are treated as a vegetable. Because they contain more starch and less oil than other nuts, they can be cooked differently. They can be eaten whole, roasted, boiled, or steamed. Once shelled, they are preserved whole in sugar or syrup as marrons glacés; chopped and used in stuffings or with vegetables; ground into a flour, or puréed for desserts. Chestnuts are available in the marketplace in the raw form. They can be packaged whole in the shell, dried whole, or canned whole in water or syrup.

Coconuts

The coconut is the fruit of the palm, native to Malaysia, which has been transplanted to all parts of the tropical and subtropical world. The coconut palm is a handsome tree that can grow to a height of 100 feet, often leaning at an angle. The fruit is 12 to 18 inches long and 6 to 8 inches in diameter. The coconut produces a milky liquid and white meat that can be grated or shredded and eaten as is or used for cooking, fresh or preserved.

Coconut is available chipped, sliced, shredded, threaded, or desiccated; sweetened or unsweetened; and domestic or imported. Coconut may also be purchased as a cream for use in baking and cocktails. It is packed in 4-, 8-, and 10-ounce, as well as 1-, 5-, and 10-pound packages. Keep unopened coconut at room temperature. Opened coconut should be stored at 32° F to 35° F in 90 percent relative humidity. To toast, spread in a shallow pan and bake in a moderate oven (350° F.) until light brown, stirring frequently. To tint coconut, place desired amount in a paper or plastic bag, add a few drops of the desired food coloring, close bag, and shake vigorously.

Filberts

Filberts, also known as hazelnuts, are drier than almonds or walnuts. Filberts are grown in clusters, and each nut is enclosed in a husk that opens as the nut ripens. They are harvested by being shaken off the bushes or gathered from the ground. Whole filberts can be salted, sugared, or eaten as is. Chopped filberts are used in candies, baked goods, and desserts. Filberts provide protein, fat, iron, and thiamine. Filberts are available whole in the shell, whole shelled, or chopped. To toast filberts, spread out in a shallow pan and bake at 400° F for about seven minutes, stirring frequently. For salted filberts, add 1 teaspoon of salt per cup of nutmeat. Filberts may be stored on the shelf if used regularly.

Peanuts

The peanut plant grows to a height of about 18 inches and bears light green leaves and white flowers. At this point, it resembles the pea plant for which it was named. When the flowers fade, the stalk bends down and into the earth. To harvest, the entire plant must be dug up. There are many uses for peanuts, peanut oil and peanut butter being two valuable products. Even the shells are pressed and used for cattle feed. There are over 300 synthetic products made from peanuts. The two types of peanuts

generally available are known as Virginia and Spanish. The Virginia peanut has larger and longer kernels, a lower oil content, and a more pronounced flavor than does the Spanish.

Peanuts are available in many forms and for many uses. They are graded by the USDA as U.S. No. 1, U.S. No. 1 Spanish, and U.S. Extra Large Virginia. The most common ready-to-use forms of peanuts include cocktail, dry roasted, and granules. Peanut butter is graded U.S. Grade A or B and is available either as fine, medium, or coarse grinds, or chunky, which is coarse chunks with fine ground. Peanuts that are vacuum packed will last indefinitely, while peanuts that have been shelled should be kept refrigerated. Peanuts are high in fat and contain a concentrated source of calories. To toast peanuts, spread in a shallow pan and bake at 300° F for about 30 minutes, stirring several times.

Pecans

A native-American nut of the pecan tree, pecans are found in the southeastern United States and in Mexico. Pecans have a very thin shell and the nutmeat has a fat content of over 70 percent. Pecans are associated with southern cooking and traditions. Store pecans covered tightly in a cool, dry place. In the refrigerator, pecans will last about nine months. Pecans are graded U.S. No. 1 and Commercial for halves and pieces. They are available whole in the shell, chopped, or half-shelled. Shelled pecans may be purchased in 3-ounce or 8-ounce cans, and in 5-, 25-, and 50-pound boxes.

Pine Nuts

Pine nuts (pignoli) are the kernels of pine cones. They resemble almonds in taste and are used in various ways, including in pesto. They are a fairly perishable nut that should be stored tightly covered in a cool, dark, dry place. They can be frozen. Pine nuts come in various sizes and are available raw or toasted. They are packaged in many forms for retail consumption, e.g., in jars, bags, cans.

Pistachios

The edible seed of a small evergreen tree, pistachios have been found growing wild in the Canary Islands, Mexico, and California, although this nut is native to Asia. The fruits of the tree grow in clusters. The pistachio is pale green to creamy white in color, with a fine texture and mild, pleasing flavor. Pistachios should be kept covered in the refrigerator.

Pistachios are available in the shell or shelled; shelled pistachios may be chopped. Pistachios are usually roasted and salted and may be dyed red or left natural. The USDA grades pistachios as Fancy, No. 1, and No. 2. They are packaged in #10 cans weighing 3 1/2 to 4 pounds, 25 cans per carton.

Walnuts

Walnuts are the edible fruit of the walnut tree. The most commonly known walnut is the English or Persian walnut. The English walnut has been cultivated for centuries in the Mediterranean region. In the United States, the species of the walnut is generally called a California walnut. The black walnut, a native-American nut, has a dark brown, deeply ridged shell covering a strongly flavored kernel. Butternuts or white walnuts are also native to America. Walnut oil, pressed from the kernel, is used in France like olive oil. Today, the United States leads the world in walnut production.

There are three sizes of walnuts: large, medium, and babies. They are available whole in the shell, shelled as halves, or chopped. Walnuts are graded as U.S. No. 1 and Commercial. Grade is based on color and condition of nuts and nutmeats. Store walnuts in a cool, dry place. To toast, spread in a shallow pan with 1 tablespoon of butter for every 2 cups of walnuts. Bake at 350° F for about 20 minutes or until a golden color.

Seeds

Seeds are multifaceted ingredients that can add wonderful flavor, texture, color, and nutrients to recipes when used as a major ingredient. Some used in cooking—for example, cumin, and coriander—are considered spices and therefore have been included in the spice section. Other seeds are used more often in cooking and baking as garnish.

Poppy Seeds

Poppy seeds are the dried seed of the poppy plant. They are used as an ingredient in many international specialties, especially in Central European, Middle Eastern, and Indian cooking. They have been incorporated into the American diet as seed garnish for rolls and breads and as an ingredient in muffins and cakes. Poppy seeds are available as whole seeds and contain about 40 to 55 percent oil.

Pumpkin Seeds

Pumpkin seeds are available in the shell or shelled. They may be toasted or raw and are often salted. Pumpkin seeds are a popular snack item or may be pressed for oil.

Sesame Seeds

A plant native to Indonesia and East Africa, it yields seeds that are used in a variety of ways in culinary and baking preparations. In Middle Eastern cuisines, sesame seeds are used raw, for oil, or mashed into a paste called tahini. In Far Eastern cooking, they are roasted to yield a darker color and stronger taste before being used primarily for flavoring various dishes. The seeds contain about 50 percent oil and 20 to 25 percent protein. Sesame seeds are often used in baked goods.

Sunflower Seeds

Sunflower seeds contain about 50 percent oil (polyunsaturated) and are grown mainly for this purpose. They are also a wonderful snack item when lightly toasted and salted. As raw seeds, they are packaged in 50-pound and in other size multiwalled bags.

Fats and Oils

Fats and oils belong to a family of compounds known as lipids. Technically, **oil** refers to a lipid that is liquid at room temperature and often comes from vegetable sources. **Fat** refers to a lipid that is solid at room temperature and often comes from animal sources. It is common, however, for the term *fat* to be used to mean *lipid*.

Fats and oils have the same chemical framework. They are made up of glycerol and three types of fatty acids: **saturated, monounsaturated,** and **polyunsaturated.** The predominant type of fatty acid determines the classifi-

Table 5–10 The Smoking Points of Different Fats and Oils

Type of Fat or Oil	Approximate Smoking Point
Whole butter	Above 250° F
Clarified butter	Above 330° F
Vegetable oils	Above 400° F (an average; olive oils are slightly lower)
Vegetable shortenings	Above 370° F (an average; due to the emulsifiers they contain)
Animal lard	Above 375° F (an average)

cation of the fat and some of its characteristics. Saturated fats are usually solid at room temperature, while monounsaturated and polyunsaturated fats are usually liquid at room temperature and have a low melting point. They also become rancid more easily when exposed to oxygen, which is called **oxidative rancidity.** Antioxidants such as butylated hydroxyanisol (BHA), butylated hydroxytoluine (BHT), or vitamin E are added to protect fats from oxygen and to extend their shelf life.

In the culinary field, chefs often choose which fats or oils to use based on their taste, saturation level, and smoking point. The *smoking point* is the maximum temperature the fat or oil can be taken to before burning occurs, the flavor is tainted, and the color changes. This is an important factor to consider because the smoking point of a fat or oil will often determine whether it can be used in conjunction with certain cooking techniques that require the fats or oils used to withstand high temperatures (often in excess of 350° F) for a particular period of time. The smoking point of a fat or oil is lowered still more if it is used repeatedly, as in the case of frying (see Table 5–10). Some breakdown occurs by simply holding the fat at moderate temperatures for long periods of time. This deterioration may also be compounded by the minute particles of food product that are left behind in the oil once the main item is cooked. The particles gradually begin to burn and impart an unpleasant flavor to the fat or oil.

Hydrogenation

Another way of protecting monounsaturated and polyunsaturated fats from oxidative rancidity is hydrogenation. *Hydrogenation* is a process that forces hydrogen into fat and

oil. This raises the smoking point of the fat or oil and makes it both more plastic and more saturated. Margarine is an example of an ingredient that is made by hydrogenating vegetable oil. Saturated fats are usually solid at room temperature; that is, they have a higher melting point. The tropical oils (coconut, palm, and palm kernel) are the exceptions; while these oils are among the few vegetable oils that are very saturated, they can be liquid at room temperature.

Growing public concern regarding heart disease has caused a dramatic rise in the popularity of monounsaturated and polyunsaturated fats in recent years. Good sources of monounsaturated fats include olive oil, canola oil, and peanut oil. Most other vegetable oils (except for the tropical oils) and fish are good sources of polyunsaturated fats. The tropical oils, hydrogenated fat, and animal fat are sources of saturated fats.

Most of the vegetable and animal fats and vegetable oils are close to 100 percent fat. Lard hydrogenated fat is 100 percent fat. Butter (approximately 80 percent fat), margarine, bacon, and salt pork contain water and nutrients in varying amounts. Reduced-fat spreads contain added air or water and can vary in fat content from 25 to 80 percent.

Economic Aspects

The cost of a fat or oil depends on the original cost of the product in which the fat or oil is found and on the processing involved. The supply of and the demand for the fat also play an important role in its cost. For example, when the fat supply is scarce, as in wartime, the cost of all fat is increased. The cost of fats with near or comparable food values varies. For example, margarine is less expensive than butter, and lard is slightly less expensive than hydrogenated fats. Olive oil is generally more expensive than other vegetable oils, and imported olive oils cost far more than those produced in this country.

Product Selection

Lipid research and product development is a billion-dollar-a-year business and is forever growing. There are hundreds of products available for use in the kitchen or dining room.

Some are as ancient as lard and others as new as canola oil blends.

To select the product that best meets the chef's needs and expectations, he or she must be able to compare the color, melting point, plasticity, smoking point, stability, emulsification value, shortening value, and, most important, flavor of the products available. Not all of these characteristics are important for each product. The following descriptions highlight some of the more important characteristics of the fats listed.

Animal Fats. *Lard* is obtained from the fatty tissues of hogs. It varies in composition and general characteristics according to the type of feed given the hog and the part of the animal from which the lard is obtained. Lard from hogs fed on soybeans or peanuts is much softer than lard from corn-fed hogs, and lard made from fat near the organs of the hog is firmer than that made from the fat of other parts of the animal. Prime steam lard comes from the fat that is stripped from the internal organs of the animal at the time of slaughter. Dry-rendered leaf lard is made from the internal fat of the hog. It is firmer than other lards and slightly grainy because of the slow chilling it undergoes after being heated during processing. Hydrogenated lards, lards to which hydrogen has been added chemically, raising their melting point, are marketed under trade names.

Suet is processed fat obtained from around the kidneys and loins of beef and sheep. It is harder than fats from other parts of the animals. Suet is marketed as oleo stearin or oleo. Suet is used in the production of baked goods and crackers.

Shortenings. *Vegetable shortening* is a lipid used for frying or baking. In baking, the effect of shortening is a crisp product that does not rise significantly. The shortening effect of fat in a flour mixture is brought about by the formation of fat layers that separate the starch and gluten particles, reducing their tendency to adhere to one another. Fat also coats flour particles and limits gluten development. Vegetable oils are used extensively in the preparation of flour mixtures. Because hydrogenated vegetable shortenings hold most of the air incorporated in mixing, they are preferred for cakes. High-ratio cake shortenings are

made by adding 2 to 5 percent monoglycerides and diglycerides to hydrogenated shortenings to improve their baking and emulsifying properties.

Fat Compounds. *Fat compounds* are produced by combining 20 percent rendered animal fats and 80 percent hydrogenated vegetable oils. A fat compound may also be any mixture of animal fats. Fat compounds are no longer widely used because of the increased public demand for unsaturated and cholesterol-free fats and oils.

Vegetable Fats and Oils. See Table 5–11 for a list of vegetable oils.

Fat Substitutes. The demand for low-fat and nonfat products has spurred the use of fat substitutes, each of which is limited in its use, function, and appeal. Table 5–12 on page 78 gives a brief overview of the fat substitutes available to the chef. They may be used as ingredients or can be found in prepared products such as cake mixes or ice cream.

Pasta and Noodles

Pasta and noodles come in an array of flavors, shapes, sizes, and colors (see Figure 5–1 on page 80). They are made from a variety of grains and flours. Dried pasta and noodles should be stored between 50° and 70° F. The best quality pastas are made from semolina, a high-protein flour. The texture of dry pasta should be hard and brittle. Pasta and noodles cook quickly; in approximately 7 to 10 minutes in boiling water from a dried state. When cooked, pasta and noodles should be firm to the bite and should retain their original shape. Table 5–13 on page 80 lists the uses of various pastas.

Convenience-Food Products

There are many products with specific uses in menu items that have not been listed or identified (see Table 5–14 on page 82). These products come under a general grocery

Table 5–11 Vegetable Oils

Item	Description
Butter-flavored	Usually blended and sometimes flavored with artificial butter; used for griddling
Canola	Low in saturated fat, high in monunsaturated and saturated fat; used in cooking and baking; light in color
Coconut	High in saturated fat; used in blended shortenings and oils; almost colorless; low smoking point
Corn	Byproduct of the manufacturing of starch, cornmeal, syrup, and hominy; light amber, clear color when fresh; used in frying and on salads; high smoking point; inexpensive
Cottonseed	Quality affected by soil fertilizer variety, season, and methods of extraction; sweet, fresh odor; amber color; dark color indicates poor quality; used in salad dressing and shortening; high smoking point
Grapeseed	Medium yellow; used in cooking, the manufacture of margarine, and salad making
Olive	Quality depends on the pressing, soil, and growing conditions; if the pits are removed before pressing, a higher quality will result; pressing must occur quickly; oil from the first pressing is referred to as virgin olive oil; refined oil comes primarily from later pressing; refined oil is called pure olive oil; light greenish to yellow; should be free of strong off-odors and flavors; used in cooking and salad dressing; low smoking point
Peanut	Extracted by expeller or hydraulic process; after the refining process, the oil has a nutty flavor and should be amber; excellent for frying and deep-frying; high smoking point
Safflower	Usually refined and golden in color; used in salad dressing, margarine, and mayonnaise; high smoking point
Salad	General name given to mild-flavored oils; used in mayonnaise and salad dressing
Sesame seed	Middle Eastern is mild and light in color; Oriental is darker in color; both are used in cooking
Soybean	Seasonal and climatic conditions, soil, and processing affect quality; yellowish clear color; used in salad dressing, margarine, and shortening; high smoking point
Sunflower	Pale yellow in color; light, almost flavorless and odorless faculties; used in salad dressing, margarine, cooking, and shortening; high smoking point
Vegetable	Vegetable oils are designated either by the name of the vegetable from which they are made or by trade names; corn, cottonseed, and soybean are examples of vegetable oils; generally have a mild flavor and high smoking point
Walnut	Highly perishable; nutty aroma and flavor; medium yellow color; used in baking and salad making

Table 5–12 Fat Substitutes

Item	Description
Microparticulated protein	Brand name, Simplesse; made from protein found in milk and eggs; gives the mouth-feel of fat; yields some calories; currently used in frozen desserts and salad dressings
Gums or gel	Soluble fibers that set up gels and thicken; provide some of the body, bulk, and mouth-feel of fat; derived from land and sea plants; some gels are produced synthetically; used in frozen desserts, cakes, puddings, custards, and nonfat dairy products, toppings, and frostings
Dried butter *buds* or powder	Dried butter solids; provide flavor only; most products contain salt to enhance flavor; sold in powder or premixed form; found in prepared foods and mixes

Figure 5–1 Various pasta shapes

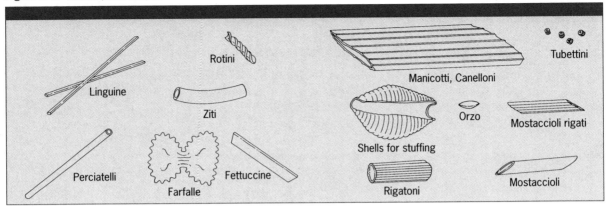

Table 5–13 Uses of Various Pastas

Item	Description	Soup	To Boil	To Bake	To Stuff
Acini de pepe (peppercorns)	Small, pellet-shaped	✓			
Agnolotti	Thin, round, curly edges, folded in half				✓
Anelli (rings)	Medium, ridges; tube pasta cut into thin rings	✓			
Cannelloni (large pipes)	Large cylinders				✓
Capellini (angel hair)	Very fine strands		✓		
Cappelletti	Thin, flat pasta, rolled up on one edge, folded to a round			✓	
Cavatappi (corkscrews)	Medium-thin, hollow, ridged pasta, twisted into a spiral		✓		
Cellophane noodles	Very fine transparent noodles; sold in compressed bunches	✓			
Conchiglie (shells)	Medium to large, ridged, shell-shaped				✓
Conchigliette (shells)	Small, ridges, shell shape	✓			
Cresti di gallo (cock's comb)	Ridged, hollow, elbow-shaped with a ruffled edge		✓		
Ditali (thimbles)	Narrow tubes cut in short lengths		✓		
Ditalini (thimbles)	Tiny narrow tubes cut into short lengths	✓			
Egg flakes	Small flat squares	✓			
Elbow macaroni	1-inch narrow, curved tubes			✓	
Farfalle (butterflies)	Flat, rectangular noodles, pinched at the center to resemble a butterfly or bow		✓		
Farfallini (tiny butterflies)	Tiny, flat, rectangular noodles, pinched at the center to resemble a butterfly or bow	✓			
Fettuccine	Half-inch wide, flat, long, ribbon-shaped		✓		
Fiochetti (bows)	Rectangular, curled pasta, pinched at the center to form bow shapes		✓		
Fusilli (twists)	Long, spiral-shaped strands		✓		
Lasagne	Large, flat noodles, 3 inches wide, usually having curly edges			✓	

(continued)

Table 5–13 Uses of Various Pastas *(continued)*

Item	Description	Soup	To Boil	To Bake	To Stuff
Linguine	⅛-inch wide, flat, solid strands		✓		
Maccheroni (macaroni)	Thin, tubular, various widths, long or cut short		✓		
Mafalde	¾-inch wide, flat, curly edged		✓		
Manicotti (small muffs)	Thick, ridged tubes; straight or angle cut				✓
Mostaccioli (small mustaches)	½-inch diameter, medium-sized tubes with angle-cut ends		✓		
Orecchiette	Half-inch, smooth, curved rounds of flat pasta	✓			
Ortzo (barley)	Small, grain-shaped	✓			
Pastina (tiny pasta)	Miniature pasta in various shapes	✓			
Penne (quills or pens)	½-inch diameter, medium-sized tubes with angle-cut ends			✓	
Ravioli	One square of thin pasta filled with assorted stuffings then a second square of thin pasta is placed on top and the edges sealed				✓
Rigatoni	Thick, ridged tubes, 1½-inch lengths		✓		
Rotelle (wheels)	Spiral shaped		✓		
Rotini (tiny cartwheels)	Tiny, round, six-spoked wheels	✓			
Ruote (cartwheels)	Small, round, six-spoked wheels		✓		
Spaghetti (little strings) or spaghettini (very thin)	Solid, round strands, ranging from very thin to thin		✓		
Tagliatelli	Same as fettuccine		✓		
Tortellini	Thin, rectangular pasta, stuffed, rolled, and twisted				✓
Tubetti lunghi (long tubes)	Small to medium, tubular, long, or cut in 1-inch lengths		✓		
Tubettini (tiny tubes)	Tubular, cut into short lengths	✓			
Vermicelli	Very fine, cylindrical		✓		
Ziti (bridegroom)	Two-inch long, ridged, thick tubes			✓	

category. Some of these items should be stocked in inventory.

Sweeteners

Sugar and Sugar Syrups

Most sugar is made from the juice of sugar cane or sugar beet, which is refined and crystallized (see Tables 5–15 on page 83 and 5–16 on page 84). Sugar syrups contain liquid that must be accounted for in the recipe. Sugar and sugar syrups are naturally occurring sweeteners that perform the following functions in food and food production:

- Impart flavor: add sweetness to cakes and candy; reduce tartness or acidity of a product; sugars, such as brown sugar, may add a characteristic flavor
- Brown: caramelization and browning in baked products and roasted meats
- Retain moisture: sugars hold water; for example, in bakery products
- Improve texture: of bakery products; used in frozen desserts, will keep ice crystals small

Table 5–14 Convenience-Food Products

Item	No. Per Package	Type of Packaging
Anchovy paste, fillets	24 each	2-oz. tubes
Anise, star		8-oz. jars
Apple butter		#10 cans
Applesauce		#10 cans
Arrowroot powder	6 each	24-oz. cans
Aspic powder	12 each	2-lb. cans
Baking powder	6 each	5-lb. cans
Baking soda	12 each	2-lb. cans
Bases, assorted		1 and 5 lb. jars
Bean paste		6-oz. can
Bouillon cubes		12, 30, or 100 cubes
Bread crumbs		1-, 5-, or 10-lb. canister
Capers	12 each	3½-oz. jars
Caviar, assorted		1- and 2-oz. jars, 2.2-lb. cans
Chili sauce		#10 can
Chocolate syrup		#10 can
Chutney	12 each	32-oz. jar
Chopped clams	12 each	#5 can
Clam juice	12 each	#5 can
Cornstarch	24 each	1-lb. boxes
Crackers, assorted		1-lb. boxes
Cranberry sauce		#10 cans
Demi-glace mix	12 each	2-lb. cans
Dressings, assorted	4 each	1-gallon jars
Escargots	12 each	2½ lbs.
Extracts	12 each	16-oz. bottles
Fiddlehead ferns		10 oz.
Garlic, chopped	12 each	1-lb. jars
Gravymaster	12 each	32-oz. bottles
Grenadine syrup	12 each	1-liter bottles
Hearts of palm	24 each	#303 cans
Hoisin sauce	24 each	#303 cans
Jelly, grape		1-lb. jars
Jelly, mint		1-lb. jars
Ketchup	24 each	14-oz. bottles
	6 each	#10 cans
Marzipan		5 lbs.
Nougat		3 lbs., 9 oz.
Olives, assorted	6 each	#10 cans
Phyllo dough	12 each	1-lb. boxes
Pickles, assorted	6 each	#10 cans
Pimentoes	24 each	#300 cans
Popcorn	36 each	3½-oz. bags
Potato chips, assorted	6 each	1-lb. bags

(continued)

Table 5–14 Convenience-Food Products *(continued)*

Item	No. Per Package	Type of Packaging
Quail eggs	24 each	15-oz. flat
Raisins, assorted	24 each	1-lb. boxes
Relish, pickle	6 each	#10 cans
Sardines	24 each	3½-oz. cans
Salsa, assorted	6 each	#10 cans
Sauerkraut	6 each	#10 cans
Sesame paste		9-oz. jars
Simple syrup		1-quart bottles
Soy sauce	6 each	1-gallon cans
Syrup, maple	6 each	1-gallon jugs
Syrup, pancake	6 each	1-gallon jugs
Taco sauce	6 each	#10 cans
Tapioca	4 each	5-lb. boxes
Tomatoes, whole peeled	6 each	#10 cans
Tomatoes, crushed	6 each	#10 cans
Tomatoes, diced	6 each	#10 cans
Tomatoes, paste	6 each	#10 cans
Tomatoes, purée	6 each	#10 cans
Tuna, canned	12 each	#5 squat
Vinegar, assorted		1-quart bottle
Worcestershire sauce	4 each	1-gallon jugs
Yeast		2-lb. cakes

Table 5–15 Common Forms of Sugar

Common Name	Other Names	Description
White sugar, coarse	Sucrose, preserving	Pure sugar in large crystals; used in baking, sauces, chutneys. Form: granulated, bulk.
White, granulated, 4X*	Sucrose, table	Pure sugar in small crystals. Form: granulated, bulk, packets, compressed into cubes.
White, superfine, 6X*	Sucrose, bar, castor	Pure sugar finely granulated; used in baking and tableside to garnish and in sauces. Form: bulk. Contains a small amount of starch.
White, confectioners, 10X*	Sucrose	Pulverized pure granulated sugar; used primarily powdered in baking. Form: powdered, bulk.
Brown sugar, raw sugar	Sucrose, turbinado	Granulated sugars in which some molasses is sucanat, muscovado left on or added to the sugar crystals; adds characteristic flavor; very little added nutritional value; moister than white sugar. Form: coarse or granular.
Fructose	Fruit, sugar, levulose	A naturally occurring sugar almost twice as sweet as sucrose; contains same number of calories as sucrose; used in the same way as sucrose. Form: granular, packets, liquid.

4X = Small crystals; 6X = Finely granulated; 10X = Fine powder

Table 5–16 Sugar Syrups

Common Name	Other Names	Description
Honey	Comb	Sweeter than table sugar, honey is used for its characteristic flavor and color; some commercial honey products are cut with corn syrup or glucose syrups
Molasses		Made from the liquor drawn from sugar crystals as they are refined; all types contain 5 to 75 percent invert sugar and sucrose; used for its characteristic flavor and color
Black strap molasses		Stronger-flavored, thicker, darker molasses; used for its strong flavor; less sweet than sugar
Nulomoline		An invert sugar used for its moisture-retaining ability; used in baking

- Add shine: to the crust of bakery products; also as glaze
- Caramelize: in candy, sauce, and frosting production
- Preserve: jams and jellies

Sugar Substitutes

Sugar substitutes replace sugar to provide sweetness. They will not perform the other functions of sugar. These substances are generally many times sweeter than table sugar. A small amount of substitute, containing a fraction of the calories of sugar, will provide an equal amount of sweetness as sugar. Sugar substitutes are often included in modified diets in which reduced calories or limited sugar intake is desired. Convenience foods containing sugar substitutes, including but not limited to beverages, light yogurts, and low-calorie candies, are widely available. Not everyone can or should use sugar substitutes. There are two primary sugar substitutes currently on the market (see Table 5–17):

- *Saccharin:* Noncaloric and far sweeter than sugar, it was discovered over a century ago and is now suspected to be a carcinogenic agent. Because this issue is still being researched by the Food and Drug Administration (FDA), the use of saccharin *must* be noted on the label in an obvious way to warn consumers. Although it is used widely in home and commercial products, it has a bitter taste, which is especially noticeable when food sweetened with saccharin is heated.
- *Aspartame:* Aspartame is an artificial sweetener that contains two amino acids: L-aspartic acid and L-phenylalanine. It is much sweeter than sugar and is not suitable for cooking or for use with acids. Some people cannot consume the amino acid phenylalanine. The use of aspartame should also be noted clearly on the label.

Table 5–17 Sugar Substitutes

Common Name	Brand Name	Description
Aspartame	Equal	Noncaloric; 180 times sweeter than sugar; made from Nutrasweet, two amino acids unstable to heat; loses sweetness during prolonged cooking, so cannot be used in baking.
Saccharin	Sweet 'n Low, Sugar Twin, and Sweet Life	Noncaloric; 375 times sweeter than table sugar. Form: powder, bulk, packets, tablets, liquid.
Acesulfame K, Ace K	Sunnette and Sweet One	Noncaloric; 200 times sweeter than table sugar. Form: powder, packets.

Food Enhancers

Food enhancers are ingredients that are added, usually in small amounts, to improve food flavor. They are divided into four categories: herbs and spices; flavorings, seasonings, and condiments. Strength, aroma, tenderness, and taste of food are affected by the use of flavor enhancers. Some enhancers may be added before cooking, others are added during cooking, and still others are added after cooking.

Many food enhancers are associated with regional and ethnic cooking. It is often the use of a particular enhancer or blend of enhancers that imparts the desired character to a food product. Becoming familiar with traditional blends of enhancers from a variety of ethnic cuisines is a great way of learning how to use them properly.

Herbs and Spices

The chef must fully understand how cooking with herbs and spices enhances the aroma and taste of certain foods.

Herbs are the fragrant leaves of various perennial or annual plants. They can be procured fresh or dried. Most fresh herbs should be stored under refrigeration at 34° to 40° F, with a relative humidity of 90 percent. Dried herbs should be stored in closed containers at room temperature, between 50° and 70° F, with a relative humidity of 50 to 60 percent.

Spices are traditionally the fruits, flowers, bark, seeds, and roots of plants and trees. Spices should be stored at room temperature (between 50° F and 70° F) with a relative humidity of 50 to 60 percent. They should be kept away from heat and sunlight (see Table 5–18).

Table 5–18 Herbs and Spices

Name	Description	Uses
Allspice (spice)	Dried, unripe, pea-sized fruit of pimiento tree; grown in Jamaica; flavor resembles a blend of cinnamon, cloves, and nutmeg.	Whole: pickles, meats, consommé, and sauces. Ground: baked goods, pâtés, puddings, relishes, and preserves.
Anise seed (spice)	Small, aromatic, licorice-flavored fruit from Spain, the East, and most subtropical countries; Italian and Spanish seeds are larger than those from Germany, Russia, and Syria.	In fish sauces, such as bouillabaisse; pastry for cakes, rolls, cookies, and candies.
Basil (herb)	Usually green leaf; belongs to the mint family; originally grown in western Europe; purchase pesto, bottled, dried, and fresh.	Soups, sauces, and salads.
Bay leaves (herb)	Aromatic, smooth, shiny green leaves of the laurel tree; grown in eastern Mediterranean.	Soups, stocks, chowders, roasts, stews, fish preparations, tomatoes, and pickles.
Caraway seed (spice)	Member of parsley family; closely related to fennel and dill; oval shaped; light to dark brown color.	Pumpernickel, rye breads; salads, vegetables, cabbage, cheeses, coleslaw, sauerkraut, goulash, and kummel schnapps.
Cardamom (spice)	Relative of ginger plant; grows nearly 10 feet high; flavor is sweet with a touch of eucalyptus.	Indian foods, curries, sweet dishes, yogurt, and baked goods.
Cayenne (spice)	Hot red peppers, ground fine; main areas of supply are Africa, Japan, and South and Central America; related to pimiento; flavor strong and pungent.	Meat, fish, egg dishes, salads, sauces, and pickles; used in making curry powder.
Celery seed (spice)	Tiny, seedlike fruit of the plant, cultivated in southern France and India.	Whole: sauces, salads and pickles. Ground: soups, fish stews, and salad dressing.
Chervil (herb)	Slightly peppery; resembles parsley; purchase dried or fresh.	Soups, sauces, and decoration.

(continued)

Table 5–18 Herbs and Spices (continued)

Name	Description	Uses
Chives (herb)	Thin, rounded shoot, resembling grass blade; grown nearly worldwide; more distinctive flavor than onions; tasty as garnishes but without dominant flavor; purchase fresh or dried.	Soups, sauces, spreads, and salads; occasionally replaces onions; garnishes.
Cinnamon (spice)	Grows in many tropical areas: Sri Lanka, southern India, West Indies, and Brazil; the tropical cinnamon evergreen can grow 30 feet high.	Curries, spicy meat stuffings, pickles, desserts, sweet potatoes, preserves, and hot beverages.
Cloves (spice)	Nail-shaped dried flower bud of clove tree; grown in Madagascar; highly aromatic and pungent; residue of clove oil provides a chemical vanilla.	Whole: hams, pickles, spiced syrups, tea, and sauces. Ground: baked goods, preserves, pickles, fruits, and sauces.
Coriander leaves (herb)	Also called Chinese parsley or cilantro; leaves resemble flat parsley; best when purchased with roots intact; store with roots in water under refrigeration.	Stir-fry dishes, soups, and chutneys; used in Chinese, Southeast Asian, Latin American, and Cajun cooking.
Coriander seeds (spice)	Grows in Asia; a member of the parsley family.	Chili, spicy dishes, pickling spices, curries, sausages, meats, baked goods, game dishes, chicken, and fish.
Cumin seed (spice)	From a plant native to the Middle East; the spicy seeds are boat-shaped and greenish-brown in color.	Chicken, fish, curries, chili, and other Mexican dishes; couscous, sausages, and hard cheese; very popular in Middle East cuisines.
Curry (spice blend)	Blend of spices including turmeric, cumin seed, coriander, pepper, pimientos, ginger, cardamom, caraway, cinnamon, mace, and cloves in fixed proportions; these powdered spices must be thoroughly blended; various combinations and amounts determine the flavor and color of curry.	Sauces, soups, meats, fish, poultry, eggs, vegetables, chowders, and rice dishes.
Dill (herb)	Highly appreciated in the cookery of all Scandinavian countries; mostly grown in western Europe; purchase fresh (dried) seeds.	Soups, salads, and fish.
Dill seed (spice)	Small, dark seed of the dill plant; aromatic, slightly sharp taste, resembling caraway.	Soups, sauces, fish dishes, salads, and for pickling.
Fennel (herb)	Grown in Mediterranean area; related to anise seed; purchase fresh and seeds.	Sauces, soups; indispensable in pickling gherkins, and onions.
Fenugreek (spice)	Fenugreek plant is part of the pea and bean family; each pod contains several ochre-brown seeds.	Indian food, pickles, chutney, poultry, and meat.
Five-spice powder (spice blend)	A combination of ground star anise, fennel, cinnamon, cloves, and Szechwan pepper.	Meat, poultry, fish, marinades, and sauces; imparts characteristic flavor to Chinese cooking.
Ginger (spice)	Fresh ginger root is easily obtained; dried ginger comes in pieces, slices, ground, or whole.	Fresh: fish, poultry, Chinese or Japanese dishes, braising and curries. Ground: gingerbread and puddings.
Horseradish (spice)	Grown throughout Europe and America; used raw, both whole and grated.	Sauces, mustard, fish, pickling gherkins, and onions.
Juniper berries (spice)	Fruit of evergreen trees that range in height from 4 to 35 feet; found throughout Europe.	Game, pork, beef stews, marinades, wines, gin, liqueurs, sauerkraut, and curing of hams and poultry.

(continued)

Table 5–18 Herbs and Spices *(continued)*

Name	Description	Uses
Lemon grass (herb)	A tall, tough, and fibrous grass that grows in tropical regions; bulbous base is used to impart a lemony flavor.	Curries and spiced dishes.
Mace (spice)	Orange-red, fleshy outer shell of nutmeg kernel, smooth, nutmeglike flavor, grown on nutmeg trees in Indonesia and Jamaica.	Ragouts, soups, sauces, preserves, stuffings, and cakes.
Marjoram (herb)	Leaves and flowering tops of aromatic herbs of mint family; grown in southern France, Chile, North Africa, and America; purchase dried or fresh.	Stews, soups, pâtés, sauces, sausages, and lamb and poultry seasonings.
Mint (herb)	Leaves of spearmint plant grown in most localities for its aromatic oil; purchase fresh (dried) extract.	Sauces, lamb, peas, tea, and pastries; popular in North African countries.
Mustard seed (spice)	Small, round, smooth seeds of annual herbacious plant of the watercress family; very common in the United States; pungent, tangy flavor.	Salads, pickles, meats, fish, sauces, and salad dressings.
Nutmeg (spice)	Dry, hard, wrinkled seed of nutmeg fruit, grown in Indonesia and Jamaica; second-quality nutmeg is sold grated.	Whole: grated as needed. Ground: ragouts, soups, sauces, and pastry.
Oregano (herb)	Dried leaves of a perennial herb of the mint family; grown in Italy and Mexico; slightly bitter flavor; purchase dried or fresh.	Soups, sauces, meats, egg dishes, and chili con carne.
Paprika (spice)	Dried, ripe, red, sweet peppers grown in Hungary, Portugal, and Spain; sold fresh, powdered, preserved whole, diced, and canned; Hungarian paprika is more pungent and markedly aromatic; Spanish paprika is sweeter and lighter in color.	Soups, sauces, fish and shellfish, stews, salad dressings, tomato dishes, and garnishes.
Parsley (herb)	Curly parsley is useful and pleasant as a decoration raw or fried; roots are indispensable in preparing fish sauces; purchase dried or fresh.	Freshly chopped leaves widely used in cookery.
Pepper (spice)	The pepper plant, a climbing shrub, is grown in all tropical regions. A distinction is made between white and black, though they come from the same shrub; the inside of the fruit of the pepper plant is the white peppercorn, from which white pepper is milled; the red skin, when dried and milled, becomes black pepper. The names of the various kinds of pepper come from the names of the growing areas. Aromatic, penetrating odor; pungent flavor.	Most generally used of all spices.
Rosemary (herb)	Aromatic, needle-shaped leaves; purchase dried or fresh.	Soups, sauces, and lamb.
Saffron (spice)	Head of dried pistil of *Crocus sativus*. European saffron generally comes from Spain, Italy, and the south of France. About 15,000 pistils are required to produce 100 grams of saffron. Saffron contains a high concentration of volatile oil and coloring matter.	Rice dishes, paella, bouillabaisse, lobster, and shrimp dishes.

(continued)

Table 5–18 Herbs and Spices *(continued)*

Name	Description	Uses
Sage (herb)	Low-growing garden herb; whitish-green leaf is dried; common in the United States; fragrant, slightly resinous flavor.	Meats, poultry stuffing, salads, soups, and egg dishes.
Savory (herb)	Strongly flavored, similar to sage; purchase dried or fresh.	Broad beans, meats, and poultry stuffing.
Sorrel (herb)	A spinach-like seasonal leaf plant, grows wild or is cultivated mainly from winter to spring; has a sour flavor; purchase dried or fresh.	Soups, sauces, and vegetables.
Star anise (spice)	Dried fruit of an oriental evergreen from the magnolia family; star-shaped fruit contains eight small brown oval seeds.	Marinades, soups, stocks, duck, pork, and fish.
Sweet marjoram (herb)	The parts used are pieces of the root and the oval leaves covered with small hairs; grown in Morocco; purchase dried or fresh.	Sausages, soups, and sauces.
Tarragon (herb)	Pungent, aromatic, anise-flavored leaves of tarragon plant.	For flavoring vinegar, mustard, marinades, soups, and salads.
Thyme (herb)	Aromatic leaves and stems of small garden perennial; common in the United States and Europe; clean, warm, slightly pungent flavor; fresh leaves have more flavor than the dried ones; purchase dried or fresh.	Sauces, especially brown sauces, soups, and meat dishes.

Table 5–19 Flavorings

Name	Description	Uses
Blanchan	Salted shrimp or prawns, dried, pounded, and fermented; never eaten raw; essential ingredients in Indonesian and Malaysian cookery	Nut sauces, vegetables, meats, poultry, and meat dishes
Capers	Small, unopened green flower buds of a spicy shrub, native to southern Europe and northern Africa	With garlic, lemon, lamb, and fish dishes
Chestnuts	Fruit of the chestnut tree	Fresh or dried in soups, sauces, and purées
Cocoa and chocolate	From pods containing cocoa beans, roasted, shelled, and ground	Desserts and alcoholic and nonalcoholic beverages
Coconut	Many forms, including coconut flesh, juice, and cream	Sweet dishes, rice, and sauces
Essences	Concentrated flavorings extracted from nuts, flowers, seeds, fruits, herbs, and spices	Widely used in cookery
Licorice	Dried root; slightly aromatic fragrance, sweet-sour flavor	Bakery products
Monosodium glutamate (MSG)	Salt of glutonic acid, derived from organic seaweed; little flavor; natural ability to enhance flavors	Meats, vegetables, soups, sauces; widely used in the Orient

(continued)

Table 5–19 Flavorings *(continued)*

Name	Description	Uses
Salt	Sodium chloride.	Preserving and sweet and savory dishes
Sugar	Sweet-tasting substances, most commonly sap of the sugar cane	Glazes, sweets, and some vegetable dishes
Tamarind	Sticky, dark brown pulp; high acidity coating	As vinegar in stews, sauces, jams, and jellies
Tomato purée	Reduced cooked tomatoes; lightly acidic and sweet	As substitute for fresh tomatoes; meat, fish, casseroles, and sauces
Truffles	Edible fungi; highly aromatic. Two types: Italian white and black	Pâté, stuffings, sauces, salads, egg dishes, and pasta
Vanilla	Essence from pod of the orchid family	Desserts, chocolate, frosting, and butter cream

Flavorings, Seasonings, and Condiments

Flavorings, seasonings, and condiments are incorporated into cooking processes to enhance the flavor of raw ingredients and to preserve and tenderize perishable foods.

Flavorings are substances commonly added to food to change and strengthen its flavor (see Table 5–19). Flavorings may also be used to tenderize and add sharpness or richness to foods. Flavorings are traditionally in the form of a liquid or paste, but they may be purchased in dry or sauce forms.

Vinegars are flavorings made when bacteria attack alcohol contained in alcoholic liquids, such as ale or wine (see Table 5–20). Oxidation takes place, and the alcoholic liquid turns into an acetic acid.

Seasonings are a blend (or combination) of herbs, spices, or salts that are used to enhance the flavor of foods (see Table 5–21 on page 90).

Condiments are traditionally accompaniments to food. Condiments take on several characteristics and may be savory, sweet, tart, hot and spicy, sour, or a combination of those characteristics. For numerous examples, see Tables

(text continues on page 92)

Table 5–20 Vinegars

Name	Description
Balsamic	Made from the must of wine grapes that is aged
Black	Similar to balsamic vinegar; sweet flavor and dark brown in color
Champagne	Produced from dry white wine from the region of Champagne, France
Cider	Made from apple cider; more acidic than white vinegar
Distilled white	Colorless, distilled in a vacuum; general-purpose vinegar
Fruit flavored	Produced by steeping fresh fruits such as raspberries and strawberries
Malt	Produced from barley that is mashed, heated by water, and fermented
Red	Sweet; pale in color
Rice	Made in Japan from rice wine; lighter than European and American vinegars
Sherry	Made in the southwestern part of Spain; excellent for salads and marinades
Wine	Used in salads; should be stored in a cool dark place

Table 5–21 Seasonings

Name	Description	Uses
Apple pie spice	Cinnamon, nutmeg, cloves, and allspice	Apple pie
Barbecue spice	Cumin, chili peppers, garlic, cloves, and salt	Barbecue sauce
Chili powder	Oregano, garlic, cumin seed, red chili pepper, and allspice	Stews, meats, and shellfish
Cinnamon sugar	Cinnamon and granulated white sugar	Sugary products
Crab oil or shrimp spice	Red peppers, mustard seed, peppercorn, and bay leaf	Seafood
Curry powder	Several spices, predominantly turmeric and fenugreek	Fish, meats, curry sauces, and vegetable dishes
Herb seasoning	Basil, chervil, oregano, and marjoram	Salad dressings
Italian seasoning	Red pepper, rosemary, oregano, and basil	Pizza and pasta
Mixed pickling spices	Red peppers, white peppercorns, mustard seed, bay leaves, dill seed, allspice, and cinnamon	Poaching fish, marinades, and brines
Poultry seasoning	Savory, thyme, sage, marjoram, and rosemary	Stuffings, salads, and poultry
Pumpkin pie	Ginger, cinnamon, cloves	Breads and pies
Seafood seasoning	Similar to shrimp spice and crab oil	Stuffings and sauces
Flavored salt	Onion, garlic, or lemon; herbs, spices, and salt	Salads, vegetables, beef, and poultry

Table 5–22 Condiments: Western

Name	Description
Barbecue sauce	Brown sugar, ketchup, chili sauce, green pepper, and vinegar
Chili sauce	Cooked fresh red chilis with spices, vinegar, salt, sugar, and garlic
Ketchup	Tomatoes, sugar, vinegar, and salt
Worcestershire	Soybean, tamarind, vinegar, anchovies, shallots, garlic, vinegar, and molasses; used in beef dishes
Steak sauce	Tomato, vinegar, raisins, salt, spices, herbs, orange base, dehydrated garlic, and onions; caramel color

Table 5–23 Condiments: Hot Sauces

Name	Description	Uses
Harissa	Very hot Tunisian sauce made from dried chili, garlic, pepper, lemon juice, and other spices	Lamb, chicken, and couscous
Indian hot	Hot oil pickles, thick chunky sauces, variety of fruits and spices	Chicken, barbecue, Indian bread, and meat
Mexican salsa	Chili peppers, onion, tomatoes, lime juice, salt, and spices	Chicken, grilled steak, tortillas, tacos, and eggs cooked to order
Nam prik	Thailand sauce made from vinegar, salt, sugar, ground chili, garlic, shallots, peanuts, fish sauce, and coconut cream	Grilled meats, noodles, rice dishes, and soups

(continued)

Table 5–23 Condiments: Hot Sauces (continued)

Name	Description	Uses
Sambals	Ground red chili peppers, sometimes with garlic	Cooked or uncooked
Sous prik	Sweeter version of nam prik; with sugar, raisins, tomatoes, and sweet jam	
Tabasco and Louisiana hot sauce	Red pepper sauce made from a variety of Mexican chilis	Soups, stews, and vegetables
Wasabi	Green horseradish of Japan; sharper than white horseradish; sold in powder or paste	Raw fish, rice, grilled meats, and chicken

Table 5–24 Condiments: Oriental Sauces

Name	Description	Uses
Duck (plum)	Plums, garlic, sweet potatoes, ginger, chili pepper, vinegar, and sugar	Dipping sauce for shrimp, spring rolls, and dumplings
Goma	Sesame and soy sauce	Beef, fondue, dipping sauce for raw vegetables, steak, and grilled chicken
Hoisin	Fermented soybeans, chili peppers, spices, flour, and garlic	Peking duck, barbecue, meats, and poultry
Ketjap manis or ketjap benteng	Indonesian soy sauce; assorted spices, sugar, and molasses	Steamed vegetables and grilled fish and chicken
Oyster	Dried oysters pounded with salt and soy sauce and other seasonings	To thicken soups; with Chinese vegetables; dipping sauce or marinade
Satay	Indonesian Chinese; coconut shrimp paste, ground peanuts, tamarind, and chilis	Good with chicken or pork kabobs
Shoyu	Japanese soy sauce; equal quantities of soybean and wheat; less salty and sweeter than soy sauce	Soups, stews, casseroles, and marinades
Soy, Chinese	Soybeans, salt, and wheat	Vegetables, rice, meat, fish, and casseroles
Sweet and sour sauce	Fruit, vinegar, and sugar	Chicken, fish, pork, and glaze
Tamari	Used in Japanese and American cooking; free from preservatives and additives; unlike soy sauce, contains very little wheat	Marinades, rice, vegetables, and meats
Tentsujy	Flavored soy sauce; significant MSG with preservatives	Tempura cooking
Teriyaki	Soy sauce, brown sugar, green onions, and fresh ginger	Vegetables, fish, beef, and chicken
Tonkatsu	Japanese version of ketchup; tomatoes, apples, carrots, and onion	Chicken, pork, and fish

Table 5–25 Condiments: Mustards

Name	Description
Dijon style	Husk of black seeds, salt, spices, and white wine
English	White and black mustard seeds, wheat flour, and turmeric
German	Vinegar, black mustard flour, tarragon, and herbs
Grainy	Vinegar, spices, and semiground seeds
Hot	Prepared with chili pepper, horseradish, and vinegar spices
Oriental	Brown mustard seed and green horseradish
Sweet	Prepared with honey and brown sugar

5–22, 5–23, and 5–24 on pages 90 and 91. Condiments are usually requested by the guests to accompany their meal. As a result, most dining rooms stock a variety of condiments. The most common condiments on American tables are ketchup and mustard.

Mustards are condiments prepared from a combination of ground white, black, or brown seeds of the cabbage family (see Table 5–25). Mustards are generally served as an accompaniment to pork, beef, salads, vegetables, cheeses, and egg dishes.

6

Seafood and Fish

6

Seafood and Fish

Seafood *can be identified as any edible animal that lives in water. This includes freshwater as well as saltwater animals. These animals are all cold-blooded. The types of animals that are considered edible are constantly increasing because the growing world population is demanding more food. The effort to satisfy this need is leading to the harvesting of a multitude of previously underutilized species.*

History

Until the 1970s, it was widely believed that the oceans absorb limitless amounts of pollution and produce large quantities of food. In certain parts of the world, technology produced increasingly efficient methods for catching fish. Each year, increasing amounts of fish and shellfish were landed by commercial fishers. Fish were plentiful and relatively inexpensive.

In the mid-1970s, many coastal areas began to suffer the effects of increased pollution caused by runoff from the land. Fish, shellfish, and wildlife began dying off. Often, what was left was unfit for human consumption. Another problem arose with deep-ocean fish that live nowhere near land and its pollution. Total catches began to decline, and the fish being caught were smaller because of overfishing. Demand for seafood continued to grow, so prices rose. With higher prices came the incentive to develop alternative sources of supply. Varieties of fish that had been discarded as *trash fish* with no previous commercial value began to appear in the cases at fish markets. Many of these fish were excellent to eat, but consumer prejudice had to be overcome. Alternative names were used to disband this mindset. For example, the market name of cape shark was substituted for dogfish. Finding legal and appealing names (nomenclature) to merchandise the unfamiliar varieties of seafood profitably became a challenge for foodservice professionals, and the FDA stepped in to prevent misbranding.

In the 1980s, to combat the diminishing supplies of seafood and fish, farming fish and shellfish became popular. Aquaculture has increased its market share each year in the seafood industry. Because of pollution, mussels and oysters are harvested increasingly from domestically developed beds. Today, pond-raised catfish, crayfish, and trout account for almost the total production of farmed fish. Pen-raised salmon account for a larger market share every year. Research is continuing for ways to farm many other types of fish, such as mahi-mahi, flounder, tuna, and swordfish.

Regulations

Declining fish stocks have prompted worldwide concern. Environmental and conservation measures are increasing to prevent the extinction of many species of fish. In the United States, commercial fishing is regulated by the National Marine Fisheries Service (NMFS), a service of the Department of Commerce. The FDA is also concerned with fisheries and has created a new Office of Seafood that will include all seafood inspection in addition to shellfish testing. Some fish farming is also regulated by the USDA, which is responsible for many other food products besides seafood. The federal inspection of seafood is voluntary for fresh seafood, not mandatory as for meat. Federal inspection, as well as product grading, are available for a fee. Frozen or canned products must be inspected and graded.

The major step in managing domestic fish populations came with the Fishery Conservation and Management Act (FCMA) of 1976. With this law, Congress extended control of U.S. coastal waters out to 200 miles and created eight regional fishery councils that set specific catch regulations.

Nutritional Benefits

Seafood contains a high-quality protein and is easily digestible because it lacks extensive connective tissue. This also contributes to its perishability, because bacteria can break fish down easily.

In general, fish is a good source of polyunsaturated fats,

and most fish is lower in fats than other animal products. Despite this, some varieties of seafood are unusually high in cholesterol: lobster, shrimp, and oysters, for example.

Fish

The first major class of seafood is marine and freshwater fish. For convenience, fish can be classified into five basic groups:

1. Anadromous fish live most of their lives in saltwater, but return to freshwater to spawn; salmon and shad are examples.
2. Ground fish live near the bottom in the relatively shallow waters of the continental shelves. They stay in particular territories and do not migrate. Cod, flounder, and haddock are common examples. Historically, this group of fish has been the most important economically.
3. Migratory fish travel great distances and feed near the surface; swordfish and bluefish are examples.
4. Catadromous fish spawn in saltwater, then live mostly in freshwater; eels are an example.
5. Freshwater fish, such as trout and catfish, are mostly farm raised.

There are other differences among fish. Not all fish have scales; shark, skate, and swordfish, for example, do not have scales. Some fish, such as sharks and skates, have cartilage instead of bones. This often makes fabrication easier, because there are no small bones to remove.

Shellfish

Shellfish is the second major class of seafood, so named because these animals have shells instead of bones. There are two main groups of shellfish: crustaceans and mollusks.

1. *Crustaceans* have exterior-jointed skeletons that they shed periodically throughout the year. Crustaceans includes shrimp, lobster, crab, and crawfish.
2. *Mollusks* are invertebrates with soft bodies that are covered by a nonjointed shell with one or more pieces. There are three types of mollusks: bivalves (clams, scallops, and oysters), univalves (abalone, conch, periwinkles, and snails), and cephalopods (octopus, cuttlefish, and squid).
   a. Bivalves are prone to contamination because they feed by pumping water through their bodies and filtering out microscopic plants called *plankton*. Bacteria and toxins are also filtered out of the seawater and collect in the bivalve's body.
   b. One well-publicized problem is paralytic shellfish poisoning (PSP), caused by a naturally occurring algae bloom called the *red tide*.
   c. Numerous illnesses, hepatitis, for example, can also occur from raw sewage in the water. There is strict monitoring of shellfish beds by the FDA, which requires that each bag of shellfish carry a tag stating from where and by whom it was harvested. Purchasers are required to keep these tags on file for 90 days.

Shellfish is available either fresh or frozen. Many varieties are only found frozen outside of their local area because of their typically short shelf life. Most shellfish carries a large percentage of waste and commands a premium price. Therefore, special attention must be given to the cost per usable portion when deciding which form to buy.

Crustaceans

Shrimp

Shrimp carry a premium price and are one of the most popular types of shellfish. Fresh frozen is the most common form available, but shrimp are also available fresh, or cooked in fresh, frozen, dried, or canned forms. Frozen shrimp are classed by range of count per pound:

Category	Count of Shrimp per Pound
U-12	Under 12
U-10	Under 10
36–40	36 to 40
21–25	21 to 25
16–20	16 to 20
Tidi	Tiny shrimp sold by the pound

Check box labels for weight, because a 2-kilogram box looks almost the same as a 5-pound box but is about 10 ounces lighter.

The term *shrimp* is usually used in markets closest to the source of the catch and refers to whole shrimp with their heads on. Most chefs buy the other four market forms:

- *Headless:* the edible portion of the shrimp with the heads removed
- *Green:* the shrimp is raw and still in the shell, with or without the head
- *Peeled:* the shell has been removed from headless shrimp
- *Deveined:* the shell has been removed and the intestinal track, a blackish-blue vein, has been removed

Crabs

Numerous types of crabs are available. The blue crab is most common. Hard- and soft-shell crabs are actually the same species and are sold alive. The soft-shell crab is a crab that has just shed (*molted*) its shell; its new shell has not had time to harden and is edible.

Cleaned crabmeat is cooked and available fresh or frozen. For a longer shelf life, it is also available pasteurized and canned. Lump crab meat is solid pieces of the whitest body meat. Flake meat is smaller pieces of body meat. Claw meat is darker and usually commands a lower price. King crab legs are cooked, frozen, and available shell on or shell off.

Mollusks

Sea scallops are the largest and most common scallop. The adductor muscle is removed from the shell and is sold either fresh or frozen. A tough fibrous strip called the *chain* is found on the side of the scallop. It should be removed before preparation.

Bay scallops are smaller scallops. They are in short supply and therefore command a higher price. Bays are about as long as they are round. *Calico scallops* come from warmer waters and are often substituted for bay scallops. Calicos do not have the characteristic sweet flavor of bays, and so they command a lower price. Beware of substitutions. The calico scallop is more tubular than genuine bay scallops. Calicos also toughen quickly when overcooked. They are slightly precooked when purchased because they must be opened with steam. Scallops take only two to three minutes to cook, so cooking time should be monitored carefully.

Hard-Shell Clams

Live, hard-shell clams are sold by the bushel, weighing 65 pounds. They are classified according to size. Average counts per bushel are as follows:

Quahogs	100 pieces
Cherrystones	200 pieces
Topnecks	300 pieces
Littlenecks	400 pieces

Shucked hard-shell clams are sold chopped (minced) and are suitable for soups and stuffings. Chopped clams are available fresh, frozen, or canned.

Soft-Shell Clams

Soft-shell clams are also known as *steamers* when sold live. The average count is 650 per 50-pound bushel. The most distinctive feature is their *foot*, which sticks out of the shell. When shucked, they are known as frying clams or clam bellies.

Oysters

When alive in the shell, a bushel weighs 60 pounds, and the average count is 240 pieces. Shucked oysters are available fresh, canned, or smoked.

Mussels

Live mussels are usually sold in half bushels weighing 25 pounds. Smoked mussel meat is either canned or fresh.

Squid

While whole fresh squid is available, the most common market form is frozen, because of squid's short shelf life. The common forms of squid are cleaned bodies, called *tubes;* tubes and tentacles and bodies cut into rings. Rings are also available prebreaded.

Manufactured Products

Manufactured products are the processed forms in which various seafood items are marketed. These include numerous varieties of frozen breaded fish and shellfish items and surimi.

- Breaded seafood is frozen to extend shelf life and to make handling easier. The amount and composition of breading will vary among manufacturers. If in doubt about the percentage of breading on a product, weigh a breaded piece, wash off the coating, and reweigh. Premium breaded products consist of solid pieces of seafood, such as whole shrimp, scallops, or fillets. Also available are reformed items such as fillets or shrimp that are a combination of pieces, chunks, or ground seafood. This form commands a lower price than its whole counterpart. Carefully reading labels will ensure that the product received is the product desired.
- *Surimi* is not one particular fish; it is a product manufactured with various fish and flavorings and is unique in its ability to mimic shellfish. A well-known example of surimi is frozen Sea Legs, a crab substitute that is made from Alaskan pollock. Surimi was first developed in Japan around A.D. 1100. Modern advances in processing equipment and food technology allow the mass production of this product in frozen form.

In the process of making surimi, ground fish is repeatedly washed to remove the water-soluble proteins and enzymes. The remaining protein is able to form a strong gel when it is cooked, making the fish elastic. Sugar, sorbitol, polyphosphates, flavorings, and salt are blended. Egg whites and starch are often added to the paste, and the mixture is blended well. The paste is extruded in thin sheets or strands and then cooked. The sheets are cut into strips of various widths, then the strips or strands are folded together to form a rope. By varying the width of the strips, various shellfish textures—for example, king crab legs—can be simulated. Surimi is nicknamed the chopped meat of the fish world because of its versatility. Even sausage-type products, such as hot dogs, are available made from surimi.

Market Forms of Seafood

Most seafood undergoes some form of processing before it reaches the market. This often entails the removal of unusable portions, such as shells, entrails, heads, or fins. The greater the amount of fabrication, the higher the price per pound. It is left to the individual purchaser to determine the most cost-effective form in which to purchase seafood products.

Fin Fish

There are six basic forms in which fin fish can be purchased (see Figures 6–1 and 6–2). Round fish are normally unfrozen, and all the other groups can be found either fresh or frozen.

Figure 6–1 Types of fillets

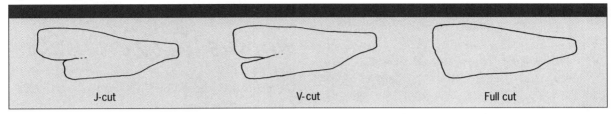

J-cut   V-cut   Full cut

Figure 6–2 Market forms of fin fish

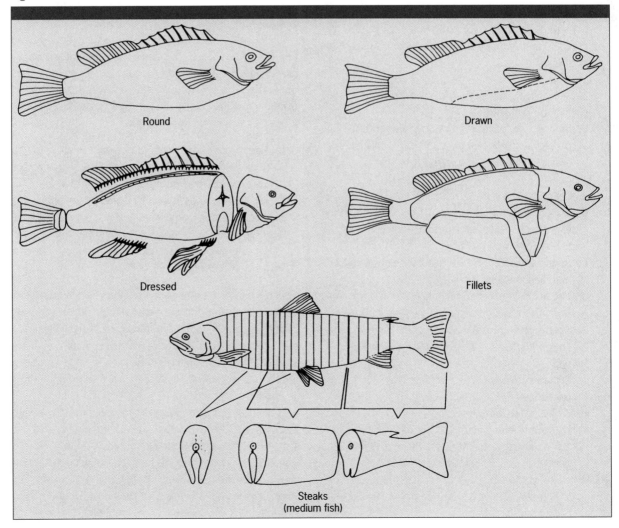

Round

Drawn

Dressed

Fillets

Steaks
(medium fish)

1. Round
   a. Whole fish as it comes from the water. Do not confuse this form with fish that are called round because of their shape.
   b. This form will have the shortest shelf life because the entrails cause bacteriological and enzymatic decay.
   c. Flat fish, such as flounder, are often sold whole, or round. The gut cavity is far enough away from the meat to cause little damage, and it is not economically feasible to remove the entrails.
2. Drawn
   a. Whole fish with entrails or gills removed.
   b. It is the best form for maximum shelf life.
   c. Gilled and gutted are two other market names for this fish.
3. Dressed
   a. Drawn fish with scales and fins removed; the head may be removed also.
   b. Smaller fish, such as trout, are referred to as *pan dressed* and are often cooked in this form. Larger dressed fish may be referred to as *logs.*
4. Fillets
   a. The most common form of fish sold.
   b. The meat is cut parallel to the backbone, and the skin may be removed. Fillets as they come off the fish are known as *full.*
   c. Boneless fillets have the pin bones removed and may be known as a *V-cut.*
   d. The fillets from round fish may have the thin flesh from the belly area, called the *nape,* removed. These are known as a *J-cut.* Larger fillets are often cut on the bias to yield individual portions.
5. Steaks
   a. Cross-section cuts of fish that may contain the backbone.
   b. Skin is often left on.
   c. Cuts from larger fish, such as tuna or swordfish, are boneless, and the preferred cut is from the center, or loin, as opposed to the tail.
6. Cubes
   a. Economical pieces that are left from the fabrication of larger fish.
   b. Suitable for stews, trim kabobs, or stir-fry.

Purchasing Fresh versus Frozen Fish

The belief that frozen fish is inferior to fresh is totally unfounded. Many other forms of seafood, such as squid, shrimp, and lobster tails, are almost always frozen, yet they are held in high esteem by the public. Considering that much "fresh" fish is several days old before it even reaches the docks, let alone the markets where consumers purchase the product, perhaps it is worthwhile to question which form is better: fresh or frozen.

Traditionally, the fishing industry was not equipped to process frozen fish. It was easier to handle fish unfrozen all through the distribution process. When freezing was done, it was in a last-ditch effort to prevent spoilage of excess product. Usually, this type of frozen fish was not a quality product for two reasons:

1. The product was frozen to prevent further spoilage. Because the quality of the product was inferior before freezing, the thawed product was undesirable.
2. The product was frozen in storage freezers, a process that took many hours or days. During that time, the product continued to age, and the formation of excessive ice crystals occurred, damaging the product by breaking up cell wells.

These problems have been overcome in the current system of fish processing. Today, many varieties of fish are being caught especially for frozen packaging. Often, these fish are processed and frozen solid within hours of being caught. This is accomplished by factory ships at sea or by shore-based plants that handle the fish directly from the boats.

Frozen fish has fewer storage requirements, longer shelf life, and will usually be less expensive than its fresh (not frozen) counterpart. Prices tend to fluctuate less with frozen products. For these reasons, the seafood industry is moving increasingly toward quality frozen products. Perhaps the foodservice professional should avoid the issue of freshness and, instead, base marketing strategies on serving *excellent* fish. Whether handling product that is frozen, unfrozen, or a combination of the two, it is important to keep in mind one important fact: All seafood is delicate. Unfrozen seafood is especially delicate. If not handled properly, fish deteriorates rapidly, maybe even within a few hours. Far too many people in the foodservice industry do not know how to handle fish. They equate the handling of fish with that of meat or poultry, and that equation can be deadly. Seafood requires lower storage temperatures than meat products; unsanitary or improper handling can result in poisoning.

Purchasing

Quality Assurance

Although there is no mandatory federal system for grading seafood, this does not mean that seafood is not safe. Processing plants are inspected by local health departments, and shellfish is routinely tested for contamination. Imported products are inspected for wholesomeness.

- The FDA is working with fishers and processors to develop a voluntary code of safe handling procedures within the domestic seafood industry. This program, the HACCP, will be enforced through spot inspections by the FDA.
- These safeguards give us reasonable assurance that seafood is wholesome and free from contamination. It does not tell us anything about its quality.

Factors Affecting Quality

The quality of fresh fin fish is affected the most by how it is handled throughout the distribution system, from the moment it is caught until it is consumed. A brief description of the methods used by New England trawlers may help illustrate how complex this system can be.

Catching the Fish

In New England, some boats may travel a day or so to get to the fishing grounds. The method of catch is with the otter trawl net. This funnel-shaped net is pulled along in back of the boat, and fish swimming in front of it are forced into it. Often, the fish die as they are pulled along in the net. How long they remain in the net depends on how long the net stays down before it is hauled up and emptied. When fish were plentiful, haul times were short because bags filled quickly. One or two hours was common. With fewer fish, some boats extend haul times for several hours. With fish (or with any animal food product for that matter), spoilage begins at death. This means deterioration begins before the fish leave the water. Bacterial action does not begin until the fish passes through *rigor mortis,* the condition of muscle contraction after death. The faster the fish is chilled after death, the longer rigor lasts, and the longer the shelf life.

Sorting

The fish are brought onto the deck of the fishing vessel to be sorted. At this stage, careful handling is critical, as overloading the deck area can cause the fish flesh to become bruised from the weight of the catch. Fish are then moved around by means of a pick, a short broom handle with a nail extending from one end at a right angle. Crews pick the fish through the head area. If the fish is picked in the meat area, a blood spot will later appear in the fillet.

Cleaning and Storing

Next, the fish must be gutted and washed. Bacteria and enzymes in the gut cavity will begin to decompose the fish if it is not gutted and washed promptly. If the bones in the stomach cavity are pulled away from the flesh, the fish was not gutted after being landed. This is known as *belly burn,* and it indicates poorly handled fish. Such fish should be rejected.

Because gutting fish is messy, the fish must be washed well and then iced down quickly in the pens in the hold. Boats with high standards will separate the iced fish every 2 feet or so with horizontal separators. This better distributes the weight of the catch and minimizes the amount of crushing of the fish that occurs.

Returning to Port

Another variable in quality depends on when the fish is caught during the trip. The first haul will be older than the haul made just before returning to port. If the boat is at sea for 7 to 10 days, this has a great effect on the variation of quality within the boat, regardless of how well the fish were handled. The premium fish is termed *top of the catch* and is caught near the end of the trip. Because they are stored toward the top of the pens, they are less likely to be damaged or bruised.

Selling the Fish

Each morning, licensed buyers who represent processors will bid on the fish from the boats that have returned that day. In the Northeast, Boston, New Bedford, Gloucester, and Portland are the auction sites. What occurs at the auction sites is an example of supply and demand economics. The *top of the catch* will bring the best price. Then buyers watch as the boats are unloaded, or lumped, to see the variation in quality. When fish of lesser quality begin to appear, the buyer of premium fish will stop taking them, and the remaining fish become sellover fish. The price of sellover fish is lowered, and another buyer may take delivery of them. This process could be repeated several times until all the fish is sold, regardless of quality. The saying on the fish pier is, "All fish is sold for a price."

Selecting a Supplier

It is necessary for chefs or managers to do their own inspecting and grading because of the complexity of the seafood supply system. This ensures the foodservice professional of getting only top-quality products. To make the job easier, it is important to select a supplier who is also concerned about quality.

Most foodservice professionals will purchase seafood through a purveyor. Each of these purveyors has its own set of standards as to the level of quality sought. Knowledge, experience, and skill will determine what level of quality is actually received.

Choose the seafood purveyor. Visit the plant, if possible. Look for a clean and efficient operation. Ask yourself the questions: "Do they respect the product? Do they buy quality fish?" No matter how well one handles the product in-house, it must have been handled properly throughout, or all efforts are in vain. Price is always a consideration, but do not buy on low bid alone.

Determining the Freshness of Seafood

Fresh Fish

Because most fresh fish is not graded for quality, it is up to the receiver at the foodservice establishment to thoroughly inspect incoming product before it is accepted. This is in addition to the normal checks for proper counts or weights. The receiver must examine three important areas when grading: smell, feel, and look.

Smell

Quality, fresh fish should have the smell of the ocean or fresh seaweed. A misconception is that fresh fish is odorless. To check whole, gutted fish, snap the head backward and sniff the gut cavity. If the fish is not at peak freshness, an off-odor will be evident. To check cut fish such as fillets or steaks, smell the surface of the fish. No one part of the fillet or steak will deteriorate faster than another.

As fish ages, the "off" or "fishy" odor will intensify. When fish is unfit for consumption, there will be an ammonia-like smell. This smell cannot be washed or soaked away. Soaking in vinegar or lemon juice or some other magic potion will not save bad fish. If this fish is cooked, the bad smell and bad taste will return.

Feel

Quality fish should be *firm*. When pushed, the flesh should spring back. The finger should not leave an indentation. If it does, this is a sign that the flesh is beginning to deteriorate. Quality fish may also be *slimy*. Dressed fish may have some original slime on it. This is a good sign and indicates that the fish was not subjected to excessive handling. However, fillets with slime suggest improper handling, spoilage, or contamination. Quality fish have scales that are firmly attached.

Look

Whole Fish

- The gills on dressed fish should be red (like blood). The condition of the gills is a sure way to determine the freshness of the fish. As a fish deteriorates, the gills turn from red to pink, then eventually to gray/brown.
- Generally, the eyes should be clear and round, but in some species and at some times of the year this may not be true. As the fish deteriorates, the eye may become cloudy and sunken into the head.

Fillets

- Fillets should have a sheen of moisture to them and should not be dry. There should not be any blood spots in the flesh.
- When the fillet is bent, the meat should not separate. If it does, this indicates that the connective tissue between the muscle has deteriorated, called *gaping.*
- Check the amount of liquid in the tub with the fillets. *Brining* is a common practice in which the fillets are put into a tank with various salt solutions. A quick dip will supposedly remove surface bacteria. However, if left in the tank for any length of time, the fish absorb extra water, which affects the flavor. When cooking fillets, watch for excessive shrinkage, which is also a sign of excessive brining.

Live Shellfish

Make sure shellfish is alive before it is accepted.

- *Lobsters and crabs:* If they move and seem lively, they are alive.
- *Mollusks:* The shell should be closed tightly or should quickly close if gently tapped. Broken shells mean dead product and indicate poor handling.

Learn quality brand names of shucked products, and use these products. There should be no off-odors.

- Oysters and steamers should be plump, clear looking, and not in an excessive amount of liquid.
- Scallops should have very little liquid and should have a sweet smell. This is another product that will absorb a tremendous amount of liquid if soaked. Beware of excessive shrinkage during cooking.

Frozen Seafood

One of the best ways to ensure good quality frozen seafood is to purchase brand names; for example, Icelandic, Icy Bay, and Gorton's.

The receiver should be aware of the quality points of frozen foods.

- Check for white cottony patches on the food product. This indicates freezer burn and is not acceptable.
- Check for odd ice formations in the product that would indicate that partial thawing occurred and then the product was refrozen.
- Individually quick frozen (IQF) products should appear as individual pieces in the package.
- Check shrimp for *melanosis,* or dark spots, on the shell. This is not harmful, but it indicates poor handling. It appears when the shrimp were not frozen quickly after being caught.
- Shrimp and lobster tails are probably the most expensive frozen product bought in the foodservice industry. The pieces are coated with a thin layer of ice, called *glazing,* to protect them from freezer burn. Beware of excessively thick ice on the product. To check, thaw in the refrigerator and reweigh. Some weight loss is normal, but not more than 5 percent.

Storage

Fresh Fish

All animal products spoil because of bacterial action. The best way to preserve the freshness of fish is to keep it well chilled and consume it as soon as possible. Because fish contains less connective tissue than meats, it deteriorates more quickly. Therefore, it is advantageous to arrange frequent seafood deliveries.

The coldest that unfrozen fish can be stored is 32° F, and the best way to achieve this is to use ice. Pellet ice is preferred, but crushed or cubed is acceptable if nothing else is available. Many fish live in temperatures around 45° F.

Whole fish can be surrounded with ice in a lug bin with holes in the bottom. It is placed over another bin to catch the drip water. Fish should not be kept in the melted water, because much of the flavor will be lost and the chance of bacterial contamination increases.

Cut fish, such as fillets or steaks, should be kept from direct contact with ice or water for the same reason. They should be stored in watertight containers that are covered on all sides by ice. The ice should be moved around daily and more ice added as needed. This prevents *cavitation,* in which the ice melts away and a cavity is formed between the ice and the product. Shelf life of fresh seafood depends on how well it is handled. Under optimum conditions, the product can be expected to last as follows:

Lean fish   14 days
Oily fish   9 days
Shellfish   14 days

These times begin when the product is taken out of the water, not when it is received. The time from the boat to the establishment may be two days or more. Obviously, the sooner fish is consumed, the better.

Poor handling will reduce the shelf life of fish. The basic rule of fish handling is the 2° rule. For every 2° F above 32° F that fish is stored for 24 hours, one day of shelf life is lost. Un-iced fish left in a hot kitchen will have a shelf life of only hours. Fish must always be kept iced.

Frozen Fish

Enzyme action continues to cause even frozen fish to deteriorate, although at a much slower rate. This action is not stopped unless the product is at 80° F below zero. Frozen fish should be stored at 0° F or below for the best shelf life. Keeping it wrapped tightly in plastic will prevent freezer burn. A change in taste and appearance is especially noticeable in freezer-burned fish. Storage time also affects the quality of frozen fish. After approximately six months, most fish will start to taste like other products stored in the freezer. After all, most fish have delicate flavor and texture and therefore are affected more by lengthy freezing times than other foods.

When possible, cook frozen fish directly from the frozen state. This is a well-established practice for a breaded product. It can be used with steaks and fillets as well. If the fish must be thawed before cooking, do so under refrigeration. As the thawing product warms to 32° F, spoilage accelerates. It is unwise to leave fish at room temperature to thaw. Bacteria grow faster as the temperature rises into the danger zone, especially above 40° F. As the outside of a piece of fish warms, it will begin to spoil, even though the center is still frozen.

As soon as fish is thawed, it has a shorter shelf life than fresh fish because of damage done in the freezing process. A thawed product should be stored in ice until cooked and should be used within a day or two. In emergencies, a quick thaw can be done under cold running water if the product is wrapped watertight. Most of the flavor in fish and shellfish comes from water-soluble protein. Thawing it in water washes away the flavor, especially on pieces with a large surface area, such as fillets.

Live Lobsters

Lobsters will not spoil while they are alive. However, as soon as they die, spoilage begins and occurs much faster than in fish, often within 24 hours.

The ideal way to store lobsters is in a storage tank, as opposed to refrigeration. This method of storage provides many benefits, as long as the water is maintained at the proper salinity and temperature (38° F to 45° F). With the water circulating continuously, preferably through a filter to keep it clean, oxygen is incorporated into the water, enabling the lobsters to breathe.

While stored in a tank, lobsters will remain almost dormant and will maintain their weight. However, they may become brittle, and, if handled roughly, claws may break off. The tank should be checked daily for dead lobsters.

A live lobster will, when picked up, thrash around, raise its claws, and arch its tail. This is a natural reaction, and it is only trying to defend itself as it would do in the wild. A dying lobster becomes lethargic and looks almost as if it is getting sleepy; such lobsters are called "sleepers." Any lobsters that are almost dead should be cooked immediately to minimize loss. When they die, they become toxic quickly because of the action of enzymes and bacteria in the digestive system. In some areas, it is illegal to use or sell lobsters once they have died.

If lobsters must be stored out of water, they can be held in a covered bin or box that is not airtight and kept in the refrigerator, away from strong drafts. They can be kept alive this way for several days and should be covered with fresh seaweed or strips of wet newspaper to maintain moisture. Because most establishments already have a refrigerator, this is the most common method of storage. When stored in refrigeration, lobsters will lose small amounts of weight due to dehydration.

Hard- and soft-shell crabs should be kept cool and damp in the same manner as lobsters that are stored out of water. Soft-shell crabs are especially delicate and are often shipped in a seaweed-lined box that is fine for storage. Their shelf life tends to be much shorter than that of hard-shell crabs, and, therefore, procuring schedules should be adjusted to account for this. It is essential to check for dead animals daily.

Live Mollusks

Like all live sea animals, mollusks must not be put into freshwater because it will kill them. They should be stored in the refrigerator away from strong drafts and kept moist with damp towels or seaweed over them. Storing mollusks in cardboard boxes or paper bags is the proper method, as opposed to plastic bags or containers, because paper storage allows them to breathe.

The shells of live mollusks should be tightly closed. It is normal for the shells of mollusks to occasionally gape partially open while in storage. However, if they do not close when moved, squeezed, or tapped lightly, they are dead and should be discarded. The foot on soft-shell clams should be firm and twitch slightly when touched. Mollusks should be treated gently because if the shells break, they will die. Discard dead mollusks daily, because the bacteria produced could spoil others.

Mussels have a beard, or byssuses threads, that should not be pulled off until just before cooking. These threads are secreted by the mussel so it can attach itself to objects in the ocean and not be swept away by tides. It is a part of the animal, and tearing it away hastens its death.

Shucked shellfish should be treated like fish fillets. Bury the containers so all sides are touching ice. Refresh the ice as it melts.

Miscellaneous Seafood Products

Many types of pickled, brined, and smoked seafood products are available. These products should be kept refrigerated because they are processed more for the purpose of imparting flavor than for preservation.

Fabrication

Fin Fish

The two most common fabrication tasks undertaken by the foodservice professional are cutting fillets and cutting steaks. Filleting a fish is not difficult, but it requires some practice so the yield of usable meat is high enough to ensure profitability. The technique for fabricating round fish is a little different than that for flat fish.

Round fish, such as salmon or cod, must be gutted when caught to ensure a quality product. The procedure for gutting a fish is rather simple:

1. Place the fish on the work surface, with the head toward the operator and the belly toward the hand holding the knife.
2. While holding the fish steady, split the belly, beginning at the gill opening and extending to the anal vent

(see Figure 6–3 for the structure of a round fish). The tip of the fillet knife should not extend into the gut cavity any more than is necessary to pierce the skin.

3. When the slit is complete, scoop out the contents of the gut cavity with the fingers. If the species contains edible roe that will be used, carefully cut or pull it away from the other organs without damaging the thin sac holding the eggs.

4. Rinse the gut cavity and the entire fish with cold water to remove any blood or stomach contents, because these will hasten spoilage of the fish.

Figure 6–3 The structure of round fish

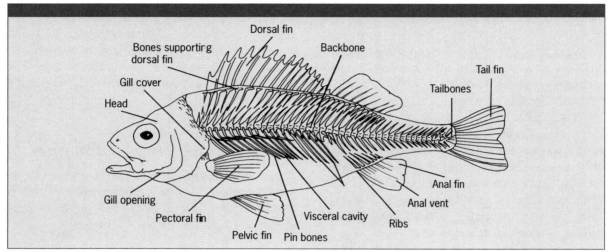

Figure 6–4 The structure of flat fish

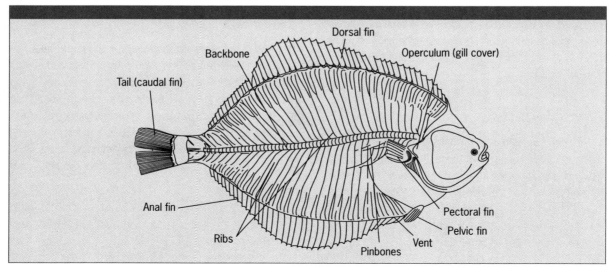

Flat fish, such as sole and flounder, must also be gutted when caught to maintain its quality. The procedure is the same for flat as it is for round fish (see Figure 6–4 for the structure of a flat fish).

To scale a round or a flat fish,

1. Place the fish in a sink and turn on the cold water.
2. Grasp the fish by the tail, allowing the head to hang into the sink.
3. Holding the fish under the cold running water, and using the back of a fillet knife or a fish scraper as a scaler, scrape the scales free from the skin by starting at the tail and working the scaler toward the head. (Scaling a fish does not have to always occur under cold running water, but using this method helps to control the amount of scales that fly in every direction as they are released from the skin. The running water washes the scales downward, and most end up in the bottom of the sink.) If the fish is very fresh, the scaling motion may have to be repeated a few times to actually remove the scales. Avoid pressing too firmly on the scaler, or the flesh of the fish may become bruised (note Figure 6–3 for cutting fillets from a round fish).
4. If the skin will be removed during fabrication, it is possible to skip the scaling process altogether. This will save time, but extra care must be taken to keep the work area and flesh of the fish clean of loose scales.

To fillet a round fish,

1. Place the fish on a cutting board with the tail toward the knife hand. Grasp the head with the other hand.
2. Cut into the fish just beyond the gill cover, but only as deep as the backbone (see Figure 6–5A). Keep the knife turned flat on the backbone, and then gently saw toward the tail, keeping the edge of the knife in contact with the backbone until the fillet is removed (see Figure 6–5B). Set the first fillet aside.
3. Turn the fish over and follow the same steps on the other side (see Figure 6–5C).

To fillet a flat fish,

1. Place the fish on a cutting board with the dark side (as opposed to the white side) facing up. Lay the tail toward the knife hand, with the head in the opposite direction, toward the opposite hand (see Figure 6–6A on page 108).
2. Remove the fillet closest to you. (Remember that a flat fish has two fillets per side; see Figure 6–6A). Begin by using the knife to cut through the flesh that runs along the backbone from gills to tail.
3. Return to the top of the incision by the gills, and begin to remove the first fillet by cutting the flesh away from the rib bones, keeping your knife flat against them while working toward the tail. Work from the middle of the fish near the backbone and toward

Figure 6–5 Filleting a round fish

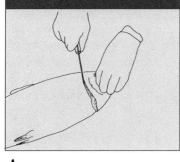

A **Cut to backbone**

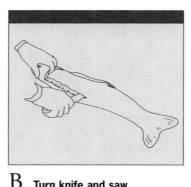

B **Turn knife and saw**

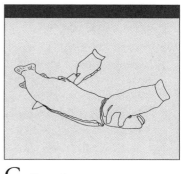

C **Repeat**

Figure 6–6 Cutting fillets from a flat fish

A

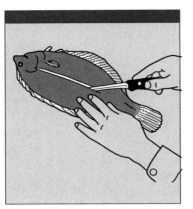

B

C

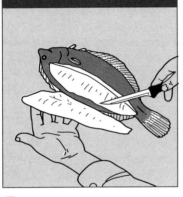

D

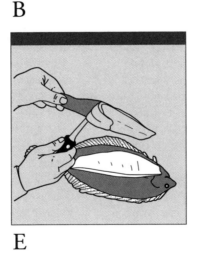

E

the fins, using long smooth strokes with the knife (see Figure 6B–6C).

4. Cut the fillet away from the fins to release it from the fish (see Figure 6–6D).

5. Repeat the process on the other side of the backbone. Turn the fish over and repeat the process on the other side (see Figure 6–6D).

6. Trim fillets, cutting off any bony edges or fins. Skin if desired (see Figure 6–6E).

7. Flat fish are normally not gutted, so try not to puncture the gut cavity during the filleting process.

8. Scrape free any flesh left on the carcass of the fish using a small blunt utensil such as a soup spoon.

The scraps of flesh can be used as filler in stuffings, salads, or even forcemeats.

Trim the fillets from a round fish. After the fillets are removed, the rib bones and the silvery skin from the gut cavity area of the fillet must be removed (see Figure 6–7). The location and thickness of these bones will vary depending on the type of fish. Following are a few examples:

- In salmon, the rib bones, referred to as pin bones, are found on the top half of the wide section of the fillet and are very pliable. Needlenose pliers are a good utensil for removing them. Rub a finger over the flesh to feel for bones and, when located, simply grasp

Figure 6–7 Removing pin and belly bones from a fillet

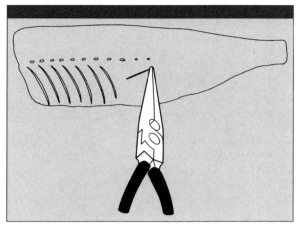

each bone, one at a time, and pull to remove. Repeat the process as needed.

- In sea bass, the rib bones are very sharp and strong and, like the salmon, are found in the top half of the wide section of the fillet. A flexible knife, like a fillet knife, must be used to remove them from the flesh. Place the edge of the knife under the end of the slightly cup-shaped bones and cut them away from the flesh, keeping the knife close to the bones to prevent excessive loss of usable flesh.
- In cod, the lateral bones are almost in the center, and it is possible to cut them out by making a V-cut into the center of the fillet. This wastes some fish, but it is necessary in order to remove the bones.

Occasionally, bones may be found in processed fillets as well, even though it is a product that is purchased with the assumption that it is boneless. Therefore, periodically check processed fillets to ensure that they are free of bones.

To skin fillets,

1. Place the fillet on a cutting board, skin side down, with the tail end near your free hand and the head end of the fillet near the knife hand.
2. Cut into the very end of the tail portion, cutting through the meat just until the skin is reached. Flatten out the knife as it reaches the skin.

3. Grasp the small piece of the tail, now near the short end of the tail, and pull tightly.
4. Keeping the knife in the same flat position and pressed slightly into the skin, begin cutting the flesh away from the skin using a slight sawing motion as the knife moves toward the head of the fillet. As the knife cuts, keep the skin pulled tight with the free hand; this will make the process easier. If the skin tends to be cut often, turn the knife over and use the back of the knife as it is pushed between skin and meat.

Yield

Minimum *yield* is the smallest percentage of usable product as skinless fillets. These yields vary with the size of the fish and are often determined by spawning conditions.

Type of Fish	Percentage of Usable Produce
Most round fish varieties (drawn)	40
Flounder (whole or round)	33
Monkfish, halibut (headless)	50
Salmon (drawn)	65
Mahi-Mahi (drawn)	60
Mackerel (round)	40

Steaks

Steaks are a cross cut of a piece of fish that usually have some skin attached and may have bones. This is often determined by the type and size of fish from which they are cut. After the fish is scaled, perpendicular cuts are made across the fish, starting at the head. When the tail section gets too small to use for steaks, it may be cut into fillets.

Cutting steaks from medium-sized fish is often easier and gives a better yield than do fillets. However, steaks cut from round fish usually have a lot of bones that are impossible to remove entirely before serving.

Larger fish, such as tuna or swordfish, must be cut into steaks because of their size. If the cross-section of the

Figure 6–8 Cutting steaks from a large fish

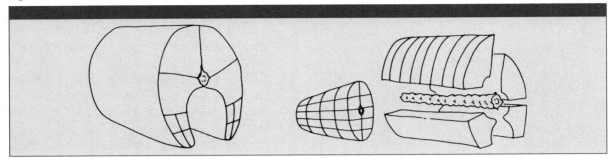

fish is larger than the size of the desired finished steak, it will be necessary to split or quarter the fish before cutting individual portions (see Figure 6–8).

When fabricating fish, the chef or manager must take particular note of both the percentage of usable portion and the number of portions obtained. Per-pound prices of gilled and gutted fish may appear favorable when compared to skinless fillets. However, should an inexperienced fabricator create excessive waste or obtain fewer usable portions than expected, there may be no economic advantage to in-house fabrication.

Shrimp

The most common form of shrimp is green (raw) headless with shell on. These are sold in 5-pound frozen blocks. The three most common in-house fabricated forms are, cleaned for cocktail, butterflied, and split for stuffing.

For each form of fabrication, the initial steps of preparation are the same:

1. Thaw the shrimp, preferably in the refrigerator.
2. Remove the shell on either raw or cooked shrimp:
   a. Grasp the tail in one hand and place the fingertips of the other hand along the belly between each set of legs.
   b. Pull underneath the shrimp between the legs to split the shell lengthwise.
   c. Peel shell and legs away in one motion.
   d. Devein shrimp (explanation follows).

The shell may or may not be left on the tail during the peeling process. The shell should be left on the tail if the final product will be eaten by picking it up with fingers or if the final product's presentation (especially the height) is greatly improved. The shell should be removed from the tail if the final product is being eaten with a knife and fork and leaving the shell on might surprise the guest. For example, a guest eating Shrimp Alfredo with Fettucine probably will not expect the shrimp to have shells (especially when they're covered with a cream sauce and because they may choke on a shell). In addition, the shell should be removed from the tail if the final product is coated with a breading or other product and fried. Here, the shell would be hidden and once again may lead the guest to believe that there is no shell on the product.

To devein the shrimp (after the shrimp has been peeled),

1. Place each shrimp flat on a cutting board with the back of the shrimp toward you.
2. Using a paring knife, make a shallow incision down the center of the back, extending from the head to the tail. Make a cut only deep enough to expose the sand vein.
3. Grasp the vein and remove it from the shrimp, making sure to remove the entire vein, from head to tail.
4. Rinse the shrimp in cold running water and keep well chilled.
5. If many shrimp need cleaning, it is best to use an assembly-line method:
   a. Make incisions on *all* the shrimp.
   b. Remove the veins from *all* the shrimp.
   c. Rinse *all* the shrimp.

Figure 6–9 Butterflying shrimp

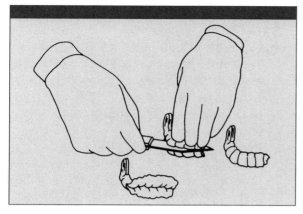

Figure 6–10 Splitting shrimp for stuffing

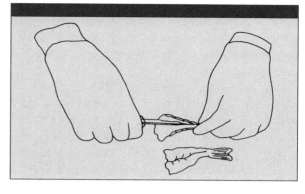

For cocktail, the shell may be removed before or after cooking.

To butterfly shrimp, the procedure is similar to the removal of the vein, except the cut is deeper. There is no need to devein the shrimp before butterflying.

1. Make an incision down the back of the shrimp, about three-quarters of the way through the flesh.
2. When all the shrimp are cut, the veins are removed and the shrimp are rinsed (see Figure 6–9).

To split for baked-stuffed shrimp, the shrimp is split from the underside. Take care not to cut the thin membrane above the sand vein, because this is all that will hold the two pieces of the shrimp together. There is no need to devein the shrimp before splitting.

1. Hold the shrimp between the thumb and forefinger with the belly up and the tail away from the knife hand
2. Insert the point of a paring knife just beneath the tail. If it goes all the way through, withdraw it until the point is in the cavity with the sand vein. Cut away from the tail and downward. With practice, the operator will feel when the blade has separated the flesh yet not cut the membrane along the back.
3. After all the shrimp have been cut, remove the veins and rinse. Store the shrimp in ice until ready to stuff (see Figure 6–10).

Raw shrimp should be stored in a container surrounded on all sides by ice and should be used within two days of thawing.

Lobster

Before preparing lobster, kill the animal humanely.

1. Place the lobster, belly side up, on a cutting board.
2. Using a side towel to protect your free hand, grasp the lobster tail and press it flat.
3. Plunge the point of a knife into the head area directly between the eyes. This will puncture the brain and kill it instantly, although the muscles will contract involuntarily for a few minutes (see Figure 6–11).

Figure 6–11 Lobster preparation

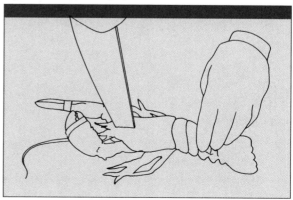

4. Save any juices that exude from the lobster and use in the recipe.

Aside from humanely killing the animal, no other advance preparation is required for a lobster that is to be boiled or steamed.

If the animal is to be split for stuffing and baking, it should first be killed humanely, as just described. Then, turn the animal on its back, and use a long knife to split the body down the center, from the tail to the head. Use care not to cut all the way through the shell on the bottom. Each half may be pried apart, and the gelatinous sac at the head should be removed. The greenish-brown tomalley—actually, the liver—should be discarded because increased pollution in many areas may make it unfit for consumption.

The body of female lobsters may contain a dark strip of coral inside the tail. These are eggs and can be used in the stuffing for enhanced flavor. The color will change from greenish-black to pink when cooked. The more experienced customer may request a female lobster when ordering because of the eggs and because they also have a wider tail than the males.

Bivalves

Clams and mussels may contain sand that is naturally ingested in the course of their feeding. Soaking the animal in clean seawater, or mixing salt and freshwater at the rate of one-third cup salt to 1 gallon cold water is a popular way to remove the sand. Adding cornmeal to the water is said to help the bivalves purge themselves of the sand. Do not leave the bivalves in the water too long or they will suffocate.

Clams

To open clams,

1. Hold the clam in the palm of the hand with the hinge away from the body.
2. Using the thumb as a brace, push the clam knife between the shells with the other four fingers.

3. When the knife is between the shells about 1/2 inch, the shells are pried apart so they are open about 1/4 inch (see Figure 6–12).
4. Do not pull apart the shells until the adductor muscles are cut on the top and bottom. This can be done by passing the tip of the clam knife across the inside surface of the top shell and then the bottom shell. The clam should be held horizontal while doing this so the juice is not lost.
5. The body of the clam should be left in one piece so it looks round and plump in the shell. All mollusks should be opened only as needed, and then kept on ice after opening, because they will spoil quickly.
6. If the clams will be used for baked items, wash them, lay them out flat, and freeze them. Then the shells can usually be pulled off quite easily. Seasoning and topping can be added while still frozen. They should be cooked from the frozen state.

Oysters

Oysters are difficult to open because the adductor muscle is often strong, and the split between the shells is not always easy to find. Oysters must be scrubbed well with a brush, because the rough shells hold dirt. To open oysters,

1. Hold the oyster with the round shell down on a cutting board. Wrap the oyster in a side towel to help protect the free hand that will hold the oyster still during opening. Wearing a safety glove on the free hand is advised.
2. Work the point of an oyster knife in at the hinge and twist it back and forth to pry the shells apart (see Figure 6–13).
3. When the shells are about 1/4 inch apart, pass the oyster knife over the top and bottom shell surfaces to cut the adductor muscle from the shell. Be careful not to puncture or tear the oyster meat, which should look plump after opening.
4. Open oysters only as needed and keep them on ice after opening.

Figure 6–12 Opening clams

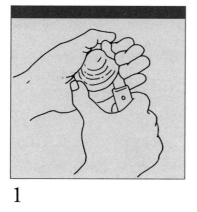

1

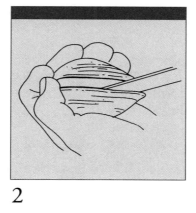

2

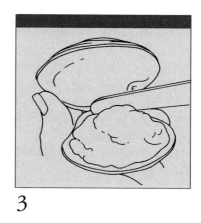

3

Figure 6–13 Opening oysters

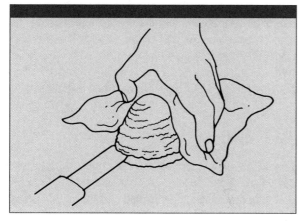

Dead clams, oysters, or other mollusks should not be served because they may cause severe illness. Before opening, inspect the animal carefully to make sure that it is alive. Dead mollusks may contain toxins, which cooking will not remove.

COOKING

Fin Fish

Fish can be cooked in a variety of ways. It may be baked, broiled, grilled, steamed, poached, sautéed, fried, and roasted. Fin fish lacks excessive amounts of connective tissue and has a generally low fat content; therefore, take care to prevent overcooking. Moderate temperatures and cooking times will help to maintain product quality and nutritional value.

Shrimp

Shrimp for cocktail may be poached in *court-bouillon* or steamed. A court-bouillon is an aromatic vegetable broth that usually includes vinegar or wine and a variety of seasonings. The most important factor in cooking any shrimp is to avoid overcooking, which causes the shrimp to become tough and rubbery. Cooking the shrimp with the shell on will retain more juice, but peeling and deveining the product before cooking will often yield a more attractive product.

The translucent color will disappear the instant the shrimp is done.

- For best results, place the thawed shrimp in simmering boiling court-bouillon that is at least double the volume of product.
- Stir briefly and allow to return to a gentle boil.
- Check for doneness at this point. The translucent color will change to white throughout the shrimp when it is fully cooked. Monitor the shrimp closely to prevent overcooking.

- Immediately drain into a colander and shock with ice water to stop the cooking. Store in a container surrounded with ice.

If using a steamer to cook shrimp, use a perforated pan and follow the manufacturer's guidelines on a small test batch. There is a strong possibility that the optimum cooking time will be different than the recommended time, so experimentation will be necessary. Keep in mind that the amount of time needed to steam the shrimp will be less than poaching it.

Lobster

No matter what the cooking method, the shell of a lobster will turn bright red when done. To boil lobster:

1. Bring to a boil at least 2 gallons of water for each lobster.
2. Kill the lobster humanely.
3. Place the lobster in the boiling water, It will require about eight minutes of boiling to cook lobsters under 2 pounds.
4. Remove the lobster from the pot when it is done cooking and serve immediately or shock to stop the cooking process.

To steam lobster:

1. Preheat a mechanical steamer or place an inch of water in the bottom of a pot, cover, and heat to boiling.
2. When preheated, add the lobster to the steaming apparatus and cover. Steaming times will vary, depending on the size of the lobster. Manufacturer's guidelines should be used for a starting point. Individual experimentation will be needed.

To bake lobster:

1. Place the prepared, stuffed lobster on a sheetpan and place in a preheated oven.
2. Bake until the stuffed lobster has reached an internal temperature of 160° F at the center of the stuffing before removing it from the oven and serving.

Bivalves

Steam clams and mussels until they open, then give one additional minute of steaming, Any clams or mussels that have not opened after this time should be discarded because these are not of the highest quality.

Scallops are one of the most delicate of shellfish and require only a few minutes of cooking, depending on the size of the product and the intensity of the heat used in the cooking technique. As with shrimp, scallops have a semi-transparent appearance (only whiter) when raw, which turns to an opaque white color when cooked. Scallops become tough and lose their flavor when overcooked.

Raw Fish

Raw fish is often eaten as sushi and sashimi, traditional Japanese dishes. *Sushi* usually contains slices of raw fish or seafood wrapped in a steamed glutinous rice (that has been cooled). It may then be, but is not always, wrapped in *nori*, a paper-thin layer of seaweed. *Sashimi* is raw fish that is sliced and eaten as is. Both sushi and sashimi are often served with condiments such as pickled ginger or soy sauce.

Because the fish is not cooked in either preparation, only the finest quality fish should be chosen. It is recommended that any fish to be eaten raw should first be frozen for at least three days at or below 0° F to kill any possible parasites in the flesh.

7

Meat Products

Meat Products

Meat is an integral part of the diet and the primary influence in the dinner selection that a customer will make. Therefore, it is necessary to acquire knowledge in meat and poultry fabrication.

Meat Composition

Meat is the flesh of domesticated or wild animals. In general, all meats are made up of water, protein, fat, and carbohydrates. The ratio of these nutrients in most meats is 75 percent water, 20 percent protein, 5 percent fat, and a trace of carbohydrates. The amount of water contained in meats will vary depending on shrinkage. Shrinkage will occur through oxidation in storage and during cooking.

The fat in meats can be seen in two major areas. The first is in the *fat cap,* or *finish,* that surrounds the muscle tissue. This fat cap is a source of insulation and energy for the animal. In many instances, this fat cap is left intact during the cooking process. The second area of fat within meat is *marbling.* Marbling is fat that is contained within the muscle tissue. The amount of marbling is related to the tenderness and quality of the meat; generally, the more marbling, the more tender and flavorful the meat will be.

Meat Structure

Meat products are made up of three types of structures: muscle fibers, connective tissues, and bones. When meat is lean, it is almost completely composed of muscle fibers. These fibers determine the texture of the meat and contribute to the flavor. Coarse-textured meats, such as bottom round, have tough, large fibers, while smooth-textured meats, like the tenderloin, have tender, small fibers.

Muscle fibers are bound by the connective tissue. There are two basic functions of connective tissue: to bind muscle fibers together and to connect muscles to bones. These tasks are accomplished by white-colored collagen connective tissue and yellow-colored elastin connective tissue. Collagen tissue will break down into gelatin and water during a slow, moist cooking process. It may also be softened by tenderizing, and there are several ways to accomplish this:

- Using acids, enzymes, and chemicals
- Physically or mechanically pounding, cubing, or grinding
- Slicing meats against the grain after they are cooked

Elastin tissue will not break down in cooking and must be removed or physically tenderized.

Bones are the skeleton of the animal. The color of the bone is an indication of how old the animal was when slaughtered. The redder the bone, the younger the animal. Older animals have white bones.

Inspection

The inspection of meat is a result of many federal food laws. In 1906, the federal government passed the Meat Inspection Act, which requires the inspection of all meats transported across state lines (see Figure 7–1). This federal law guarantees that the meat is wholesome and fit for consumption, and that the animal was not diseased. This is not a mark of quality.

Inspection is a necessary evaluation of wholesomeness performed by the USDA. There are five major functions of

Figure 7–1 Sample meat inspection stamp

the inspector. Detection and destruction of diseased and unfit meat is but one of them.

Grading

Federal and Private

Federal grading was developed as a result of the formation of the USDA Federal Grading Service in 1927 (see Figure 7–2). This service was the yardstick for measuring quality that was part of the law that developed the service. Graders graded the meat for quality, usually 24 hours or more after slaughter and federal inspection. Federal grading is an optional evaluation of quality based on three criteria:

- *Conformation:* the shape, size, and yield of the animal
- *Finish:* the surface fat that covers the animal as well as the organ fat
- *Quality characteristics:* flesh color, meat texture, firmness of the meat, age, and marbling of the animal

Private grading usually does not have the consistency of federal grading. Unlike federal grading, private grading is not under the supervision of the USDA. A private grade stamp used by a company usually does not indicate high quality. Product with a federal stamp is what to demand from purveyors if the chef or manager is after consistent quality. The federal grades are as follows:

Meat	Federal Grade
Beef	Prime, choice, select, standard, commercial, utility, cutter, and canner
Lamb	Prime, choice, good, and utility
Veal	Prime, choice, good, standard, and utility
Pork	1, 2, 3, 4, and utility
Chicken	A, B, C, and utility

Figure 7–2 Sample meat quality grade stamp

Prime grade is usually the most expensive grade of any meat. It is the most desired grade because of its palatability and is produced from younger animals. The age and feeding practices of the animals contribute to the high quality of the marbling. Juiciness and flavorful meat result.

Choice grade is widely accepted within the foodservice industry and is most preferred by consumers because of the flavor and tenderness. Choice meats are a good value because the quality and price are both acceptable.

Select grade is considered by customers to be a good buy. The quality is still acceptable, and usually the price is lower. This grade lacks marbling and is therefore less juicy.

Standard grade has very little marbling and is sold to those who are more concerned about yield and cost factors than about flavor.

Commercial grade comes from older cattle and lacks tenderness. This is principally used in a slow, moist cooking process and most likely will require tenderization.

The lower grades of *utility, cutter,* and *canner* are used primarily for processed meat products. The *yield grade* is the amount of boneless meat obtained from a side of beef. Primal cuts used for the yield-grade test are arm chuck, rib, short loin, sirloin, and round. The yield-grade system is used in conjunction with the first three grades of beef: prime, choice, and select. There are five yield grades of beef:

Yield Grade	Edible Meat Specifications (percentage)
1	52.3
2	52.3–50.0
3	50.0–47.7
4	47.7–45.4
5	Less than 45.4

Aging

Aging is the process by which meat is tenderized through enzymatic action (lactic acid), which causes the meat to further ripen. After the animal is slaughtered, rigor mortis sets in. This condition stiffens muscles and is caused by chemical changes in the flesh. The meat is softened, or ripened, in a short period of time after rigor mortis. Aging is performed under refrigeration, causing the meat to develop flavor and become tender.

There are three methods of aging meat under refrigeration:

- *Dry aging:* Temperature, relative humidity, and air flow are monitored to control bacteria.
- *Fast aging:* Meat is aged at higher temperatures to reduce required time. Ultraviolet lights are used to control bacteria.
- *Vacuum-packed aging:* Meat is placed in a heavy plastic bag with the air exhausted, and the bag is sealed and refrigerated. This is also called cryovac aging.

Handling and Storage

Fresh meat is best stored at temperatures of 32° to 34° F with a high relative humidity of 80 percent. Cryovac-aged meat should remain sealed in the plastic bag until it is ready to be used. Meats should be stored separately from other foods, as well as prepared in separate areas to avoid cross-contamination. Refrigerated fresh meats should be used within two or three days of delivery for best results. Ground meats should be used more quickly because of possible bacteria contamination.

Frozen meats should be well wrapped to avoid freezer burn and oxidation and should be stored at or below 0° F. Rotation of stock is important; FIFO (First In, First Out) is the best method to use. The recommended shelf life of frozen meat is from four to six months.

Frozen meats should be defrosted carefully. The best method for defrosting is in the refrigerator. Microwave defrosting and defrosting under cold running water, if the product is totally wrapped, are sometimes used but are not recommended. A significant loss of moisture occurs in the thawing process. Therefore, refreezing meats after they have thawed is inadvisable.

Meat Cuts

The breakdown of animals to be used as meat products in foodservice operations has been standardized (see Table 7–1). Most purveyors of meat use the Institutional Meat Purchase Specifications (IMPS). This is the same system used by the National Association of Meat Purveyor Specifications (NAMPS). The cuts, numbers, and name are contained in NAMPS' *Meat Buyer's Guide.*

Table 7–1 Meat Fabrication and Cooking Chart

Primal Cut	Common Cuts	Cooking Method
Beef		
Forequarter		
Chuck	Shoulder clod, blade roast/steak, boneless chuck, chuck short ribs, chuck tenders, cubed steaks, stew beef, and shank	Moist heat
	Ground chuck	Dry or moist heat
Brisket	Boneless brisket and corned brisket	Moist heat
	Ground beef	Dry or moist heat
Primal Rib (7 × 10 and/or 7 × 10 rib)	Rib steaks and rib roast	Dry heat
	Short ribs	Moist heat
Short plate	Skirt steak rolls, short ribs, and stew beef	Moist heat
	Ground beef	Dry or moist heat

(continued)

Table 7–1 Meat Fabrication and Cooking Chart *(continued)*

Primal Cut	Common Cuts	Cooking Method
Hindquarter		
Short loin	Top loin steak, T-bone, strip, and New York strip	Dry heat
Sirloin	Top sirloin, bottom sirloin, tenderloin butt, shell steaks, and kabobs	Dry heat
Round	Sirloin tip, top round, bottom round, eye of the round, shank, and heel	Dry heat
		Moist heat
Flank	Flank steak	Dry or moist heat
Veal		
Foresaddle	Shoulder roast, cubed steak shoulder roast, steaks	Dry heat
Shoulder/chuck	Chops, ground, shank	Moist heat
Hotel rack	Rib roast and rib chops	Dry heat
Breast (not a wholesale	Boneless breast	Dry heat
primal cut)	Cubed steaks and ground veal	Dry or moist heat
Hindsaddle		
Loin	Loin chops and saddle (roast)	Dry heat
Leg	Leg roast	Dry heat
	Cutlets and osso buco from the shank	Moist heat
Lamb		
Foresaddle		
Shoulder and/or chuck	Shoulder roast and shoulder chops	Dry heat
Hotel rack	Crown roast, rib chops, and rib roast	Dry heat
Breast (not a wholesale	Breast, riblets, and stew meat	Moist heat
primal cut)	Ground lamb	Dry or moist heat
Hindsaddle		
Loin	Loin chaps, and loin roast	Dry heat
Leg	Leg roast, leg chops, sirloin chops, and sirloin roast	Dry heat
	Shank	Moist heat
Pork		
Picnic shoulder	Fresh or smoked shoulder and shoulder hocks	Moist heat
	Ground pork	Dry or moist heat
Boston butt	Butt steaks, shoulder roast, ground pork, and sausage meat	Dry or moist heat
Ham	Fresh ham and ham hocks	Dry or moist heat
	Smoked hams and ham steaks	Dry heat
Loin	Boneless loin	Dry or moist heat
	Loin roast	Dry heat
	Canadian bacon	Dry or moist heat
Belly	Bacon and spare ribs (not a wholesale primal cut)	Dry or moist heat
Spareribs	Spareribs	Dry or moist heat

The primary types of meat—beef, lamb, veal, and pork—can be purchased as carcasses, partial carcasses, primal cuts, or fabricated cuts. The fabricated cuts may be broken down further into portion cuts. All of these cuts have been assigned numbers for clarity in purchasing and production.

The carcass is the whole animal after it has been slaughtered and eviscerated. The head, feet, and hide are removed except for pork, which retains the feet. The use of carcasses and partial carcasses is not feasible in most foodservice operations. The cost of labor, equipment, and facilities for processing carcasses and partial carcasses can only be supported by the largest of operations. Most operators do not purchase their meats in these market forms.

Primal, or wholesale, cuts are one of the most popular forms that are available to foodservice operations. Primal cuts are the most easily handled by foodservice operators. Using primal cuts rather than portion cuts allows operators to develop a variety of uses and sizes for their operations. These cuts are also easier to handle and store.

Portion, or fabricated, cuts are primal cuts reduced to menu-portion sizes. The guidelines for these cuts are set by the IMPS/NAMPS specifications. If preferred, purchasers may have portions cut to their own specifications. This allows for the development of special menu items.

Variety Meats

Variety meats are traditionally internal organs of the animal that are removed during the processing of the carcass. The classes of variety meats are

- Brain
- Kidney
- Oxtail
- Sweetbread (thymus gland)
- Heart
- Liver
- Tongue
- Tripe (stomach)

Traditionally viewed as ethnic food items, variety meats have found their way onto American menus in limited quantities. American chefs have found a need to present customers with a variety of ingredients, allowing for the further acceptance of these products. Variety meats are high in protein, vitamins, and iron.

Poultry

Poultry is considered to be large domestic birds raised for human consumption. This category includes chicken, turkey, ducks, and geese. The composition and structure of poultry products is similar to that of meats.

Inspection and Grading

All poultry, like meats, must be inspected and most are graded. The process of poultry inspection is similar to that of meat inspection (see Figure 7–3).

Most poultry is graded, but, unlike meats, the grading stamp is not used on the carcass. Traditionally, a wing tag is attached to the bird to denote grade. This grading is voluntary and is based on quality. The quality grades of poultry depend on the following areas:

- Body shape or conformation
- Amount of flesh
- Amount of fat
- Presence of pinfeathers or cleanliness
- Condition of the bird (no broken bones, tears in the skin, or blemishes)

The grades of poultry are assigned letters rather than descriptions. The letters A, B, and C are used to denote the quality grades (see Figure 7–4 on page 122).

Figure 7–3 Sample chicken inspection stamp

Figure 7–4 Sample chicken quality grade stamp

Handling and Storage

Fresh poultry is highly perishable and should be used within 24 hours of receipt. Poultry should be received packed in ice from purveyors and should be repacked for storage in the refrigerator. The risk of a food-borne outbreak of salmonella is a serious threat when handling poultry. All surfaces that come into contact with the poultry must be thoroughly cleaned and sanitized before being used for other products to eliminate the possibility of cross-contamination.

Frozen poultry should be stored at or below 0° F and should be thawed in the original packaging. Thawing should take place under refrigeration or in the microwave. It is inadvisable to refreeze poultry items.

Poultry Market Forms

Poultry is available in several forms based on whether it is chicken, turkey, or duck. The subdivision of kind (broiler, fryer, or roaster) is often used to further differentiate products in poultry. Another way to describe poultry products is by the amount of processing (see Table 7–2): live versus slaughtered, dressed, and ready to cook (RTC) as a whole, parts, or cut up.

Table 7–2 Poultry Classification and Cooking Chart

Product Type	Description	Cooking Method
Chicken		
Cornish hen	Young bird (5 to 6 weeks); ¾ to 1¼ lbs.	Dry heat
Fryer	Young bird (9 to 12 weeks) of either sex; smooth skin and tender flesh. 1½ to 2½ lbs.	Dry heat
Broiler	2½ to 3½ lbs.	Dry heat
Roaster (light and heavy)	Young bird (3 to 5 months) of either sex; smooth skin and tender flesh; cartilage is less flexible; 3½ to 5 lbs. (light) or 5 to 12 lbs. (heavy)	Dry heat
Capon	Very expensive male chicken that has been castrated; good flavor and very tender; under 8 months; 5 to 8 lbs. (a type of roaster)	Dry heat
Stewer	Coarse skin and tough flesh; fowl or hen; mature female, over 10 months; 3½ to 6 lbs.	Moist heat
Goose		
Young goose	Tender flesh; under 6 months; 6 to 10 lbs.	Dry heat
Mature goose	Tough flesh; over 6 months.	Dry or moist heat
Guineas		
Young guinea	Under 6 months; relative of pheasant; ¾ to 1½ lbs.	Dry heat
Old guinea	Up to 12 months; 1 to 2 lbs.	Dry heat
Pigeon		
Squab	Tender, light meat; young, 3 to 4 weeks.	Dry heat
Pigeon	Tough, dark meat; old, over 4 weeks.	Dry heat
Pheasant	Old, 6 to 12 months; females are more tender.	Moist heat

Game

In addition to the traditional meats and meat products that have been described, game is another class of animals that is appearing more frequently on menus in America. These animals may be categorized as:

- *Furred:* rabbit, venison, hare, bear, wild boar, elk, squirrel, moose, opossum, woodchuck, beaver, muskrat
- *Feathered:* guinea fowl, squab, pigeon, pheasant, woodcock, ostrich, teal, quail

This classification is further broken down into two categories:

- *Domestic game:* animals and birds that are raised in a farmlike environment
- *Wild game:* animals that grow and are hunted in their native environment

The most popular of the furred game animals include rabbit, venison, and hare. The most popular of the feathered animals—guinea fowl, squab, pigeon, and pheasant—have been added to the poultry chart. In addition, woodcock and teal are sometimes consumed.

All wild game has a very strong flavor and the meat is dark. These wild animals are very active and, therefore, their flesh tends to be tougher and drier (because of a lower fat content) than most other animals. The farm-bred game varieties have a more subtle flavor and lighter flesh.

Hanging Game

Before cooking, game is often hung for varying lengths of time to aid in the maturation of the meat. During the hanging process, the carbohydrates in the tissue are converted into lactic acid, thus tenderizing the meat and imparting a stronger flavor. The hanging process is completed by eviscerating the animal (with the exception of woodcock and thrush) and then hanging it in a cool, dark place with plenty of air circulation. A refrigerator works well for the hanging process. Game animals that live on the ground are hung by the hind legs, while birds are hung by the head. The plumage or coat is left intact until the hanging process is complete and the animal is ready for cooking. The length of hanging time depends on the age and type of game:

Woodcock or pheasant	4 days
Thrush or duck	3 days
Hare	2 days
Large game	6 to 8 days

Game sold commercially is often matured before being sold.

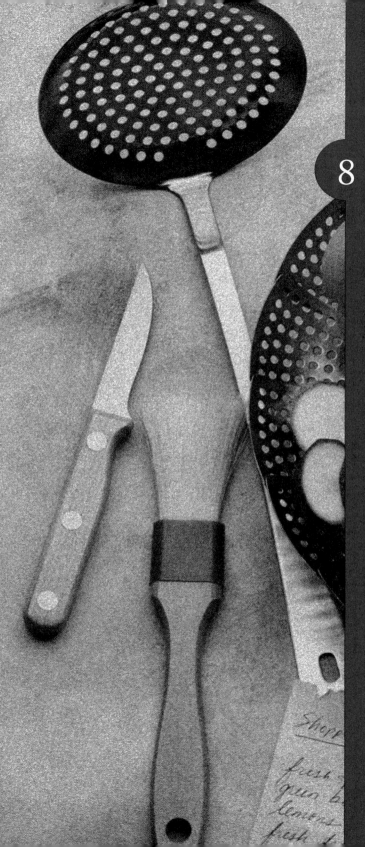

Equipment and Smallwares

8

Equipment and Smallwares

*Food cookery requires proper equipment and **smallwares.** The chef or manager should be familiar with all equipment and smallwares to make sound decisions in selection and purchasing because equipment is relatively expensive. Operating and maintaining equipment effectively is vital to ensure safety in the kitchen and to maximize the life of the equipment.*

The Cooking Line

The arrangement of the equipment in most commercial kitchens is called the *cooking line*. There are several configurations:

- *Single straight-line arrangement:* The simplest design for arranging equipment in foodservice establishments, the straight-line arrangement can take the shape of an island or be placed along a wall.
- *Ell-shaped arrangement:* The ell-shaped arrangement generally separates two major areas of equipment or workspace. For example, one side of the line may be used primarily for prep, while the second side may contain the equipment used for service and production. An ell-shaped arrangement is shown in Figure 8–1.
- *U-shaped arrangement:* The U-shaped arrangement is ideally used in establishments where space is limited and few employees will use the space. The arrangement is popular in the bar or dishwashing area in many establishments. A U-shaped arrangement is shown in Figure 8–2.
- *Parallel, back-to-back arrangement:* The parallel, back-to-back arrangement is comprised of two lines of equipment that are placed back to back. The lines may be divided by a wall and could possibly be designed to separate the prep and service areas. One advantage to such a configuration is that utility lines are centralized. A parallel, back-to-back arrangement is shown in Figure 8–3 on page 128.
- *Parallel, face-to-face arrangement:* The parallel, face-to-face arrangement configures two straight lines of equipment facing each other and separated by a work aisle. Unlike the parallel, back-to-back arrangement, two separate utility lines are needed. A parallel, face-to-face arrangement is shown in Figure 8–4 on page 128.

Grills, Broilers, and Salamanders

Broilers are either top-fired, where the flame and source of heat is above the foods being cooked, or bottom-fired, in the case of a grill, where the heat source is below the

Figure 8–1 Ell-shaped arrangement

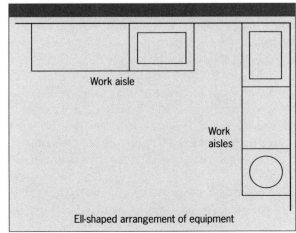

Ell-shaped arrangement of equipment

Figure 8–2 U-shaped arrangement

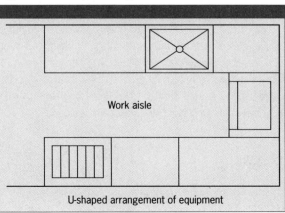

U-shaped arrangement of equipment

Figure 8–3 Parallel, back-to-back arrangement

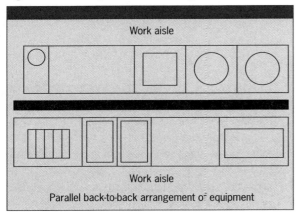
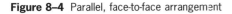

Work aisle

Work aisle

Parallel back-to-back arrangement of equipment

Figure 8–4 Parallel, face-to-face arrangement

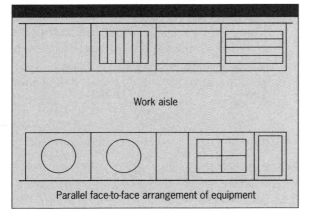

Work aisle

Parallel face-to-face arrangement of equipment

Figure 8–5 Broiler

Figure 8–6 Center or wall-mounted salamander broiler

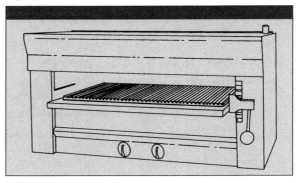

foods being cooked (see Figure 8–5). A broiler is designed to cook the food from start to finish. A salamander is a smaller broiler, usually mounted on the cooking line over a range, that is used for browning or glazing the tops of some food products (see Figure 8–6). The heat source for broilers and salamanders is either gas or electric; while grills may use gas, electric, charcoal, or wood.

Ranges

Ranges are the most used piece of equipment in today's kitchens. Braising, sautéing, and poaching are some of the cooking techniques performed on the range. Two types of conventional cook tops are used on ranges: open burners (see Figure 8–7) and flat tops (see Figure 8–8). Open burners have the advantage of using either an open gas flame or an electric element in the cooking process; thus, the amount of heat being used can be regulated more easily than with flat tops. Flat tops are used to distribute heat over larger areas, which create a more uniform transfer of heat.

Graduated heat tops are designed similarly to flat tops, although areas on the surface contain graduated rings that can be removed to regulate the heat more easily.

Figure 8–7 Open-burner range

Figure 8–8 Flat-top burner range

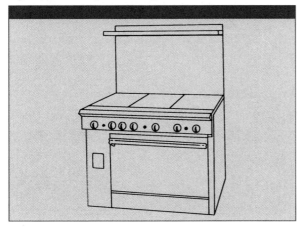

Graduated heat tops generally give the chef or manager more control of the heat compared to flat tops.

Induction differs from conventional electric cook tops, which are often slow to heat, to recover heat, and to cool down. Magnetic induction cook tops are electric and characteristically have a smooth ceramic surface that remains cool to the touch even at intense temperatures and is easy to clean. Heat is immediate and evenly distributed, with great flexibility from a rapid boil to a gentle simmer in a short amount of time. For instance, two cups of water, placed on high heat, will come to a boil within 30 seconds.

Induction cook tops come in single-burner countertop, and two or four tops. Induction is a faster, more efficient way of cooking than is cooking on conventional electric cook tops.

The griddle is another type of range top (see Figure 8–9). A griddle is a smooth, flat surface on which foods are cooked directly. It is usually constructed of nickel-plated metal. Breakfast and luncheon items are often prepared on this piece of equipment.

Modern technology provides the chrome griddle, which has several advantages to the nickel-plated griddle. In the chrome griddle plate, the heat is more uniformly retained, therefore emitting less radiant heat to the air and ventilation systems. Other advantages of the chrome surface is its smoothness, which repels flavor transfer and ease of cleaning over conventional models. According to testing data at the University of Illinois, the chromium griddle requires 44 percent less time to clean. The chromium griddle is available in liquid propane, gas, and electrical versions. Its general appearance is similar to that of a conventional griddle.

Figure 8–9 Griddle

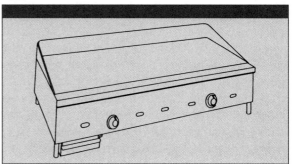

Deep-Fat Fryers

Deep-fat fryers (see Figure 8–10 on page 130) are operated by either electric or gas heat and are easy to maintain and clean. Thermostatically controlled temperatures and quick recovery of heat between basket loads allow food to cook evenly while keeping the fat from burning or getting too cool. Oil in conventional deep fryers is heated from

Figure 8–10 Deep-fat fryer

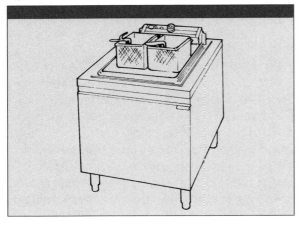

below by either an electric element or a gas flame, which has to achieve high temperatures exceeding 750° F to heat the oil to temperatures between 340° F and 375° F. As a result, hazardous conditions exist because the smoking, oxidation, and flashpoints of the fat are exceeded. Also off-odors and a mist of oil are released into the air over the equipment and into the general production area. Deep-fryers can be equipped with timer devices that mechanically lower and raise the food, eliminating the chance of over- or undercooking. Filtering devices can be attached to the fryolators to remove particles even while cooking. Continual filtration helps to extend the longevity of the fat.

The appearance of induction deep-fat fryers is similar to the conventional fryolator. The two large metal cylinders in the center of the fry vat supply the heat to the fat by means of induction. Unlike the conventional fryolators, the induction cylinder needs only to be heated to temperatures of 500° F to bring the fat to the correct temperature. The heat cylinders are not located at the bottom of the vat, so the fat temperature remains only 140° F at the bottom while the rest of the fat may be operating at 350° F. Therefore, small particles of food that fall during the frying process do not have as great a chance of burning during extended use. The *recovery time,* the time needed for the fryolator to return the temperature of the fat to its preset temperature after cold foods have been added, is 25 percent less than that of conventional fryers.

Steam Table

The steam table (see Figure 8–11) is used to hold hot foods for service. Foods should be cooked completely or preheated before being placed on the steam table. All food items should be maintained at a temperature of 140° F. The steam table is designed with separators that allow foods to be placed in various-sized hotel-pan inserts (see Figure 8–12). Depths of inserts may be 2, 4, or 6 inches.

Figure 8–11 Steam table

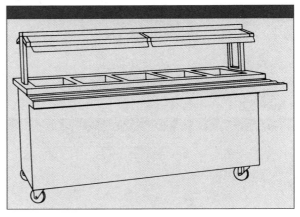

Figure 8–12 Steam-table inserts

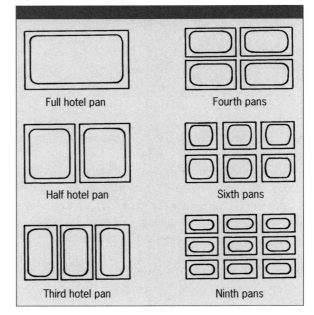

Full hotel pan

Fourth pans

Half hotel pan

Sixth pans

Third hotel pan

Ninth pans

Ovens

Conventional Ovens

The conventional oven (see Figure 8–13) is usually mounted underneath a range top and can be heated by either gas or electricity. It provides a source of heat for roasting, baking, and braising.

Convection Ovens

A convection oven (see Figures 8–14 and 8–15 on page 132) is one equipped with a blower fan to circulate the air for rapid and even heating. Reduced cooking times and energy savings have made the convection oven popular in foodservice operations. If a recipe does not specify convection baking temperature, a good rule of thumb is to decrease the oven temperature by approximately 50° F and reduce cooking time approximately 30 percent. Cooking time will depend on the product recipe, number of items baked at one time, and the type of pan used.

FlashBake Oven

The FlashBake oven (see Figure 8–16 on page 132) cooks food using infrared and visible light rays. Unlike conven-

Figure 8-13 Conventional oven with graduated heat top

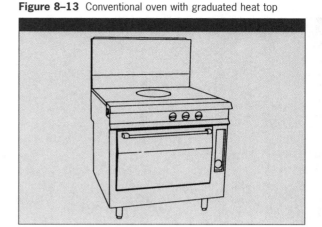

tional and convection ovens, the FlashBake is smaller and requires only four square feet of space. The cavity of the oven is only 14 inches in diameter and can cook a variety of foods. For example, it can cook a 9-inch raw-dough pizza with toppings in just 3 minutes, and if a par-cooked crust is used, the pizza will cook in just 95 seconds. The resulting product has crispy crust and bubbling cheese, just as if it had been cooked in a deck, or rotary, oven. A strip steak can be cooked in 2 minutes and an angel food cake in just 4 minutes.

The FlashBake oven cooks food using two zones of heat: five quartz tubes underneath the cooking area and five

Figure 8-14 Standard convection oven

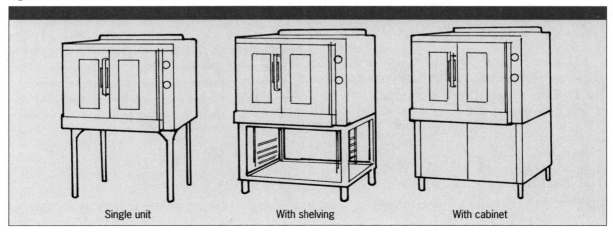

Single unit   With shelving   With cabinet

Figure 8–15 Double convection oven

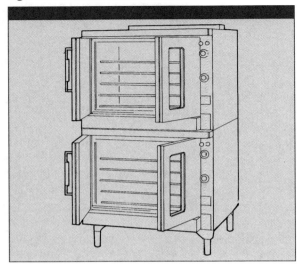

Figure 8–17 Holding oven

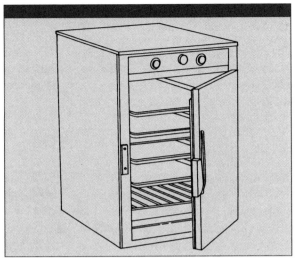

Figure 8–16 FlashBake oven

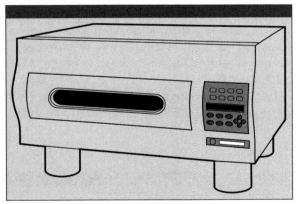

above, both areas of which can be controlled separately. The oven has several advantages: it requires no preheating, it can be used continually, and it requires no venting.

a probe that allows the chef or manager to monitor oven and internal product temperatures. Roasting foods slowly in holding ovens results in less shrinkage and greater yields. Holding ovens are often used in institutional foodservice operations.

Microwave Ovens

The microwave oven (see Figure 8–18) converts microwave energy into heat energy within the food product. The energy is emitted by electronic microwave tubes located in the cooking chamber. As the energy radiates from the tubes, it is absorbed by the food product and transformed into heat. Foods cooked in a microwave oven cook from the inside out, and the cooking time is drastically reduced compared to that of conventional and convection ovens. In the foodservice industry, microwave ovens are used primarily to reheat or to thaw small amounts of frozen foods.

Holding Ovens

Holding ovens (see Figure 8–17) can be used to either cook or hold food for service. The oven design may feature

Reel Ovens

A reel oven (see Figure 8–19) has rotating shelves and a large capacity. It uses the same times and temperatures

Figure 8–18 Microwave oven

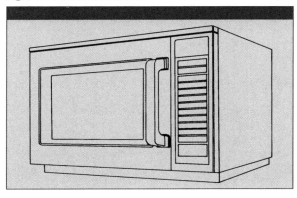

Figure 8–19 Reel oven

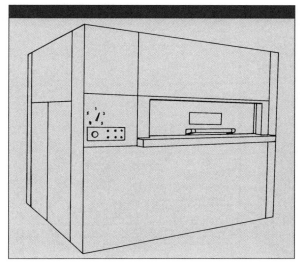

as a conventional oven and will hold up to 12 to 15 baking pans. Types of reel ovens include direct gas fired, indirect gas fired, indirect-direct gas fired, indirect oil fired, and electric. Advantages of the reel oven are that heat is distributed more evenly because of rotation of shelves (see Figure 8–20), large quantities can be baked simultaneously, and height is excellent for loading and unloading. Disadvantages of the reel oven are that the oven occupies a lot of space and the oven is expensive.

Deck, or Stack, Ovens

Deck, or stack, ovens (see Figure 8–21 on page 134) are placed directly on top of one another and operate in much the same way as conventional ovens. Deck ovens can have two baking controls, one regulating heat in the top oven and the other regulating heat in the bottom oven. The two types of deck ovens are gas fired and electric.

Rotary Ovens

Rotary-type convection ovens (see Figures 8–22 and 8–23 on page 134) were originally constructed for the bakery trade because of their high-volume production and specific requirements. These ovens have one or more rotating racks and maintain an absolutely uniform temperature from top to bottom. Baking trays are commonly used, but perfo-

Figure 8–20 Heat distribution in a reel oven

Figure 8–21 Deck, or stack, oven

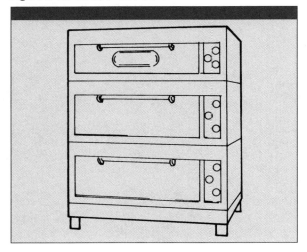

Figure 8–23 Rotary oven with automatic steam generator

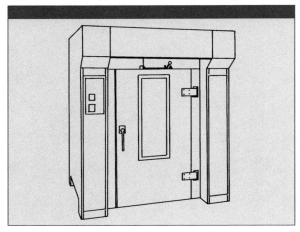

Figure 8–22 Rotary oven

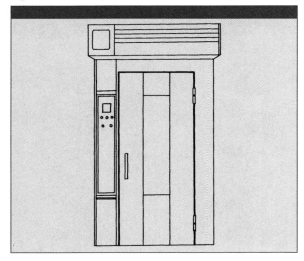

1. Set the thermostat at the desired temperature and preheat.
2. Wheel in the rack with the trays ready for baking.
3. When a glaze on the bread caused by steam is desired, set the electric timer for the built-in automatic steam generator to about three minutes. After one-half minute, open the door, wheel the rack into the oven chamber filled with steam, and close the door. The steaming will automatically begin.
4. Set the timer for the suggested baking time.

Steam Pressure Cooker

A steam pressure cooker (see Figure 8–24) works on the principle of steam under pressure that is in direct contact with the food product being cooked. Food is exposed in perforated hotel pans and placed into the cooker compartments. The pressure door is then secured and the steam valve is opened, allowing the chamber to fill with pressurized steam that surrounds the food.

Steam heat is hotter than boiling water and cooks foods more quickly. Steamed vegetables lose less color and vitamins, seafoods cook without losing their moisture and delicate flavor, and meats cook quickly with less shrinkage.

rated trays recommended when a crust is desired on foods, such as with loaves of bread. Oven temperatures vary from product to product, but the average is approximately 425° F. Rotary ovens can be heated by electricity, gas, or oil.

The following steps are recommended when using rotary rack ovens with an automatic steam generator:

Figure 8–24 Steam pressure cooker

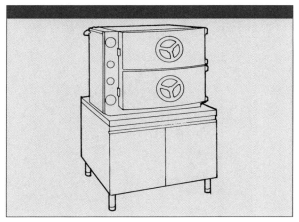

Convection or Tabletop Low-Pressure Steamers

Convection or tabletop low-pressure steamers (see Figure 8–25) are similar in design to steam pressure cookers but are smaller and use less pressure: 4 to 6 pounds per square inch (psi). The convection steamer replaces the pressure with a fan to transfer the heat.

Figure 8–25 Convection or free-standing low-pressure steamer

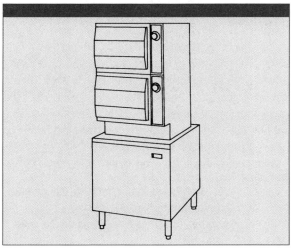

Pressureless Steamer

Pressureless steamers (see Figure 8–26) are small units that require less energy to operate than do larger steamers. The steam-chamber temperature will remain just above 212° F. Pressureless steamers are practical and most cost effective for a low-volume food operation. The quantity of food that can be steamed at a time is limited. The steaming process can be interrupted or stopped at any time because no pressure is present.

Tilting Skillet

The tilting skillet is one of the most versatile pieces of equipment available and can be found in many high-volume commercial kitchens (see Figure 8–27). A tilting skillet is

Figure 8–26 Pressureless steamer

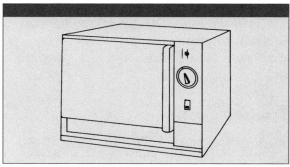

Figure 8–27 Tilting skillet

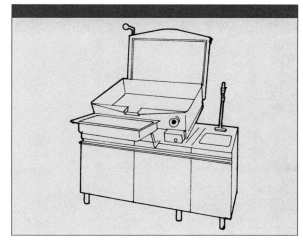

equipped with a lever that allows the cooking surface to tilt for convenient removal of foods. It can be used for cooking a variety of foods ranging from scrambled eggs, vegetables, stir-fried rice, braised meats, to fried chicken.

Steam-Jacketed Kettle

Steam kettles (see Figure 8–28) are double-walled stainless-steel kettles that allow steam pressure to build between the walls, heating the inner chamber. Unlike steamers, the steam makes no contact with the food, but, by controlling the amount of steam entering the chamber, even temperature can be achieved for quick boiling or slow simmering. This double-boiler effect is excellent for simmering sauces, and the large cover allows the chef to braise meats or to bring large quantities of water to a boil in a short time. Some steam kettles tilt for pouring, while others have valves at the base for draining liquids more easily. Steam kettles are available with hermetically sealed lids, enabling them to convert into pressure cookers. This lid option is commonly desirable in large-volume operations.

Trunion Kettles

Trunion kettles (see Figure 8–29) are similar to steam-jacketed kettles but are usually smaller in volume and capacity.

Figure 8–28 Steam-jacketed kettle

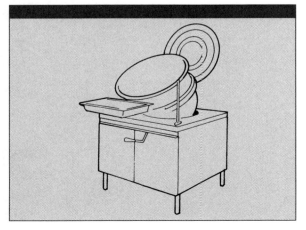

Figure 8–29 Trunion kettles

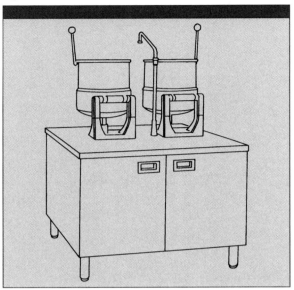

Kitchen Machinery

The equipment that is used in the preparation of food is referred to as *kitchen machinery.*

Mixer (Universal Kitchen Machine)

Mixing machines (see Figure 8–30) can perform many tasks, such as mixing batters and doughs or aerating by whipping. With the use of other attachments, mixing machines can grind, grate, shred, slice, and dice. The mixing machine has three basic parts: the motor and control box, the carriage that holds the bowl and raises or lowers it to the beater, and the frame.

Mixers come in the following sizes:

5 quart	For small quantities: to whip or mix creams or incorporate flavoring or color
20 quart	Also has attachment for use as a 12 quart
30 quart	Floor model

Figure 8–30 Standard mixer and various attachments and agitators

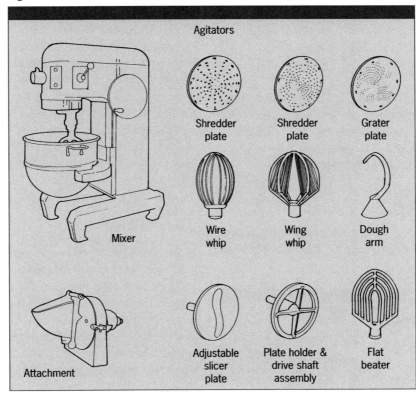

60 quart   Also has attachment for use as a 40 quart
80 quart   Also has attachment for use as a 40 to 60 quart
140 quart   Also has attachment for use as a 60 to 80 quart

Figure 8–31 Vertical cutter mixer

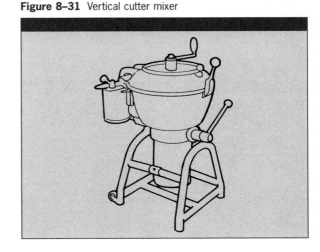

Vertical Cutter Mixer

The vertical cutter mixer (VCM) (see Figure 8–31) is used in foodservice operations that must produce large volumes of food quickly. The larger cutters are capable of cutting a dozen heads of lettuce for salad in less than two seconds; making over 60 pounds of meat loaf, oven-ready, in seconds; or mixing over 60 pounds of heavy bread dough in about one minute. The large, top-loading cover makes it easy to fill, and the tilting action of the unit makes unloading and cleaning a simple task. Because of the nature of the design, the machine may cut various foods unevenly, and foods can easily be overworked if forgotten.

Food Processor

The food processor (see Figure 8–32) is similar in design to the VCM, only this version is used to produce smaller quantities of foods. Multifaceted, the food processor is equipped with many different blades, which are designed to chop, grind, slice, grate, and blend.

Food Chopper

There are three basic parts to a food chopper, also known as a buffalo chopper (see Figure 8–33). The *bowl* rotates

the food into the *blade* that chops it as it passes through. The more the bowl passes the food through the blade, the finer the pieces become. The *motor*, the power source for the chopper, is also capable of powering attachments for grinding, shredding, grating, and slicing. Food choppers are useful in kitchens of all sizes. By shutting off the motor and removing the safety shield, the blade and bowl can be removed for easy cleaning. Because of the simple, solid design, choppers can give excellent service for many maintenance-free years. The food chopper has generally been replaced by the VCM and food processor in modern kitchens.

Food Slicer

Slicers (see Figure 8–34) are designed to slice primarily meats and cheeses in uniform sizes and quantities. There are three basic parts to a slicer: the *body*, or *base*, which contains the motor and holds the blade; the *blade guide*, which adjusts the thickness of the cut; and the *carriage with the food holder*, which holds the product securely and passes back and forth over the blade. Some slicers operate with an automatic carriage that moves the food across the blade. Care should be taken when using a slicer to ensure safety. Food slicers should be cleaned and sanitized after each use. Some delis use separate slicers for cheese versus meat to prevent cross contamination.

Figure 8–32 Food processor

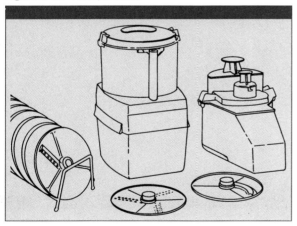

Figure 8–33 Food chopper

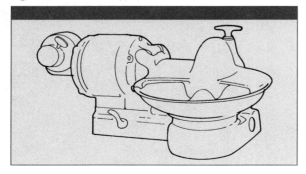

Figure 8–34 Food slicer

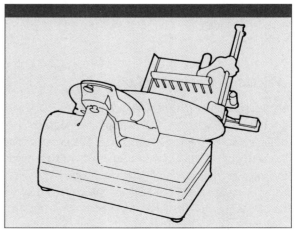

Automatic Potato Peeler

Automatic potato peelers (see Figure 8–35) are designed to wash potatoes and remove the peels with the use of friction. The inside of the peeling compartment has a turntable that whirls the potatoes around, bouncing them off the rough walls, stripping the peel from the potato like sandpaper smooths a board. At the same time, a spray of water washes the peel scraps into a perforated basket in the base, which is emptied later.

Much care must be used when operating this machine to prevent waste, as the sanding effect will reduce large potatoes to the size of radishes if the potatoes are not removed in time. Peelers of this type are not designed to remove potato eyes.

Figure 8–35 Automatic potato peeler

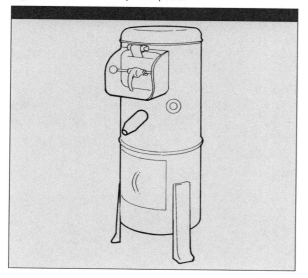

Figure 8–36 Free-standing meat grinder

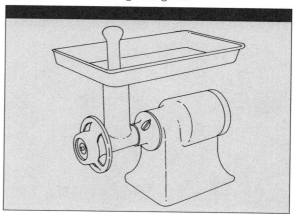

Meat Grinder

The meat grinder (see Figure 8–36) may take two forms: either a free-standing unit or an attachment for a mixer. It is used to prepare any meat or fish item that needs to be ground into various sized grind. The meat grinder comes with different-sized faceplates. The appropriate faceplate should be chosen to control for the size grind desired.

Smallwares

Pots and pans are made of a variety of materials: aluminum, copper, stainless steel, stainless steel and aluminum clad, cast iron, and ceramic. Usually the chef will select pots and pans based on personal preference. Utensils, on the other hand, are either stainless steel, plastic, or wood. Most chefs prefer stainless steel because of durability and longevity. See Figure 8–37 on page 140 for illustrations of pots and pans and Figure 8–38 on page 141 for illustrations of kitchen utensils.

Figure 8–37 Smallwares: pots and pans

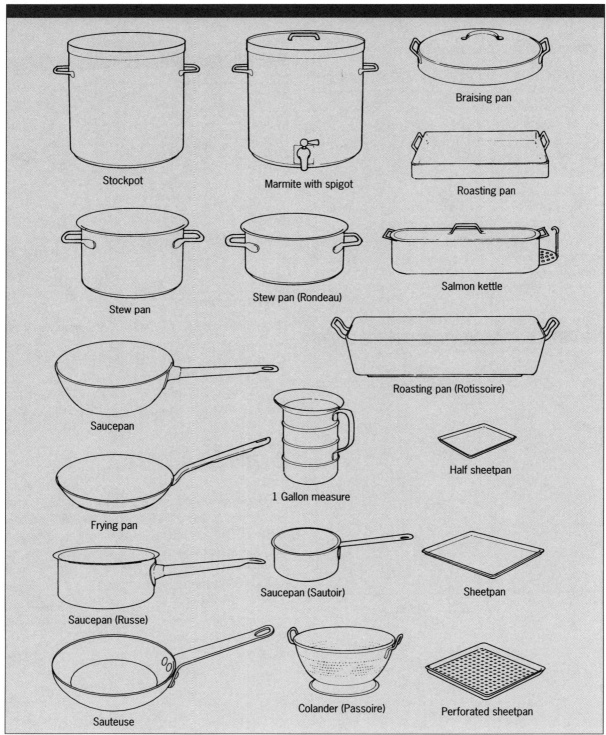

Stockpot

Marmite with spigot

Braising pan

Roasting pan

Stew pan

Stew pan (Rondeau)

Salmon kettle

Saucepan

1 Gallon measure

Roasting pan (Rotissoire)

Half sheetpan

Frying pan

Saucepan (Russe)

Saucepan (Sautoir)

Sheetpan

Sauteuse

Colander (Passoire)

Perforated sheetpan

Figure 8–37 Smallwares: pots and pans (continued)

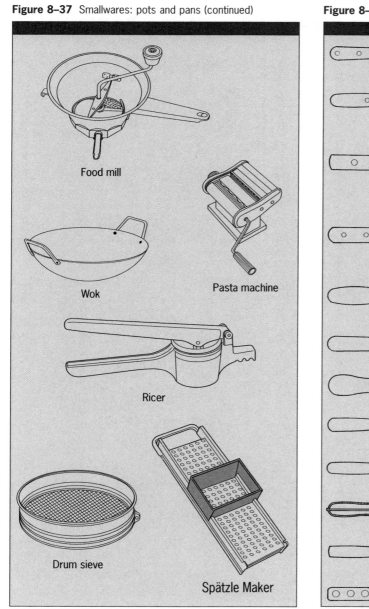

Food mill

Wok

Pasta machine

Ricer

Drum sieve

Spätzle Maker

Figure 8–38 Smallwares: utensils (continued)

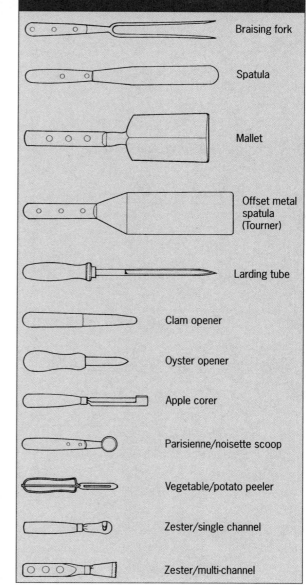

Braising fork

Spatula

Mallet

Offset metal spatula (Tourner)

Larding tube

Clam opener

Oyster opener

Apple corer

Parisienne/noisette scoop

Vegetable/potato peeler

Zester/single channel

Zester/multi-channel

(continued)

Figure 8–38 Smallwares: utensils (continued)

Kitchen ladle (louche)

Deep fat skimmer
(écumoire pour friteuse)

Bain-Marie spoon (cuillère à Bain-Marie)

Bouillon strainer (passe-bouillon)

Pouring ladle (cuillère à verse)

Sauce sieve (chinois fin)

Sauce sieve (chinois gros)

Lifter (pelle a frire)

Fine mesh sieve (chinois mousseline)

Perforated lifter (spatule a reduir)

Skimming ladle (écumoire)

Whisk, heavy duty
(fouet, extra-fort)

Fish server (pelle a poisson)

Gravy or piano whisk (fouet à sauce)

Potato masher (presse purée)

Potato nest fryer
(corbeille pour nids de pommes
de terre)

Kitchen fork (fourchette à viande)

Metals in the Kitchen

Heat Efficiency of Metals

In the efficiency of cooking, heat transfer is important. Silver, the most efficient metal, has a 100 percent rating for heat transfer; but, because of its high cost, care, and maintenance, it is mainly used for chafing dishes and serving platters. In comparison, the following metals are rated in heat transfer efficiency percentages: copper, 73 percent; aluminum, 31 percent; iron or steel, 11 percent.

Copper

An advantage of using copper in cooking is its high melting point of 1,985° F. When copper is exposed to the air, however, a thin, poisonous, bluish-green skin of verdigris material forms. Therefore, the inside of the vessel is lined with another metal. This prevents the oxidation of the metal. Much care and attention is necessary to maintain copper vessels in good working condition.

Aluminum

Aluminum is a soft metal that is low-priced, light, and rust-free. Heat conductivity is relatively high; thus, aluminum has been used successfully in cooking vessels. However, caution is advised when using stainless-steel utensils with aluminum cookware. These utensils can remove a microscopic layer of the aluminum, causing discoloration of various food products. Foods high in acid, such as tomatoes, vinegar, or lemon juice, should not be cooked in aluminum because chemical reactions occur.

Stainless Steel

Stainless steel is costly to manufacture and conducts heat poorly. Stainless-steel pots are often made with conductivity plates on the bottom. The plates are usually made from aluminum or copper encased in a thin layer of stainless steel. The combination of metals in the cookware improves the low conductivity rating of stainless steel.

Iron

Iron has low heat conductivity and a tendency to rust. Use is restricted to frying, where cleaning is accomplished by simply wiping the vessel dry.

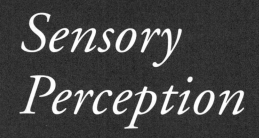

9

Sensory Perception

Sensory Perception

The study of sensory perception is the study of how our eyes, ears, nose, mouth, and skin detect and evaluate the world around us.

Understanding sensory perception is important to chefs who wish to improve their ability to taste, and who strive to increase their customers' enjoyment of food. Chefs with heightened sensory awareness are better able to

- Identify flavor imbalances and correct them.
- Detect off-flavors in food before it reaches the guest; for example, off-flavors may be found in burnt or spoiled foods.
- Create imaginative and interesting flavor combinations.

Factors such as genetics, gender, and health all influence the extent of an individual's sensory perception. Experience is the most important factor, however, because, regardless of current abilities, they can always be improved by consciously paying attention to details of food when eating.

What Is Sensory Perception?

All five of the sense organs are active during the eating process. Special receptors detect changes in the environment. When a receptor is stimulated (see Table 9–1), nerve impulses carry the signal to the brain, where the informa-tion is processed. The organ that actually senses stimuli is the brain, not the skin, eyes, ears, nose, or taste buds.

Taste and smell do more than increase our enjoyment of food. They increase the production of saliva and certain hormonal and gastric secretions important for proper digestion and nutrient uptake (Schiffman, p.2). An evolutionary advantage to having well-developed senses is to better detect danger. Many poisonous foods are bitter or otherwise unpleasant, while many healthful foods, such as ripe fruit, are sweet or otherwise pleasant.

The Senses

The sensory properties of food include color and appearance, flavor, and texture. Each is detected by four of our five sense organs: the taste buds, nose, skin, and eyes. Sometimes these sensory properties are called *organoleptic properties*.

Color and Appearance

The appearance of food is usually the first indication of how it will taste. Based on appearance alone, the brain processes information about flavor and texture and makes decisions about likes and dislikes. This occurs because

Table 9–1 The Sensory Properties of Food

Sense Organ	Receptor	Stimuli	Sensation
Taste buds	Taste cells	Sugars, salts, acids, amino acids, and alkaloids	Taste
Nose	Olfactory cells	Odor chemicals	Smell
Skin	Free nerve endings	Common chemicals	Feeling factors and pain
Skin	Skin receptors	Heat and pressure	Touch
Eyes	Rods and cones	Light energy	Sight
Ears	Hair cells	Sound vibrations	Hearing

Adapted from Mader, p. 324.

humans have a highly developed sense of sight; so highly developed, in fact, that messages received from the other senses are often ignored (Freedman, p.70). For example, we expect yellow candy to be lemon flavored, green to be lime, and purple to be grape, and we get confused when they are not. We expect a darker yellow candy to be more lemony, and if the candy holds it shape and looks smooth and hard, we expect it to be hard to bite. This is what is meant by the expression "we eat with our eyes." Because the sense of sight is so important to the overall perception of food, chefs should be sure that the color and appearance of food are appealing.

Factors that Affect Our Perception of Color and Appearance

Several factors affect how we perceive the color and appearance of food:

- *Chemical:* When the extent of cooking or the quality of raw materials differ, appearances will vary. For example, fresh spinach, which contains more chlorophyll than old greens, will have a brighter, greener color when cooked. Properly cooked greens will have a brighter color than if overcooked. The duller, olive-green hue of the overcooked vegetable is caused by the chemical changes that occur in the natural color, caused by the pigment chlorophyll. The way air and liquids are physically distributed throughout a product affects its color and appearance.
- *Physical:* For example, raw spinach and other greens are made of plant cells that contain a large amount of liquid and are surrounded by air pockets. When greens are cooked, air escapes from the pockets, the plant cells burst, and the pockets fill with liquid. Because light reflects off liquids differently than it does off air, the cooked greens—and other cooked vegetables—appear translucent rather than opaque. Ideally, serve the greens during the time *after* air leaves the pockets but *before* they are filled with liquid. It is at this point that they are brightest and most attractive.
- *Lighting:* Different types of lighting will affect the perception of color. For example, greens viewed under

a regular incandescent bulb will appear more yellow than the same greens viewed under fluorescent lighting. Chefs should be aware that what they see in the kitchen may not be what the customer sees under restaurant lighting.

Flavor

Taste, or flavor, is a combination of three sensory experiences: basic tastes, odors or aromas, and feeling, sometimes referred to as pain or irritation. Our perception of these three sensory experiences are chemical in nature. Salt, for instance, changes the chemistry of certain taste receptor cells. This change in chemistry triggers a signal to the brain that travels through nerve fibers. The brain translates this signal into the perception of saltiness.

Basic Tastes

Perception of the basic tastes is relatively simple because there are only four: sweet, salty, sour, and bitter. The Japanese include umami as a fifth basic taste, but most Americans consider it a feeling factor. *Umami* is the taste of MSG, a flavor enhancer used in many Asian dishes, and is most often translated into English as *savoriness* or *tastiness.* Umami is a taste that can occur naturally in foods, such as mushrooms, or it may be added by using MSG, for instance.

Taste cells, the receptors of the basic tastes, are hidden in skinfolds on the tongue as opposed to being located on the surface. As a result, saliva plays an important role in taste perception. Without saliva, which is mostly water, the taste molecules—the acids, sweeteners, salts, and bitter components—could not reach the taste cells.

Taste buds are located throughout the mouth and over the entire tongue, but the perception of sweetness is strongest on the tip of the tongue, saltiness and sourness on the sides, and bitterness toward the back (Mader, p.325).

Odor or Aroma

The perception of aroma is much more sensitive, complex, and not as well understood as the perception of the basic tastes. Humans can identify only four basic tastes, but they can identify hundreds, even thousands, of distinctly different aromas. Many distinct aromas themselves are complex. For example, there is no one single coffee molecule. Instead, coffee aroma consists of hundreds of separate chemicals that evaporate and together bombard the olfactory cells at the top of the nasal cavity. These molecules are perceived either directly from the food to the nose or by evaporation in the back of the throat. The brain processes all this information simultaneously and concludes that the smell is of coffee.

When humans have colds, the nasal passages become blocked, thereby preventing the odor chemicals from reaching the top of the nasal cavity where the olfactory receptor cells are located. As a result, it seems that we cannot "taste" when we have colds. Strictly speaking, we can still taste the basic tastes, but we cannot smell any odors. Without the perception of smell, it is impossible to differentiate between similar flavors, such as a peach versus an apricot or beef versus pork.

Interestingly, the part of the brain that receives and processes information about aromas is wired to the same part responsible for memory and emotions (Freedman, p.73). As a result, smells of certain foods may trigger memories of years past or even strong emotional feelings. Not surprisingly, a great merchandising technique for selling barbecued chicken or cinnamon buns is the smell of the product wafting through the air. The aromas naturally draw customers to buy the familiar foods.

Communicating information about food and beverage aromas requires common terminology. Like the wine industry, food manufacturers have attempted to standardize terminology to simplify understanding. Table 9–2, lists a

Table 9–2 Off-Flavors Found in Coffee

Description of Off-Flavor	Cause
Soapy, wet wool, wet dog	Chemical changes to oils in coffee
Acrid, kerosene	Chemical changes to acids in the coffee
Green, hay, wet paper	Loss of organic material
Burnt, charred, cereal-like	Improper roasting
Yeasty, mildewy	Absorbed moldy or musty odor

few representative off-flavors identified in coffee by the Specialty Coffee Association of America. In the table, the off-flavors are categorized by what is likely to cause them.

Feeling Factors

This third chemical sensory system is a series of raw nerve endings running just below the skin throughout the mouth and nose. It is separate and distinct from taste and aroma, and it is sometimes called the *common chemical sense,* or the trigeminal nerve system. Chemicals that stimulate these raw nerve endings are more likely to be oil soluble than water soluble, and persons who have lost their sense of taste and smell often can still detect the presence of these feeling factors (Mela and Mattes, p.6). For example, the cooling of menthol in peppermint, the heat or burn of capsaicin in hot peppers, the effervescence of carbon dioxide in carbonated beverages, the pungency of piperine in black pepper, and the astringency of tannins in cranberry juice are all feeling factors perceived through this third chemical sensory system.

Texture

Texture, like taste or flavor, represents many characteristics evaluated simultaneously. It is useful to define each textural characteristic individually and specifically, although doing this well takes practice. For example, cooked, buttered rice can be described as rough or smooth, sticky or slick, hard or soft, moist or dry, chewy or crumbly, mouth coating or not, and more. Sometimes, one textural characteristic predominates, but, as professionals, it is important to practice analyzing food as completely as possible.

To systematically evaluate texture, consider the following:

1. How does the food feel against the soft tissue in the mouth. For example, is it rough or smooth?
2. How does the food react to a force such as squeezing, pulling, biting, or chewing? Does it resist the force? In other words, is it hard, firm, or thick? Does it bounce back like gelatin? Is it rubbery or springy?

Does it shatter into many pieces? Is it crumbly? Understand that how food reacts to the squeezing of your hand is not necessarily the same as how it reacts to biting. For this reason, evaluate only finger foods with your hand.

3. How does the food react to the warmth of the mouth? For example, gelatins, fats, ice cream, and chocolates are all foods that respond to body heat. The smooth textural characteristics depend in part on how quickly and completely they melt.

4. How much remains coating the mouth and throat after swallowing? For example, shortenings, especially those with high melting points, tend to leave a waxy coating in the mouth, while oils tend to leave a slick, greasy coating.

5. How does the food sound when chewed? Think about it. Potato chips are not actually crispy and tortilla chips are not crunchy unless you can *hear* the crisp or crunch. Scientists believe that the difference between crispiness and crunchiness depends on how long and how high pitched the sound is during chewing. Specifically, crunchy products sound louder longer; crispy products sound higher pitched for a shorter period of time (Stone, p.89).

The Importance of Time in Flavor and Texture Perception

Our perceptions of flavor and texture are time-dependent. That is, what we taste and feel when food is first placed in our mouths is different from what we taste and feel as we swallow. The following illustration should help explain the importance of this point.

Certain flavors, such as sweetness, are perceived right away. Others, such as the pungency of black pepper and ginger, are perceived somewhat later and may linger from one bite to the next. The most full-bodied, satisfying flavors combine a mixture of ingredients that are perceived at different stages. If a food seems to have a weak flavor, it is probably missing a strong initial taste or aroma because flavor strength is typically evaluated immediately after placing it into the mouth. If a food appears "thin" in flavor or lacking body or substance, it is probably missing ingredi-

ents perceived later in the tasting process. If a product has flavor that "peaks and valleys," the food will appear disjointed or unbalanced.

Sensory Evaluation of Food

What is sensory evaluation? Sensory evaluation, or sensory analysis, is the systematic tasting of food by typical consumers and/or by trained and experienced food professionals. Many food companies and restaurant chains conduct consumer taste tests to determine what their customers like and dislike. Because it is the customer that will ultimately eat and pay for the food, these companies strive to design the taste to the customers' likings.

When trained food professionals evaluate food products, it is not to express their likes and dislikes. Rather, it is to objectively describe the sensory characteristics. Descriptive panels of about 8 to 12 experts train together for many hours, tasting a wide array of food products and discussing their characteristics until they are able to agree on terminology and adequately describe products in similar ways. The process is similar to a wine tasting and, as with wine tasting, the best environment for evaluating food is well-lit, clean, well-ventilated, and quiet. To increase the objectivity of the evaluations, food products should be tasted *blind;* meaning the samples should be coded so the tasters are not biased by prior knowledge of the product.

Much practice is needed to be able to successfully recognize and identify the many interrelated sensory characteristics of food. While culinary skills involve a process of synthesizing, or putting flavors together, the process of sensory evaluation is one of analysis, or taking things apart.

Product Factors Affecting Flavor Perception

What makes one version of a food product taste or smell different from another? For example, why might one vinaigrette taste more sour than another, *when they both contain the same amount of acid?* Several factors influence the characteristics of a food product:

- *Type of ingredient:* The vinaigrettes may contain the same amount of acid, but if they contain different *types* of acid, they will not be perceived as equally sour. For example, if one contains primarily acetic acid (vinegar) and the other citric acid (from lemons), the vinaigrette made from vinegar will seem more acidic.
- *Product temperature:* In general, products have a stronger taste and aroma when they are warmed, so a chilled vinaigrette will taste less sour than one at room temperature. There are two exceptions: First, flavor strength diminishes above a certain temperature. This may be because the taste and aroma molecules are moving around too quickly to be "captured" by our taste and olfactory receptor cells. Second, saltiness may be perceived differently at varying temperatures; salt seems stronger at lower temperatures than at higher temperatures (Bennion, p.10). Therefore, it is important to season products at their appropriate serving temperatures.
- *Product thickness or consistency:* Flavor molecules take longer to dissolve or evaporate in saliva when food products are a thicker consistency. This translates into less flavor for thicker products, at least initially. Thick soups, sauces, and vinaigrette are all examples of thick foods that may cause this phenomenon.
- *Presence of other taste, aroma, and feeling factors:* Combining tastes, aromas, or feeling elements in foods can suppress the ability to perceive flavor. For example, add a little sugar to a vinaigrette and it will taste less sour, even if you have added so little that it does not quite taste sweet. This trick works for other basic tastes, feeling factors, and aromas. An acid may be added to make food taste less sweet, sugar to make it taste less bitter, and salt to make it taste less sour. It is unknown whether this suppression of taste perception occurs at the site of the taste cells, where the messages are received and

transmitted to the brain, or in the brain, where the messages are decoded (O'Mahony, p.11). The following pairings of food are probably linked to our intuitive sense of modulating one taste with other basic tastes: pairing salty peanuts or pretzels with beer, possibly to reduce the bitterness of the beer, salting of fresh fruits to reduce their sourness, or pairing sweet desserts with bitter coffee, to reduce the overwhelming sweetness of the dessert.

- *Flavor enhancers:* Flavor enhancers modify or harmonize flavor *without necessarily adding a flavor of their own.* How they work is largely unknown, but it is likely that they interact with certain taste chemicals and receptors, making it easier for the two to bind and produce a taste perception. For example, a vinaigrette that contains a flavor enhancer such as MSG should taste smoother, less sharply acidic than one that doesn't. Free glutamate, the part of MSG that acts as the flavor enhancer, is a natural amino acid present in many foods (see Table 9–3). Free glutamate is particularly high in aged, fermented, and dried foods. Adding aged cheeses, fermented soy sauce, or dried mushrooms and fish to foods for flavor means complementing foods with natural flavor enhancers.
- *Amount of oil and water:* Taste, odor, and common chemicals are completely soluble in water, in oil, or partially in each. A taste chemical that dissolves in oil will not fully dissolve in saliva and, as a result, little will reach the taste buds. To the extent that an *odor* chemical dissolves in water *or* oil, it will not evaporate to the olfactory cells where it can be smelled. The amount of oil and water in foods, in this case, the amount of oil in a vinaigrette, will affect the perception

Table 9–3 Free Glutamate Content of Foods

Product	Amount of Free Glutamate (mg/100 g)
Fresh mushrooms	180
Fresh tomato juice	260
Parmesan cheese	1,200
Roquefort cheese	1,280

Source: Glutamate Association.

of sourness; the more oil, the less sour the vinaigrette. This will be true even if the amount of vinegar added to each is the same.

Factors Affecting the Ability to Taste

When it comes to eating, each individual has likes and dislikes. There are many reasons for this. One is simply that each of us *perceives* characteristics in food differently. One person may like food that is bitter not so much because that person likes bitterness, but because that person does not taste much bitterness. Another reason someone may like bitter foods is because that person has become accustomed to the taste. Bitter foods are an acquired taste.

Everyone has taste buds that detect bitterness in foods, so why is it that everyone does not taste it to the same degree? Why are spicy foods not at all hot to some and unbearable to others? The following factors help explain differences in the perception of basic tastes, odors, and feeling factors.

- *Genetics:* People vary in their abilities to taste and smell partly due to the varying number of receptors (taste buds, olfactory cells, and free nerve endings) that run throughout the mouth and nose. For example, some people have as few as 500 taste buds while others have as many as 10,000 (Pennisi, p.110). The number of receptors each person has may be genetically programmed or may have to do with age and health. According to Linda Bartoshuk, a researcher at Yale University, 20 percent of the population, those she labels "supertasters," have an unusually high number of taste buds and a highly sensitive ability to detect basic tastes and feeling factors, including the burn of hot peppers. Another 20 percent, the "nontasters," have few taste buds and a proportionally dull sense of taste. The rest, about 60 percent of the population, fall in between (Levenson, p.14).

  Chefs would benefit from knowing whether they are supertasters or nontasters. Supertasters tend to underseason foods for the rest of the population; nontasters tend to overseason. According to Bartoshuk (IFIC, p.4), one simple way to test whether you are a supertaster or nontaster is as follows: Taste salt substitute (potassium chloride) and saccharin. If both seem bitter, you are probably a supertaster. If neither seems bitter, you are probably a nontaster.

- *Gender:* About two-thirds of supertasters are female (IFIC, p.4), suggesting a strong link between gender and the ability to taste. Recall that supertasters have an increased sensitivity to tastes and feeling factors because they have a greater number of receptors throughout the mouth.

- *Smoking and alcohol:* Nonsmokers are more sensitive to taste and smell than are smokers (Hirsch, p.96). Many ex-smokers report that their ability to taste and smell greatly increased shortly after they stopped smoking. Preliminary studies suggest a genetic link between alcoholism and taste perception (IFIC, p.5). The studies indicate that alcoholics and children of alcoholics may be more likely to be nontasters than the general population.

- *Emotional condition:* Conditions of stress, fatigue, or social deprivation (battlefield, dormlife) may reduce the perception of food flavor. This may possibly be related to the reduced output of saliva that occurs during these conditions (Hanni, p.3).

- *Experience:* Experience comes from exposure to a wide variety of foods and by conscious attention to the details of those foods. Experienced tasters do not necessarily have better taste buds or noses. Instead, they have simply learned to notice small details and to understand and describe these details. Like any skill, it requires practice. Yet, solid experience overrides many of the other factors that affect peoples' abilities to taste and smell.

- *Focus:* Food is a complex mixture of sensory characteristics, so it is likely that people focusing on different characteristics of the food will obtain different overall perceptions (O'Mahony, pp.11–12). For example, if the color of food is the focus, then odor, taste, and texture information may be missed. The perceptions made may not be incorrect, but they are also incomplete. Experienced tasters may simply be those who have the learned ability to focus and interpret more messages simultaneously, therefore gaining a more complete analysis of the food product.

- *Age:* Taste buds are most numerous in children under age 6 (Lewis, p.32). The number of taste buds and olfactory cells decreases with age. Therefore, a progressive loss in the perception of the basic tastes and smells occurs. These losses become measurable, although not necessarily a problem, at approximately 60 years of age (Schiffman, p.1). Compared with health, age is a minor factor in explaining taste and smell deficiencies. Still, it is important for chefs to be aware that, at present, the only solution to age-related losses is to increase the flavor intensity of foods served to the elderly. This is especially true for sweetness, saltiness, and odor.

- *Disease, malnutrition, and medical treatments:* More than 2 million Americans suffer from a significant loss of their sense of smell (Freedman, p.76). Many of these losses are caused by disease, malnutrition, and medical treatments. Common causes include head trauma, multiple sclerosis, hypertension, vitamin (niacin and riboflavin) and mineral (zinc) deficiencies, allergies, viral infections, chemotherapy, radiation therapy, and the use of certain prescription drugs (Freedman, p.76; Schiffman, p.1).

  People with Alzheimer's disease have a significantly reduced ability to detect odors, even though their ability to detect basic tastes remains undiminished. As the disease progresses, the sense of smell continues to decline. The likely cause of this impairment is neurological damage to the brain rather than damage to the olfactory cells. Measurement of this loss may be useful in the future as a means of monitoring progression of the disease (Anonymous, p.300).

- *Adaptation:* The sensory system is very efficient. The brain receives only information from the senses of *new change* taking place; not information about *no change* taking place. Imagine what would happen if this were not the case. You put your clothes on in the morning, and your touch receptors sense the feel of the cloth against your skin. Throughout every minute of the day, you are conscious of the presence of your clothes against your skin. This would be distracting and mentally tiring, so the sensory system minimizes the processing of unnecessary information through *adaptation.* It is easy to see how important adaptation is to the brain, as the brain already has a very large and constant flow of information to process (O'Mahony, pp. 13–14).

In terms of food, however, the first bite of a dish is perceived to its fullest, only to have subsequent bites not so easily tasted or smelled. As soon as we adapt to a meal, it becomes less interesting. To minimize adaptation, present contrasting flavors, textures, and colors to continually stimulate the senses. Moving or rolling food and drink around the mouth and cleansing the palate with water or plain crackers are other ways to maintain a high level of taste and odor awareness.

Plate Composition

The objective behind plate composition is to maintain a high level of visual, textural, and flavor interest throughout a meal. This is done by presenting contrasts within each of the following design components. In doing so, the guest's pleasure will be increased by minimizing sensory adaptation to each of the components. The first impression a guest gets of the food is through its presentation. Such an impression can be so strong that it may influence whether the food is liked or disliked, even before a bite is eaten. Plate composition should be carefully planned even before the food is cooked to ensure success. As with sensory development, increasing skills of plate presentation require much practice. Like building a library by slowly acquiring volumes of books, developing strong plate-presentation skills requires creating a repertoire of skills and ideas from which to work.

Color and Appearance

The colors in food presented on a plate should be vibrant and contrasting. Rather than using only three different shades of green for instance, other colors should be chosen to create diversity on the plate. The colors used in a presentation should not only be planned conceptually and must be followed through in the cooking process to ensure that the plan comes to fruition.

Color can also be attained by carefully choosing the plate on which the food will be served. The china may also add color and design, but should not have such a striking appearance as to detract from the food presentation.

The overall food presentation should be neat, revealing that care was taken in the planning and assembly of the plate. Avoid placing food on the rim of the plate, even when garnishing. The rim of the plate should be a neutral zone, acting both as a frame for the artful presentation of the food and an area for the service staff to pick up the plate. For example, if a scattering of finely chopped herbs is desired to add color around the presentation, rather than sprinkling the herbs on the rim where they will likely be disturbed while the plate is carried to the guest, plan the presentation so that there is a narrow margin of clean china between the inner rim of the plate and the food.

The appearance of the food should create excitement in the guest, developing a high level of perceived value. Avoid overcrowding the plate with food, and at the same time, make sure there is just enough food to satisfy the guest, depending on what course has been ordered. This can be an especially difficult skill to develop, and attaining knowledge of how many courses the average guest orders in a dining period is important. Remember that the goal is to satisfy the guest's hunger with creative preparations while charging a reasonable price for the food.

Height

Often one of the most difficult elements to achieve in plate composition is ensuring that varying heights of food occur on a plate. Achieving this requires careful planning. Current industry trends suggest the need for height variations, although the concept is often taken to the extreme. As an example, a poorly planned presentation of a grilled 8-ounce sirloin steak, mashed potatoes, and buttered corn on the cob might consist of simply placing each food product on the plate with the steak at the 6 o'clock position; the potatoes, dropped on the plate with a large spoon, at 10

o'clock; and the ear of corn stuck in the 2 o'clock position or wherever there is room.

A more effective presentation that incorporates height may be organized differently. The mashed potatoes are neatly piped onto the plate in the 10 o'clock position in a circular pinnacle using a piping bag fitted with a star tip. The grilled steak is then placed in approximately the 6 o'clock position, with the left end of the meat leaning slightly on the front side of the mashed potatoes for height. The cob of corn is then cut on a mild diagonal in half, seasoned and buttered, and stood on each cut end at the 12 and 1 o'clock positions. The new presentation has both height and color, but if another contrast is desired, a dollop of red-onion chutney may be added to the presentation to accompany the meat. If added texture is needed, a bit of potato, cut into a paille, could be fried and placed on top of the mashed.

Shape

Vary the shape of foods in every presentation. For example, serving meatloaf in the form of a round patty with sautéed peas and parisienne potatoes would create a dull presentation because all of the shapes are round. Serving the meatloaf with snow peas and diced, roasted potatoes instead would create a better variation of shape.

Texture

Include a variety of textures in each plate composition by carefully choosing foods that may have soft, hard, chewy, crunchy, creamy, or meaty textures. Food textures often play as important a role in likes and dislikes of foods as taste does. When the plate of food is first presented, the guest looks at the food and unconsciously compares the different textures in each element based on knowledge provided by previous dining experiences. This informal audit influences whether the guest will enjoy the food, even before taking a bite.

Flavor

Each element of food in a plate presentation should contribute a variety of basic tastes, seasonings, and aromas that lend to the overall flavor of the food. Flavors and seasonings used should be varied and should complement each other. In planning, the flavors used should be considered not only in the raw ingredients but also in other preparations and cooking methods used.

Temperature

Foods should be served at the appropriate temperature. For example, hot foods, such as soup, should be served scorching while cold foods, such as fresh vegetable salads, should be ice cold. Such a practice not only will ensure a more satisfied guest but will maintain HACCP requirements. (See Chapter 3 for more information on HACCP.)

Foods should be served on plates or in bowls having a similar temperature; that is, hot food should be served on hot plates, while cold food should be served on chilled plates. The temperature of foods may change significantly by heat or cold lost through the air during the process of service. Maintaining the dishware at the appropriate temperature can help maintain the integrity of the food until it reaches the guest.

Garnishing

A garnish is an optional, decorative, edible accompaniment that is placed on food to improve its visual appeal. It should be the same temperature as the food on which it is served. Hot foods should be served with hot garnishes, and cold foods should be decorated with cold garnishes. If carefully planned, not all food presentations should require a garnish. Creating garnishes can be costly from the standpoint of raw ingredients and the labor needed to prepare them.

Garnishes should only be used *after* careful thought has been put into the plate presentation. If the elements of color and appearance, height, shape, texture, flavor, and temperature have all been achieved in the presentation and it is still lacking visual appeal, then those elements should be re-examined and organized before any garnishing takes place. Garnishing should not be used to fix a poorly planned presentation, but rather should be the crowning touch on a magnificent plate of food.

The Special Flavor Challenges of Fat-Free Foods

Fats and oils serve as solvents to many important tastes, odors, and common chemicals. Such chemicals release slowly from fats and oils into saliva or to the nose. This provides full-fat foods with a sustained and balanced flavor profile and a pleasant aftertaste (Hatchwell, p.99).

With fat-free foods, however, flavor chemicals move into the saliva and evaporate to the olfactory cells in a fast rush (Stauffer, p.28), if they have not already been lost to evaporation during cooking or baking. Such characteristics of fat-free foods can create several problems:

- Fat-free foods often are harshly overflavored, yet may lack "lasting power," depth of flavor, or a pleasant aftertaste. If this occurs, try a wider variety of spices and seasonings and use them at lower levels.
- When cooked or baked, fat-free foods lose flavors to evaporation and may be bland and underflavored (Stauffer, p.26). If possible, add spices and seasonings later in the cooking process when reducing the amount of fat.
- Fat-free foods often exhibit flavor peaks and valleys, discussed earlier as a major cause of disjointed or unbalanced flavors. If this occurs, other ingredients may help smooth out this imbalance. Flavor enhancers and protein foods (eggs and milk) can sometimes help smooth out flavor profiles in fat-free foods (Hatchwell, pp.99–100).
- Off-flavors are more noticeable in fat-free foods, probably because they evaporate to the olfactory cells more easily than when fat is present (Hatchwell, p.98). To prevent the problems presented here, use only the highest-quality ingredients in fat-free foods.

The more fat removed from food, the more difficult the flavor challenge. For this reason, it may make more sense to *reduce* rather than to eliminate fat altogether in many foods. A realistic goal is a 25 percent fat reduction, which would require minimal flavor adjustments in most foods.

10

Culinary Skills, Cooking Techniques, and Preparation

Culinary Skills, Cooking Techniques, and Preparation

Great chefs have their own unique, creative styles of cooking, yet they all have a common knowledge and mastery of culinary skills, cooking techniques, and preparation techniques. Obtaining an understanding of the use of knives, learning proper techniques, and safety in handling knives is essential to becoming a chef.

Knife Skills

The use of knives is one of the most important skills a chef needs to refine over time. Learning proper techniques is essential to increasing production speed and quality. Proper maintenance of and safety in handling a knife is crucial.

Safety

Knives can be dangerous tools and should be handled very carefully. Following are safety guidelines to consider when using knives:

- Hold the point of the knife down when walking.
- Do not try to catch a falling knife.
- Never leave a knife in the pot sink.
- Always use a knife on a cutting board.
- Never check the sharpness of a knife on the arm or fingers.
- Wipe the blade carefully, from the back/dull side
- Always wash, sanitize, and wipe knives before storing them in the knife kit.
- Always use sharp knives.
- Do not use knives to open cans.
- Always use the proper knife for the task.
- When passing a knife to another person, carefully grasp the blade from the back/dull side, extending the handle outwards.

Sharpening Stone

To keep a fine edge on knives, a sharpening stone is essential. There are a number of different sizes and kinds of sharpening stones in use. Today, the most common material used to make sharpening stones is carborundum.

The standard size of a sharpening stone is 8 inches by 2 inches by 13/16 of an inch. A large sharpening stone has a greater surface, making it easier to work with. A small stone is more difficult to work with, less expensive, and easier to store.

A tri-stone (see Figure 10–1) is composed of three separate stones, each with a different surface grit: coarse, medium, and fine. The size of this tri-stone can vary, but all have a turntable design with a locking mechanism that allows for easy use. Mineral oil should be the only oil used to lubricate the stones. There is an oil reserve at the bottom in which the two stones not in use will rest. Each stone can be removed and replaced as it becomes worn out. For safety, always place a damp cloth or rubber mesh under the stone housing before beginning to sharpen a knife to prevent the stone from moving.

Rules for Sharpening a Knife

- If the knife is dull, start with the coarse stone, then go to the medium stone, then to the fine stone.
- Hold the knife at a 20- to 25-degree angle to the stone.

Figure 10–1 Tri-stone sharpening stone

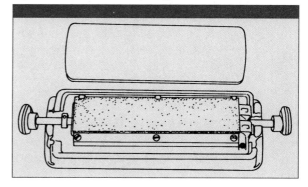

- Sharpen in a cross-direction, using a partial circular motion.
- Make the strokes on each side of the blade equal stress and number.
- Use the fine-textured stone primarily for finishing purposes.
- Apply the newly sharpened knife to a steel to remove burrs resulting from the sharpening process.

Types of Knives

Knife Alloys

Carbon Steel

Carbon steel is a soft alloy, with an easy-to-maintain edge, but it often rusts and stains. Foods high in acid can acquire a metallic taste from carbon steel because of the soft composition of the alloy.

High Carbon Steel

This is the most expensive of all knife alloys. It does not rust, stain, or transfer a metallic taste to foods as do carbon steel knives. These knives can be honed to a sharp edge. They maintain their edge, but not as well as carbon steel knives. This alloy has a good appearance and shine.

Stainless Steel

Stainless steel is a hard, strong metal. Properly maintained, a stainless-steel knife will not rust, stain, or transfer a metallic taste to foods. However, it is difficult to sharpen and must be ground at regular intervals.

Super Stainless Steel

Super stainless steel is so hard it cannot be sharpened. Super stainless steel knives are sold as domestic knives with the claim that they never need sharpening and will

last a lifetime. The blade will dull with use. The critical difference between stainless steel and super stainless steel knives is the higher carbon content of the super stainless. Stainless steel has more chromium and nickel. See Figure 10–2 for the parts of a knife and Figure 10–3 for illustrations of various knives.

Figure 10–2 Parts of a knife

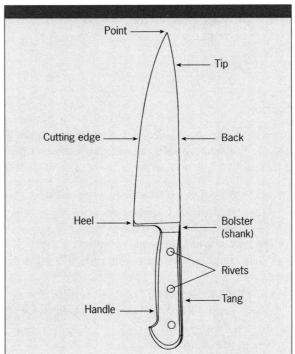

Steel

A steel's purpose is to maintain the straight edge on a knife, not to sharpen it. The magnetized tip of the steel captures tiny particles of steel from the edge of the blade in the process of straightening the edge. Figure 10–4 shows the parts of a steel. Figure 10–5 illustrates how to use a steel.

Figure 10–3 Knives

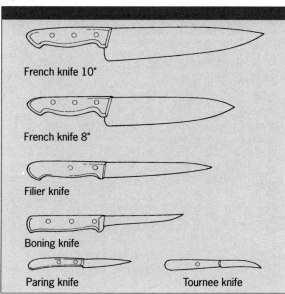

French knife 10"

French knife 8"

Filier knife

Boning knife

Paring knife

Tournee knife

Figure 10–4 Parts of a steel

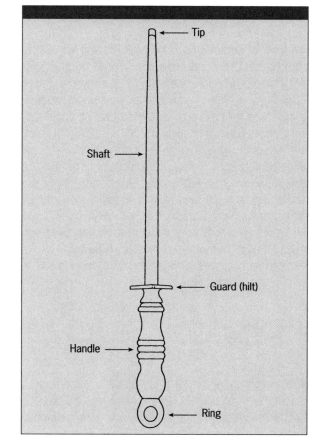

Tip

Shaft

Guard (hilt)

Handle

Ring

1. Hold the steel in the nondominant hand by the handle beneath the guard collar. The arm should be outstretched in front at a 60-degree angle. The steel should be held stationary.
2. Hold the knife in the dominant hand and angle the blade at approximately 20 degrees on the tip of the steel.
3. Maintaining the 20-degree angle on the knife, pull the knife, in contact with the steel, from the tip of the steel to the guard collar. The heel of the knife should be in contact at the tip of the steel, while the knife should be slowly pulled outward as it moves down the steel so the tip of the knife now touches the steel as it reaches the bottom by the guard collar.
4. Repeat the process on the other side of the knife before alternating sides of the knife. Continue process until the edge is straightened.

Figure 10–5 How to use a steel

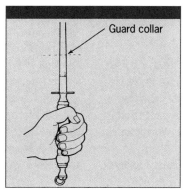

Guard collar

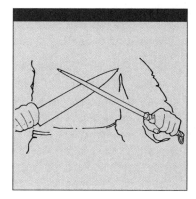

Various Cuts

A variety of cuts are used for potatoes and vegetables (see Figure 10-6), and there are different purposes for each cut. For example, a mirepoix is a rough cut or dice used if the vegetables will not be included in the final food product and will be used only for flavor during cooking or if the vegetables will be pureed. The size of the cut is significant, not only because the cooking time may be affected but also because it is important to produce an overall balance and visual appeal. However, there are also some cutting techniques that are traditionally used for particular food products. For example, the *frite* is used for French fried potatoes, and care should be taken with regard to the uniformity of the cut. Experience in the proper use of knives will help the chef develop skill in preparing and using each cut.

Cooking

What is cooking? A master chef's definition of cooking is: a matrix of knife skills, cooking techniques, and preparation techniques. Cooking is producing safe, palatable, tasteful, digestible food products by using heat energy in a most creative way.

Cooking Techniques

Cooking techniques can be categorized by the medium used. They are classified as moist, dry, or a combination of both (see Table 10–1).

- *Moist technique:* The moist technique uses liquid other than oil to transfer heat. A good example is boiling. In the case of sweating, where no additional water or liquid are added, the natural moisture that exudes from the food product during the cooking process becomes the cooking medium.
- *Dry technique:* The dry technique uses metal, radiation of air or hot gases, oil, or fat to transfer heat. No

Table 10–1 Cooking Methods and Medium

Technique		Medium
English	**French**	
To boil	Bouillir	Moist
To simmer	Mijoter	Moist
To poach	Pocher	Moist
To steam	Cuisson a la vapeur	Moist
To bake	Cuire au four	Dry
To roast	Rôtir	Dry
To sauté	Sauter	Dry
To deep fry	Frire	Dry
To grill	Griller	Dry
To broil	Griller	Dry
To braise	Braiser	Combination
To stew	Étuver	Combination

moisture is used in the cooking process, and any moisture exuding from the food product is allowed to evaporate. A good example of a dry technique is baking.
- *Combination technique:* Combination cooking uses both the moist and dry techniques. Two stages of cooking occur, beginning with one technique and finishing with another. A good example of this technique is braising.

Moist Technique

To Boil / Bouillir, 212° F

To boil is to bring a liquid (water, stock, or court bouillon) to the boiling point (212° F at sea level) and maintain the temperature. As soon as the liquid is boiling, food products may be added and cooked (see Figure 10–7 on page 165). Because of the characteristic rapid convection movement, relatively few ingredients are actually boiled. For example, although the rapid convection movement is crucial in keeping pasta from sticking as it cooks, such movement may be too violent to cook a piece of fish without breaking it.

Boiling is often used to *blanch,* or partially cook, raw ingredients. Blanching is a two-step process:

(text continues on page 165)

Figure 10–6 Approximate measurements and cuts and shapes of potatoes and vegetables

Potatoes			
Frite	French fry	½ × ½ × 3 inches	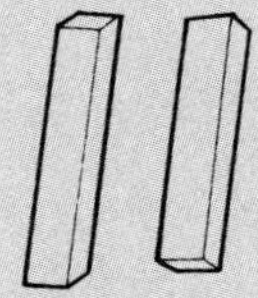
Pont-Neuf	Steak fry	Larger than frite	
Mignonettes	Stick	⅜ × ⅜ × 2 inches	
Batonnet	Small stick	¼ × ¼ × 3 inches	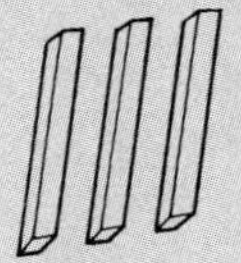
Allumette	Matchstick	⅛ × ⅛ × 3 inches	
Paille	Straw	Finely shredded	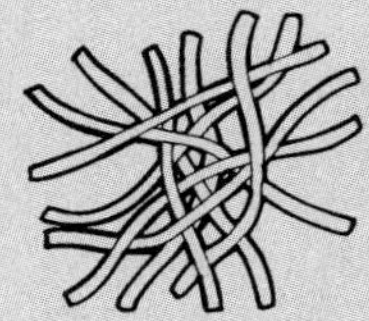
Carre	Square	¾ x ¾ x ¾ inch	
Parmentier	Dice	½ × ½ × ½ inch	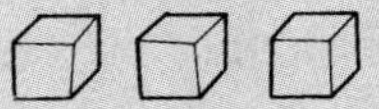
Chips	Chip	⅛ inch thick; slice	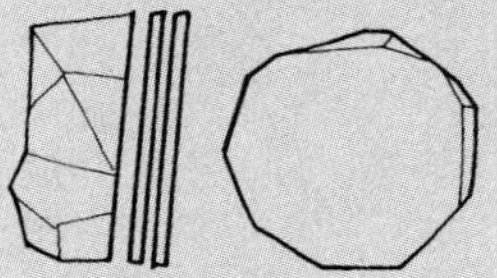
Gaufrettes	Waffle	⅛ inch thick; perforated	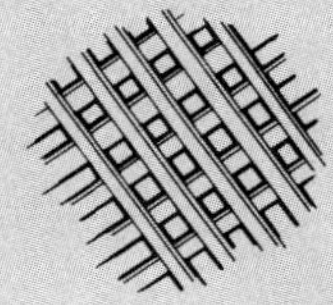

(continued)

Potatoes (continued)

Parisienne	Paris style	Sphere shape; 1 inch average	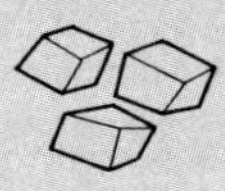
Noisette	Hazelnut	Sphere shape; ½ to ¾ inch average	
Tourne Olivette	Olivelike	7-sided; 1 to 2 inches	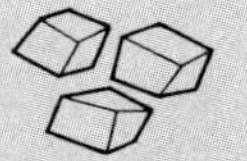
Tourne Château	Castlellike	7-sided; 2 to 2½ inches	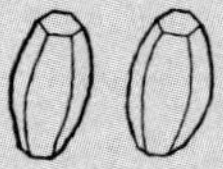
Fondante	Castlellike	Jumbo tourne; 3 inches or more	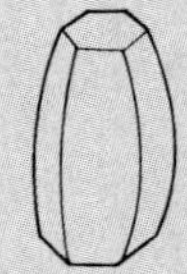

Vegetables

Brunoise	Fine dice	⅛ × ⅛ × ⅛ inch	
Macédoine	Small dice	¼ × ¼ × ¼ inch	
Julienne	Short, thin stick	⅛ × ⅛ × 1½ to 2 inches	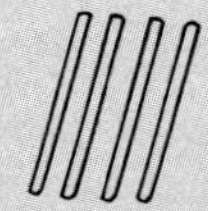
Vichy	Slice of carrot	⅛ inch thick; slice round or biased	
Mirepoix	Rough cut	½ inch average	
Paysanne	Rough cut	1 inch average	
Carre	Square	¾ × ¾ × ¾ inch	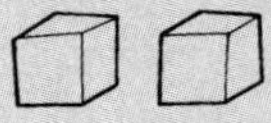
Parmentier	Dice	½ × ½ × ½ inch	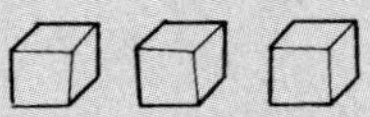
Chips	Round, thin slice	⅛ inch thick; slice	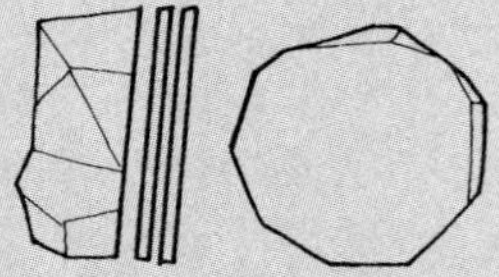
Gaufrettes	Waffle	⅛ inch thick; perforated	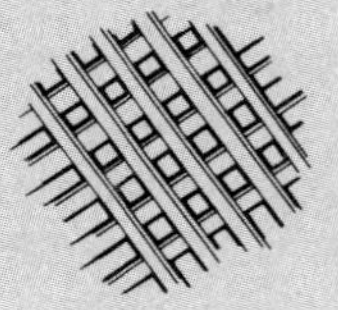

(continued)

Figure 10–6 Approximate measurements and cuts and shapes of potatoes and vegetables (continued)

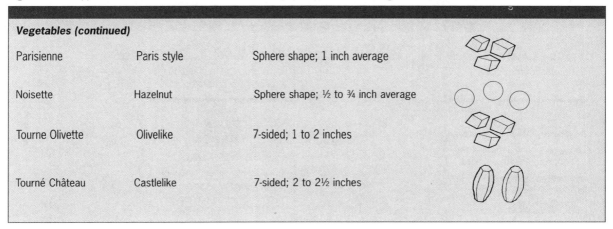

Vegetables (continued)		
Parisienne	Paris style	Sphere shape; 1 inch average
Noisette	Hazelnut	Sphere shape; ½ to ¾ inch average
Tourne Olivette	Olivelike	7-sided; 1 to 2 inches
Tourné Château	Castlelike	7-sided; 2 to 2½ inches

Figure 10–7 The boiling process (212° F at sea level)

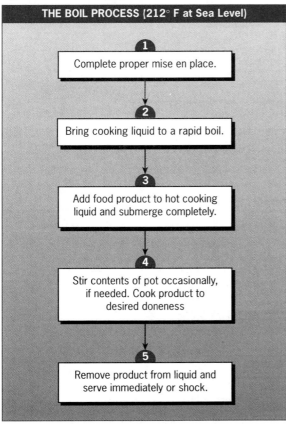

- Step 1: Blanching can be achieved by boiling, whereby the food product is completely submerged into a boiling liquid to lightly cook it. When *al dente,* or cooked but still firm to the bite, the blanched food is removed from the boiling liquid and shocked. *Rafraichir,* to refresh or shock, means to plunge a cooking product into an ice bath to completely and immediately stop the cooking process. This first stage of blanching can also be achieved by simmering, steaming, or frying. *Monder* is a term specifically devoted to the process of lightly blanching fresh tomatoes to facilitate skin removal. After blanching, the tomatoes are shocked before peeling and removing the seeds.
- Step Two: A blanched, or partially cooked, food product is often finished by a second stage of cooking, such as sautéing, before serving.

To Simmer / Mijoter, 185° to 200° F

To simmer is to cook food slowly and steadily in a liquid at 185° to 200° F (see Figure 10–8 on page 166). Foods being simmered should be fully submerged in the liquid. A gentle convection movement is characteristic and there are several advantages of simmering versus boiling:

- Less shrinkage of food product
- Less evaporation and better control over evaporation that does occur
- Less breakup of fragile-textured food such as fish

Figure 10–8 The simmering and poaching process (185° to 200° F)

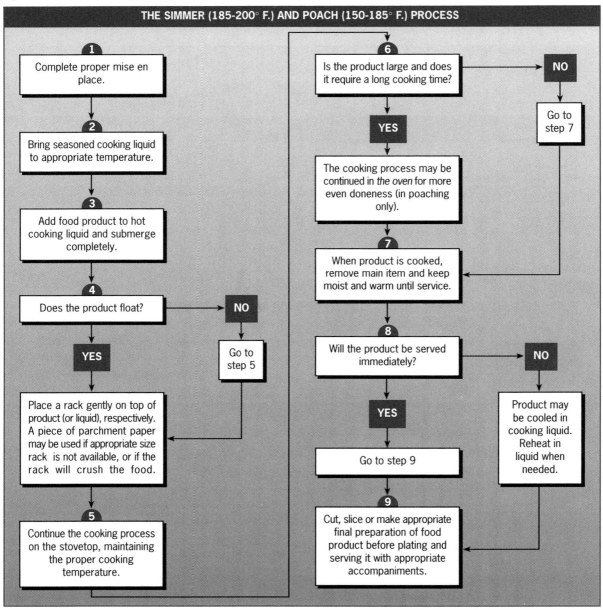

Simmering may also be used to simply reduce a liquid, such as a sauce. For foods with delicate textures and little connective tissue, simmering is a viable blanching method .

To Poach / Pocher, 150° to 185° F

Poaching is the technique of cooking foods in a gently simmering, flavorful liquid. Generally, tender or delicate foods such as fish or eggs are poached in just enough liquid to cover the product. The temperature should range from 150° to 185° F. In many recipes, the cooking liquid will often be used to produce a sauce that will be served with the food. Poaching may occur on the stove top or in the oven.

To Steam/ Cuisson a la Vapeur, Above 212° F at Sea Level

Steaming is the technique of cooking foods in a closed environment that is filled with steam (see Figures 10–9 and 10–10 on page 168). Steam is created as a result of water reaching the boiling point and vaporizing. If the vapor

Figure 10–9 The conventional steaming process, with pressure

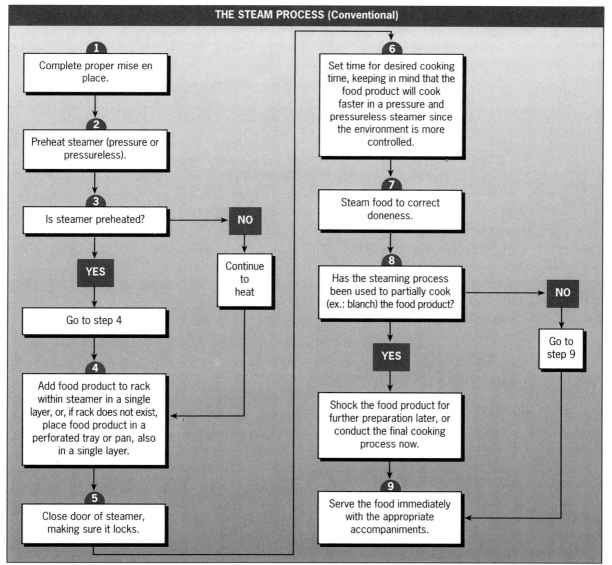

Figure 10–10 The traditional steaming process, pressureless

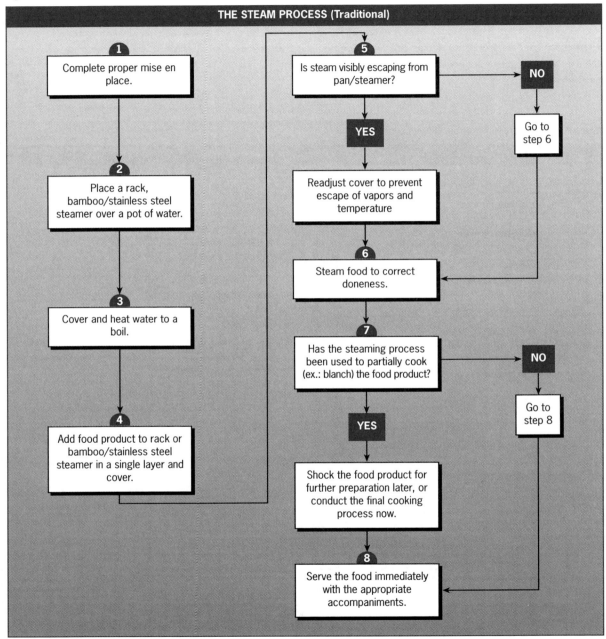

is enclosed in a cooking environment, the heat will rise, thus cooking the food. If pressure is added to the steaming process, the temperature will increase. For example, 5-psi pressure allows the steam temperature to rise to 227° F. At 15 psi, the steam temperature rises to 250° F. Today, there are two commercial types of steamers: the pressure steamer

Figure 10–11 The steaming process, en papillote

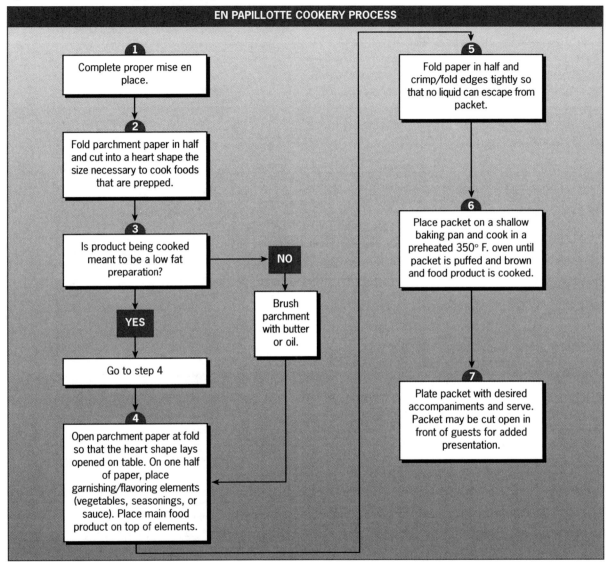

EN PAPILLOTTE COOKERY PROCESS

1 Complete proper mise en place.

2 Fold parchment paper in half and cut into a heart shape the size necessary to cook foods that are prepped.

3 Is product being cooked meant to be a low fat preparation?

NO → Brush parchment with butter or oil.

YES → Go to step 4

4 Open parchment paper at fold so that the heart shape lays opened on table. On one half of paper, place garnishing/flavoring elements (vegetables, seasonings, or sauce). Place main food product on top of elements.

5 Fold paper in half and crimp/fold edges tightly so that no liquid can escape from packet.

6 Place packet on a shallow baking pan and cook in a preheated 350° F. oven until packet is puffed and brown and food product is cooked.

7 Plate packet with desired accompaniments and serve. Packet may be cut open in front of guests for added presentation.

and the pressureless steamer. Steaming may be used as the cooking technique for the first stage of blanching. Pressureless steamers are common equipment in commercial kitchens.

The classic process of steaming involves placing 1 to 2 inches of water or flavorful liquid in the bottom of a pan or casserole and then placing a rack that just clears the surface of the liquid into the pan. (Pacific Rim cookery uses a bamboo steamer that sits on top of the pot or wok, instead of the rack.) The pan is then covered, and the contents are brought to a boil. As soon as steam is created, the food product can be placed on the rack and cooked, covered. The steaming of food, even in a pressureless steamer, is generally faster than other moist cooking methods.

En papillote cookery (see Figure 10–11) is an application of steaming. Cooking en papillote involves sealing a food product, often seafood, with aromatics and liquid in nonporous (parchment) paper. The packet is then baked in a hot oven. The moisture in the food product begins to turn to steam as the heat in the packet increases. Because the edges of the paper are sealed tightly, the steam is retained, thus cooking the food product. Aluminum foil may be used instead of paper, although attention should be given to possible chemical reactions between acidic ingredients and the aluminum.

Dry Technique

To Bake/ Cuire au Four

Baking is a cooking technique using dry convected heat in a closed environment, usually an oven (see Figure 10–12). No perceptible fat or liquid is used as the cooking medium, and any moisture that is released from the food in the form of steam is allowed to evaporate in the heat of the oven.

To Roast/ Rôtir (Convection/Radiation)

Roasting is a cooking technique using dry convected heat in a closed environment, usually an oven (see Figure 10–13). Meat, poultry, fish, or game are foods that are commonly roasted. At the beginning of the roasting process, the outside of the food product, primarily meat, is seared. *Searing* may be done in two ways:

- *Manual searing:* Heat a pan on high heat on the stove top. When hot, add a small amount of oil. Add the food product, such as a pork roast, to the pan and let brown on one side before turning. Continue to turn the pork roast until all surfaces are brown. When done searing, transfer meat to the oven and finish cooking by roasting.
- *Oven searing:* Heat the oven to 550° F, place pork roast on a pan, and place in the oven. Leave the roast in the oven, approximately 15 to 20 minutes, or until the outside has begun to turn a golden brown. This method, often preferred to manual searing because it requires fewer steps, sears the roast by means of the hot air. As soon as the searing process is done, the temperature should be reduced,

Figure 10–12 The baking process

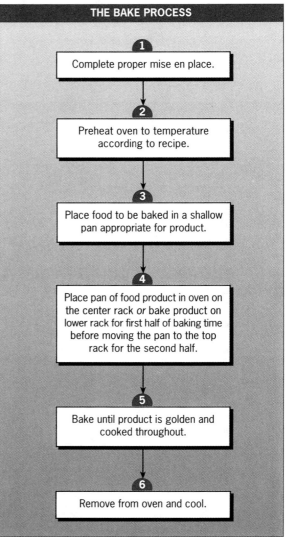

THE BAKE PROCESS

1 Complete proper mise en place.

2 Preheat oven to temperature according to recipe.

3 Place food to be baked in a shallow pan appropriate for product.

4 Place pan of food product in oven on the center rack *or* bake product on lower rack for first half of baking time before moving the pan to the top rack for the second half.

5 Bake until product is golden and cooked throughout.

6 Remove from oven and cool.

generally to 325° to 350° F, so the meat cooks more slowly and evenly.

When the food product has reached the desired doneness, usually determined by the internal temperature, it should be removed from the oven. If the food product is meat, carryover cooking should be taken into consideration. *Carryover cooking* is the continued cooking that

Figure 10–13 The roasting process

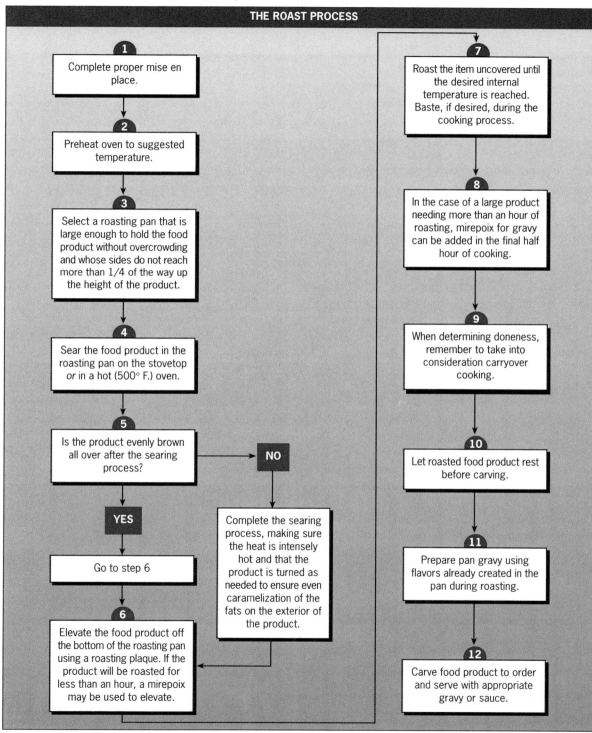

THE ROAST PROCESS

1 Complete proper mise en place.

2 Preheat oven to suggested temperature.

3 Select a roasting pan that is large enough to hold the food product without overcrowding and whose sides do not reach more than 1/4 of the way up the height of the product.

4 Sear the food product in the roasting pan on the stovetop *or* in a hot (500° F.) oven.

5 Is the product evenly brown all over after the searing process?

NO → Complete the searing process, making sure the heat is intensely hot and that the product is turned as needed to ensure even caramelization of the fats on the exterior of the product.

YES

Go to step 6

6 Elevate the food product off the bottom of the roasting pan using a roasting plaque. If the product will be roasted for less than an hour, a mirepoix may be used to elevate.

7 Roast the item uncovered until the desired internal temperature is reached. Baste, if desired, during the cooking process.

8 In the case of a large product needing more than an hour of roasting, mirepoix for gravy can be added in the final half hour of cooking.

9 When determining doneness, remember to take into consideration carryover cooking.

10 Let roasted food product rest before carving.

11 Prepare pan gravy using flavors already created in the pan during roasting.

12 Carve food product to order and serve with appropriate gravy or sauce.

occurs even after large food products are removed from the oven. Generally, a large piece of meat will continue to cook for 5 to 15 minutes after removal from the oven, and a rise in internal temperature is not unlikely during this time.

Barding and larding are two techniques that may be performed before cooking to help lean meats retain their flavor and moisture during roasting. *Barding* involves wrapping a lean meat with fat, commonly bacon or fatback, then roasting it. The fat is removed a few minutes before the meat is removed from the oven to allow the surface to brown. *Larding* involves inserting long thin strips of fat (or sometimes vegetables) into the center of the lean meat to add moisture and sometimes visual appeal.

Open-spit roasting involves cooking food, especially meats, over an open fire. The food product is placed on a metal rod or long skewer and slowly turned over the heat source. A drip pan may be placed under the roast to catch the juices escaping from the roast.

To Sauté/Sauter

Sautéing is a dry-cooking method that cooks or reheats food quickly in a shallow pan with minimum fat or oil (see Figure 10–14). The pan should be preheated on high heat before the fat or oil is added. When the fat or oil is near the smoking point, the food is placed in the pan. If the fat is too cold, the food product will absorb the fat or oil, and the result will be a poor-quality product. A higher temperature will result in proper coloration and sealing of the product. After the initial sealing, the temperature should be lowered to allow for even cooking. Sautéing is generally used with delicate food products that cook relatively quickly; for example, fillets of fish, scallops, tender cuts of meat, vegetables, or fruit.

A version of sautéing is sweating. *Sweating* is a cooking technique that may begin by sautéing the product, but that transfers the mode of heat from dry to moist before any browning occurs. The transformation may be achieved by covering the pan, or overcrowding the pan with food product and lowering the heat. Both covering and overcrowding the pan allow the moisture to collect, thereby changing the original dry technique of sautéing to a moist technique of sweating. For example, vegetables cooked for a light-colored pureed soup may be sweated as opposed to sautéed to develop sweetness and to avoid carmelization (and coloration) of the food product.

Stir-frying is the Asian version of sautéing in which a wok is used instead of a sauté pan (see Figure 10–15 on page 175). Similar to sautéing, stir-frying involves cooking small pieces of food over intense heat, using a minimal amount of fat. Because of the size, metallic composition, and shape of the wok, the potential heat intensity and cooking surface area is much greater than in a sauté pan, therefore requiring constant, brisk movement of the food. Stir-frying is just one of the cooking techniques that can be performed in the wok. The wok can also be used to steam, boil, poach, deepfry, and shallow fry.

To Deep Fry/ Frire

Food that is deep fried is cooked by complete submersion in heated fat or oil at a temperature between 350° and 375° F (see Figure 10–16 on page 177). As a result, the outside of the food product is sealed when placed in contact with the heated fat or oil. Frying is a dry cooking technique, and as soon as the food is submerged in the non–water-based fat or oil, the natural moisture in the food turns to steam, which escapes as bubbles via the surface of the fat.

Fried foods are often coated with batter or breading before frying to add texture, add flavor, and aid in coloration of the fried product. A *batter* is a semiliquid mixture usually containing common ingredients such as flour, milk, and eggs. The food is dipped into the batter immediately before submerging it in the hot fat. If a food is breaded, as opposed to dipped in batter, then it goes through a four-step process referred to as the *standard breading procedure*. This procedure involves completion of a sequence of steps to coat the food product with ingredients that alternate between wet and dry characteristics:

1. Mise en place the (*wet*) food product.
2. Dredge the food product in seasoned (*dry*) flour. Dredging is done by dipping the product into flour and coating it evenly on all surfaces, shaking off the excess. Avoid dredging foods in advance; dredging

Figure 10–14 The sautéing process

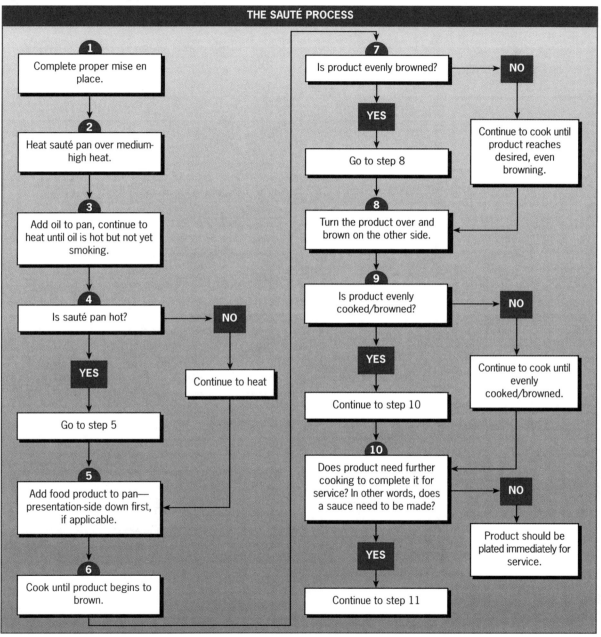

(continued)

Figure 10–14 The sautéing process (continued)

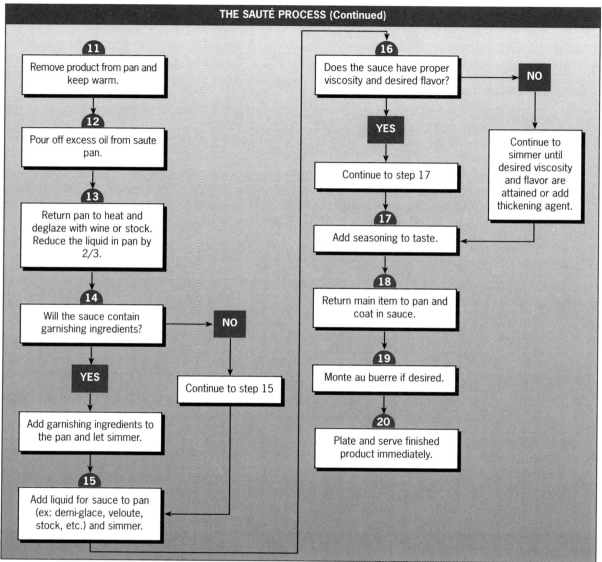

THE SAUTÉ PROCESS (Continued)

11 Remove product from pan and keep warm.

12 Pour off excess oil from saute pan.

13 Return pan to heat and deglaze with wine or stock. Reduce the liquid in pan by 2/3.

14 Will the sauce contain garnishing ingredients?

NO → Continue to step 15

YES → Add garnishing ingredients to the pan and let simmer.

15 Add liquid for sauce to pan (ex: demi-glace, veloute, stock, etc.) and simmer.

16 Does the sauce have proper viscosity and desired flavor?

NO → Continue to simmer until desired viscosity and flavor are attained or add thickening agent.

YES → Continue to step 17

17 Add seasoning to taste.

18 Return main item to pan and coat in sauce.

19 Monte au buerre if desired.

20 Plate and serve finished product immediately.

Figure 10–15 The stir-frying process

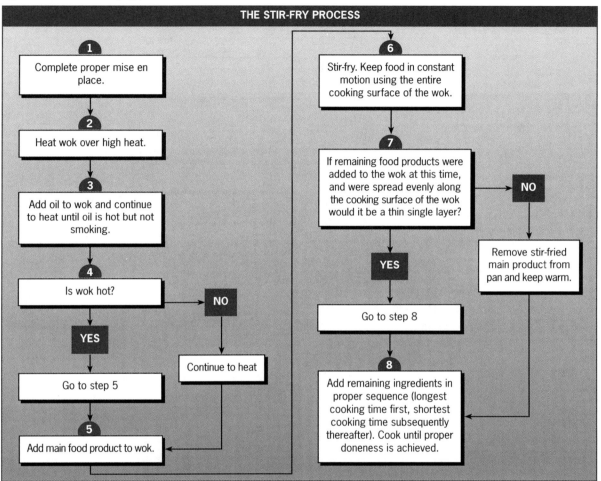

(continued)

should be performed immediately before dipping in egg or other liquid. Stacking or overlapping dredged food product will result in the dry, floured surface becoming pasty. The purpose for dredging a food product in the standard breading procedure is to create a dry surface to which the next liquid step can adhere.

3. Dip the dredged food product into a (*wet*) egg wash or other liquid, coating completely and shaking off the excess.

4. Immediately place the egg-washed food product into a container of (*dry*) crumbs; often made from bread, ground nuts, cereal, crackers, and sometimes shredded fruit such as coconut.

Fried foods should be drained well on an absorbent surface immediately after frying. If needed, the foods should then be seasoned on the draining surface, not over the fat. Fried foods are the best quality when served immediately; however, if holding is necessary, the fried product should be stored in a hot oven. When doing so, the following rules are crucial to maintaining the crispy texture:

Figure 10–15 The stir-frying process (continued)

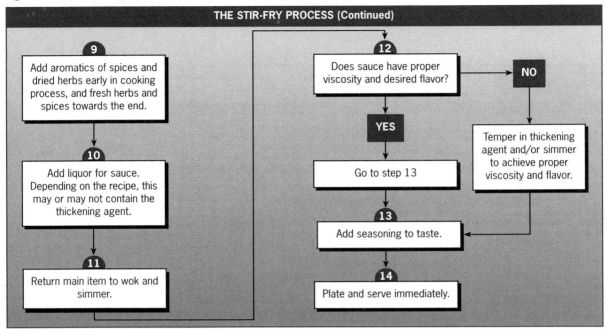

- Never cover containers holding fried foods.
- Lay the fried foods in a container in a single layer; stacking foods causes the fried coating to become soggy because moisture cannot escape.

In the foodservice industry, deep frying is usually conducted in commercial fryers although traditionally a deep pan was once used. Like all cooking techniques, frying must also take into account *recovery time,* the time it takes for the fat to return to the preset temperature after food has been submerged. Commercial fryers may have a much shorter recovery time than pan frying methods and commercial equipment is designed to maximize the life of the frying fat. Today pan frying is still done, but, because of the convenience of fryolators, it is used for frying with moderate amounts of fat. Commonly referred to as *shallow frying,* the method involves cooking in hot fat (350° to 375° F) that covers the food only half to three-quarters (see Figure 10–17 on page 178). As a result, when the first side of the food is fried to a golden hue, the product must be turned to allow for even cooking and coloration.

To Grill/ Griller

Grilling is a method of cooking food on a gridlike surface that sits *above* a heat source (see Figure 10–18 on page 179). For example, gas, electric, charcoal, or wood can be used as heat sources. Grilling is a dry method of cookery for tender foods that cook relatively quickly.

Properly grilling foods involves preheating the grill while mise en place is prepared. The food product is lightly brushed with oil before placing it on the grill. Once placed on the grill, the food should remain in the same position until distinct grill marks are established. If a cross-hatch marking is desired, the product should be lifted and turned in a 90-degree angle, placing it on the grill in a new, hot area. When the cross-hatch marks are established, the product may be turned and cooked to completion on the other side.

Griddling is a version of grilling that uses equipment manufactured with a solid, flat surface as opposed to a grid. Griddles use gas or electricity as the heat source. Griddling is a common, dry, radiant cooking technique used in preparing breakfast and luncheon items. Pancakes, eggs to order, and sandwiches are commonly prepared on a griddle.

Figure 10–16 The deep-frying process

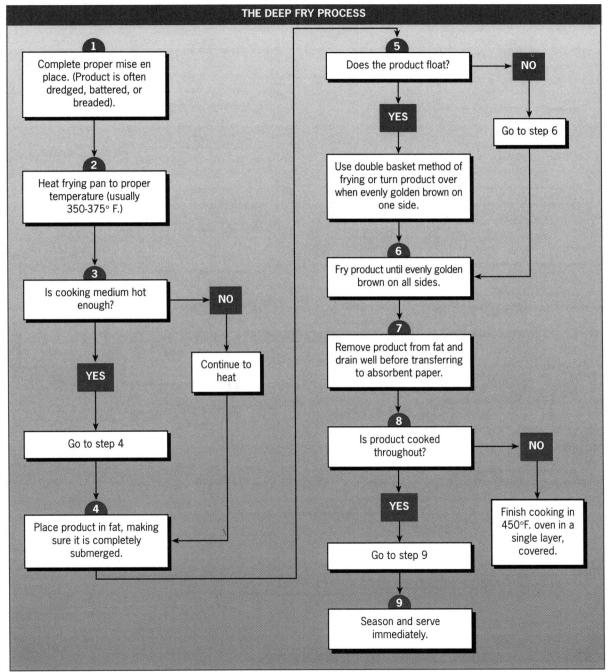

Figure 10–17 The shallow-frying process

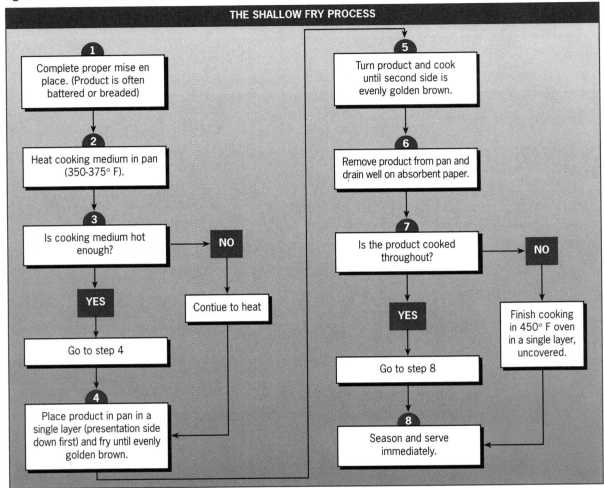

THE SHALLOW FRY PROCESS

1. Complete proper mise en place. (Product is often battered or breaded)

2. Heat cooking medium in pan (350-375° F).

3. Is cooking medium hot enough?
   - NO → Contiue to heat
   - YES → Go to step 4

4. Place product in pan in a single layer (presentation side down first) and fry until evenly golden brown.

5. Turn product and cook until second side is evenly golden brown.

6. Remove product from pan and drain well on absorbent paper.

7. Is the product cooked throughout?
   - NO → Finish cooking in 450° F oven in a single layer, uncovered.
   - YES → Go to step 8

8. Season and serve immediately.

Figure 10–18 The grilling/broiling process

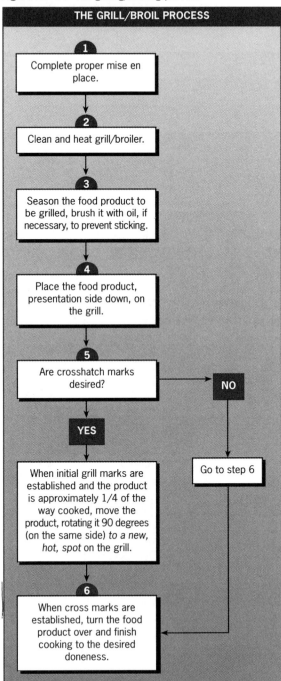

THE GRILL/BROIL PROCESS

1. Complete proper mise en place.

2. Clean and heat grill/broiler.

3. Season the food product to be grilled, brush it with oil, if necessary, to prevent sticking.

4. Place the food product, presentation side down, on the grill.

5. Are crosshatch marks desired? — **NO** → Go to step 6

YES

When initial grill marks are established and the product is approximately 1/4 of the way cooked, move the product, rotating it 90 degrees (on the same side) *to a new, hot, spot* on the grill.

6. When cross marks are established, turn the food product over and finish cooking to the desired doneness.

To Broil/ Griller

Broiling is a similar cooking technique to grilling (see Figure 10–18) except the gridlike cooking surface sits *below* the heat source. Commercial kitchens are usually equipped with a grill *or* a broiler. Broilers are heated by gas or electricity only, and therefore do not offer the possibility of adding additional flavor to food by burning charcoal or wood.

Combination Technique

To Braise/ Braiser

Braising is a combination cooking method that begins by searing a food product in a frying or roasting pan (see Figure 10–19 on page 180). The food product is then removed from the pan, and the pan is deglazed. The seared product is returned to the deglazed pan and a liquid (wine, stock, or sauce) is added to cover the product by two-thirds. The pan is then commonly placed in a 350° F oven, and the food product is cooked slowly until the meat is fork tender. Braising produces a very flavorful liquid medium, because the flavors extracted from the food products become concentrated during the long, slow cooking process. Braised foods are always served with the cooking liquid that has been refined, often by straining, thickening, and seasoning.

To Stew/ Braiser

Stewing is a version of braising (see Figure 10–20 on page 181). Also a combination cooking method, stewing usually begins by searing a food product in a medium-sized pan. The pan may be deglazed, and the food product is barely covered with liquid. The stew is then brought to a simmer, most commonly on the stove top, and cooked until tender. Vegetables may be added at the point during stewing that will ensure doneness but not overcooking at the end. Stewing produces a very flavorful liquid because the extracted flavors of the food products become concentrated during the long, slow cooking process. Stewed foods are always served with the cooking liquid that may be seasoned but generally not thickened. See Table 10–2 on page 182.

Figure 10–19 The braising process

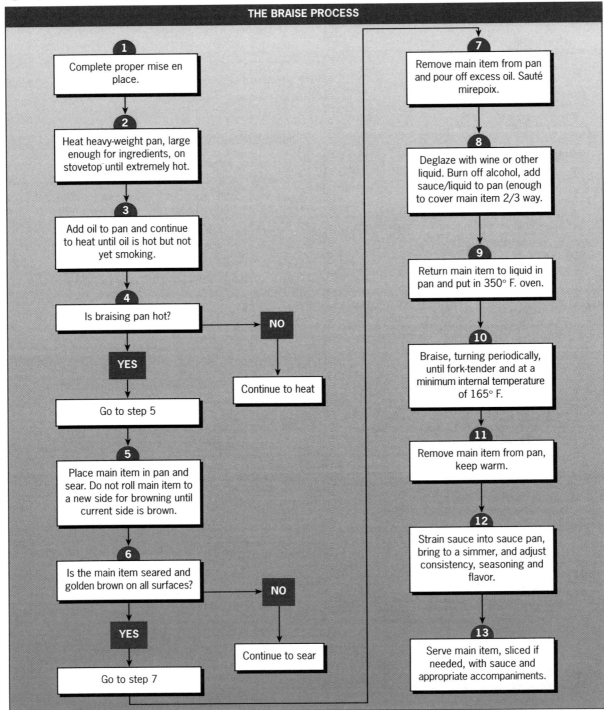

THE BRAISE PROCESS

1. Complete proper mise en place.

2. Heat heavy-weight pan, large enough for ingredients, on stovetop until extremely hot.

3. Add oil to pan and continue to heat until oil is hot but not yet smoking.

4. Is braising pan hot?
   - NO → Continue to heat
   - YES → Go to step 5

5. Place main item in pan and sear. Do not roll main item to a new side for browning until current side is brown.

6. Is the main item seared and golden brown on all surfaces?
   - NO → Continue to sear
   - YES → Go to step 7

7. Remove main item from pan and pour off excess oil. Sauté mirepoix.

8. Deglaze with wine or other liquid. Burn off alcohol, add sauce/liquid to pan (enough to cover main item 2/3 way.

9. Return main item to liquid in pan and put in 350° F. oven.

10. Braise, turning periodically, until fork-tender and at a minimum internal temperature of 165° F.

11. Remove main item from pan, keep warm.

12. Strain sauce into sauce pan, bring to a simmer, and adjust consistency, seasoning and flavor.

13. Serve main item, sliced if needed, with sauce and appropriate accompaniments.

Figure 10–20 The stewing process

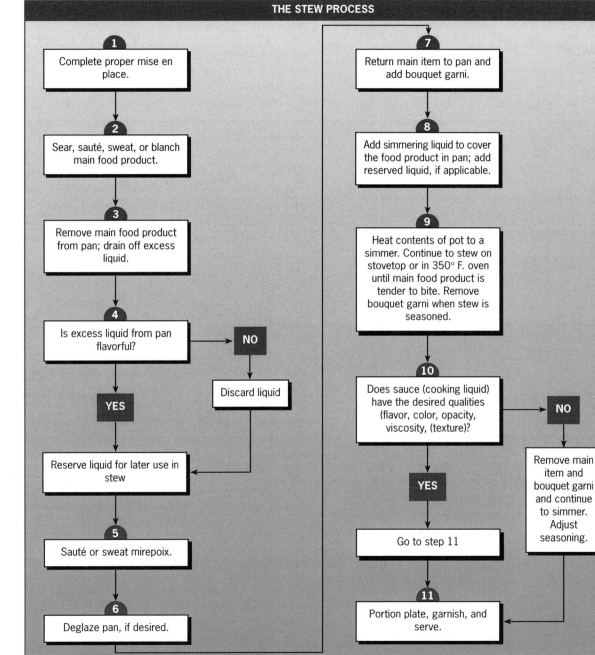

THE STEW PROCESS

1. Complete proper mise en place.

2. Sear, sauté, sweat, or blanch main food product.

3. Remove main food product from pan; drain off excess liquid.

4. Is excess liquid from pan flavorful?
   - NO → Discard liquid
   - YES → Reserve liquid for later use in stew

5. Sauté or sweat mirepoix.

6. Deglaze pan, if desired.

7. Return main item to pan and add bouquet garni.

8. Add simmering liquid to cover the food product in pan; add reserved liquid, if applicable.

9. Heat contents of pot to a simmer. Continue to stew on stovetop or in 350° F. oven until main food product is tender to bite. Remove bouquet garni when stew is seasoned.

10. Does sauce (cooking liquid) have the desired qualities (flavor, color, opacity, viscosity, (texture)?
    - NO → Remove main item and bouquet garni and continue to simmer. Adjust seasoning.
    - YES → Go to step 11

11. Portion plate, garnish, and serve.

Table 10–2 The Basic Differences between Braising and Stewing

Braising	Stewing
Large, tough cuts of meat are braised.	Tough cuts of meat are often cubed when stewed.
The cooking liquid covers the food product by two-thirds.	The cooking liquid covers the food product completely.
The cooking liquid is comprised of wine, stock, or sauce and may contain an acid.	The cooking liquid is comprised primarily of the natural juices from the food product but may also contain wine, stock, sauce, or an acid.
The cooking process of the large cuts of meat most commonly occurs in the oven, where the heat is indirect.	The cooking process of the small cuts of meat most commonly occurs on the stove top, where the direct heat is appropriate.
Braised foods, such as meats, may require slicing before serving.	Stews may be served "as is" and generally require no slicing for presentation.
The cooking liquid requires refinement by straining, seasoning, and thickening.	The cooking liquid is seasoned and served "as is."

Applications and Reactions

Cooking will produce various changes in food products. The most common are changes in texture, color, odor, and nutritive value. The degree of change will depend on the length of cooking time, the temperature, and the cooking technique used.

Texture

The texture of foods changes during the cooking process because of the coagulation of proteins, the breakdown of tissue, and the loss of moisture. When heat is applied to proteins, the proteins toughen, or *coagulate*. The longer proteins are subjected to heat, the tougher they become. For example, when comparing the textural differences be-

tween a medium-rare steak and one cooked well done, it is easy to apply the principal of coagulation. Loss of moisture during the cooking process also lends to the difference in textures in this example. Following coagulation, proteins will eventually begin to break down, also referred to as *denaturation*. The tenderizing of tough meats that occurs during the stewing and braising processes are good examples of denaturation.

Vegetables and fruits are affected more by the loss of moisture than by coagulation. As produce cooks, moisture is extracted from the cells of the product. Simultaneously, the fiber that gives structure and texture to the produce begins to cook, thus softening, and, as a result, denaturation occurs. The fiber contained in fruits and vegetables that grow above ground will generally soften more than the fiber found in vegetables that grow below the soil.

Color

As with texture, color is affected by the cooking process. As meat cooks for extended times and moisture is extracted, the myoglobin that gives meat tissue its color both extracts and oxidizes. For instance, a medium-rare steak will have a much redder, visually appealing color than a brownish-gray, well-done steak.

The color of produce is also affected by the cooking process. Each fruit or vegetable gets its unique coloration from the naturally occuring pigments it contains. Pigmentation compounds differ from product to product, and each is affected differently by cooking. Certain ingredients commonly used in vegetable cookery, such as acids (wine, lemon juice, and vinegar) and alkalis (baking soda), can also have varying effects on different pigments. See Table 10–3.

Aroma and Nutritive Value

The odor of food, especially meats, will change as a result of cooking. Cooking techniques that use fats, either as an ingredient or as a medium, create an especially appealing aroma. As the heat cooks the food product, the fat aids in caramelization. The aroma created from cooking various foods can be as appealing as the flavor and presentation of the final product.

The nutritive value of raw food diminishes the longer it

Table 10–3 Effects of Cooking on Pigments

Pigment	Color	Solubility		Avoid Acids?	Avoid Alkalis?
		Oil	Water		
Chlorophyll	Green	Yes	Yes	Yes	Yes
Carotenoids	Orange/Yellow	Yes	No (generally)	No	Yes
Flavones	White/pale	No	No (generally)	No	Yes
Anthocyanins	Red	Yes	Yes	No	Yes

cooks, and certain cooking techniques may accelerate the loss. Blanching green beans by boiling, for instance, not only destroys nutrients by means of the heat, but dilutes the nutrients into the cooking medium as well. Because the water the beans are cooked in is not served, valuable nutrients are lost. Steaming, however, may cause some nutrient loss from the application of heat, but because the food is cooked in a medium of vapor, nutrients are not lost through dilution in the medium.

Guidelines for Cooking Various Food Products

Vegetables

Vegetables can be blanched using a variety of cooking techniques, but if boiling or simmering are used, then certain rules apply.

1. *Below-ground or root vegetables* are often dense, fibrous, and starchy. A gradual cooking process ensures even cooking. Start cooking the vegetables in cold, seasoned liquid and gradually bring to a boil, reduce to a simmer, and cook to desired doneness.
2. *Above-ground vegetables* are often less dense, fibrous, and starchy than root vegetables and therefore may be cooked more quickly. Start cooking above-ground vegetables in a boiling, seasoned liquid. The heat may be reduced to allow for a simmer, often required for more delicate vegetables.

3. *The size and the cut of the vegetable may cause the first two rules to vary.* For example, if a root vegetable is small, such as a new potato versus an all-purpose potato, then it may be cooked by starting it in a boiling seasoned liquid. Due to its large size, the all-purpose potato would be cooked by starting it in a cold, seasoned liquid and gradually bringing it to a boil before reducing it to a simmer. However, if the all-purpose potato is washed and diced macédoine, it will cook much more quickly and therefore may be cooked by starting it in a boiling, seasoned liquid.

Rice

Although there are about 7,000 varieties of rice in the world, rice is divided into three categories: long grain, medium grain, and short grain. The same technique or recipe is used for cooking both medium- and short-grain rice because they both absorb about four times their bulk in liquid. Long-grain rice, however, will absorb one and one-half to two times its bulk in liquid. Wild rice is not a grain but a water grass that is cooked similarly to rice. Unless rice is precooked or pretreated, it should always be rinsed under cold running water and drained well before cooking. The ratios for cooking rice are:

Shorter medium grain: 4:1 (liquid to rice)
Long grain: 1½–2:1 (liquid to rice)

Methods of Cooking Rice

Steamed

Measure the quantity of rice and liquid (usually water) needed according to the ratio above. Rinse the rice under cold running water and drain. Place rice and measured amount of water in a pan, bring to a boil, cover tightly, and reduce to a simmer. Cook until all water is absorbed. Steamed rice is eaten plain or as a garnish.

Boiled

Measure the quantity of rice desired and wash thoroughly under cold running water; drain well. Place rice in a pan with five parts seasoned liquid and bring to a boil; maintain convection movement until rice is al dente. Drain excess liquid.

Pilaf

Measure the quantity of rice desired and wash thoroughly under cold running water; drain well. Sauté the rice in fat or oil before adding boiling, measured liquid. Bring mixture of rice and liquid to a boil, reduce to a simmer, and cover. Finish cooking on low heat on the stove top or in a 350° F oven for 16 to 20 minutes until all the liquid is absorbed. A side or main dish, pilaf may be made with rice or bulgur wheat, and thousands of variations are possible by adding various chopped meats, seafood, game, or vegetables to the sautéd rice at the beginning of the process. The seasoning may range from very mild to heavily spiced.

Risotto

Traditionally an Italian rice dish because of the arborio rice used in its preparation, risotto is an accepted method of cooking any short-grain rice. When done, a properly made risotto is a creamy mixture where the tender texture of the rice grain is faintly noticeable. The process for making risotto involves sautéing the rice in fat or oil, then reducing the heat and adding the hot liquid slowly. The proportion of hot, flavorful liquid used to the rice is approximately 3–4 to 1, and the liquid is added a cup at a time. As soon as a cup has been added, the mixture is stirred continuously until all the liquid is absorbed. Another cup of liquid is added, and again the mixture is stirred until it is absorbed by the rice. This process continues until all of the premeasured liquid is added to the pot. The risotto gets its creamy texture from the starches that exude from the grains of rice while stirring during the cooking process. Risotto can be flavored in a variety of ways and may be served as a side dish or as a more substantial part of the meal. It should be made in small

batches and served immediately because the consistency is very important to the dish. Risottos that are held on a steam table quickly become heavy and overly thick, with texture loss in the grains.

Grains

Grains such as barley, corn, millet, and oats are generally used as garnish in soups. Often rinsed before cooking, the grains are barely covered in a flavorful liquid and then simmered until al dente. Cereals such as polenta, bulgur, sago, and semolina are generally boiled or steamed.

Pasta

In Italian, pasta means *paste* and refers to a dough made by mixing *semolina flour,* which is made from grinding durum wheat; and a liquid, often water or milk. Pasta may be given a richer, more tender texture by adding fat to the dough, often in the form of oil or eggs or both. Pastas cooked from a dried state require a much longer cooking time, often 7 to 10 minutes, than fresh pastas, which need a shorter time of only a minute or two. The general process of cooking pasta includes the following steps:

1. Cook pasta in plenty of liquid, usually a ratio of 1 part pasta to 5 parts salted water.
2. Bring the water to a boil, and season it with salt. Salt should be added an average of 1 ounce to 1 gallon.
3. Plunge the pasta into the boiling water.
4. Stir the pasta with a braising fork or serving spoon, and continue to do so during the cooking process. The combination of the rapid convection movement, the large proportion of water to pasta, and the stirring should keep the pasta from sticking together.
5. Test the pasta to determine doneness. Pasta should be *al dente,* tender yet slightly firm to the bite.
6. When the pasta is done, strain at once and serve immediately or refresh in ice water to stop the cooking.
7. Pasta not served immediately should be tossed lightly in oil and refrigerated for use at a later time.
8. Reheat pasta in boiling salted water.

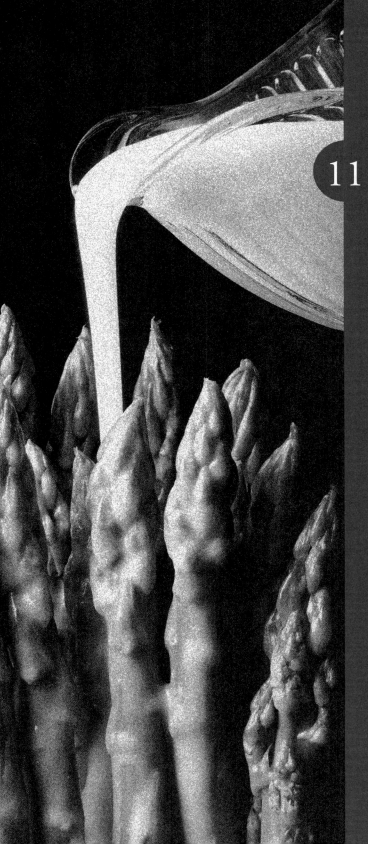

11

Stocks,
Sauces,
Emulsions,
and Soups

Stocks, Sauces, Emulsions, and Soups

Today many chefs and managers are using bases instead of stocks.

Fonds/Stocks

Fond is the French word for *stock* and means bottom, ground, or basis. In use since the 16th century, stocks are the basic liquids used in the preparation of soups and sauces. Stocks are the result of extracting flavors from various food items using liquid as a base. Bones, vegetables, herbs, and spices are simmered in a liquid, often water, to produce a stock. The production of stocks can be a time-consuming process.

Care in preparing stocks must be given the highest priority. Simmering stocks result in the extraction of flavor from the ingredients while allowing reduction to take place. *Reduction* occurs when a liquid is simmered for increasing lengths of time, reducing the amount of water in the stock and concentrating the flavor.

Base was invented after World War II as a substitute for stocks. When the paste or powder was mixed with water, a stock was produced that saved time, labor, and money. Bases quickly became popular in the industry, but chefs and managers needed to make adjustments in their recipes to account for the high sodium content and lack of flavor intensity. If not used as a total substitution for stocks, many chefs and managers use bases as an additional ingredient to fortify the flavor of soups and sauces made from stocks.

Composition of a Stock

A stock is composed of four elements: the nourishing element, mirepoix, bouquet garni, and liquid.

Nourishing Element

The most important ingredient used in the production of a stock is the *nourishing element*. The primary purpose of the nourishing element is to provide flavor, nutrients, and color. Some nourishing elements may add other beneficial characteristics to the stock, as in the case of bones, which add gelatin. Nourishing elements may include any one or a combination of the following ingredients:

- Fresh bones (beef, veal, lamb, chicken, fish, game)
- Meat trimmings from butchering
- Fish heads and trimmings for fish stock
- Vegetables for a vegetable stock

Mirepoix

A *mirepoix* is a mixture of diced vegetables that is used in the stock to add flavor, nutrients, and color. It consists of the following ingredients, but may vary depending on the recipe:

- Onions
- Celery
- Carrots
- Leeks

Bouquet Garni

A *bouquet garni* is a collection of aromatics that may be added directly to a simmering liquid or can be tied together in a sachet. A *sachet* is a permeable container that holds the aromatics and may be made out of cheesecloth, celery stalks, or leek greens that are tied together with twine. Enclosing the aromatics in a sachet enables the cook to easily remove the aromatics when the stock is properly seasoned.

A standard bouquet garni consists of thyme leaves, bay leaves, whole black peppercorns, and parsley stems. Other spices and herbs can be added or substituted depending on the recipe.

The liquid used to make a stock should be cold at the onset of the cooking process to allow for the maximum extraction of flavor from the ingredients. When all ingredients are assembled for the stock, the ratio of the liquid to the other ingredients should be approximately 2:1. The liquid used to make the stock is commonly water or remouillage.

Remouillage means to re-wet. A remouillage is a weak stock made from the solid ingredients that are leftover after a stock has been strained, therefore maximizing flavor that may be remaining. The use of remouillage naturally improves the taste of the new stock while reducing simmering time. Remouillage can also be used as a liquid for braising meats, preparing soups, or moistening stuffings.

After a stock has been completed and strained, water is once again added to the three remaining elements (bones, mirepoix, and boquet garni) and brought to a simmer. Usually about one-half of the original amount of liquid is sufficient. Simmering time is approximately one-half of the original time.

Some chefs add salt to stocks to aid in the extraction process or to extend the holding period under refrigeration. This practice should be avoided when the stock is to be reduced to a glaze. Types of stock are:

French Terminology	English Translation
Fond de boeuf	Beef stock
Fond de veau	Veal stock
Fond de volaille	Poultry stock
Fond de légume	Vegetable stock
Fond d'agneau	Lamb stock
Fond de poisson	Fish stock
Fond de gibier	Game stock

Classification of Stocks

Stocks are further classified as to color and method of preparation of the nourishing elements and mirepoix under the following two categories:

French Terminology	English Translation
Fond blanc	White stock
Fond brun	Brown stock

In kitchen terminology, stocks may be specifically referred to using both the type and classification. For instance, requesting 1 gallon of fond blanc de volaille is much different from 1 gallon of fond brun de volaille. In the first, 1 gallon of white chicken stock has been requested, but 1 gallon of brown chicken stock was stated in the second. Chefs and managers must be familiar with both French and English culinary terminology.

Production of Stocks

There are four important steps to producing a good stock: cold liquid, natural clarification, skimming, and temperature.

Cold Liquid

Starting with cold liquid allows for the slow release of flavor from the solid ingredients and helps to prevent cloudiness.

Natural Clarification

Albumin is a protein that is soluble only in cold water. It is found in muscles, blood, and many vegetable tissues, especially leeks. Once released slowly into the water, albumin has the ability to naturally clarify the liquid by coagulating with impurities. Gently simmering the stock, as opposed to boiling it, aids the albumin in the natural clarification process.

Skimming

During the simmering process, the chef should dépouiller the stock. *Dépouillage* means to skim the fat, scum, and impurities off the surface of the stock. A liquid should be dépouillaged while it is simmering because the convection movement forces the fats and impurities to the surface so they accumulate in a smaller area, thus making the process easier (see Figure 11–1). All the fat is easily removed using a ladle. The fat can be reserved and clarified for future use.

Figure 11–1 Types of convection movement and skimming area

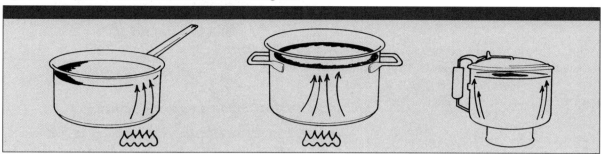

Maintaining the Proper Simmering Temperature

To allow for proper clarification and fortification of the cooking liquid, the stock should be simmered. Simmering involves heating the liquid to a temperature between 185° and 200° F, so a slow convection, or bubbling, movement occurs. If allowed to boil, the fat and impurities will simply revolve back into the body of the stock, thus preventing the opportunity to dépouillage. If the stock is cooked at a temperature below the simmering point, the convection movement is not strong enough to push the impurities to the surface. The chef or manager also risks allowing the stock's temperature to fall into the TDZ.

Glace/Glaze

Glace is the French term for *glaze*, a stock that is reduced by 85 to 90 percent of its original volume. The end result should be a thick and syrupy liquid that is highly flavored. The glaze may also have a naturally high sodium content caused by the extreme removal of water from the stock. Types of glazes include the following:

French Name	English Translation
Glace de viande	Meat glaze; often made from veal or beef stock
Glace de veau	Veal glaze
Glace de boeuf	Beef glaze
Glace de volaille	Poultry glaze

French Name	English Translation
Glace d'agneau	Lamb glaze
Glace de poisson	Fish glaze
Glace de gibier	Game glaze

Preparation of a Glaze

Prepare a glaze according to the following steps:

1. Place a large quantity (for example, 5 gallons) of stock in a heavy-gauge pan.
2. Bring the stock to a simmer and dépouillage the fat and impurities as needed. As the stock reduces and becomes syrupy, the sides of the pan can be cleaned with a natural bristle brush moistened lightly with water.
3. Transfer the stock into a smaller pan as the process progresses to ensure a controlled and even reduction.
4. When the glaze is finished, strain through a chinois mousseline, cool, label, and refrigerate.

Uses of Glazes

Glazes are used to

- Fortify a weak stock or sauce, soup, or other food item that lacks the desired flavor.
- Make a light-bodied yet flavorful sauce.
- Add shine to food items such as chateaubriand, tourne potatoes, or showpieces for food competitions.

Fumet

A *fumet* is a flavorful liquid that has been reduced by 50 percent. Seasonings are sometimes used to enhance the flavor. A fumet is made from vegetables, fowl, poultry, fish, or game that have been simmered in stock or wine.

Uses of Fumets

Fumet are used to make a light-bodied, flavorful sauce and to give additional body and richness to various sauces and stocks.

Essences (Extracts)

Essences are strongly reduced liquids. Neutral liquids, such as wine, stock, vegetable juices, or water, are simmered with the addition of a primary element, until the strength of the primary element dominates. The liquid essence is then strained and used as needed. The primary element is the main flavor to be produced. For example, mushrooms are the primary element used to produce a mushroom essence.

Uses of Essences

Essences fortify food products with similar flavors, add a particular flavor to a food product, and are sometimes incorporated with whole butter or flavored oil to make a light-bodied sauce.

Sauces

A *sauce* is a flavored, thickened liquid that is served with such foods as entrées and accompaniments. Generally, sauces are derived from stocks. The sauce should comple-ment the item being served. Balance should be created between the flavor and the consistency of the sauce so it does not detract from the flavor of the main item.

Mother or Leading Sauces

There are many theories about basic sauces, often termed *mother sauces* or *leading sauces*. All six mother sauces are made in the same general way; they are a result of combining a liquid with a thickening agent. Generally, only six hot sauces are categorized under the name of mother sauce.

1. *Sauce espagnole* is a thickened basic brown stock with the addition of a tomato product and limited seasonings for flavor.
2. *Demi-glace sauce* is a sauce derived from combining half espagnole sauce and half brown stock, which is then reduced by half and flavored with Madeira wine. Demi-glace is used as a base sauce for brown compound-reduction sauces.
3. *Tomato sauce* is a sauce made from simmering a tomato product with flavorings, seasonings, and a liquid (such as stock). Basic tomato sauce is completely vegetable based, but variations may include meat.
4. *Béchamel sauce* is a simmering milk that is thickened with a white roux, flavorings, and seasonings.
5. *Velouté*, literally meaning velvety, is a sauce made with a light-colored stock thickened with a light-colored roux. The type of stock used to make the velouté indicates the name of the product. For example,
   a. Chicken velouté is prepared with a white chicken stock.
   b. Fish velouté is prepared with a fish stock.
   c. Veal velouté is prepared with a white veal stock.
   d. Vegetable velouté is prepared with a white vegetable stock.
6. *Hollandaise sauce* is a hot permanent emulsion sauce made by beating egg yolks with a reduction, clarified butter, and seasonings over a bath of hot water.

Methods of Thickening Liquids

Liaison

A *liaison* is a thickening agent used to alter the viscosity of sauces and soups. The most common liaisons used are starches, although liquids may also be thickened by means of emulsions and reduction. The viscosity, or thickness, of the liquid will vary depending on the percentage of thickening agent added. Viscosity is classified as follows:

- Minimum viscosity: 10 percent
- Medium viscosity: 11.5 percent
- Maximum viscosity: 13 percent

To determine the amount of thickening agent required for a sauce, use the following viscosity formula:

Ounces of thickening agent = Viscosity percentage
× Liquid, in ounces

Applying Liaisons

Starches used for thickening need to be handled in a particular way:

1. Dilute powdered starches with a cool liquid, such as stock, water, milk, or oil, before they are added to the sauces or soups that need to be thickened.
2. After the starch is diluted in the cool liquid, add the mixture to the hot sauce or soup by tempering. *Tempering* is the process of equalizing the temperatures of two liquids before adding them together. This is done by gradually adding small quantities of the hot to the cool liquid, slowly raising the temperature until they are almost equal. Tempering should be done to prevent the following:
   a. *Lumping:* If the diluted starch mixture is added directly to the hot sauce or soup without tempering, the starches may cook in the form of lumps as opposed to being evenly distributed throughout the liquid.
   b. *Breaking:* The mixture may break if a final liaison containing a dairy product is used. Some dairy products have a low fat content and will be more susceptible to breaking when quickly introduced into a hot liquid.
3. As soon as the mixture is added to the hot liquid, the sauce or soup should be brought back to a simmer. Starches require heat to activate the thickening process. Some thickening agents will take a longer simmering time than others in order to thicken. For example, cornstarch will thicken the hot liquid completely as soon as it comes back to a simmer, whereas a roux requires 10 to 15 minutes of simmering to fully thicken.

Starches

A starch is a carbohydrate naturally found in fruits, seeds, roots, tubers, and the pith of stemmed plants. Wheat, corn, rice, potatoes, and arrowroot are common examples of starches used as thickening agents.

Flour

The most common flour used in the kitchen is wheat flour. As a thickening agent, flour can be used in three different ways:

- *As is,* the flour may be used to *singer,* a process in which a pan that may have been used to sauté an entrée is dusted with flour. The fat in the pan absorbs the flour, instantly forming a thickening agent known as a roux.
- *Roux* is a cooked thickening agent made by combining equal parts by weight of flour and a clarified fat or oil. The most common fat used when making a roux is clarified butter or margarine. All-purpose flour is the most common type used. When making a roux, the flour is sprinkled into the warm clarified fat or oil in a pan and whisked to incorporate. The mixture is then cooked by placing the pan on low to medium

heat and stirring constantly. Cooking time for the roux varies depending on its use. Following are cooking times for the various types of roux:

French Terminology	English Translation	Cooking Time
Roux blanc	White Roux	5 to 6 minutes
Roux blonde	Pale Roux	5 to 6 minutes
Roux brun	Brown Roux	15 to 20 minutes.

or mix fat with toasted flour and cook for 5 to 6 minutes.

- *Beurre manié* is an uncooked thickening agent made by combining equal parts of flour and whole butter. The butter should be just melted before it is blended with the flour. The mixture is then added to a hot sauce or soup by tempering at the end of the cooking process and should not be brought back to a simmer. Beurre manié was used in classical times as a "quick fix" for a soup or sauce that was not the desired consistency at the time of service. It is seldom used in modern applications because cornstarch and arrowroot are now available, thickening a liquid quickly and easily. The drawback to using a beurre manié is that, although the final product may be the correct consistency, the flavor of the soup or sauce remains starchy because the flour cannot be cooked properly.

Cornstarch

Cornstarch is a dense powdery flour made from the endosperm of corn. It is applied to hot liquids the same way as all thickening agents. Cornstarch imparts a different characteristic to a liquid than does roux, as it creates a translucent appearance. When using cornstarch,

1. Combine the cornstarch with an equal amount of cold liquid, and temper.
2. Pour the diluted cornstarch into the hot liquid.
3. Bring the hot liquid back to a simmer.
4. Do not simmer for more than 10 minutes or the cornstarch will begin to break down, resulting in the loss of thickening properties.

Arrowroot

Arrowroot is a thickening agent made from drying and grinding the rootstalks of arrowroot into a fine powder. Its thickening power is about twice the strength of flour. The best of the purified starches, arrowroot is used like cornstarch except it will not lose its thickening property during the cooking process. Similar to cornstarch, arrowroot imparts a transparent appearance to the sauce or soup.

Potato or Tapioca

Potato flour or starch is made from cooked, dried, and ground potatoes. Tapioca is made from the ground root of the cassava plant and can be purchased in the form of granules, flakes, pellets (pearls), and flour. Both potato and tapioca are gluten-free. They are added to hot liquids using the same procedure as all thickening agents. These starches are seldom used in the foodservice industry because they break down very easily, losing their thickening properties.

Emulsions

Emulsions are another way of thickening sauces and are made by mixing two or more liquid ingredients that normally do not combine, with the aid of an emulsifying agent. Oil and water are examples of two liquids that do not naturally combine. An example of an emulsifying agent is *lecithin*, an element found in egg yolks. Lecithin is a fatty substance that may also help to preserve and add moisture to food products.

Emulsification is achieved by blending one liquid containing the egg yolks to another (often oil, added drop by drop) while whisking briskly. In the case of a permanent emulsion, the molecules of lecithin separate during the whisking and bond to the molecules of oil, thus suspending the oil molecules in the liquid mixture. The resulting sauce becomes thick and creamy.

There are three types of emulsions:

- A *permanent* emulsion will last for a period of time, usually several days or more. Mayonnaise, an example of a permanent emulsion sauce, contains an emulsifying agent among other ingredients.
- A *semipermanent* emulsion will last for a period of time, usually several hours or more. A semipermanent emulsion sauce is classified as such because of sani-

tary restrictions. An example of a semipermanent emulsion is hollandaise. Caution must be taken when producing a hollandaise sauce because the eggs will cook at a temperature above 140° F. Because eggs are considered a potentially hazardous food, hollandaise sauce should not be held for more than 20 minutes; therefore categorizing it as a semipermanent emulsion.

- A *temporary* emulsion will last for a short period of time, usually several minutes. A temporary emulsion is classified as such because it *does not* contain an emulsifying agent. An emulsion of the two liquid ingredients can be attained by briskly whisking the ingredients, although the emulsification will not last long. During the whisking, the air bubbles incorporated into the liquid cling to each molecule of oil, allowing them to remain suspended temporarily. The air bubbles will dissipate after a few minutes, however, and the liquid will have to be reblended to bring back the emulsion. An example of a temporary emulsion is a vinaigrette.

Reduction

The third way of thickening sauces is through natural reduction. During this process, water is evaporated from the liquid (often stock), resulting in a concentration of the flavor, color, and gelatinous content, thus naturally thickening the liquid. When reduction is used as a primary method of thickening, no starches are incorporated.

Liaison Finale

A liaison finale is done to enhance flavor or to make liquids, such as soups or sauces, smoother and richer. The most commonly used liaisons are generally high in fat and cream; cream, egg yolk, and whole butter are examples. The liaison is tempered and added to the hot liquid at the end of the cooking process and is not usually allowed to come back to a simmer. If butter is used, small pieces are added at a time and whisked briskly to incorporate. This is known as *monter au beurre*. Puréed vegetables, sour cream,

coral, yogurt, foie gras, and giblets are other food products that can be used as a final liaison.

In some traditional classical cooking, fresh blood of pork, game, or fowl is used as a final liaison. Before using this method, check with the state health department. The use of fresh blood may not be allowed in foodservice operations in some states.

Quality of a Sauce

A good sauce will be judged by the following factors:

- *Taste:* The flavor of the sauce should be distinct and well rounded, complementing the food product it accompanies. Proper seasoning is an important element in developing a balanced flavor. Sauces containing thickeners should be free of any starchy taste.
- *Color:* The color of the sauce should be distinct and natural. For instance, a cream sauce should be white, not gray; and a velouté should be a pale ivory. Brown sauces should be rich and deep, while tomato should be robust.
- *Luster:* All sauces should have a good shine. The correct amount of fat in a sauce can contribute to the shine, while too much can detract from it.
- *Texture:* Most sauces should have a smooth, creamy texture that is free of lumps or other particles. The creaminess of a sauce depends on the amount of fat in it. The higher the fat content, the creamier the texture. However, when adjusting a sauce for nutritional soundness, take care not to remove too much fat for fear of destroying the texture.
- *Opacity:* A sauce should have the correct degree of opacity, which is often determined by the thickener used and the amount of reduction that has taken place. For instance, the brown sauce served with osso buco should be thickened with a roux, giving the sauce a high degree of opacity. The sauce should have a rich, dense-brown color that complements the braised veal shank. The degree of opacity would be incorrect if the sauce were thickened with cornstarch, which would produce a brown, semitransparent sauce.

- *Viscosity:* The more a sauce is thickened, the more viscous it becomes. A sauce has an appropriate thickness, or viscosity, when it can lightly coat the back of a metal spoon.

Compound Sauces

All classical sauces are made from the six mother, or leading, sauces. Compound sauces are made by combining a mother sauce with additional flavorings and seasonings. Although there are only a few mother sauces, they are the basis for numerous compound sauces (see Table 11–1).

Classifications

Compound sauces are classified according to the following categories:

1. *Sauce espagnole,* although rarely used alone, is an important ingredient in making demi-glace.
2. *Sauce demi-glace* is an espagnole sauce *taken to the limit of perfection,* according to Escoffier. A basic brown sauce, demi-glace may use different wines to produce compound sauces.
3. *Béchamel sauce* is a basic cream sauce of butter, flour, and milk or cream.
4. *Velouté sauce* is made by thickening a white stock with a white roux. The compound sauces that derive from veloutés differ not only with the additional ingredients, but with the type of white stock used.
5. *Tomato sauce* is a basic tomato sauce consisting of olive oil, onions, garlic, red wine, basil leaves, rosemary, anise, crushed red pepper, tomato paste, crushed tomatoes, and stock, beef, veal, or chicken.
6. *Hollandaise sauce* is a hot emulsion of egg yolk, reduction, and clarified butter.

Cold Emulsion Sauces

Mayonnaise is a permanent emulsion of egg yolk and oil. Some compounds are Bagration, Anglaise, Verte, Russe, Rémoulade, Tartar, and Tyrolienne.

Vinaigrette is a temporary emulsion of acid and oil, generally with a ratio of one part acid to three or four parts oil. Some compounds are Pecheur, Ravigote, Indienne, Marseillaise, and Norvegienne.

Independent, Nonderivative Sauces

Independent, nonderivative sauces are sometimes referred to as English sauces. They can be hot or cold. Examples of hot sauces are applesauce, bread sauce, moutarde, and Soubise. Cold sauces include cranberry, Cumberland, Chantilly, raifort, oxford, échalote, and cocktail sauce.

Compound Butters

A *compound butter* is butter with one or more ingredients added to change the color or flavor. The ingredients that are added may be either puréed or finely chopped first. Sometimes, instead of using a sauce to complement a food product, a chef might opt for a smaller flavoring element. Such a flavoring element may be referred to as a cold or hard sauce; an example would be compound butters. Compound butters may also be used as a *monter au beurre.* There are two types of compound butters: simple and complex.

Simple Compound Butters

Simple compound butters are merely softened butter combined or mixed with one, two, or three flavoring elements. Common examples of simple compound butter are as follows:

Almond butter	Pound almonds to a paste with a little water to prevent their turning oily. Blend with soft butter; pass through a sieve.

Table 11–1 Description of Mother, or Leading, Sauces

Name of Sauce	Additional Ingredients	Wine/Stock Used	Uses	Sauce Espagnole	Sauce Demi-Glace	Béchamel Sauce	Velouté Sauce	Tomato	Hollandaise
Albufera	Sauce suprême, meat glaze, red pepper butter	Chicken	Chicken, duck				✓		
Allemande	Mushroom essence, egg yolks, lemon juice	Especially beef (may use veal)	Offal, vegetables, eggs				✓		
Aurore	Tomato purée, heavy cream, butter (*optional*: vinegar)	Any white stock	Veal, chicken, eggs				✓		
Béarnaise	Tarragon reduction	NA	Grilled meat, grilled fish						✓
Bercy	Sauce normande, shallots, white wine, parsley	Fish	Fish				✓		
Bigarade	Orange zest, duck stock, cognac	Vinegar	Duck	✓					
Bolognaise	Ham, various vegetables, beef, lean pork, chicken livers, white wine	NA	Pasta dishes, gratins					✓	
Bonnefoy	White wine, shallots, garlic, tarragon	Any white stock	Fish				✓		
Bordelaise	Shallots, peppercorns, thyme, bay leaf, lemon juice, poached marrow	Red wine	Grilled meat	✓					
Cardinal	Fish stock, heavy cream, lobster butter, truffle	NA	Crustaceans, fish			✓			
Chasseur	Mushrooms, shallots, cognac, tomato concasse, chervil, tarragon	White wine	Chicken	✓					
Choron	Béarnaise with tomato	NA	Grilled fish, tournedos, eggs						✓
Crème	Heavy cream or crème fraîche, lemon juice	NA	Vegetables, seafood, poultry, veal			✓			
Creole	Onion, celery, peppers, garlic, lemon zest, thyme	NA	Meat, poultry					✓	
Curry	Curry, onion, coconut milk, cream (*optional*: cilantro, lemon juice)	Veal or any white stock	Meat, chicken, fish	✓			✓		
Diable	Shallots, vinegar, cayenne	White wine	Grilled chicken or other poultry	✓					
Duxelles	Shallots, mushroom essence, tomato purée, duxelle	White wine	Game, meat, vegetables	✓	✓				
Financière	Madère sauce, truffle	Madeira wine	Chicken, veal, game				✓		
Foyot	Béarnaise with meat glaze	NA	Meat						✓
Hussarde	Shallots, onion, tomato purée, cured ham, garlic, horseradish	White wine	Grilled red meats	✓	✓				

(continued)

Table 11–1 Description of Mother, or Leading, Sauces (continued)

Name of Sauce	Additional Ingredients	Wine/Stock Used	Uses	Sauce Espagnole	Sauce Demi-Glace	Béchamel Sauce	Velouté Sauce	Tomato	Hollandaise
Italienne	Duxelles, tomato purée, parsley, chervil, tarragon, lean ham	White wine	Meat, fish, vegetables, eggs	✓	✓			✓	
Madère	None	Madeira wine	Chicken, veal, game		✓				
Maltaise	Blood orange juice, orange zest	NA	Fish, vegetables						✓
Meurette	Shallots, parsley, thyme, bay leaf, mushrooms (beurre manié)	Red wine	Meat, fish, eggs		✓				
Mornay	Grated Gruyère and Parmesan cheeses (egg yolks optional)	NA	Souffles, gratins			✓			
Mousseline	Whipped heavy cream	NA	Fish, vegetables						✓
Nantua	Crustacean butter, heavy cream	NA	Crustaceans, fish			✓			
Noisette	Brown butter	NA	Salmon, trout, turbot						✓
Normande	Mushroom essence, egg yolks, heavy cream, butter	Fish	Fish				✓		
Paloise	Mint	NA	Meat						✓
Piquante	Shallots, white wine, gherkins, parsley, chervil, tarragon	Vinegar	Grilled meat, pork		✓				
Poivrade	Mirepoix, meat/game trimmings, white wine, marinade, peppercorns	Vinegar	Red meats, game		✓				
Porto	None	Port wine	Duck		✓				
Portugaise	Onions, garlic, meat glaze, parsley, butter	NA	Meat, poultry, fish, eggs					✓	
Poullette	Sauce allemande, lemon juice, chopped parsley	Chicken, veal	Chicken, fish, mussels, offal, snails				✓		
Provençale	Olive oil, onion, garlic, white wine (*optional:* sliced mushroom)	NA	Vegetables, eggs, poultry, fish					✓	
Rouennaise	Bordelaise sauce (without marrow), thickened with puréed duck liver	Red wine	Duck, eggs		✓				
Ravigote	White wine, white vinegar, shallots, chervil, chives, tarragon	Veal	Calves' head and brains, boiled fowl				✓		
Salmis	Brunoise mirepoix, meat trimmings	White wine	Game, small birds, meats		✓				
Soubise	Onion purée	NA	Veal, seafood			✓			
Suprême	Heavy cream, butter (*optional:* mushroom essence and lemon juice)	Chicken	Poultry				✓		

Anchovy butter	Pound fish to a paste.
Caper butter	Finely chopped capers, anchovies, and lemon and orange juice; top with three whole capers after piping into balls.
Chivry butter	Blanch parsley, chives, tarragon, chervil, and fresh burnet. Pound with chopped, blanched shallots. Add to butter; pass through fine sieve. Sometimes referred to as beurre ravigote.
Curry butter	Curry paste or powder and sugar.
Green butter	Combine spinach juice, celery salt, nutmeg, and white pepper. Sprinkle or blend in chopped parsley.
Herb balls	Pinch pepper, sugar, lemon juice, and fresh chopped mixed herbs. Blend; form balls; cool; roll in more herbs.
Maître d'hôtel	Lemon juice and chopped parsley.
Mushroom butter	Slice, sauté briefly, season, pound, add to butter, pass through fine sieve.
Orange butter	Combine orange juice, grated zest, and rough-chopped green peppercorns, if desired.
Paprika butter	Paprika of choice combined with whipped butter.
Pepper butter	Combine freshly ground black pepper, celery salt, and garlic salt. May be used as a curl.
Printanier butter	Purée blanched green vegetables, such as peas, beans, and asparagus tips. Add to equal quantity of butter. Pass through fine sieve. Can be used for soups and sauces.
Salmon butter	Smoked salmon blended with whipped butter using the same method as anchovy butter.
Salmon and dill butter	Mix cayenne, finely chopped onion, and chopped salmon. Spread on plastic wrap, chill, sprinkle with chopped dill, roll.
Tarragon butter	Same as chivry butter.
Tomato butter	Concentrated tomato purée. Can be used for soups and sauces.

Complex Compound Butters

Complex compound butters are clarified butter combined with flavoring ingredients. The flavoring ingredient may be edible or inedible. An example of an inedible flavoring may be the shells of shrimp or lobster. This mixture is placed over a double boiler, and the flavor is slowly extracted. The butter is then strained and cooled. In the case of complex compound butters, only the flavor of the ingredient is present in the butter, as in shrimp butter.

Soups

Soup sets the tone for the meal. In some cases, it is the meal itself. In parts of rural France, *la soupe* has been the name of the evening meal for centuries, from which is derived the word *supper*. La soupe comes from the word *sop*—the crust of bread over which *le potage*, soup, is poured. The French have long considered soup a source of nourishment and sustenance.

Classification of Soups

Soups can be divided into five categories:

1. *Clear soup* is made with a clarified liquid or a consommé; it is unthickened.
2. *Thin soup* is a soup using water, milk, or a stock as a liquid. It is unthickened. Beef and vegetable soups are examples.
3. *Thick soup* is a soup using stock or broth. It is thickened. Cream, velouté, and puréed soups are the three types of thick soup.

4. *Specialty soups* are made from particular ingredients reflecting a specific region. They can be clear, thin, or thick. Examples are chowders or a gumbo.
5. *International soups* are soups of foreign origin. The preparations are varied. Examples are French onion soup or Polish borscht.

General Methods for Making Soups

Consommé

Consommé is a clarified *and* fortified soup made from a meat stock and additional ingredients. Consommés are simmered, not boiled, to achieve a richly flavored, highly aromatic, full-bodied, thin but clear soup. Consommés should contain no visible fat. The distinctive features of consommés are perfect clarity and gold to amber color. See Appendix D for a list of classical garnishes for consommés.

Functions of Ingredients for the Clarification of a Consommé

- A *cold, flavorful stock* that is free of all visible fat is the main ingredient of a consommé. The stock must be cold to prevent premature coagulation of albumin, which is a type of protein. The flavor of the stock should be the same as that of the finished soup. For example, if a crayfish consommé is desired, then a crayfish stock should be used.
- *Egg whites,* which contain large amounts of the protein albumin, are the primary clarifying agent in consommé. When albumin is heated, it coagulates, trapping particles floating in the stock. This clarifies the stock by attracting and holding impurities in the raft. The recommended number of egg whites to use per gallon of stock is eight to ten.
- *Lean ground meat* adds flavor, color, and structure (to the raft), and is a minor clarifying agent because of the small amount of albumin it contains. The meat must be ground to allow even disbursement throughout the soup at the beginning of the process.

- The *mirepoix*—celery, carrots, onions, and sometimes leeks—contributes to flavor, color, and structure (to the raft). Because the vegetables will be discarded when the soup is finished, cutting a rough chop of the vegetables is adequate. There is no need to spend excessive amounts of time cutting the mirepoix into fine cuts such as a brunoise or julienne.
- The *acid ingredient* acts as a catalyst, helping the albumin to clarify more quickly. Wine and tomato products, such as purée, are the most common ingredients used for this purpose. Because the acid product also adds color and flavor to the consommé, an ingredient that best complements the finished product should be chosen. For instance, if a fond blanc de volaille is used to make a chicken consommé, then a tomato product could make the resulting consommé pink; an undesirable color. A white wine with complementary flavor may be a more appropriate acid ingredient.
- *Seasoning* adds flavor to the consommé. The bouquet garni is the most common seasoning used when making a consommé. However, chefs also commonly season the consommé with salt *before* the soup is cooked. This allows the salt, which usually makes the soup cloudy if seasoned after straining, to be clarified by means of the raft. The result is a soup with clarity and good seasoning. Because a consommé simmers approximately 2 hours after the raft is formed, take care to slightly underseason the soup with salt so that, as reduction occurs, the soup does not become overseasoned.

Technique for Making a Consommé

1. Assemble mise en place.
2. Select a marmite, preferably one with a spigot, and mix all ingredients together in the pot with a whisk so everything is well disbursed.
3. Place the marmite on a burner on high heat and *stir constantly* with a wooden spoon until the soup is just about to simmer. Stirring the soup at this point is crucial to prevent burning. Because the heat from the burner is most intense on the bottom of the marmite, if the stirring motion stops, the solid ingredi-

ents, such as meat and vegetables, will settle and burn.

4. When the first, consistent, gentle bubbling occurs (as indicated by a simmer), stop stirring the soup and reduce heat. At this point, the heat in the soup has intensified enough so albumin begins to fully coagulate, gathering together the particles that cause cloudiness.

5. As the soup continues to softly simmer, the meat, vegetables, acid, seasonings, and impurities will begin to rise to the surface, thus forming the raft. The raft will begin to look like a circular loaf of meat floating on top of the soup. Notice that, by this point, the soup is already extremely clear.

6. Lower the heat enough to maintain the gentle simmering. The correct amount of simmering is that which allows the stock to bubble up through the raft for fortification but does not break it.

7. Monitor the consommé to maintain proper convection movement during the fortification process. Simmer the consommé for approximately 2 hours after the raft has formed, and, in the meantime, mise en place the garnish.

Straining Techniques for Consommé

1. When the consommé has simmered for 2 hours and is clarified and the flavor is fortified, then it is ready to be strained.

2. Mise en place a chinois mousseline lined with cheesecloth and place it over the vessel in which the consommé will be held. Set the marmite spigot over the chinois in preparation of straining.

3. Open the spigot and allow the consommé to drain in a thin stream from the marmite. When the pot is almost empty, with the exception of the raft, close the spigot. The consommé should be completely clear. If any particles are floating in the soup, clean the chinois mousseline, re-line it with a fresh piece of cheesecloth, and repeat the straining process. If the consommé is strained by laddling from the top, separate the raft and proceed as in #2 under Special Notes.

4. Remove any visible fat from the surface of the soup by chilling and removing the solid pieces of fat, or by gently wiping the surface of the hot soup with a clean towel or cheesecloth.

5. Heat the soup thoroughly before serving. Garniture should be prepared and held warm, separately from the consommé. When serving, place the hot garnish in the soup cup and top with consommé.

Special Notes

1. When straining a consommé, avoid picking up the marmite and dumping its contents, raft and all, into the chinois. All previous efforts made to achieve a solid raft and avoid particles in the consommé will be ruined. The clarification process will have to be repeated.

2. If a spigot is not available on the marmite, the consommé can still be made. The only step of the consommé process that will change is the straining process. There are a couple of alternatives for straining, and the secret in each one is to avoid breaking the raft as much as possible. As with the straining process explained earlier, mise en place a chinois mousseline lined with cheesecloth, remove the marmite containing the finished consommé from the stove, and choose one of the following methods:

   a. Using a paring knife, carefully cut a piece out of the raft large enough for a ladle to fit through. The raft will be firm, almost like the texture of a delicate meatloaf, and should cut easily. Using a slotted spoon, very gently remove the cut piece from the remaining raft and set aside. Ladle the consommé through the hole in the raft into the chinois lined with cheesecloth.

   b. Choose a clean, flat plate or lid slightly smaller than the diameter of the marmite and place it gently on top of the floating raft. Using two long-handled serving spoons, slowly press on the flat object, thus pushing the raft to the bottom and allowing the consommé to rise to the top of the pot. The more slowly the raft is lowered, the fewer particles will end up in the consommé. The soup can then be ladled through a chinois mousseline lined with cheesecloth.

3. Avoid holding consommé hot for many hours. Overreduction of the finished soup will cause the color and flavor to become overly concentrated. Consommé should have an amber hue so the garnish can clearly be seen in the bottom of the soup cup.
4. If the consommé is not clear after the raft is fully formed, then the liquid should be strained and cooled. Once chilled, the consommé process should be started again, beginning with the mise en place of the ingredients. Use the chilled stock saved from the previously failed consommé to make the new soup.

Thin Soups

Thin soups are generally simple to prepare and depend on the high quality of their ingredients for success. The steps for making thin soups are as follows:

1. Sauté, sweat, or boil the solid flavoring ingredients to the soup. Vegetables and meats are examples of ingredients that may be used to flavor and thus garnish the soup.
2. *Optional*: If a dry method of cookery was used in the first step, the pan may be deglazed with wine, stock, or other flavorful liquid to capture the flavor and particles that may be stuck to the pan.
3. Add simmering seasoned liquid, often stock, to the cooked flavoring ingredients, and return the entire contents of the pan to a simmer.
4. Continue to simmer the soup until the ingredients are cooked and the desired flavor is achieved.
5. *Dépouiller* the soup as it simmers.
6. Adjust seasoning before serving in a hot soup cup, and garnish with additional garnish if desired.

Puréed Soups

Puréed soups are easy to prepare, but they require a few more steps than when making thin soups:

1. Sauté, sweat, or boil the flavoring ingredients to the soup. Vegetables and meats are examples of ingredients that may be used to flavor and thus garnish the soup.
2. *Optional: Singer* is dusting the sautéed or sweated ingredients with a starch such as flour. Puréed soups get their thick consistency from both the puréed vegetables and a starch that helps the purée to remain suspended in the soup. If the pan is not dusted with a starch, a thickening agent may be added later in the cooking process. Dusting at this stage in the preparation may save work later on in the process.
3. If desired, deglaze the pan with wine, stock, or other liquid.
4. Add the simmering, seasoned liquid that will make up the bulk of the soup to the pan. Bring the entire contents back to a simmer and cook until the flavoring ingredients are very soft. Dépouiller as the soup simmers.
5. Purée the soup; two different methods may be used: (a) Insert the blade of a hand blender, often referred to as a magic wand, into the pot of soup and purée until no solid particles remain. Never submerge the motor below the surface of the soup or any other liquid. This type of equipment is available in the foodservice industry, and making puréed soups is simplified with them. *Or* (b) strain the solid ingredients from the soup liquid and purée in the bowl of a food processor until very smooth. Using a small amount of the soup liquid in the puréeing process may lead to acquiring a smoother consistency. When puréed, return to the pot of soup liquid.
6. Bring the puréed soup back to a simmer and adjust the consistency (thickness).
7. Add final seasonings to the soup and remove *dépouillage* if needed.
8. If a liaison finale is used, temper and add to the soup.
9. Serve hot in warmed soup bowls, garnishing as desired.

Garde-Manger

Garde-Manger

Garde-manger, *literally translated, means keeper of food to be eaten. Once used as a way of protecting food from rodents and preserving food prior to the invention of refrigeration, garde-manger now plays a very different role in the foodservice industry. Garde-manger includes the preparation and artistic presentation of cold food items such as appetizers, salads, pâtés, mousses, galantines, smoked meats, and seafood. It also includes ice and vegetable carvings. Most garde-manger departments exist in large hotels, fine restaurants, and some catering companies.*

Duties of the Chef Garde-Manger

The formal chef garde-manger supervises the creation of the following:

- Formal and informal parties (testimonials and standard parties)
- Buffets: light and full (wide assortments of items such as meats and salads)
- Cocktail parties (canapés and hors d'oeuvre)
- Appetizers (hot and cold items)
- Cold plates (assorted meats, salads, and molds)
- Cold sauces for salads (dressings)
- Displays (pièces montées)
- Fruit, ice, or vegetable carvings

Kitchen Equipment Needed by the Chef Garde-Manger

The properly equipped garde-manger requires special preparation surfaces and storage areas:

- Cold (refrigerated) surfaces where items are prepared
- Walk-in refrigerators and freezers
- Reach-in refrigerators
- Ice-cube maker
- Adequate stoves and ranges
- Smoker
- Air-conditioned room
- Food slicer
- Food processor
- Blender (small)

Tools Commonly Used by the Chef Garde-Manger

In addition to the tools that are commonly used by a working chef, the chef garde-manger should also have the following equipment:

- Aspic cutters (small, specially shaped metal designs to create motifs)
- Large cutters in different motifs
- Small individual molds (such as timbales, tartlets, darioles, and barquettes)
- Egg wedger and slicer
- Larding needles of different sizes
- Serrated knives
- Pastry bags and assorted pastry tubes
- Offset spatulas

Garde-Manger Brigade

The garde-manger brigade is composed of the following:

- *Boucher* (butcher): the person in charge of all meats except preserved meats
- *Poissonnier*: the person in charge of fish and shellfish cleaning, preparation, and storage

- *Buffettier:* the person in charge of the buffet
- *Hors d'oeuvrier:* the person in charge of hors d'oeuvre
- *Charcutier:* the person in charge of sausage and smoked items
- *Commis:* the apprentice

Menu Planning for Parties and Garde-Manger Functions

Menu planning has four main aspects: gastronomic, economic, practical, and language.

Gastronomic Aspects

The menu should be planned as a whole meal, rather than a succession of independent, unrelated courses. This is achieved by avoiding repetition of ingredients and color and texture.

Ingredients

A wide variety of ingredients will enhance the overall menu presentation. For example, if a menu begins with a grapefruit cocktail, then it should not end with a fruit salad. If a menu begins with a pâté and toast, then it would be wrong to finish the meal with canapés Diane. No major ingredient used in a previous course should be used as a garnish. For example, if a mushroom soup is featured, then mushrooms should not be used as a garnish for a subsequent dish of grilled meat.

Color and Texture

Contrasts are important. There should be no fewer than three different contrasting colors in the presentation of a meal. In addition, there should be a variety of textures throughout the courses in a menu. For example, after a consommé, sole bonne femme, or spaghetti Bolognese, the guest should be presented with something crisp and crunchy; a crème caramel, while not being totally unacceptable, would be much less welcome than a firm apple with cheese biscuits.

Economic Aspects

The menu needs to be costed as it is being planned, and considerable skill is often needed to meet both gastronomic and economic criteria. Economy is another reason for avoiding too many elaborate dishes because time costs money.

Practical Aspects

When planning a function, available equipment, skill level of the staff, and type of service must all be considered. The following are common rules for planning a function:

- Carefully consider the people for whom the party is to be catered. Various religions and ethnic choices should be considered.
- Do not prepare dishes that have not been produced before without proper thought and testing prior to the event.
- Plan a menu with food items of varying labor intensity. There should be at least two dishes with no final preparation stages before service to allow adequate timing.
- Avoid serving a totally cold menu, regardless of the season.

Language

Language and terminology used in writing menus should be understandable by the people for whom it is intended. When preparing a French classical menu for a group of Americans, the food item should be in the original language and the descriptive copy should be in English. For example:

Terrine de la Maison The Terrine of the House is a slice of light, savory pork, onions, and parsley pâté, served chilled with cranberry compote.

Salads

Originally, the salad course was made of green leaves mixed with a dressing and served after the main course to cleanse the palate. A vinaigrette was the most popular dressing. Presently, salad is a very loose term referring to a mixture or combination of ingredients. Some of the food used includes items such as fish, vegetables, meat, and leafy greens.

Components of Salads

A salad is made of four components: foundation, body, garnish, and dressing.

Foundation

In most cases, the foundation of a salad consists of leafy greens such as romaine, Bibb, Boston, radicchio, or iceberg lettuce. These may be used as whole leaves or cut into a chiffonade. Occasionally, other vegetables may be used, such as a julienne of red pepper or brunoise of red onion.

Body

The body is the main component of a salad. The main element of the body usually supplies the identity and sometimes the name. For example, a garden salad will be composed of garden-fresh vegetables. A protein salad will contain protein, such as meat, fish, or lentils. The body of the salad should be attractively presented to minimize the need for extensive garnishing.

Garnish

The garnish gives aesthetic quality to the salad and should be edible, colorful, and the same temperature as the salad. The garnish should not overpower the presentation of the salad. In some cases, the makeup of a salad—for example, fruit salad—will require no garnish at all.

Dressing

The dressing should be added to the salad just before service time to give it a unique flavor. In most cases, delicate greens—cos or radicchio, for example—should be crowned with a light dressing such as a vinaigrette. Fruit salads can be topped with sweet dressings like Chantilly cream, and vegetables should be accompanied by a tart dressing.

Types of Salads

Although the green salad is the most recognized type, a great variety of salads can be featured on menus.

- *Green:* The main ingredient of a green salad is one or more types of green, leafy vegetables.
- *Vegetable:* The main ingredient of a vegetable salad is one or more types of nonleafy green vegetables that are usually served raw but are sometimes lightly blanched. These salads are commonly marinated in vinaigrettes.
- *Fruit:* The main ingredient of the fruit salad is fruit that is raw, canned, or cooked. The fruit salad can be dressed in a variety of ways.
- *Cooked:* The main ingredient of the cooked salad is any cooked food product. Often referred to as protein or bound salad, examples of main ingredients may include but are not limited to chicken, tuna, egg, turkey, salmon, pasta, or potatoes. A cooked salad is commonly bound with a mayonnaise-based dressing.
- *Gelatin:* A gelatin salad is made of food products that are set in a flavored gelatin. The classical garde-manger would commonly serve these as salads. An example would be tomatoes in aspic. A common gela-

tin salad prepared in American households is fruit set in Jello.

- *Combination:* The combination salad is a mix of two or more types of salad listed above. Examples of a combination salad include Chicken Caesar Salad, Salade Nicoise, Salmon Pasta Salad with Herbs, and Waldorf Salad.

Salad as a Variety of Courses

Today, salad can be served in different courses and is classified as appetizers, main course, accompaniment, salad course, or dessert

Appetizer

As an appetizer, a salad is generally a combination of fish, blanched vegetables, or meat, and is dressed with a vinaigrette or mayonnaise. A shrimp salad is an example of an appetizer. The appetizer salad is designed to whet the appetite.

Main Course

Cooked and combination salads are well suited as a main course.

Accompaniment

Salads as an accompaniment of a main course complement the food being served and should be relatively light bodied. For example, Parisienne salad complements cold poached salmon nicely.

Salad Course

Depending on the type of service, the salad course may be served either before or after the main course. For instance, in American service the salad is served before the entrée, while in French service the salad is served after the entrée. Green salads are the most popular type, although a vegetable or fruit salad is also appropriate.

Dessert

Fruit salads are some of the most popular salads served for dessert. They may contain liqueurs, cream, or nuts.

Salad Dressings

Following are some of the most common types of dressings:

- *Vinaigrette:* The basic vinaigrette dressing consists of three parts oil and one part vinegar. Examples include Italian or French vinaigrette.
- *Fatty:* Mayonnaise and dairy-based dressings are most commonly served with green, fruit, and cooked salads. French, Thousand Island, Ranch, Blue Cheese, and Creamy Italian are examples of fatty dressings.
- *Cooked:* Cooked dressings contain a cooked element with the addition of a vinaigrette. Examples include hot bacon dressing and hot Dijon mustard dressing.
- *Fruit:* Fruit dressings use fruit, often puréed, and are flavored according to what they accompany. These dressings may by sweet, tart, or piquante.

Hors d'Oeuvre

Hors d'oeuvre are small, bite-sized appetizers usually served before a meal. Cold hors d'oeuvre are usually served before soup, while hot hors d'oeuvre are served either in lieu of or following the soup. It is common to serve cold hors d'oeuvre for lunch and hot hors d'oeuvre for dinner. The three classifications of hors d'oeuvre are: a single food, hors d'oeuvre varies, or a finger food.

A Single Food

Served before the main course to the seated customer, the single-food hors d'oeuvre usually consists of one garnished item. The hors d'oeuvre may be served hot or cold on a plate, in a coupe, or in another appropriate dish. Examples include seafood cocktail, pâté, galantine, frog legs, mussels marinière, and salade composée.

Hors d'Oeuvre Varies

Served before the main meal, hors d'oeuvre varies are an assortment of light, tasty items that can be presented plated, on a platter, or on a guéridon. For plated hors d'oeuvre varies, the assortment is preplated and garnished for each guest. Seafood, charcuterie, and antipasto are examples. Hors d'oeuvre varies on a platter are especially made for ravier dishes. *Ravier dishes* are small glass or crystal dishes that hold eight small portions of each item. Hors d'oeuvre varies on a guéridon are served in larger raviers, bowls, or platters. The cart can be prepared in the kitchen before service and then left in the dining room. The guéridon may be decorated with napkin folds and a centerpiece. The customer selects directly from the guéridon.

Ravier Dishes for the Guéridon Cart

Ravier dishes may contain the following items:

- Shrimp salad, Marie-Rose sauce on chiffonade, or feather decoration with tomato ketchup
- Prosciutto ham with figs or melon boats
- Melon cocktail with port wine
- Tomato salad, thin slices of brunoise shallots, vinaigrette dressing, and chopped parsley
- Pâté sliced with garniture, Cumberland sauce, or aspic
- Avocado, stuffed with shrimp salad and vinaigrette
- Waldorf salad with romaine
- Smoked bay scallops with citrus sauce
- Cherry tomatoes stuffed with lobster mousse
- Smoked pork or duck garni
- Cucumber salad, sour cream, and dill sauce
- Smoked salmon: thin slices enveloping shrimp Marie-Rose, simple lemon, olive, and parsley garnish
- Smoked salmon sliced with capers, horseradish sauce, onion rings, parsley, and lemon

- Gravlax served with toast points and dill syrup
- Salade niçoise: fresh seared tuna loin, olives, potatoes, green beans, tomato, and eggs
- Mousse, either ham or salmon, stuffed in barquettes, tartlets, or artichoke bottoms
- Smoked lamb-rosemary sausage with peach salsa

A Finger Food

Finger foods are bite-sized hot or cold hors d'oeuvre that are served at cocktail parties or prior to a meal. Hot and cold hors d'oeuvre should be presented on separate platters. The platters can be arranged on a table or passed by the serving staff. Chicken teriyaki, spanikopita, clams casino, and stuffed mushrooms are some hot finger hors d'oeuvre. Examples of cold finger hors d'oeuvre are deviled eggs, cheese balls, canapés, crudités, shrimp, barquettes, and tartlets.

Hot Hors d'Oeuvre
Bacon-Wrapped Hors d'Oeuvre

Bacon-wrapped hors d'oeuvre are very popular and may be made with fish, seafood, meat, or blanched vegetables. They are broiled or pan fried. Variations include chicken livers, scallops, shrimp, oysters, and cubed tenderloin.

Barquettes or Tartlets

Barquettes and *tartlets* are made from a savory pie crust or short dough in tartlet or barquette molds and filled just before serving.

Bouchées and Vol-au-Vent

Bouchées and *vol-au-vent* are shells made from puff pastry that are filled in numerous ways. They are baked ahead of time, cooled, and filled just before serving so the crust remains crisp. The various sizes of these hot hors d'oeuvre include:

- *Bouchette* is a smaller bouchée, about 1 to 1½ inches in diameter, and always served as a finger food. The term *bouchées* means "mouthful."
- *Bouchée* is 1½ to 2 inches in diameter and is usually served as an appetizer eaten with a fork and knife.
- *Vol-au-vent* (flying in the wind) may be made into various shapes and sizes and are usually a minimum of 4 inches in diameter. Vol-au-vent may be served as a plated appetizer or as an entrée. As an entrée, vol-au-vent can serve one, four, or eight people.

If the vol-au-vent is filled with a salpicon before cooking, it can be served tableside straight from the oven. Cut the top off and spoon the salpicon onto the plates. When the filling is served to more than one guest, the pastry case can be equally divided.

If the vol-au-vent is blind-baked, it may be stored at room temperature for a few days before using. To serve, cut off the top and remove the filler. Heat in the oven for a few minutes, then remove it, place it on a silver platter or plate, and fill it with a hot salpicon.

The following fillings may be used to fill bouchées or vol-au-vents:

1. *Ragoût:* A thick, well-seasoned stew made of meat, poultry, or fish, and may or may not contain vegetables.
2. *Creamed chicken and mushrooms.*
3. *Fricassée:* A thick, chunky, light-colored stew often flavored with wine
4. *Cheese fondue:* Melted cheese (usually of Swiss origin) that is combined with wine and seasonings.
5. *Salpicons:* One or more ingredients cut in fine dice or brunoise and bound with sauce. Salpicons are usually served hot, but may also be served cold. Cold salpicons are bound with mayonnaise or a vinaigrette. Examples of hot salpicons, are
   a. *Salpicon à l'américaine:* Diced lobster or langoustino flesh bound with American sauce.
   b. *Salpicon à la Saint-Hubert:* Finely diced game meat bound with reduced demi-glace made with game fumet of the same flavor.
   c. *Salpicon à la marinière:* Mussels bound with a white wine sauce.
   d. *Salpicon de légumes à la crème:* Vegetable brunoise of artichoke hearts, asparagus, or eggplant bound with a béchamel sauce.

Examples of cold salpicons are listed on page 212.

Spanakopita

Spanakopita is phyllo dough stuffed with spinach, feta cheese, dill, and onion. It is baked and served hot.

Blinis

Blinis are small buckwheat pancakes made from a yeast batter and served hot, usually with caviar.

Cheese Balls

Cheese balls are a seasoned mixture of grated cheeses bound with a thick cream sauce. Shaped into spheres and breaded, cheese balls are then fried and served hot with a dipping sauce.

Croissant Miniatures

Croissant miniatures are made of vienna dough filled with a variety of stuffings, and baked. They are always served hot. Variations include

- Black forest ham with Gruyère cheese and Dijon mustard
- Ragoût of wild mushrooms and fine herbs
- Grilled eggplant with Niçoise olives and sun dried tomato

Croûtes

Croûtes are thick, hollowed-out pieces of toasted bread or rolls that are filled with a variety of stuffings and baked. They are served hot. Shrimp en croûte is an example.

Croquettes

Croquettes are made of cooked meats, fish, or vegetables that are diced very fine and mixed with a thick cream sauce and egg yolks. Formed into a variety of shapes that are breaded and fried, croquettes are often served hot with dipping sauces. Sweet potato croquettes served with a jalapeño-onion relish are a fine example.

Meatballs

Meatballs are made from veal, beef, lamb, pork, or any combination of meats. Seasonings such as curry, paprika, garlic, marjoram, oregano, and chili powder can be used. Meatballs may be baked or fried and served hot with a cold or hot dipping sauce. For example, cilantro-curry chicken served with a cucumber yogurt sauce is flavorful.

Hot Hors d'Oeuvre Suggestions

- Toasted Virginia ham finger sandwiches
- Clams casino
- Oysters Rockefeller
- Oysters Lincoln (lobster sauce gratinée)
- Stuffed mushroom caps
- Rumaki
- Frito misto (breaded fried vegetables with garlic butter)
- Phyllo bundles with hot salpicon
- Quiche
- Souvlaki
- Coconut shrimp
- Cantonese egg rolls
- Spring rolls
- Frog legs
- Small stuffed cabbage
- Assorted croquettes
- Chicken wings, barbecued
- Cheese fritters
- Asparagus wrapped in ham, breaded, and fried
- Fried mushrooms
- Fritters with Madeira
- Fried oysters
- Clams bourguignonne, garlic butter, and bread
- Crabmeat fritters
- Clam cakes
- Mini pizza

- Small coulibiac of salmon
- Barbecued spareribs
- Buffalo chicken wings
- Goujons of sole Orly
- Batter-fried chicken fillets with duck sauce
- Sautéed shrimp and garlic butter
- Crêpes with crab
- Mussels marinière or bourguignonne
- Snails in mushroom caps ramekin
- Fried ravioli

Cold Hors d'Oeuvre

Crudités

Crudités are inexpensive appetizers consisting of fresh raw vegetables usually served with a dip. The most common vegetables used are carrots, celery, broccoli, cauliflower, cherry tomatoes, and green peppers. Olives and pickled vegetables can be added for richness and variety. Crudités are very popular in the United States because they are low in calories and high in vitamin content.

To maintain freshness, keep the prepared vegetables in ice water. If the vegetables are to be placed immediately on the platter, cover or wrap with a wet cloth until service. Select a colorful variety of vegetables, cut into bite-sized pieces, and arrange in an attractive presentation.

Caviar

Caviar comes from sturgeon, a fish that lives in the Caspian Sea. About 98 percent of all real caviar harvested in the world comes from the Caspian Sea. Of the 24 species of sturgeon, only 3 are selected for the harvesting of caviar. The sturgeon can weigh up to 2,000 pounds, and 10 to 12 percent of their body weight consists of eggs, which are extracted from the white stomach of the female. Some sturgeon can hold up to 4 million eggs in the womb. A sieve is used to separate the eggs from the membrane that holds them together. The eggs are then lightly salted. Salt is a vital ingredient to preserve the caviar and to extract flavor. The word *malossol* on the label does not describe the type of caviar, but rather the fact that the roe is lightly salted.

Species of Sturgeon Producing Caviar

The female sturgeon produces eggs, or roe, the color of which varies from grey to hazelnut. The three major species of sturgeon that are harvested for caviar are

- *Beluga,* the largest species. The female weighs an average of 800 to 2,000 pounds. Her size ranges from 6½ to 26 feet. It takes nearly 20 years for the female to mature and to be able to reproduce. The eggs are more or less dark grey, heavy, well separated, and firm.
- *Ossetra,* a medium-sized species. The female weighs an average of 400 to 700 pounds. Her size ranges from 4 to 7 feet. It takes nearly 13 years for the female to mature and to be able to reproduce. The eggs are a golden yellow to brown color and have more even grains that are more oily. The flavor of ossetra is considered by many to be the best caviar, some saying it has almost a fruity taste.
- *Sevruga,* the smallest of the small-sized species, characterized by its long, pointed muzzle. The female weighs an average of 80 to 120 pounds. Her size ranges from 3 to 5 feet. It takes about seven years for the female to mature and to be able to reproduce. The eggs are medium sized, with varying shades of grey ranging from light to dark.

A special preparation of these three types of caviar is called *pressed caviar,* which is made from the ripest eggs, which are pressed into a black paste, giving it a concentrated taste. Pressed caviar characteristically has a strong, oily taste, and some connoisseurs consider it too salty. One pound of pressed caviar is equivalent to four pounds of fresh.

Other Fish

Other fish that produce caviar include salmon, whitefish, and lumpfish. The caviar from these fish is relatively inexpensive and of lesser quality than roe from sturgeon. The color of the salmon roe is orange; the whitefish is yellow; and the lumpfish is translucent, colored black or red.

Rules of Service for Caviar

- Refrigerate at a temperature between 32° and 36° F; never freeze.
- Ensure that caviar is consumed within 24 hours of opening the container.
- Serve caviar in its own jar on a bed of crushed ice.
- Do not present caviar in direct contact with silver, as the reaction with the silver destroys the flavor of the caviar.
- Caviar can be placed on tortoise shell, ivory, mother of pearl, and gold without detriment to the quality of its flavor. A gold serving spoon is the most appropriate flatware to accompany caviar service.
- Present caviar using attractive plates, bowls, and napkins. The lid from the caviar tin or jar should accompany the presentation to show authenticity of product.
- Do not use chopped eggs, herbs, onion, or lemon for garnish, as these negatively affect the flavor of the caviar. Although many of these ingredients are classical garnishes, recent research has shown their negative effects on maximizing the flavor of the caviar.
- Caviar goes well with lightly buttered toast, which reveals its flavor well.
- Blinis served hot with crème fraîche or sour cream is a perfect complement to fresh caviar.
- Remove pressed caviar from refrigeration 1 to 2 hours before serving to improve flavor.
- The suggested serving portion is 50 grams per person.
- Pressed caviar is best served with brut Champagne or great Russian vodka, such as Moskovskaya or Stolichnaya.

Sandwiches

According to the history of gastronomy, sandwiches were named after John Montagu, the fourth Earl of Sandwich. A compulsive gambler who refused to leave the tables while gambling, he had the habit of requesting sliced meats placed between two slices of bread. It was such a practical concept that it immediately became popular throughout England and quickly spread to other parts of the world.

There are three types of sandwiches: open sandwiches; covered, or club, sandwiches; and canapés.

- *Open sandwiches* are comprised of one slice of bread, either plain or toasted, with a thin coat of compound butter or spread, plus the appropriate toppings and garniture. Open sandwiches can be square, rectangular, oval, round, or triangular.
- *Covered, or club sandwiches* consist of two slices of bread or toast, plus the appropriate coating and topping. A triple-decker sandwich contains three slices of bread or toast, the coatings, and toppings. The covered, or club, sandwich is usually square or triangular.
- *Canapés* are small, bite-sized open sandwiches, with assorted toppings and artistic garnishes.

Canapés

The word *canapé* means sofa. The sofa is a platform with cushions to lay and rest on. The canapés platform is usually a crouton, a crustless piece of bread cut into geometric shapes that are toasted or fried. Flavored butter or spreads are applied to the platform to hold a topping as well as to prevent the base from becoming soggy. For salami or other spicy meats, a mustard-flavored butter should be used. Classical canapés are usually covered with a thin layer of aspic to prevent drying or discoloration.

Canapés are light and generally used for cocktail parties or for predinner gatherings for the purpose of stimulating the appetite. Canapés are generally served cold. The average allowance for a function is 8 to 10 canapés per hour per person.

Parts of a Canapé

Base The base of a canapé may be made of bread, such as whole wheat, rye, or pumpernickel. The bread is usually toasted to make croutons by baking in an oven at 375° F for three to five minutes or until crisp and golden brown. The croutons should be cooled and bagged and set at room temperature for future use.

Crackers or firm vegetables may also be used. The most common shapes for the base are rounds, rectangles, right

Figure 12–1 Common canapé shapes

triangles, squares, ovals, and isosceles triangles (see Figure 12–1).

Spread. The spread is a seasoned mixture consisting of mayonnaise, cream cheese, butter compounds, or sour cream. The spread is used for three main reasons:

- In the case of croutons or crackers, to keep the base from becoming soggy.
- To enhance flavor.
- To help secure food product onto the base.

Suggestions for plain mixture spreads include mayonnaise, cream cheese, compound butter, and sour cream.

Liner (optional). The liner is most commonly made with leafy vegetables. Lettuce adds an attractive background for canapés with bland color. The liner, providing it is well dried, will provide a barrier between the moisture in the nourishing element and the base.

Nourishing Element The nourishing element occurs in the largest proportion compared to all other ingredients and contributes flavor, texture, color, and nutrients. It should be the main part of the canapé, yet still bite sized. It should be simple, light, and palatable. Fish, meat, cheese, salads, vegetables, or fruits are examples of nourishing elements.

Canapé Garnishes. The *garnish* is a decorative, edible accompaniment to the canapé. Garnishes may be used to add color, flavor, and texture. Not all canapés will require garnishes. Creating garnishes can become expensive because of the ingredients used or the labor required to make them. Some inexpensive garnishes are

- Chopped parsley
- Lemon zest
- Orange zest
- Sprigs of parsley or watercress
- Black olives, slices, rings, or quarters
- Pimientos, strips or bows diced
- Red onions, sliced
- Capers
- Butter compound, piped through a star or rose tube using a pastry bag
- Carrots, cooked
- Peas

Examples of Canapés

- *Cheese crab canapé:* Combine minced crab, grated sharp cheese, and béchamel sauce. Chill several hours. Place on small toasted croutons, sprinkle with grated cheese, and brown under a salamander.
- *Pâté de foie gras:* Spread rectangular croutons with pâté de foie gras. Garnish with gherkins.
- *Chicken canapé:* Mix cooked, cooled chicken with mayonnaise, salt, pepper, and lemon juice. Spread mixture on croûton; garnish with slivered almonds and sliced red grapes.
- *Watercress canapé:* Spread croûton with garlic butter. Place a thin slice of cucumber on the croûton. Top with watercress.

Other Cold Hors d'Oeuvre Suggestions

- Gravlax
- Watercress pinwheel roll (bread and cream cheese)
- Ham or salmon mousse pinwheel roll
- Melon pieces with prosciutto
- Nim chow
- Shrimp on ice
- Crab claws on ice
- Caviar with garnishes.
- Oysters and clams
- Assorted sushi or sashimi

- Bouchettes (puff paste filled with cream cheese, chives, and scallions)
- Bouchettes with pastry roquefort, salmon mousse, or liver pâté
- Hearts of palm slices and salmon mousse
- Tuna tartare on toast with wasabi
- Steak tartare on toast
- Seared gravlax with dill syrup on pumpernickel
- Marinated artichoke hearts stuffed with tapenade
- Barquettes or tartlets with smoked bluefish, cream cheese, and horseradish
- Barquettes or tartlets with mousse en gelée
- Chicken salad bound with curry and mayonnaise
- Seafood salad bound with dill vinaigrette

Zakuski

Zakuski, known as canapés à la russe, are made up of specified ingredients. Zakuski are essentially dinner hors d'oeuvre that may be served hot or cold and are larger than the average canapé. Sometimes called a meal before a meal, this type of canapé originated in Russia during the 17th and 18th centuries. An example of zakuski is toast covered with smoked fish and finished with a thin gelée or aspic.

Forcemeats

Forcemeats are ground or finely chopped, puréed seasoned meats, poultry, fish, vegetables, or fruit. The following French terms are used when referring to forcemeats:

- *Farce:* Stuffing or forcemeat
- *Farci:* Stuffed
- *Farcir:* To stuff

Elements of Forcemeats

Forcemeats are made up of four basic elements: nourishing elements, fats, binders, and seasonings.

Nourishing elements occur in the largest proportion compared to all other ingredients in forcemeats and contribute flavor, texture, color, and nutrients. Common nourishing ingredients include meat, fish, poultry, fruit, or vegetables.

Fats are used in forcemeats to improve moisture and enrich flavor. Butter, cream and natural animal fats such as pork fat, egg yolk and jowl fat are commonly used.

Binders are added for shape and smoothness. They include panadas, egg whites, gelatin, and velouté.

Seasonings help to heighten flavor; they vary according to the recipe.

Types of Basic Forcemeats

Straight Method

In the *straight-method forcemeat*, the meats and fat are cut into small pieces and are further processed through curing or seasoning before being ground, sieved, and bound.

Country Style

The *country-style forcemeat* usually denotes a coarse ground mixture of pork and pork fat with varying percentages of liver and other garnishing ingredients.

Gratin Method

The *gratin method* indicates that a portion of the main flavoring element, usually liver, has been sautéed and chilled before being ground and used. The gratin usually does not exceed 25 percent of the total farce weight.

Mousseline

The *mousseline* is a fine forcemeat with cream added. It is used to make mousses and quenelles.

Godiveau

Godiveau is made with veal and suet, and is used primarily to make pâtés and galantines.

Forcemeat Derivatives

Eight derivatives are produced from the five types of basic forcemeats. The differences in the derivatives are sometimes in their respective molds or cooking and serving methods.

Pâté

A *pâté* is a smooth or coarse forcemeat mixture usually enclosed in a thin layer of fat or plastic wrap.

Cooking vessel	Metal, cast iron, ceramic, or earthenware mold.
Cooking method	Cooked in an oven in a hot water bath. Allowed to cool in the mold overnight.
Uses	Served as a cold appetizer or as a buffet item.

Pâté en Croûte

Pâté en croûte uses the same forcemeat mixture as pâtés. However, instead of being encased in a layer of fat, the pâté is placed in pastry dough that lines the metal mold. When cooked and cooled, the pâté en croûte is carefully removed from the mold and filled with flavored aspic.

Cooking vessel	Metal mold whose sides are detractable by removing pins. A similar design to a spring-form pan, this makes it easier to remove the cooked pâté en croûte from the mold without breaking.
Cooking method	Cooked in a dry, hot oven. Allowed to cool in the mold overnight.
Uses	Sliced, garnished, and served as a cold appetizer or as a buffet item.

Terrine

A *terrine* is a smooth or coarse forcemeat mixture. The mold may be lined with a thin layer of fat or plastic wrap.

Cooking vessel	Earthenware or ceramic dish or mold.
Cooking method	Cooked in an oven in a hot water bath. Allowed to cool in the mold overnight.

Uses	*Served cold as an appetizer.*
Special note	Natural shrinkage occurs during cooking, but, if overcooked, the terrine will shrink excessively, and a dry, rubbery product will result. If the product is still dry when cooked to the correct internal temperature, more fat should be added to the recipe. If too much shrinkage occurs when the terrine is cooked correctly, the amount of fat in the recipe should be decreased.

Galantine

A *galantine* is made from poultry or game that has been boned and stuffed. The entire galantine may then be wrapped in the skin, before enclosing it in plastic wrap or cheesecloth and tying the ends with twine.

Cooking vessel	Any pan filled with enough seasoned cooking liquid to cover galantine.
Cooking method	Poached. Allowed to cool in cooking liquid overnight.
Uses	Slice, garnish, and serve as a cold appetizer, entrée, or buffet item.

Ballottine

Originally a meat item, a *ballottine* may also be made with poultry or fish. Its preparation is the same as a galantine, except a ballottine must be wrapped in the skin before it is enclosed in cheesecloth tied at the ends. It is braised and served hot as an entrée or cold as an appetizer.

Cooking vessel	Any braising pan filled with enough cooking liquid to cover the ballottine at least by two-thirds.
Cooking method	Braised. If served hot, slice and plate as soon as it is done cooking. If served cold, allow ballottine to cool in cooking liquid overnight before serving.
Uses	Slice, garnish, and serve as either a hot entrée or cold appetizer.

Quenelle

A *quenelle* is a fine forcemeat mixture in a three-sided football shape that is formed by using two spoons.

Cooking vessel	Any pan filled with enough seasoned cooking liquid to cover the quenelle completely.
Cooking method	Poached. If served hot, plate as soon as it is done cooking. If served cold, allow quenelle to cool in cooking liquid thoroughly before serving.
Uses	Plate and garnish as either a hot or a cold appetizer, entrée, or garnish (as for a soup).

Mousse

A *mousse* differs from a pâté in that a mousse is always a very fine, sieved mixture. The nourishing element should be foods that have a relatively small amount of connective tissue, such as poultry, fish, and vegetables. This fine mixture also has semiwhipped cream or egg whites that are incorporated while the mixture is submerged in an ice bath. There are two types of mousse: raw mousse and cooked mousse.

Raw Mousse

A *raw mousse* is made with a finely ground, raw, nourishing element that is bound with a panada or egg whites. Egg yolks, cream, butter, or animal fat may be used as the fat element. The raw mousse may be shaped in plastic wrap or poured into a container such as a timbale before cooking.

Cooking vessel	If mousse is in a container such as a timbale, it should be cooked in the oven in a hot water bath. If it is shaped and wrapped in plastic wrap, the mousse may be poached in a pan on the stove top.
Cooking method	Baked or poached. If served hot, plate and garnish immediately. If served cold, cool in cooking liquid overnight before serving.

Uses	Plate and garnish as either a hot or a cold appetizer or entrée.

Cooked Mousse

A cooked mousse is prepared with a nourishing element that is cooked and cooled before making the mousse. Therefore, a cooked mousse is a good way to use leftovers. Gelatin, aspic, or velouté may be used as the binding element, and cream is generally the fat.

Cooking vessel	Whatever is initially needed to cook the nourishing element.
Cooking method	Except for the initial cooking of the nourishing element, no cooking is needed for the final mousse.
Uses	A cooked mousse is always served cold as an appetizer or an entrée.

Sausage

Sausage is a forcemeat enclosed in a natural or synthetic casing. Sausages may be smoke-cured, dried, or cooked.

Note: All forcemeats should be cooked to an internal temperature of 165° F.

Guidelines

Keeping all the elements cold is essential when working with forcemeats. Take the following precautions in order to work in a sanitary manner and to prevent curdling of the food product:

- Work in a cold room.
- Use cold food products.
- Use clean, cold utensils.
- Avoid overworking the food.
- Work over an ice bath.
- Wash hands frequently.

Assembling Forcemeats

When assembling forcemeats, follow the steps below:

- Pass the meat through a grinder, using a large or medium grinder plate.
- Pass the meat through the grinder a second time using a smaller grinder plate.
- Add fat during the second grind.
- If a finer forcemeat is needed, transfer the ground mixture to a Robot coupe or VCM and process to the desired consistency.
- Mix by hand and add seasonings, random garnish (nuts, olive, shrimp), and the binder. Finally, add cream.

Table 12–1 on page 216 gives approximate proportions of classical forcemeat ingredients in various types of farce.

Panadas

Panadas are used in forcemeats to

- Bind.
- Tenderize.
- Give a smooth texture.
- Add moisture.
- Produce a higher yield.

Panadas should be neutral in color and flavor. They are composed of two basic elements: starch (flour, potato, rice, or bread) and liquid (water, stock, or milk). All panadas, except for the potato panada, are cooled completely before they are added to forcemeats.

The five basic kinds of panadas are

Bread	Crustless bread is added to boiling milk and cooked until all the liquid is absorbed. It is used in meat loaf, fish, forcemeats, and hamburger.
Flour	Flour is added to boiling water and butter, or stock and butter, and is cooked a few minutes to increase the smoothness of the mixture. It is used in quenelles.
Potato	Potatoes are cooked and mashed, and milk is added to create a smooth consistency. When the panada is still warm, add it to the forcemeat. It is used in white meat quenelles.
Rice	Cook short-grain or pudding rice in white stock; purée. It is used in various forcemeats.
Frangipane	Frangipane is a flour panada with the addition of egg yolks. It is used in chicken or fish forcemeats.

Table 12–1 Approximate Proportions of Classical Forcemeat Ingredients

Type of Farce	Nutritional Element	Fat	Binder	Seasoning
Any meat farce	2 parts any meat	1 part fat	1 to 2 eggs per pound	Appropriate pâté spice
	1 part lean meat, 1 part fatty meat	Optional	1 to 2 eggs per pound	Appropriate pâté spice
	3 parts lean meat	1 part fat	1 to 2 eggs per pound	Appropriate pâté spice
Pork or sausage farce	1 part lean pork	1 part pork fat	1 to 2 eggs per pound	Appropriate pâté spice
Pork and veal farce	1 part lean pork, 1 part lean veal	2 parts pork fat	1 to 2 eggs per pound	Appropriate pâté spice
Poultry farce	1 part poultry, 1 part lean veal, 1 part lean pork, 1 part liver (optional)	2 parts pork fat	1 to 2 eggs per pound	Appropriate pâté spice
Game farce	2 parts lean game, 1 part lean pork	2 parts pork fat	1 to 2 eggs per pound	Appropriate pâté spice
	2 parts lean game and pork combination	1 part pork fat	1 to 2 eggs per pound	Appropriate pâté spice
Gratin farce	Add sautéed, sieved liver to enrich a meat farce. The amount of the prepared liver added to the meat farce should not be greater than one-quarter of the farce weight.			
Mousseline	2¼ lb. meat or fish purée	2½ to 3 cups heavy cream	4 egg whites	As needed
	1 lb. fish meat	5 ozs. heavy cream	½ lb. (or less) panada *and* 2 to 3 egg whites	As needed
Cold mousseline	4 parts cooked meat or fish	¾ parts heavy cream	1 part melted aspic	As needed
Mousse		¾ parts unsalted butter	1½ parts velouté	
Vegetable mousseline	1½ to 2 pounds vegetable	1 cup heavy cream	3 to 4 eggs and 2 tablespoons unflavored gelatin	As needed
Farce with panada	2 parts meat or fish farce	¼ part heavy cream (optional)	1 part panada (or less)	Appropriate pâté spice

Food Preservation

Preserving food dates back to the early ages of humankind. Hunting and, later, gathering were the primary means of attaining food. Because early humans did not fully understand the need for food preservation, it was often spoiled when consumed. By chance, they discovered that when winter approached and animal meat froze, it was preserved for longer periods. As time went on, drying and smoking processes were introduced as a way of preserving meat. Primary preserving methods continued today in garde-manger include curing, brining, salting, marinating, and smoking.

Preserving Techniques

Curing

A food product is *cured* by preserving it either by immersing it in a brine (salt solution) or by drying it in granular salt. Table 12–2 lists various types of salt used for preserving.

Brining

A *brine* is a solution of sea salt, water, spices, aromatics, sugar, or honey. It preserves and gives flavor to products such as meat, fish, poultry, game, and some vegetables. The ingredients are combined and brought to a boil to dissolve the salt and sugar, and then cooled. The food product is then immersed into the cold brine and refrigerated.

Some common examples of brined meats include bacon, tongue, brisket, corned beef, and pastrami. If the cut of meat is large, it may be perforated with a sharp knife to shorten the time it takes the brine to reach the center.

Following are the steps involved in the modern curing method of brining:

1. Soak the food product, fully immersed, in the brine for the required time (2 to 48 hours).
2. Wash the food product.
3. Cook (usually boil, bake, or poach) the food product or choose maturation, of which there are two types:
   a. *Drying* at 60° to 70° F (e.g., bacon, pastrami)
   b. *Smoking:* cold at 50° to 95° F (1 hour to 4 days) or hot at 140° F or above (for the desired amount of time).

The time-consuming brining process may be shortened using one of three other methods:

- Artery pumping (minimum time). This method requires filling an artery in the meat with the curing solution. This allows complete distribution of the cure throughout the meat.
- Spray pumping (24 hours). The curing solution is injected directly into the cut of meat by inserting a hand-held device into the meat and air spraying the pressurized solution into the meat.
- Pickle injector (instantaneous commercial process). This is the fastest method used to shorten curing

Table 12–2 Types of Salt Available for Preserving

Type of Salt	Basic Characteristics	Description
Table salt	Fine-grained and refined	• Has additives to make it free-flowing • Mainly used in cooking and as a table condiment
Iodized salt	Fine-grained and refined	• Table salt with added iodine (sodium iodide) • Important in areas that lack natural iodine • Important preventative for hypothyroidism
Kosher salt	Coarse-grained	• Additive free • Used in preparation of meat by religious Jews • Used by gourmet cooks who prefer its texture and flavor
Sea salt	Can be purchased as fine-grained or larger crystals	• Used widely through the ages • Made from evaporating sea water, a costly process
Pickling salt	Fine-grained	• Used to make brines for pickles, sauerkraut, pearl onions, pickled pigs feet, etc. • Contains no additives and therefore will not make brine cloudy
Seasoned salt	Fine-grained and refined	• Table salt with addition of seasonings. Examples include onion salt, garlic salt, celery salt.

times. This mechanical machine is used primarily by large pork-producing companies.

Salting

During the *salting* process, salt is rubbed evenly onto the meat. Then the meat is packed in more salt. The salt absorbs moisture, so the juices are drawn from the meat. This preserves the meat because, without moisture, the bacteria cannot survive.

An example of meat that is cured by salting is prosciutto ham. The ham is left approximately four weeks in salt, washed, then hung to mature, allowing the curing process to continue. Meats preserved with salt or in a brine are referred to as *salaisons*. See Table 12–2 for a description of the types of salt used for preserving.

The steps involved in the classical curing method of salting are as follows:

1. Wash the food product.
2. Rub salt on the surface.
3. Place food product in a container and pack in salt.
4. Cure food product in salt for the required time under refrigeration. (It can be kept up to eight weeks.) Larger food products requiring lengthier curing times may need to be repacked with additional salt as moisture extracted from food melts the original salt away from the surface.
5. Wash salt from the product.
6. Cook food product or choose maturation (three types):
   a. Drying at 60° to 70° F (2 to 4 weeks)
   b. Storage (aging) at 50° to 60° F (4 to 6 weeks)
   c. Smoking: cold at 50° to 95° F (I hour to 4 days) or hot at 140° F or above (for the desired amount of time).

Marinades

Marinades are seasoned liquids in which foods such as meats, fish, game, poultry, or vegetables are soaked (marinated) for varying lengths of time. The purpose of marinating food is to add flavor: to tenderize: and, to some degree, to preserve. A marinade is a temporary emulsion that should be cold when the food product is added to it. If the product is not completely immersed in the marinade, then it should be turned frequently to ensure even absorption for flavoring and tenderizing.

Marinades are composed of

- Acids, such as vinegar, lemon juice, and wine. Acids add flavor but, more specifically, help to break down tough connective tissues, thus tenderizing.
- Oils of various types. Oils may add flavor.
- Aromatics, herbs, and spices, which are used primarily to create flavor in marinades.

The two main types of marinades are raw marinades and cooked marinades. In *raw marinades,* all raw ingredients are blended together. The marinade is used only once. In, cooked marinades, the ingredients are cooked before combining. For instance, vegetables or aromatics may be sautéed before the acid and oil are added and brought to a boil. The mixture is cooled completely before marinating any food product in the marinade.

Smoking

Smoking was originally used as a means of preserving food. The main chemical, components of smoke are tar, creosote, alcohol, and formaldehyde, which impart flavor and preserving agents in small quantities. Smoking alone is not enough to preserve. A food product should be treated with salt or a brine solution before smoking to ensure a longer shelf life. Only a food product already processed—cheese, for example—can be smoked without salt treatment.

The product to be smoked should be dry to the touch before smoking and rubbed with oil to prevent a crust from forming. The preheated smokehouse should be filled with smoke, allowing for a slight circulation of air.

The smoke can be produced by burning either sawdust or wood chips. Types of wood used for smoking are low in resin content and include mainly hardwoods. The type of wood used is determined by the flavor desired in the food product. Some woods commonly used include the following:

- Hickory
- Cherry
- Apple
- Maple
- Oak
- Alder
- Mesquite
- Pecan

Four Types of Smoking

There are four types of smoking: fast, slow, pan, and liquid.

Fast, or Hot, Smoking

In *Fast, or hot, smoking,* the product is cooked at the same time that it is smoked. This method is generally used in commercial settings. Temperatures for fast smoking range from 140° F to above. The smoking time of the food product depends on the size of the item. For example, chicken can be smoked anywhere from 20 minutes to two hours, while a pork loin will take much longer.

Slow, or Cold, Smoking

Slow, or cold, smoking is the best and only true method, according to the definition of smoking. The process only imparts flavor and does not cook the food product. Food products that are cold smoked should be either cured before smoking or cooked after the smoking is completed. Food products should be cold smoked at a temperature ranging from 50° to 95° F. The amount of time required to cold smoke an item will vary greatly depending on the size of the item and the specific equipment used. For example, scallops or shrimp may be smoked in one hour, whereas a ham may need to be smoked for up to four days. Generally, an outdoor smokehouse uses smoke created outside the building, and a longer time is required to smoke the food product. Indoor cold smokers smoke food products more quickly.

Pan, or Roast, Smoking

Pan, or roast, smoking is generally considered a hot smoking method, and therefore the temperature may range from 140° F to above. To prepare the smoking station, you will need the following:

- A 4-inch deep (prefereably disposable) hotel pan with cover
- 5 ounces of wood chips to start; more may be needed dependin on the length of the smoking process.
- A hotel-pan-sized roasting rack

The steps for completing the smoking process are as follows:

1. Line the bottom of the hotel pan with the wood chips.
2. Place the pan on burner or flat top and set heat on high.
3. Place food product on the roasting rack.
4. When wood begins to smoke, place rack into hotel pan and cover, sealing edges well.
5. Smoke food product to desired doneness, generally 7 to 15 minutes.

Liquid Smoking

Liquid smoking imparts a smoky flavor to food without subjecting it to an actual smoking process. The liquid containing the smoke flavor can be purchased premade or can be produced in-house. The solution of liquid smoke is made by rubbing resin, which builds up on the walls of the smokehouse or chimney, with a liquid.

The process for liquid smoking foods is simple. The smoke-flavored liquid is rubbed into the scored skin or flesh of the food product, which is then allowed to marinate for a few hours. As soon as the smoke flavor penetrates the food, it is slow-roasted at 325° F until done.

Buffets and Buffet Catering

A *buffet* is a selection of food that is presented, often decoratively, on one or several tables. The food is usually presented in chafing dishes, on platters, or in bowls, and may be served hot or cold. Buffets are frequently used for such occasions as weddings, and they provide an alternative way of feeding the guests without great demands on the service staff. Buffets may contain very informal finger foods or can be an elaborate multicourse meal. The food may be served by the guests, waiters, or chefs. Buffets can be classified as formal or informal, which is mainly determined by the extent of service, cost of ingredients, and type of seating available.

Different Types of Buffets

Breakfast or Brunch Buffets

Many hotels offer patrons breakfast and brunch buffets with a wide selection ranging from hot to cold dishes. Such buffets are usually self-serve with the exception of beverages, which are ordered from the server. The selection of food may vary widely from one region to another and from one continent to another. Included on the buffet may be breads and rolls with butter, cheeses, jams and marmalades, danish and other breakfast pastry, cold meats and fish, eggs, pancakes, waffles, hot and cold cereals, and fresh or stewed fruit. Brunch buffets may also include luncheon selections, because brunch is designed to serve as either breakfast or lunch.

Full Buffets

A full buffet is a main meal and, as with all buffets, is displayed in the dining room. For a full buffet, tables and chairs are essential for all guests, and the tables should be fully set with china, cutlery, napkins and glassware. The food is displayed on the buffet table, giving the chef the additional opportunity to decorate and garnish the food. Service may be performed either by the guests or by the staff.

Fork Buffets

A fork buffet is a meal that can be eaten standing up with a plate in one hand and a fork in the other. These buffets are ideally suited for events occurring where space is limited or where the guests are encouraged to mingle. Regardless of the reason for serving a fork buffet, some seating is recommended for those guests wishing or needing to sit while dining.

A fork-buffet table should look just as attractive as a full buffet, but the variety of foods will not be as great. Foods presented at a fork buffet should be easily eaten with a fork without the need for cutting. For instance, meat finger sandwiches or meat salads are more appropriate than offering a carving station of meats. The former are easily consumed, while the sliced meats may require the guest to cut and assemble them with bread before eating. A menu at the buffet is suggested because dishes are not always easy for guests to identify. Hot dishes are suitable, and curries, ragoûts, and sautés are all popular. A fork buffet is generally less formal than a sit-down buffet, and guests tend to eat less. The planning of fork buffets should include plenty of service staff to clear soiled plates and replenish the buffet with fresh china and flatware. There should also be numerous good-quality napkins available.

Finger Buffets

Finger buffets are the least formal type of buffet and, like fork buffets, they are suitable for an occasion where the host wants the guests to mingle. A finger buffet may take the place of a main meal, may occur between meals, or is only the prelude to heavier dining. Foods for finger buffets must be planned so they are bite-sized pieces that can be eaten without cutlery. With a finger buffet, numerous large napkins are essential, and finger bowls are permissible. Although the food can readily be eaten standing up, it is still advisable to have adequate seating for the convenience of guests who want or need to sit.

Creating and Planning the Buffet

Most buffets should have a theme, a centralized idea or concept that the buffet is intended to convey. The theme should be easily identified and constant throughout numerous elements on the buffet. For instance, the menu items, centerpieces, and accompaniments should all support the theme. When creating the theme, the meal period, reason or occasion, season of the year, and budget should be considered.

When planning a buffet menu, gastronomics, economics, and practicalities should be taken into consideration. Additional planning considerations should support the theme and may include the following:

- Placement of the table and available table space
- Number of zones
- Types of centerpieces and placement on the buffet

- Decor
- Space needed around tables for service
- Distance from the kitchen for the purpose of servicing

Zones

A *zone* is an area on a buffet that is distinguished in some way from adjoining parts. The number of zones on a buffet is often determined by the configuration that will ensure an efficient flow of patron traffic (see Figure 12–2). A small buffet, serving 75 to 125 people, may be comprised of one zone, while a larger buffet could have several. Planners of multizoned buffets should ensure that each zone has the same selection of food.

The size and shape of the buffet table is often dictated by the configuration and seating arrangement in the dining room. Strategically placing tables of varying shapes in the dining room can influence the initial visual impact by the guest. Several table layouts are possible, depending on availability of equipment and how the buffet will be replenished during the event.

Figure 12–2 Examples or service flow for a buffet

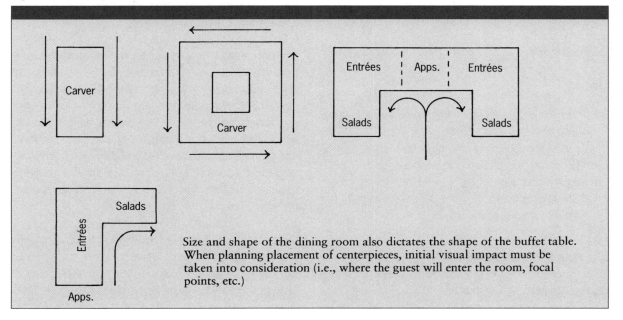

Size and shape of the dining room also dictates the shape of the buffet table. When planning placement of centerpieces, initial visual impact must be taken into consideration (i.e., where the guest will enter the room, focal points, etc.)

Preparation Schedule of Food-Related Buffet Elements

The order of mise en place for cold buffets includes:

- Day 1 (2 days prior to the event): preparation of force-meats, grosse pièces (edible platter centerpieces), centerpieces (ice, salt dough, vegetable carvings)
- Day 2 (the day before the event): Decoration of grosse pièces, garnishes for platters, accompaniments
- Day 3 (day of the event): slicing of meats, platter assembly, and presentation.

Centerpieces (Pièces Montées)

A *centerpiece* is an adornment on the buffet table. The centerpiece, the major focal point when the guests first enter the room, should support the theme. The centerpiece is often in the form of a tray, sometimes lined with a mirror, where baskets of fruits, vases of flowers, ice carvings, sculptures, and candelabra are presented. Centerpieces were widely used starting in the Middle Ages and still continue today. Some factors to consider when planning a centerpiece are color contrast, shape, size, medium used, and cost.

The centerpiece should generally be prepared several days prior to the buffet, and proper mise en place is required:

- Research a concept according to the buffet theme.
- Develop the concept.
- Acquire the necessary raw materials.
- Plan production of the centerpiece.
- Begin production.
- Store in an appropriate space that will ensure integrity of the centerpiece until the buffet.

Available Centerpiece Media

Some of the most often used media for centerpiece production include ice, vegetables, salt dough, sugar pastillage, chocolate, and marzipan. The cost is affected by the availability of the product, the ease with which a product can be stored and transported, and the high percentage of breakage.

Ice carvings are excellent for room and buffet-table centerpieces and are one of the most attractive and sought-after decorations. The large size of finished ice carvings is often one of the characteristics that makes them so intriguing. The cost of producing ice carvings can vary greatly, depending on the availability of the ice, skilled artisans, and proper storage. The cost of attaining ice carvings for buffets can increase greatly when not produced in-house.

Vegetable carvings can be very attractive and are also popular centerpieces. Production costs depend on the availability of produce, the variety of vegetables used, and the skill of the culinarian. Unlike ice carvings, vegetable carvings are fairly limited in size and therefore are used to decorate small areas on a buffet, a dining table, or a platter.

Salt-dough centerpieces are versatile, may suit any theme, and can vary greatly in size. The medium for salt-dough sculptures is inexpensive and comprised of a mixture of finely ground salt, cornstarch, and water. Salt-dough sculptures should be stored in a container of silica gel (which removes moisture from the air) to ensure repeated use at various buffets.

Sugar pastillage, chocolate, and marzipan centerpieces are appropriate for pastry buffets and are produced in the bakeshop. Pastillage consists of a gum paste made from sugar, cornstarch, gelatin, and water. Marzipan consists of a doughlike mixture made from almond paste, sugar, and sometimes egg whites. Chocolate is made of carefully tempered chocolate or temper-free chocolate. All three can be made into varying sizes and themes, but only pastillage is inexpensive to produce. Appropriate storage is essential to ensure repeated use of the centerpieces made from these media.

Guidelines to Making Ice and Vegetable Centerpieces

Ice Carvings. The art of ice carving was made popular by Georges Auguste Escoffier when he presented a pair of swans to Madame Melba of the Lonhengrin Opera House. The swans, carved of ice, accompanied his famous classical dessert, Peach Melba.

Ice carvings are generally prepared from one solid block of ice. The sculpture's design is usually simple and requires a few basic skills. The standard block of ice selected for ice carving weighs 300 pounds and measures 10 inches deep, 20 inches wide, and 40 inches high. A block of ice this size takes about 50 hours to freeze and about 30 hours to melt at room temperature. Depending on the size and shape, many ice carvings will last for five to six hours. A block of ice is formed in a mold surrounded by circulating ammonia solution, which has a much lower freezing point than water. At the base of the block is a small air hole. Air is pumped through this hole, causing the water to circulate continuously, forming ice that is free from crystals, resulting in ice that is clear instead of cloudy. The last part of the block that is frozen is the center. The last part of the center to freeze is cloudy and is referred to as the feather. It is the weakest point of the ice and should be carved with care. The smaller the feather, the better quality the ice.

Ice can be carved outdoors provided the area is shaded and at a temperature of 60° F or below. Carving indoors should be in a well-ventilated walk-in refrigerator. Before carving, the ice must be tempered, otherwise it will be very brittle and break easily. Ice tempers in about a half hour, or when the block begins to clear. Tempering should occur in a relatively cool environment of 40° to 68° F.

Ice-Carving Tools. Tools required for ice carving include

Safety goggles	Made of plastic; protect the eyes from flying pieces of ice.
Safety gloves	Made of carbon mesh; protect the hands from being cut, but will not prevent impalement by sharp implements.
Steel-toed boots	Heavyweight, water-resistant boots, preferably with steel toes.
Ice tongs	Used to move large blocks of ice.
Ice pick	Used for splitting the block into smaller pieces or for removing large parts not needed in the design.
Ice chipper	A six-pronged implement used to carve and cut around small areas of the ice.
Chisels	Wood and V-shaped; used for fine grooving and channeling.
Saw	A single-handled tree saw with coarse teeth makes it possible to remove large pieces from the block of ice without damaging the design.
Yardstick	Assists in laying out the design.

Carving the Ice. Draw a template. A *template* is a pattern for the design of the carving and should be drawn on a piece of paper the size of the block of ice. This can be easily done by using the grid method of copying. When duplicating the design, the template should be drawn slightly larger than needed to allow for the melting that occurs while finishing the centerpiece. Every design should include a substantial base to ensure stability of the centerpiece when it is carved. The steps involved in carving include:

- Adhere the template to the block of ice with water.
- Transfer the design onto the surface of the ice by using an ice shaver. Remove the paper template from the block of ice and hang it nearby to serve as a useful reference while carving.
- Determine the largest unwanted areas and remove them. Be sure to make all cuts completely through the block of ice so that the front looks the same as the back.
- Once the unwanted areas are removed and the carving begins to resemble the template, remove the "boxy" shape by carving the edges smooth and round. This will give the carving a three-dimensional shape.
- Using a chisel, add the fine details to the carving. This is best left as the last step of the carving because if done prematurely, the details will melt away.
- Return carving to the freezer, and store until needed for the buffet.
- On the day of the buffet, remove the carving from the freezer and temper it before placing on display. Due to melting that may occur during tempering, detailing may need to be redefined with a chisel before presenting.

Ice carvings must be handled with special care since they are actually more fragile and brittle than glass. Any sudden jarring or bumping may cause the carving to break or shatter.

Mending Breaks

Small breaks may be mended by simply placing the broken piece back on the carving and applying pressure until the two pieces fuse together. Larger breaks may be fixed by applying with pressure carbon dioxide (CO_2) gas, salt, snow, or shaved ice to the break.

Advanced Ice Carvings

Advanced or compound carvings are sculptures that use one or more blocks of ice and require additional skills. There are three processes associated with advanced carving:

- Fusing   Fusing parts of a single block or multiple blocks of ice together to form a larger size block or different shape is performed the same way as mending breaks. Fusing allows the advanced carver to complete more intricate and difficult carvings. An example of such a carving would be a castle made from fusing more than 60 blocks of ice together.
- Notching   Notching is the process of carving a cavity in the main block of ice and inserting another carved piece. On an ice carving of a bird in flight, for instance, wings are a common element that may be added using the notching method. The skill of notching allows an advanced ice carver to add greater intricacy to a carving.
- Slushing   Slushing is a process often used in conjunction with notching. The notched area is packed with slush which acts as an adhesive as it solidifies and gives structure to the wings, as explained above.

Themes

Blocks of ice can be designed to match any theme, and numerous books are available that provide detailed infor-

mation about the art of ice carving and include design templates. Common carvings include:

- Spring (flower basket)
- Valentine's day or wedding (love birds on a heart)
- Anniversary (letters or numbers)
- Sporting events (sailboat or automobile)
- Thanksgiving (turkey or horn of plenty)
- Christmas (Santa Claus or Christmas tree)

In addition to being used as centerpieces, ice carvings may be used to present canned or bottled beverages, bowls of caviar, or raw bars.

Presentation

Ice carvings should be presented on a raised socle that also acts as a drip pan. The most desirable drip pans are equipped with a drain, rubber hose, and a light. The drain carries away the melted ice while the light illuminates the carving. Additional colored lights can be placed at the back or under the ice carving. If such lights are used, the electric wiring must be well insulated so that melting water does not cause a short circuit. Greenery and in-season floral decorations may also be used to bring attention to the centerpiece.

Vegetable Carving

Vegetable carvings can vary in size, color and shape. Reusing vegetable centerpieces after soaking them in ice water can decrease the initial cost.

- Be sure all raw vegetables are washed well.
- Vegetables should be at room temperature before carving.
- After carving, the vegetables should be immersed in ice water to facilitate crispness.

Vegetable Carving Tools

Intricate vegetable carvings can be created using such simple tools as a vegetable peeler, a paring or tourne knife, a French knife, and a channel knife. Specialty carving tools can also be purchased but add unnecessary expense to learning this simple skill. Numerous books are available that detail the procedures for various vegetable and fruit carvings. Those that include step-by-step sequences illustrated with color photographs are the most helpful.

Bouquet Arrangement

The most common carved vegetable centerpiece is the bouquet which should be proportionally sized to the display area. A carved vegetable bouquet is comprised of several parts:

- *Vase:* A hollowed out acorn or butternut squash can be used as the base of the bouquet and should be decoratively carved. Before filling the vase with carved vegetables, be sure to cut a flat surface on the bottom of the squash to ensure stability.
- *Wooden skewers or toothpicks:* The skewers or toothpicks are inserted into the back of each carved vegetable and serve as the stem of the flower. The height of the finished centerpiece determines the length of skewer or toothpick to use.
- *Scallion greens:* Cover the toothpicks or skewers with scallion greens. Since all visible parts of the centerpiece should be edible, the scallions complete this requirement.
- *Foliage:* Leek greens can be cut into the shape of leaves to take the place of foliage
- *Flowers:* The various carved vegetables serve as the flowers in the arrangement. Diversity of colors, sizes, and shapes should be included to create an interesting centerpiece.

Examples of carved vegetables and their uses include the following:

- Carrots (flowers, tiger lily, tulip)
- Cucumbers (leaves)
- Gherkins (fans)
- Leeks (leek daisy)
- Onions (water lily)
- Potatoes (roses)
- Radishes (assorted flowers)
- Tomatoes (flowers)
- Turnips (carved flowers, sculpture)

Equipment for Food Display

Platters are often used as the primary container for displaying foods on a buffet. Due to the great variety of foods that may be served, platters are made in numerous shapes and sizes and out of varying materials.

Certain steps should be followed before actually presenting the food on the platter:

1. Based on the buffet menu, select the platter(s) that will be used to present the food. The size of each display platter available will determine the size of the food placed on it.
2. Develop the platter blueprint. A *platter blueprint* is a design or drawing of what a platter will look like when the food is displayed on it. A blueprint should be designed for each platter that will be presented on a buffet and should do the following:
   a. Detail exactly what foods will be presented on the platter.
   b. Aid visualization of the finished foods.
   c. Detail how the platter will be lined and decorated.
   d. Aid visualization of positioning foods on the platter. There are two types of platters: bordered and borderless (see Figures 12–3 and 12–4 on page 226).

Figure 12–3 Silver plater with border

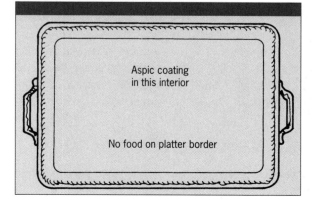

Aspic coating
in this interior

No food on platter border

Figure 12–4 Borderless platter

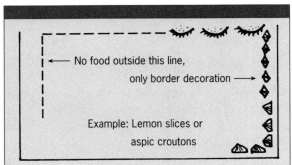

No food outside this line, only border decoration →

Example: Lemon slices or aspic croutons

e. Ensure that food is never placed on the border of a platter.

f. On borderless platters such as formica, plexiglass, marble, or mirrors, show an imaginary 2-inch border, with no food displayed on this border.

g. Establish space requirements based on the size of the platter.

h. Determine proper size and shape of garnishes.

i. Ensure use of diverse shapes.

j. Ensure use of diverse heights.

k. Ensure color contrasts.

l. Facilitate production by various staff members.

3. Clean and sanitize the platter, removing any dust, dirt, food, or fingerprints from the surface. Some metallic platters may become tarnished while in storage and, therefore, should be polished before use.

4. Line and decorate the platter. Platters, with the exception of formica, marble, plexiglass, or mirrors, are commonly lined with an edible coating, such as aspic, before the food is presented. The edible coating may be tinted with natural coloring or decorated with blanched vegetable cuts, herbs, or spices to add to the overall presentation. Aspic and other edible coatings also protect foods from tarnishing metals.

Advanced Platter Design

Foods prepared and presented on buffet platters should have

- *Function:* The food should meet the requirements of the menu.
- *Flavor:* The food should taste delicious.
- *Utilization:* The salads, accompaniments, and garnishes should utilize ingredients used in other preparations that would normally go to waste.
- *Creativity:* Numerous skills and ideas should be presented in the food displayed.
- *Design:* The chef or manager should plan attractive designs of food presentation.

Five Basic Elements of Food on a Balanced Platter

1. *Main piece:* The main pâté, terrine, or galantine. This item is usually a solid or semisolid choice cut of meat.
2. *Utilization piece:* Usually composed of the trimmings and extra pieces from the main piece. Its texture is usually ground or puréed.
3. *Enhancing salad:* A salad that is designed to add flavor, balance, texture, and color to the platter.
4. *Garnish:* The various garnishes on the platter should be flavorful, functional, and colorful.
5. *Starch:* The starch is often a cracker, croûton, or socle added to an element of the platter for nutritional balance and texture.

Confirming Balance

As soon as the chef or manager has determined the five basic food elements for the platter blueprint, the presentation should be tested for balance. The following questions should be asked:

- *Is the presentation balanced?* Does the platter include foods that are both simple and complex to prepare?
- *Is there a variety of color?* Does the layout of the food maximize the use of contrasting colors used in the foods?
- *Are there a variety of cooking methods used to prepare the basic food elements?* Would adding or removing the use of a particular cooking technique or method improve the platter?

- *Do the basic food elements contain a variety of textures?* For example, are all of the elements containing meat ground fine, or has the natural texture or grain of the meat been maintained in at least one piece? Are foods containing crispy texture contrasted with those containing soft?
- *Are the flavors of the food elements complementary?* Use the concept of flavor opposites. Are the number of rich foods balanced with the leaner preparations? Are hot and spicy foods balanced with foods seasoned with milder aromatics? Are cured, smoked foods balanced with sweet or acidic accompaniments? Are sweet flavors balanced with sour? Are spicy flavors balanced with sweet?
- *Is there nutritional balance?* Are proteins, carbohydrates, and vegetables well represented in the five basic elements of the platter?

Rules of Platter Layout

Carefully planning and assembling food on the platter is vital to the success of the resulting presentation. Note the following rules:

- Maintain a natural frame on the platter.
- On bordered platters, keep the foods at least one inch away from the inner edge.
- On borderless platters, keep the foods at least two inches away from the edge.
- Use the one-quarter concept. Visualize an imaginary grid over the platter blueprint and later over the finished presentation (see Figure 12–5). Are the five

Figure 12–5 Visualize an imaginary grid over the platter

basic food elements equally distributed in each quarter of the grid? If not, the presentation should be rearranged to ensure this.
- Confirm the alignment and order of sliced foods. Be sure the slices of food are neatly shingled in a row (see Figure 12–6 on page 228). The slices should be displayed in the exact order in which they were sliced and should shingle toward the guest.
- Do not under- or overcrowd the platter. Does the amount of food presented on the platter look appetizing? Avoid putting too much food on the platter. A platter can be replenished during service or a second platter with identical layout can be made for backup.

Checking for Practicality

Foods should be arranged not only for eye appeal, but for ease of service as well. The following are basic rules to note:

- Place taller food items toward the rear of the platter.
- Make portions consistent. For example, if there are eight portions of the main item, then there should also be eight portions of every other element.
- Confirm that the portion size is correct. Slices should be no more than one-quarter of an inch thick.

Aspic

Aspic is made from gelatin, which is an amorphous, colorless solid without any odor. Aspic can be produced from many foods:

- *Meat:* A classical aspic is produced by cooking bones, cartilage, and tendons for several hours. The liquid aspic is then cooled, and the substance turns into a gelatinous mass. More modern preparations of aspic are made by mixing bouillon or consommé with gelatin. Today, aspic is prepared from ready-made gelatin leaves or powders, avoiding the necessity of the lengthy cooking process.
- *Fish:* Gelatin obtained from fish is called *isinglass.*

Figure 12–6 The alignment and layout of sliced food

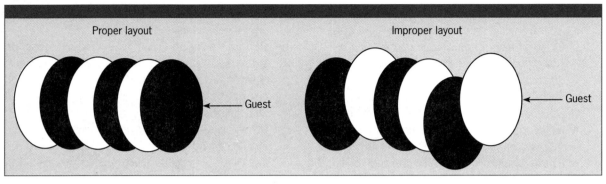

- *Vegetables or seaweed:* If gelatin is derived from vegetables or seaweed, it is called *agar-agar*.

Reasons for Using Aspic

Aspic is used

- As a binder, to give structure.
- For flavor, to complement the food being coated.
- To preserve and protect by coating the food, thereby preventing oxidation and drying.
- To decorate the borders of platters, using colored aspic.
- For coating, to achieve a brilliant shine to improve the appearance of food.
- As a lining, for coating metal platters to protect food against contamination and discoloration.

Various Methods of Applying Aspic

The firm, chilled aspic is heated in a double boiler until it melts. Before applying aspic to foods, it should be tempered over an ice bath to a temperature below 85° F. During this process, stirring or agitation should be minimized to prevent the formation of bubbles in the liquid aspic. After coating the foods with aspic, they should be refrigerated so the aspic coating will solidify before reapplying multiple coats. Aspic that coats foods should be completely clear and without bubbles, food particles, streaks, or finger-

prints. There are four common ways of applying aspic to chilled foods:

- *Spray:* The tempered aspic is placed into a spray bottle and misted over the chilled food products. Care must be taken to keep the spray bottle in a hot water bath to prevent the aspic from cooling and solidifying within the spraying mechanism. Because of this complication, spraying is not used extensively
- *Ladle:* The tempered aspic is ladled over the food product as it sits on a coating rack. This method is especially appropriate for coating large pieces, such as gros piéces.
- *Brush:* The tempered aspic is brushed onto the food product using a natural bristle brush. Brushing is one of the least-used methods of applying aspic because the coating created is commonly streaked. Brushing is a good method if the food requires only a thin coating and time before service is limited.
- *Dip:* The food product is dipped into a tempered container of aspic before placing it on a clean surface and refrigerating. Dipping foods into the aspic is one of the best ways to achieve a clean, smooth coating.

Steps for Using Aspic

When using aspic, follow these steps:

1. Slice or lay foods needing aspic coating neatly on a coating rack.

2. Chill food thoroughly while preparing the aspic for coating.
3. Melt the aspic in a double boiler. Heat only the amount of aspic that can be used in a 15- to 20-minute period.
4. Clean and sanitize utensils that will be used for dipping.
5. Temper aspic over an ice bath, bringing it to a temperature below 85° F.
6. Carefully stir or swirl aspic while tempering to avoid creation of air bubbles.
7. Coat the food product with the aspic, starting on one side of the coating rack and moving to the opposite end. Avoid dripping.
8. Refrigerate the coated food.
9. Prepare aspic for second coating by bringing it to the appropriate temperature.
10. Should the aspic become cloudy or contaminated with food particles, strain it through cheesecloth or other fine apparatus before reusing. Avoid mixing new, clean aspic with aspic that has already been used.
11. Repeat coating process as needed to create a clear, even coating on all food. One even coating is usually adequate for a buffet that will be consumed quickly, while two to three coatings is necessary for a buffet that will be presented for several hours. Foods presented for culinary competition should be coated with a minimum of three layers of aspic.
12. When handling foods coated with aspic, avoid using bare hands. Latex gloves should be worn to handle and plate the foods onto the platters.

Figure 12–7 on page 230 illustrates aspic molds and how to cool them prior to covering them with aspic. Figure 12–8 on page 230 shows slicing, dicing, and chopping of aspic.

Chaud-Froid Sauce

A *chaud-froid sauce* is a hot sauce or a product served cold. A classical garde-manger preparation, chaud-froid sauce is used to coat pieces of poultry, game, fish, or meat before a final coat of aspic is applied. Traditionally, chaud-froid was used to mask the poor appearance of a food product or to create a nice color base for later decoration. The color and flavor of the sauce are determined by the type of food to be coated. Brown chaud-froid sauce is served with roasted or red meats, white chaud-froid sauce with white meats or poached items such as fish. Sometimes mayonnaise collée is substituted as a coating for fish products.

Types of Chaud-Froid

The four types of chaud-froid sauce include the following:

- *Classical brown:* demi-glace, Madeira brown stock, and aspic (for various brown meats)
- *Classical white:* béchamel sauce, white wine, white stock, and aspic (for white meats and fish)
- *Orange:* demi-glace, brown stock, Madeira, orange juice, blanched julienne or orange zest, and aspic
- *Tomato:* tomato pulp, cooked and reduced, and aspic

Reasons for Using Chaud-Froid

Chaud-froid sauce is used for the following reasons:

- *Flavoring:* Chaud-froid sauce adds a savory element to foods.
- *Decoration:* Colored chaud-froid sauce may be used to add color to foods and platter linings.
- *Coating:* A brilliant shine and colorful appearance are achieved with chaud-froid; it is often used to mask the appearance of foods.
- *Lining:* Chaud-froid may be used to coat the inside of timbales or to line platters.

Points to Remember When Using Chaud-Froid

Chaud-froid sauce is handled much the same way as aspic, although it is slightly more temperamental because of the

Figure 12–7 Molds and how to cool them before covering with aspic

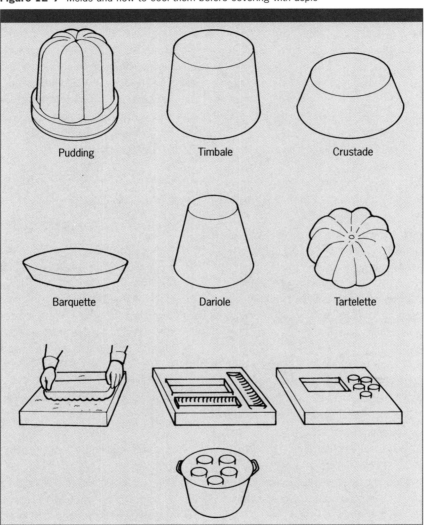

Pudding

Timbale

Crustade

Barquette

Dariole

Tartelette

Figure 12–8 Slicing, dicing, and chopping aspic

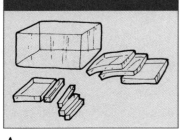

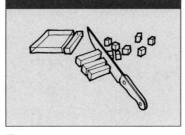

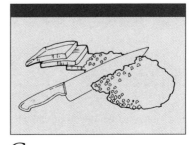

A **Slicing**

B **Dicing**

C **Chopping**

additional ingredients. Ingredients coated with chaud-froid are first coated with one layer of aspic. When coating with chaud-froid,

1. Lay aspic-coated foods needing chaud-froid neatly on a clean surface.
2. Chill food thoroughly while preparing the chaud-froid for coating.
3. Melt the chaud-froid sauce in a double boiler. Heat only the amount of sauce that can be used in a 15- to 20-minute period.
4. Clean and sanitize utensils that will be used for dipping.
5. Temper chaud-froid over an ice bath, bringing it to a temperature below 85° F.
6. Carefully stir or swirl chaud-froid while tempering to avoid creation of air bubbles.
7. Coat the food product with the chaud-froid, starting on one side of the coating rack or tray and moving to the opposite end. Avoid dripping. The first coating of chaud-froid should be thinner than subsequent ones.
8. Refrigerate the coated food.
9. Prepare chaud-froid for second coating by bringing it to the appropriate temperature.
10. Should the chaud-froid become contaminated with food particles, strain it through cheesecloth or other fine apparatus before reusing. Avoid mixing new, clean chaud-froid with sauce that has already been used.
11. Repeat coating process as needed to create an even coating on all food. Two to three coatings are recommended to achieve a solid color.
12. After the food is coated with the desired amount of chaud-froid, chill thoroughly before coating with a final layer of aspic.
13. When handling foods coated with chaud-froid, avoid using bare hands. Wear latex gloves to handle and plate the foods onto the platters.

Mayonnaise Collée

Mayonnaise collée is a sauce made by combining mayonnaise with aspic. The preparation is a way of increasing the stability of the emulsion. The ratio of mayonnaise to aspic will vary, depending on the required consistency. A 7:1 ratio, with 7 representing the mayonnaise, will be fairly loose, and a 1:1 ratio will be extra strength. Presently, the sauce is used as a chaud-froid, generally for fish, eggs, and salads.

Preparation of Buffet the Day of the Event

Foods are arranged on the platters, and final garnishing is performed in the kitchen, while the dining-room staff prepares the front-of-the-house presentation. The buffet is set up according to the following order:

1. Check table placement and table size.
2. Drape tables with linen.
3. Set up socles for pièces montées (centerpiece on a platter or tray) and drape.
4. Arrange pièces montées.
5. Set up ice with underliners, lights, flowers, and ferns.
6. Place largest platters on table.
7. Arrange smaller platters, salads, and appetizers around the large platters.
8. Place sauceboats, underliners, and ladles on the table.
9. Arrange final decorations on the table. For example, small flower arrangements, event-appropriate props, vegetable carvings, and folded napkins may be added.
10. Arrange service utensils next to each platter on underliners.

13

Introduction to Baking

Introduction to Baking

Bread's origin, and consequently the origins of the first baking techniques, are vague. The first breads were unleavened and were similar to present-day flatbreads such as the pita and the tortilla. There is no question as to the influence and importance bread has had on civilization, particularly Western cultures; it has played an important role in the development of many rituals, both religious and metaphorical, throughout history.

The History of Bread and Baking

Bread is one of the most widely eaten foods in the Western world. It has a fascinating history that dates back to the Stone Age, when humans first began to grind seeds of barley and millet with stones to make the first rudimentary flatbreads. Because the flour obtained was coarse, and leavening had not yet been discovered, the resultant bread was flat and heavy. The bread was more than likely a paste that was cooked on hot stones—much like the tortilla or Native North American johnnycake—both of which are descendants of the flatbreads common to everyday life in the Stone Age.

The quality of bread improved with the accidental discovery by a young Egyptian around 4000 B.C. that the uncooked paste would ferment and become aerated, if left to stand for a few days. However, it took the domestication of wheat to truly advance the technique for baking bread; wild wheats needed to be parched to separate the grain, which also denatured the properties of the gluten or protein. It was not until the improvement of grinding materials by the Egyptians around 800 B.C. that raw wheat could be obtained and used to alter bread's texture dramatically. The Egyptians can also be credited with the introduction of an enclosed baking container and later the oven. Ovens were conical in shape, made of baked Nile clay, and divided into two sections: the upper for the bread and the lower for the fire. The Egyptians also promoted the control of fermentation through the use of a day-old piece of dough—the basic *levain* still used by French bakers today.

From Egypt, the history of bread can be traced to Greece, where the adoption of the new wheat did not take place until around 400 B.C. As the Egyptians became more expert in growing wheat in quantity, they began to export the surplus to the Greeks, who, in turn, became the master bakers of their time. The Greeks also became specialists in baking cakes and pastries. A plain cake made of oat flour, spices, cream cheese, and honey was commonly made to celebrate the theatre or to recognize religious festivals. The Greeks made many types of cheesecakes and fritters; in addition, some Greek brides gave their bridegrooms a wedding cake—probably the first in Western civilization.

The Romans eventually adopted most of the techniques developed by the Greeks and, during the second century B.C., many Romans, except for the wealthy, started using professional bakers rather than making their own bread. Under the *Flavians*, a college was organized to teach and refine the knowledge of these professionals; it had government rules and regulations that all were required to follow and became the first corporation of bakers in Western civilization.

The Romans continued to improve their baking skills. During the reign of Augustus around 30 B.C., there were 329 bakeries in Rome; most were run by Greeks with Gauls from the north as assistants. The first mechanical dough mixer, attributed to Marcus Virgilius Eurysaces, of Greek origin, consisted of a stone bowl with wooden paddles that were pulled in circles by a donkey. Eurysaces had a monument depicting the different stages of bread making erected for him after his death.

Romans also graded their grain in order to provide finer and whiter bread for the nobility; whole wheat for the masses; and rough (Cibarus) for slaves, convicts, and their navy. Like the Greeks, the Romans developed many types of bread and cake; among them, a flaky pastry (similar to modern phyllo) filled with cheese and honey. Fritters were even more popular with the Romans than with the Greeks, and the Romans also adopted a type of wedding cake from the Greeks as well.

During the Arabic invasion of Europe that took place during the Middle Ages, the Arabs brought many new foods and food practices to Europe, among them, the windmill. With windmills to advance the milling of the wheat, the profession of bread making was established, and bakers specialized in the making of either brown bread (for the lower classes) or white bread (for the upper classes).

The Norman invasion of Britain brought with it renewed activity in baking. Early Norman bread tended to be large, round, and flat, indicating use of a less-refined grain that did not react well to fermentation. These bread rounds were useful, however, as they could serve a dual purpose—as a plate, called a *trencher,* and a food. These trenchers soaked up the fats and juices from the various meats and either were eaten last or given to the poor.

The number of bakeries in Britain steadily increased, and guilds became popular. The first of these guilds was known as the Fraternity of St. Clement of the Mistery of Bakers. St. Clement was the patron saint of bakers. The guild set and maintained standards in the bake shops. It had strict apprenticeship rules that protected the *misteries* of baking and lasted throughout the seven years of apprenticeship and journeyman status until one could be called a master baker. Those bakers found to be cheating the public were tried by the guild; if found guilty, they were often hauled through the streets with their loaves of bread tied around their necks. Customers were then free to get their revenge by throwing both abuse and rotten produce at them.

As the guild grew in size and importance, the bakers applied for and obtained a charter from King Henry VII in 1486 and purchased a hall for meetings. To protect their reputation, they agreed to bake an extra loaf, known as the *makeweight loaf,* for every dozen. Hence, the expression "baker's dozen" was born.

By the 16th century, pastry cooks throughout Europe, especially France and Italy, had developed meat and fish pies as well as pear tarts made with pastry cream. Flaky pastries similar to the early Roman cakes were developed, but they were made with the use of butter between the layers rather than cheese. When Catherine de Medici of Italy married King Henry II of France, she brought a brigade of accomplished bakers and pastry chefs to Paris. These bakers brought with them formulas and skills for the baking of cream puffs, cream custards, eclairs, tarts, sorbets, frozen creams, and other developed pastries. Croissants

came from Vienna, along with ices; the former were supposedly shaped in the form of a crescent to celebrate the Hungarian defeat of the Turks. Hungarian bakers were given the privilege of making the crescent-shaped rolls after they had alerted the city to an attack by the Ottoman Turks. The crescent, being the emblem of the Turkish flag, was thought to be a suitable symbol for a celebratory bread. Later, in 1780, a school was opened in Paris, and pastry baking became a specialized art, setting itself apart from the art of bread baking.

Because Eastern cultures and other regions predominantly grew rice and other starchy roots rather than wheat, breads were less common; although the Chinese pancake is an excellent example of an early flatbread. However, the history of baking through the 16th century is not restricted to Western cultures—the Chinese made biscuits, dried compotes that contained rice flour; fritters; and sugar pastries. Apparently, thin-layered dough was first made in the Near East to create *baklava*—paper-thin sheets of dough piled in layers and filled with honey and nuts. As the Turks moved westward into Hungary, so did this dessert. It was later carried into Germany and Austria. When Hungary became a part of the Austro-Hungarian Empire, this pastry developed into what we know today as *strudel.*

History in America

Over many years, Native Americans had cultivated wild grass presumed to come originally from the Mexican highlands. This was gradually developed into a valuable crop called corn or maize. For the first white settlers, the value of this crop was immense, as wheat was not an easy crop to grow throughout the eastern coastal regions. Corn, however, being suited to many soils and conditions, became an important part of the colonists' diet. Although wheat was difficult to grow, some was indeed grown during the early settlers' time, as evidenced by recipes such as Ryes's Injun Bread.

The first explorers to the New World were pleasantly surprised and encouraged to find the sophisticated agriculture of the Native Americans, who used their land efficiently and managed to plant and reap three crops per year.

Agriculture was not the only skill the white settlers borrowed from the Native Americans. They also shared recipes as well as ways of preparing corn. The johnnycake, probably a corruption of "journey cake," originated from the provisions of cornmeal carried by the Native Americans while on hunting expeditions.

The pilgrims learned how to pound corn in stone mortars or in scooped-out parts of a great log. They later established grist mills, which allowed for finer flour to be ground. Gradually, white flour became much more accessible as the settlers ventured out toward the west, and wheat was successfully grown across large areas.

The easiest way to leaven bread was with the fermentation of bacteria and wild yeast that would grow within the dough. Cowboys would make their starters by mixing flour and potato water in a keg that would be left in the sun or taken to bed at night to keep warm. Fermentation would then take place. Yet another way of starting a dough was to mix together cornmeal, water, and sugar. The following day, this would be blended with flour, salt, and other ingredients to yield a salt-rising or sour-dough bread.

During the days of fireplace cookery, the dough would be put into a bake kettle, lined with green oak leaves, and allowed to rise twice. More oak leaves were added, and an iron cover placed on top. The kettle would then be moved onto a bed of equal parts embers and hot ashes about three to four inches thick, then covered with more of this hot mixture. Halfway through this baking, the top covering would need to be removed and fresh embers and ashes added. Baking time would be 1½ hours.

Another method was to fill two large iron basins with the prepared dough. These would be placed together to make an enclosed container, joined as one loaf, set in the middle of the fireplace, covered with the hot ashes, and left to bake overnight.

The first American "pyes" were created during the first hard years. Pumpkin fibers and seeds could be scooped out and the shells filled with milk and baked on the open hearth. The first American pie pans were round and shallow, to stretch the food. Soon, however, large and richly crusted pies became common. Various regions of this newly settled land created pies that reflected not only the ingredients at hand but also the country of origin of the settlers.

Technological advances were also seen. In 1784, a young inventor, Oliver Evans, developed the process of milling flour. He designed a completely automatic flour mill that not only carried the grain into the mill but conveyed it through every grinding operation and delivered the flour already bagged, all without having to be touched by hand. For the next century, the Evans mills needed to be built around waterpower centers, regardless of the locality or access to wheat fields. Evans was one of the first to apply for a federal patent from the newly established Patent Office. From this invention, Evans went on to construct a steam engine large enough to run a flour mill, making it possible for milling centers to be constructed close to the wheat fields regardless of the availability of waterpower.

In the 19th century, new leavening products were introduced: baking powder in 1856, then commercial yeast as an offshoot from byproducts from the brewery industry in 1868.

Baking technology now began to develop rapidly. Ingredients became purer, thus improving the functional qualities of the dough. This, along with the improvement in mechanized equipment, reduced the need for a large labor force, increased production, decreased costs, and expanded the availability of low-priced baked products.

The 1930s produced the first mixes for the nonprofessional, and professionals began using doughnut mixes. It was during this era that emulsifiers were added to produce high-ratio shortenings, making it possible for batters to carry greater proportions of shortening, sugar, milk, and eggs.

Today's bakeries are factories where highly developed mechanization and technical baking allow for extensive production. Pastry professionals must be knowledgeable in science and business.

Basic Ingredients in Bread Making

There are four basic ingredients to bread dough: wheat flour, water, salt, and yeast (see Table 13–1 on page 238). An enrichener, or improver, is any ingredient other than the basic four ingredients or conditioners that affect the

Table 13–1 Basic Ingredients in Baking Bread

Ingredient	Purpose	Effect
Flour	Structure binder. Holds other ingredients. Toughener and dryer.	Largest constituent. Source of gluten. Base of formula. Development possible.
Water	Controls temperature. Forms gluten. Regulates consistency of dough.	Makes gluten possible. Determines consistency. Distributes ingredients. Makes yeast development possible.
Yeast	Leavening. Tenderizer. Enhances flavor. Makes product digestible.	Raises and aerates. Improves flavor and taste. Adds nutrition. Digestible.
Salt	Brings out flavor. Strengthens gluten. Prevents bacteria.	Imparts flavor. Gluten stabilized regulates fermentation time. Gluten forms strands, and salt strengthens those strands.
Sugar	Tenderness. Sweetness. Color.	Food for yeast. Color, smoother texture, flavor, and softness. Improved keeping qualities.
Shortening	Preservative. Shortens gluten.	Improved crust, grain, and tenderness. Softer crumb. Finer texture. Improved keeping quality.
Dry milk solids	Color, flavor, and nutritional value.	Texture is softer. Improved keeping quality.

color, texture, and flavor of the dough. These may include fats, sweeteners, milk products, or eggs.

Wheat Flour

Wheat flour is the only flour that contains both components of gluten, the protein formed when the flour is mixed with liquid. These components are very important in the making of a bread dough because they are what give the dough its strength and elasticity. The two components are

1. *Glutenin:* the component that gives the dough the strength and ability to retain the gases given off by the yeast, and
2. *Gliadin:* the component that provides the dough with its elasticity.

When another flour, such as rye, potato, or whole wheat, is used in the bread-making process, at least 20 percent of the formula's flour total must be made up of wheat flour—otherwise the dough will not be strong enough or elastic enough to be usable (see Table 13–2).

Wheats are generally classified according to the hardness of the kernel. They may also be classified according to the time in which they are sown and harvested.

Table 13–2 Protein Content of Flour

Flour	Types of Flour	Percentage of Protein
Hard wheat flour	First clear	14.5 to 15.5
	High gluten	13.5 to 14.5
	Patent	13
	Whole wheat	11 to 13
Soft wheat flour	Cake	6 to 8
	Pastry	7 to 9.5
Rye flour	Meal or pumpernickel	Up to 12
	Dark rye	12 to 16
	Medium rye	9 to 10
	White rye	6 to 9

Hard-Wheat Flour

Hard wheat has kernels that are hard, tough, and difficult to cut. This type of wheat produces the best bread flour. Characteristically, hard-wheat flour

- Is creamy or creamy-white in color.
- Is sharply granular in feel.
- Does not pack easily when squeezed.
- Dusts the bench easily.
- Has a heavy wheat smell.
- Is usually a winter wheat.

Hard-wheat flours are used specifically in the making of yeast-raised products because of their high gluten content. Hard wheat is known as southwestern wheat because it is grown in Kansas, Texas, and Nebraska. It is used for bread, rolls, and special sweet yeast products. There are four types of hard-wheat flours classified according to their gluten content: first-clear flour, high-gluten flour, patent or second-clear flour, and whole-wheat flour.

First-Clear Flour

First-clear flour uses only the endosperm of the wheat kernel, which gives softness and spreadability to the dough. Straight flour is the flour obtained after the wheat has been washed and the bran and the germ have been removed, leaving the endosperm. It then goes through one milling process and yields first-clear flour, which is slightly gray. The protein content of first-clear flour is 14.5 to 15.5 percent. The higher the protein content, the more gluten development will occur in the dough. The gluten properties of the flour are inconsistent. Because of the increased amount of protein in the flour, it may be necessary to add more water and perhaps more fat. First-clear flour is used where strength is needed. It is used in wheat, whole-wheat, and rye breads because these flours have poor gluten-forming and gas-retaining ability. In hearth bread, there is no pan to give the loaf shape, and this flour helps the loaf hold its own shape. In multigrain breads, it gives strength and lift to the multigrains.

High-Gluten Flour

High-gluten flour is a product of washing out the starch from patent flour, resulting in higher protein than patent flour. The protein content is 13.5 to 14.5 percent. The gluten properties of high-gluten flour are more consistent than those of first-clear flour.

Patent or Second-Clear Flour

Patent flour is the most-used flour. Less than the entire endosperm is used. Patent flour is also used where strength is needed.

Whole-Wheat Flour

The entire wheat kernel is used in making whole-wheat flour. The protein content of whole-wheat flour is 11 to 13 percent. Whole-wheat flour has poor structure and poor gas-retention abilities and must be used in combination with first-clear flour. It also has poor absorption abilities and must be soaked overnight before use.

Soft-Wheat Flour

Soft wheat has a comparatively soft kernel. It is suitable for cakes, pastries, and crackers. This type of wheat produces the best cake and pastry flour. Soft-wheat flour

- Is creamy to white in color.
- Feels soft.
- Packs easily when squeezed.
- Does not flow or dust over the bench easily.
- Has a light wheat to sweet smell.
- Is usually a spring wheat.

Soft-wheat flours are used specifically in making cake and pastry products because of their low-gluten, high-starch content. The two types of soft-wheat flour are cake flour and pastry flour.

Cake Flour

Cake flour is the softest flour because it has a high-starch content and a low-protein content of 6 to 8 percent. Because of the starch and protein content, cake flour has little resistance and results in a lot of height. Cake flour is white because it has been chemically bleached. It absorbs water quickly and packs easily. Cake flour is used for high-ratio cakes, which have a higher ratio of sugar to flour. This flour is able to carry increased amounts of shortening and sugar, which is important for aeration.

Pastry Flour

Pastry flour, which has a protein content of 7 to 9.5 percent, is off-white in color. It is used for low-ratio cakes, where the amount of flour is greater than the amount of sugar. It is used for cakes only if cake flour is unavailable because pastry flour has a greater amount of protein. Pastry flour is used for cookies, such as ice-box, oatmeal, and chocolate-chip cookies, which are high in fat and sugar; and it is used in pastries, as well as for pie doughs and short doughs.

Flour Blends

There are two flours that are between the hard- and soft-wheat flours: all-purpose flour and cookie flour. These lean more toward the soft-wheat flours.

All-Purpose Flour

All-purpose flour is called family flour or blend flour because it is a blend of cake flour and bread flour. It is used in the home as a multipurpose flour.

Cookie Flour

Cookie flour is similar to all-purpose flour. It is also a blend of hard- and soft-wheat flours, but contains less starch than the other flours.

Classified According to Time of Harvesting: Winter or Spring

Winter wheat is sown in the fall and harvested the following summer in climates where winters are not severe enough to kill the sprouted grain.

Spring wheat is sown in the spring and harvested in late summer and fall in climates where frost will not kill it before it has a chance to ripen.

Purposes of Flour

Flour is the basis and structure of all baked goods that contain it. There are five important reasons for using flour in a baked good:

1. It is the backbone and structure of baked goods, chiefly because of its gluten content.
2. It acts as a binding and absorbing agent.
3. It affects the keeping quality of products and retards staleness because of its ability to absorb and retain moisture.
4. It provides important flavor to baked products.

5. It adds nutritional value to the baked product through the vitamins, carbohydrates, and minerals it contains.

The selection of flour is tantamount to the success of the finished baked product. Professional bakeries stock many types of flours according to their needs. It is imperative that flours in a bake shop are stored dry and out of direct sunlight and that they do not become contaminated with flours of a different type; this could dilute the original flour's characteristics.

Make-Up of Flour

Flour consists of starch particles, protein particles, moisture, fat, ash, and enzymes. The group of enzymes, called *diastase,* is a very small, but very important component. These enzymes break down some of the starch into sugars, which can then be acted on by the yeast in a yeast-raised dough.

Starch Particles

Starch is the major component of flour, making up about 70 percent of its total weight. The starch in flour aids in gas production by furnishing sugar for the yeast. Damaged starch granules are attacked by the enzymes, converting them into sugar that is used by the yeast as food. Starch assists in providing structure in the baked products. This is done when the starch particles come into contact with moisture from the water in the formula and the moisture it absorbs from the gluten. It then gelatinizes during baking, causing the gluten to set but still maintain a permeable film that keeps the loaf from collapsing while allowing gas to escape.

Protein Particles

The protein in flour primarily affects the baking quality of the flour. The hardness or softness of a flour is determined by the proportion of protein to starch in the flour. In the grinding process, starch is processed into a fine powder, while the protein usually remains in larger, coarser particles that feel gritty. Proteins determine the gluten content of the flour, which subsequently determines what the flour will be used for. The quality of the protein in the flour is as important, if not more so, than the quantity; quality is relative and must be determined through use and experimentation of various flours for specific needs.

Bleaching the Flour

Bleaching refers to both the whitening and the aging of flour. Flour requires proper aging to produce the best results in baking. A flour that is newly milled is called a *green flour.* There are two ways to age a green flour. It can be stored for several months to allow the oxygen in the air to react slowly with the color pigments in the flour; this is called *aging,* which naturally bleaches the flour. Because the storage of flour for natural bleaching can be a very time-consuming and costly process and produce inconsistent results, another method of aging flour—artificial chemical bleaching—was developed. These chemicals can also be called *gluten-oxidizing agents* because they cause the gluten to be more elastic and stretchable and thus able to hold more gas, resulting in an end product with greater volume. The two most common bleaching agents are chlorine and benzoyl peroxide. Benzoyl peroxide is used solely as a bleaching agent, while chlorine is used to both whiten and mature the flour. Chlorine treatment changes the characteristics of the protein and starch molecules, which improve the flour's volume, grain, and texture. In bleaching, the flour is changed from yellow to white through the oxidization of the carotenoid pigments. At the same time, the gluten in the hard-wheat flours is matured, and the end result is a stronger flour with better gas-retaining abilities.

Ascorbic acid, potassium bromate, and azodicarbonamide (ADA) are all used as maturing agents in hard-wheat flours; all work without bleaching. These three agents react principally within a bread dough to increase loaf volume and to improve grain.

Bleaching and maturing of flours is determined by the mill; for this reason qualities of flour vary from mill to mill throughout the country.

Anatomy of a Kernel

Understanding the parts of a kernel of wheat (see Figure 13–1) aids in the understanding of the difference in flours.

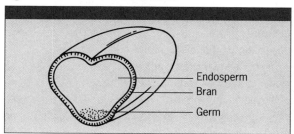

Figure 13–1 Parts of a wheat kernel

Endosperm
Bran
Germ

The largest part of the wheat is the endosperm. Around the outside of the kernel is the bran. If the entire kernel is ground, whole-wheat flour is produced. White flour is made by using only the endosperm. During the milling process, the kernel is broken up into a meal and sifted. The bran is lifted off by air and then the germ is separated. On average, from 100 pounds of wheat, the yield is about 72 pounds of flour and 28 pounds of animal feed.

The various parts of the wheat kernel offer considerable nutrition:

- The bran is a good source of insoluble fiber and B vitamins.
- The endosperm is a good source of complex carbohydrates.
- The germ is high in vitamin E and fiber.
- Whole-wheat and enriched flours are good sources of the B vitamins, thiamin, niacin, and riboflavin.

Special Types of Flours

Whole-Wheat Flour

In whole-wheat flour, the entire wheat kernel (the endosperm, the bran, and the germ) is used. The types of whole-wheat flour are refined whole-wheat flour, cracked-wheat flakes, and rustic-wheat flakes. Refined whole-wheat flour is similar to bread flour, but it has the bran and germ. The bran and germ do not take away from or tear the gluten as much as in other whole-wheat flours. Refined whole-wheat flour forms a smooth mass of dough. Refined whole-wheat flour is the most commonly used of the whole-wheat flours. Cracked-wheat flakes need the addition of vital wheat gluten (VWG), conditioners, or emulsifiers to produce good volume and structure. Rustic-wheat flakes are very coarse, large flakes. Cracked-wheat flakes and rustic-wheat flakes may be associated with the same name, depending on the milling process.

The bran and the germ in the whole-wheat flour tear the gluten in the flour as the dough is being mixed, so some of the gluten properties are lost. Therefore, certain adjustments must be made to provide sufficient gluten when making whole-wheat doughs and rye doughs as well. A combination of the proper ratio of whole-wheat flour to first-clear flour is used in making whole-wheat dough.

First-clear flour is used because it has a high-protein content, which the whole-wheat flour lacks. Use one-third whole-wheat or rye flour to two-thirds first-clear flour, or 50 percent whole-wheat to 50 percent first-clear flour. The first-clear flour has a slightly gray color, which does not take away from the wheat or rye dough. Using whole-wheat flour with first-clear flour yields a product of good volume because of the gluten of the first-clear flour. It also produces a product of good flavor because of the flavor of the whole wheat.

If using 100 percent whole-wheat flour, certain adjustments must be made. Cracked- and rustic-wheat flakes must be soaked. When using cracked-wheat flour, the percentage of water used in the soaking process must be increased. Sufficient shortening, 6 to 8 percent, must be used to lubricate the gluten that is trying to form and to protect, to some degree, the gluten from the bran and germ. Molasses or honey may be used to add moisture, promote color, and sweeten the product.

Soaking the Whole-Wheat Flour

The primary goal of soaking the flour is to soften the wheat flour to yield a smooth mass of dough and to prevent the dough from drying when mixed. Refined whole-wheat flour is so fine that, when it is subjected to moisture, it immediately absorbs the water; therefore, it does not need to be soaked. Gluten forms faster because of the bran and germ being smaller. It is especially important to soak cracked-wheat and rustic-wheat flours. Cracked- and rustic-wheat flours should be soaked overnight with most of the water and all of the salt called for in the formula. In soaking, the protein is pulled out of the flour. The wheat flakes enlarge

as they absorb water. A stringy, white material will also be noted. This is the protein that is brought out. Soaking also allows for maximum water absorption, which in turn makes the dough easier to handle, similar to the sponge-dough mixing method. The protein that has been pulled out of the flour is now hydrated and gluten is formed. Finally, the salt used in soaking helps to strengthen the gluten proteins while the wheat flour is soaking.

The cracked- or rustic-wheat flakes use 65 to 75 percent water, rather than the 50 percent of water normally used in bread dough. Because of the composition of the flakes, they require an extensive soaking to put them in a useable form. Rancidity will develop, however, if the whole-wheat flakes are soaked for too long because of the fat in the wheat.

The mixture is usually left to stand but can be mixed on low speed for 40 minutes. This speeds up the process and gluten development. After the soaking process is complete, the final mixing begins. If any water is left, the water temperature must be calculated. Multiply the desired dough temperature (DDT) times 4, subtract the temperature of the soaked mix, then subtract the room temperature, then subtract the temperature of the remaining flour, and, finally, subtract the friction temperature. The result is the temperature of the remaining water for the final formula. If there is no water to be added to the formula, mix the dough to the DDT.

Whole-wheat doughs have a 30 percent lower fermentation tolerance because of the lack of structure. Rye doughs have an even lower fermentation tolerance.

As the dough is being mixed, the proteins on the outside are taking in the oxygen, making the dough lighter in color. Whole-wheat doughs may need steam because the bran and germ cause the doughs to be tight.

Rye Flour

Rye is mostly grown in Europe and Russia. In the United States, the predominant states that produce rye flour are North Dakota, Minnesota, and Wisconsin, but it is also grown in Michigan and Illinois. Rye flour is not classified as a wheat flour, but as a grain flour. It does not have all the properties found in wheat flours and thus yields a weaker dough. Rye flour lacks glutenin, so the dough lacks strength and structure. This flour has practically no gliadin, which means that the dough has little or no elasticity.

Because rye flour has protein and starch but lacks gluten-forming properties necessary for strength, structure, and elasticity, the following factors should be considered when working with rye flours for dough:

- A strong flour, such as first-clear flour, must be added to the rye flour to give the dough some gluten-forming properties.
- Rye-flour doughs require less mixing. The more rye flour used, the less mixing will be required. A low mixing speed is used to avoid tearing the gluten. The more the dough is mixed, the more it will break down.
- The fermentation tolerance of rye-flour dough is low, 30 to 40 percent less than regular dough, because of the lack of gluten to hold the carbon-dioxide gas in the dough. The more acidity in the dough, the less proof will be required.
- Rye flour is soft and tends to absorb water or moisture very quickly, but it cannot hold the moisture for long because the rye flour comes from grain, not from wheat, and lacks gluten. The moisture works its way back out of the flour, giving this dough a wet texture.
- When shaping the rye dough, it cannot be handled as dough normally would because it cannot be stretched. The dough should be handled gently to prevent tearing during rounding and forming. Also, the rye dough may burst in an oven that is too hot because of the lack of gluten.

Types of Rye Flours

There are four types of rye flours: light rye, medium rye, dark rye, and rye meal. Light-rye flour is milled from the center of the rye berry. It is composed mainly of fine starch particles, is low in protein, and is used for light-rye bread. It is the best flour for sours. Medium rye, or straight flour, is composed of all the flour after the bran and shell are removed. Dark rye may be compared to clear flour milled from regular wheat. It is the flour remaining after the starch is removed. Smaller particles of bran are present in dark rye, and it is used for darker, heavier rye breads. Rye meal, or pumpernickel flour, is made by grinding the entire rye berry. It is coarse and dark, and is used for pumpernickel bread. Rye meal may be considered the whole-wheat version of rye.

The proper ratios of rye flour to first-clear flour are 1:1 or 1:2. That is, half first-clear flour, half rye flour, or one-third rye flour to two-thirds first-clear flour. The further apart the ratios, the more volume in the product.

Ingredients of Rye Bread

Rye bread contains the following ingredients:

- Yeast
- Water
- Rye flour
- First-clear flour
- Salt
- Molasses
- Caramel coloring
- Sugar, small amounts; it is better to use molasses for sweetening
- Regular shortening; to lubricate the gluten, making the dough easier to shape
- Caraway seeds
- Dry-milk solids, for soft rye rolls
- Buttermilk, for sour rye breads

Rye-Flour Characteristics

Rye flour has the following characteristics:

- It lacks glutenin.
- It deteriorates rapidly; rye flour has a short storage time because of its high fat content.
- It ferments quickly.
- Its flavor is enhanced by salt, which also controls fermentation.
- It has low tolerance to mixing and becomes sticky. The lower the quantity and lighter the rye flour in a dough, the more tolerant the dough is to development. The higher the quantity and the darker the rye flour, the less tolerant it is to development.
- It has an increased absorption quality, compared to wheat flour. The greater the amount of rye flour and the darker the flour, the stiffer the dough.

Making a Rye Dough

A sponge and a sour can be used to make rye bread doughs. Instant yeast is excellent with rye doughs because it allows for less fermentation.

When mixing, add the molasses and the caramel color with the liquids and mix on low speed to fully color. If the coloring agents are mixed with the flours, the flour will bind and will not color. The result will be streaking of the product.

Steam can be used with rye dough, but it does not have to be. If the dough is underproofed, use steam. Rye breads tend to have a longer shelf life because the starch keeps the moisture in.

Water

Water is the liquid that makes possible the formation of gluten by hydrating the protein in the flour, which gives structure to the product. Milk and eggs can also aid in the formation of gluten. The three functions of water are to regulate the consistency of the dough, to control the temperature of the dough, and to help form gluten. Too much water will cause the product to be runny and too moist. Too little water will cause the product to be dry and crumbly. Generally, water that is used for baking is of medium hardness and slightly below 7.0 pH.

The mineral content, or acidity, of the water affects the end product. Acidity and alkalinity determine the rate of fermentation. Alkaline, or hard, water slows fermentation. Hard water is caused by the presence of calcium carbonate in the water. The degree of hardness is related to the degree of acidity/alkalinity, or pH. The pH is expressed as a value between 0 and 14. Pure water has a pH of 7.0. A pH below 7.0 is said to be acidic, and a pH above 7.0 is said to be alkaline. Excessively hard water may retard fermentation by toughening the gluten. The minerals present in the hard water prevent the proteins from absorbing water.

There are three things that can be done if the water to be used for baking is too hard. Reduce the pH by adding vinegar or another harmless acid, use more yeast, or decrease the dough improvers. Dough improvers contain minerals and tend to increase the alkalinity of the dough.

Soft water has very little concentration of calcium carbonate. Water that contains no minerals, or soft water, has a pH of 7.0 and is said to be neutral. Water that is too soft causes the dough to be too sticky. This is seldom a problem because the dough improvers and yeast foods add minerals to the water.

Yeast

Yeast is a microorganism of the fungus type. It is a biological leavener, which means that it is a living organism that thrives on various foods in various conditions. Yeast converts fermentable sugar and some starches in the dough or batter into carbon-dioxide gas and alcohol and provides desirable and controllable fermentation.

History shows that the Greeks used some fermented dough to make fresh doughs, but fermentation was not always controlled. The discovery of the nature of yeast and fermentation is credited to Louis Pasteur in 1859, and the first company to commercially produce yeast was the Fleischmann's Company in the 1870s.

Yeast is composed of proteins, carbohydrates, fat, mineral matter, moisture (which may constitute from 68 to 73 percent of the yeast), and enzymes. The original yeast cell was selected from a strain that could be used for baking, brewing, and wine making. There are now two major varieties of yeast: brewer's yeast, which gives flavor and lightness, and baker's yeast, which gives lift or height to the products through alcohol and carbon-dioxide leavening.

Ideal growth conditions for yeast include a proper environment and supply of food. The environment must have plenty of moisture, water or humidity, must maintain temperatures between 85° and 95° F, and must have a high concentration of dissolved oxygen in the air. Yeast requires food, in the form of a constantly maintained concentration of carbohydrates, starch, and sugar; proper concentration of hydrogen ions; and other nutrients, which include nitrogen, potassium, and phosphorus. Under these favorable conditions, the yeast cells multiply rapidly through a pro-

Figure 13–2 What yeast does

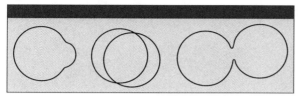

cess called budding (see Figure 13–2). Budding occurs when each cell develops to the full size of the parent cell. As soon as the cell reaches full size, it breaks off and budding continues. This process must be controlled for uniform leavening power.

Functions of Yeast

Yeast feeds on sugars and starches and produces alcohol and carbon dioxide as waste products. This is achieved through enzymes found in the yeast. Enzymes are organic catalysts, substances that cause changes to take place without changing themselves (see Figure 13–3). Changes that take place in the dough as a result of enzymatic action start slowly, then increase as fermentation progresses.

Major enzymes in yeast are diastase, invertase, and zymase. Diastase feeds on the starch and converts it to disaccharides, or complex sugars such as sucrose. More simply, diastase breaks down starch in flour and converts it to sugar. Invertase takes the disaccharides, or complex sugars, and breaks them down into monosaccharides, or simple sugars (sucrose into glucose and dextrose). If there is any malt sugar in the formula, the enzyme maltase feeds on the maltose sugar and breaks it down into the simple sugars dextrose and glucose (see Figure 13–4 on page 246). There are two types of malt sugar: diastatic and nondiastastic. The nondiastastic malt sugar is used in pastries. Zymase takes the monosaccharides and breaks them down into alcohol and carbon dioxide. Lactose, or milk sugar, is not fermented by yeast. It is a tenderizer and gives color to the crust.

Purchase Forms of Yeast

There are three purchase forms of yeast: compressed, or fresh-cake, yeast; dry active yeast; and instant dry yeast.

Figure 13–3 Enzymatic actions of yeast

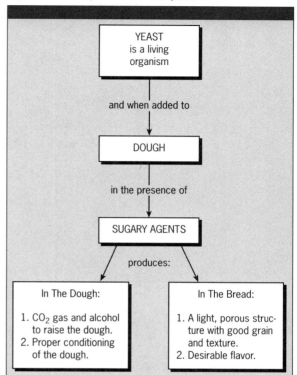

- *Compressed, or fresh-cake, yeast* has been available longer than the other types of yeast. It must be refrigerated and should be kept only for one or two weeks. It does not freeze well. If compressed yeast is to be frozen, it should be wrapped in the portions in which it is used to allow for faster freezing and thawing. Fresh yeast is dry, crumbly, and breaks crisply. Frozen yeast is soft and mushy and collects moisture, and the starches in the product break down. It should be broken before being dissolved in water not hotter than 120° F. Use between 4 and 6 percent in a formula, depending on room conditions, the time frame, and the end use.
- *Dry active yeast* (DAY) is a dehydrated form of compressed yeast and must be reactivated in 105° F to 110° F water for 3 to 5 minutes. Use two to three times the weight of the water to yeast. For example, for 4 ounces of yeast, use 8 to 12 ounces of water.

Figure 13–4 The sugar-refinement process

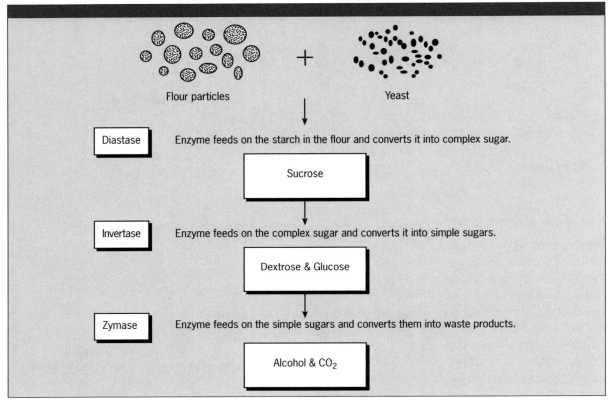

Flour particles + Yeast

Diastase — Enzyme feeds on the starch in the flour and converts it into complex sugar.

Sucrose

Invertase — Enzyme feeds on the complex sugar and converts it into simple sugars.

Dextrose & Glucose

Zymase — Enzyme feeds on the simple sugars and converts them into waste products.

Alcohol & CO_2

- *Instant dry yeast* One of the most popular dry yeast products is SAF. The dough produced by this product should not be bulk fermented. Bench rest for about 30 minutes. These products contain ascorbic acid and sometimes an emulsifying agent so they condition the dough slightly during mixing. After the dough has been mixed, this instant dry yeast will produce a dough with little aeration compared to doughs produced with compressed yeast. However, the dough will be soft and pliable for shaping. Add the yeast after all the liquids have been absorbed during the pick-up stage in the center of the bowl because the yeast will not react if it comes into direct contact with ice or with very cold water. If the dough is to be frozen, the yeast should be dissolved in warm water tempering it before adding it to the dough. The key is to freeze the dough rock hard as quickly as possible.

Salt

Common salt is sodium chloride and is present in many everyday foods. Commercial salt is produced from two different sources; dissolved in the water of saltwater oceans, seas, and lakes; and deposited in the earth in the form of rock in salt beds. To obtain salt from water, the water is evaporated, leaving behind salt crystals, which are then purified, dried, crushed, and graded. Salt is mined from the earth, crushed, and graded. Rock salt must be purified to make it edible. Refined salt is almost pure sodium chloride. The impurities present in the salt are mainly calcium and magnesium salts.

Salt adds flavor to foods, but, when added in proper amounts, the salt also brings out the flavor of other ingredients, such as sugar. Breads that lack salt have a flat taste. Dietetic breads are made without salt, but VWG is used instead. These breads have an off-white crumb. Too much salt results in an unpleasant taste.

Salt also retards or slows fermentation. It inhibits the yeast growth, so it should not be allowed to come into direct contact with the yeast in the formula, which would cause the fermentation period to be too long, or it might even prevent fermentation altogether. Using too little salt in bread making will result in fermentation not being controlled.

Salt strengthens gluten formation and structure by chemically breaking the water so the proteins in the wheat flour combine with the water. This makes the gluten strong and increases the stretching ability, making for good texture in the end product. This action of salt also has a bleaching effect, and the result is a white crumb. If too little salt is used, the gluten strands are weakened and the end product loses shape during baking. Finally, salt prevents the growth of bacteria and aids in digestion.

Dough Improvers

Dough improvers, also known as dough conditioners, help to maintain consistency in yeast-leavened products. This is important, especially when time, labor costs, and customer satisfaction are demanding issues.

There are five elements to improvers: fats, oxidants, biological substances, emulsifiers, and sugars. The fats lubricate the gluten. Oxidants, or trap dioxide, strengthen the gluten because of the trapped dioxides, while ascorbic acid, or vitamin C, makes the dough stronger. The biological substances in the form of enzymes slow the secondary fermentation. Emulsifiers from vegetable, plant, and animal sources develop gluten, creating superficial tension. Finally, the sugars, or dextrose, act as yeast food and provide color.

The dough improvers allow the chef to work with the dough less and they reduce fermentation time. They make the dough more pliable and stronger, improving its tolerance to machinery. Dough improvers also help produce an end product that is lighter, has a better crust color, and has an extended shelf life. Some improvers will increase the retarding or freezing tolerance of the dough.

Some of the claimed advantages are that they may be used to produce one or more of the following characteristics:

- Increased absorption
- Dough conditioning
- Drier and better handling doughs
- Increased yield
- Bread whitening
- Improved texture
- Improved grain
- Improved keeping quality
- Softer loaf
- Better flavor

Common Ingredients Used in Baking

Sweeteners

Sugar and sugar syrups are available in a variety of forms, some of which have commercial importance. Sweeteners are pleasing because they taste sweet; however, their importance as an ingredient in a baked good goes beyond flavor. Sugar serves many purposes in the production of baked goods:

- It adds sweetness.
- It acts as a principle moisture retainer and consequently affects texture and keeping qualities of the product.

- It acts as food for fermentation in doughs.
- It creates crust color through caramelization.
- It acts as a base for many icings.
- It aids in the creaming and whipping process of mixing.

FYI

Sugar has a rich history. Sugar cane apparently originated somewhere in the South Pacific and was carried to Asia by humans through early migrations. The ability to make sugar by pressing out the cane juice and boiling the juice down to make dark crystals was known as early as 500 B.C. in India. Sugar spread to the Tigris-Euphrates through the Persians around the sixth century A.D.; the Arabs, in their domination of Persia in A.D. 640 spread the use of sugar and the sugar cane plant to northern Africa and Spain through the 1100s. It was not until the crusades, during the 12th century, that sugar was introduced to Europe. Europeans first treated sugar the same as they treated any other spice—it was mostly used for medicinal purposes. Sugar was mainly used by druggists to make small medicinal candies and to bind and disguise the taste of other ingredients. When sugar began to be used by the Europeans as a luxurious sweetener is not certain; a French druggist reportedly used sugar to coat almonds in a candy as early as 1200, but it was not until the 1700s that sugar was being used by the average person.

In baking, there are two categories of sugar:

1. *Simple sugars, or monosaccharides* are directly digestible by living organisms. Monosaccharides include the following:
   a. *Fructose* (sometimes referred to as levulose)—the sugar found naturally in fruits and vegetables
   b. *Dextrose* (sometimes referred to as glucose)—the sugar that is most commonly derived from the starches in corn
   c. *Galactose*—one of the monosaccharides found in lactose, or milk sugar
2. *Double, or complex, sugars called disaccharides* must be broken down by enzymatic reaction into monosaccharides before they can be digested by living organisms. These sugars include the following:
   a. *Maltose*—made up of two glucose molecules; derived from the starches found in malt
   b. *Lactose*—made up of glucose and galactose; the sugar found in milk
   c. *Sucrose*—made up of glucose (dextrose) and fructose; the sugar derived from sugar cane and sugar beets

It is sucrose that is most often used in the production of baked goods. It can be purchased in several forms for use in the bake shop.

Granulated Sugar

Granulated sugar is refined through a series of complicated steps (see Figure 13–5). Basically, the sugar cane or sugar beet is clarified through the use of heat and lime and then boiled down to concentrate the sugar. The juice is then crystallized through the use of centrifuges to draw off the molasses and then decolorized with the use of granular carbon. After the granular carbon removes the last remaining impurities, it is filtered out. Final crystallization is controlled to give the final sugar crystals uniform size. Molasses and brown sugar both result from various stages of the refinement process.

Granulated sugar is available in several grain sizes for use in the bake shop:

- *Coarse sugar:* Coarse sugar has the largest granule size; because of this, it is used for decorative purposes only, for example, to add color to a product such as a sugar-sprinkled muffin or cookie.
- *Regular granulated sugar:* Although granule size differs from manufacturer to manufacturer, regular granulated sugar is most commonly used in baked goods and is what is referred to as "table sugar."
- *Fine and superfine:* Both fine and superfine sugars have granules that have been refined to a much smaller size. These sugars are often used in the making of delicate items where the sugar needs to be readily dissolved and absorbed.
- *Confectionery, or powdered, sugar:* Powdered sugar has been pulverized to create a powder and contains 3 percent cornstarch as an anticaking agent. Confectionery sugars are available in various forms of fineness classified by the number of Xs found on the

Figure 13–5 Cane sugar production

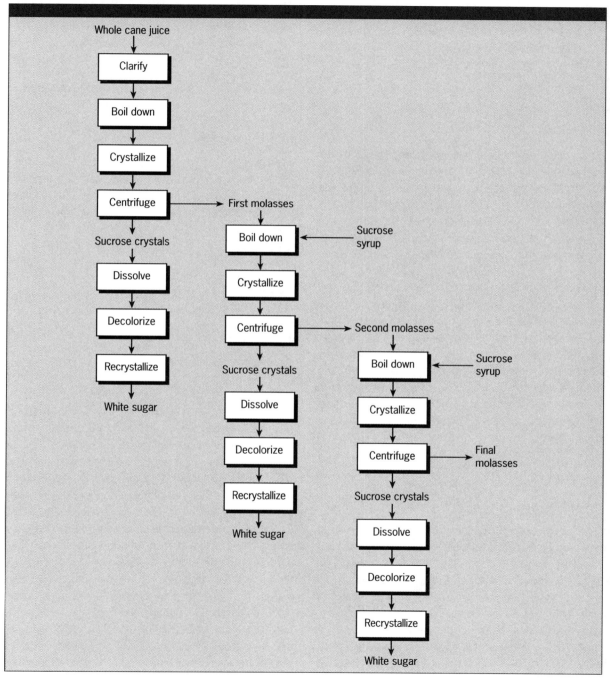

package, starting with 2x as the least fine, 4x, 6x, and 10x, which is the most fine. Confectionery sugars are most often used in the preparation of icings and cake mixes, in some candies, and sprinkled on finished products as decoration.

Molasses

During the refinement process, three basic liquids are derived: dark, cloudy, and clear. It is from the further refinement of these liquids that molasses, brown sugar, and granulated sugar are made. Molasses is derived from the dark liquid and is basically the syrup left after the available sucrose has been crystallized. Molasses is derived from sugar cane only; beet molasses has too unpleasant an odor to be used. As the sugar goes through the stages of crystallization and refinement, different qualities of molasses are obtained. The molasses from the first crystallization has a high sugar content. The molasses obtained from the second and third crystallization have a lower sugar content and are lighter in color. Molasses is made by blending clarified cane syrups with first molasses to produce a product that is uniform in color, flavor, and body. Generally, final molasses is so full of impurities and minerals that it is unfit for human consumption and is used most often for animal feed.

Brown Sugar

Brown sugar is derived from the cloudy liquid of the refining process and is basically a mixture of white sugar and molasses. Syrups that still contain molasses are added to refined, redissolved sucrose, then crystallized. Brown sugar is highly valued for the special flavor it imparts to many dishes, especially cakes, cookies, and breads, and certain pie fillings. Brown sugars can be light or dark in color. The more refined the sugar, the lighter the color. Brown sugar can replace white sugar in any formula where its characteristic flavor will not affect the final product.

Liquid Sweeteners

Invert sugars are sugars that are inverted to liquid form through the use of heat, acid, or enzymatic reaction. This breaks the sucrose partially into its two monosaccharides, fructose (levulose) and dextrose (glucose). This process can occur naturally in nature, as in the case of honey and maple syrup, or it can be manufactured, as in the case of commercial syrups such as nulomoline. Inverts and other liquid sweeteners are valued for their excellent moisture-retaining, or hygroscopic, capabilities and are usually between 15 and 18 percent water. Some liquid sweeteners, such as glucose, are used to prevent crystallization and improve elasticity in candy and sugar showpieces. Types of invert sugars include nulomoline, honey, and maple syrup.

Nulomoline

Nulomoline is an invert syrup having excellent hygroscopic properties. It can retain more moisture than other sugars in the baked foods in which it is used. Ten to 20 percent of the granulated sugar used in current formulas may be replaced by nulomoline. Because invert sugar contains approximately 15 percent moisture, the quantity of water used in the formula must be reduced by about 2½ ounces for every pound of invert used. If invert syrup is already an ingredient in the formula, the amount of water has already been corrected. Add the invert sugar along with the liquid to the batch; it is not necessary to dissolve it in the liquid. When stored for long periods of time, invert syrup tends to separate with the dextrose, or glucose (dextrose)—the white material—settling to the bottom, and the fructose (levulose)—the liquid portion—rising to the top. Should this occur, mix and blend the two together before using. Invert, like most other syrups, will caramelize at a lower temperature than sugar, so products containing invert sugar will tend to color more rapidly than other sugars during baking.

Honey

Instead of dirt and poison we have rather chosen to fill our hives with honey and wax; thus furnishing mankind with the two noblest of things, which are sweetness and light.
— *Jonathan Swift*, The Battle of the Books

Honey is basically the nectar collected by bees from various flowers; the type of honey is determined by the type of flower. The most important sources of nectar are orange blossoms, clovers, sunflowers, dandelions, and linden trees. Other honeys, such as tupelo and buckwheat, are more rare but are highly valued because of their distinctive taste. In honey, sucrose is converted by bees during ripening almost entirely to fructose and glucose; the honey also undergoes many changes in flavor and color. Before honey can be placed on the market, it must be freed of all foreign material and dirt. To accomplish this, the honey is heated to about 155° F to destroy sugar-fermenting yeasts that may cause spoilage. The heated syrup is then carefully strained to remove wax and dirt and then filtered under pressure to remove air bubbles. Honey is produced in nearly every country in the world and lends distinct flavor to traditional sweets such as baklava and nougat. Like other inverts, honey is more hygroscopic than granulated sugar and can tenderize and keep baked goods moister for longer shelf life.

Maple Syrup

Maple syrup is obtained from boiling the sap of certain varieties of maple trees. The density and color of the syrup are controlled and determined by how long and at how high a temperature the syrup is boiled; the darker the color of the syrup, the denser and heavier its taste will be. Syrups are graded according to their color, flavor, and sugar density—the lighter and less dense the syrup, the higher grade it will receive. Products that are labeled pure maple syrup do not contain any other sugar syrup. Like honey, maple syrup lends a unique flavor to baked goods and has excellent hygroscopic qualities.

Maple syrup was the first sweetener, other than fruits and berries, known in North America. Many Native North American tribes had established methods of sugaring long before the European settlers came; it was these tribes that taught the early settlers their processes and techniques.

Corn Syrup

Corn syrup is derived from the starch found in corn; the starch granules are extracted from corn kernels and treated with an acid or certain enzymes to invert the starch into a thick, sweet syrup of glucose molecules. Because of its thick viscosity, corn syrup can interfere with recrystallization of sucrose during sugar boiling for candies and pulled sugar showpieces, as well as improve elasticity. It also has excellent hygroscopic capabilities that tenderize and provide the product with longer shelf life. Corn syrup is available in both light and dark forms; the dark syrup contains added flavorings and colors and is not used as extensively as the light syrup in the bake shop.

Glucose

Glucose is derived from the starch found in corn, potatoes, rice, or wheat; in the United States, its derivation is most commonly corn. It is more viscous than corn syrup but is used for many of the same purposes, most often in sugar artistry and boiled syrups and sauces to prevent crystallization and increase elasticity.

Malt Syrup

Malt syrup is derived from barley and is most commonly used to flavor yeast-raised breads. It contains diastase, an enzyme used by yeast during fermentation to break its starch into sugars, which provide food for the yeast. Nondiastasic malt contains no diastase because it is boiled at a higher temperature than is diastasic malt. Although it is mostly used only in bread products, it retains moisture and gives distinct flavor to other baked goods as well.

Eggs

Eggs are a very important and costly ingredient in baked goods; they are second only to flour as a structural component and can represent nearly half the cost incurred in cake production. Although most bake shops use hen eggs, other types of eggs, such as duck or quail eggs, could theoretically be used, and are in fact used in some countries. Brown eggs and white eggs are virtually the same, the difference lies in the breed of hen. Discussion here is limited to that of hen eggs.

Eggs serve many purposes in baking:

- *Leavening:* Whipped or beaten eggs entrap air that expands when heated.
- *Creaming:* Eggs increase the number of air cells formed and coat these cells with fat that allows expansion.
- *Color:* The rich yellow color of the yolk provides a distinct color to baked goods.
- *Flavor:* Eggs impart a distinct odor and flavor to baked goods.
- *Nutritional value:* The albumen (egg white) is a valuable source of protein.
- *Richness:* The yolk is 30 percent fat; this, combined with other solids of the egg, provide shortness to a mix and also act as tenderizers.
- *Freshness:* Because eggs contain close to 75 percent moisture and can bind and retain moisture, eggs improve the shelf life of the product.
- *Structure:* Because of their high moisture content, eggs have a natural ability to act as a binding agent.
- *Emulsification and thickening:* The lecithin (an emulsifier) found in the yolk of the egg allows fillings and sauces to come together, bind, and thicken.

There are four forms of eggs that can be used in the bake shop:

1. *Fresh eggs* are probably the most common form of egg used. Eggs that have been previously cracked and then packaged can save time in high-volume bake shops but are no longer widely used in the United States because of contamination risks. Eggs begin to deteriorate almost immediately upon cracking; great care must be taken that they are properly handled, not only for sanitary reasons, but also so they do not lose their valuable qualities. Eggs should be stored below 40° F when not in use. Fresh eggs generally have a shelf life of up to four weeks.

2. *Frozen eggs* are broken, strained, mixed, and most often pasteurized. Pasteurization requires that the egg be heated to 145° F and kept there for 3½ minutes to help destroy pathogenic bacteria, particularly salmonella. The eggs are then quickly frozen at 10° F to 15° F. Frozen eggs are best thawed by ordering them in advance so that thawing may take place under refrigeration; however, a cool water bath may be used if necessary. Very convenient to use, frozen eggs can be substituted for fresh eggs in many items, although their use in cooked fillings and custards should be avoided to prevent the formation of yellow spots in the final product—fresh eggs are recommended for these items. Frozen yolks are available but contain 10 percent added sugar to prevent gelling and to act as a preservative. When using sugar yolks, in which the sugar is above the usual 10 percent, allowance should be made for the extra sugar and lesser amount of liquid. If this is not done, the mix will be thicker and bake with a deep color and loss of volume. Adjusting sugar and moisture helps to produce a closer grain and moist texture. To illustrate, if 1 pound of eggs is replaced by 1 pound of sugar yolks containing 20 percent sugar, then the sugar in the mix should be reduced by 20 percent of 1 pound, or approximately 3¼ ounces of sugar. In addition, because the yolks contain 8 ounces of moisture instead of 12 ounces, an additional 4 ounces of liquid, water, or milk should be added. Frozen whites often contain small amounts of whipping aids, usually in the form of triethyl citrate.

3. *Dried eggs*, eggs with the water removed, became important during World War II when they were developed for use in field rations for the military. They principally are used in cake mixes and rarely used as an egg substitute. Meringue powders are commonly used, however, with excellent results. If used in a dough, it is best to reconstitute dried eggs to prevent moisture absorption and stiffening.

4. *Liquid eggs* are cracked from the shell, then pasteurized. After pasteurization they are packed in sanitary

cartons and sold in liquid form. Liquid eggs were once widely used; now they are rarely seen in bake shops.

Composition of the Egg

Figure 13–6 shows the composition of the average chicken egg.

The Yolk

The yolk of the egg, the more solid part, contains most of the fatty material in a finely emulsified state. The approximate amount of lecithin fat in the yolk is between 7 and 10 percent of total fat content. The yolk makes up approximately one-third of the egg's shelled weight. Yolks improve creaming and emulsification, create volume because of their ability to hold air cells, and act as thickeners in creams and sauces. When egg yolks are heated to a temperature exceeding 175° F, they begin to lose moisture and the proteins within them squeeze closely together, causing curdling. Care must be taken to heat sauces and desserts where the egg is the main ingredient very carefully over a baine marie.

The White

The egg white contains proteins that are both thick and thin. The white close to the yolk is generally thick, while that portion closer to the shell is thin. Whites are fibrous

Figure 13–6 Composition of a chicken egg

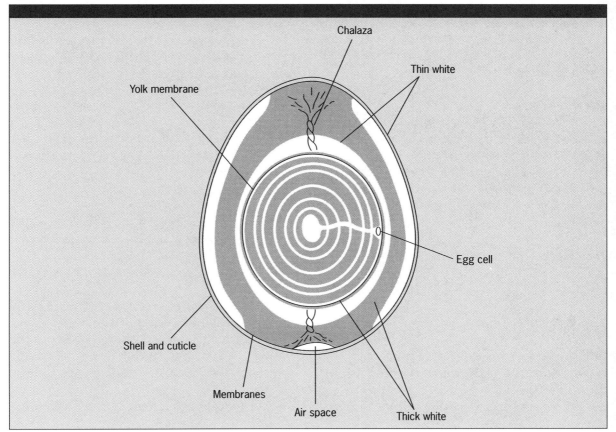

and tend to hold together; they make excellent foams that can be increased by nearly eight times their original volume when whipped. When an egg white is whipped, the protein molecules are redispersed into a foam of air and water that bond with one another to create a stable foam. Fats reduce the volume of egg-white foams by interfering with coagulation of the proteins—this means that any yolk present in a foam could potentially reduce or even prevent a stable foam from occurring. Likewise, plastic bowls should not be used when whipping egg-white foams because of plastic's capacity for retaining fatty substances on its surface. Acid, in the form of cream of tartar, is often used to stabilize egg-white foams by lowering the pH level of the albumen; copper bowls are often used in making egg-white foams for the same reason.

The Shell
The shell of the egg acts as a protective vessel. The shell is hard and porous, but it allows the egg to breathe by giving off carbon dioxide and taking in oxygen. Most eggshells are coated with a thin film of mineral oil to retard aging and improve shelf life.

The Air Pocket
Attached to the shell at the larger base of the egg is the air pocket. As the egg loses carbon dioxide and moisture with time, it gets smaller; the air pocket, conversely, gets larger. The size of the air pocket is a direct indication of the freshness of the egg: the larger the air pocket, the older the egg; the smaller the air pocket, the younger and fresher the egg.

The Chalazae
The chalazae is the twisted white cord that holds the yolk in place.

Quality of Eggs

While government standards grade eggs in terms of depth or thickness of the air pocket, movement of the yolk, and the yolk's position with respect to the center of the egg, firmness of the egg whites, clarity of the yolk and white, and condition of the shell, freshness is the most important factor. *Candling* is used to determine the quality of an egg.

In candling, the egg is held up to a light source in a darkened room or positioned so the contents and condition of the egg may easily be seen. If the yolk is in the center, the air pocket is small. If the yolk is held firmly by the white when the egg is turned and the shell is unbroken and clean, then the egg is of good quality.

Smell and odor are not revealed readily unless the shell is broken. Bad odors are caused by bacteria or mold and may be present even when the shell is not broken. Because the shell is porous, moisture or washing will permit entry of bacteria and mold spores. Any questionable egg or eggs should be discarded. Spots in eggs are generally due to blood fragments in the ovary and are found as spots on the yolk or suspended in the whites. Such eggs are edible and may be used.

Sanitation

Eggs are a fine medium for the development of bacteria and molds, particularly salmonella. Following are some proper tips for handling and storing eggs:

- Immediately upon receipt, refrigerate eggs below 40°F.
- Never leave eggs at room temperature for more than one hour, including delivery, storage, preparation, or service time.
- Store shell eggs in their case.
- Rotate stock; first in, first out.
- Do not thaw frozen eggs at room temperature. Thaw in the refrigerator or under cold running water in watertight containers.
- Keep defrosted egg products under 40° F. Use within three days.
- Immediately refrigerate leftover egg products below 40° F. Keep airtight and use within six days.
- To ensure that salmonella bacteria have been killed, heat the food product to 145° F and cook for 3½ minutes, the time and temperature conditions for pasteurization.
- Discard eggs that have even the smallest of cracks.
- Never mix shells with egg content or crack eggs at the mixer.

- Cook thoroughly, until there is no visible liquid egg, especially yolk. When cooking egg mixtures, bring the temperature to 140° F and hold for at least 3½ minutes. This may require recipe adjustment. It is not safe to serve any product that cannot be prepared according to this guideline.
- Thoroughly wash equipment, utensils, and countertops that have been in contact with raw eggs before preparing other foods.
- Never prepare egg dishes on a wooden cutting board.
- Wash hands thoroughly after handling raw eggs and before handling other foods.
- Hold at 140° F or higher for no longer than 30 minutes.
- Do not combine eggs that have been held in a steamtable pan with a fresh batch of eggs. Always use a fresh steam-table pan.
- If the product is to be served cold, after cooking, chill quickly over an ice bath and hold below 40° F.

Milk

The unqualified word *milk* refers to fresh, raw milk as it is taken from the cow. Milk is treated in many ways to increase keeping qualities and to facilitate handling because of its high perishability. Milk is sold in many forms, all of which are subjected to various forms of pasteurization, homogenization, and vitamin fortification.

Milk contains butterfat, proteins, lactose (milk sugar), vitamins, minerals, salts, and water. Milk is rich in calcium; the butterfat contains vitamin A, and the other milk solids contain vitamin B. Milk is fortified with vitamin D. Government standards require liquid whole milk to contain at least 3½ percent butterfat and 8 percent nonfat solids. The butterfat and the proteins in milk are the most valuable components to the baker, although because it contains vitamins and minerals milk is also of great nutritional value.

Lactose intolerance is common in humans throughout the world. Western cultures and a few nomadic African tribes are the only people among most humans to produce the enzyme that breaks down lactose, allowing them to drink milk into adulthood. People in most other cultures do not produce the enzyme after the age of

about three. Cheese, yogurt, and other fermented or cultured dairy products are enjoyed by many cultures because the fermenting bacteria used to make them use up most of the lactose as fuel during the fermentation process.

Purposes and Uses of Milk

Milk has many uses for the baker. Its protein, fat, and sugar content give it unique qualities that enhance baked goods, custards, ice creams, and dough. Milk is also a good source of protein, vitamins, and minerals.

- Milk increases absorption in bread doughs (because of the protein casein, see below) providing a strengthening effect and increasing fermentation tolerance in the dough.
- Milk aids in creaming because of casein's ability to absorb moisture, which in turn aids in preventing curdling.
- Milk provides richness and shortness to cakes because of its fat content.
- Milk aids in crust color because of the caramelization of lactose (milk sugar).
- Milk produces better texture in baked products because of its fat and sugar content.
- Milk helps maintain freshness in a baked good because of its high moisture content.
- The emulsified butterfat in dried milk solids (DMS) aids in creaming to improve cell structure of the product.
- Milk imparts flavor to baked goods.
- Milk is a nutritionally valuable source of vitamins, minerals, and protein.

Pasteurization of Milk

Milk is a very favorable medium for the growth of bacteria, many of which are harmful. Unless great care is taken in handling milk, it can be the source of serious illness. The many bacteria in milk thrive at temperatures of 70° F to 100° F. When the temperature is kept below 70° F, the activity of the bacteria decreases. Milk should be stored under refrigeration at below 40° F.

Because milk is such a hospitable host for so many microbes, it is almost always pasteurized before being sold for human consumption. Pasteurization was developed by

Louis Pasteur during the 1820s as a way to heat beer and wine to prevent spoilage without destroying flavor. His theory was to heat a substance just hot enough for just a long enough period of time for most of the bacteria to be destroyed, preserving the substance. There are two standard methods of pasteurizing milk:

1. *The Holder Process:* Milk is heated to 144° F and held there for 30 minutes.
2. *High Temperature, Short Time (HTST) method:* Milk is heated to 161° F and held there for 15 seconds.

In both methods, the milk is cooled after heating to below 50° F and bottled within 3 to 5 minutes. Ultrapasteurization, where the temperature is taken to 280° F and held there for 1 to 2 seconds, is reserved usually for cream and unrefrigerated shelf milks, such as Parmalat, which are used less and kept longer.

Homogenization of Milk

In addition to pasteurization, most commercially sold milk is also homogenized to prevent the separation of the fat; this separation is commonly referred to as *creaming*. Homogenization forces the milk at high pressure through a very small nozzle onto a hard surface; this reduces the size of the fat globules and allows them to stay suspended, rather than rising. Developed in France around 1900, homogenization prevented the baker from having to try to redisperse the risen fat globules unevenly into the remaining milk.

Homogenization makes milk blander, whiter, and more sensitive to spoilage by light.

The Composition of Milk

As previously discussed, milk contains many components. The fat, lactose, and proteins are the most valuable components in baking. Whole milk is made up of almost 90 percent water, 3½ percent butterfat, approximately 3 percent protein, and 4½ to 5 percent lactose.

Although many proteins are found in milk, the two most important for baking are casein and lactoglobulin.

- *Casein* is the protein in milk that clumps and curdles because of the addition of acid, too high heat, or too much salt. Casein has good moisture-absorbing—a quality that can be very valuable in the creaming process (see Purposes and Uses of Milk). Commonly, casein is referred to as the *curd*.
- *Lactoglobulin* is the protein that remains suspended throughout the liquid. It is commonly referred to as the *whey*. Unlike casein, it is strongly resistant to curdling.

Types of Milk

Liquid Whole Milk

Liquid whole milk is used in the bake shop for various items, including rich bread doughs, cakes, pastry cream, and sauces such as crème anglaise. It contains 3½ percent butterfat.

Liquid Low-Fat Milk

Milk is readily available with reduced fat. The most common are 1 and 2 percent fat milk. These products have the advantage of a quality milk taste with lower fat and calories than whole milk.

Liquid Skim Milk

Skim milk is milk with all fat removed and is used in low-fat baking.

Evaporated or Condensed Milks

Evaporated milk is made by rapidly evaporating close to 60 percent of the water by vacuum. The resulting liquid is sterilized, homogenized, and then canned. Because of this process, evaporated milks can keep almost indefinitely (unopened) and they take up less storage space than liquid milk. Evaporated milks can be reconstituted to make whole milk for use in formulas by mixing their amount with the same amount of water by volume.

Sweetened condensed milk has 40 to 50 percent of the water evaporated, then approximately 50 percent sugar is added. This level of sugar makes the milk uninhabitable for microbes; therefore, sweetened condensed milk usually is not sterilized.

Evaporated milks are available in both whole and skim forms, and are labeled as such according to the amount of butterfat they contain. As soon as they are exposed to air, evaporated milks can spoil; they should be covered and refrigerated for storage upon opening.

Evaporated milks (including sweetened condensed milk) may appear off-color upon opening. This is normal; the high temperature reached during sterilization, together with the concentrated levels of lactose and other sugars cause both caramelization and maillard browning (similar to the browning of a roast, where both sugar and protein are present).

Powdered, or Dry, Milk

Powdered, or dry, milk is made similarly to evaporated milks; the milk is rapidly evaporated by being forced through heat cylinders, removing all but a tiny fraction of the water. The words *powdered* or *dry* are used interchangeably when describing dry milk solids, commonly referred to as DMS. There are three kinds of dried milk: dry whole, dry skim, and dry buttermilk, although skim is the preferable choice because of its low fat content. DMS made with skim milk will not spoil as quickly and reconstitutes with water more readily than DMS made with whole milk or buttermilk. A basic formula for reconstituting any DMS is 1 quart of water to 4 ounces of DMS. Dry milks are valuable in bake shops because they

- Do not require refrigeration and can be stored in bulk.
- Are economical.
- Keep for several months in dry, cool surroundings.
- Are easy to handle.
- Can be used in climates that make liquid milk impractical.

Fermented Dairy Products

Liquid buttermilk, yogurt, and sour cream are thickened and curdled by acid-producing bacteria. Because of this, they lend a unique flavor to the finished product.

Liquid Buttermilk

Originally, buttermilk was made from either sweet or sour milk that had been churned to remove the butterfat; the result was the solids—butter—and the liquid—buttermilk. Commercially produced buttermilk (cultured buttermilk) is made from *skim milk* that has either an acid or bacteria introduced into it; which converts the lactose into lactic acid and sours the milk. Liquid buttermilk is sometimes used in baked products because it produces a distinct, tart flavor in the finished product. Because of its high acidity, it is usually used in conjunction with baking soda (an alkaline) to produce carbon-dioxide gas and to create leavening.

Yogurt

Yogurt is made from either whole or skim milk. It is soured with two specific types of bacteria that consume the milk's lactose as an energy source and give off lactic acid as a waste product. Yogurt is made by heating milk to 185° F; a mixed culture of the two bacteria are added to the milk when it cools to 113° F. The temperature is dropped to 110° F and held there for at least four hours, causing the milk to ferment and to coagulate into a custardlike consistency. Like buttermilk, it provides a tangy flavor to fillings and sauces; it is also commonly used to make frozen yogurt. Yogurt is often substituted for sour cream to significantly reduce fat content.

Sour Cream

Sour cream can be made with or without bacteria; often an acid is used instead. Sour cream is made with cream, not milk, and is required to have a minimum of 18 percent butterfat. The cream is soured with bacteria that, as in yogurt and buttermilk, consume lactose and give off lactic acid. As soon as the bacteria are introduced into the cream, the cream is left to culture for up to two days. Stabilizers and emulsifiers are often added to help produce the cream's thick, smooth texture. Sour cream is often used in fillings or to dress cold fruit soups.

Crème Fraîche

Crème fraîche has a similar taste and consistency to that of sour cream. It is made commercially by adding an acid to culture and thicken the cream. It can be made tradition-ally by allowing unhomogenized milk or cream to separate (this requires a few hours) and then skimming off the risen cream and allowing it to stand for further thickening. "Mock" crème fraîche is often used instead and is usually a combination of buttermilk or sour cream and heavy cream that is heated and left to thicken.

Cream

Cream is a form of milk in which the fat globules are larger and more concentrated than they are in milk. Traditionally, cream was made by letting unhomogenized milk separate, with the cream rising to the top. Today, modern dairies use centrifuges to skim off the cream. There are four grades of cream:

- Half-and-half, with a butterfat content of 10 to 18 percent
- Light cream, with a butterfat content of between 18 and 30 percent
- Light whipping cream, with a butterfat content of be-tween 30 and 36 percent
- Heavy whipping cream, with a butterfat content of between 36 and 40 percent

As with milk, these grades of butterfat can vary according to the state or dairy in which they are produced and, consequently, can cause confusion. To avoid confusion, the dairy or supplier can provide a list of products according to their name and butterfat content.

Cream is used in baking as either a liquid ingredient, as in a custard, sauce, or ice cream; or it can be whipped, as in a Chantilly cream, Bavarian cream, or mousse. Whipped creams are often piped for use as decoration. For more information on the proper method or procedure for whip-ping cream, refer to the section on creams starting on page 356.

Handling and Storage of Milk and Cream

Both milk and cream are highly susceptible to spoilage. They should always be stored under refrigeration below 40° F. Never leave milk at room temperature unless under controlled circumstances (such as in the making of crème fraîche). Milk should be used within one week to ten days of purchase.

Fats and Oils

Chemically, fats and oils have the same makeup; they are both in the same class of chemical compounds known as *triglycerides*. They differ only in the temperature of their melting points: Fats are solid at room temperature and oils are liquid at room temperature. Fats and oils are commonly used in baked goods (see Table 13–3); they can be of either animal or vegetable sources. Fats should be gener-ally neutral in taste unless the flavor (as in butter or lard) can enhance the product. Fats are often blended by the baker to develop a desired flavor and, because some fats (such as butter) can be costly, keep costs down.

Fats and oils play an important role in baking. They

- Impart shortness and tenderness to the product by means of lubricating gluten strands.
- Aid in creaming, resulting in aeration of the product.
- Contribute greatly to the flavor of the product, particu-larly if butter or lard is used.
- Promote a desirable grain and texture through cream-ing.
- Provide flakiness in laminated doughs by creating steam upon melting.
- Help emulsify (especially during creaming) and hold liquids

The melting point of a fat is the temperature at which that fat turns from a solid to a liquid state; the plasticity of a fat is how "workable" it is at room temperature before it begins to melt. If a fat has a high melting point, it will also have a high plasticity, or plastic, range.

Types of Fats

Lard
Lard is nearly 100 percent refined pork fat, rendered from the hog. One of the finest-quality lards is called *prime steam lard.* This fat directly surrounds the internal organs

Table 13–3 Common Fats Used in Baking

Type of Fat	Source	Color	Odor and Flavor	Consistency	Fat Content (%)
Vegetable shortening	Vegetable oil	White	None	Solid	100
Butter	Animal (milk)	Yellow	Sweet and pleasant	Solid	80
Oil	Vegetable	Neutral to yellow	None to mild odor	Liquid	100
Lard	Animal (hog)	White	Mild odor	Solid	98
Margarine	Animal or vegetable	White to yellow	Neutral to milk, butter flavor	Solid	80 to 85
Puff paste	Animal or vegetable	White	None to mild, salt taste	Solid	80 to 85
Cocoa butter	Vegetable (cacao bean)	Cream to yellow	Sweet, chocolaty	Solid	92

of the animal. A good-quality lard is white, contains little or no odor or taste, and has a smooth texture. The further away from the internal organs, the lower the quality of the lard; the color will appear more yellow, the texture will tend to be gritty, and a slight odor and flavor may be noticeable. Because of this possible odor and flavor, lard is not used in delicate pastries. It is usually reserved for such items as pie dough, because lard produces a flaky pie crust; a flavorful filling camouflages the possible flavor of the lard. Lard's high melting point is similar to that of shortening and makes it very valuable to the baker because it creates a flavorful, flaky crust. Because it comes from an animal, which means it is higher in cholesterol than fats from a vegetable source, lard is not used as often in bake shops as it once was. It is on the average more economical to use than other fats, however, so some bakeries use it in certain pastries (such as pie dough) to keep costs down.

Butter

To make butter, cream is removed from whole milk and then churned, or agitated. Eventually, the butter granules form, get larger, and stick together. This creates a mass of butter with liquid left over, known as buttermilk. The USDA requires that butter be at least 80 percent butterfat. Quality butter should have no more than 15 percent water, with butter's remaining 5 percent made up of nonfat milk solids and minerals. Butter's chief value in baking and cooking is its flavor. Because butter has a low melting point of 80° F (i.e., lower than body temperature), it "melts

in your mouth." Butter's low melting point, flavor, and aroma make it paramount to the success of delicate pastries such as puff pastry, buttercreams, and certain cakes and cookies.

Butter is susceptible to spoilage and oxidation and should be wrapped airtight for storage under refrigeration below 45° F; it should not be held at room temperature for more than six to eight hours. Butter can keep for months in the freezer if properly wrapped.

Butter comes in two forms: Salted or unsalted. Because salted butter contains anywhere from 6 to 8 percent salt, unsalted, or sweet, butter should be used in the bake shop. This will prevent unnecessary altering of formulas.

Margarine

Margarine is a blend of refined animal or vegetable fats that are usually churned with skim milk. It can be made without any animal fat or cream. It was basically developed as a butter substitute and is divided into two main types: oleomargarine, which is made chiefly of beef fat and a blend of other oils, and vegetable margarine, which is made from a blend of vegetable oils, usually corn or soybean. The oils are pressed from the source, purified, hydrogenated, and then colored and fortified with vitamins. Vegetable margarine, with or without added milk products, is most commonly found in the United States. Margarine contains approximately 80 percent fat; 15 to 20 percent water; and 2 to 5 percent solids, salt, preservatives, and emulsifiers. Different types of margarine are available to the baker:

Baker's margarine, which is cakelike, is excellent for creaming; puff pastry-type margarines are used as roll-in fats in laminated doughs. Both have a considerably higher melting point than that of table margarine, which begins to turn soft and melt at around 75° F. Butter and margarine blends are now available and are made mostly of vegetable margarine but contain small amounts of butter to improve flavor and assist in melting.

Shortenings

Shortenings are made from purified oils that are heated and then injected with hydrogen while the oil is still hot. The hydrogen causes the liquid oil to change into a solid; the more hydrogen injected, the firmer the fat will become. This process is called *hydrogenation,* and it causes the resulting shortening to have a higher melting point and plasticity. Margarine is also hydrogenated to a small degree. There are different types of shortenings:

- *High-ratio shortening* is shortening with the addition of emulsifiers (mono- and diglycerides) that enable the fat to absorb and retain moisture. This type of fat is usually used in cakes that contain high ratios of sugar and in icings, so the fat can absorb the moisture that the high ratio of sugar will create.
- *All-purpose shortening* is also emulsified but absorbs less moisture than do high-ratio shortenings and is therefore used in pie doughs and other doughs where there is no danger of an excess of moisture that the fat would retain.
- *Liquid shortening* is a form of high-ratio shortening that is only partially hydrogenated. It is left in a semiliquid state to enable it to be used in one-step mixing procedures. It is often referred to as a micro-emulsified shortening. It cannot be replaced by any other fat because of its unique composition. Cake batters most often use liquid shortening.
- *Puff-pastry shortening* is super hydrogenated and therefore has a high melting point and plasticity. This makes it excellent for creating steam during the physical leavening process, but the high melting point creates a tremendous flavor loss. It is used in laminated doughs such as puff pastry to create flaky layers, but,

because of its poor flavor, puff-pastry shortening is often blended with another fat, such as butter, to produce the best product.

Oils

Many refined oils are available for baking, including corn, soybean, peanut, and coconut. Oils are obtained from their sources through pressing or by solvent extraction, or by both. Oils are primarily used in doughs and quick breads and for frying. Most oils are generally lower in saturated fat than are fats. Some oils, such as sesame and olive oil, retain much of the flavor of their source—this flavor will be imparted to the baked good if these oils are used (sometimes this flavor is desired). Most often, an oil of neutral taste and flavor, such as corn or salad oil, is used in the bake shop.

Leavening Actions

Leavening actions aerate mixtures or doughs and lighten their textures; this results in a light and porous product with good volume and tenderness. There are three leavening actions: physical, chemical, and biological. Each of these actions is brought about through the use of specific leavening agents:

Physical Action

- *Air* is considered a physical leavening agent because it is applied to or occurs in products as a result of a physical action taken by the baker to leaven the product. Air is introduced into a mixture through sifting dry ingredients, creaming and mixing batters, and incorporating whipped eggs or egg whites. To some degree, all mixtures (yeast-leavened breads, cakes, and cookies) depend on air for leavening. Usually air is not sufficient and additional leavening agents are used. The basic formula for shortened cake usually directs that some chemical leavening agent be used, although extensive creaming of the fat and sugar is recommended for aeration. This creaming action leads to the formation of air cells into which the carbon-dioxide gas formed by the baking powder can diffuse. When foam cakes—angel food and sponge—are heated, the air trapped in the cells expands and the volume of the cake increases. Angel food cakes are leavened by the incorporation of air cells into the mixture by whipped egg whites, and air is whipped into egg yolks or whole eggs for yellow sponge cakes. Chiffon cakes depend on whipped eggs for a large part of their leavening, but baking powder also can be used.

- *Steam* is created when the moisture of a product evaporates in the oven, pushing its layers up and leavening the product. Steam is created in the leavening of laminated doughs, such as croissant, Danish, and puff pastry, by the evaporation of the many layers of fat that have been rolled into the dough, creating flaky layers. Pie dough also uses steam through the evaporation of the fat used. A fat with a high moisture percentage, such as butter, is valuable for physical leavening. Fats with high melting points and the use of a high oven temperature will also ensure a flaky product, although fats with these qualities tend to be low in moisture and flavor. Pastries such as cream puffs and eclairs, because of their high moisture content, also use steam (in addition to a chemical leavener).

Chemical Action

Chemical leaveners use carbon dioxide given off during the mixing or baking of the product. Chemical leavening agents include baking powder, baking soda, and ammonium carbonate.

Baking powder, a basic composition of baking soda (an alkaline), cream of tartar (an acid), and starch (to prevent caking), is used frequently in cakes, cookies, and quick breads. When baking powder comes in contact with heat or liquid, the alkaline and acid react and give off carbon dioxide, which expands and leavens the product. The three types of baking powder are fast-acting, slow-acting, and double-acting. Fast-acting baking powder reacts to the liquid in the formula. Slow-acting baking powder reacts to the heat of the oven. Double-acting baking powder reacts

to both heat and liquid, and is the type of baking powder most commonly used in the bake shop. Baking powder should be measured very accurately; too much will cause an undesirable aftertaste and change the texture and volume of the final product.

Baking soda, or sodium bicarbonate, is an alkaline and must be used in conjunction with an acid to give off carbon dioxide. It is most often used in formulas that contain an acid, such as chocolate or buttermilk, to create the desired leavening action. It reacts to the liquid in a formula, so products in which it is used should be handled quickly. Like baking powder, it can leave an undesirable aftertaste if measured inaccurately. In addition to leavening, it also darkens the color of the product. Unlike baking powder, which causes mostly a rising and spreading action, baking powder creates more of a spread than a rise in the final product.

Ammonium carbonate reacts to heat and moisture and gives off water, ammonia, and carbon dioxide. Like baking soda, it reacts immediately, and products in which it is used must be handled quickly. It is most often used in pâte à choux to ensure the puffiness of the final product; however, it gives off a strong ammonialike odor until the internal temperature of the baked item reaches 140° F.

Biological Action

Yeast is a living microorganism, a one-celled fungus that multiplies very quickly under favorable conditions: a warm, moist environment. Yeast, through enzymatic action, converts certain sugars and starches it finds in the dough into carbon dioxide and alcohol. The carbon dioxide expands and leavens; the alcohol is eventually baked off with the rise of the internal temperature of the product. This leavening action of yeast is known as *fermentation*. Yeast gives bread a distinctive flavor and is available in compressed, dry, or instant forms.

- *Compressed (or fresh) yeast* is a moist mixture of yeast and starch. It should have a pleasant smell and crumble easily. It must be kept refrigerated to retard deterioration—its shelf life is generally two weeks maximum. Dried out, dark compressed cakes with a cheesy flavor may be ineffective and may produce a product that is unpalatable. Compressed yeast can be frozen, but it will lose some of its strength and should be thawed slowly and used the same day.

- *Dry yeast* contains no water and therefore is less apt to deteriorate during storage. The manufacture of both is similar. Dry yeast is passed through dryers, cutting the moisture content to about 8 percent, making the cells dormant and refrigeration unnecessary. Dry yeast must be soaked in warm water, 110° F, for 5 to 10 minutes before it can be used. Dry yeast becomes inactive after prolonged storage. Packages of dry yeast show an expiration date; the yeast should not be used after the date indicated. To substitute dry yeast for compressed yeast, cut the total amount of yeast used in half.

- *Instant yeast* is similar to dry yeast, but it has already been activated, then dried. This allows the yeast to be added to the dough at any stage without needing to be activated in warm water, which can reduce fermentation time.

Thickening Agents

Thickening agents create a fuller body in many sauces, fillings, and puddings. There are many types of thickening agents, each derived most often from the starch molecules found in the roots or seeds of certain plants or in tubers. Chemically, most starches are made up of thousands of glucose sugar molecules produced by plants during photosynthesis. Some starch granules are not soluble in a liquid at room temperature and must be heated to dissolve; others, because of their chemical structure, can be added directly to liquid without heating. Most starches are used to thicken fillings, glazes, and sauces, and perform valuable functions for the baker:

- They thicken fillings and sauces quickly.
- They produce a gloss to fillings and glazes.
- They sometimes offset the action of acids (particularly fruit acids).
- They maintain fruit flavor and color in fruit fillings, sauces, and glazes.

- They maintain thickness and consistency in the filling or sauce upon cooling.

Each starch has a specific method in which it should be used.

Cornstarch is one of the most commonly used thickeners in the bake shop. To prevent lumping, it should be dissolved in a small portion of cold liquid before it is used. Because cornstarch begins to thicken only after it has been heated to between 140° F to 170° F (where it begins to gelatinize), it must be heated with the formula's liquid ingredients and cooked until it is translucent, or it will leave an unpleasant aftertaste (depending on the formula's ingredients, this cooking time could be anywhere from 1 to 3 minutes). Because cornstarch begins to break down three to four days after cooking, items thickened with cornstarch will begin to weep and separate. Fruits high in acid can fragment the starch granules in cornstarch and cause thinning; sugar in the formula will most often decrease this effect and is usually calculated accordingly to do so.

Flour is also used as a thickener, particularly in the form of roux for sauces, in much the same manner as cornstarch. It must be predissolved and then heated with the liquid from the formula. Because it contains wheat protein, its thickening power is diluted to almost half that of cornstarch. These proteins also cause an opaqueness in the final product, unlike the glossy shine produced by cornstarch. Flour will also leave an unpleasant aftertaste and mouthfeel if not cooked long enough.

Arrowroot is derived from the root of a native Caribbean plant. Unlike cornstarch and flour, arrowroot's chemical makeup is such that it is almost tasteless, so it leaves no unpleasant aftertaste. But, perhaps more importantly, it thickens at a much lower temperature than cornstarch so is sometimes easier to use. In addition, it has almost the same strength as cornstarch but can be used in less quantity. Arrowroot can be used in conjunction with fruits that contain high levels of acid because its granules are not broken down by the high acidity.

Potato starch is used less often than other forms of starch in most bake shops, but can be used with great success. Like arrowroot, it leaves no unpleasant aftertaste and has a lesser tendency to break down. Its strength is less than that of cornstarch, so it must be used in greater quantity and is often used in conjunction with other starches. It provides a high gloss and shine to the finished product.

Tapioca is derived from the root of the cassava plant native to South America and is most often used in puddings. It comes in several forms: granules, flakes, or pearls; all are cooked only until they are softened. Tapioca flour is also available and is cooked in the same manner as cornstarch.

Modified food starches are most commonly used in food processing to thicken canned fruit fillings, for example. They have been modified with acid or other chemical or physical treatments to enhance or repress certain characteristics of the starch so that it will perform specific applications without rupturing, losing viscosity, or weeping. These starches are not commonly used in the food industry.

Pregelatinized starches, such as Instant ClearJel, are precooked and therefore require no heating to enable the starch to absorb water and gelatinize. They are combined with the sugar and then added to the liquid in the formula. These types of starches are excellent for use in thickening sauces quickly. They can also be used to thicken coulis-type sauces so the coulis can remain uncooked and still reach the desired consistency.

Gelling Agents

Gelling agents, like thickening agents, are used to thicken certain fillings and desserts in the bake shop. They can also be used to stabilize unstable foams, such as whipped cream, and to make glazes and jellies. Gelling agents come from a variety of sources—plant and animal—and can vary in strength. Gelling agents are handled differently than most starch-based thickeners.

Gelatin is derived from the collagen found in the connective tissues of animals. Commercial, culinary gelatin (type A) is made from pigskins. When making gelatin, the collagen is separated from the other animal components, then purified and converted into gelatin. The gelatin is then purified, refined, and ground into granules or cut into sheet or leaf gelatin. Gelatin is fairly strong in its gelling power and, when used in the right quantity, can allow certain desserts, such as Bavarian creams, to hold the shape of

their mold after they are unmolded. The strength of gelatin is measured by a Bloom Gellometer (named after the French scientist who developed it). A tool is placed in the gelatin to read its gelling ability on a scale from 50 to 300. The gelatin used for baking is most often between 200 to 250 bloom. The term *bloom* is also used to describe the rehydration of gelatin. Gelatin must be rehydrated in cold liquid and then dissolved with heat for use in a formula. It comes in either powdered or sheet form; these forms can be substituted in equal weights for each other (generally, there are ten sheets of gelatin to every ounce of powdered gelatin), but care must be taken because more water may need to be added to the formula when substituting sheet gelatin for powdered gelatin. Some fruits, such as pineapples, kiwi, figs, and other tropical fruits, contain bromelian or papain enzymes that, if used raw, will break down gelatin's protein structure; these fruits must be heated to destroy the enzyme before they can be used with gelatin.

Agar-agar is extracted from Japanese seaweed. Because it is purely vegetable, it is of great use in kitchens where dietary restrictions such as vegetarianism or keeping kosher are of concern. It is also used widely in the making of some candies. Agar-agar is eight times as strong as gelatin and comes in powdered, flake, or strip forms. It should be heated with liquid and simmered over low heat to dissolve it. Unlike gelatin, it is not protein-based and will not break down when used with tropical fruits containing bromelian or papain enzymes.

Pectin occurs naturally in many fruits, especially blueberries, cranberries, apples, and citrus fruits. It is also derived from plant cells. It is the substance most responsible for thickening and gelling jams, jellies, and preserves. It can also be used to make glazes for fruits. Pectin can be purchased in either powdered or liquid form

Vegetable gums are being used increasingly in many forms of food processing, particularly in ice creams and in low-fat or calorie-reduced foods. Gums can retain water, reduce evaporation rates, modify ice-crystal formation, and improve the consistency and flow of certain foods. By dissolving or dispersing in water, gums produce a thickening or texture-building effect. Common gums used by the food industry are agar, guar gum, carrageenan, and gum tragacanth.

Herbs and Spices

Herbs and spices add flavor, color, and aroma when used for culinary purposes (even though most often they are used in small quantities), and are often the life of the product in which they are used. Each has a rich history all its own and most have played an important role in history. Spices were valued first for their medicinal uses, as well as for their use in incense, perfumes, and ancient cosmetics. The ancient Greeks used many herbs and spices to season foods and developed many interesting myths about each of the herbs and spices they used.

Spices are grown mostly in hot, humid environments. They were first imported to the West from India, China, and Southeast Asia, and were instrumental in establishing trade and encouraging exploration. Both Marco Polo and Christopher Columbus were in search of spices and new trade routes when they set out on their historic journeys. Spices were once so highly valued that they were used as currency, and many wars were fought over them.

Today, most spices are imported to the United States from Southeast Asia, Central and South America, and the Mediterranean. They are still relatively expensive to use because many of the countries that cultivate them are underdeveloped, so most spices are still cultivated by hand.

Most spices are derived from the bark, roots, buds, flowers, or seeds of aromatic tropical plants. Their flavor and aroma chiefly come from the volatile oils found within these sources. Herbs are generally the leaves or stems of soft- or woody-stemmed plants that grow in moderate climates.

Both herbs and spices should be stored in airtight containers out of sunlight in a cool, dry place. If properly stored, they will remain aromatic for several months. Fresh herbs should be wrapped and stored under refrigeration. Spices that are in crushed or powdered form release their flavor almost immediately when added to the cooking process, so it is best to add them last. Whole spices are used so their flavor may be extracted over long cooking periods, as in poaching. Spices must be measured accurately because some strong spices, such as clove or cardamom, can overpower the flavor of a product. Crumbling and toasting some spices just before using them will enhance their flavor. Herbs are best if used fresh, but dried herbs are adequate (twice the amount of fresh minced herb is sometimes used when substituting for dried).

Spices

Allspice

Allspice is the dried, unripe berry of the pimiento tree, a tropical evergreen tree found in the West Indies and in Latin America. The berries are dried and either left whole or ground. The flavor of allspice seems to combine the flavors of nutmeg, clove, and cinnamon. It is most often used in pickling, cakes, sweet and savory soups, and some meat dishes.

Angelica

Angelica is a large plant native to Northern Europe that can grow up to six feet tall and is a member of the parsley family. The leaves, roots, and stalk can all be used to flavor and infuse. The green candied stalk is often used to decorate cakes and pastries and as an ingredient in fruitcakes.

Anise Seed

Anise seed is the dried green-brown seed of the parsley family with a strong, licorice-like aroma and flavor. It is an important flavoring in liqueurs such as anisette, ouzo, and Pernod, and it can be used to flavor a variety of dishes, both sweet and savory. Native to the Middle East, today its chief producer is Mexico.

Caraway Seed

Caraway seed is the seed of an herb in the parsley family. It is native to the Middle East and grown throughout northern and central Europe and Asia. Caraway has a warm, spicy odor and flavor. Rye bread gets its characteristic flavor from caraway seed. Caraway seed can also be used to infuse poached fruits.

Cardamom

Cardamom is the seed from the fruit of a perennial herb of the ginger family. It is native to India and used to flavor many Indian dishes, both sweet and savory. Scandinavian sweet breads often use cardamom as well. It is highly aromatic with a sweet, pungent but almost pepperlike flavor and aroma. It is expensive, the third most-expensive spice in the world behind saffron and vanilla.

Cinnamon

Cinnamon is used more in the baking industry than perhaps any other spice. It is the thin, dried inner bark of two related evergreen trees of the laurel family found mostly in Southeast Asia. One is true cinnamon, the other is more properly termed *cassia*. Cinnamon has a warm, spicy pungent aroma and flavor, and is used in many cakes, cookies, and pies. True cinnamon is referred to as Ceylon cinnamon and was at one time falsely considered superior to cassia; however, today most of the cinnamon used is either cassia or a blend of both. Ceylon is usually lighter in color than the darkish-brown cassia and has a sweeter but less-powerful flavor.

Cloves

Cloves are the dried flower buds of an evergreen tree of the myrtle family that is native to the Molucca Islands, often referred to as the Spice Islands. The best cloves are large and plump, somewhat wrinkled, unbroken, and a light purplish-brown color. They have a warm and spicy flavor and aroma, and can be used either ground or whole. They are used in many baked goods, for pickling, and for infusing fruits and sauces.

Coriander

Coriander is the fruit of perennial plants native to the south of Europe and Asia. It is also cultivated in southern England. The taste and odor of coriander seed is mildly spicy; it is used in some baked goods and for pickling and infusing. There is evidence that coriander has been in use since 5000 B.C.; it is mentioned in Egyptian Sanskrit dating from that time.

Cumin

Cumin seed is the dried, ripened fruit of an annual herb of the parsley family. It looks very much like caraway seed but has a much different flavor and aroma. It is the spice most commonly associated with chili and lends chili its distinct flavor. It is also used to flavor some Scandinavian and German breads.

Fennel Seeds

Fennel seeds are from a tall, hardy perennial of the parsley family native to the Mediterranean. In addition to the fennel seed, the fennel plant is used widely in cooking; both have a mild aniselike flavor but should not be confused with anise. Fennel seed is used in many ethnic breads, crackers, and sausages.

Ginger

Ginger is the underground stem of a tropical plant native to Asia but now grown extensively in tropical climates, particularly Jamaica. It can be used fresh or dried; dried is most often used in baking to flavor cookies and cakes. Fresh ginger has a stronger flavor than dried and should be peeled before it is used. Ginger has a strong, aromatic, sweet, peppery flavor that goes well with many baked goods and fruits; it is also used in a wide variety of Asian dishes.

Mace

Mace is the fibrous growth that forms around the shell enclosing the nutmeg seed. It is usually sold in dried form and tastes similar to nutmeg, although it is not as strong.

Nutmeg

Nutmeg is the kernel of the fruit or seed of the evergreen nutmeg tree that is native to the Molucca Islands. Nutmegs are dried, removed from the shell, and either ground or kept whole for grating. Nutmeg has a sweet, warm, spicy flavor that lends itself to many baked items as well as to a variety of savory dishes. Freshly ground nutmeg is superior in flavor to ground nutmeg.

Pepper and Peppercorns

Pepper is arguably one of the world's most important and widely used spices, native to India. Pepper is now cultivated in many tropical regions, including South America and Malaysia. Pepper is a smooth woody vine that climbs tree trunks to produce grapelike clusters of small berries. The berries start green then turn to red as they ripen. Pepper is available in both ground and whole (peppercorn) form.

- Green peppercorns are harvested before they are ripe and are usually sold packed in brine. They are milder in flavor than black pepper.
- Black peppercorns are harvested when green, are fermented, and then dried. Their black skin is due to a fungus. The most common of the peppers, black pepper is also the strongest in flavor.
- White peppercorns are harvested when the berries are completely ripe; the skins are removed before they are dried. White pepper is often used in classic white sauces so that their presence is noted only by the tastebuds, not the eye.
- Pink peppercorns are not related to pepper at all— they are actually the dried berries of a type of rose plant grown in Madagascar. They have a spicy, pungent flavor and aroma and are sometimes difficult to obtain, which makes them relatively expensive.

Poppy Seeds

Poppy seeds are the dried, ripened seed of the opium poppy native to the Middle East. They have a nutty flavor and are used in many breads as well as in Middle Eastern and Indian dishes.

Saffron

Saffron is the most expensive spice in the world—and for good reason: It is the stigmas of a type of crocus plant native to the eastern Mediterranean; each of the threads of stigmas must be handpicked. In addition, it takes 13,000 stigmas to make up a pound. Saffron is used in baking mainly to lend color and flavor to certain breads and rolls; it is more widely used in savory dishes and is the traditional flavoring in such classic dishes as French bouillabaisse and Spanish paella. Ground, it is often adulterated with turmeric, which is why it is best to purchase it in thread form only.

Sesame Seeds

The sesame seed is the small honey-colored seed of a tall annual herb native to Africa, where it is still widely grown, as well as to Asia. Sesame seeds impart a delicious roasted-nut flavor to hard rolls and breads and are used in a variety of Middle Eastern and Asian dishes. Sesame seeds are close to 50 percent oil—the oil is extracted to produce sesame oil.

Star Anise

Star anise is botanically unrelated to anise; it is actually the fruit of a tree in the Magnolia family. It has a strong licoricelike flavor and is used to infuse flavor in poached fruits and compotes.

Turmeric

Turmeric is the underground stem of a tropical herb. It has a mild, peppery flavor and is used in curry powders, mustards, and condiments.

Vanilla

Vanilla is the most widely used flavoring in the bake shop— its delicate flavor lends itself to almost every other flavor. Vanilla is native to Mexico, where it was discovered by the Spaniards during their exploration of the New World. Vanilla is second only to saffron as the most expensive spice in the world, largely because in many areas it is still hand-pollinated and the growing and sweating process to produce the bean is so long—up to a year. Vanilla is actually the liana of an orchid that, after flowering and pollination, produces a long green bean that can take nearly eight months to mature. As soon as the beans are picked, they must be sweated, or cured, to produce the delicate flavor desired. There are several new methods used to cure vanilla beans, but the most common is the sun method— which can take nine months to a year to accomplish and which in part accounts for its high price. There are three types of vanilla, all with distinct flavors:

- Madagascar, or Bourbon, vanilla is produced on the island of Madagascar off the coast of South East Africa. It is widely used for extracts.
- Mexican vanilla is the same species of vanilla as Madagascar but with a more raw, pungent flavor and aroma.

- Tahitian vanilla is cultivated in Tahiti and is a different species than the Mexican and Madagascan varieties; Tahitian vanilla has a more floral aroma and flavor.

Extracts of vanilla, lemon, orange, and almond are obtained through the use of alcohol; at its most basic, a vanilla extract can be made by placing three to five beans in a quart of white spirit (such as vodka) and allowing it to sit, guarded from direct sunlight, for three months. The longer the "extract" sits, the more of the essential flavor will be extracted and the stronger the extract will become.

Flavorings and Seasonings

Flavorings and seasonings have been incorporated into cooking processes to enhance the flavor of raw ingredients, to preserve perishable foods, and to nationalize the presentation of different cuisines.

Flavorings

Flavorings are substances commonly added to food to change the flavor and to strengthen the flavor. Flavorings may also be used to tenderize or to add sharpness or richness to foods. Flavorings are traditionally in the form of a liquid or paste, but they may be purchased dry or in sauce form. See Table 13–4 for a listing of flavorings used by the pastry professional.

Seasonings

Seasonings are a blend of herbs, spices, or salts that are used to enhance the flavor of foods. See Table 13–5 for a description of seasonings frequently used by the pastry professional.

Herbs

Basil

Basil is an annual herb of the mint family with tender, leafy stems. It is grown in moderate climates. It is available in many varieties and has a pungently mild licoricelike flavor. It is used in many Mediterranean dishes and some Asian dishes.

Table 13–4 Flavorings

Name	Description	Uses
Chestnuts	Fruit of the chestnut tree.	Ready made paste used in pastries.
Cocoa & Chocolate	From the pods containing cocoa beans, roasted, shelled, and ground.	Desserts, alcoholic beverages.
Coconut	Many forms, including coconut flesh, juice, and cream.	Desserts.
Essences	Concentrated flavorings extracted from nuts, flowers, seeds, fruits, herbs, and spices.	Widely used in cooking and baking.
Licorice	Dried root; slightly aromatic, sweet-sour flavor.	Bakery products.
Salt	Sodium chloride.	Bakery products.
Sugar	Sweet tasting substances, most commonly sap of the sugar cane.	Bakery products.
Vanilla	Essence from the pod of the orchid family.	Sweets, chocolate, icing, and buttercream.

Table 13–5 Seasonings

Name	Description	Uses
Apple pie spice	Cinnamon, nutmeg, cloves, and allspice.	Apple pie.
Cinnamon sugar	Cinnamon and granulated sugar.	Sugary products.
Mixed pickling spices	Red peppers, white peppercorns, mustard seed, bay leaves, dill seed, allspice, and cinnamon.	Poaching fruit, marinades, and dessert sauces.
Pumpkin pie spice	Ginger, cinnamon, and cloves.	Breads and pies.

Chives

Chives are the long cylindrical leaves of a perennial in the onion family. Chives have a delicate onion flavor and can be used to flavor breads and soft rolls as well many savory dishes.

Dill

Dill is a feathery-leaved herb of the carrot or parsley family. It has a strong distinct flavor that is commonly associated with pickling. It is also used in many breads and to flavor various vegetables.

Marjoram

Marjoram is a perennial of the mint family with a warm, pungent flavor similar to that of oregano but milder. It is used to flavor soups and stews as well as many poultry, fish, and meat dishes.

Mint

Mint grows in many varieties, the most well-known being peppermint and spearmint. It is widely used in many cultures to flavor both sweet and savory dishes. It is the source of menthol, which is used to produce cigarettes, candy, mouthwash, and many other products. Its soothing effect on the mouth when eaten makes it popular in many hot Asian and Indian dishes. In the United States, it is most often used in sweet dishes and ice creams, often paired with chocolate.

Mint gets its name from Minthe, a beautiful nymph adored by Hades, the Greek god of the underworld (also known as Pluto); when Hades's wife Persephone found out, she was put into a rage and turned the innocent Minthe into a lowly sprawling plant for everyone to walk on. Pluto could not undo his wife's spell; instead, he gave Minthe one of the sweetest of smells, and each time she was tread upon her smell became even sweeter.

Oregano

Oregano is sometimes referred to as wild marjoram and has a similar but stronger flavor. Oregano is a perennial that grows in moderate climates and is native to the Medi-terranean, which explains its popularity in so many Italian, Spanish, and Greek foods and breads.

Parsley

Parsley is grown in many varieties; like mint, it has a soothing effect on the taste buds. It is used widely in Middle Eastern and Mediterranean cuisines.

Rosemary

Rosemary, an evergreen shrub with needlelike leaves, is a member of the mint family. It grows in moderate climates and is native to the Mediterranean. It has a strong, pungent flavor and aroma that complements many savory dishes as well as many baked goods.

Sage

Sage is a perennial shrub of the mint family with many varieties, all of which produce a soft down on its leaves. It is fragrant and warm and is most often used in soups, stews, and sausages, and as a seasoning for poultry and pork.

Savory

Savory is another member of the mint family with a spicy taste that lends itself to meat and fish dishes, as well as to many baked goods.

Tarragon

Tarragon is a perennial herb from the daisy family. Its flavor is a cross between mint and anise and is what gives sauce béarnaise its characteristic flavor. It is also used to flavor salad dressings and other condiments, particularly vinegar.

Thyme

Thyme is a shrub of the mint family. Its sharp and pungent, spicy flavor is used in meat and poultry dishes as well as in many cream dishes and baked goods.

Nuts

Many baking recipes call for the use of a variety of nuts. Nuts are classified as the kernels of fruits with hard, dry layers rather than fleshy ones, although this is misleading because some nuts, such as almonds and walnuts, are actually surrounded by a fleshy layer while on the tree and others, such as Brazil and pine nuts, are actually seeds. However misleading their botanical classification, nuts are widely used in baked goods to add flavor, texture, and color. Nuts are grown mostly on trees that bear them as fruit, although some, like the peanut, grow underground on a sprawling plant. It is estimated that nut-bearing trees existed some 60 million years ago; nuts have played an important role in the history of the survival of humans.

Most nuts are generally nutritious as they are a good source of B vitamins and protein; unfortunately, most are also nearly 70 to 80 percent fat. This high fat content makes them particularly susceptible to rancidity. They also easily can absorb odors from their surroundings. Nuts should be stored in cool, dark, dry areas in glass or plastic containers, not metal.

Roasting nuts will bring out a more intense flavor that may or may not be useful to certain dishes and baked goods. When grinding nuts, place them in the freezer for 10 to 15 minutes first to prevent loss of their volatile oils and, consequently, their flavor. Most nuts can be purchased with the skin on (natural) or with the skin off (blanched).

Almonds

Almonds are perhaps the most popular of common nuts. They are used widely in breads, cakes, and pastries, and also as decorations, as well as to make almond paste and marzipan. Grown on the almond tree (a relative of the peach and plum), the nut is covered with a medium-brown skin and is white inside. There are two kinds of almonds: sweet and bitter. Sweet almonds are eaten, and bitter almonds are used as a source of almond flavorings and extracts. In the United States, almonds are grown commercially in California, where their cultivation is second in acreage only to grapes. They are available whole, sliced, slivered, ground, and in flour or meal form.

Brazil Nuts

Native to the Amazon, the Brazil nut—which is actually a seed—is cultivated on commercial plantations and grown

in the wild; the tree's habitat is increasingly threatened by destruction of the Amazon Rain Forest, a factor that makes the nut relatively expensive. The large nuts grow in a pod that contains around 15 seeds. Brazil nuts have a mild flavor and a high fat content; because of their cost, they are not widely used in baking, although their flavor is superior.

Cashews

The cashew is the edible seed of a tropical evergreen tree, native to the Amazon but cultivated widely in India and East Africa. The tree is related to poison ivy, which is why the nut is never sold in its shell; the shell's irritating oils must be removed with heat and the oils are used in making paints and varnishes. The cashew tree produces an apple-shaped fruit with the nut being the fruit's single seed. The fruit is eaten by the natives, but rarely is it seen outside cultivation areas; instead, it is used to make vinegar and a liqueur called Kaju. Cashews are also relatively expensive and, consequently, not commonly seen on bake-shop shelves—indeed, because of their high fat content (up to 74 percent). They should be stored under refrigeration. They have a delicious, smoky flavor that is excellent in many baked goods.

Chestnuts

The sweet chestnut is the seed of the chestnut tree; the tree grows in almost any moderate climate and has been grown for many centuries for use in soups, cereals, stews, and stuffings. The chestnut trees in North America were almost completely wiped out early in the 20th century because of a devastating blight. Most chestnuts are imported from Europe (where they are widely popular, especially in marrons glacé, where they are preserved in a sweet sugar syrup.) The nut grows inside a prickly green husk and is surrounded by a dark-brown leatherlike shell, which is usually removed by roasting or boiling. Chestnuts are ripe in North America in early October. Chestnuts contain more starch and less oil than other nuts. They can be eaten whole, roasted, boiled, or steamed. As soon as they are shelled, they can be purchased dried; canned in brine, as chestnut paste; chopped and used in stuffings or with vegetables; or ground into a flour. They are used to flavor buttercreams and fillings, and as decoration for cakes and cookies. In Central Europe they are served as "Marron au Chantilly," chestnut pureé with cream.

Coconuts

The coconut is the fruit of the coconut palm, native to Malaya, but it has been transplanted to all parts of the tropical and subtropical world. Like the almond, the coconut is actually the seed of a type of fruit called a drupe—the same type of fruit as a plum, peach, and apricot. Coconuts are not only prized for their culinary uses: The trees provide materials for thatching roofs, weaving mats, and making ropes, and they provide valuable lumber. Because the trees produce fruit year round, fresh coconut is inexpensive and is readily available. Coconut milk is available canned and is popular in many Thai and Southeast Asian dishes, as well as in fresh coconut cake. Coconut is also available in grated or flaked form, in cans or packages, and may be dried or moist, sweetened or unsweetened. Desiccated, or macaroon, coconut is dried, unsweetened coconut that has been ground to a fine meal. Keep unopened coconut at room temperature and opened coconut tightly covered in the refrigerator. To toast coconut, spread in shallow pans and bake in a moderate oven (350° F) until it is light brown, stirring frequently.

――――――――――*FYI*――――――――――

To choose a fresh coconut, check its weight; if it feels heavy for its size and the milk can be heard splashing around inside, it is probably ripe. To open it, first drain the milk by piercing one or all of the three eyes at the end of the coconut. After the milk has drained off, smash the coconut with a mallet or throw it on the floor monkey style. Warming the coconut in a 350° oven for a few minutes will allow its dark outer skin to peel off more easily.

Filberts, or Hazelnuts

Filberts, also known as hazelnuts, are drier than most other nuts and native to most temperate regions in the Northern Hemisphere, but they are grown mostly in Turkey, Italy, and the northwestern region of the United States. Filberts are grown in clusters, and each nut is enclosed in a husk that opens as the nut ripens. They are harvested by being shaken off the bushes or gathered from the ground. Whole filberts can be toasted, salted, sugared, or eaten as is; their flavor is greatly improved by toasting them. Chopped filberts are used in candies, baked goods, and desserts; they are essential in Linzer dough and can also be made into a paste for flavoring buttercream and fillings. Filberts provide protein, fat, iron, and thiamin. Filberts are available whole in the shell, whole shelled, or chopped.

Macadamia Nuts

Macadamia nuts are the nut of an evergreen tree native to northeastern Australia; they were introduced to Hawaii during the 1890s, which is where they now mostly are grown. They have a wonderfully smooth, buttery flavor and are very popular in cakes, cookies, and ice creams. They are very expensive and are usually reserved for signature items. Often they can only be purchased roasted and salted; to remove the salt, blanch and dry the nuts.

Peanuts

The peanut is a common nut in North American and Asian cuisines; it is native to South America but was brought to East Africa by the Spanish and Portuguese explorers and to North America via the slave trade. Peanuts became a significant crop in the South after the Civil War as a substitute for pest-ridden cotton. The peanut is actually a member of the legume family; the plant pushes its fruit capsules underground as they mature. To harvest, the entire plant must be dug up. There are many uses for peanuts; peanut oil and peanut butter are two valuable products. Even the shells are pressed and used for cattle fodder. Over 300 synthetic products are made from peanuts. Two types of peanuts generally available are known as Virginia and Spanish. The Virginia has larger and longer kernels, a lower oil content, and a more pronounced flavor than the Spanish. Vacuum-packed peanuts will last indefinitely, while peanuts that have been shelled should be kept refrigerated because of their high fat content (75 percent). Peanuts are particularly popular in American pastries and candies such as peanut brittle; peanuts are often paired with chocolate—this flavor combination is very popular in American culture.

Pecans

A native American nut of the pecan tree, pecans are found in the southeastern United States and Mexico. Pecans, like walnuts, are part of the hickory family and have a very thin shell; the nutmeat has a fat content of over 70 percent. Pecans are associated with southern and southwestern cooking, such as pecan pie and pralines. They have a delicate flavor and can be purchased shelled in either halves or pieces. They are relatively expensive compared to other nuts but can easily be substituted in any formula that calls for nuts.

Pine Nuts, or Pignoli

Pine nuts are the seed of a variety of species of pine, and they are widely cultivated in Italy and Spain. These kernels of pine cones, which resemble almonds in taste, are used in many savory Mediterranean dishes, including pesto. Because of their high fat content, they are fairly perishable and are best if stored under refrigeration. Pine nuts come in various sizes and are available raw or toasted, which enhances their delicate flavor. They are used in some breads, in some cookies, and as decoration for some pastries.

Pistachios

The edible seed of a small evergreen tree native to central Asia, pistachios are valued highly for their delicate flavor, low fat content, and distinctive green color. They are cultivated mostly in the Middle East, but the United States has grown to be the world's second-largest producer since the first harvest of pistachios there in 1976. The fruits of the tree grow in clusters; the clusters produce an outer red shell that is removed before packing and an inner thin shell that should be slightly open to indicate that the nut is ripe. The pistachio is pale green to creamy white in color and has a fine texture and a mild, pleasing flavor. The nut is used in a variety of cakes and pastries, to flavor buttercreams and ice creams, and as a garnish for cakes and petits fours.

FYI

Pistachios were supposedly dyed red by Middle Eastern merchants to hide blemishes caused by the harvesting methods used.

Sunflower Seeds

Sunflower seeds are actually complete fruits called *achenes*, similar to the seeds on the exterior of a strawberry. Native to North America, today the world's leading producer is Russia. In addition to enhancing the flavor and texture of some breads and other baked items, sunflower seeds are the source of most vegetable oils.

Walnuts

Walnuts are the edible fruit of the walnut tree native to Asia, Europe, and North America. Like its relative, the pecan, it is actually the seed of a drupe. Only almonds prove more popular in baking than the walnut, which is used in cookies, brownies, ice creams, cakes, and muffins. The most commonly known walnut is the English or Persian walnut, now grown mainly in California. The black walnut, native to the Appalachians, has a dark-brown, deeply ridged shell that is difficult to husk, with a strong-flavored kernel that is very popular in black-walnut cake, a southern delicacy. Butternuts, or white walnuts, are also native to America. Walnut oil, extracted from the kernel, is used in France like olive oil. Today, the United States leads the world in walnut production. Walnuts can be purchased in halves, used mostly for decoration, and in pieces.

14

Yeast-Raised Doughs

Yeast-Raised Doughs

Here is bread, which strengthens man's heart,
and therefore called the staff of life.
—*Matthew Henry, from* Commentaries

The making of bread in some form is very important to most Western cultures; many traditions are centered around the baking of special breads or rolls for everyday use as well as for special occasions and holidays. Bakeries have taken over this process for most households, at least on a daily basis, although baking bread still remains a great hobby for many.

Understanding the ingredients that go into various types of breads and rolls is imperative; in addition, as in all formulas, the scaling and measuring of bread formulas must be accurate.

There are two basic methods of fermentation in yeast-raised doughs: the straight-dough method and the sponge method. In the straight-dough method, the ingredients are mixed together during one mixing phase until the proper gluten structure is formed. In a sponge dough, a very soft dough is made from 50 percent to 75 percent of the flour and 60 percent to 70 percent of the water (more water is used for stronger flours) and the yeast; sometimes malt or sugar are also added. The sponge is covered and left to rise in a warm place, usually until it has doubled in volume (from three to four hours). The sponge is then placed in the mixer, the remaining ingredients are added, and the dough is mixed until proper gluten development is formed.

The sponge-dough method allows the yeast to ferment and develop strength without the interference of other ingredients; this gives the bread a strong flavor and good texture. Items made using the sponge method are usually lighter in volume, have a slightly open grain with a smooth texture, and have a strong yeastlike flavor. This method is used in making many hearth breads and breads that have a high sugar content. The straight-dough method is used for many basic breads, such as lean doughs and soft rolls.

A variation of the sponge method is what is sometimes referred to as the *predough method*. In this method, a firmer sponge is made. A small percentage of the yeast is mixed with flour and water to form a firm, smooth dough. This mixture is then covered and left to rise, usually overnight; after this fermentation, the remaining ingredients are added and mixed as with a regular sponge. The French use a starter of this nature in many of their breads to add flavor and structure to their doughs—stolen from the ancient Mesopotamians—they simply add a piece of old dough from the previous day during the mixing of a fresh dough.

The Temperature of the Dough

When working with yeast-raised doughs, a specific temperature is needed for proper fermentation. A warm, humid environment is ideal for proper fermentation, ideally around 78° F to 82° F, with a humidity of approximately 85 percent. Each dough has its own particular desired dough temperature (DDT). The average dough temperature is 80° F. The three varieties of dough most frequently used, and their DDT, are

Lean dough   75° to 78° F (cool)
Soft-roll dough   80° F ± 1°
Sweet/rich dough 81° to 82° F ± 1°

Sweet doughs have higher fat percentages and need warmer temperatures; generally, the higher the fat percentage in a bread formula, the higher the DDT will need to be.

Calculating the DDT

When it is stated that the DDT is 75° F, this means that when the dough has finished mixing, the temperature should be

75° F. In the bake shop operating under perfect conditions, no calculations would be necessary because the room temperature, flour temperature, and water temperature would all be 75° F. If the friction temperature of the mixing process were not to be considered, then the dough temperature would also be 75° F.

Because most bake shops are not operating under perfect conditions and the temperature of the friction from the mixing process must be taken into consideration, the water temperature is the only variable that can be controlled by the baker and its temperature must be calculated. The steps to calculating the water temperature are

1. Know the DDT.
2. DDT $\times$ 3 = total temperature factor (TTF).
3. TTF − flour temperature − room temperature − friction temperature = water temperature.

In some instances, as with sponge dough, high amounts of scraps in the dough, sour starters, or soaking stages (rustic wheats), the multiplication factor in step 2 will be increased. Flour temperature is usually 66° to 68° F. The friction temperature depends on the mixer used. Because the average dough should be approximately 80° F and because 80 × 3 = 240, this method of calculating the DDT is sometimes referred to as the 240 Factor. For example,

$$DDT = 75° F$$

$$75 \times 3 = 225$$

$$\text{Flour temperature} = 66° F$$

$$\text{Room temperature} = 70° F$$

$$\text{Friction temperature} = 30° F$$

$$225 - 66 = 159$$

$$159 - 70 = 89$$

$$89 - 30 = 59$$

Therefore, the DDT is 59° F.

It is necessary to calculate water temperature because different doughs thrive best at different temperatures. The temperature of the water can be adjusted by using ice to cool the water.

The Ten Steps of Bread Making

There are 10 steps in the baking process when using a straight-dough method. If a sponge or predough method is used, these ten steps are usually followed from the mixing stage (step 2) *after* the mixing and fermentation of the sponge. Although formulas vary, if the ten steps to baking bread are understood, they can be used as a guideline for making any yeast-raised product.

Step 1. Scale Ingredients

The exact scaling of ingredients is an integral part of the baking process. If ingredients have not been scaled properly, an inconsistent and often inferior product will result. The proper use of a baker's scale can ensure that amounts of ingredients conform to a given formula.

Eggs, oil, liquid shortening, malt, honey, molasses, and other heavy liquids with a viscosity denser than milk or water should all be weighed on the baker's scale. Water and milk can be measured with liquid measures: one pint equals one pound (see Table 14–1).

Table 14–1 Yeast-Dough Percentages

Refined Whole-Wheat Flour (percentage)	Ingredient	Cracked-Wheat Flour (percentage)
100	Flour	100
58	Water	70
9	Molasses or honey	5
2	Salt	2
6.5	Regular shortening	8
(2% instant) (4% water)	Compressed yeast	(2% instant) (4% water)

Step 2. Mixing Yeast-Raised Dough

Mixing accomplishes two major objectives: It evenly and thoroughly distributes ingredients, and it allows for maximum development of the gluten. The procedure for mixing doughs can vary with the type of yeast used. The method described here uses compressed, fresh yeast. If instant yeast is used, it must be added just *after* the liquids have absorbed into the flour. For a straight dough, the water and fresh yeast are mixed together.

Overmixing will give a letdown, or complete breakdown, of the dough. The dough will be warm and sticky and will come apart easily. There are four stages in the mixing process: pickup, cleanup, development, and final clear.

Pickup

A low speed is used to mix the flour and dry ingredients together, then the water and yeast are added. Any other wet ingredients are usually added to the water and yeast just before they are added to the dry ingredients. All the water should be added before the kneader is accelerated to medium speed. Any solid fats that are used in the formula are added last; oils are usually added at the beginning of the mixing process, just after the water and yeast.

Cleanup

During the cleanup stage, the ingredients come together and the bottom of the bowl can be seen clearly. At this point, the kneader is accelerated to medium speed.

Development

This is the longest stage in the mixing process. It is called the development stage because the gluten is being developed. Oxygen is being absorbed into the dough. The starch will come to the surface as gluten is forming, and the dough will be whiter. The dough will tear easily, and the color will be uneven.

Final Clear

The final-clear stage occurs when the proper development of gluten has been obtained; when a small piece of dough is cut from the mass, it is stretched to such a thinness that light will shine clearly through. The dough also can be stretched a few times without tearing. As soon as the dough reaches this stage, it is properly developed and can be removed from the mixing bowl.

The dough should be lightly coated with oil before floor fermentation to prevent the dough from sticking to its container (usually a bulk proof box or trough) and from developing a skin. If dough improvers or instant yeast are used, bulk fermentation (step 3) is not necessary. If conditioners are used, bulk fermentation is eliminated, and the dough may be divided immediately.

Step 3. Bulk, or Flour, Fermentation

During the fermentation process, yeast cells act on sugary agents in the dough and produce carbon dioxide and alcohol. The gluten structure, formed by mixing, will contain the carbon dioxide produced by the yeast. The gluten is conditioned and mellowed and becomes more elastic as a result of the effect of the alcohol given off by the yeast and the lower acidity in the dough. The important factors for good fermentation are

- Properly developed dough.
- Proper humidity of between 75 percent and 85 percent. The dough should be kept covered and away from drafts. Bulk fermentation is done in a proof box where the humidity can be controlled and observed.
- Dough temperature should be between 78° F and 82° F for optimum fermentation.

Fermentation must be regulated throughout to ensure proper flavor and conditioning.

In many bake shops, fermentation time is cut considerably with the use of dough conditioners; these chemically conditioned additives

eliminate the need for bulk fermentation and save on labor costs. Unfortunately, the rich yeast flavor of bulk-fermented breads is lost in this type of product. In addition, the texture and crumb of a bread or roll made with conditioners is not of as high a quality as that of bulk-fermented bread.

Step 4. Dividing the Dough and Punchdown

When bulk fermentation has caused the dough to rise (in most cases, close to double in volume or 50 percent fermentation), it is tested for punchdown—the fingers are inserted into the dough to the knuckles and the dough is observed to see if the finger marks leave a slight indentation and then close very slowly; if so, the dough is ready for punchdown. Punchdown is done by folding the sides of the dough into the middle and turning the dough over. Punching keeps the dough at an even temperature by turning the dough inside out; it also releases some of the carbon dioxide, which, if allowed to stay concentrated, will eventually restrict fermentation; it introduces fresh oxygen to the dough to help with fermentation, and it helps develop gluten.

Dividing the dough should be done as quickly and accurately as possible. The dough continues to ferment during dividing, and delay will cause overfermentation of the last unit scaled. The dough is divided using a bench scraper and weighed to the desired weight, either for a dough press or for individual loaves. Leftover dough from inaccurate scaling should be divided evenly among the number of large pieces and tucked under. Smaller pieces will ferment faster and must be incorporated properly.

Step 5. Rounding or Folding Over

Rounding or folding the dough over are ways for the newly divided and scaled dough to be shaped into better condition for further shaping that will come after the second fermentation. Rounding also prevents too much gas loss by providing the dough with a thin skin that entraps the gas. Folding over allows old gases to escape and new gases to be created. When rounding or folding over, the pieces of dough should be kept in order—the first piece rounded or folded should be the first piece shaped after having been bench rested, so all the rounded pieces of dough will receive the proper fermentation time.

Step 6. Bench Rest or Intermediate Proof

Bench rest or intermediate proof is a short resting period in which the rounded or folded pieces of dough are relaxed. Fermentation continues, and the pieces become gassy; the gluten relaxes in this step, which makes future handling of the dough easier. The dough must be covered to keep in moisture and prevent crust formation; usually the dough is put back in the proof box, even for this short period, to ensure that the proper humidity and temperature is maintained. Sometimes it is left in the dough troughs; the troughs cover each other as they are stacked and prevent crust formation. It is during this rest period that the dough will begin to feel lighter and softer, and more yeast flavor will develop.

Step 7. Shaping

Shaping is the step in which the properly rested dough is formed into the desired shape. Shaping should be done quickly, with as little dusting flour as possible to prevent the dough from drying. If a seam is a part of the finished product, it should be placed on the bottom; a proper seam should be straight and tight because the seam is the weakest part of any shaped product and could open during baking. Rolls, braids, and other rustic loaves are all shaped at this stage. The first piece of dough that was rounded or folded over is the first piece of dough to be shaped.

Step 8. Panning

At this stage, the proper pan is selected and prepared according to the type of bread being made: pullman loaves, French baguettes, soft rolls, and so on. (Bread formulas will indicate the proper mise en place for panning.) All washes and appropriate garnishes should be applied after panning. Generally, lean doughs are placed on perforated pans with cornmeal and are water washed; soft or medium doughs are placed on sheet pans with parchment or in lightly greased loaf pans and are egg washed.

Step 9. Final Proof

This stage should achieve maximum fermentation prior to baking the product. Final proofing should occur in a proof box, which produces a warm and humid environment. The proof box should be maintained at a temperature of 90° F to 95° F, with a humidity of 80 to 90 percent. In most cases, a properly proofed product should be nearly doubled in volume, should be light and airy to the touch, and will close around a finger indentation slowly without collapsing.

Proofing time is affected by the type of dough and the size and shape of the product. Sweet doughs should be proofed only partially before they are baked to prevent the richness of the dough exerting extra weight on the gluten strands and compromising the final structure of the item.

Some items, particularly hard or lean doughs, are stippled (cut) before, during, or after final proof. *Stippling* is the term used for the characteristic and decorative cuts made on the top of certain types of bread. Stippling improves the look of the product by making it more visually interesting; it also lightens the product by allowing the crumb to move upward and expand during baking. If done correctly, stippling cuts will look like a scar on the surface of the product (see Figure 14–1).

For most breads, stippling is done during the last 20 percent of the final proof or when the loaf has reached three-quarters of its maximum volume. The loaf will then expand more by moving up. A razor is better than a serrated knife for stippling because the knife tends to drag

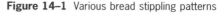
Figure 14–1 Various bread stippling patterns

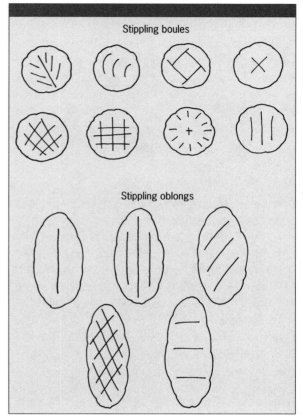

across the dough. If the dough is fairly dry, the razor blade should be dipped in warm water. If the dough is very wet, using light rye flour will help the knife cut cleanly. In either case, the blade should never be dragged across the dough; a clear, sharp cut is desired. To stipple the bread dough,

- Hold the blade almost parallel to the length of the dough.
- Cut just under the surface of the dough, not deep, and make a straight cut.
- Overlap the cuts by one-third the length of each cut.
- Make all cuts of equal lengths.
- Make the cuts cover the full length of the dough.
- Use both hands, one to steady the product and the other to cut.

Step 10. Baking

Baking changes and transforms the dough into an appetizing, desirable product. Baking times and temperatures are determined by the type of dough, the size of the unit, the richness of the unit, the crust color desired, and often by the weather. Generally, the leaner the dough, the higher the oven temperature and the shorter the baking time; richer doughs usually require lower oven temperatures and longer baking periods. As the product is baked, the internal temperature rises, and four major changes take place, in the following order:

1. Natural oven spring is a sudden rise and expansion caused by the last effort of the yeast, reacting to the heat of the oven, to ferment before it is killed at 138° F to 140° F and the rapid expansion of the carbon dioxide created during the proofing process. This process occurs during the first five minutes or so of baking. Some reasons for the failure of this reaction include the following:
   a. There is too much salt in the dough.
   b. The product was overproofed.
   c. Not enough yeast was added during mixing.
   The dough is very soft at this stage and will collapse if touched.
2. At 130° F, the starch granules will begin to swell from a transfer of moisture from other ingredients; as they swell, they will become fixed in the gluten structure. At 150° F, the starches will gelatinize and become the chief structure of the dough, rather than the gluten, which begins to dry out and coagulate at 165° F and continues to coagulate until the product is finished baking. The structure will begin to finalize in the crumb.
3. The crust will be formed at 165° F because of the exposed starch and sugar at the surface of the dough. This finalizes the structure of the product. At this point, the product will begin to appear done, but the taste will still be heavy with alcohol because evaporation of alcohol has not yet taken place.
4. The alcohol given off by the yeast as a byproduct will be burned off from the product at 176° F. The finished bread will have an approximate internal temperature of 220° F.

Baking with Steam

Some breads, such as French and Italian loaves, require a thin, hard crispy crust. Most professional bakers accomplish this through the use of steam in the oven during baking. Steam provides a moist environment that prevents a crust from forming too soon; the sugar present in the dough mixes with the moisture on the surface of the product and caramelizes. When the steam is released by the opening of the oven's damper, a crispy crust is formed. All ovens have different steam pressures and timing must be adjusted to each situation (i.e., how many seconds of steam will actually be applied). Older ovens and deck ovens may need to be loaded with steam prior to placing the product in the oven. Steam has a few major effects on a product:

- The moisture helps improve natural oven spring by creating a proof-box type environment. This keeps the product soft and creates a glossy shine.
- Steam prevents cracking of the crust during baking.
- Starches and sugars mix with the steam, caramelizing to create crust color. The damper is then opened to let the steam out and prevent overbrowning. In older products (old dough), the yeast will have digested a large amount of sugar and the product will have less color.

Staling and Storage

Staling is the process of the firming of starch particles after a product is baked. Staling starts immediately after baking. Moisture is taken in by the starch after it has gelled. Two factors can postpone the staling action: the type of packaging and the ingredients in the dough. Keeping starch at one consistent temperature also helps to delay the staling process.

The two distinct areas of staling are the crust and the

crumb. The crumb produces a drying effect as the moisture leaves the crumb, going to the crust. The crust becomes more moist and tough with a loss of flavor and taste caused by the transfer of moisture from the crumb to the crust. If the staling process has not proceeded too far, it can be reversed by heating. Staling is not as rapid in richer doughs, such as sour rye, raisin, and cinnamon breads.

There are five ingredients that can be added to help delay the staling process: milk powder, malt syrup, soy flour, fat, and high-gluten flour. Milk powder retains moisture, and reduces the rate of starch retrogradation. Malt syrup retains moisture, which delays staling. Soy flour retains a higher moisture level, which in turn slows down the drying of the crumb. Increase of fat retains the tenderness of the loaf. High-gluten flour also retains moisture and absorbs more liquid while mixing. Rye flour absorbs starch particles and tends to retain the moisture gel. The higher amount of starch results in a longer time for retrogradation. Finally, proper proofing is essential in maintaining freshness; breads that are overproofed will stale faster than properly proofed breads.

If bread is to be kept for more than a day (which it generally should not be), it should be wrapped as airtight as possible and stored in the freezer to retard staling. Breads that will not be frozen should be wrapped and stored at room temperature; storing bread in the refrigerator speeds the staling process considerably. Usually, breads should be made and sold (and consequently eaten) on the same day to ensure maximum freshness.

Young Dough versus Old Dough

A young dough is one that is underfermented or that lacks fermentation. It has low volume, is drier, lacks flavor, is more tough, and can be harder to work with. Young dough is drier because its dense structure (due to lack of fermentation) has not had time to draw moisture from the ingredients. If there is inadequate proofing time, young dough

must be used at cooler oven temperatures, higher humidity, and a longer baking period to ensure that the product is properly baked. Sometimes bakers who use convection ovens put the product in the oven and steam it, then turn the oven off for a couple of minutes to extend the natural oven spring. Young dough will not reach the volume during baking of a properly proofed dough.

An older dough is overfermented. It has excessive volume, is very moist, is soft, has a weak structure, and has a strong odor of alcohol. The gluten strands are stretched too far and may collapse in their weakened state. The crumb of an old dough may be grayish or uneven because of the yeast's digestion of the starches leaving gray proteins behind. Older doughs will also lack crust color because of the increased consumption of sugar (which aids in crust color) by the yeast (the exact opposite of a young dough). If an old dough has to be used, lower humidity and steam should be used as well as higher oven temperatures and shorter baking times.

Types of Doughs
Lean Dough

The basic four ingredients in a lean dough are wheat flour (bread or high gluten), water, yeast, and salt. Lean dough traditionally uses little or no fat or sugar. Eggs, if used, provide color, fat, and moisture, while egg whites provide protein and moisture. Fat or shortenings, when used in a lean dough, give the product a soft crumb, but oil will make the dough more easily workable. Conditioners and acid oxidants can also be used for emulsifying and gluten strengthening.

If a stronger flour than desired is used, there are ways to adjust the strength: Add more water, use less flour, introduce large amounts of starch to increase the starch percentage and decrease the protein percentage, or tenderize by adding of fat or sugar.

Some of the items produced with various types of lean doughs are bagels, hard rolls, Vienna rolls, Kaiser or grinder rolls, Italian bread (oblong, boulé, Vienna braids), batard (a short, fat cylinder-shaped loaf with a hard crust), and French baguettes (a long, slim cylinder-shaped loaf with a hard crust).

Makeup of Items Made with Lean Dough

French and Italian Breads

Both French breads and Italian breads and rolls are made from lean dough. They sometimes contain a small amount of malt and sugar to maintain the dough's characteristics without producing excessive tenderness or crust color; they also have a high-gluten content to withstand strong fermentation, large proofing, and strong oven spring. The French bread is long and cylindrical, while Italian bread is short and oblong. French breads have a thin, crisp, hard crust, and Italian breads have a slightly thicker, crisp crust. The crumb of French bread is soft, light, and porous, and the crumb of Italian bread is soft, chewy, and less porous. Stippling is necessary for both of these types of bread.

Baguette and Batard

A batard and a baguette are scaled to the same weight and are basically produced using the same production method at the beginning. The batard, however, will be crustier and have a thicker crust. The method of preparation is to start by patting out the dough. Start the batard with a square and the baguette with a rectangle. Fold the top down two-thirds and the bottom one-third over. Pat down. Roll up, starting with the top, using your left hand, and sealing with the heel of your right hand as you roll. The effect is a spiraling of the dough. The seam is the weakest part of the product. It should be straight and, when the loaf is formed, the seam should be at the bottom so it will not open during proofing and baking. The baguette is rolled straight, while the batard is rolled curved, with the ends rolled up more quickly than the center, making it oblong.

To prepare the loaves for baking, wet the bottom of the loaf and roll it in cornmeal. The cornmeal provides flavor and makes the crust on the bottom bake more quickly, mimicking the action of a hearth oven. Place them on a perforated baguette pan. Steam also helps to achieve the same results as a hearth oven. Make sure you stipple these products.

Baguettes are by far the most popular bread in France and French-speaking countries; the French have many provisions for the baking of the loaves. Because of the differences in flours in the United States and Europe, baguettes made in the United States, while excellent, do not quite duplicate the delicacy of the crumb and crispiness of the crust produced in France.

Hearth Breads

Hearth bread is a lean-dough bread with a thin, hard, crispy crust and a soft, chewy crumb. Authentic hearth breads use a lean dough and are peeled (placed onto the oven floor using a wooden or metal paddle) and baked directly on the brick or stone. High gluten flour is used because the dough must be strong enough to withstand shaping, fermentation, and peeling. The hearth oven is heated with bricks or stones on which the dough is placed. This causes the dough to move up and helps produce a hard crust. Cornmeal is usually used on the bottom of most hearth breads; it gives flavor and helps to keep the dough from sticking. It also helps the bottom of the dough bake faster. When an authentic hearth oven is not used, perforated pans are used to allow the heat and steam to get through the product faster.

There are many different types and makeups of hearth breads; many sourdoughs and multigrain breads are baked using the hearth method as well.

Bagels/Bialys

Bagels are traditionally a ring-shaped, yeast-leavened product that have an extremely chewy consistency because of their composition. The name is a derivation from Yiddish of the German word *boug*, meaning ring. Bagels are made from a very lean dough. The dough is based on the use of high-gluten flour, water, salt, and a low level of yeast. After mixing to full development, the dough can be processed in different ways. The majority of the bagels' relaxing and conditioning occurs during the extensive retarding periods that they are subject to prior to the boiling/steaming/baking process. Traditionally, a bagel is boiled in a water-malt mixture to liven the bagel, for lift and to allow the malt to linger on the outer crust, and for improved crust color in the oven. Boiling the bagel reduces the starch, which helps to give the bagel its characteristically chewy texture.

Egg bagels are also popular; they are less chewy and not boiled before they are baked. They are often topped with various seeds—poppy, sesame, caraway—as well as onions and garlic. Cinnamon-raisin bagels have also become very popular.

In today's market, some bagels contain dough conditioners or improvers, which are necessary to satisfy production time and quality concerns. These bagels are usually proofed in a proof box, followed by baking with steam to simulate the technique of boiling.

Kaiser Rolls

Kaiser, or Vienna rolls, are named after the Kaisers, emperors of Austria from 1804 to 1918. Kaiser rolls are made from a lean dough and should have a crispy crust with a characteristic fanlike stipple on their tops. Often the Kaiser roll is topped with poppy seeds. In today's bake shop, the special stippling is made either with a special Kaiser press or by machine.

Soft-Roll Dough

The most common dough found in the United States is the soft-roll dough. It produces a soft crumb and a soft crust. This dough has more elasticity than a lean dough and tears easily. Soft-roll dough incorporates the use of enricheners along with the lean dough's basic ingredients of flour, salt, yeast, and water. The most common enricheners used in the soft-roll dough are

- Granulated sugar
- All-purpose shortening
- Dry milk solids
- Eggs and egg yolks, which give a rich color and appearance to the crumb and crust

Variations of soft-roll dough (see Table 14–2) are used to make

- Single knots (see Figure 14–2 on page 284).
- Onion rolls.
- Double knots (see Figure 14–3 on page 284).
- Cloverleaf rolls.
- Figure-8 knots.
- Pullman breads.
- Parker House rolls.

Table 14–2 Soft-Dough Chart

Roll or Bread Variety	Press Weight	Garnish or Shape	Panning
Single, double, or figure-8 knots	3 lb.	As demonstrated.	6 × 6 per sheet.
Round, or finger, rolls	3 lb.	As demonstrated. With or without seeds.	5 × 7 per sheet.
Snowflake rolls	3 lb.	Dusted with cake flour.	5 × 7 per sheet.
Parker House rolls	3 lb.	Brushed with melted butter before and after baking.	5 × 7 per sheet.
Onion rolls	3 lb.	Onion, oil, and poppy seeds.	5 × 7 per sheet.
Clover	2 lb., 4 oz.	Each will be cut twice.	Three small roundups per muffin tin.
Pullman loaf	1 lb., 13 oz.	Loaf—not divided.	Pullman loaf pan.
Buttercrust	1 lb., 12 oz.	Loaf—not divided.	2 lb. loaf pans.

Figure 14–2 Making a single-knot roll

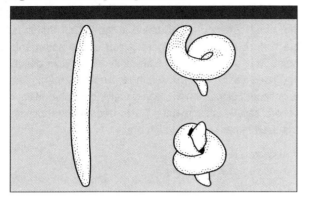

Figure 14–3 Making a double-knot roll

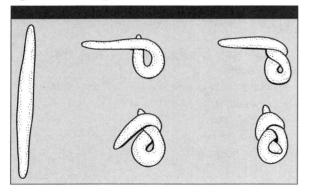

- Hamburger buns.
- Butterflake rolls.
- Hot dog buns.

FYI

No steam is used in baking soft-roll dough unless the dough is underproofed. Soft-roll dough, which is made with bread flour, has a higher percentage of enricheners, is elastic but tears easily, and requires a DDT of 80° F to 81° F. In contrast, lean doughs use a combination of bread flour and high-gluten flour. Steam is used in baking lean doughs. This dough is also elastic, but it is strong and will not tear easily. Lean dough requires a DDT of 75° F to 78° F. In comparing soft-roll dough to lean dough, the percentage of sugar and shortening in the lean dough is only 1 to 2 percent, while in a soft-roll dough the sugar and shortening percentage is 6 to 9 percent.

Rich Dough and Sweet Dough

Rich sweet doughs are used to make certain sweet breads and breakfast pastries; they generally contain as much as 25 percent sugar as well as 25 percent fats. The choice of flour depends on the use of the dough and the quantity of enricheners used. For bread shapes, less fat and sugar is used. In addition, high-gluten flour is used to support all the enricheners used. The more fats and sugars that are included in a formula, the more difficult it will be for the product to hold its shape.

Most rich doughs are wet and sticky. Do not be tempted to add more flour. This slackness gives the product its tenderness and is caused by the enricheners added. Use a minimum amount of flour in dusting and handling to preserve these qualities.

A sponge may be used for rich dough to give more flavor through fermentation. Fermentation in a sweet dough is slowed by the increase of enricheners and so the flavor of the sponge balances the sweetness of the dough. A sponge is also used to make dough handling easier. Some bakers make this dough days in advance and freeze or retard it to dry the exterior for easier handling.

Traditionally, rich and sweet doughs have a yellow color to their crumb. However, a great many eggs must be added to give this color, which adversely affects gluten formation and weighs down the dough. In many commercial operations, egg shade is added to provide the color, and shortening is used to compensate for the richness. Brioche, Portuguese sweet bread, and cinnamon-raisin bread are all excellent examples of sweet-dough products.

FYI

Of all yeast doughs, brioche is the richest in butter and eggs—a delectable dough with an incredibly smooth taste and texture. Rich in history as well, it is more than likely the "cake" to which Marie Antoinette referred in her now immortal words to France's peasants. Although during her time brioche was more than likely an indulgence of the upper classes, it has since become a delicacy enjoyed by all.

The French take great pride in their brioche, and they have dozens of ways to shape and serve it. The classic way is to bake it in a fluted brioche mold—giving it its flared body and characteristic ball, or head, on top—this is known as brioche Parisienne. The dough itself can be used in any number of ways, all of which are a delight to the palate.

Brioche dough should be made a day in advance, allowed to rise once, and then should be punched down (deflated) and allowed to rest in the refrigerator overnight. This slow fermentation brings out the rich flavors of the dough and makes it easier to handle. The next day the dough can be shaped into a number of different shapes: brioche mousseline (a cylinder), brioche nanterre (shaped in a loaf pan), and, of course, the classic brioche Parisienne. Great care should be taken in the handling of the dough—use a marble table if possible to keep the dough cool during handling and work in a cool, unventilated area. As soon as the brioches are shaped, bake them in a hot oven, 425° F, until they begin to brown, then reduce the heat to 400° F. Brioche is best enjoyed directly from the oven but can also be frozen for later use.

Babas and Savarins are rich but light yeast cakes that are made with a dough similar to brioche and soaked with a syrup, usually heavily laced with rum. The baba supposedly originated in Poland, where, in the 1600s, King Stanislas Leczyinski doused his gugelhuph (baba) in syrup, feeling it was too dry. So delighted with his innovation was he that he named it after the main character, Ali Baba, in his favorite story, A Thousand and One Nights. *Later, when the dessert was introduced to France, the name was shortened to* baba. *Babas can be baked in a variety of shapes, including brioche molds, but the classic is always a tall cylinder. When the same or similar dough is baked in a ring mold, it is called Savarin. Savarin can be baked large, the center filled with freshly soaked fruits, or it can be baked in small, individual molds.*

Whole-Wheat Breads

Rustic breads are breads that use coarsely ground or stone-ground flours; they are often baked in the same manner as a hearth bread. Whole-wheat breads may include whole wheats and rye flours. When using cracked whole wheat, it is advantageous to soak the wheat overnight with an equal quantity of water and salt in the formula. This allows the wheat to absorb the water and to release the starches and proteins. It also softens the kernels so they will not damage the gluten when the dough is kneaded. Do not soak the flour for more than 8 to 12 hours at room temperature, which may cause the oils to be released from the grain and damage the product. The bran and the germ will continuously tear the dough as you knead it. Slower and longer mixing time must be used to minimize the tearing of the gluten that could occur if the dough is mixed on higher speeds. Salt in the formula helps the gluten formation as the proteins are released from the flour. With the finely milled whole wheat stone-ground products, soaking is not necessary. The starches are plainly visible, as are the proteins, and gluten will be developed immediately.

In most cases, first-clear flour is mixed with whole-wheat flours in various ratios to give a lighter and easier-to-manage product. The most common ratio for rustic products is one-third weaker, fibrous flour to two-thirds first-clear flour. A 100 percent rustic flour product may be made, but great care in mixing must be used to give a good bread. Experiment with flour ratios to create the product you wish to achieve. First-clear flour is preferred to high-gluten flour because of its strength and economy. If high-gluten flour is used instead of first clear, the bread will be a lighter color than that from the first clear. As the quantity of white wheat flour is increased, so will the volume and structure of the bread be increased. As the quantity of whole-grain or weaker flour is increased in the formula, the denser and heavier the product will be.

When using 100 percent whole-wheat flours, many companies use 5 to 10 percent vital wheat gluten (VWG) to strengthen the dough. This product is very expensive because it totals only 12 to 15 percent of the whole-wheat kernel.

The total water content of a formula may be greater than 70 percent because whole-wheat flours need much more water to become properly hydrated. The more the starches and proteins are hidden, the more liquids and the more extensive soaking are required.

Either an instant yeast or a smaller amount of compressed yeast should be used when making whole-wheat breads because the weaker dough may not handle the activity of the compressed yeast over time.

A liquid sweetener is used to add moisture, usually molasses or honey, which also darkens the color of the product. Granulated sugar will give a drier product; brown sugar is a good compromise between using granulated sugar and a liquid sweetener. Brown sugar adds some dark coloring and moisture while still tenderizing the dough. A solid fat is recommended to lubricate gluten for less damage by bran and germ, and for better volume, moisture, and manageability. Oils can be used, but they do not provide high levels of lubrication to the gluten strands.

Rye Breads

Rye flours will weaken the bread two to three times as much as whole-wheat grains. Rye berries are cereal grain; they have bran, germ, and endosperm. Rye has no glutenin and little or no gliadin. There will be some elasticity caused in part by the small amount of gliadin, but this is mainly because rye flour is very high in starch. One hundred percent rye dough would have no gas-retaining properties, and the baked product would be a dense, flat, heavy product. For this reason, rye flour is always combined with wheat flour, the backbone of all baked goods, to produce rye breads. Rye breads have a longer shelf life because of their high starch content. The shelf life of rye breads is twice as long as that of most other bread products.

Rye flours can be very difficult to handle. Special handling considerations include the following:

- Mixing time should be reduced by 25 percent because of the lesser amounts of gluten in the flour. Rye flours absorb moisture very quickly because of the starch content, and they release the moisture during mixing. Starch does not retain moisture as well as does gluten.
- Fermentation time is decreased by about 25 percent because the weakness of the flour cannot maintain its structure if too much gas is present.
- The amount of yeast must be reduced by about 25 percent, or instant yeast used, to lower total fermentation.

- Rye dough requires careful handling during mixing, rounding, and shaping. These doughs should not be overhandled, or they will tear.
- Rye dough *must* be docked, or stippled, before baking. If it is not, the dough will form a crust early because of its high starch content, which will impede crumb movement and cause the loaf to burst through this early crust development due to natural oven spring.
- Rye breads are baked with steam to prevent some early crust development.

Most commercial rye breads made in the United States contain only between 5 percent and 10 percent rye flour. In Europe, 60 percent rye flour must be used for the product to be considered rye bread. The more rye flour included in a formula, the softer and weaker the product will be. To simulate rye, many bakers use 5 percent rye flour, add caraway seeds, caramel coloring, and vinegar, and call the product pumpernickel; some bakers also use an industrial-grade dough-conditioning mix that is concentrated in rye flavorings.

Rye Flours

There are four types of rye flour: light or white rye; medium rye; dark rye; and rye meal, rye chops, or pumpernickel.

- Light or white rye, sometimes called cream rye, is very white in color, soft, and very high in starch. It is made predominantly from the endosperm portion of the grain only.
- Medium rye includes some of the bran and germ. It is a little darker than white rye, but the bran and germ are not visible because the wheat is finely ground.
- Dark rye is very dark in color. More of the rye berry is used in dark-rye flour than in the lighter-colored flours. Dark rye should be stored in the refrigerator.
- Rye meal, rye chops, or pumpernickel flours are made from the entire rye berry. This is the weakest of the rye flours. This product should be refrigerated.

Sourdough Rye

The term *sour,* as it applies to rye bread, indicates that this product has a lower pH than other types of yeast-

Table 14–3 Sample Schedule for Making Sour Starter

	Monday A.M.	Monday P.M.	Tuesday A.M.	Tuesday P.M.	Total
	Example: For Wednesday Production				
Flour	2 lb., 8 oz.	2 lb., 8 oz.	2 lb., 8 oz.	2 lb., 8 oz.	10 lb.
Water	2 lb.	2 lb.	2 lb.	2 lb.	8 lb.
Yeast	4 oz.	—	—	—	4 oz.
					18 lb., 4 oz.

raised breads. A starter is prepared using a light-rye flour, water, and a one-time addition of yeast. This will be fed in stages with flour and water to achieve a mature starter. The high acidity of this starter is caused by the production of lactic and acetic acids during fermentation as the rye flour is digested by enzymatic activity. The formula for making sour starter is as follows:

Light rye flour	2 pounds, 8 ounces (3 pounds in high-humidity areas)
Water	2 pounds
Compressed yeast	1 ounce
Onion, quartered (optional)	1

Light-rye flour is preferred because of its high starch content and its lack of bran and germ to interfere with acid production. The yeast is added only at the beginning to start the fermentation and to lighten the mixture. Further addition of yeast will interfere with the production of lactic acids. The onion, which is optional, adds flavor and removes bitterness. The onion is decomposed by the sour. Some bakers chop some of the onion for use in the sour and use the rest in the final bread formula.

To make a sour starter, simply mix all the ingredients together. The starter should be mixed in a plastic, food-grade container. Ceramic or glass may be used, but care should be taken that it is not chipped, or does not become chipped during use. Metal should not be used. The container should be covered with plastic wrap or with a plastic lid. The starter should be kept at 85° F to 90° F. A higher temperature will cause rancidity, and a lower temperature will lend poor flavor production. Feed the starter as necessary after it has exhausted its fermentation capabilities.

The starter will rise, then fall, as early as four hours after it is set up. The number of feedings may vary. An average of three to five feedings is usually sufficient.

The starter is built over time to obtain a smooth flavor. For example, if 18 pounds of starter are needed for a formula, you must begin at least three days in advance, making additions in three to five parts (see Table 14–3). In the beginning, the starter will be very bitter because it is beginning to produce acids, and the rye flour is somewhat bitter to begin with. The more time the starter has, and the more regulated the feeding of the product, the better, more mellow flavor will be obtained.

You now have 18 pounds, 4 ounces of starter available for Wednesday morning's production, assuming you do not want any left over for future production. You may make any amounts you wish, as long as you keep the water and flour proportions the same. If you want to start a sour for future use, you should make sure you set a par level for your bucket of sour. Never dip below your par stock to ensure an even product and flavor every time you make bread, and to ensure you have enough sour to meet excess production demand.

The starter may be used for leavening and flavor or just for flavor. If it is used for a leavening effect as well, you may not use additional yeast because the alcohol and lactic-acid fermentations do not work well together. In addition, it is an extremely lengthy process and very time and temperature dependent. The temperature of the starter should be 85° F to 90° F, and the DDT should be 80° F.

Working Sours into a Formula

Sours generally range from 25 percent to 50 percent in any given formula (see Table 14–4 on page 288). As the

Table 14–4 Adding Sours: Rye

	Original Formula	Sour 25%	Final Dough
Light rye	15 lb.	7 lb., 8 oz.	7 lb., 8 oz.
First clear	30 lb.	—	30 lb.
Water	24 lb.	6 lb.	18 lb.
Salt	14 oz.	—	1 lb., 1½ oz.
Compressed yeast	1 lb., 10 oz.	4 oz.	1 lb., 6 oz.
Carraway	6 oz.	—	6 oz.
All-purpose shortening	2 lb., 10 oz.	—	2 lb., 10 oz.

Table 14–5 Adding Sours: Wheat

	Original Formula	Sour 35%	Final Dough
High gluten	24 lb.	5 lb., 11 oz.	18 lb., 5 oz.
Water	13 lb.	4 lb., 9 oz.	8 lb., 7 oz.
Salt	8 oz.	—	11 oz.
Oil	10 oz.	—	10 oz.
Compressed yeast	1 lb., 5 oz.	3 oz.	1 lb., 2 oz.

percentage of sour is increased, the taste and density or texture of the bread also increase. Remember, this is not only a rye-flour product, but the rye flour in the sour has been worked and digested and does not hold moisture well.

There are four rules for calculating starters:

1. Sour water equals the original water weight multiplied by the sour percentage desired.
2. Sour flour equals sour water multiplied by 125 percent (humidity × 150 percent).
3. Sour yeast equals sour flour multiplied by 3 percent (humidity × 2 percent).
4. Adjust salt. Increase by sour percentage to help counteract some of the acidity of the flavor and to strengthen the dough.

These calculations result in a dough of equal weight to the original, except for the increase in salt. A total weight of sour to be added, based on your decided percentage, will

be reached. The addition will simply replace part of the original flour/water/yeast with the *sour* flour/water/yeast to preserve the generally intended textural qualities of the bread, but add the flavor of sourdough.

To make a sourdough rye, the dry ingredients listed in a formula are placed in a mixing bowl with the 13 pounds, 12 ounces of sour. Then the formula procedure for the rye dough is followed; that is, add the water, then the all-purpose shortening, and so on.

Sourdough Wheat

The discussion of sourdough rye also applies to sourdough wheat. The sour will be a little less acidic when wheat is used than when rye is used because there will be little or no acetic-acid production. High-gluten flour and the same proportions of ingredients are used for sourdough wheat. Sour wheat starter can be used for lean doughs.

The formulas for sourdough rye and for sourdough wheat have been converted from compressed yeast to instant yeast in the laboratory for better handling (see Table 14–5).

Appendix 14A

Bake-Shop Conversion for Straight Doughs

Changing a formula in pounds to percent

1. Add weight of all flour to arrive at total flour weight.
2. Divide weight of each ingredient by the weight of the total flour and multiply by 100 to change the formula to percentage.

Ingredient	Pounds	Ounces	Calculation
Flour	80	—	(80 ÷ 80) × 100 = 100%
Water	50	—	(50 ÷ 80) × 100 = 62.5%
Yeast	1	9½	(1.6 ÷ 80) × 100 = 2%
Yeast food	—	3¼	(0.2 ÷ 80) × 100 = 0.25%
Salt	—	12¾	
Malt	—	12¾	(0.8 ÷ 80) × 100 = 1.0%
Shortening	2	6½	(2.4 ÷ 80) × 100 = 3%
Sugar	3	4	(3.25 ÷ 80) × 100 = 4%

Changing a formula from percentages to pounds

1. Change the percentage to a decimal (move the decimal point two places to the left).
2. Multiply the weight of total flour by the formula percentage of each ingredient expressed as a decimal.

Ingredient	Percentage	Calculation	Pounds/Ounces
Flour	100	1.0 × 150 = 150 lb.	150 lb.
Water	63	0.63 × 150 − 94.5 lb.	94 lb., 8 oz.
Yeast	2	0.02 × 150 = 3.0 lb.	3 lb.
Yeast food	0.25	0.0025 × 150 = 6 oz.	6 oz.
Salt	1.5	0.015 × 150 = 2.25 lb.	2 lb., 4 oz.
Shortening	3	0.03 × 150 = 4.5 lb.	4 lb., 8 oz.
Sugar	5	0.05 × 150 = 7.5 lb.	7 lb., 8 oz.

Appendix 14B

Conversions for Sponge Doughs

Changing a Formula in Pounds to Percent

1. Add weight of all flour to get total flour weight.
2. Divide weight of water in the sponge by weight of flour in the sponge and multiply by 100 to obtain percent sponge absorption.
3. Add weight of water in the sponge to weight of water in the dough to obtain total weight of water. Divide this total weight of water by total flour weight and multiply by 100 to obtain total or final percent absorption.
4. Divide weight of each ingredient by the weight of the total and multiply by 100 to obtain the percent of each ingredient.

EXAMPLE: Convert the following formula in pounds to percentages.

Ingredient	Lb.	Oz.	Calculation
		Sponge	
Flour	400	—	(400 ÷ 500) × 100 = 80%
Water	252	—	(252 ÷ 400) × 100 = 63%
Yeast	10	—	(10 ÷ 500) × 100 = 2%
Mineral yeast food	1	4	(1.25 ÷ 500) × 100 = 0.25%
		Dough	
Flour	100	—	(100 ÷ 500) × 100 = 20%
Water	68	—	(320 ÷ 500) × 100 = 64%
Salt	12	8	(12.5 ÷ 500) × 100 = 2.5%
Sugar	20	—	(20 ÷ 500) × 100 = 4%
Milk solids	30	—	(30 ÷ 500) × 100 = 6%
Shortening	15	—	(15 ÷ 500) × 100 = 3%

Total Flour	Total Water
400 lb. (sponge flour)	252 lb. (sponge water)
+ 100 lb. (dough flour)	+ 68 lb. (dough water)
= 500 lb. total flour (100%)	= 320 lb. total water

Changing the Formula in Percent to Pounds

Given the weight of flour. Method:

1. Change the percent into decimal.
2. Multiply weight of total flour by formula percent of each ingredient expressed decimally, except sponge water.
3. Multiply weight of sponge flour by formula percent absorption of sponge to get amount of water in sponge.
4. Multiply weight of total flour by formula percent absorption of dough to get total amount of water. Subtract from this the amount of water already used in the sponge to get amount of water to add to the dough.
5. We must know eight pounds of flour or pounds of dough required to convert the formula.

EXAMPLE: Change the following percent formula into pounds to give us a dough using 500 lb. of flour.

Ingredient	Percentage	Calculation	Lb./Oz.
		Sponge	
Flour	55	55 = .55 × 500 =	275 lb.
Water	64	64 = .64 × 275 =	176 lb.
Yeast	3	3 = .03 × 500 =	15 lb.
Yeast food	0.25	0.25 = 0.0025 × 500 =	1 lb., 4 oz.
		Dough	
Flour	45	45% = .45 × 500 =	225 lb.
Water	61	61% = .61 × 500 =	129 lb.
Salt	2	2% = .02 × 500 =	10 lb.
Malt	1	1% = .01 × 500 =	5 lb.
Sugar	4	4% = .04 × 500 =	20 lb.
Shortening	2	2% = .02 × 500 =	10 lb.
Milk	3	3% = .03 × 500 =	15 lb.

$$500 \times 0.61 = 305 \text{ lb. Total water}$$
$$- 176 \text{ lb. Water in sponge}$$
$$= 129 \text{ lb. Water to add to dough}$$

Given the Weight of the Dough in Pounds Method

1. Total the formula percent, exclusive of the percentage sponge water.
2. The total weight of dough divided by the total formula percentage and multiplied by 100 gives the weight in pounds of flour needed.
3. Proceed as when given the weight of the flour.

EXAMPLE: Using 1,125 lb. of dough and the following formula, convert from percentage to pounds.

1,125 lb. dough × 100 = 636 lb. flour necessary

Ingredient	Percentage	Calculation	Lb./Oz.
		Sponge	
Flour	70	0.70 × 636 =	445 lb.
Water	63	0.63 × 445 =	280 lb.
Yeast	3	0.03 × 636 =	19 lb., 1¾ oz.
M.Y.F.	0.25	0.0025 × 636 =	1 lb., 9½ oz.
		Dough	
Flour	30 =	0.30 × 636 = 191	191 lb.
Water	60 =	0.60 × 636 = 101	101 lb.
Salt	1¾ =	0.0175 × 636 = 11.1	11 lb., 1½ oz.
Sugar	5 =	0.05 × 636 = 31.8	31 lb., 12¾ oz.
Shortening	3 =	0.03 × 636 = 19.08	19 lb., 1¼ oz.
Milk	4 =	0.04 × 636 = 25.44	25 lb., 7 oz.
Total Formula	177%		

$$636 \times 0.60 = 381 \text{ lb. Total water}$$
$$- 280 \text{ Water in Sponge}$$
$$= 101 \text{ lb. water to add to dough}$$

Given the Number of Loaves with Scaling Weight

EXAMPLE: Given the formula below, find the size of dough batch necessary to produce 2,000 loaves, scaled at 18 oz. each loaf.

1. Find the lb. of total dough necessary by multiplying the number of loaves times the scaled weight of each loaf in ounces and dividing by 16.

     (2000 × 18) ÷ 16 - 2,250 lb. of dough

2. Total the formula percentage exclusive of the percentage of sponge water.

3. Total the amount of the dough divided by the total formula percent and multiplied times 100 gives the weight of the flour necessary.

     (2250 ÷ 175) × 100 - 1,323.5 lb. of flour.

4. Proceed as when given flour weight.

Ingredients	Percentage	Calculation	Lb./Oz.
		Sponge	
Flour	60	0.60 × 1,323.5 =	794 lb.
Water	62	0.62 × 794 =	492
Yeast	2	0.02 × 1,323.5 =	26 lb., 8 oz.
Yeast food	0.25	0.0025 × 1,323.5 =	3 lb., 5 oz.
		Dough	
Flour	40	0.40 × 1,323.5 =	529 lb., 8 oz.
Water	60		302 lb.
Salt	1.75	0.0175 × 1,323.5 =	23 lb., 4 oz.
Sugar	4	0.04 × 1,323.5 =	53 lb.
Shortening	2	0.02 × 1,323.5 =	26 lb.
Total	170		

15

Laminated Doughs

Laminated Doughs

I do like a little bit of butter to my bread!
— *A.A. Milne,* The King's Breakfast

Laminated doughs are doughs that are layered with many layers of fat. The layers of fat not only provide great flavor but also leaven the dough through a process known as *physical leavening*. In a laminated dough, the many layers of fat that have been folded into the dough melt and evaporate with the heat of the oven, creating steam; this steam has the strength to push the layers of dough up to create height and flakiness.

Laminated doughs are valued for their flakiness—they are some of the most challenging doughs to make in the bake shop. There are three basic laminated doughs: puff pastry, which is leavened only with fat; croissant, which is leavened with both fat and yeast; and Danish pastry, which is also leavened with both fat and yeast. Many variations of croissant and Danish are popular in Europe as well as in the United States.

Puff-Pastry Dough

Puff pastry dough is a basic dough that is used widely in the bakeshop to create a variety of items. Although it is a basic dough, it takes great skill to master the making of it. Puff pastry is a non-yeast, laminated dough composed of hundreds of layers of butter and dough that when baked create a light, buttery-flavored pastry. There are many stories as to the dough's origin, but the most popular is the story of the chef's apprentice who forgot to add the butter to his dough. Fearing the chef's wrath, but not wanting to go to the trouble of remaking the dough, he spread the butter on the dough and flattened and turned it several times to hide his mistake. The chef was so pleased with the flaky result that he insisted on knowing the method by which the apprentice created the dough.

Actually, flaky doughs such as puff pastry originated as early as the ancient Romans. By the year 1311 puff pastry dough was well-known to chefs. By the seventeenth cen-

tury, the great French painter and pastry chef Claude Gelée, le Lorrain had popularized the pastry in France. Marie Antoine Carème is credited for developing the method of turns or folds that is required to make the pastry. The French word for puff pastry is a *feuilletage,* a derivation of *feuilles,* meaning "leaves." *Mille feuilles,* or "a thousand leaves," is the appropriate name for the pastry Americans call napoleon.

Ingredients of Puff Pastry

Puff pastry is a basic mixture of water, salt, butter, and flour (the flour and water mixture is classically referred to as *detrempe*). The flour used can be a mixture of hard and soft flours—some chefs feel this produces the best effect—or a hard flour such as bread flour. The flour must be strong to support the high percentage of roll-in fat and to withstand the repeated rolling and folding done to create the flaky layers of the dough—bread flour is usually used. Eggs are sometimes added as enricheners, although they can cause the dough to be chewy; if they are used, some of the fat in the formula is usually eliminated. As in a pie dough, many chefs add a very small amount of acid, such as vinegar or lemon juice, to relax the gliadin in the gluten; this makes the rolling of the dough easier and quicker and will cause less shrinkage when the pastry is baked. Salt, in addition to providing flavor, strengthens gluten strands.

The fat used as roll-in in puff pastry is of great importance. Butter is the most widely accepted fat used for this type of pastry, largely because of its incomparable taste to that of other fats. In addition, butter contains a great deal of moisture, which will create steam when the pastry begins to bake. Butter's only downfall is that it has a low melting point—80° F. This can sometimes cause the fat to melt out of the pastry before it has a chance to create the flaky layers. For this reason, some chefs use a combination of puff-pastry shortening with real butter. The high melting point of the puff-pastry shortening will ensure flakiness, and the butter will provide superior flavor. Classically, butter is the only fat used for roll-in in a puff pastry.

Making the dough correctly is of great concern; if the detrempe contains too much flour or is worked too much, the dough will be rubbery and difficult to work with; in addition, it will shrink when baked. The dough must always be rested for at least 30 minutes before the first fold is put into it.

Great care must also be taken in the making of the roll-in fat. Creating a structure of even layers can be accomplished only if the butter and the dough are close to the same consistency. To accomplish this, a small percentage of flour is added to the roll-in fat to make the fat easier to handle. If rolled out properly, puff-pastry dough will have a layer of butter between each layer of dough and, depending on the number of folds given, these layers can number between 500 to 1,500.

Roll-in Methods

Block, or French, Method

After the dough has rested for a period, it is laminated with roll-in fat. There are many different methods of rolling the fat into the dough; the most common method, often referred to as the block, or French, method, is one in which the dough is rolled out on the bench, and the roll-in fat is placed over two-thirds. The roll-in fat is formed into a block before it is placed on the dough; it should not be too soft, or it will be impossible to handle; if it is too cold, it will be too brittle and will break or tear the dough. As soon as the fat is spread over two-thirds of the dough, the dough is ready for its initial fold. Another version of the block method is to roll the dough into a square that is just slightly larger than the block of fat. The block of fat is then placed diagonally on the square dough (see Figure 15–1). The flaps of the dough are then folded toward the center and gently sealed; now the dough is ready for its initial turn. This method is very commonly used.

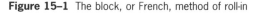

Figure 15–1 The block, or French, method of roll-in

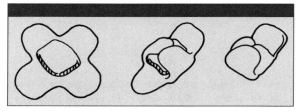

Blitz Method

Another method for roll-in of the at is the Scottish, or blitz, method. The term *blitz* comes from the word *blitzkrieg*, which originated from World War II and means lightening speed. The dough is developed, and the fat is added and mixed only enough to be incorporated, as is done in a pie dough. The fat is quite visible in large pieces throughout the dough. This dough then can be folded according to the same procedures as in the block method. The blitz method is popular in high-volume bake shops because it can be produced quickly, reducing procedure time. However, the block method allows more even distribution of the fat with a reduced amount of dusting flour; if too much flour is absorbed into the dough during rolling and turning, the consequent flour absorption can create a toughness in the dough. The blitz version will also produce a slightly more compact product when compared to the block method.

After the initial roll-in, the pastry is folded, with resting periods between each fold using either a single turn (or threefold) or a double turn (or fourfold). A combination of both folds can be used as well (see Figure 15–2). Generally for puff pastry, either two double turns or fourfolds are used or a threefold/fourfold/threefold/fourfold method is used. Too many folds will result in a compact product, while not enough folding will result in too few layers to produce the desired flaky texture. It is important to not

Figure 15–2 Rolling-in methods: the 3-fold and 4-fold

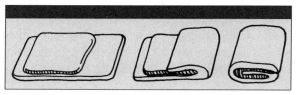

roll the dough too thin or too hard because this can damage the structure of the layers. However, if the dough is too thick, the fat will have a tendency to melt during baking and thus reduce flakiness.

Guidelines for Puff Pastry

- Enough dusting flour must be used to prevent the dough from sticking to the table during the roll-in process; however, it is important to brush the excess off the dough between each fold. If the flour is not removed, the dough will be tougher and will not rise properly in the oven.
- When rolling the dough, care must be taken that the structure of the layers is not ruptured with the use of too much force—the dough should be handled very gently during rolling and folding.
- It is of the utmost importance that puff-pastry dough have proper rest periods between folds to maintain a good finished product. After the detrempe is made, the dough needs to rest as long as 30 minutes before the initial fold is executed to relax the gluten. The dough should also rest for 10 to 15 minutes between each fold, and some rest period is required before the actual formation, or makeup, of the pastry item. When resting the dough, keep it covered with a damp cloth or plastic wrap to prevent crusting.
- Knives and other tools needed to form puff-pastry items must have sharp edges to cut the dough. A dull knife or cutter will press edges together and result in lower volume and uneven baking. The knife or cutter should be held at a sharp 90-degree angle so the edges of the dough remain perfectly straight for baking.
- If egg wash is used for puff items, the wash should never drip over the sides, or it may seal the dough and cause it to rise unevenly.
- Puff-pastry items should be rested again before being placed in the oven. The necessary rest time will vary, depending on the item. A large vol-au-vent, for instance, needs at least 45 minutes of resting before baking. Other items, such as those that are rolled in sugar, require a short rest period before baking because long rest periods would cause the sugar

Table 15–1 Troubleshooting Puff Pastry

Problem	Reason
Not enough volume.	Flour too soft. Old dough. Too many folds. Low oven temperature.
Shrinkage during baking.	Too much pressure during folding. Not enough rest period.
Shortening dissipates.	Roll-in fat too hard and cold. Not enough folding. Low oven temperature.
Uneven product.	Uneven roll-in. Not enough rest period. Dusting flour not removed. Uneven oven temperature.

to melt. Items should always be refrigerated during resting.

- Puff pastry should ideally be made with all folds during one production period and left refrigerated overnight before makeup of the items the next day. If this is not possible, at least two folds in addition to the initial fold can be given with the remaining folds the next day. If not enough folds are given before overnight refrigeration, the butter layer will be too hard and thick and will break when the dough is rolled out the following day.

See Table 15–1 for troubleshooting puff pastry.

Oven Temperatures

Low oven temperature leads to problems with puff pastry; if the oven is not hot enough, the butter will melt before it has a chance to create the steam needed for flakiness. Puff pastry needs a uniform oven temperature that does not fluctuate—the oven door should not be opened frequently during baking. Uneven temperatures result in butter dissipation, poor coloring, and poor volume. Small puff-pastry items should be baked at 415° F to 425° F, and slightly lower temperatures are used for larger items. The oven temperature should never be set below 400° F. Begin baking large items at high temperatures to set the structure, then lower the temperature to complete baking.

Storage of Puff Pastry

After puff-pastry dough is made up, it should be kept no longer than a week. As in pie dough, the flour and water will begin to ferment and oxidize, turning the dough gray and giving it an off-taste. The dough should be kept well covered at all times. Puff-pastry dough freezes very well in either dough form or as finished pieces, as long as it is well-wrapped.

Scraps

Scraps of puff-pastry dough will not be as flaky as fresh; however, for some pastries that do not require as much height, scraps can be used. When using scraps, the pieces should never be kneaded together—this will destroy the structure of the layers. Instead, scraps can be laid on top of each other and gently rolled together.

Items Made from Puff Pastry

Vol-au-Vents and Bouchées

Both vol-au-vents and bouchées are patties of puff dough made with a rim; the rim rises during baking to make a shell or cup of puff dough that can be filled with a variety of cream and fruit fillings. Vol-au-vents are classically larger than bouchées. Vol-au-vents were given their name by the famous French chef, Antonin Carême, who proclaimed "s'envola au vent" (they are "flying in the wind") upon removing his light and airy creation from the oven.

Napoleons, or Mille Feuilles â la Crême

Napoleons are among the most well-known puff items in the United States; as mentioned, the name means "thousand leaves." This pastry is docked heavily before it is baked and cut into rectangles, which are then filled with a pastry cream, or chiboust.

Docking is the act of creating small holes in the surface of a dough. This has a duel purpose: the first is to create vents for steam within the product (as in a pie crust) and to promote even baking; the second is to prevent the dough from rising as much as it would without docking (as in a napoleon).

The top of the pastry is always decorated with fondant.

Palmiers

Palmiers are commonly referred to in the United States as elephant ears. These pastries can be large or the size of petits fours. They are delicately rolled out with granulated sugar and folded in a fourfold to look like a palm leaf.

Sacristains

Sacristains are twisted to resemble a corkscrew and are usually coated with almonds. They received their ecclesiastical name because of the necessity of the corkscrew in opening wine for church services.

Turnovers

Turnovers are fruit-filled pastries that resemble slippers. In French, *"chaussons,"* meaning slippers.

Pithiviers

A pithiviers is a large, dome-shaped gateau made from puff pastry and filled with soft frangipane (almond cream). The top of the gateau is characteristically docked with slits resembling a sun. The town of Pithiviers is located about 50 miles south of Paris.

Laminated Yeast Doughs

Croissants and Danish are the two main types of laminated yeast doughs. Variations exist throughout Europe of the croissant—the Germans and Swiss make a version called *gipfels,* which is more pronounced in its crescent shape than the French version. In Austria and Germany, *plunder* is made—which is sort of a combination of a croissant and a Danish. Many of the same procedures and guidelines used for making a puff pastry are used for making croissants and Danish—the characteristic difference is the yeast and in how they are folded and made up into individual pastries. Also, a true French croissant does not contain eggs; Danish pastry usually does. In Europe, Danish contains nearly twice as much fat as a croissant dough, although in the United States both pastries usually contain close to the same amount of roll-in fat.

Croissants and Danish are popular throughout Europe and the United States; croissants are often filled with chocolate or almond creams and left flat rather than rolled into a crescent—this designates that they are filled. In the United States, savory croissants filled with meats, cheeses, and vegetables have become very popular. Danish dough can be made into bear claws, or *kamm* (comb in Danish).

The croissant supposedly originated from the attempt of the Turks in 1686 to lay siege to Budapest by tunneling into the city late one night. A group of bakers working to make the next day's breads heard the Turks' tunneling noise and alerted the city to the invasion. The Turks were defeated, and the bakers were given the honor of making a commemorative pastry; they made a sweet dough and rolled it into individual rolls shaped like the crescent on the Ottoman flag. Eventually, the shape found its way to France, where the French, probably following the procedure they were using to laminate puff pastry, made the croissant with its now characteristically flaky layers.

Guidelines for Laminated Yeast Doughs

- Laminated doughs should not be overmixed. The ingredients should be mixed into a smooth mass of dough without overdeveloping the gluten. Gluten development takes place mainly during the rolling-in process, rather than in mixing. If the dough is mixed too much, gluten is developed, and the dough will be hard to roll out. The final product will be tough and chewy. Laminated doughs can be mixed by hand or by machine on low speed with the paddle or hook. The paddle implement incorporates fats in the dough better. If using the hook, the gluten should be allowed to form a little, then the fat is added.

- Laminated doughs should be kept cold during folding and makeup for three important reasons: to keep yeast activity down (making the dough easier to handle), to help relax the gluten strands, and to keep the roll-in fat in condition and maintained in its appropriate place. If the dough becomes warm, the roll-in fat will melt out from between the layers when laminating.

- As with puff dough, the dough and roll-in fat should be of the same consistency. The reason for maintaining the same consistency of dough and roll-in fat is that when the product is baked, the layers of dough and roll-in fat should move together. If the dough is too stiff, the fat will melt, and the product will lose its flakiness.

- Enough dusting flour must be used to prevent the dough from sticking to the table during the roll-in process; however, it is important to brush the excess off the dough between each fold. If the flour is not removed, the dough will be tougher and not rise properly in the oven.

- When rolling the dough, care must be taken that the structure of the layers is not ruptured with the use of too much force—the dough should be handled very gently during rolling and folding.

- Both croissant and Danish dough will be easier to work with if the dough is allowed to rest for several hours between the roll-in procedure and the actual makeup of the individual pastries.

- Knives and other tools needed to cut croissants and Danish must have sharp edges to cut the dough. A dull knife or cutter will press edges together and result in lower volume and uneven baking. The knife or cutter should be held at a sharp 90-degree angle so the edges of the dough remains perfectly straight for baking.

- Because croissant and danish doughs contain yeast as a leavening agent, they are proofed. They should never be overproofed—most products receive a three-quarter proof at the most. If a laminated product is overproofed, the dough and roll-in fat will not stay properly layered; the shift in layers causes the fat to melt out, or the dough may simply collapse. Proof at temperatures lower than 80° F to 85° F. Unsalted butter has an 80° F melting point. Higher proofing temperatures will cause the roll-in fat to melt and run out of the product during proofing.

Croissants

Croissant dough is a wet or soft, bland laminated yeast dough containing 25 to 50 percent roll-in fat. The fat percentage is based on the weight of the dough. It is calculated by adding the weights of the ingredients of the dough and then taking 25 to 50 percent of that weight. The dough is wet or soft because of the close ratio of the flour and water. Many formulas call for the use of milk, rather than water, in the dough to enrich and flavor it.

A classic croissant uses unsalted sweet butter for the roll-in fat, although other fats, such as baker's margarine or shortening, can be used—with a great deal of flavor loss. As in puff pastry, the fat must contain a high percentage of moisture to help create steam in the oven, which in turn provides flakiness.

Croissants should be light and flaky, with a moderately open grain and a distinctly layered texture. Well-developed doughs that are rich in fat will provide these characteristics. The ingredients for croissants include bread flour, to keep the dough strong enough for shaping; *cold* water or milk, to retard yeast action and keep gluten relaxed; yeast, as the primary leavening mechanism; and salt, for flavor, for gluten strengthening, and to retard yeast action. Dry milk solids are used when milk is not, and along with granulated sugar; both soften the crust and give it color. Butter or shortening is added in the dough stage to lubricate gluten strands. Eggs may be used for additional color and richness, although they are not used classically.

Croissants usually receive an initial threefold (see Figure 15–2 on page 296), or single turn, and then three more threefolds to complete the roll-in procedure. Too many folds in a croissant can make the pastry heavy and chewy, rather than light and flaky.

To form a croissant, follow these steps:

1. After mixing, place the dough on a lightly floured sheet pan and place in the retarder to relax for 30 minutes.
2. Soften and mix the roll-in fat. Place the dough on a papered sheet pan and roll out to two-thirds the size of the pan. Retard to stiffen slightly.
3. Roll out the dough to ½-inch thickness. Shape into a rectangle, approximately the size of a sheet pan and three times as long as it is wide.
4. Place the roll-in fat over two-thirds the length of the dough, leaving 1-inch edges. As soon as the fat is on the dough, fold the edges in to keep the fat from running out.
5. Fold over one-third of the dough with no fat; then fold over one-third of the dough with fat, making three layers of dough and two layers of fat.

6. Turn the dough one-quarter and roll out to the size of the sheet pan. This is the first fold. The quarter turn allows the gluten to be stretched in all directions, not just lengthwise.
7. Allow the dough to rest for 20 to 30 minutes, refrigerated. This gives the gluten strands a chance to relax.
8. After the rest, take the dough to the bench and position as above, roll into a rectangle approximately the size of the sheet pan. Rolling is done from the middle, out to the opposite side. Fold in thirds again. The rolling can be done with a sheeter. Dust the surface with flour as needed. If rolling out with a rolling pin while on the sheeter, do it on the right side of the sheeter. To lift the dough, fold into an S shape.
9. Allow the dough to rest between rolls and folds to relax the gluten. Mark the number of turns done each time by indenting the dough with the fingers, one indention per turn.

10. When all turns are done, rest the dough in the retarder overnight. Cover the dough to prevent crusting.

11. Cut the dough into 5-inch strips. Take one to work with, and return the remainder to the retarder, covered. Lightly flour and, either manually or with the sheeter, flatten or thin the strip to the desired width.

12. Keep the dough floured to prevent sticking. Thin out to desired thickness. If the dough rides the roller, it is too thin.

13. When the desired thickness is reached, take the dough to the unfloured bench, and dust off all the flour from the dough. Begin to cut the dough using a sharp pastry wheel or a French knife or a special roller designed for this purpose. Trim the dough evenly.

14. Beginning at a slight angle, make isosceles triangles. Remember that the width of the strip determines the size of the triangle. The length should be twice the width. A wide triangle yields a flat crescent. A narrow triangle yields a short, fat crescent, in which the dough is wrapped around itself, leaving the inside unbaked.

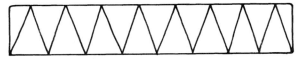

15. Weigh each triangle. Add any scrap dough to the triangles to make them the proper weight.

16. Notch the center of the wide end of the triangle to allow the dough to roll out more and keep it in a crescent shape when formed.

17. Begin to roll the dough toward the point, either toward or away from you. Stretch the point.

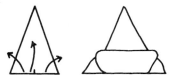

18. Finish rolling. The point should be placed underneath so it does not pop out when baked. The wide bands should be on the outside of the crescent, and the point of the dough should be toward the inside of the crescent.

19. The ends of the croissant may be overlapped before baking. This is good for croissant sandwiches.

20. Pan the croissant on papered pans, in rows of 5 × 5.

21. Proof the croissants to a three-quarter proof.

22. Lightly egg wash each croissant or brush each with milk.

23. Bake at 425° F to 430° F until golden and baked through. To check the croissant for doneness, look for a light, golden brown color on the top and the bottom and lift the croissant to see that it feels light.

Danish Pastry

Danish pastry was originally made in Denmark and was brought to the United States by Scandinavian pastry chefs around 1919. There are five basic differences between Danish and croissants. Danish is more flaky, has more flavor, has more roll-in fat, is more tender, and is softer.

The amount of roll-in fat in a Danish dough is of great importance in terms of appearance of the finished product. In the production of real, high-quality Danish pastry, the mixed dough is weighed, and then enough roll-in fat is used to equal half the dough's weight. For example, if the total Danish dough weight is two pounds, one pound of roll-in fat will be required. However, the pastry may be made with anywhere from 10 to 50 percent roll-in fat and still be acceptable Danish pastry.

Danish, like croissant, is a wet dough—both use between 50 to 60 percent liquid in their formulas. Danish dough is semisweet to sweet; the dough is rich in eggs and further enriched with the use of DMS or milk. Cardamom is characteristically used to flavor Danish dough.

Ordinary bread flour gives a good result in making Danish pastry. If the bread flour is too strong in gluten content, a small percentage of pastry or cake flour may be added. A 75 percent bread and 25 percent pastry or cake flour may be sufficient.

Butter or baker's margarine is usually used as the roll-in fat in Danish pastry, or a combination of the two; the fat should have a plastic consistency for even distribution of the fat between the layers, without having the layers break apart during the roll-in procedure.

Sugar is used to sweeten and moisten the dough, but care should be taken that excessive amounts are avoided. If too much sugar is used, the Danish will appear flat and unbaked because of the added moisture the excess sugar provides the dough. Generally, 3 to 5 ounces of sugar is used per quart of liquid.

Milk and eggs are both used to enrich the dough. Eggs are added at no more than eight per quart of liquid; the more roll-in fat per quart of liquid, the more eggs can be used.

Salt enhances the flavor of Danish and gives the dough better consistency while it controls fermentation and helps to relax gluten strands. One-third ounce per quart of liquid is sufficient.

It is important that all ingredients are kept cold before mixing to retain a cold dough. The dough itself should not be overmixed. As with other laminated doughs, the dough and the roll-in fat should have the same consistency for best results.

There are several methods of folding the dough, but the threefold (3×3) method is the most popular. When folding dough, do not press hard on the dough. Maintain even distribution of the roll-in fat by rolling firmly and carefully. This will result in a good, flaky Danish pastry.

The folding in of the fat is an important factor affecting the appearance of the finished product. Not enough folds result in the fat running out of the pastry during baking. Too many folds and the fat becomes part of the dough, and flakiness is lost. As with puff pastry and croissant, the incorporation of the fat into the dough before the actual folding occurs is not counted as one of the dough folds.

As with all laminated doughs, during the make-up period of the Danish, use a minimum of dusting flour. All dusting flour should be brushed off before panning or freezing.

A desired proof temperature for Danish pastry is 80° F to 85° F. If the temperature in the proofing cabinet is too high, the fat will melt and dissipate out of the dough. Too much steam and too high a temperature in the proofing cabinet can cause problems in the finished product. For example, the fat will melt out of the dough during proofing and the stretching of the gluten strands due to the high heat will cause the dough to collapse, all of which will result in a dense, heavy pastry.

A sufficient baking temperature for Danish pastry is between 375° F and 420° F. The more sugar in the dough, the lower the baking temperature. The higher the percentage of roll-in fat, the higher the baking temperature at the beginning of the baking process because the roll-in fat needs to be transformed into steam quickly. As a general rule, American Danish is baked at low heat to slowly caramelize the high sugar levels. European Danish is baked at moderate, or average, temperatures. Scandinavian Danish begins with high oven temperature.

Most Danish will feel light after baking, with the exception of American Danish, which feels heavier because of the richer, sweeter dough consistency. After baking, Danish are often finished with simple syrup or glaze and sprinkled lightly with fondant.

Types of Danish

The three types of Danish are American, Scandinavian, and European. The basic difference among these types is the amount of roll-in fat used in their production. American Danish is 10 to 20 percent roll-in fat; European Danish is 25 to 40 percent roll-in fat; and Scandinavian Danish, which is considered to be the best Danish, is 45 to 55 percent roll-in fat.

American Danish

Because there is a low amount of roll-in fat in American Danish, the flavor of the dough must be obtained through other ingredients. American Danish generally has a large amount of sugar and salt and an increased amount of

Figure 15–3 A Bear Claw

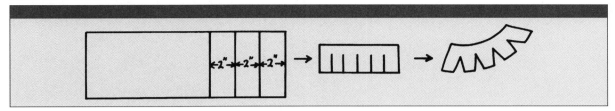

yeast. Spices, shortening or margarine, and eggs are added to the dough for added flavor. To keep the cost of American Danish lower, DMS and water, rather than milk, are used and the roll-in fat is butter-flavored shortening, rather than butter.

Because there is such a high percentage of fats and sugar in American Danish, the creaming method of mixing is used. The dough will only need three to four turns, as more turns will only hinder the dough. American Danish is baked at 375° F because the oven spring is not as important given the low percentage of roll-in fat.

Scandinavian Danish

Scandinavian Danish is a wet (soft), bland, laminated yeast dough containing between 45 and 55 percent roll-in fat. Butter, or sometimes puff-pastry shortening, is usually used as the roll-in fat, to produce a very crispy, flaky dough. Scandinavian Danish should be proofed at a lower temperature so the butter does not melt and run out; it should be baked at a higher temperature, between 425° F and 450° F, for the same reason. The dough will take four to six turns. It is much more like a puff-pastry dough than the other types of Danish. Care should be taken to see that the dough is not overmixed; it should be removed from the mixer as soon as it comes together.

European Danish

European Danish is less crisp than Scandinavian. European Danish is baked at moderate temperatures, slightly above 400° F.

Items Made from Danish Dough

Snecken

Snecken means snail in German. In this type of Danish, the dough is rolled out to ¼-inch thickness and sprinkled with cinnamon sugar or cinnamon oil, then rolled to form a long snake. Thin 1-inch slices are cut from the snake and filled with a fruit or cheese filling.

Filled Danish Twists

The dough for filled Danish twists is rolled out as in snecken, but filled with a filling. Then the dough is folded in half over itself, lengthwise. One-half-inch strips are cut, then twisted together and rolled into a snail. The Danish can be filled, as the snecken is filled, if desired.

Bear Claw

Bear claws, probably the most well-known of Danish items, get their name from the characteristic cuts made after they have been filled with a frangipane, or almond cream, and shaped to resemble a bear's claw. The Scandinavian name for them, *kamm*, means comb and refers to a cock's comb (see Figure 15–3).

Quick Breads, Tea Cakes, and Coffee Cakes

Quick Breads, Tea Cakes, and Coffee Cakes

Should I, after tea and cakes and ices,
Have the strength to force the moment to its crisis?
    —*T.S. Eliot,* The Love Song of J. Alfred Prufrock

Quick breads, tea cakes, and coffee cakes have a breadlike texture but contain no yeast products; instead their heavy batters use baking powder or baking soda for leavening.

Quick breads, tea cakes, and coffee cakes were originally created to replace the need for yeast-leavened breads because of the latter's time-consuming process. Variations of these cakes have since become popular in most Western cultures, particularly in Europe and the United States. They are usually heavily flavored with nuts, fruits, or chocolate chips, and, because their batters are so heavy, they are baked in either loaf or bundt pans. They often use a flour, such as bread or pastry, that contains a high gluten content to hold the structure of the bread or cake. Care must be taken that the batter is not overmixed; this would overwork the gluten and make the bread or cake tough and rubbery with low volume and a dense crumb.

There are many forms of quick breads, all of which taste good with coffee or tea and are often served as breakfast breads or afternoon tea snacks. Banana bread or cranberry bread are what are traditionally considered quick breads, but there are many other types of quick breads that do not appear in the familiar loaf shape. Scones, baking-powder biscuits, buttermilk biscuits, corn bread, and muffins are all examples of quick breads. Quick breads can be served plain, lightly glazed, or sprinkled with confectionery sugar.

Mixing Methods

There are three basic mixing methods for producing a quick bread: creaming; blending; and rubbing, or biscuit. These methods are not always used in the same manner as they would be for a cake.

Creaming Method

The creaming method is used in many muffin formulas when solid shortening is required. To properly cream, the fat must be in the softened state. The sugar and shortening are mixed on low speed with a paddle only until light and fluffy in texture, about 3 to 4 minutes. Overcreaming this mixture will result in poor texture of the finished product. The eggs are then added slowly, one at a time, so they may properly emulsify. Dry ingredients are added alternately with the liquids until all ingredients are in the bowl, beginning and ending with the dry. The creaming method gives muffins a soft, cakelike crumb (for more explanation of the creaming method, see page 332).

Blending Method

The blending method is also used with muffins, as well as with banana bread and carrot-raisin bread. It is sometimes used when oils or liquid fats are called for in a formula. When the blending method is used, all dry ingredients are sifted, then combined on low speed; then the eggs and liquid are added. The liquid fat is carefully blended in last. The blending method requires the mixer to stay on low speed and uses the paddle as the mixing implement.

Rubbing, or Biscuit, Method

The rubbing, or biscuit, method is used most often for scones and biscuits. This method is done by hand, but it can be accomplished in a mixer on low speed if done carefully. With this method, the shortening is rubbed into the flour, forming large pieces of fat. The eggs and liquid are whisked together, added to the flour mixture, and mixed lightly. The mixture will be very wet when finished, and caution should be taken to avoid overmixing. This is the same method used in making a pie dough.

Tips

There are three tips that help to produce a high-quality quick bread: do not overmix, do not overflavor, and do not overbake.

Do Not Overmix

Overmixing quick breads, especially after the addition of the flour, will produce a tough end product. The product will resist leavening and expansion during baking.

Do Not Overflavor

Adding excessive flavorings can damage a quick bread in many ways: one, the product can become too potent and bitter, especially with citrus flavors; and, two, depending on the flavoring, a change in the mixture's consistency can occur, which in turn may affect the structural integrity of the final product.

Do Not Overbake

Overbaking reduces the overall moisture level of the product, causing the staling process to begin earlier than usual.

A toothpick or knife inserted at the center of the product should come out clean, and the product should have proper browning.

Classic Quick Breads, Tea Cakes, and Coffee Cakes

Scones are British tea biscuits similar to American biscuits but with a slightly heavier texture. Scones may contain soaked fruits, usually currants or raisins. Mixing of scones is identical to that of mixing biscuits, but the shapes are traditionally wedges or triangles.

Banana bread is a traditional American favorite baked in loaves. The batter is heavy and should be made with overripe bananas to produce the fullest flavor.

Gingerbread cake is a traditional coffee or tea cake served at afternoon coffee or tea breaks; it is strong and spicy with a delicate crumb.

Pound cake, also called English cake, was made in England as early as the 1600s. These cakes were originally mixed with a pound each of butter, sugar, flour, and eggs, and often fruits, nuts, and spices. Pound cake is quite possibly the first quick bread and is most definitely the forerunner of latter-day sponge and butter cakes. Many variations, with often considerably less poundage in the ratios of ingredients, have been popular for hundreds of years.

17

Cookies

Cookies

I am still convinced that a good, simple, homemade cookie is preferable to all the store-bought cookies one can find.

—James Beard

The word *cookie* comes from the Dutch word *koekje*, meaning small cake, a fitting description for a word that encompasses such a variety of offerings. There are more varieties of cookies than any other type of baked good, mainly because cookies can be made in so many different ways.

Cookies are some of the most tantalizingly ubiquitous sweets in the world; almost every culture has some form of what could be deemed a cookie. Perhaps this is because they are so small, easy to eat, and full of flavor. Many cultures have traditions centered around cookies: afternoon teas and coffee breaks, holiday cookie-making parties, midnight snacks of cookies and milk. As with so many other baked items, it sometimes seems that all that is good with the world is mixed into these bite-sized wonders.

Cookie Textures

The texture of a cookie is perhaps one of its most identifying characteristics: No one would want to eat a soft, chewy biscotti anymore than one would want to crunch on a crispy, hard coconut macaroon. Some cookies, such as chocolate chip cookies, can be either chewy or crunchy, depending on which texture is desired. To develop different textures in cookies, it is important to understand the effects the ingredients in them have on the finished product.

Crisp-Textured Cookies

Crisp cookies need a relatively low moisture content. They should also be high in fat and sugar; if they are not high in fat and sugar, they will usually have a lot of flour compared to other cookies. They are crispiest if they are baked in small, thin shapes so they may dry as they bake. Because they will absorb moisture from the air and the refrigerator, it is best to store them unrefrigerated in airtight containers.

Chewy-Textured Cookies

For cookies to have a chewy texture, they must be high in moisture; they must have a high ratio of eggs or other liquid to dry ingredients. Chewy cookies usually contain less fat (although fat is the chief tenderizer, it also provides crispiness in such a compact product) than their crispy counterparts. Strong flours are often used in conjunction with softer flours if a chewy cookie is desired.

Cake-Textured Cookies

The soft texture that is required in a cakelike cookie means that the batter must be high in moisture and relatively low in fat, just as in a chewy cookie. This type of cookie is usually thick and large, which enables it to keep its moistness throughout the baking process. Often these cookies will contain invert sugars that are extremely hygroscopic. These cookies should be slightly underbaked.

Ingredients

Sugar

Creaming is a primary method for making cookies; if the sugar used during the creaming process is too coarse or the cookies are overcreamed, the cookie will spread too much during baking. For this reason, many chefs like to use a combination of granulated sugar and confectionery sugar. (Confectionery sugar alone will absorb too much moisture from the batter.) A fine-granulated sugar is excellent for cookie making, especially if spreading is a problem. (Fine-granulated sugar can be made from regular granulated sugar by placing the sugar in the robot coupe and processing it until it is of a fine consistency.)

Fat

Most cookies have high levels of fat compared to other baked goods, regardless of their texture. This is especially true in American-style creamed cookies such as chocolate chip and oatmeal raisin. Because most cookies undergo the creaming process, a shortening is used, usually in conjunction with butter, to improve flavor. Some cookies use all butter.

Eggs

Eggs are the chief source of liquid, and therefore moisture, in a cookie. Eggs also provide structure to the batter and, consequently, contribute to the shape of the cookie. They also impart a great deal of taste as they enrich.

Flour

Flour (along with the eggs) provide structure in a cookie, as it does in all baked goods that contain it. Because of the high fat content in most cookies, a strong flour is needed to be able to support the fat and maintain the cookie's structure. Strong flours can develop too much gluten, however, so oftentimes a blend of hard and soft flours is needed. Pastry flour works well in many cookie formulas, but it is important to experiment with blends, if warranted, to achieve the desired effect.

Leaveners

Most cookies use chemical leaveners in the form of baking powder and baking soda; baking powder creates more of a rise, while baking soda creates a spread. If these effects are not desired, cookies will not contain them. Cookies are also leavened by physical leavening through the creaming process, which is why overcreaming can create havoc with the shape of a cookie. Baking soda and ammonium carbonate, because of their mellowing effect on the gluten in flour, add spreadability and tenderness to cookies.

Forming Cookies

Cookies can be formed and placed on sheet pans using one of two basic methods.

Deposit Cookies

A pastry bag or scoop is used for making deposit cookies. The pastry bag allows the baker to pipe a variety of shapes that can be piped directly onto paper-lined sheet pans. Small ice-cream scoops can be used to deposit cookie batter directly onto sheet pans as well. A variation of this method is to roll cookie dough out to a desired thickness and cut shapes from the dough (as in a Linzer cookie), then the shapes are carefully placed on paper-lined sheet pans.

Rolled/Refrigerated Cookies

A specified amount of dough is rolled into a log, wrapped in parchment paper, and stored in the refrigerator to make rolled/refrigerated cookies. When the cookies are to be baked, designated-size slices are cut from the roll and placed on paper-lined sheet pans. This method lends itself to high-production kitchens—a large batch of dough can be made, then stored and used for several days; whenever cookies are needed, they can be cut and baked with ease. A variation of this method is to bake the entire log and cut the cookies immediately after they are removed from the oven (as in a biscotti).

Baking Cookies

Regardless of what method is used to get cookies onto the sheet pan, it is imperative that they are of equal size and shape and that they are placed in uniform rows, either staggered or straight. This will promote even baking throughout the product and reduce waste. Because most cookies contain a lot of sugar, they will brown faster than other baked goods—it is a good idea to always double pan cookies to prevent them from browning too much on the bottom. Cookies will continue to bake and brown on a hot sheet pan—called *crossover baking.* To prevent this, the cookies should be transferred to a cool sheet pan as they come out of the oven (this is easily done by lifting the entire baking sheet and placing it on a cool pan). Baking temperatures for most cookies are between 350° F and 375° F, although ladyfingers and macaroons require a high heat of 400° F.

Decorating Cookies

Because there are so many varieties of cookies, there are also many different ways of decorating them. They may be dipped in chocolate, sandwiched with preserves, or sprinkled with confectionery sugar—each type of cookie usually has a specific way in which it is decorated.

Types of Cookies

Creamed Cookies

Most cookies, regardless of their makeup, fall into the category of creamed cookies: chocolate chip, peanut butter, oatmeal raisin, short dough, and butter cookies, even most biscotti. They are creamed cookies because the creaming method is used in their preparation. The creaming method also applies to some cake batters, but, because cookies contain little or no liquid (less than for a cake batter), the method differs slightly for their preparation:

1. The fats are creamed with a paddle on low speed until they are pliable.
2. The sugars are added, and the mixture is creamed until it lightens in color, texture, and volume. The mixing bowl should be scraped frequently to ensure proper incorporation of the ingredients. If the mixture is over- or undercreamed, it will have a dramatic effect on the finished product: less volume and poor

texture, and overcreamed batters will spread during baking.
3. The eggs are added, one at a time, until they are incorporated. If the eggs are added too quickly, the fat will not be able to absorb the moisture in the eggs, and the ingredients will not emulsify, causing curdling. The emulsified mixture is referred to as a *water-in-fat emulsion.* The emulsifier lecithin, found in the egg yolk, aids in creaming. The bowl should be scraped frequently during this process.
4. The sifted flour is added in two or three stages, depending on amounts. The batter should be mixed just until the flour is absorbed unless strong gluten development is desired. Chocolate chips, nuts, and so on, are added last.

Shaped, or Formed, Cookies

These cookies are fun and exciting to make because they are shaped not only before, but after they are baked. They lend an interesting effect to plated desserts and cookie platters. Most often, a template is used to spread the cookie batter onto the sheet pan (silpats are excellent for making formed cookies) in the desired shape; the hot cookie is usually placed around a dowel, cone, or cup to create a dramatic effect. When the cookie cools, it retains the shape of what it was formed in, on, or around. Some form pastes can be piped into strips and designs and formed around dowels to make corkscrew shapes. There are several types of form cookie batters.

- Hippen paste is an almond wafer paste that is used to make a variety of formed cookies, including cups and especially butterflies. The batter must be mixed properly, with no lumps in the almond paste, for the cookie to be successful.
- Tulip, or Cigarette, paste is very versatile because it can be piped or spread with a template with great success. It is used to make the classic French petits fours sec, *les copeaux,* which means corkscrew. Tulip paste is made with butter, confectionery sugar (to reduce spreading), egg whites, and bread flour. If this batter is overmixed, it will incorporate too much air

and spread during baking—ruining the design of the cookie. Often, it is made by hand on the table using fraisage to prevent overmixing.

- Almond lace cookies are made from a batter of thinly sliced blanched almonds, flour, sugar, butter, and glucose. These cookies do not use a template and spread dramatically, because of the glucose, during baking. They can be shaped while hot, reheated, and shaped again to form a variety of cups, triangles, halos, and so on. This batter can be used to make the classic *florentine* cookie: The batter is formed into a ball, baked, and, while warm, wrapped around a dowel. The cookie is then filled with chocolate buttercream. *Tuiles*, or cookie cups, are also made from this batter.
- Sandwich cookies are thin cookies that are sandwiched together with ganache, chocolate, fondant, or preserves. They are often dipped or piped to add flavor and to create color contrasts. Window cookies are sandwich-type cookies with a window cut from the top cookie to allow the filling to peek through. Two classic window cookies are *Linzer* cookies, fashioned after the Linzer torte, and almond ring cookies.
- Sponge cookies are made using the whipping method (which is fully described on page 357). This method is also used to make many types of sponge cakes. Sponge cookies use the incorporation of air into the egg whites and egg yolks in the formula as physical leavening. They contain relatively low amounts of sugar and flour and usually very little fat.
- Ladyfingers are a classic sponge cookie that is piped into a finger-sized cylinder and baked. They are used in the making of many desserts, such as charlottes.
- Madeleines are a classic French cookie that are baked in the shape of a scallop shell. They are richer than ladyfingers and often contain honey or orange flavorings. They were supposedly invented by a woman named Madeleine who was a pastry chef in the region in France known as Lorraine. They are quite a delicacy; the French writer Proust immortalized them when he described them in his most celebrated work, *Remembrance of Things Past*:

Once I had recognized the taste of the crumb of madeleine soaked in her decoction of lime flowers which my aunt used to give me . . . immediately the old gray house upon the street, where her room was, rose up like the scenery of a theater.

Twice-Baked Cookies

Twice-baked cookies are made with doughs fairly high in flour, rolled into logs, and baked until done, then cut into strips and baked again. They can be sweetened or unsweetened and are often flavored with almonds, almond oil, or anise. Most are very dry and are meant to be eaten with a strong cup of coffee or espresso: Italians make many varieties of *biscotti,* the French have *biscotte,* the Germans make *zwieback,* and a favorite Jewish cookie is *mandelbrot.*

Brownies

Brownies are not actually a type of cookie, they are an entity all their own. They are quintessentially American and, over the years, a number of variations have been invented to satisfy the American palate. There are two basic types, categorized according to their texture:

- Cake brownies have a cakelike texture because they are made with an average amount of sugar.
- Fudge brownies are rich, dense, and chewy because they are made with a higher amount of sugar compared to cake brownies.

Either type of brownie can be served with a fudge or cream cheese icing.

Petits Fours

Petits fours are small, bite-sized pastry items, measuring no more than 1 and 1½ inches. The term *petits fours* is the French translation of little oven, and the concept of petits fours originated in France. Originally, small cakes were baked in the solid fuel-stoked ovens, which were cooling down at the end of the day. Thus, the petits fours were baked at lower temperatures to dry them.

The art of producing petits fours is an achievement of sight, as much as taste. The basic items are chosen carefully to offer suitable body to maintain form and to minimize crumbling. When fondants are used, white, pale pastels and chocolate are appropriate. Bright, artificial colors should be avoided. Decorations, usually consisting of tiny buttercream flowers and designs, or chocolate lines and patterns, are carefully planned to maintain a simple yet elegant appearance.

Petits fours are usually served at high tea, formal coffee service, or as part of a buffet. The terms *friandise* and *mignardise* are French menu terms for various assortments of petits fours and candies, often complementary to a meal.

There are four types of petits fours: petits fours glacés, petits fours sec, petits fours demi-sec, and petits fours variés.

Petits Fours Glacés

Petits fours glacés are cake-based petits fours coated with fondant icing, glazes, or chocolate coating. A single layer of cake may be used, or several layers assembled with a small amount of warm jelly or jam. Frangipane, a dense almond pound cake, is the cake commonly used for petits fours glacés because it can be cut into shapes with clean lines without crumbling, but any type of firm, dense cake can be used. The frangipane is baked in a flat sheet pan and inverted onto a surface dusted with granulated sugar to prevent sticking. A thin layer of apricot or raspberry preserve is spread on the cake, which is then topped with a thin layer of marzipan. The sheets are cut into various shapes. Squares, rectangles, and diamonds are the most cost-effective shapes for petits fours because they use the greatest amount of cake, producing few scraps.

Fondant is normally used to cover the petits fours glacés, but chocolate coating or glazes can also be used. To achieve the desired consistency, fondant must be warmed and sometimes it must also be thinned. The fondant is heated to 100° F (blood temperature) over a double boiler or a hot-water bath. Because the fondant at 100° F is slightly warmer than blood or body temperature, it will begin to feel warm to the touch and can easily be judged ready for use. If the fondant is heated to over 100° F, it will lose its shine when dry, giving the product a spotty, dull appearance. Egg white may be added for additional shine, but if egg white is added, the fondant must be kept refrigerated to prevent spoilage.

To adjust the consistency of fondant, water, simple syrup, flavorings, liqueur, or liquor are used. Fondant can be flavored with alcohol, liqueur, liquor, fruit compound, or fruit purée. When dipping or coating petits fours, care must be taken to coat the item completely and evenly. An item that requires a second coating to fill voids will develop ripples, spoiling the desired effect.

Petits Fours Sec

Petits fours sec are petits fours that are prepared using a method similar to that of petits fours glacés. The difference between the two is that the basis for petits fours sec is a dry, bite-sized cookie, such as a macaroon. Petits fours sec may be garnished in the same manner as petits fours glacés, dipped in chocolate glaze, or simply decorated with fine lines of chocolate.

Petits Fours Demi-Sec

Petits fours demi-sec also use cookies as their base, but these confections are created using an assembly of layers. In their simplest form, petits fours demi-sec may be two small, thin layers of cookie, such as hippen paste, joined with a filling of jam, buttercream, or chocolate. The sandwich may then be dipped or coated and decorated. More elaborate petits fours demi-sec are made by producing the individual layers of varying items, assembling them, and garnishing as described for petits fours glacés. The pastry chef may choose a thin layer of lining paste or 1-2-3 dough for a base, then layer jelly or jam with a layer or two of cookies. Top these with marzipan and finish with appropriate garnishes. When multiple layers are used, they must be relatively thin to maintain the symmetry of the finished product.

Petits Fours Variés

Petits fours variés are any bite-sized pastry items not categorized as a glacé, sec, or demi-sec. They may consist of items such as pâte à choux, meringue, tartlets, partially glazed cake, or candies. Chocolate ducats, lace cookies, and tuiles can be prepared as petits fours variés.

Tips for Cookie Production

- Use a canvas cloth or tablecloth to reduce the amount of dusting flour needed when rolling out cookies.

- Pipe dough from a pastry bag rather than dropping it to create more uniform shapes.
- Store soft cookies in cookie boxes and cover them to retard drying.
- Ensure that the oven temperature is not too high, as an oven temperature that is too high will prevent cookies from spreading properly.
- Cool baked items slowly and away from drafts to prevent the tops from cracking.

18

Pies and Tarts

Pies and Tarts

The best of all physicians is apple pie and cheese!
—Eugene Field, from Apple Pie and Cheese

Both pies and tarts are favorite pastries throughout Western culture; pies are deemed typically American, while tarts have a particularly European style. Pies are generally deeper than tarts due to more filling and are made with an unsweet crust (valued for its flakiness). Tarts are usually made with any one of a variety of shortdoughs.

Although they date back to Europe, particularly England (Shakespeare alludes to them) from as early as the 16th century, pies have been synonymous with American baking. Brought by the early settlers, sweet and savory pies were simply prepared dishes used to feed many and to extend ingredients. They were also easy to cut and eat and, because of the high sugar content in their fillings, could be easily kept. Through Colonial times, many versions of pies, cobblers, slumps, and crisps were among the most popular of pastries.

Pies used then, as they still do today, seasonal fruits as fillings. Many types of syrup pies made of maple syrup in the north and molasses or cane syrup in the south became popular; these pies were referred to as "cheese" pies because they often curdled like a cheese when baked because of the amount of eggs and butter used. Over the years, the term *cheese* denigrated into *chess* the name is still used for these deliciously rich custard-style pies.

Although pie making has become more sophisticated through the centuries, pies are still considered to be some of the simplest and most delicious of desserts and should be treated as such.

Pie Dough

Pie dough is arguably the most important element in making a good pie; its flakiness and tenderness are tantamount to the success of the pie, regardless of how well the filling is made.

Pie dough is basically composed of flour, fat, cold liquid, and salt. Sugar or DMS may be used to sweeten and enrich the dough. The method used to distribute the fat in the flour determines the flakiness of the crust; fat lumps in the dough produce flakiness through physical leavening. Just as in a puff-pastry dough, the fat in the dough melts to create steam and, in turn, produces a flaky crust.

There are three types of pie dough: long flake, short flake, and mealy pie dough. Long flake pie dough is used only as a top crust pie dough. The fat is broken up into half-dollar-sized pieces. Short-flake pie dough is an all-purpose dough, used as either a top crust or a bottom crust. The fat is broken up into quarter-sized pieces. In a mealy pie dough, the fat is broken into pea-sized bits; it is used only for a bottom crust because it does not flake and is more water tight. The fat is completely incorporated into the flour, leaving no lumps of fat in the dough.

Ingredients in Pie Dough

Flour

Pastry flour is used in pie dough. It contains a relatively low amount of gluten, but enough to hold the dough together and give it enough elasticity to be rolled out. Bread flour is too high in gluten content and would absorb most of the liquid, making the dough rubbery and tough. Cake flour is too low in gluten content—there would not be enough gluten to hold the dough together for rolling out—causing the dough to crack and crumble.

Fat

All-purpose shortening, butter, and lard are generally the types of fat used in a pie dough.

- Butter has an excellent flavor, but a low melting point (80° F) and high water content that will cause the crust to lose its shape during baking; the baked crust will be mealy and crumbly. If butter is used, it should be used in combination with another fat that has a higher melting point, either shortening or lard. Three parts shortening or lard to one part butter will produce a flavorful, flaky crust that will not fall apart during baking.

- Lard is an excellent fat for making pie dough because of its high melting point (90° F to 100° F). It creates a light, flaky crust. Unfortunately, lard can also impart undesirable flavor at times to the crust, largely because of the inconsistency of its quality. Lard is rendered from the hog and is therefore high in cholesterol and unacceptable for use in kosher and vegetarian diets.

- All-purpose shortening is the best fat to use for a pie dough. It has a high melting point similar to that of lard, which produces a light, flaky crust. It imparts no flavor to the dough, and the quality of shortening is very consistent. Unlike puff pastry, where the flavor of butter is paramount, the flavor of a pie dough is often overshadowed by the sweetness of the filling; however, many chefs still prefer to mix shortening and butter together to create optimum flakiness and flavor.

FYI

It is important to use all-purpose shortening, *and not* high-ratio shortening *in a pie dough. The latter contains emulsifiers in the form of mono- and diglycerides, which enable it to absorb moisture. If used in a pie dough, it will cause the crust to absorb too much moisture and to become heavy and soggy.*

Cold Liquid

Milk or water used in combination with DMS is sometimes used to enrich the dough and contribute to crust color. Unfortunately, the added sugar and fat in milk can create a heavy, soggy crust. If DMS is used, it should be reconstituted in the water before adding it to the flour, or it will cause the dough to stiffen and become tough.

Water is most often used as the liquid in a pie dough; it provides the moisture required without adding extra components that will adversely affect the crust. Water (or milk, if used) should be ice cold when used in a pie dough—this

will preserve the solid state of the fat and help retard gluten development. It is important to always use the entire amount of water specified in a formula to prevent mealiness in the dough.

Salt

Salt is used in a pie dough to bring out flavor and to aid in retarding gluten development. Too much salt can break and tear gluten strands and ruin the flavor of the dough.

Sugar

Sugar is sometimes used in pie dough to provide flavor through sweetness. Unfortunately, because of sugar's hygroscopic qualities, it can also absorb moisture and create a soggy crust. Sugar is best sprinkled *on top* of the dough to create caramelization.

Making a Pie Dough

The biggest error to be made when making a pie dough is overmixing. It is important to keep the fat in large lumps for flakiness and to not overwork the gluten in the flour. Although large amounts of dough can be done in the mixer, unless the amount is overwhelmingly large, it is always best to mix pie dough by hand. The method for making a pie dough by hand is called the *rubbing*, or *biscuit method*. In this method, the flour and salt are sifted together and placed in a bowl. The fat is cut into the flour either by hand or with a pastry cutter until it is well distributed, but still in large pieces. The cold water is sprinkled over the mixture, a little at a time, and the mixture is tossed until all the water has been completely incorporated, and a ball can be formed with the dough. A basic ratio of ingredients for pie dough is three parts flour to two parts fat to one part liquid.

Pie dough should be wrapped airtight and refrigerated; it is best to let it rest overnight before use to allow the gluten to relax. As with puff-pastry dough, pie dough should not be kept longer than a week, or it will begin to oxidize and the flour and water mixture will begin to ferment, turning the dough gray.

Just as in laminated doughs, too much flour used on the bench for rolling out will affect the flavor and flakiness of the dough. Any excess flour should be brushed away with a bench brush. Scraps from pie dough should be treated the same as puff-pastry scraps—never knead them together—layer them on top of each other to roll out a second time.

Pie dough can be successfully frozen; it should be divided into 8- to 10-ounce portions and wrapped airtight. To defrost, let it rest in the refrigerator overnight.

As with puff pastry, pie dough must be baked in a hot oven, 425° F to 450° F, to ensure that the fat does not melt out of the dough before it has a chance to evaporate and create the steam needed for flakiness. Pie crust should also rest after makeup in the freezer or refrigerator for 10 to 20 minutes before baking to relax the dough and solidify the fat to reduce shrinkage.

Types of Pies

A pie is categorized according to the type of filling it has. There are five basic types of fillings for pies:

- *Fruit pies* are made with fresh, canned, frozen, or dried fruit that is mixed with sweeteners and thickeners. Apple, peach, and cherry are good examples.
- *Cream pies* have a smooth cream filling that are made using a method similar to that for pastry cream. Chocolate cream, banana cream, and coconut cream are good examples.
- *Custard (soft) pies* are generally thickened with eggs (and sometimes starch) and sweetened with syrups; there are a wide variety of different custard-style pies. Pumpkin pie, pecan pie, and chess pie are all good examples.
- *Chiffon pies* have fruit-based fillings with a *chiffon* folded into them after cooking to lighten and aerate them. The term *chiffon* is used when whipped egg whites (and usually sugar to prevent drying of the whites) is added to a batter or filling. These pies are

usually very low in fat. Strawberry chiffon and lemon chiffon are good examples.
- *Specialty pies* use special crusts, such as cookie or graham cracker crusts, and are filled with ice cream or cheese-type fillings.

Procedures for Pie Fillings

Fruit Pies

There are three types are fruit pies: cooked juice, cooked juice and fruit, and homestyle. The first two types have precooked fillings that use cornstarch as a thickening agent. Homestyle pies are not precooked and use flour as a thickening agent.

Cooked Juice

A cooked-juice filling uses fresh, canned, or frozen fruits that are soft and will lose shape and structure if overcooked.

1. Drain juice well from fruit. If fresh fruits are used and there is not enough juice, use water in the same amount.
2. Reserve a small amount of juice to dissolve the cornstarch. Use approximately 3 to 4 ounces of starch per quart of liquid.
3. Bring sugar and remaining juice to a rolling boil.
4. While the mixture is boiling, vigorously whisk in the dissolved cornstarch.
5. Bring the mixture to a second boil, allowing it to thicken. The mixture should begin to lose its cloudiness and turn translucent; when this occurs, remove it from the heat.
6. Gently fold in the fruit. Do not overmix at this point, or the heat from the filling will overcook the fruit.
7. Let the filling cool, covered and unrefrigerated.
8. Fill an unbaked pie shell to the rim of the pie tin, not to the rim of the pie or the filling will bubble over during baking.
9. A top crust, either full or lattice (see Figure 18–1 on page 322) is always used for fruit fillings. Seal the crust with an egg wash. For a full crust, vent

Figure 18–1 Lattice pie crust

holes should be cut into the dough to allow excess steam from the filling to escape.

10. Freeze or refrigerate the pie for 10 to 20 minutes.
11. Remove the pie from the freezer, and egg wash the top crust before baking.
12. Bake at 425° F until golden brown.

Cooked Juice and Fruit

A cooked juice and fruit pie filling is used for firmer fruits, such as fresh apples or canned cherries. Because part of the fruit is cooked, the fruit must be able to withstand the heat of the cooking process. This procedure can also be used for fillings in which the final state of the fruit is not important. The filling is made using the same procedure as a cooked-juice filling; the difference is that in a cooked juice and fruit filling, approximately two-thirds of the fruit is cooked.

1. Dissolve starch in a small portion of the cold liquid, either juice or water, from the formula.
2. Reserve about one-third of the fruit.
3. Bring the remaining two-thirds of the fruit, the granulated sugar, and any liquids to a boil.

4. When the mixture reaches a boil, vigorously stir in the dissolved cornstarch mixture.
5. Bring the mixture to a second boil, allowing it to thicken and turn translucent.
6. As soon as it is thickened, remove from heat and gently fold in the remaining fruit. Allow the filling to cool, covered and unrefrigerated.
7. Fill, chill, and bake as in a cooked-juice pie.

Homestyle Pies

Homestyle pies usually use firm, fresh fruit, such as apples, peaches, and blackberries. Other types of fruit may be used, although fresh fruit produces the best results. The fruit is dredged in sugar, spices, and cake or pastry flour. The amount of the coating is not specified, but rather feel, taste, sight, and experience determine the amount used. The general procedure for homestyle apple pie is

1. Peel, core, and prepare fruit.
2. Cut large fruit into large slices. Leave small fruits whole.
3. Dredge the fruit in sugar (the sugar will create a syrup that will allow the mixture to absorb the flour), then spices, and finally cake flour.
4. Fill, chill, and bake as before.

Purchase Forms of Fruit

Canned Fruit

Canned fruit comes in three forms: solid packed, water packed, or syrup packed. Solid-packed fruit, such as apples, is canned with very little or no added water. Water-packed fruits, such as red-tart cherries, are washed, pitted, seeded, and cored. The fruit is par-boiled, with no sweeteners added, and canned with water. Syrup-packed fruit, such as peaches, is the most expensive type of canned fruit because the fruit is already cooked with sugar and packed in a sugar syrup. It is used more for finishing and decoration than for fillings. Syrup-packed fruit is of a higher quality than solid or water-packed fruits. Syrup-packed fruits are also available with low or no sugar in their syrups.

Frozen Fruit

Frozen fruit is available as individually quick frozen (IQF) or frozen canned fruit. IQF fruit uses a flash method of freezing that retains the original shape of the fruit. Raspberries, blueberries, and cranberries are readily available IQF. Frozen canned fruits contain a high amount of sugar and water, and are used for chiffon pies or pies where bleeding is not a major consideration. Frozen canned fruit is generally purchased in a #10 can, or in 6½-pound plastic containers.

Fresh Fruit

Fresh fruit is an excellent choice for making pies and desserts if high-quality fruit is purchased when it is in season. Seasonal availability is carefully monitored by successful pastry chefs; many chefs are using only locally grown produce from their area to ensure freshness, ripeness, and availability. For some areas of the country, this can limit a menu considerably in the fall and winter months. For this reason, some chefs order fruits from other hemispheres—such as from Chile, Australia, or New Zealand—where the out-of-season fruits they are looking for are growing during winter. These fruits can be expensive, and their quality is sometimes questionable because there is no way to tell if the fruit was picked at the peak of its ripeness, or if it has been stored in cold storage for too long. Most purveyors will ship fruits overnight to almost anywhere in the world to ensure freshness and quality, but the cost of doing so can sometimes outweigh the profit.

Good chefs get to know local farmers and purveyors and understand what fruits are indigenous to their area and when they are available. (California has a long growing season, which is one reason why California has become such a culinary mecca.) Many chefs prefer produce that is organically grown, and feel the extra costs involved in buying organic produce is well worth the quality.

Fresh fruits should be used at the peak of their ripeness; appearance and taste should be the factors in determining what to buy. Good chefs know seasonal availability of various fruits and they plan their menus accordingly.

Grade Standards of Fresh Fruits

Most fresh fruit is sold by wholesalers on the basis of the USDA grades, although not many are identified by grade when sold by retailers. These voluntary grade standards provide a common basis for wholesale trading and a means by which prices may be determined. One or more of the parties of a wholesale fruit transaction may request and pay for grading of the shipment by an inspector who is licensed by the USDA. The grades for fresh fruit are U.S. fancy, U.S. No. 1, U.S. No. 2, and U.S. No. 3.

U.S. fancy is a premium quality fruit. This grade covers only top-quality range produce. U.S. No. 1 is the chief trading grade and also represents good average quality. U.S. No. 2 is practical to pack under commercial conditions and covers the bulk of the quality range produce. U.S. No. 2 is of an intermediate quality. It is noticeably superior to U.S. No. 3, which is the lowest grade that is practical to pack under normal commercial conditions.

Most grading is visual, but internal and external qualities of many products are also examined. Models, color guides, and color photographs are available for graders to check samples for shape, degree of coloring, and degree of defects or damage.

Some of the other functions of the grade standards are to help establish loan values for produce in storage; to ensure that products purchased by the military services and various government agencies are acceptable in quality; to provide purchasing specifications that might be used by restaurants, shipping lines, and other feeding establishments; and to establish a basis for the trading of fruit crops on the futures market.

See Table 18–1 for guidelines of the availability of some commonly used fruits in the bake shop.

Dried Fruit

A wide variety of dried fruit is available for use in pies, compotes, chutneys, and other desserts: Apples, pears, apricots, figs, cherries, cranberries, and blueberries are just a few, in addition to the more common raisin and prune. Dried fruits add an interesting flavor and texture to desserts.

Table 18–1 Seasonal Availability of Commonly Used Fresh Fruits

Fruit	Availability
Apples (Granny Smith, Greening, Jonathan, Macintosh, Rhode Island, Rome, Winesap)	Late summer, fall, and winter Available cold storage year around (Red Delicious, Golden Delicious, Granny Smith)
Apricots	Spring through mid-summer
Bananas	Year round
Blackberries	Mid-to-late summer
Blueberries	Early to mid-summer
Cantaloupe	Throughout summer
Carambola	Winter through early spring
Cherries	Late spring, early to mid-summer
Clementines	Winter, early spring
Cranberries	Mid- to late fall, early winter
Currants (red and black)	Late fall through winter
Figs (Mission and Smyrna)	Summer through early fall
Gooseberries	Mid- to late summer, early fall
Grapefruit	Florida: Mid-fall through early summer California: Late winter through late summer
Grapes (Thompson, Emperor, Cardenal)	Early summer through late fall
Guavas	Spring, summer
Honeydew	Early spring through summer

Dried fruits are usually "plumped," or rehydrated, before using them in formulas. This is done by placing the fruits in boiling water and allowing them to sit for 30 seconds to 1 minute.

Maceration is another way of plumping fruits (dried, fresh, canned, or frozen) in sugar and alcohol rather than water. The alcohol and sugar are absorbed into the fruit and give it a distinct flavor and texture.

Procedures for Pie Fillings (continued)

Cream Pies

Cream-pie fillings use some of the same ingredients and the same basic procedure as that of pastry cream (see page 357), although there can sometimes be minor variations. Cream fillings are thick, smooth, and thickened with cornstarch; gelatin is sometimes added to ensure that the pie cuts cleanly.

There are some problems inherent in cream pies:

- Cream fillings can be inconsistent; they can become lumpy because of improper dissolution of the starch. The starch should always be mixed with a small portion of the sugar and then whisked together with a small amount of the liquid (usually milk) to make a slurry. This will rid the filling of lumps caused from starch.
- Undercooked cream fillings have a starchy taste; the starch must be cooked long enough to become translucent (1 to 3 minutes) to ensure that the filling will not retain a starchy taste and mouth feel.
- If not cooked properly, the eggs will curdle. The eggs should be whisked and then added to the slurry mixture so the eggs can be more readily absorbed by the starch, which helps protect them from overcooking. The egg mixture should be tempered by whisking a small stream of the hot liquid into them to avoid cooking the eggs.
- Overcooking and not properly whisking the filling while it is thickening will cause the filling to burn around the sides of the pan and create a scorched flavor that can sometimes penetrate the entire filling.

Prebaked pie shells should always be used for cream pies.

Prebaked pie shells should not be refrigerated because the humidity in the refrigerator will cause them to become soggy. When they are cold and a hot filling is added, condensation will form. Pie shells are best if filled when they are piping hot to help form a bond between the filling and the crust, and to give the pie a longer shelf life.

The filling should also be hot when put into the crust to

bond the filling and the crust and to ensure maximum fluidity of the filling; if the filling is allowed to set, it will not pour easily into the shell and will create a lumpy, uneven appearance. As soon as the cream filling has been added to the pie shell, the pie should be covered with food film (plastic wrap) to prevent a skin from forming on the filling. The pies should be allowed to come to room temperature before refrigeration to prevent a crack or tear on the surface of the filling.

Cream pies do not last as long as fruit pies. After about two days, cream pies will dry out, and the filling and crust will begin to separate from one another. The crust will lose some of its flakiness because of the humidity in the refrigerator. Cream pies should be consumed or sold within two days of production.

Custard Pies

Pumpkin, squash, pecan, custard, and sweet potato are examples of soft pies. They are baked with the crust, not poured into prebaked crust. Soft pies and cream pies are called *open pies* because they have no top crust.

There is no set procedure for preparing custard pies—each is unique in its production, and the formula should be carefully followed. Many custard pies use a variation of the creaming method of mixing.

Soft pies are baked in an unbaked pie shell; the filling is poured to the rim of the pie tin, not the rim of the crust. Soft pies are usually done when the filling extends past the rim of the pie and the pie is firm but jiggly in the center. To set the crust, custard pies are baked at 425° F for approximately 10 to 15 minutes, then the oven temperature is reduced to 350° F to 375° F so the delicate custard filling does not overbake. The filling will tear if it is overcooked.

Pumpkin and squash pies are best if the filling is made and poured into the crust the day before they are baked to give the filling time to thicken and develop flavor.

Chiffon Pies

Chiffon pies are light, airy pies as a result of the chiffon, which is folded into the filling at the end of the makeup procedure. They are most often fruit based, and use a cooked-fruit or cooked-fruit-and-juice method of procedure that is sometimes combined with the method of procedure for pastry cream. Other pies, such as pumpkin or cream pies, can be made with a chiffon added as well. Chiffon pies are usually thickened with a combination of cornstarch and gelatin. Chiffon pies are placed in a prebaked shell that has been allowed to cool.

Following is the general procedure for making chiffon pies.

1. Bloom the gelatin in cold water. Powdered gelatin or gelatin sheets may be used. When using gelatin sheets, soak them in cold water. Set aside.
2. Dissolve the cornstarch in a small portion of the cold liquid.
3. Place the sugar, flavorings, salt, liquid, and two-thirds of the fruit in a pan and bring to a boil.
4. Add the dissolved cornstarch, and stir until the mixture has thickened and become translucent.
5. Remove the filling from the heat, and add the bloomed gelatin.
6. Fold in the remaining fruit. Set the filling aside, covered and unrefrigerated.
7. Whip egg whites and granulated sugar to a medium peak, and fold into the mixture. Some mixtures, such as strawberry chiffon, need a fairly cool filling to add the chiffon. Others, such as lemon chiffon, should be hot when the chiffon is added, or they will get lumpy.
8. Place the mixture into a prebaked pie shell, let cool and set, and garnish as desired.

Specialty Pies

Specialty pies are usually made of ice-cream or cream-cheese mixtures; they usually have cookie or cracker crusts that have been sweetened with sugar and spices and have just enough melted butter added to them to allow them to stick together. There is no set method of procedure for specialty pies because there are so many different varieties.

Tarts

"The friendly cow all red and white,
I love with all my heart:
She gives me cream with all her might,
To eat with apple tart."
—Robert Louis Stevenson

While pies have become American in nature, tarts are particularly European; tarts filled with pastry cream and poached pears have been traced to as early as the 1400s in Italy and France. Tarts share a few similarities to pies: They both have crusts and can be filled with a variety of fillings. However, the similarities stop there.

Tarts are baked in shallow tins that are either fluted or unfluted; the crusts have no lip or rim in contrast to that of a pie, and the sides of the tart are straight, not angled like a pie's. This is because tarts are made to be served lifted from the pie tin, whereas pies are served in the tin and cut when served; if a pie were to be unmolded from the tin as a tart is, its heavy filling would collapse. So tarts are shallow and hold less filling.

Tart dough is usually made from some form of short dough (although pie dough and puff-pastry dough can also be used). A short dough is a mixture of butter, sugar, pastry flour, and eggs. *Short dough* refers to how the butter shortens and tenderizes the gluten strands in the flour.

The French have many types of short doughs: pâte sablé, pâte sucrée, pâte brisée; all are rich in butter and eggs and are mixed by hand using a method known as *fraisage* (this method can be used in the making of other doughs as well). Fraisage is done on the table and helps to prevent overmixing. It is done by sifting the flour and salt together and then rubbing the butter into them, using a bowl scraper. When the butter is sufficiently coated with the flour and is still in relatively large leaves, a well is made in the center of the ingredients, and the liquid (usually eggs and a little water or milk) is placed in the well. The mixture is then worked with the hands—moving from the inside of the well to the outside—until it is cohesive.

American short dough is referred to as 1-2-3 dough because it contains sugar in one part, butter in two parts, and pastry flour in three parts; eggs are usually added according to the amount of sugar used (1 to 3 eggs for every pound of sugar). Short dough can be mixed using the fraisage method or by mixer using the creaming method. Either way, if the dough is overmixed, it will shrink during baking and be tough and rubbery, just as a pie dough would be. Short-dough shells are much richer than pie shells and, although the butter provides some flakiness because so much sugar is present in the dough, these shells are never as flaky as a pie dough. However, short dough is so flavorful that it is also used as the basis for many types of cookies.

Because they are so shallow, tart shells should be rolled out to no more than ⅛ of an inch thick. Tart shells can be baked with a filling or without. Baking a shell without the filling is known as *blind baking*; the shell must be lined with baking paper or aluminum foil and weighted with beans or rice to prevent the shell from moving during baking. Most tart shells are prebaked, even if only partially, to prevent the crust from absorbing fluid from the filling and becoming too soggy.

Many of the same principles of making a pie dough apply to short doughs as well:

- Pastry flour is used to provide enough gluten for rolling out, but not enough to make the dough tough. It is sometimes best to combine pastry flour and cake flour to obtain the correct consistency needed from the flour.
- The biggest error to be made when making a short dough is overmixing or overcreaming. It is important to keep the fat in large lumps for flakiness and to not overwork the gluten in the flour.
- Short dough should be wrapped airtight and refrigerated; it is best to let it rest for at least 30 minutes before use to allow the gluten to relax. As with puff-pastry dough, pie dough should not be kept longer than a week, or it will begin to oxidize.

- Just as in laminated doughs, too much flour used on the bench for rolling out will affect the flavor and flakiness of the dough. Any excess flour should be brushed away with a bench brush. Scraps from short dough should be treated the same as puff-pastry scraps—never knead them together—layer them on top of each other to roll out a second time.
- Short dough can be successfully frozen; it should be divided into 8- to 10-ounce portions and wrapped airtight. To defrost, let it rest in the refrigerator overnight.
- *Unlike* pie and puff doughs, short doughs are baked at lower oven temperatures—325° F to 350° F. The high sugar content in the dough would turn the crust too dark before it was fully baked if baked at higher temperatures.
- If the filling and the crust are baked separately, the crust is usually painted with chocolate to prevent the moisture from the filling absorbing into the crust.
- The filling of a tart is often baked with or covered with fruit; the fruit is usually glazed to protect it and give it shine.

———————————————(FYI)———————————————

Cobblers and crisps are popular variations of fruit pies and have evolved into being just as uniquely American. Cobblers are deeper versions of pies that are served in square pans with lattice crusts or sweet biscuit dough baked on top of their fruit fillings. Crisps are similar, but are usually baked with a streusel-like topping to cover their fruit. Some chefs bake cobblers and crisps with no bottom crusts, although this practice varies from region to region. No matter how they are made, like fruit pies, they are an excellent way of utilizing delicious, seasonal, fresh fruit.

Glazes

Glazes are used for two basic purposes: to add shine, enhance color, and improve overall appearance; and to seal and protect. In addition, because they seal whatever they are applied to, they also help extend the shelf life of the product.

Glazes can be applied in three basic ways: with a pastry brush, by pouring the glaze over the product, and by using a glaze sprayer or paint gun. The first two methods are the most traditional and time consuming. The latter allows for a more even flow of glaze, which results in a more uniform product. Sprayers also tend to reduce waste and labor costs.

Some manufacturers of quality glazes include:

- Patis France
- Puratos—Harmony Glazes
- Napstar
- Grandmother—Apricoatings
- Dreidoppelgel A

Depending on manufacturer's recommendations, most glazes must be heated before use. Some must be mixed with water (Harmony, for example, has a 2:1 ratio of Harmony glaze to water), others can simply be melted down (Apricoatings). Glazes such as the Dreidoppel A, which are in powder form, are formulated first, then heated. Most manufacturers agree that the glaze should be brought to a boil to remove lumps and should be applied while still hot. Glazes may have color or flavor added to them to enhance their appeal.

Because most glazes are pectin-based, glazes can also be made from preserves or fruit purées and juices. These are particularly colorful when used on items like mirror tortes and Bavarians. Gelatin can be added to ensure that the glaze sets properly. Fruits with a high acid content can break down the gelling quality of most glazes and gelatins, so they should be avoided unless they are cooked first.

Glazes should, as mentioned, be applied while hot. This ensures a more uniform distribution of the glaze over the product and prevents lumping. Glazes that are allowed to cool before application will clump and cause an uneven and unattractive appearance (pouring glazes over mirror tortes is an exception). Depending on the thickness of the glaze, most begin to boil at approximately 190° F to 195° F.

Examples of Tarts

Fruit tarts come in many forms; unlike pies, there is no designation of type when it comes to their fillings. Following are some of the most classic examples of tarts.

- The *fruit tart* is the most classically known of all tarts and, although many variations have come about over the years, a fruit tart basically consists of a blind-baked short-dough shell, a pastry cream-type filling, fruit arranged decoratively on the top of the filling, glaze, and nuts (usually toasted almonds) on the sides of the tart for a more finished look.
- The *Linzer torte* is actually a *tart* not a *torte*. This classic originated in the town of Linz, Austria. Its crust is traditionally made with hazelnuts, although almonds and even walnuts are often used, and it is filled with sweet raspberry jam. The Linzer torte is traditionally made with a lattice-style top crust.
- *Swiss apple flan* is a mixture of tart apples and custard. Variations of this tart are made with other fruits and variations in the flavor of the custard.
- The *Tarte Tatin* is one of the most classic of all tarts. This upside-down tart was created by the sisters demoiselles Tatin at their restaurant in the Loire Valley outside of Paris over 100 years ago. The tart is made with apples that caramelize with sugar covered with puff pastry; when the pastry is golden brown, the tart is turn upside down to reveal the beautifully caramelized apples.

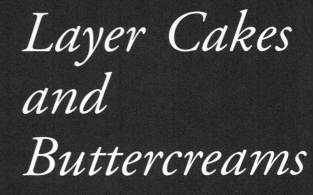

19

*Layer Cakes
and
Buttercreams*

Layer Cakes and Buttercreams

Pat-a-cake, pat-a-cake, baker's man,
Bake me a cake as fast as you can;
Pat it and prick it, and mark it with a B,
Put it in the oven for baby and me.
—Anonymous Nursery Rhyme

Layer Cakes

Cakes of cheese and honey have been in existence since the early Greeks and Romans; over the centuries, their ideas developed into yeast cakes and sponge cakes. The Italians and French, during the time of Catherine di Medici in the mid-1500s, elevated the mixing methods of the sponge used to make the layers in layer cakes and tortes. Many classic cakes are derived from their efforts.

Cakes provide the structure, texture, and flavor to many desserts, ranging from a simple pound cake garnished with a light dusting of confectionery sugar to the rich chocolate cake used to produce a Black Forest Torte. Cakes are differentiated not only by the flavorings or added ingredients such as walnuts or chocolate chunks, but also by the mixing method used to make them. The mixing methods, together with the ingredients, determine the texture and characteristics of the cake. There are two basic types of cake batters: shortened cakes, in which fat is used to lubricate, tenderize, and, with the sugar, create air cells for leavening; and foam cakes, where liquid fat is used in small quantities with the eggs or egg whites to create air cells for leavening. The first type generally uses a chemical leavener and is made through the creaming method or the blending method. The latter type uses little or no chemical leavening and incorporates the use of the whipping method to produce the batter.

Ingredients in Cake Making

Flour

Because the flour used for cakes should be low in gluten content, cake flours are used. If high gluten flours are used, the cake will have a tough, rubbery texture and will not rise to full capacity. If it does rise, it will more than likely fall in the center when the cakes are removed from the oven. Cake flours are bleached and provide the whiteness needed for some cakes. Flour is the chief binding and absorbing agent in a cake. Flour should always be sifted to aerate and rid it of lumps and foreign matter before using it in a cake formula.

Sugar

Sugar provides flavor through sweetness and, because of its hygroscopic ability, is one of the principle tenderizers in cakes. Sugar is the chief tenderizer in foam cakes that are low in fat or contain no fat, except for the amount found in the egg yolks. In shortened cakes, sugar helps the fat hold air cells for aeration and leavening. In foam cakes, sugar provides a more stable egg foam for folding. Sugar also contributes to crust color.

Fats

Fats tenderize and lubricate gluten strands making the cake tender with a better crumb. In shortened cakes, the fats used are solid, usually butter or shortening. These fats combine with the sugar to hold air cells, which lighten and aerate the batter. The fats used in foam cakes are liquid; either oil or melted butter is used and provides tenderness and softness to the crumb of foam cakes. Fats retard staleness through tenderization of the crumb.

Eggs

Eggs bind ingredients and provide moisture, which helps retard the staling. In shortened cakes, they aid in creaming by helping to emulsify the mixture as they are added to the fat(s) and sugar. In foam cakes, they are the chief source of leavening—the air trapped within their cells expands with the heat in the oven and makes the cake rise. Eggs also provide rich flavor and color in cake batters.

Liquids

Liquids are used to provide moisture and expansion. Milk or water are most often used, although melted chocolate, coffee, or water infused with flavor are also used. The moisture provided by the liquid contributes to the keeping quality of the cake.

Chemical Leaveners

Baking powder and baking soda, or a combination of the two, are often used in cake batters, particularly shortened cake batters. Soda is used in conjunction with cocoa and chocolate, buttermilk, and any other batter that may contain an added ingredient with a high acid content.

Mixing Methods

Many an excellent formula has been condemned by bakers because the end product was poor. Ordinarily, little thought was given to the possibility that the handling of the formula may have been at fault. The formula represents only the raw materials; knowing how to mix them together is the difference, along with the use of the best ingredients possible, between success and failure. Proper mixing of cakes should accomplish the following purposes:

- Achieve a uniform and complete mixture of all ingredients in the formula.
- Form and incorporate air cells, the amount depending on the method of mixing suited to the formula.
- Develop a desirable grain and texture in the baked product.

The four cake-mixing methods are sugar-shortening or creaming, blending, whipping, and a combination of creaming and whipping.

Creaming Method

In the creaming method, the sugar and fat (butter or shortening or both) are blended together first, and then creamed by mixing. During this stage, small air cells are formed and incorporated into the mix. The mix takes on added volume and becomes softer.

The exact length of time for proper creaming at this stage is controlled by several factors, one of which is the temperature of the shortening or fat. Shortening or fat that is cold must be brought to a temperature of 70° F before the best creaming potential will be achieved. Cold shortening is not sufficiently plastic to quickly incorporate and hold air cells. This applies to butter and margarine as well. Therefore, cold fats require a longer mixing time for maximum creaming. Fats that are warm, above 75° F, will not be able to hold as much air or give as much volume because they are soft and will not tolerate the friction of the machine and the constant mixing.

The temperature of the bake shop is another factor. Creaming takes place faster in warm weather than in cold weather. If the shop temperature is affected by seasonal temperatures, allowances must be made for mixing time.

The speed of the mixing machine must also be considered. Too often, inexperienced bakers allow the mixer to turn at a high speed and find the mix has not creamed properly. Not only does high speed create friction, but it also tends to destroy or reduce the number of air cells that are formed and incorporated during the early stages of mixing. The sugar and fats are best creamed at low, or first, speed to blend them; the speed should then be increased to medium, or second, speed until the mixture is soft and light.

During the second stage, the eggs are added in several portions. This does not mean that the eggs are added as they are absorbed. Very often, an inexperienced baker will have the mix curdle before all the eggs are incorporated. It is the yolk of the egg, which contains the lecithin, that coats the surface of the cells formed in creaming and allows the cells to expand and hold the liquid (egg whites, milk, and so on) without curdling. Curdling is the result of having more liquid than the fat-coated cells have the capacity to retain. A creamed mixture that has been carefully mixed and does not curdle is called a *water-in-fat emulsion*. Adding the eggs too quickly or adding all the other liquids at once will cause curdling. The addition of a small portion of the flour at the start of the mix will help eliminate curdling in mixes with high liquid content. Addition of flour alternately with the liquid when the mix is creamed will also eliminate the tendency to curdle.

The steps of creaming are as follows:

1. Cream together the fats with a paddle on low speed until they are pliable.
2. Add the sugars, and cream the mixture until it lightens in color, texture, and volume. Scrape the mixing bowl frequently to ensure proper incorporation of the ingredients. If the mixture is over- or undercreamed, it will have a dramatic effect on the finished product: less volume and a poor texture; overcreamed batters will spread during baking.
3. Add the eggs, one at a time, until incorporated. If the eggs are added too quickly, the fat will not be able to absorb the moisture in the eggs, and the ingredients will not emulsify, causing curdling. The emulsifier lecithin, found in the egg yolk, aids in creaming. Scrape the bowl frequently during this process. The mixture will also curdle if the fat is allowed to get too warm during mixing, either by the temperature of the room or by the overmixing of the mixture.
4. Add the sifted flour, alternating with the liquid, beginning and ending with the flour. The flour is added first to absorb excess liquid and to prevent curdling.

Blending Method

The blending method of mixing is primarily used in the making of high-ratio cakes. In this method, most of the ingredients, including some of the liquid, are placed in the mixing bowl at the same time. The mixer is run for a few minutes on medium speed until the ingredients are blended. The eggs and additional milk are added, and the mix is blended for another few minutes. Air cells are formed and incorporated, but there are not as many cells and they do not become as large and extended as they do in the creaming method, so the final grain of the cake layer will be tight and firm.

The ingredients must be blended properly and have a smooth mix that is not curdled. Curdling takes place as a result of improper mixing or through the use of unsuitable ingredients. For example, in a high-ratio mix, a high-ratio shortening must be used. This is an emulsifier. This fat enables the cells formed in mixing to hold the large percentage of moisture and sugar without curdling. A regular hydrogenated vegetable shortening will not be able to absorb the high percentage of moisture in the mix and, consequently, the mix will curdle. If butter is used, curdling can occur easily because of the fat's inability to absorb the moisture; therefore, great care in mixing should be taken when butter is used for the blending method. The temperature of the fat or other shortening is important. For example, hard or chilled fat must first be softened or made pliable by mixing before the other ingredients are blended into it. If this is not done, the fat will break into brittle pieces, which will not become dispersed in the liquid of the mix. Because of this, blending will not take place properly.

Where high percentages of sugar are used, it is best to dissolve the sugar in the liquid and then add it to the mix. This will eliminate the possibility of incomplete blending of the sugar and result in a more tender crust in the baked product.

Following are the steps of blending:

1. With a paddle, blend the sifted flour, sugar, and chemical leaveners or other dry ingredients for 30 seconds.
2. Add the softened fat(s) and half the liquids.
3. Mix on low speed until the ingredients are moistened.
4. Increase the speed to medium, and aerate the mixture for one minute.
5. Scrape the sides of the bowl, then add the remaining liquids.
6. Blend on low speed for one more minute.

Whipping Method

The whipping method of mixing is used mostly in the preparation of sponge and angel food cakes. In whipping eggs, air cells are formed and incorporated into the mix. In fact, in pure sponges these cells affect the entire leavening; no chemical leavening is used.

The eggs and sugar are warmed to about 100° F before whipping. This softens the egg yolks and allows quicker whipping and greater volume. The egg yolks contain fat, which surrounds the cells in the foam. This permits a greater number of cells to be formed containing a larger amount of air. It has been found that an additional 20 percent whole eggs will improve the foam during the whipping of the eggs.

For some types of sponge cakes, it is advisable to whip the yolks and part of the sugar as a type of pâte à bombe, then the egg whites and remaining sugar are whipped separately, and the two whipped products are combined. This has the added advantage of producing maximum aeration of the foam formed in the whipping of the eggs. Where large amounts of sugar are used compared to the amount of eggs, part of the sugar is dissolved in the liquid (water or milk) and then folded in after the eggs have been whipped. For example, if the sugar is above 100 percent, the extra part, over 100 percent, is dissolved in the liquid. In leaner-type sponge cakes, where lesser amounts of eggs are used, the liquid is added after the eggs are almost completely whipped and the whipping completed.

A one-step method for making a sponge cake is the liquid-shortening sponge cake. This mixing method is streamlined and foolproof. The ingredients are whipped together using the blitz method; all the ingredients are added into one bowl and whipped first on the highest speed and then on medium speed using a whip. This formula has a maximum of seven minutes of mixing time. The cake produced using this method is light but firm, is easy to cut, and has excellent keeping qualities.

Water should be added in a steady stream while the mixer is running and not after the flour has been added. In the case of hot milk and butter sponge, the milk and butter are heated to about 140° F and added after the flour has been gently folded in. The flour should be sifted and folded in gently in stages; often, cornstarch is used in conjunction with the flour to stabilize the mixture. Loss of aeration results from mixing too much of the flour at one time. This will have an adverse effect on the volume and texture of the final product.

Whipping Eggs

When whipping egg whites, as for angel cake, best results and maximum volume are obtained from egg whites that are cool, about 60° F. In this procedure, the whites are whipped slightly to a foam, and then the sugar is added in a steady stream while the mixer is running on high speed. In cakes where a large percentage of sugar is used, not all the sugar is whipped into the whites because it would be too heavy. Too much sugar prevents maximum aeration in whipping. The additional sugar is sifted with the flour or cornstarch, and then folded in gently; for some cakes, it is whipped together with the yolks in the same manner as it is whipped into the whites.

Egg whites are usually whipped to a wet rather than dry peak, which makes folding easier. A wet peak is usually determined by the shiny appearance of the egg-white peaks; the addition of sugar to the whites during whipping and the proper amount of mixing will ensure a wet peak. If the egg whites dry out, they will be difficult to fold into the remainder of the batter, and volume and texture will be lost. Over- and underwhipping are the most common problems in the whipping of eggs. The quality and condition of the eggs are important; a poor grade of egg will not result in maximum aeration. Deterioration and aging of the egg is often the cause of poor results in whipping. This leads to weakening of the protein in the whites and their ability to aerate is lessened. Off-flavors may also result from the use of eggs that have been stored too long.

Although most bakers whip egg yolks right from the container or after the egg yolks have been broken and separated from the shell, the temperature of the eggs affects the amount of time necessary for greatest aeration. The condition of the yolk and fat naturally present in the yolk determines the speed of whipping. For this reason, eggs are warmed. This is even more important when melted fat is added to the mix, as in a *genoise*.

Genoise is a classic French sponge cake that contains a higher ratio of eggs than American-type sponges; it always has melted butter (usually clarified) added to it during the last stage of mixing. It is used to build many different types of tortes.

A cool mix may cause the fat to solidify before it is fully mixed in. The speed of the mixer is an important factor; best results are obtained by running the mixer on high speed until the eggs are almost completely whipped and then slowing to a lower speed for maximum aeration. Loss in volume may be the result of mixing at high speed in the final stages of mixing because air cells formed may be ruptured at high speed, and the volume will be deflated.

There are many variations of the whipping method; the following method for genoise is commonly used:

1. Sift the flour and starch, if used, together and set aside.
2. Place the eggs, egg yolks, sugar, and flavorings in a bowl; place the bowl over a water bath and whisk the mixture lightly until it has reached 110° F.
3. Place the egg mixture on a mixer and whip to full volume.
4. Using a hand sifter, sift the flour mixture again as it is being folded into the egg mixture.
5. Fold in the melted butter gently.

Combination Method (Creaming and Whipping)

The combination method is very often used in the making of old-fashioned pound cake. The flour and shortening are creamed together until soft and light. The eggs and sugar are whipped as for sponge cake. The two are then gently combined by folding the whipped eggs and sugar into the creamed flour and shortening. Maximum aeration is the basic means of leavening; little, if any, other leavening is used.

The combination method is also used in some types of cheesecake. In this type of cake, care must be taken in folding in the whites. Undermixing results in the formation of large holes in the cake and uneven grain. Overmixing results in a loss of volume. The whites should be whipped to a set peak so they are more easily folded. If in a dry peak state, the whites will tend to break up into pieces and they will be difficult to fold. This leads to excessive mixing and loss of volume and possible toughness in the mix and in the resulting product. The problem of under- or overmixing is always present. The baker must learn how to determine complete and thorough mixing no matter what the method of mixing may be.

Baking Cakes

Most cakes are baked at moderate oven temperatures, between 350° F and 375° F. Cakes are done when the center of the cake springs back when it is lightly touched. Because some cakes are chocolate and dark in color, crust color alone cannot be relied on to determine doneness.

Storage of Cakes

Baked cakes can be stored by wrapping them airtight and refrigerating them until they are needed. Undecorated cakes freeze very well for up to one month if they are wrapped airtight. If cakes are decorated with buttercream or another type of icing, they should be stored in the refrigerator until used. Decorated cakes must be covered or boxed for storage because the odors in the refrigerator can be absorbed easily by the buttercream and, consequently, give the cake an off-flavor. Decorated cakes should be brought to room temperature before serving.

Classic Cakes and Tortes

What is the difference between a cake and a torte? The answer is hotly debated. Webster's defines a torte as a "cake made of many eggs and often grated nuts or dry bread crumbs and usually covered with a rich frosting." It defines a cake as a "sweet batter or dough usually containing a leaven (as baking powder) that is first baked and then often coated with an icing."

Baumkuchen

Baumkuchen, a German pound cake originated as spit cake in Greece during the 1600s and was brought to Germany in the 1700s as the Ottoman empire collapsed and the Austro-Hungarian empire gained power. The modern version of the cake is baked using a roller in a special oven. The roller is dipped into a trough to cover it with the batter and then baked; the procedure is repeated until the roller has approximately one to two inches of batter baked on it. When removed from the roller and cut horizontally, the cake reveals the rings created during baking; because the rings resemble the year rings of a tree, the Germans appropriately named the cake *baumkuchen,* or tree cake. Baumkuchen has many variations in Germany and is a popular cake to fill with creams and to decorate for use as a centerpiece. If a special baumkuchen oven is not available, the layers can be flash baked in a sheetpan and used to make petits fours or parkay designs for cakes.

Black Forest Torte

This classic torte comes from the Black Forest of Germany. *Schwartz Walder Kirsch Torte* is made with chocolate sponge, whipped cream, cherries, kirschwasser, or kirsch liqueur, and chocolate. Many variations exist as to how these five basic components of the torte are assembled, but the torte is so popular, it can be found almost everywhere in western cultures.

Boston Cream Pie

Boston cream pie is not a pie at all, but a sponge cake filled with custard and topped with chocolate glaze. Early settlers in America often baked their cakes in pie tins because cake tins were not available to them. This *pudding pie cake* was popularized by Harvey D. Parker of the famous Parker House Restaurant in Boston in 1856 (the origin of Parker House rolls as well).

Dobos Torte

This classic Hungarian torte was invented by the famous Hungarian chef Jozsef Dobos in 1887 in Budapest. It is an impressive torte of many thin layers of vanilla sponge (how many is debatable) and filled with chocolate buttercream. The top layer of sponge is spread with caramel and cut into the appropriate number of slices for the torte. Each wedge or slice of sugar is then propped up on the top of the torte with a chocolate rosette, to designate the slices. Traditionally, the sides of the torte are never iced, so the many layers can show; however, many modern versions have the sides of the cake either iced or dipped in chocolate.

Opera Torte

The opera torte, a multilayered torte of thin sponge cake, chocolate buttercream, and ganache, is a popular torte in Paris, where it is sold by weight; for this reason, the torte is traditionally prepared in a square form rather than a round one and, like the Dobos torte, the many layers are usually exposed.

Sacher Torte

During the 1800s, Vienna rose out of Europe to become the center for confections and pastries. Franz Sacher created the Sacher torte for Prince Fuerst Metternich of Austria to entertain the prince's guests at the congress of Vienna in 1814. The torte consisted of two slices of a dry chocolate cake that were put together with whortleberry preserves, a sweet native berry. The torte was glazed with a layer of apricot preserves and covered with a chocolate glaze. As time passed, Franz Sacher came to open his own hotel, all the while producing his torte. The hotel's business had begun to fail and the famed Demel's Patisserie offered to purchase the cake formula. After considering the offer, Franz sold it, unknowingly propelling the creation to fame. Needless to say, Franz Sacher was unhappy and decided to take the Demels to court, claiming that only he could call the torte the "Original Sacher Torte." The ensuing court battle lasted seven years and was dubbed the "Sweet Seven-Year War." The outcome of the trial was in favor of the Hotel Sacher, stating that they had the sole patent to produce the Original Sacher Torte. Today, the Hotel Sacher is still in operation in Vienna, Austria. A more current version of the Sacher Torte is produced where individual chocolate disks, on which the torte's name is written, have replaced the original style. Daily, 300 to 400 Sacher tortes are produced at the hotel, some of which are shipped to other countries. Most often, the torte is served *mit schlag* (with cream) and strong coffee on the terrace of the hotel, which overlooks the Vienna opera house.

Buttercreams and Icings

Icings are used to fill and frost cakes and tortes and to decorate cookies and various dessert items. Icings have three main functions:

- To improve the keeping quality of the cake by trapping moisture
- To improve the taste of the item
- To enhance the eye appeal and make the cake a more attractive item for sale

Proper combinations of flavorings are imperative and only the best flavorings should be used for icings. Pure extracts and fresh fruit or fruit compounds should be used. Delicate pastel colors enhance eye appeal; bright colors are generally reserved for children's cakes. Color combinations must be carefully blended to ensure compatibility; too little color is easier to correct than too much.

There are four basic icings: buttercream, fudge, boiled, and royal.

Buttercream

Buttercream is usually used to make tortes and desserts taste better and look more attractive. The following suggestions are important to produce good buttercreams that will appeal to the eye as well as to the palate:

- The fat used in buttercream should be unsalted butter; shortenings or margarines with a high melting point

can be used in some percentage to stabilize the mixture, especially if the cake is to be iced and served in a hot climate.
- The temperature of the butter or margarine used is also important. For best results, a desired temperature of 75° F is recommended.
- When using a three-speed mixer, buttercream should be whipped at medium speed for 10 to 20 minutes to produce high volume and good consistency. A smooth consistency is necessary to maintain a smooth design.
- Different types of extracts and fruit compounds are used to flavor buttercreams. The best results are achieved when natural products are used as flavoring, such as coffee for mocha flavor, or melted chocolate or pure liquors like rum, cherry, or orange liqueur. Fat-based flavorings, rather than water-based, should be used to prevent curdling.
- The colors used should be light and delicate rather than deep and harsh. Colors should harmonize with each other and with the flavor of the dessert. Limit the number of colors used on one dessert item.

Types of Buttercreams

There are five basic types of buttercream:

- *American* is made with a combination of butter, shortening, and confectionery sugar. This buttercream does not produce as smooth a texture as the others because the sugar is never dissolved. Milk, egg whites, or sugar syrups are sometimes added to improve texture and shine.
- *German* is made with butter, some shortening, and fondant.
- *Swiss* is made with Swiss meringue and butter.
- *French* is made with pâte á bombe and butter. It is sometimes referred to as *mousseline*.
- *Italian* is made with Italian meringue and butter.

Sometimes a buttercream will separate in the mixing bowl. There are several reasons why this may occur; the buttercream may be too cold, in which case the buttercream must be heated slightly over a double boiler. A microwave oven can also be used very successfully for this warming process. The buttercream may get overheated; additional butter or slow whipping can sometimes bring it back together.

Fudge Icing

For fudge icing, the sugar is cooked into a syrup to obtain the smoothness required. When this hot syrup is added to the balance of the ingredients in the formula, it creates a rather heavy body. Before the icing is applied to the cake, it should be heated slightly in a water bath. When it is not in use, fudge icing should be covered and stored to prevent spoilage and drying. Fudge icing is generally used on cupcakes, cakes, and brownies.

Boiled Icing

Boiled icing is made by cooking a syrup of sugar, water, and glucose or corn syrup, which is then added to whipped egg whites while hot. A heavy or thin icing depends on the heaviness or thinness of the syrup. Boiled icings may be flavored with vanilla and colored lightly. Boiled icing should be applied generously and left in peaks on the cake. This icing will break down if stored overnight and should be made only in the required amounts, as needed. Boiled icing is also called "Seven Minute" or "White Mountain Icing." By adding gelatin as a stabilizer, a marshmallow icing can be made and applied in the same manner as boiled icing.

Royal Icing

For royal icing, confectionery sugar, egg whites, and cream of tartar or another acid agent are creamed together into a smooth, fluffy consistency. This icing is used primarily for decorating, for flower making, and for assembling gingerbread houses and pastillage show pieces. It is also used to decorate dummy cakes for display purposes. It may be colored as desired and should be covered for storage with a damp cloth and wrapped airtight with plastic wrap to prevent it from drying out.

Fondant

Fondant is a heavy, white syrup made of glucose, sugar, and water, cooked to 240° F. It is then cooled to approximately 108° F and agitated quickly (which crystallizes the sugar) until it is creamy, white, and smooth. Because fondant is difficult to make consistently, it is usually purchased ready-made. The fondant is kept in buckets and should be covered with water to prevent it from drying out.

Fondant is used for two purposes. Its primary use is as a coating or glaze. It may also be used as an ingredient. When fondant is used as a coating or glaze, the desired quantity should be removed from the container, and a small amount of water or simple syrup (egg whites and liqueurs can also be used) is added; the fondant is heated to 98° F to 100° F over a warm water bath while stirring constantly. This thins the icing and causes it to flow freely. If it is heated over 100° F, fondant will lose its shine and have a grainy, dull finish. If it is still too heavy, add water or simple syrup to thin to the desired consistency. Flavorings or pastel colorings may be added to fondant.

Methods of Building Tortes

Building a Torte by Hand

Cutting the Layers

1. To trim the sponge layers, find the lowest outside edge of the cake to begin.
2. Place the serrated knife on the sponge; make sure the knife is parallel to the table.
3. Using a light touch and without forcing the knife, make a cut path by turning the cake counterclockwise using your opposite hand as you push the knife through the cake.
4. Following the original cut mark, cut into the cake about one-half inch, making sure to keep the knife parallel to the table.
5. Use this channel to continue cutting the sponge until it has been cut completely through.
6. Each layer should be cut in exactly the same manner; measure each layer to be three-eighths of an inch thick (see Figure 19–1).

Figure 19–1 Cutting layers of sponge cake for a torte

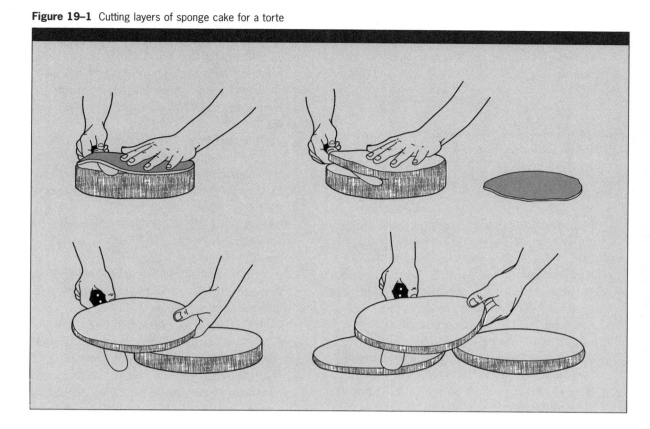

Note: If the layer is convex after cutting, too much downward pressure is being put on the knife. If the layer looks concave after cutting, the knife is not parallel during cutting. If the layer is scalloped with rough edges, the cut path is not being followed and the cake layer is uneven. If the layer is wedge-shaped, the cake is not being turned enough with the opposite hand during cutting.

Filling the Torte

1. Place a flat 9-inch cardboard cake circle on the table.
2. Adhere the first layer of sponge to the cake circle with a small dab of buttercream.
3. Imbibe the sponge layer with a small amount of appropriately flavored simple syrup.
4. Spread an even layer of buttercream over the bottom layer of the sponge using an icing spatula.
5. Place the second layer of sponge cake over the buttercream and align it evenly with the first layer of sponge. A flat cardboard cake circle can be used to flatten the sponge layer into the buttercream.
6. Imbibe the second layer with a small amount of appropriately flavored simple syrup.
7. Spread another layer of buttercream evenly over the second layer of sponge using an icing spatula.
8. Place the final layer of sponge over the evenly spread buttercream. Make sure that all the sponge layers are stacked evenly on top of one another. Press the layers again with a cardboard cake circle to ensure that the layers are even.
9. Imbibe the last layer with the appropriate simple syrup.
10. Check the assembly of the torte to see if all the sides are even with one another and that the top

of the torte is flat (the cardboard should extend out from the torte layers approximately 3/16 of an inch; if not, trim the layers to allow for the clearance.

FYI

Simple syrups are frequently used to imbibe torte layers because they add flavor to the torte and provide moistness to the layers.

Finishing the Torte:

1. Spoon approximately 12 ounces of buttercream on the top of the torte and spread it out evenly using an icing spatula. Keep the buttercream straight across the top layer without rounding the buttercream over the edges of the torte. The buttercream should be approximately ½-inch thick.

2. Lift the torte off the table and place it in your dominant hand. Spread your fingertips to place them in contact with the cardboard, and the torte will remain stationary. By pushing your palm up and fingers away and down (from the cardboard) at the same time, the torte will rotate on your hand. Now the torte can be rotated on your palm by first gripping with your fingertips, then flicking your wrist counterclockwise as you push your palm up and fingers away (as described above). The weight of the torte will actually help pull it into motion. Stop the torte by touching your fingertips back into the cardboard and relaxing your palm.

3. Cover the sides of the torte by applying buttercream a little at a time from the tip of the icing spatula. The torte should be held at a 5-degree angle sloping

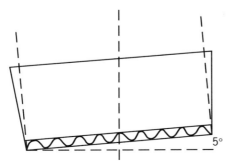

from the right to the left if using your right hand, or the left to the right if using your left hand. Use the edges of the spatula to smooth the sides, using a back-and-forth motion. Apply the buttercream on the sides by making sure that it exceeds the top layer of the torte, making an edge on the top of the torte.

4. Continue the procedure until all the sides of the torte are covered. Use the edge of the icing spatula to smooth the sides uniformly, using the cardboard circle on the bottom of the torte as a guide to pivot the spatula and angle the sides.

5. Level the top of the torte in hand or by placing the torte back on the table. If leveling in hand, keep the torte at eye level.

6. Begin leveling the torte by using the edge of the spatula to straighten the sides. Keep the handle of the spatula directly under the torte. Never press the face of the icing spatula directly into the side of the torte (it may pull the buttercream off), and always use the cardboard as your guide.

7. Place the torte on the table, allowing approximately 1½ inches of the torte to hang over the edge of the table. This will allow you to move the torte more easily with your hand.

8. Grasp your serrated knife and, using the smooth edge and both hands, smooth the top of the torte by pulling it over the top of the torte at a 40-degree angle, moving from left to right, outside to inside. This should remove the high peaks of buttercream and establish a smooth, level top. After each pass, move toward the center of the torte and turn the blade in a sweeping motion, from left to right to remove any excess buttercream. Give the torte a slight turn, and repeat until all the peaks are removed. Never continue across the entire surface of the torte.

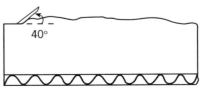

9. Remember, leveling the torte is a gradual process. Rushing the procedure will only lead to problems.

10. Pick up the torte and straighten the sides. Remember, each time the top of the torte is leveled, the sides will need to be smoothed again.

11. Return the torte to the table, and continue to level and smooth the top. Keep the blade at a 20-degree angle and parallel to the table at all times. Check the depth of the buttercream layer on top with a small pocket ruler. There should be no more than ⅛ of an inch of buttercream on the top of the torte. Check the torte from the sides to see if the center is mounded; if so, remove the buttercream from the center.

12. Pick up the torte once more, and straighten and correct the sides and top edge. *Note:* As the process continues, less and less buttercream will be removed, and great care should be taken to maintain and perfect the top edge.

13. Return the torte to the table for the last time for final corrections and for smoothing of the top.

Note: If the torte is less than satisfactory, it can be placed in the refrigerator until the buttercream is firm, and then it can be realigned although setting the buttercream in the refrigerator may cause discoloration.

Building a Torte in a Ring

1. Cut a cardboard cake circle to fit the inside diameter of a metal cake ring. It should be measured and cut to fit the inside of the ring exactly.

2. Cut sponge layers, using the method for cutting used above in Building a Torte by Hand to ⅜ of an inch thick. Stack the layers and trim them to allow approximately ³⁄₁₆ of an inch of space between the ring and the layer of sponge. This is to allow space for the buttercream.

3. Place the ring around the trimmed sponge layer to check for spacing.

4. Remove the ring, and ice the inside edges with about ³⁄₁₆ of an inch of buttercream using an icing spatula.

5. Hold the ring parallel to yourself using your dominant hand. The ring should be grasped between your thumb and index finger and supported by your pinkie finger,

6. *OR,* the ring can be stood up on its side on the table with its opening facing you; roll the ring from side to side as you apply the buttercream using an icing spatula,

7. *OR,* place the ring flat on the table and turn it with your left hand as you apply the buttercream up against the sides of the ring.

8. After the inside of the ring is iced, place the cardboard cake circle under the ring and press and squeeze the ring to cover the cardboard completely.

9. Cut the sponge layers in half across the diameter so you have two halves of sponge.

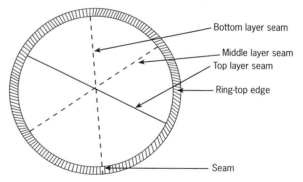

Bottom layer seam
Middle layer seam
Top layer seam
Ring-top edge
Seam

10. Place the bottom layer in the ring by pressing the curved part of the sponge half toward the curve of the ring, against the buttercream. Use the seam in the metal ring as a guideline for placing the sponge halves.

11. Rotate the ring 180 degrees, and place the second half against the buttercream. The center seam of the two sponge halves should come together smoothly. If the sponge doesn't fit, never press it into the buttercream; instead, trim the sponge to fit, or remove some of the buttercream.

12. Now spread or pipe a layer of buttercream onto the sponge halves to fill the torte.

13. Find the seam in the ring, rotate the ring by one-third (120 degrees), and place the second sponge layer the same as the first; spread or pipe buttercream to fill the layers. Remember to imbibe the layers of sponge before icing them with simple syrup if desired.
14. Rotate the ring another one-third, or 120 degrees, and continue as above. Rotating the seam in the sponge layers ensures that they are not aligned and gives structure to the built torte.
15. At this point, only the top layer of buttercream needs to be applied. If more than ⅛ of an inch of space exists between the top of the torte and the ring, use a spacer under the bottom cardboard to raise the cake to the proper height.
16. Finish the top of the torte by filling the space with buttercream and leveling the torte with a straight edge. Use the top edge of the ring as your guide and smooth out the buttercream.
17. Refrigerate the entire torte, in the ring, until firm.
18. To remove the ring, place the torte on a platform and heat the outside of the ring slightly using a hand-held torch or a hot towel. Carefully slide the ring down, not up, and remove it away from the torte. *Note:* The platform should be approximately three times the height of the torte and smaller in diameter so the ring can slide down. Take care not to touch the top edge of the torte with your fingertips.
19. The torte can now be finished and decorated.

Building a Torte Using a Turntable

1. Cut the layers of the torte as described above.
2. Place a cardboard cake circle on a turntable.
3. On the cardboard cake circle, place a slice of sponge cake; imbibe the sponge layer if desired.
4. Spread buttercream over the sponge layer using an icing spatula to approximately ¼-inch thickness.
5. Repeat steps three and four until the torte is built with three layers.
6. Cover the top layer of the torte with buttercream, using an icing spatula, evening out the layer of buttercream and spreading it to cover over the outside top edge.
7. Spread buttercream over the sides of the torte, using the icing spatula. Smooth the sides of the buttercream by holding the spatula at a 90-degree angle to the turntable and rotating the turntable as you press the face of the spatula into the side of the torte. This can also be done using a bench scraper. As you turn, an edge should be formed on the top of the torte.
8. Remove the edge of buttercream on the top of the torte by pulling the buttercream toward the center of the torte with an icing spatula.
9. Check the sides and center of the torte to make sure it is smooth and not mounded in the center; if it is not smooth or if it is mounded, correct using the above techniques.
10. After the torte is iced, the torte can be decorated.

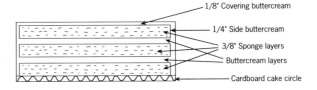

Appendix 19A

Bake Shop Conversion for Cake Formulas

Changing a Formula in Pounds to Percent

1. Add weight of all flour to arrive at total flour weight.
2. Divide weight of each ingredient by the weight of the total flour and multiply by 100 to change the formula to a percentage.

(When constructing a formula given a certain measure of water, convert that measure to pounds; i.e., 1 gallon of water weighs 8.4 pounds.)

Ingredient	Pounds	Calculation (Total flour weight = 100%.)
Cake flour	20	$(20 \div 85) \times 100 = 23.5\%$
Bread flour	65	$(65 \div 85) \times 100 = 76.5\%$
Water	5 (gallons)	$(42 \div 85) \times 100 = 49.5\%$
Yeast	5	$(5 \div 85) \times 100 = 5.9\%$
Sugar	10	$(10 \div 85) \times 100 = 11.8\%$
Salt	1	$(1 \div 85) \times 100 = 1.2\%$
Malt	2½	$(2.5 \div 85) \times 100 = 2.9\%$
Shortening	15	$(15 \div 85) \times 100 = 17.7\%$
Eggs	10	$(10 \div 85) \times 100 = 11.8\%$

Changing a Formula from Percentages to Pounds

In order to change a cake formula in percentages to pounds, one of the following four conditions must be given or known: 1. weight of flour, 2. weight of batter, 3. number of layers with scaling weight, or 4. weight of any ingredient (other than flour).

1. *Weight of Flour*
   Change the following percent formula into pounds to give a batter using 27 lb. of flour.
   Method: Multiply the weight of total flour by the formula percent of each ingredient expressed decimally.

Ingredient	Percentage	Calculation	Lb./Oz.
Flour	100	$1.0 \times 27 = 27$ lb.	27 lb.
Shortening	40	$0.4 \times 27 - 10.8$ lb.	10 lb., 12¾ oz.
Sugar	120	$1.20 \times 27 = 32.4$ lb.	32 lb., 6½ oz.
Whole eggs	50	$0.5 \times 27 = 13.5$ lb.	13 lb., 8 oz.
Milk	100	$1 \times 27 = 27$ lb.	27 lb.
Salt	3.5	$0.035 \times 27 = 0.945$ lb.	15 oz.
Baking Powder	4.5	$0.045 \times 27 = 1.22$ lb.	1 lb., 3½ oz.

2. *Weight of Batter*
   Change the following percent formula into pounds to give a formula making 133.75 lb. of batter.
   Method: When we are given the pounds of batter, we must add up the formula to find total formula percent.

   The pounds of batter divided by the total formula percent and multiplied by 100 gives pounds of flour to use in the formula. When you find amount of flour to use, proceed as in example 1, weight of flour.

Ingredient	Percentage	Calculation
Flour	100	1.0 × 32 = 32.0 lb.
Shortening	40	0.4 × 32 = 12.8 lb.
Sugar	120	1.2 × 32 = 38.4 lb.
Eggs	50	0.5 × 32 = 16.0 lb.
Milk	100	1.0 × 32 = 32.0 lb.
Salt	3.5	0.035 × 32 = 1.12 lb.
Baking powder	4.5	0.045 × 32 = 1.44 lb. Total: 133.76 lb. batter

3. *Number of Layers with Scaling Weight*
   Given the following formula, find the size of the pans necessary to make 360 two-layer cakes scaled at 12½ oz. per layer.

   360 × 2 = 720 layers necessary;
   (720 × 12½) ÷ 16 = 562.5 lb. of batter.

Ingredient	Percentage	Calculation
Flour	100	1.0 × 134.5 = 134.5 lb.
Shortening	40	0.4 × 134.5 = 53.9 lb.
Sugar	120	1.2 × 134.5 = 161.3 lb.
Whole eggs	50	0.5 × 134.5 = 67.3 lb.
Milk	100	1.0 × 134.5 = 134.5 lb.
Salt	3.5	0.035 × 134.5 = 4.7 lb.
Baking Powder	4.5	0.045 × 134.5 = 6.06 Total batter: 562.16 lb.

4. *Weight of Any Ingredient*
   Given the following formula percentage, find the weights of all the ingredients necessary to make a balanced formula if 35 lb. of eggs are to be used.
   Method: Making a ratio between eggs and flour, we

   can find the weight of flour necessary to satisfy the conditions. Then proceed as in 1.

   $$\frac{\% \text{ Eggs}}{\text{Wt. Eggs}} \quad \frac{\% \text{ Flour}}{\text{Wt. Flour}} = \frac{55\%}{35 \text{ lb.}} \quad \frac{100\%}{\text{X lb.}} \quad \text{X} = 63.6 \text{ lb.}$$

Ingredient	Percentage	Calculation	
Flour	100	X = 63.6 lb.	63 lb., 9½ oz.
Shortening	40	63.6 × 0.40 = 25.44 lb.	25 lb., 7 oz.
Sugar	120	63.6 × 1.2 = 76.32 lb.	76 lb., 5 oz.
Eggs	55	35 lb. (given)	35 lb.
Milk	100	63.6 × 1.0 = 63.6 lb.	63 lb., 9½ oz.
Salt	3.5	63.6 × .035 = 2.23 lb.	2 lb., 3¾ oz.
Baking powder	4.5	63.6 × 0.045 = 2.86 lb.	2 lb., 13¾ oz.

Appendix 19B

Chocolate/Cocoa Substitutions

Chocolate to Cocoa Substitution

Chocolate in Formula		Cocoa Needed		Shortening to Add
Pounds	Ounces	Pounds	Ounces	Ounces
1	0	0	5	2
1	4	0	13	4
1	8	0	15	5
1	12	1	2	5
2	0	1	4	6
2	4	1	7	7
2	8	1	9	8
2	12	1	12	8
3	0	2	1	9
3	4	2	3	10
3	8	2	6	11
3	12	2	8	11
4	0	2	11	12
4	4	2	13	13
4	8	3	0	14
4	12	3	0	14
5	0	3	2	15

Cocoa to Chocolate Substitution

Cocoa in Formula		Chocolate Needed		Shortening to Reduce	
Pounds	Ounces	Pounds	Ounces	Pounds	Ounces
0	8	0	13		2
1	0	1	10		5
1	4	2	0		6
1	8	2	6		7
1	12	2	13		8
2	0	3	3		10
2	4	3	10		11
2	8	4	0		12
2	12	4	6		13
3	0	4	13		14
3	4	5	3	1	0
3	8	5	10	1	1
3	12	6	0	1	2
4	0	6	6	1	3
4	4	6	13	1	4
4	8	7	3	1	6
4	12	7	10	1	7
5	0	8	0	1	8

20

Slow Baking

Slow Baking

Slow baking is a term that encompasses the making of many desserts; the term refers to a lengthy baking time with a low oven heat. Many basic desserts are slow baked: custards, cheesecakes, clafoutis, some soufflés, and meringues. There are two forms of slow baking: wet and dry.

Wet Slow Baking

Wet slow baking uses a water bath to insulate the product during baking. The item is usually baked in a ramekin that has been placed in hot water; it is then baked in a low-temperature oven, between 300° F and 325° F. The water bath protects the delicate ingredients in the product through insulation, promotes even baking of the product, prevents the drying out of the product, and prevents cracking on the surface of the product. It is important that the water be constantly monitored and replenished during baking if necessary. Many items require the use of a water bath during baking.

Custards

At its most basic, a custard is a combination of eggs, sugar, milk, or cream. Custards use the coagulation of the egg protein from the heat in the oven to make them firm. Custards are one of the simplest desserts to prepare, but one of the hardest to bake because of their delicacy; if they are overbaked, they become chewy and full of pockets; if they are underbaked, they are runny and textureless. To keep the custard well-insulated in the oven, hot water is used to create the water bath, and it is usually best to double pan the ramekins, if possible.

The final texture of the custard is determined by the egg-to-liquid ratio in the formula. If a custard is to be unmolded after baking, such as a flan or crème caramel, it needs a higher ratio of eggs to liquid—two eggs per cup of liquid is the standard. If a custard is to be served in its ramekin, as in a crème brûlée, fewer eggs are used, and heavy cream is used rather than milk—this will give the custard its characteristic soft, rich texture.

There are many types of custards, many of them classic:

- *Crème caramel*, a basic custard of milk, sugar, and eggs, crème caramel is the classic French version of a flan. Caramelized sugar is placed in the ramekin before it is filled with the custard. After baking, the custard is unmolded to reveal that a portion of the sugar has melted to create a sugar-syrupy sauce.
- *Flan* is perhaps the forerunner of the crème caramel; it is made in a similar fashion, although the flan tends to have a higher ratio of cream to milk and sometimes contains cream cheese. The caramel is usually mixed with a sugar syrup just before pouring it into the ramekin to make a stickier syrup that melts better than straight caramel. Flans were invented by Spanish nuns; they were seeking a way to utilize the abundance of egg yolks donated to them by the makers of the Spanish sherry, Jerez, in which the egg whites were used to clarify the sherry, but for which the wine makers had no use. Spanish flan spread to many parts of Central and South America during the conquests of the Spanish after the discovery of the New World and are popular desserts in many of these cultures.
- *Crème brûlée*, burnt cream, has been a popular English dessert since the 1600s. The French popularized the dessert in the late 19th century, calling it *crème brûlée*. It is a thicker custard than a flan or crème caramel, made with all heavy cream, eggs, and egg yolks rather than milk and whole eggs. Because it is so soft after baking, it is served in the ramekin. The sugar in a crème brûlée is broiled on the top of the custard after it has baked and been left to set overnight; early kitchens used a hot broiler oven to caramelize the sugar—modern kitchens use the blow torch.
- *Pots de crème* is a rich custard made with both eggs and egg yolks, milk, and heavy cream. This custard is baked in special pots de crème molds that cover the tops completely during baking—with the exception of one tiny hole for steam. If the molds are not available, covering a ramekin with foil and punching a steam

hole through the foil will suffice. Pots de crème are different from crème caramel and crème brûlée because they contain no caramelized sugar.

- *Bread pudding* was invented in England in the 13th century as a way to use up old or staling bread, bread pudding was brought to the United States by the early colonists. Variations such as hasty pudding, made with corn bread rather than wheat bread, became popular in the colonies because of an early lack of wheat. By the 1800s, bread puddings were popular throughout the country. They are basically a custard that is poured and cooked over stale breads—many variations now exist—and they have become increasingly popular on menus because of their rustic appeal. Large hotels and cafeterias still utilize the original intention of the dish, which was to use stale breads as another product. Restaurants tend to use more trendy breads, such as brioche or croissant, that are often made specifically for the making of the pudding. Regardless of the type of bread used, it should be stale—at least a day old—or it can be dried in a low-temperature oven for an hour or so to stale it. The drier the bread, the more it will soak up the custard, which in turn will create a more tender pudding.

Soufflés

The term *soufflé* comes from the French verb *souffler,* which means to blow up. A soufflé is made of two basic parts, the base and the egg whites. The base contains all the elements that give the soufflé its flavor. The egg whites are whipped, resulting in the incorporation of air, then folded into the base just before baking. Because the air expands with heat, the soufflé rises dramatically in the oven as it bakes. The moisture in the base will also form steam and assist in the leavening of the soufflé.

Soufflé bases consist of a pâte à choux typebase, where milk is brought to a boil and softened butter and flour are added, then eggs are beaten in. When the batter is still warm but not hot, the whipped egg whites are added. This batter lends itself well to fruit soufflés because the heaviness of the batter can support the weight of the fruit.

The other method is to create a custard-type base from a procedure similar to crème anglaise or pastry cream, then, while the cream is warm but not hot, the whipped egg whites are folded in. This method often uses a liqueur, such as Grand Marnier or Chambord, as a way of flavoring the soufflé; the alcohol evaporation aids in the leavening of the soufflé.

Soufflés are classically made in round ramekins with striated sides. The striations, or grooves, on the outside of the dish help to ensure proper distribution of heat through the whole batter. If a soufflé dish is not available, a charlotte mold or heat-proof glass casserole dish can be used.

Soufflés are baked in a moderate oven. The cooking time varies, depending on the soufflé size and style, savory or sweet. When the soufflé is cooked, it must be served without delay or it will collapse. Soufflés can collapse in as little as 3 minutes from the time they are removed from the oven. For this reason, in restaurants soufflés are always baked *a la minute,* or by the minute. Timing with the dining room is crucial for the proper service of a soufflé: It should always arrive at the table before it has collapsed. The soufflé should, however, eventually collapse; if it keeps its height, it has probably been overbaked and dried out or made with too heavy a base.

As long as the proper dish for the amount of batter is used, the soufflé will rise to a beautiful crown. If the dish is too small, the batter will rise out of the dish and spill down the sides. Soufflé dishes are usually filled three-quarters of the way to the top of the ramekin. If a greater amount of batter is needed, a paper collar is useful to contain the soufflé. A collar can be made by cutting a piece of parchment paper twice as high and 1⅓ times the diameter of the dish. The surface of the paper is buttered and wrapped around the outside of the dish. The lower edges of the paper should be touching the workbench, and the buttered side should be facing inward toward the soufflé dish.

Soufflés can be quite versatile; they can be made sweet or savory, served as an entrée or a dessert, and their sizes can range from large enough to serve a group or small enough for individual servings. To ensure that the soufflé is evenly cooked, bake it in a moderate oven, at about 325° F—it is imperative that the oven be preheated to the correct temperature or the soufflé will fall. For a French-style soufflé, which has about 1½ inches of crisp batter enclosing a soft, creamy center, the soufflé is baked at a high temperature of 400° F. Soufflé batters can be made ahead, and just before service the egg whites can be added for baking.

Note: Not all soufflés are baked in a water bath; most custard-style soufflés do not need the added insulation and are baked in a hot oven of 400° F to 410° F, as described above.

Cheesecakes

Cheesecakes were one of the very first cakes; the Greeks and Romans both made dense cheesecakes sweetened with honey and nuts—in a way, the cheesecake is the forerunner of all baked cakes. By the 1400s, various forms of cheesecake were popular all over Europe; the type of cheese used was what was indigenous to the locale. German, Austrian, and Scandinavian cheesecakes are usually made from soft fresh cheeses, while Italian and other Mediterranean cheesecakes are usually made with ricotta cheese. In the United States, cream cheese is most often used.

In the United States, cheesecakes fall into two basic categories: New York, or deli-style, and French-style. New York, or deli-style, cheesecake is rich and dense. It is most often made with a graham-cracker or cookie crust. French-style cheesecake is a lightly textured cheesecake, using a chiffon to provide a lighter grain and texture. The pans used in making French cheesecakes are usually prepared with a thin layer of baked sponge cake on the bottom of a greased cake pan to serve as a crust.

Most cheesecakes fall into one of these two styles, with many variations having been popularized in the last 20 years. Cheesecakes are well-loved and are almost always found on dessert menus and buffets.

Cheesecakes use a variation of the creaming method of mixing. The batter must contain no large lumps after mixing. Softening the cheese(s) with the butter (if it is used), adding the eggs very slowly during mixing, and

scraping the bowl constantly during mixing will ensure that the batter is lump free. Overmixing the cheesecake to rid the batter of lumps will result in too much incorporation of air—this will result in holes or cracks on the surface of the cake during baking. If lumps occur, the batter can be smoothed by processing it in the robot coupe for a few seconds.

Cheeses

A quality cheesecake usually contains one of the following cheeses: cream cheese; baker's cheese; or Neufchâtel cheese, a soft, white, French cheese. All work well in cheesecake, but each has its own distinctive flavor and texture.

- Cream cheese is more expensive than other cheeses, but it is readily available in all areas. Cakes that contain cream cheese freeze very well because of the high butterfat content in the cheese.
- Baker's cheese is approximately 75 percent water and has a rather bland flavor. Therefore, many bakers choose to blend cream cheese with baker's cheese for added flavor. It is recommended that baker's cheese be used fresh rather than frozen to maintain the best possible flavor and mixing properties.
- Neufchâtel cheese is a soft, white, French cheese that gives a wonderful flavor to cheesecake. Because of its lower fat content, Neufchâtel cheese is usually less expensive than cream cheese and helps to create a lower-fat pastry item.

Dry Slow Baking

Dry slow baking includes one item only: meringue. However, meringues can be made in several different ways and, once made, can be piped into many decorative items for use as desserts or decorations for or on desserts.

Meringues are made from egg-white foams; these foams can increase in volume up to eight times when whipped because of the teamwork of the albumen and ovalbumen proteins. When the egg whites are agitated, air bubbles are incorporated; the albumen proteins present in the egg white stabilize the air bubbles while also forming a network around them that holds the water of the foam in place. This redispersion of protein is known chemically as *denaturization*. When the foam is heated, as it often is, the ovalbumen protein coagulates from the heat, preventing the expansion due to air from collapsing the structure of the meringue.

Meringues are a ratio of two parts sugar to one part egg white; meringues that contain sugar in other ratios are often referred to as chiffons (although technically a chiffon does not contain any sugar). Sugar plays an important role by not only flavoring and sweetening the meringue but also stabilizing the egg foam, particularly when the meringue is heated. It bonds with the meringue's protein structure and creates a more smooth, stable foam and also helps prevent overcoagulation of the proteins. Sugar can also hinder the foam and decrease volume; for this reason, it should always be added only after the meringue has begun to increase in volume, and it should be added to the meringue in a slow, steady stream. Adding the sugar too early or too fast can prevent the foam from whipping.

Acids, in the form of lemon juice or cream of tartar, are sometimes added to meringues during whipping because they change the pH level of the foam, which stabilizes it. Too much acid will prevent the coagulation of the proteins during baking and alter the taste of the meringue. Copper bowls have long been used to whip egg whites; it was thought that the copper had the same stabilizing effect that an acid does. This theory is under debate at present, so the best way to stabilize would be to use an acid. Aluminum bowls will change the color of the meringue to a grayish tint; plastic bowls retain fats that will hinder whipping; therefore, a stainless steel bowl is best.

Fats will interfere with the coagulation of the proteins and reduce volume drastically. Any yolk present in the whites should be removed. Plastic bowls, as mentioned, retain fats that also hinder whipping and should never be used.

For easy measuring:

1 Cup egg whites = 8 egg whites
1 Cup whole eggs = 4 whole eggs
1 Cup egg yolks = 12 egg yolks

Note: All eggs are large size.

Types of Meringues

There are three basic types of meringue. All have a 2:1 ratio of sugar to egg whites; the difference between them is in their method of procedure:

1. *Common, cold,* or *French:* This is the easiest of the three types of meringues to make. The egg whites are beaten at high speed until frothy, then the granulated sugar is added in a slow, steady stream until the volume desired is reached. Because this meringue is not heated, its structure is weaker than the other meringues, and the texture is more grainy. It is the quickest to prepare.
2. *Swiss:* In this meringue, both the sugar and the egg whites are heated to 110° F over a water bath while lightly whisking. At this temperature, the mixture will feel warm to the touch, and the sugar granules will have mostly dissolved. As soon as the mixture is heated, it is whipped at high speed until the desired volume is reached.
3. *Italian meringue:* This is considered to be the finest of the three meringues. It is made by heating the sugar in a sugar syrup to 245° F to 250° F. A small handful of the sugar is usually reserved to aid in whipping the egg whites. The egg whites are beaten to full volume when the sugar syrup reaches approximately 238° F. When the syrup has reached final temperature, it is poured in a thin steady stream into the whipping egg whites; the mixing speed should be reduced to medium. The mixture is beaten until cool.

Because Swiss and Italian meringues are heated, they form a stronger bond and structure, and their texture is smoother than a French meringue.

A variation of a meringue is japonaise; this is a meringue with ground, blanched almonds added to it. It is often piped into disks that are used as torte layers.

Baking Meringues

Meringues can be dried out with two basic methods:

- The meringue can be baked in the oven at a low oven temperature of 200° F to 225° F until the structure is set. This method is fast, but it tends to slightly color the meringue.

- The meringue can be left overnight in a gas oven with just the pilot light for heat. This method requires more mise en place because it takes longer, but the color usually remains white.

Storage of Meringues

Because of their high sugar content, meringues are very susceptible to moisture. After baking, they should be used immediately if possible or stored in airtight containers.

Items Made from Meringue

- *Vacherin:* Vacherin is a classic French term for a meringue that is piped into a basket shape to hold mousses, creams, fruits, and so on.

- *Filligrees:* Like chocolate and royal icing, meringue can be piped into delicate ornaments and used to decorate cakes, pastries, and desserts.
- *Swans:* Meringue can be piped into swans and filled with mousse or chantilly cream for an elegant dessert.
- *Pavlovas:* A classic Australian dessert created in Sydney to celebrate a performance of the famous prima ballerina, Anna Pavlova. The dessert is a meringue cup filled with a pastry cream or cream diplomat and topped with fresh fruits.

21

Basic Desserts

Basic Desserts

There are many items made in the bakeshop that are used alone or as components to create other, more elaborate desserts. This chapter concentrates on many of them, with a focus on their method of preparation as well as how many of them are utilized

Creams and Mousses

There are a variety of creams that comprise many desserts; they may be a component or filling, as in a pastry cream, or they may stand alone, as in a bavarian cream. The term *cream* encompasses a vast array of mixtures that use cream as a major ingredient. Most have many applications, so to master them is to begin to master other items in pastry that are built on them.

Pastry Cream

Pastry cream is one of the most basic creams, with many applications in the bake shop. It serves as a filling for many pastries, such as cream puffs, éclairs, napoleons, cakes, and pies. It is basically an egg custard similar to the classic crème anglaise; the difference is that pastry cream contains cornstarch as a thickening agent. Not only does the cornstarch thicken the cream to a much thicker consistency than that of a crème anglaise, it also is absorbed by the eggs and allows them to be cooked to the boiling point without curdling. Many of the same concerns for cream pie fillings apply to pastry cream because these fillings are based on pastry cream:

- Pastry creams can be inconsistent; they can become lumpy because of improper dissolution of the starch. The starch should always be mixed with a small portion of the sugar and then whisked together with a small amount of the liquid (usually milk) to make a slurry. This will rid the filling of lumps caused by the starch.
- Undercooked pastry cream will have a starchy taste; the starch must be cooked long enough to become translucent (1 to 3 minutes) to ensure that the filling will not retain a starchy taste and mouth feel.
- If not cooked properly, the eggs will curdle. The eggs should be whisked and then added to the slurry mixture so they can be more readily absorbed by the starch, which helps protect them from overcooking. The egg mixture is always tempered by whisking a small stream of the hot liquid into it to avoid cooking the eggs.
- Overcooking and not properly whisking the filling while it is thickening will cause the filling to burn around the sides of the pan and create a scorched flavor that can sometimes penetrate the entire filling.

To eliminate cholesterol and fat, use only egg whites in place of the whole eggs and egg yolks. Also eliminate the butter. This low-fat version is especially useful in the summer months when pastry cream is very susceptible to spoiling because of the high fat content of the egg yolks and butter.

After cooking the pastry cream, it is best to place it in a mixer over an ice-water bath and paddle the mixture on low speed until cool. Cooling the mixture this way reduces the chance of food-borne illness and, at the same time, produces a smoother cream that will be less likely to form a skin. As soon as it is cool, the pastry cream should be spread on a sheet pan to no more than 2 inches thick and covered with food film immediately. Skins form on milk products because of the bonding of the calcium found in the milk and the milk proteins. If left exposed to air, the skin will become heavy and cause lumps. Always cover these products airtight. Pastry cream should be used within 2 to 4 days.

Chantilly Cream

Chantilly cream is whipped cream with the addition of sugar and flavorings; its name comes from the château of Chantilly where the famous French chef Vatel worked in the 1800s. To understand Chantilly cream, it is important to understand whipped cream and its uses.

Whipped cream is used not only as a garnish, in the form of chantilly cream, for many desserts, but also as a lightening ingredient for a huge range of creams and chilled desserts. There are two forms of whipped cream:

1. *Stiff peak:* This form is whipped to maximum volume and used for decorations, such as rosettes and shells.
2. *Soft peak:* This form is whipped to between one-half to three-quarter volume and is used as a lightening ingredient for desserts such as mousse and bavarian cream.

Like whipped egg whites, whipped cream is a foam of air and water that is stabilized by the proteins in the cream. The proteins redisperse when agitated; some are caught in the walls of the bubbles, others form a film surrounding the bubbles that make it cohesive and allow volume to occur. Unlike egg-white foams, fat stabilizes a whipped cream and because fat is more stable cold than it is at warmer temperatures, keeping cream cold for whipping will stabilize the whipping process. The amount of fat is also important: Thirty percent or more is best to create a stable foam. If agitated quickly enough, even milk will produce a thick foam, but most bake-shop mixers do not have the velocity to accomplish this.

Cream can be overwhipped easily, curdling and creating butter. If a cream is whipped to the point of even the slightest separation into butter, it cannot be altered; the butter lumps will remain in the cream and cause an unsightly appearance and texture. Therefore, care must be taken when whipping cream.

- Make sure the cream is as cold as possible to stabilize the foam.
- If possible (and this is not likely in a busy bake shop), freeze the utensils used for whipping.
- Always whip small amounts of cream, let the cream become viscous, then add more liquid cream until the desired peak is reached. Pouring a large amount of cream in the mixer at once not only takes too long, it also can cause curdling.
- Never walk away from cream while it is whipping.
- Add flavors at the end of whipping, just before the

cream has reached desired volume. For a standard Chantilly cream, 2 ounces of confectionery sugar are added to 1 quart of whipping cream; vanilla can be added to taste. Compounds and liqueurs can also be added to flavor whipped cream—the acid content in a compound should be relatively low, or it will curdle the cream.

Crème Diplomat

Crème diplomat is a composite cream consisting of a 1:1 ratio of pastry cream and whipped cream. To make it, the whipped cream and pastry cream must be free of lumps and of similar consistencies; a firm pastry cream will cause the cream to lump and volume and texture will be lost from the overstirring produced while trying to get out the lumps. Use a pastry cream that has the minimum amount of cornstarch, or one that is thickened only with flour, and use it at room temperature. Crème diplomat can be used in place of pastry cream to fill many pastries, such as Gateaux Saint Honore, napoleons, and choux pastries.

Crème Chiboust

A chiboust is a light composite cream made of pastry cream and Italian meringue (usually equal parts of both, as in a diplomat). Again, a soft pastry cream should be used and the temperature of the pastry cream should be warm but not hot. If the pastry cream is too hot, it will melt the meringue and volume and texture will be lost. If the cream is too cold, lumps will occur when the two are folded together.

Bavarian Cream

Although it is not known, it is believed that Bavarian cream got its name from the area in the south of Germany known as Bavaria. Bavarian creams are very versatile and can be used as a dessert or as a component in a cake or pastry. They are the basis for charlottes, which consist of molding the cream with a sponge lining of some sort.

Bavarian creams are basic custardlike creams, with the addition of gelatin for setting and whipped cream for lightness. They can be made with two different bases: a crème anglaise-type base or a pâte à bombe base.

- A *crème anglaise base* uses a basic custard of milk, heavy cream, sugar, and eggs or egg yolks that is cooked to napper over a water bath. The gelatin is bloomed and then dissolved with the heat of the cooking custard. The mixture is cooled over an ice bath while mixing and, just as the gelatin is about to set, the whipped cream is folded into the mixture. The mixture is immediately poured into molds. This is the more popular of the two methods and is the one most often used.
- The *pâte à bombe base* is a mixture of whipped egg yolks and sugar syrup. It is made using the same method of procedure as that of an Italian meringue. To use it for a Bavarian cream, the pâte à bombe is made and the gelatin is bloomed and dissolved separately, then added to the bombe mixture, and then the whipped cream is folded in while the mixture is still soft. The advantage to using pâte à bombe for a base is that it can be made up ahead and refrigerated, then reheated slightly so that the gelatin and whipped cream can be added.

The timing in making a Bavarian is crucial: If the gelatin begins to set too much before the whipped cream is added, the mixture will lump badly; if the gelatin has not thickened the mixture enough, the whipped cream will disintegrate into the mixture and it will lose volume and texture. The amount of gelatin used is also important. Too much will make the cream tough and rubbery; too little and the dessert will not be able to hold its shape when it is unmolded.

After the base is made, Bavarian can be flavored with chocolate, fruits, nuts, or liqueurs, or combinations. Some fruits contain enzymes that will inhibit the setting of the gelatin; either cook the fruits and purée them before use or use a vegetable-based thickener such as agar-agar.

After the cream has set (at least 2 to 3 hours), it can be unmolded either by dipping the upside-down mold into hot water for a few seconds or by heating it with a blow torch. Because the process can be messy, it is best to

unmold the Bavarians onto parchment paper and transfer them onto plates or serving dishes for service.

Items Made from Bavarian Cream

- *Charlotte russe* is a Bavarian cream filling surrounded by lady fingers, usually molded in a large brioche mold. The mold is lined with the ladyfingers, then the Bavarian cream is poured in and the charlotte is allowed to set.
- *Charlotte royal* is a Bavarian cream filling lined with a jelly-roll sponge cake filled with jam or preserves and rolled. The cut pieces from the roll are placed to fit around the outside of a hemispherical mold (a bowl will do), and the Bavarian filling is poured inside and allowed to set.

The term charlotte comes from the original charlotte aux pommes, an apple compote baked inside a mold lined with toast slices. This dessert was created for and named after the wife of King George III of England during the 1700s. In the 1800s, famed French chef Marie Antoine Carême radically redesigned the concept of the original charlotte because of a mishap in the kitchen: His Bavarian cream would not set up because of a lack of gelatin; Carême innovated by supporting the sides of the cream with lady fingers and adopted the name charlotte russe (since the banquet was to celebrate the return to Paris of Louis XVIII from Russia) for his innovation.

Ganache

The two main ingredients in ganache are chocolate and a water-based liquid: milk, cream, teas, or orange juice. Any other ingredients, such as fat, flavorings, or alcohol, are optional. Additional sugars can also be added, such as glucose, corn syrup, and granulated sugar, to improve the texture and shine of the ganache. Egg yolks are sometimes used to make a richer ganache.

Ganache is prepared by bringing the liquid to a boil. The liquid is removed from the heat and added to a finely chopped chocolate. The mixture is whisked until all the ingredients are well blended, the chocolate has completely melted, and the mixture is smooth. A rubber spatula should be used to scrape the sides of the bowl to ensure that all the chocolate is incorporated.

Any fats to be added to a ganache should be added with the chocolate or at a later point and not boiled with the liquid; this prevents overheating the chocolate. Additional sugars should be brought to a boil with the liquid to prevent graininess in the final product. Flavorings or liqueurs should be added after the mixture is completely smooth to avoid the evaporation of the alcohol and loss of flavor. The cold liquor can also interfere with the melting of the chocolate, if added too soon. Egg yolks, if used, are heated with the liquid until they are thickened—as in a crème anglaise.

Ganaches are used as fillings for tortes and pralines when firm, or as a glaze for tortes and other desserts when liquid. Ganache may have fat-based or water-based flavorings added to it. It can also have nuts, candied fruits, praline paste, crushed nougat, or dried fruit added to it. Ganache will stay fresh for approximately two weeks if handled properly. After this time, a flavor change will occur.

Mousses

Mousses are made from whipped cream, beaten egg yolks, beaten egg whites, and flavorings. Mousses are very popular and versatile; they can be served as an individual dessert or as filling for tortes and pastries. The word *mousse* means foam in French and, if a mousse is made correctly, it will seem like a light foam to the palate.

Mousses are fairly simple to prepare, although the timing in making them is like that of a Bavarian cream. Mousses other than chocolate require the addition of a thickening agent, usually gelatin, to allow them to set.

When egg yolks are used, they are usually made into a pâte à bombe with part of the sugar and any flavorings used are added to them. Egg whites are whipped with the remaining sugar and folded into the yolk mixture alternately with the whipped cream. Chocolate mousse is probably the hardest mousse to make because the consistency depends on the tempering of all the different textures; if not tempered into the ingredients properly, the melted chocolate will seize and create lumps.

Some mousses need to be allowed to set for a few hours or overnight to thicken. If this type of mousse is to be served individually, it should be piped into the serving glass or dish before storing to prevent the mousse from setting in a mass.

Items Made from Mousse

Mousses can be used alone or as components for other items:

- *Marquise:* Although most often chocolate, this term encompasses any variety of box cakes that use mousse as a filling. The cakes are usually glazed and decorated with ganache.
- *Semi-freddo:* This is an Italian frozen dessert made from a semi-frozen to completely frozen mousse. It is usually frozen in molds and sliced for serving.
- *Mousse cakes:* These firm mousses have become popular fillings for various tortes and cakes throughout Europe and the United States.

Crêpes

The pancake is one of the earliest forms of putting eggs, flour, butter, and milk together; the German version, *pfann-kuchen,* is one of the oldest and most basic of foods in Europe. Since its elevation to use in many elegant desserts, the French term, *crêpe,* has been used.

The crêpe started out hundreds of years ago as the simplest of breakfast favorites. The French version, which is very thin, has become what is used as an elegant dessert filled with fruit or cream and doused in liqueur.

Crêpes are easy to make but can be time-consuming; it is best to have special crêpe pans that are just the size of the pancake for making them. The batter is usually made at least one day before the crêpes to allow the flour to absorb the liquid ingredients. The batter will keep for several days if refrigerated. Often, crêpes are made in advance and frozen, then used when needed.

There are many varieties of crêpes, some of which are classic:

- *Crêpes Suzette* is a classic crêpe flavored with oranges, sugar, and spices; traditionally flambéed with orange liqueur and cognac.
- *Crêpes Jacques* are filled with sautéed bananas and seasoned with butter and spices.
- *Crêpes Empire* are filled with pineapple macerated in kirsch or cherry brandy.

Fruit-Based Desserts

There are only 10 minutes in the life of a pear when it is perfect to eat.—Ralph Waldo Emerson

Fresh, ripe fruits in season provide the pastry chef with an abundance of almost limitless choices in planning dessert items. There are many ways to prepare fruit for the table, but, for most, fruit-based creations are simple and classic forms of presenting a dessert with color, flavor, and style.

Simple presentations with the focus of the plate's components relying more on flavor than on architecture are an underlying theme in today's desserts. Fruit, in almost any form, provides this simplicity and is extremely popular on dessert menus and, while some chefs order off-season fruits from South America and New Zealand, most stress the importance of using locally grown produce. Some never use any shipped or cold-storage fruit and stress also the importance of knowing the way in which the produce is grown; they use organic produce if possible, but not always. Many chefs change their menu nightly depending on what was available earlier in the day at the farmers' market, so their menu relies heavily on what fruits they can get on a daily basis and their knowledge of what fruits are in season. Developing a relationship with local vendors is also advantageous.

Today's chefs are also willing to pay higher prices for a better, riper product, although most chefs agree that even expensive or exotic locally grown produce can end up costing *less* because of the price tag associated with shipped products and the waste involved when the shipped product often turns out to be inferior in flavor.

Poached Fruit

Poaching fruit is an excellent way to use firm fruits that can withstand the heat and cooking time involved. Poaching imparts delicious flavor to the fruit through the use of a poaching liquid that is based on a sugar syrup (usually four parts liquid to one part sugar); the syrup can be fruit, water, or wine based and is flavored with herbs and spices.

In addition to flavoring the fruit, poaching also tenderizes the fruit and makes it more palatable. Depending on the color of the poaching liquid (red or white wines are often used with or without the addition of fruit juices), the finished fruit will also change color.

For poaching, the fruit is usually left whole, so the shape and condition of the fruit is tantamount to the success of the dessert; it is especially nice to leave the stem on certain fruits such as pears or figs. Firm fruits such as pears, apples, peaches, figs, pineapples, and oranges lend themselves particularly well to poaching because they do not fall apart as easily as fleshy fruits such as strawberries, kiwis, and raspberries.

To poach fruit, follow these steps:

1. Peel, core, and prepare the fruit. Some fruits (such as apples and pears) should be kept covered in water and lemon juice to prevent oxidization (browning).
2. Prepare the poaching liquid, and bring it to a boil in a pot large enough to hold all the fruit without stacking one on top of another. Reduce the heat to a simmer.
3. Put the whole fruit into the hot liquid and cover it with a plate that is covered with cheesecloth. The plate keeps the fruit from bobbing up out of the liquid during cooking, ensuring even doneness and color. The cheesecloth makes it easier to pick the plate out of the pot.
4. Let the fruit simmer, checking it periodically for doneness by piercing it in the core's cavity (this is so the mark of the knife will not be seen) with a paring knife.

The fruit should give to the knife but still be slightly firm. Different fruits will take different amounts of time to cook.

5. When the fruit is done, remove it from the heat.
6. Cool the mixture over an ice bath, if necessary, to prevent further cooking.
7. Let the fruit sit in the poaching liquid, refrigerated, overnight. Make sure that the plate is in place to prevent bobbing.
8. Remove the plate. Carefully pick the fruit out with a slotted spoon and let it drain on paper towels.
9. The poaching liquid may be used again for poaching, or it can be used to make a sauce to accompany the fruit. It can also be used as a base for other fruit desserts or sorbets.

Compotes

Compotes are made in almost the same manner as the method of procedure for poaching fruits; the difference is that in a compote, the fruit is cooked until it begins to lose its shape and fall apart. This actually more accurately describes *stewed* fruit because, in stewing, as in poaching, the fruit is usually left whole. More often than not, compotes are made by selecting several fruits and cutting and dicing them before cooking. Fresh or dried fruits can be used; if canned or frozen fruits, or even soft, fleshy fruits are used, they should be added after the cooking process, while the compote is cooling, so they do not lose all their texture and color.

Compotes should be served hot; used as a garnish, they provide wonderful texture, temperature, and color contrasts for plated desserts. Cold compotes can be made by cooling a hot compote after cooking or by macerating soft fruits in alcohol and sugar.

To make a compote,

1. Follow the procedure for poaching, noting the above guidelines.
2. Omit the use of the plate and cheesecloth; simply stir the compote periodically as it cooks. It should simmer until the fruits are completely soft.

3. Compotes can be left overnight to absorb flavor and color, or they can be used immediately.

Salads and Salsas

Fruit salads and salsas are both excellent ways to use fresh fruits when they are at the peak of their ripeness. Like vegetable salads, fruit salads are decoratively cut fruits with a light dressing; the fruit can also be tossed simply with sugar and a complementary liqueur. Fruit salads can be the basis for a dessert, used as garnish for a dessert, or presented at buffet tables.

Fruit salsas are derived from their savory counterparts. They are diced and julienned fruits that are served with a variety of herbs, spices, and other flavorings that complement the flavor of the fruit; their bright color and flavor make an excellent garnish for many plated dessert presentations.

Although both salads and salsas are most often made from fresh fruits, dried, frozen, or canned fruits can also be used, provided the appearance and texture of the fruit is acceptable. In addition, poached fruits can be used, sliced or diced, and served chilled.

Fruit Chutneys

Chutneys can be vegetable or fruit based; the former has been around for centuries and consists of pickling a variety of vegetables with spices and onions. Mincemeat is the forerunner to the first fruit chutney; it was a way to make the suet and other discarded parts of meat palatable. Centuries later, without the suet, fruit chutneys are excellent ways to add color, texture, and flavor to a dessert. Often made with dried fruits, fruit chutneys are pickled by macerating the fruits in alcohol and sugar for an extended period of time. They can be made to taste, and because of the high alcohol and sugar content, will keep almost indefinitely. Chutneys can be served hot or cold.

Fritters

Fritters are another way to utilize ripe, fresh fruits; dried fruits such as prunes and apricots can also be used. Fritters are fruits that are dipped in batter, then deep fried. The word *fritter* comes from the denigration of the term frying in batter. The fritters can be served as a main item or as a garnish for a plated dessert, but that should always be served hot.

As in poaching, the fruits used in frying should be of a firm enough consistency to withstand the heat of the frying process. The oil used for frying should be neutral in taste and have a high enough smoke point to be used for deep frying. The proper temperatures for deep frying are 350° to 375° F. If the oil is too hot, the fritter will get too dark or possibly burn on the outside before it has a chance to cook on the inside; conversely, if the temperature of the oil is too cold, the fritter will become saturated with oil.

The batter is a basic mixture of flour, sugar, liquid, sometimes eggs, spices, and seasonings. Sweet wines are often used to impart flavor.

To fry fruit fritters, follow these steps:

1. Peel, core, slice, and prepare the fruits. Do not submerge them in water and lemon juice.
2. Prepare the fritter batter according to the formula.
3. Dredge the fruit in the batter.
4. Carefully drop the fruit into the hot oil. The fruit will sink and then rise; it should be turned during frying for even doneness.
5. Lift the fritter out of the oil with a slotted metal spoon or hot tongs.
6. Drain the fritter on paper towels to soak up and remove excess oil.
7. Dredge the fruit in cinnamon and sugar, or let it cool somewhat and dredge it in chocolate shavings.
8. Serve while hot.

Flambéed Fruits/Tableside Desserts

Flambéed desserts are prepared tableside on a guèridon by a waiter or at buffet tables by a chef or pastry cook; their presentation is impressive because of the height of the cooking flames. Flambéed desserts use fresh fruits and a liqueur or spirit to ignite the flame. Then burning off of the alcohol both reduces and intensifies the flavor of it. Surprisingly, most flambéed desserts are simple in ingredients and simple to prepare; it is the dramatic presentation and, of course, the simplicity of their flavors that make them so popular.

Classic items served tableside include

- *Crêpes Suzette,* arguably the most famous of all flambéed desserts. It consists of crêpes served with oranges and sugar that have been flambéed with Grand Marnier and cognac.
- *Cherries jubilee,* which are macerated bing cherries flambéed in Kirschwasser traditionally served with vanilla ice cream.
- *Bananas Foster,* the New Orleans classic consisting of flambéed bananas with sugar and spices traditionally served with vanilla ice cream.

Pâte à Choux

Pâte à choux is the versatile pastry paste used for making cream puffs, éclairs, profiteroles, swans, and croquembouche. It is also used in combination with puff pastry to create the classic Saint Honore and tarte Alsacienne. Pâte à choux literally translates to "cabbage paste"—a reference to what cream puffs resemble before and after they are baked.

Pâte à choux is composed of bread flour, water or milk, fat, eggs, and salt: basically a roux with the addition of eggs. High-production bakeries often add a chemical leavener to ensure the characteristic puffiness of the product. The paste is piped into desired shapes and baked until it has expanded and the center is no longer wet.

Pâte à choux items are considered specialty products and are very popular in all foodservice areas from retail bakeries and hotel restaurants to institutional baking. The season of the year and the merchandising facilities govern their production and sales. Cool weather or refrigeration is a must in the making and selling of these products because most of them are filled with cream-based fillings.

Ingredients

Flour

A good bread flour is recommended for making pâte à choux. Cake and pastry flour are too weak, and a clear flour is usually too strong. Sometimes a mixture of bread flour and cake flour is used, if the bread flour is too strong. Stronger flours are generally used for large items such as Paris Brest and Saint Honore, and mixtures of bread and cake flours are used for small items such as profiteroles.

Fat

The fat used is butter; its excellent flavor makes its high price worthwhile. Some chefs prefer to use oil because it is more easily dispersed in the liquid at the beginning of the cooking procedure.

Eggs

Eggs are one of the most important ingredients in pâte à choux. When combined with the flour, eggs form the structure of the shell; they also provide most of the leavening and moisture. Eggs are also a variable; the amount of eggs stated in the formula will vary, depending on how long the mixture is cooked, how much evaporation takes place, and the dryness of the flour. Sometimes not all the eggs are used, while at other times extra eggs are needed—generally as many eggs as the paste can absorb without losing its shape when piped. The paste will appear slightly shiny if it contains the correct amount of eggs.

Liquid

Either water or milk can be used in a pâte à choux; the latter will provide a richer batter with better flavor and crust color. However, a pâte à choux made with water is less dense and tends to be lighter and puffier.

Chemical Leavening

Some pâte à choux formulas call for a small amount of baking powder or ammonium carbonate to ensure leavening. These chemical leaveners are not necessary and are seldom recommended.

Salt

Salt provides flavor and helps relax gluten.

Cooking

Thoroughly cooking the flour-paste mixture is an important step in making good shells. The sifted flour and salt are added to the milk or water just as the mixture reaches a boil. Vigorous stirring is necessary to properly cook the mixture. The cooking helps to gelatinize the starch in the flour and mellow the gluten. If the fat is not properly dispersed in the liquid before the flour is added, the mixture will not properly emulsify and will have a tendency to separate.

The mixture is removed from the heat and placed on the mixer; using a paddle on low speed, it is mixed until it begins to cool. If it is overmixed at this point, some of the fat may separate and come to the surface of the batter and, when the eggs are added, the mixture will curdle. It is best to mix on low speed and turn the mixer off and on from time to time to prevent overmixing.

When the mixture is no longer hot—do not wait until it is cold—the eggs are added one at a time so they can properly emulsify. Add enough eggs until the mixture is sticky and has a slightly shiny appearance. The texture of the paste is very important; if it is too wet, it will not hold its shape when piped and subsequently when baked. If it is too dry, the baked pastries will be low in volume and unbaked in the center.

Baking

The piped pâte à choux should be placed in the oven as soon as possible (if this is not possible, they should be wrapped and frozen immediately) to prevent skin formation. If this is not done, a crust will form, which will result in low volume, or the surface will crack which will produce undesired shapes. Some pastry chefs wash the shells with water, milk, egg wash, or melted shortening before placing them in the oven to obtain a somewhat smoother shell, although if the paste is made correctly it will be smooth and shiny without the need for a wash.

Pâte à choux is baked in a hot oven of 425° F with the damper closed until the desired color and volume are achieved. Steam from the moisture in the eggs leavens pâte à choux; the hot oven will ensure that the pieces rise rapidly and create a hollow center—this takes approximately 10 to 15 minutes. At this point, the damper is opened and some chefs find that reducing the oven temperature to between 375° F and 400° F for the final baking time helps to ensure that the product becomes firm and dry, without too much browning.

The oven should not be opened for at least half of the baking time to prevent the product from collapsing. Pâte à choux is done when it is golden brown on the top and bottom of the shell, when the moisture has evaporated from the outside, and when the inside is no longer wet.

Storing

Pâte à choux shells can be stored for a day or two, if covered or frozen. If filled, the pastries should be served the same day.

Items Made from Pâte à Choux

- *Éclairs and cream puffs:* Although different in shape (éclairs are oblong and cream puffs are round), both are usually filled with a pastry cream, cream diplomat, chantilly cream, or chiboust. Often the tops are glazed with chocolate glaze or fondant.
- *Cygnes or swans:* One of the most beautiful of the choux pastries, swans are made by cutting a shell-shaped puff in half horizontally and filling it with a decorative cream. The remaining top is cut in half

vertically and placed into the sides of the filling to resemble wings. Special necks are piped and baked separately and placed at the front of the filled shell. The entire pastry is usually dusted with confectionery sugar.

- *Paris-Brest:* For this, the pâte à choux is piped in the form of a wreath and baked with almonds on top. The filling is traditionally praline flavored.
- *Saint Honore:* Named for the patron saint of pastry chefs (and the street in Paris that is home to so many *patisserie,* or pastry shops), this classic gateau is made with a puff-pastry base that has a ring of pâte à choux piped around its edge. It is filled with a cream filling, usually a crèma diplomat, and decorated with a chantilly cream that is piped using a special tip that creates a woven pattern. The sides of the gateau are decorated with profiteroles that have been filled with cream and dipped in light caramel.
- *Profiteroles:* Basically a small cream puff, these tiny pastries form the basis for the classic French wedding cake, croquembouche. Each of the tiny choux are filled and dipped in caramel and arranged in a tall pyramidlike tower. The croquembouche is often decorated with spun and pulled sugar pieces.
- *Religieuses: Religieuse* means nun, evidently what the French feel this finished pastry looks like. Two small, filled choux are decorated with fondant and stacked. The bottom choux has a decorative teardrop of buttercream piped around it where the two choux fit together.
- *Beignets:* A deliciously sweet pâte à choux that is deep fried and dredged in cinnamon and sugar. These French fritters have been immortalized by the Café du Monde in New Orleans, where they are popular served with the café's famous coffee.

Spoon Desserts

Spoon desserts are rustic desserts that are usually served in a large bowl and spooned out to be eaten. They exist in many varieties and are popular for buffets because they can serve many at a time. Recent restaurant trends have placed these desserts in the spotlight, and often they are served nontraditionally as individual servings. The offerings here are among the best known, but by no means represent the whole.

Trifle

Trifle is a spoon dessert of English origin; it originated in the 1600s as nothing more than whipped-cream flavored with sugar, spices, and Madeira wine. During the Victorian era, the dessert became popular with the addition of biscuits or ladyfingers soaked in sherry and a custard; the dessert took on a layered look and was consequently served in a large glass bowl so that the layers could be seen. It was also known to the Victorians as "tipsy pudding"—they enjoyed the spirit-laden layers at a time when drinking openly was frowned upon—and were often inebriated by it.

Today it consists of layers of ladyfingers or sponge cake (trifle is an excellent way to use leftover cake scraps), pastry cream or custard, and macerated fruits. It is still served in a large bowl so the intricacy of the layers can be seen. Chefs have capitalized on its appeal by creating a multitude of variations.

Zuppa Inglese

Zuppa Inglese is an Italian version of English trifle. *Zuppa Inglese,* or English soup, as most of these delicacies are sometimes called, are usually rum- or liqueur-soaked cakes or cookies layered with a cream-type filling, often including ricotta or mascarpone cheese. They are traditionally served in large bowls to be spooned out by the diner. *Tiramisu* is the most well-known of these Italian spoon desserts. Tiramisu is best when made with the traditional *savoiardi* (ladyfingers) that have been soaked in an espresso-flavored simple syrup laced with rum. Mascarpone and cream cheeses are usually creamed together to create the filling. Tiramisu has taken on many different forms in the United States, and many pastry chefs use

their own original variations to interpret the dish. Some use a light sponge cake soaked in espresso and Kahlua and fill the tiramisu with a mousse of *zabaglione* and mascarpone or ricotta cheese. Other versions use a dense sponge that holds liqueurs (such as amaretto or crème de cocoa) and espresso better. Some chefs serve tiramisu in innovative single servings, such as molding the layers in muffin tins, or rolling the filling into a jelly-roll sponge from which they cut cylindrical serving shapes.

Most Americans would probably be surprised to find how much more simple the Italian version of tiramisu is than what is most often seen in the United States. Orange-flavored tiramisu is a favorite dessert in Rome at Easter; indeed, special occasions and holidays are when these rich desserts are most often enjoyed in Italy—the communion of spooning the dish brings family and friends together in true Italian tradition.

Gratin

Gratin is a French dessert (of Italian origin) of fresh fruits laced in flavored syrups and topped with a sabayon. The fruits are placed in a large baking dish and the sabayon, which is often mixed with cream or yogurt, is broiled until it is light brown. A variety of fruits can be used, and many versions have evolved in the United States.

The term *gratin* is used for any savory dish that is topped with cheese and bread crumbs and broiled to melt the cheese. The dessert version evolved from the savory one.

Clafoutis

Clafoutis originated in the Limousin area of France and is traditionally made with fresh, dark cherries (although any fruit can be used). Clafoutis is an excellent way to use fresh fruits when they are in season. It is a simple, rustic dish made by preparing a soufflé or casserole dish and lining it with the fresh fruit, then pouring a light sponge over it. More fruit is placed on the top of the sponge, and the mixture is baked until done, often in a water bath to ensure moistness.

Clafoutis is similar to New England-style cobblers in how it uses fresh fruits baked in a deep dish with a batter on top. Cobblers and crisps are excellent examples of American spoon desserts.

Banana Pudding

Probably a variation of the trifle, banana pudding is a southern tradition in the United States. It uses all the components of a trifle, excluding the sherry, of course. Modern versions are made with vanilla wafers—any substitute is forbidden—and banana pudding layered in a large bowl. It is a favorite at reunions, homecomings, and other special occasions.

Stretched Doughs

This category of fine pastries includes three basic doughs—phyllo, strudel, and cannoli—the success of which are all derived from one basic factor: They are stretched to a thinness that makes them crispy, light, and delicate. Baklava and strudel doughs are stretched to a paper-thin quality that accounts for the delicacy of the pastries they make up. Cannoli dough is not stretched as thin; although most Italians stretch it with a pasta machine, a rolling pin will work just fine.

Phyllo Dough

Phyllo dough is a whisper-thin pastry dough that, when layered and baked, produces an extraordinarily crisp, golden-brown crust of delicious flakiness. The word *phyllo* actually translates into the word leaf. These leaves of pastry more than likely originated in Turkey and spread to gain popularity throughout the eastern Mediterranean and Near East, particularly Greece. Although phyllo dough is used for sweets such as baklava, it is also commonly used to make the savory Greek dish, spanikopita—phyllo triangles filled with feta cheese.

Current concerns in health and nutrition have given new importance to phyllo dough because it is a low-fat, low-cholesterol dough that can replace traditional pie crusts and puff pastry, both of which are high in saturated fat. Puff-pastry dough, for example, can be as high as 50 percent fat. In comparison, phyllo dough contains virtually no fat. It has a small amount of vegetable shortening to bind the dough. Products that substitute phyllo dough for puff-pastry dough are lighter in texture, are flakier, and have little or no greasy aftertaste.

Phyllo dough is often shredded and made into kataifi; both are used to make not only pastries but also decorative cups and holders for various plated dessert presentations. Although still made by hand in the Middle East, most phyllo dough in the United States is made by machine and bought by chefs for use in the bake shop.

Phyllo dough will dry out in less than 3 minutes if it is left exposed to the air. When working with phyllo dough, keep it covered with a lightly moistened cloth. Wrap it airtight, and refrigerate or freeze it for future use.

Most desserts made with phyllo dough, particularly baklava, are soaked with rose or citrus-scented honey syrups that are traditional in Middle Eastern and eastern Mediterranean cooking styles. The nuts used to fill these pastries are indigenous to the region as well: Walnuts and pistachios are the nuts most commonly used.

Baklava

Perhaps the most well-known to westerners of these desserts is baklava. Baklava is made by layering many layers of phyllo, each sprinkled heavily with melted butter, with a mixture of ground pistachios and walnuts. The layering of the dough is debatable; some chefs layer five layers of dough, then top it with nuts, then another five layers of dough that is topped with nuts, and so on, until 15 to 20 layers of dough are in the pastry. Other chefs layer 10 layers of dough, top these layers with all the nuts, and complete the pastry with another 10 layers of the dough.

The butter provides even more flakiness to the dough

because it evaporates and creates steam that pushes the layers apart. Traditionally, the pastry is cut into triangles before it is baked in a 400° F oven. When it is removed from the oven, the hot honey syrup is immediately poured over it. Baklava will keep for several days; it should be left overnight after the first day of baking to allow the syrup to absorb into the layers.

Strudel

Strudel is the most famous of all Austrian pastries. It was brought to Austria by the Hungarians, who learned to make it from the Turks, fashioned after the Turkish phyllo dough. After the Ottoman Empire (which included Vienna) folded, the defeated Turkish pastry chefs found work in the new Austro-Hungarian Empire and brought their knowledge of this paper-thin dough to the kitchens of the Viennese aristocrats, where the Austrian version was born. The pastry was soon a popular menu item in the many coffeehouses that were soon to pop up all over Vienna.

The key to making the dough is to be sure that it is properly developed: A strong flour, such as bread flour is used, and vinegar is used in the dough to relax the gliadin (the component of gluten that provides elasticity). The dough is developed and then allowed to rest for an hour or so before stretching it out. If properly made and rested, it will stretch over an entire pastry bench. The traditional test of thinness for a strudel dough is if a newspaper can be read through it after it has been stretched. For strudel,

like baklava, the dough is sprinkled with melted butter for added flavor and flakiness, then filled. It is then rolled, snakelike into a long log; the log is curved in an S to fit on a sheetpan and baked at 400° F. Strudel should be served hot and is traditionally sprinkled with confectionery sugar.

Both Baklava and strudel are fun to make, but they require patience and dedication, as most worthy things do, to acquire skill at making them. The doughs can be difficult to work with for beginners. They should be worked quickly so they do not dry out; therefore, mise en place must be in place before beginning.

Cannoli

The word *cannoli* means pipes, which is an accurate description of the shape of a cannoli. Cannoli, a popular dessert from Sicily, are cylinders of sweet, crispy pastry with fillings that vary from sweet ricotta cheese to pastry-cream fillings with dried fruit and nuts. The pastry is stretched or rolled and wrapped around tubes, then deep fried to a crispy, golden brown. The pastry shells can be fried ahead of time and stored until needed.

Cannoli is a traditional Sicilian delicacy filled with sweetened ricotta cheese; in Palermo, it is common for the filling to be laced with chocolate chips. Cannoli was brought by Sicilian immigrants to the United States, as pizza was, at the turn of the century. It can be found in many Italian-American bake shops and coffeehouses.

Ice Creams and Frozen Desserts

Ice Creams and Frozen Desserts

My advice to you is not to inquire why or whither, but just to enjoy your ice cream while it's on your plate—that's my philosophy.—Thorton Wilder, from The Skin of Our Teeth

Ice creams and frozen desserts have a universal appeal. Because of their versatility they are enjoyed by almost every culture in the world. Ice cream and frozen desserts are popular not only because they are cold and refreshing, but also because they are diverse and can accompany a variety of items. Ice cream is often used as an ingredient, served as a main item, or used to complement the flavor or texture of other items.

Ices can be dated back to the Chinese hundreds of years before Christ; they enjoyed pouring flavored syrups over chipped ice. They invented a device that used snow and salt packed over containers filled with the flavored syrups. Because there was no churning involved, the resulting product was hard and therefore had to be chipped or scraped (the Italians later borrowed this idea to make their beloved *granita*). This idea spread throughout the Far and Middle East, where the Arabs enjoyed crushed ices flavored with fruit and honey that they called *sharbat*—the predecessor of sorbet and sherbet. Eventually, the idea gained respect in Italy, where Catherine di Medici and her brigade of chefs elevated the churning process, and the Italian *sorbetti* was born. She brought the idea with her to France upon marrying Henry II in 1533. The French loved their *sorbet* so much that it eventually (over almost 300 years) spread from the nobility to the working classes through the rise of popularity of the coffeehouse in the 1800s, where it was often served—and still is. The French are also credited with adding cream to these ices— Charles I, early in the 17th century, is the first on record to have served ice creams at his lavish dinner parties.

By the 1700s, there is a record of ice creams in middle-class English cookbooks, and the idea had spread to the colonies. In 1846, the most important advance in the making of ice cream was created by an American woman named Nancy Johnson—little else is known of her—who invented the hand-cranked freezer. This single accomplishment elevated the quality of ice cream a thousandfold—

with a steady addition of air and the constant moving of the mixture, the resulting ice cream was much smoother with less grit—a favorite American pastime was born. Other than the Italians, who still pride themselves on their sorbetto, granita, and of course their gelato, Americans eat and love ice cream more than any other culture on earth.

Types of Ice Cream

There are two basic types of ice cream, based on their ingredients:

- French ice cream is a thick, custard ice cream that contains eggs and is made with a crème anglaise or pâte à bombe base. Because of the eggs, this ice cream is always heated.
- American ice cream contains no eggs. It is a basic mixture of milk, cream, and sugar. It can be heated or not heated.

Qualities of Ice Cream

The chief component that determines the quality of an ice cream is the butterfat found in the milk products used. It is this butterfat that provides richness, smoothness, and body and is responsible for an ice cream's velvety-smooth texture. FDA requirements state that vanilla ice cream must contain at least 10 percent butterfat and chocolate ice cream must contain at least 8 percent.

Texture of an ice cream can also be altered with the addition of gums, gelatins, and chemical additives, which also stabilize the ice cream. Additives are often used in the manufacturing of ice cream to create smooth texture and body without using costly ingredients, such as cream and eggs. Premium ice-cream brands rarely use additives, relying more on the quality of ingredients to create texture and body. Ice creams are graded on three general areas:

- *Smoothness of texture* is determined by the size of the ice crystals and the butterfat content as well as the whipping and churning.
- *Body* is determined by the amount of total solids, butterfat, and the amount of overrun.
- *Richness and flavor* are determined by the ingredients used in the making of the mix or base. Dried milk should not be used in the making of an ice cream.

Freezing and Overrun

After preparation of the ice-cream mix, it must go through two important steps: (1) The mix must be frozen, and (2) air must be incorporated. The freezing process takes place at 0° F. In the ice-cream processing, overrun is the increase in volume of the ice cream over the volume of the mix caused by the incorporation of air. It is expressed as the percentage of the volume of the mix. The freezing process must take place quickly to keep the ice crystals as small as possible; but too fast a freezing process has a negative effect on the overrun. The air can only be absorbed when there are enough liquid components still contained in the mix.

In the freezing process, one-third of the water changes into ice. Not enough air causes the ice cream to be heavy and feel very cold in the mouth. Too much air gives a foamy, snowy texture. The overrun should be between 70 percent and 100 percent. Overrun is determined by

- The freezing equipment used
- Freezing or churning time

- The amount of mix related to the size of the freezer capacity; for maximum overrun, the freezer should be filled only halfway
- The amount of total solids in the mix, which should total approximately 40 percent

An example of overrun: Scale 1 cup of ice-cream mix. For example,

1 cup of ice-cream mix	= 8 ounces
1 cup of ice cream	= 4 ounces
Weight loss	= 4 ounces
Increase in volume	= 100 percent

The ice cream comes out of the freezer at a temperature between 22° F and 26° F. The product is now most tasty and can be served directly. It can also be stored for up to one week in a subzero hardening cabinet. It must be packed airtight to prevent ice crystals from forming on the surface and to prevent absorption of odors from the freezer. Fluctuations in temperature during storage can cause coarseness of texture and shorten the shelf life of the product.

The hardening process happens when the ice cream is taken out of the freezing machine and put into a hardening cabinet, which has a constant temperature of 6° F to 22° F. Another one-third of the water changes to ice crystals under these conditions. After the hardening period, the ice cream can be placed into serving cabinets of 46° F to 50° F.

The percentage of sugar in a French ice-cream mix should be around 15 percent of the total weight of the mix, while the percentage of egg yolks should be in a range between 5 and 50 percent. If, for example, a French ice-cream mix with a dairy-fat content of 12 percent is desired, the calculation would be as follows:

percentage of heavy cream (30 percent fat)
percentage of milk (whole, 3 percent fat)
15 percent granulated sugar
5 percent egg yolks
100 percent total

The heavy cream and milk represent 80 percent of the total formula, and the fat content desired is a combined

Figure 22–1 Pearson square

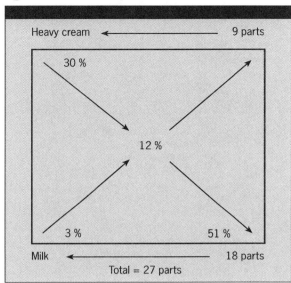

Heavy cream ← 9 parts

30 %

12 %

3 %   51 %

Milk ← 18 parts

Total = 27 parts

(9 ÷ 27) × 80 percent = 27 percent cream

(18 ÷ 27) × 80 percent = 53 percent milk

The 27 percent cream and the 53 percent milk totals the 80 percent (27 + 53 = 80), which is required by the formula. The completed formula percentages are

27 percent heavy cream
53 percent milk
15 percent sugar
5 percent egg yolks
100 percent total

Ingredients in Ice Cream

Milk and Cream

The butterfat found in the milk and cream are the chief contributors to the texture, body, and richness of the ice cream. Butterfat percentages generally run between 14 and 16 percent; the percentage should never total more than 22 to 25 percent, or the extra butterfat will adversely affect the whipping ability of the mix and overrun will be impaired. Too much fat will also freeze separately during churning and produce frozen grains of butterfat that give the ice cream a grainy texture. Solids found in the milk and cream other than the fat are referred to as *serum solids*. These should total at least 20 percent. Milk solids contribute to whipping capabilities, but too much can cause the lactose in the milk to crystallize and give the ice cream a sandy texture.

total of 12 percent. To solve this problem, the Pearson square is used (see Figure 22–1). This is a method used to determine the amounts of two products—in this example, milk and cream—with different percentages of fat needed to give the necessary fat content of the formula.

To start, draw a square. In the middle of the square, write the percentage of fat desired or called for in the formula. In the upper left corner, write the percentage of fat in the cream. In the lower left corner, write the percentage of fat in the milk. Now, subtract the lower left number from the middle number (12 − 3 = 9). Write that number in the upper right corner (9 parts). Subtract the upper left number from the middle number (30 − 12 = 18), and write that number in the lower right corner (18) parts.

Read the answer from right to left on the top (9 parts of 30 percent cream), and read from right to left on the bottom (18 parts of 3 percent milk). This will give a 12 percent milk-fat content.

But, what percentage of 12 percent cream and milk make up the 80 percent needed for the formula?

Nine parts of cream plus 18 parts of milk equals a total of 27 parts, so

Eggs

Eggs contribute to overall flavor and fat content. The color of an ice cream is also affected when eggs are used. Because they contain the emulsifier lecithin, eggs contribute to the body of the ice cream. When eggs are used in an ice-cream base, the mixture should be heated to at least 145° F.

Sweeteners

Sugar is used to enhance sweetness and flavor; in ice creams, total sugar content runs between 14 and 16 percent. Sugar enhances the smoothness of the ice cream, but because it is a freezing inhibitor, can also prevent firmness; sugar content should never be more than 18 percent.

Total Solids

Total solids are the combination of the fat, sugar, nonfat milk solids, and egg solids; their makeup should total approximately 40 percent of the mix. Total solids contribute to flavor, texture, color, and body and can reduce the "head freeze" that ice cream can cause when eaten too fast. Total solids are expensive, and gums and stabilizers are sometimes used in manufacturing as a cheaper way of producing the same effects. See Table 22–1.

Flavoring

More flavor has to be used when making ice cream than when making other products. When cold, the taste buds

Table 22–1 Commonly Used Binding Agents

Binding Agent	Percent
Eggs	5 to 20
Starches	2 to 6
Gelatin	1 to 2
Agar-agar	0.3 to 0.6
Tragarant	0.3 to 0.65
Arabisch gum	1 to 2
Dextrine	0.2 to 0.5
Carageen	0.5 to 0.8
Fruit Ice	—
Pectin	0.5 to 1

Table 22–2 Ice-Cream Flavors

Flavor	Ingredients
Chocolate	1 qt. French ice-cream mix. 6 oz. semisweet chocolate.
Mocha/coffee	1 qt. French ice-cream mix. 1 oz. instant coffee, dissolved or 2 oz. coffee paste.
Praline	1 qt. French ice-cream mix. 5 oz. praline paste.
Nougat	1 qt. French ice-cream mix. 2 oz. praline paste. 5 oz. ground nougat.
Strawberry	1 qt. French ice-cream mix. 2 pt. chopped strawberries. 1 oz. strawberry compound.
Banana	1 qt. French ice-cream mix. 1 lb. banana purée. Juice of ½ lemon.
Rum and raisin	1 qt. French ice-cream mix. *3 oz. raisins macerated in rum. *rum to taste.
Eggnog	1 qt. French ice-cream mix. ¼ tsp. nutmeg. Rum and brandy to taste.
Almond	1 qt. French ice-cream mix cooked with 3 oz. almond paste and 2 oz. ground, toasted almonds.
Chocolate chip	1 qt. French ice-cream mix *3 oz. chocolate chips (chopped couverture).

*Incorporate ingredients after the mix has been whipped and frozen in the ice-cream machine.

are less sensitive. Also, because of the higher fat percentage, a part of the flavoring is captured by the milk fat and is more difficult to release. If the ice-cream mix is to be heated, the flavoring should be added after it has been heated and cooled. See Table 22–2.

Ice-Cream Products

The variety of ice-cream products is extensive. Following is a description of the most common types:

Coupes or Sundaes

Coupes or sundaes (see Table 22–3) are one or more types of ice cream, which, together with a fruit or nut garniture and a sauce, such as fudge, are served in a glass or silver dish. For a coupe, pat the ice cream into a dessert glass. Top with a circle of whipped cream. Add fruit or sauce.

Table 22–3 Sundaes/Coupes

	Components
Butterscotch	Caramelized walnuts. Butterscotch ice cream. Vanilla ice cream. Butterscotch sauce. Whipped cream. Decorate walnut halves.
Carribean	Fresh pineapple chunks, soaked in white rum and sugar. Pineapple ice cream. Whipped cream.
Cherry	Cherries soaked in syrup or brandy. Cherry ice cream. Vanilla ice cream. Whipped cream. Decorate with fresh cherry halves.
Chocolate Fudge	Chocolate ice cream. Vanilla ice cream. Chocolate fudge sauce. Toasted hazelnuts. Whipped cream.
Coffee	Coffee ice cream. Dark chocolate sauce. Cappuccino ice cream. Tia Maria or more chocolate sauce. Whipped cream. Decorate with grated chocolate or toasted nuts.
Honey Melon	Melon & ginger ice cream. Melon sherbet. Honey sauce. Whipped cream. Decorate with crystalized ginger.
Praline	Praline ice cream. Caramel syrup. Caramel ice cream. Whipped cream. Decorate with toasted almonds.
Strawberry	Sugared fresh strawberries. Lemon ice cream. Strawberry ice cream or sorbet. Whipped cream. Decorate with fresh strawberries or toasted almonds.

Parfait Glace and Soufflé Glace

Parfaits are made from a pâte à bombe or crème anglaise base that has a lightly whipped cream folded into it. Flavors can be added as well. Neither is frozen in an ice-cream machine; therefore, they contain no overrun and are referred to as *still mixtures*. Parfaits are frozen in glasses or molded in terrines; soufflé glace is frozen in a ramekin with a collar. When the mixture is hard, the collar is removed to reveal a frozen parfait that resembles a baked soufflé.

Ice-Cream Bombes

Originally, ice-cream bombes were spherical or dome-shaped, hence the name bombe. Today, however, ice-cream bombes vary in shape, but their contents remain basically the same. Bombes are generally made with layers of ice cream; when the bombe is cut, it reveals the intricate layers. The outside layer of a bombe is best if made with a custard or French-style ice cream; the last inside layer is usually filled with a parfait mixture. The bottom of the bombe may or may not be lined with a thin layer of cake. Bombes are almost always decorated after unmolding with an Italian meringue—the meringue is piped into decorative patterns and then browned with a torch. One of the most classic bombes is the Baked Alaska. Two ice-cream bombes include the bombe Carmen and the strawberry bombe. To make the bombe Carmen, line a bombe mold about ½-inch thick with vanilla ice cream. Fill the center with a raspberry mousse. Freeze. To make the strawberry bombe, line a 2-quart bowl, about 1-inch thick with strawberry ice cream. Make a second lining of lemon ice. Fill with strawberries that have previously been soaked in kirsch. Freeze.

Semifreddo

A *semifreddo* is an Italian specialty made with a semi- to completely frozen mousse. It is usually frozen in molds and sliced for serving.

Classic Ice-Cream Presentations

Pears Belle Hélène

Pears Belle Hélène, a simple but classic dessert, consists simply of a poached pear or pear half with a scoop of vanilla ice cream and is served with a rich chocolate sauce. Escoffier is often mistakenly credited with the innovation, to which he added candied violets; his dessert was named for Helen, the Duchess D'Acosta. The origin, however, is more than likely from the operetta *La Belle Hélène* by Offenbach about the Trojan War and written in 1864. Helen of Troy's abduction by the Trojan prince Paris prompted the Trojan War. Offenbach's burlesque rendition of the war became so popular that the name Helene became very popular on menus at the time, and many savory dishes are classified as Hélène or Belle Hélène. This classical French style of cooking always includes asparagus and truffles.

Peach Melba

Peach melba is a classic ice-cream dessert invented by Escoffier in 1892 for Dame Nellie Melba; the dessert consisted of ice cream and peaches presented inside a swan made of ice and topped with spun sugar. It was to celebrate the dame's (a great opera diva) success in the opera *Lohengrin*. The modern version is usually made with a slice of sponge cake, vanilla ice cream, peaches, and melba sauce.

Baked Alaska

Baked Alaska supposedly originated in China, and the idea was brought to France by a visiting Chinese chef who taught the French chef Balzac how to prepare ice creams baked in a pastry crust. Balzac capitalized on the idea and named his dessert Surprise Omelette. Later, in the United States, it was discovered that a meringue was a much better insulator for the ice cream. The idea of the dessert was improved upon at the famous New York restaurant Delmonico's, where it was called "Alaska and Florida" to represent the temperature contrasts within it. Fannie Farmer is credited with the name "Baked Alaska," to celebrate America's purchase of Alaska. The modern version usually consists of vanilla, chocolate, and strawberry ice cream layered in a bombe and lined on the bottom with a thin layer of sponge. The bombe is decorated with an Italian meringue and is often served flambéed in a waiter's parade.

Sorbets and Other Ices

Sorbets, sherbets, and spooms are all made from sugar-syrup bases with the addition of fruit, fruit juice, and sometimes alcohol. The sugar syrup is cooked to a certain density to ensure that the product freezes well and has enough body; the density of the sugar is usually measured with a baumé scale, or hydrometer.

Because they lack the total solids of ice cream, sorbets and other ices can be difficult to produce. Sorbets and sherbets are basically made from the same type base, but a sherbet contains the addition of a milk product. Spooms are made just as sorbet, but an Italian meringue is folded into them during freezing; they are often made from wine or champagne. In addition to a lack of total solids, sorbets, sherbets, and spooms differ from ice cream in the following ways:

- They have a high fruit-acid content, a minimum of 0.35 percent, which produces a tart flavor.

- They have a much lower overrun, usually 25 to 45 percent.
- They have a much higher sugar content, between 25 and 35 percent, which gives a lower melting point.
- Because of the lack of solids, particularly butterfat, they have a coarser texture.
- They have a greater cooling characteristic while being consumed because of the coarser texture and the lower melting point.

A baumé scale, or hydrometer, is a device that measures the amount of sugar in a sugar syrup. The denser in sugar the syrup, the higher the reading will be (sorbets are generally between 14° F and 18° F). The syrup must be at room temperature for the scale to read accurately. If a baumé scale is not available, an egg can be placed in tepid syrup; when it floats, the area of the egg that peaks through the syrup should be between the size of a dime and a quarter.

Special Problems with Sorbets, Sherbets, and Spooms

Sales analysis of sherbet in the United States shows that the popular flavors for this product are orange, raspberry, lime, and lemon. The fruit-flavoring ingredients specified for ice cream may also be used for sherbets and ices. Citrus sherbets must contain a minimum of 2 percent fruit. Berry sherbets must contain a minimum of 6 percent fruit. Other sherbets must contain a minimum of 10 percent fruit. Water ice has the same flavoring provisions as fruit sherbets.

Separation of the Concentrated Sugar Syrup

Separation of the concentrated sugar syrup is one of the most common problems, especially if the ice is wine- or alcohol-based. This is caused by

- Too much sugar in the base mixture.
- Too much overrun.
- The lack of total solids to bind the mixture.

To control for this separation,

- Reduce the amount of sugar in the formula.
- Use proper freezing techniques.
- Add stabilizers in the form of gelatin, agar-agar, pectin, or egg whites to the base mixture. The amount of gelatin is generally 2 teaspoons per quart of sorbet base mixture. Fruits high in pectin, such as citrus fruits, blueberries, cranberries, and apples, should not need the use of a stabilizer.

Sugar and Ice Crystallization

Sugar and ice crystallization is usually caused by

- Exposure to air in the freezer.
- Fluctuation of storage temperatures.
- Use of granulated sugar to make the sugar syrup.

To control for this crystallization,

- Store sorbet in airtight containers.
- Ensure that the cabinet temperature is constant and maintained.
- Replace granulated sugar, at least in part, by an invert sugar such as glucose or honey. Granulated sugar can cause the extraction of water onto the surface of the mixture as soon as it has been frozen, causing ice and sugar crystals to form; the use of an invert will help prevent this.

Coarse or Crumbly Texture in the Final Product

Coarse or crumbly texture is caused by

- Too low a sugar content in the base mixture.
- Inefficient freezing methods—the process is too slow.
- An overrun that is too high.

To control for coarse or crumbly texture,

- Adjust the sugar content, and add an invert to the total percentage of sugar.
- Use efficient freezing techniques.
- Freeze the base mixture with less overrun.

Stabilizers

Most of the basic stabilizers used in ice cream may also be used in sherbets and ices. The amount of basic stabilizers needed to stabilize sherbets and ices is approximately as follows:

Gelatin (200 bloom)	0.45 percent
Agar-agar	0.20 percent
Pectin	0.18 percent

Stabilization in sherbets and ices is even more important than for ice cream because of greater danger of sugar separation and crumbly texture.

Sugar Content

In general, the sugar content of these products is about double that of ice cream. The range may be from 25 to 35 percent. Sources of sugar include cane or beet sugar, corn-syrup solids, honey, and other invert sugars. In making good sorbets, it is necessary to control the sugar content and overrun. Overrun also controls the firmness of sorbets and ices. Overrun in sorbets is usually 30 to 45 percent, while for ices it is 25 to 35 percent.

Granita

Granita, or the French *granite*, is an Italian ice made with a sugar syrup and fruit or fruit juice just as in a sorbet, sherbet, or spoom. With a granita, however, the density of the sugar syrup is thinner, about 10 degrees to 12 degrees baumé (usually three or four parts water to one part sugar). The syrup is cooked, then mixed with the fruit and other ingredients (wine or champagne are often used); it is not frozen in an ice-cream machine, but is still frozen in a shallow pan. The mixture is usually stirred two to three times during freezing. Granitas, unlike their sister ices, sorbets, are nothing more than puréed fruit, sugar syrup, and sometimes fruit juice or alcohol. While this could also

describe a sorbet, the difference lies in the freezing process: Sorbets are churned during freezing, while granitas are still frozen and then scraped after they are solid. The result is an icy-cool treat similar in texture to a snow cone or crushed ice. Granitas can also contain less sugar than sorbets. Granita gets its name from the Italian *grana*, meaning grainy.

Granitas are easy to make and invent. Decide on a favorite fruit, purée it, and then sweeten with a sugar syrup. The sugar syrup can be infused with herbs to create an added dimension to the flavor of the fruit chosen, as can wines, champagne, or liqueurs. It is important that not too much sugar or alcohol is added to the puréed mix because both can inhibit freezing. Make the sugar syrup in advance so it has time to cool. As soon as the ingredients are combined, place them in a shallow rectangular dish, cover, and freeze. Remember that some fruits contain higher levels of water and sugar, so taste testing the mix as well as adjusting the amount of water in the sugar syrup to the water content of the fruit is important to the final outcome. Although most granitas can be left for a day to freeze, some should be checked to make sure the mixture is not separating (too much water in the fruit or too much sugar in the mixture can cause the mixture to separate). If it does, stir it every hour or so during freezing until the mixture comes together. As soon as it is frozen, scrape the mixture with a large metal spoon. Once scraped, the granita is ready to eat.

Frozen Yogurt

Dessert items such as frozen yogurt are in great demand because of increased public concern over nutrition and healthy eating. There are, however, problems associated with producing this item. Sometimes there is an inability to obtain commercially used gums and additives for small-scale production of frozen yogurt. In their place, corn-starch, gelatin, or heavy cream can be used to prevent the product from freezing rock hard. Any flavor can be created from different fruits, flavorings, or liqueurs. A tasty, nonfat version of frozen yogurt can be prepared by using a nonfat yogurt and skim milk.

23

Chocolate

Chocolate

All bitter things conduce to sweet,
  As this example shows;
  Without the little spirochete
  We'd have no chocolate to eat,
  Nor would tobacco's fragrance greet
  The European nose.
  —*Richard Purdy Wilbur, from* Pangloss's Song: A Comic
    Opera Lyric

Chocolate is perhaps one of the most well-loved foods in the world. Cole Porter reportedly loved chocolate fudge so much that each month he had 10 pounds of it sent to him from his favorite confectioner in his hometown of Peru, Indiana. He was, and is, not alone in his love of this new-world discovery: Chocolate is a thriving $10-billion industry in the United States, with Americans consuming more than 2 billion pounds of it a year. For Valentine's Day alone, Americans spend between $400 and $500 million on this creamy, complex-tasting (over 400 flavor components exist in chocolate—more than in any other food) confection that apparently acts as a mood enhancer, while at the same time relaxing the lucky indulger. Many of the reasons why chocolate is so well loved remains a mystery, even to food scientists, but whether or not anyone can explain the legendary, almost drug-like qualities of chocolate, the bottom line is that it tastes great, which in turn means that pastry chefs must utilize its luscious flavor in everything from cakes to croissants and have a deep understanding of how this complex food should be handled and used.

The story of chocolate begins in South America, where the valued cocoa beans have grown for centuries and were carried north to Mexico by the Mayans before the seventh century A.D. Drinks of chocolate and water that were flavored with vanilla and various chiles were drunk by the Aztecs, Mayans, and Toltecs. These civilizations valued chocolate so much they used it as a form of currency. Columbus brought cocoa beans back to Spain in 1504, but the Spanish conquistador Hernando Cortez is credited with understanding and popularizing chocolate—he supposedly enjoyed a hot chocolate drink with the Aztec emperor Montezuma. The Aztecs believed chocolate to be an aphrodisiac and mood enhancer, and Aztec men drank it from golden cups. This "hot chocolate" was brought back to Spain, where sugar was added to it to enhance its flavor; indeed, the Spanish were soon enjoying many hot chocolate drinks that they flavored with vanilla, cinnamon, saffron, chiles, and rose petals.

By 1580, the Spanish had devised a method (taken from Mexican natives) of drying the chocolate, spices and all, into a paste that could be wrapped and allowed to harden; these tablets could then be sold easily for mixing with water. In spite of Spain's effort to keep chocolate to itself, by around 1650, its use had spread through most of western Europe, and chocolate houses were becoming important social meeting places, particularly in London.

Chocolate was rarely enjoyed as anything but a drink until 1828, when Conrad van Houten, a Dutchman searching for a way to make the chocolate drink less oily and filling, developed a screw process that removed most of the cocoa butter from the bean. In the process, van Houten "invented" cocoa powder. The excess cocoa butter that was extracted from the beans was added back to the original cocoa paste, greatly improving the texture. This single accomplishment made possible the development of chocolate candy.

The first chocolate developed specifically for eating enjoyment was introduced by the English firm of Fry and Sons in 1847; within 30 years, chocolate candy would be almost as much a rage as it is today. Milk chocolate was developed in 1876 by a Swiss confectioner, Daniel Peter, by using Henri Nestle's new development of dried milk. Soon after, in 1879, Rodolphe Lindt developed the technique of conching (named after the trough Lindt used to hold the chocolate, which was shaped like the conch shell.) This technique slowly kneads the chocolate and produces a smoother texture—a development that greatly impacted the popularity of chocolate. In 1913, Swiss confectioner Jules Sechaurd developed the world's first molded and filled chocolates. By World War II, the chocolate bar was so popular that it was given to American GIs as part of their field rations, resulting in a huge shortage of it on store shelves. GIs were known to hand it out (along with silk stockings) wherever they went—an act that made them uniquely popular. Today, chocolate continues to gain popularity, particularly in the United States and Europe. Although the United States consumes the largest share of the world's chocolate, the Swiss eat the most per capita—21 pounds per person annually.

The Making of Chocolate

Cocoa, which comes from the cocoa tree, is the main component in chocolate. The cocoa tree is a large evergreen that grows to approximately 30 feet in height and flourishes in warm climates close to the equator. The name *cacao* is a corruption of the Aztec word *cocao,* meaning "cocoa water" or "bitter water." The cocoa tree must have the right amount of moisture and heat for proper growing. Banana trees are usually planted between cocoa trees to shield them from too much sunlight, which can kill the cocoa tree.

Cocoa is grown around the world between 20° north and 20° south latitude. Most of the world's cocoa plantations are found in western Africa and in South and Central America. At this time, over 70% of the world's supply is grown in western Africa. Cocoa trees also flourish in some of the islands of the West Indies, in Sri Lanka, the Philippines, and other South Pacific islands. The leading cocoa-producing countries are Ghana, Brazil, Nigeria, Cameroon, and Ecuador. Every year, people in the United States consume more than one third of all the cocoa grown.

The Cocoa Bean

The cocoa tree is an evergreen that blooms all year around. Its tiny flowers may be white, pink, yellow, bright red, or two-toned, depending on the variety of tree. The fruit of the cocoa tree is called pods, which, when ripe, resemble small red, orange, or gold footballs. They grow directly on the trunk of the tree, as well as on the older branches. Some pods are smooth, some are deeply ridged, and many are flecked with dark brown or black.

The harvesting of the pods is conducted twice a year.

When they are ripe, they are picked and split open. Inside the pods are the cocoa beans.

Cocoa beans are oval, the size of an almond, and there are usually 50 beans in each pod, nestled in the white pulp. These beans are the main substance used in making chocolate. They are fermented and dried and go through many processes before they are transformed into chocolate bars and candies, chocolate ice cream, fudge sauce, hot chocolate, and other chocolate-flavored favorites.

Producing Chocolate

After the cocoa beans have been removed from the pod, the beans are fermented for approximately 6 days. The beans are placed in large piles and covered with banana leaves or burlap. Fermentation enhances and develops the flavor of the beans, takes away some of their bitterness, and destroys their ability to germinate or sprout. After fermentation the beans are sun-dried to prevent spoilage before, during, and after shipping. Drying lowers the moisture content of the beans and develops flavor that makes possible the transformation into chocolate. The beans are packed into large bags and shipped to processing plants all over the world.

Cleaning and Roasting

At the processing plant, the beans are cleaned utilizing brushes, air, and gravity. They are brushed, blown, and shaken over screens to remove dirt and foreign particles. Water is never used to clean cocoa beans. Next, the beans are roasted in special ovens at up to 300° F for 15 to 20 minutes. Roasting the beans enhances their flavor, darkens them, further dries them, and loosens the shell for removal. The beans are then cracked, and the shell is removed through the use of air. The pure bean without the shell is referred to as the nib.

The nibs, now in small pieces, are placed into a liquor mill and finely ground to produce a liquid mass, which is called chocolate or cocoa liquor. The nibs contain up to 55% cocoa fat, and the heat from the friction of the mill causes the dry cocoa to liquefy. The liquor is very bitter and can be sold as chocolate liquor or chocolate mass and as unsweetened chocolate (used to manufacture cocoa powder and cocoa butter), or can be used primarily as an ingredient in the making of sweet, eating chocolate.

Ingredients

To produce chocolate, the liquor is put in a mixer (mélangeur), and various ingredients are added to produce the different types of chocolate: dark chocolate (sweet, semi-sweet, and bitter), milk chocolate, and white chocolate. The ingredients for each are as follows:

Dark: Chocolate liquor, extra cocoa butter, granulated sugar, vanilla or vanillin, and soy bean lecithin.
Milk: Same as dark chocolate with dried or condensed milk. Fresh milk is seldom used because it contains a moisture content that is too high.
White: Cocoa butter, granulated sugar, vanilla or vanillin, lecithin, and dried or condensed milk. There is no chocolate liquor in white chocolate.

Note: In the United States, white chocolate cannot be sold under the name *chocolate.*

Lecithin emulsifies the components of the chocolate and gives the melted chocolate a more fluid consistency. Before lecithin was used in chocolate, extra cocoa butter was added in a great amount to make it fluid enough to work with when dipping or molding. Adding cocoa butter drove up the cost of the chocolate and caused a loss of flavor in the chocolate. Cocoa butter and lecithin also can be added during the conching.

After mixing, the chocolate is still harsh and gritty, so it is put into a refiner. It is sent through a roll press that crushes the particles and gives the chocolate a finer texture.

Conching

After the initial refining, the chocolate is conched. Conching further refines the chocolate by kneading, shaking, and pressing it for up to 72 hours. Conching affects the flavor and texture of the chocolate; the constant pressing reduces the ingredients to minute particles and creates a smooth texture. It is important to remember that the particles are ground, not dissolved. The shaking, sometimes referred to as kneading, further emulsifies the ingredients, so each particle will be surrounded with a layer of cocoa butter, which increases the smoothness of the chocolate and allows for even melting when eaten. Conching also aerates the chocolate.

Aeration of the chocolate is important because it helps evaporate unwanted volatile acids. This reduces the harshness of the flavor and mellows it. Aeration also removes some of the water that is still present in the chocolate, helping the chocolate to become more fluid. The more water removed, the more fluid the chocolate.

Conching, therefore, creates a chocolate that is smoother in texture, more fluid, better melting, and smoother in flavor. When conching is complete, the chocolate is tempered. After tempering, the chocolate is poured into molds, cooled, unmolded, and wrapped.

Cocoa Butter and Cocoa Powder

The chocolate liquor, containing up to 55% cocoa butter, is pressed by hydraulics to extract a large amount of the cocoa butter. The remaining liquor is now dry and disk-shaped; it is called a cocoa press cake. This cake is broken into small pieces and pulverized into cocoa powder. The *Dutch process* is a procedure that, through the use of alkaline chemicals, neutralizes some of the acids in the cocoa. The pure cocoa butter that is extracted can be used in the making of chocolate or sold as cocoa butter for confectionery, pharmaceutical, and cosmetic products.

Couverture

Couverture is a bulk chocolate that is used in the making of confections, pralines, and fine pastries. Couverture is a finer, higher-grade product than regular chocolate and is, therefore, more expensive. It is largely used in the dipping, enrobing, and molding of chocolate products, and in the making of special fillings. It is produced in the same way as chocolate, except that the percentage of cocoa butter is higher. The high percentage of cocoa butter provides more fluidity when the couverture is melted and a better shine when it sets, as well as a harder set (or snap) when the chocolate cools. Couverture is sold in dark, milk, and white forms, with a varying amount of cocoa butter in each.

FYI

Melting Chocolate:

1. *Clean the work area completely.*
2. *Set up the work area with a handled mixing bowl, white rubber spatula, a serrated knife, and a side towel.*
3. *Fill a large sauce pan with 1 quart of water, and place it on medium heat.*
4. *Remove the chocolate from its packaging, and chop across the block with medium strokes, using the serrated knife.*
5. *Continue chopping the chocolate until it is finely chopped.*
6. *Place the chocolate in the bowl, and place the bowl over the saucepan.*
7. *Begin to stir the chocolate with the white spatula; stir the chocolate constantly, but never beat it.*
8. *When about one third of the chocolate has melted, remove the bowl from the heat, taking care not to get any moisture droplets from the bottom of the bowl into the chocolate (wipe the bowl bottom with the side towel).*
9. *Continue stirring the chocolate—the residual heat will continue melting it.*
10. *Never fully melt the chocolate over the heat—it will be overheated.*
11. *Return the chocolate to the heat from time to time to keep it fluid, or hot chocolate (113° F to 122° F) can be added to it if it begins to get too cold.*

Chocolate also can be melted using a microwave; it should be placed in a microwaveable container and melted using a short time pulse so that it does not burn. The chocolate should be stirred between each pulse.

To melt chocolate using a warm oven, heating cabinet, or melting machine, adjust the temperature of the unit to the desired melted temperature of the chocolate. Let the chocolate fully melt; then stir well.

Tempering

Tempering chocolate is very important because it provides the chocolate with a nice, shiny, appealing appearance and smooth texture. Whenever chocolate is used for showpieces, for coating, or for molding, it must be tempered because of the cocoa butter in the chocolate. Cocoa butter is a fat comprising many different glycerides that have different melting and setting temperatures.

If the chocolate is not tempered before use, it will have negative effects on the product. When the chocolate sets, the cocoa butter will crystallize unevenly and improperly, causing the chocolate to take longer to set. The cocoa butter will not remain homogenized with the other ingredients and will separate, and some will flow to the surface, layering it. When the chocolate sets, the cocoa butter will turn grayish or whitish and appear in the form of a film, streaks, circles, or dots. This is called fat bloom or cocoa butter bloom. The chocolate also will have a grainy texture because of the improper crystal formation of the cocoa butter.

Tempering, therefore, is done to allow proper crystallization of the cocoa butter to occur and to allow it to set evenly and properly. Tempered chocolate will set more quickly than untempered chocolate and will not allow the cocoa butter time enough to separate and rise to the surface. The tempering process keeps the cocoa butter well emulsified with all of the other ingredients. There are six methods of tempering

- Table method
- Vaccination or shaving method
- Resting method
- Microwave method
- Machine method
- Cold-water bath method

Table Method

Heat the chocolate over a double boiler, stirring constantly, to 113° F, the temperature at which the cocoa butter will melt completely. Stirring the chocolate not only reduces the chance of overheating the chocolate, but also ensures that the chocolate melts evenly. Never heat dark chocolate higher than 122° F, and do not heat milk or white chocolate higher than 115° F.

Cool two thirds of the chocolate on a marble slab, moving it around with an offset spatula and bench scraper until it is pasty and is 80° F, for dark chocolate; 78° F, for milk chocolate; and 76° F, for white chocolate. Add the paste back to the remaining third of the chocolate, stirring well to prevent lumping. Slowly reheat the chocolate back to 90° F, for dark chocolate; 88° F, for milk chocolate; or 86° F, for white chocolate. The chocolate also can be reheated with more hot chocolate, if necessary. Always check the temperature before reheating the chocolate.

After the chocolate has reached its proper temperature, check to see if it sets properly and quickly. Also check the evenness of the setting and the appearance of the chocolate. Keep the chocolate at its maximum temperature for maximum fluidity and shine, to prevent the chocolate from needing retempering.

Vaccination Method No. 1

Vaccination is a very common and popular method of tempering. Use a mixer with a grating attachment to make chocolate shavings. Heat the chocolate to 113° F. Put enough additional shavings in the melted chocolate to make it pasty. Slowly reheat the chocolate to the proper temperature by either heating it over a double boiler or by adding more hot chocolate to it.

Vaccination Method No. 2

Melt the chocolate to 113° F. Slowly cool the chocolate by gradually adding chocolate shavings, while stirring constantly. Cool the chocolate to 90° F, for dark chocolate; 88° F, for milk chocolate; or 86° F, for white chocolate.

Resting Method

The resting method is used only for small amounts of chocolate. The chocolate is heated to 113° F. It is then allowed to rest, stirring occasionally, until it cools and becomes pasty. It is then reheated to the proper tempered temperature. A large piece of chocolate can be added to the melted chocolate to speed the cooling procedure. This piece is removed when the chocolate begins to paste.

Microwave Method

The tempered, set chocolate is chopped finely and placed in a microwaveable bowl. Slowly melt the chocolate, using short time pulses, stirring well between pulses, until the chocolate reaches, without exceeding, the proper tempered temperature. The microwave method is called a direct tempering method.

Machine Method

The machine method is also a direct tempering method. The tempering machine slowly melts the chocolate to the proper tempered temperature without exceeding it, thus preventing the chocolate from becoming untempered.

Cold-Water Bath Method

Chopped chocolate is heated to 113° F. The chocolate is cooled over a cold-water bath until it reaches a pasty consistency. It is then reheated to the proper tempered temperature. This method works particularly well for white chocolate. Ensure that no water from the bath is splashed onto the chocolate.

During tempering, the cooling chocolate builds the proper cocoa butter crystals needed in the chocolate. Reheating the chocolate brings it to a fluid consistency but still allows the crystallized cocoa butter to remain in its proper form. The crystallized cocoa butter acts as a base for the entire cocoa butter to crystallize evenly and properly. This base is called the seed.

If the chocolate is reheated higher than the proper temperature, the heat melts and destroys the seed, which is used by the remainder of the cocoa butter to act on; in turn, the cocoa butter will not crystallize properly. If dark chocolate is heated to 95° F or higher, the proper crystal structure is destroyed completely, and the chocolate must be tempered again to build a new seed. If dark chocolate is overheated but remains below 95° F, the chocolate can be "fixed" by cooling it a bit and then reheating it to the proper temperature. This cooling can be done by using either a cold water bath, a marble table top, or the addition of chocolate shavings or a colder tempered chocolate. Fixing a tempered chocolate may not always prove successful and sometimes results in a chocolate that appears tempered but is not as shiny; in this case, the chocolate should be retempered.

Chocolate Compound (Compound Chocolate)

Chocolate compound, also called summer coating, confectioner's coating, nontempering chocolate, or simply coating, is not real chocolate and does not need to be tempered. It contains other fats, such as vegetable shortening, and sometimes a small amount of cocoa butter and, therefore, is not true chocolate. It is less expensive than real chocolate, and although many excellent coatings exist, all are inferior to real chocolate in taste and strength. Coatings or compounds were developed as labor savers to prevent the necessity of tempering. Compound chocolates, however, should not be used in the making of pralines and chocolate showpieces.

Enemies of Chocolate

Moisture

Melted Chocolate

If moisture droplets get into melted chocolate, it will paste up and become thick and sluggish. Moisture surrounds sugar particles in the chocolate, increasing the friction between particles and causing them to move more slowly, which, in turn, increases the viscosity of the chocolate. This does not affect the taste or appearance of the chocolate when it is set. Once chocolate has moisture in it, however, it will remain pasty and can be used only for fillings.

Set Chocolate

In set chocolate, moisture will form water droplets on the surface of the chocolate and will begin to dissolve some of the sugar in the chocolate. The chocolate may be covered with a layer of sugar syrup, which eventually dries and forms a crust of sugar on the chocolate. This is called sugar bloom. Sugar bloom looks similar to fat bloom but, unlike fat bloom, does not dissolve when the chocolate is remelted. Sugar bloom is always due to moisture on set chocolate, not moisture in melted chocolate. It should be scraped off before the chocolate is melted. To prevent sugar bloom, chocolate should never be stored in a refrigerator.

Excessive Heat

Melted Chocolate

Chocolate is very sensitive to high temperatures and when overheated, will paste up, become grainy, and lose flavor. The graininess is due to the sugar crystals in the chocolate lumping together when it gets too hot. If the chocolate is not too grainy, it can be strained and used for fillings of lower quality. If the chocolate has too much graininess, it must be thrown away.

Set Chocolate

Excessive heat in set chocolate is usually due to improper storage temperatures. Because cocoa butter melts at a lower temperature than does body temperature, the heat of the human hand occasionally can also melt set chocolate. In either case, the cocoa butter will start to melt and soften and then separate and rise to the surface, causing fat bloom.

Storage

Chocolate must be wrapped properly and protected from light, strong odors, and foreign particles such as dust. It should be kept cool (at temperatures of 60° F to 65° F) and dry; the humidity in the room should not exceed 50%. Chocolate should never be stored in a refrigerator, or moisture will collect on its surface, causing sugar bloom.

Chocolate must be protected from light and, therefore, should be stored in a dark place. Light causes chocolate to spoil faster due to the cocoa butter's reaction to the light.

Chocolate can be frozen, but it must be done delicately. It should be wrapped airtight and must be frozen very quickly in a very cold freezer that keeps a constant temperature. The thawing of the chocolate should be done very gradually to prevent condensation, which will cause sugar bloom.

Texture Changes in Melted Chocolate

Cold

If melted chocolate becomes too cold, it will turn thick and pasty. The chocolate should be heated slightly to return it to the liquid state. Also, cold chocolate should not be

stirred too much without reheating it, or the chocolate will retain a large percentage of air bubbles. Chocolate will not shine as much and will have a dull appearance if it is used at too cold a temperature.

Overheating

Melted chocolate will turn pasty and grainy and lose some flavor if it is overheated or burned. If this happens, it can be strained and used as a flavoring for sponges, creams, and fillings. Chocolate that has been overheated cannot be used for pralines, fine fillings, or coatings.

Air

If chocolate is mixed incorrectly or mixed when it is too cold, too much air will be incorporated. The chocolate will show a lot of bubbles on its surface and will have a dull appearance when set; therefore, a whipping motion should never be used when stirring melted chocolate. If air bubbles are present, the warm chocolate can be placed in a warm area until air is released and the chocolate returns to a liquid consistency. For tempered chocolate, when time will not allow the chocolate to sit for a while, it should be reheated just to 113° F and then retempered.

Moisture

If melted chocolate comes into contact with moisture, it will become thick and pasty and cannot be used for coating. If the melted chocolate is not tempered, it will separate. These chocolates can be used for ganaches, flavoring, sauces, and some fillings.

Overuse

If chocolate is reused again and again without the addition of fresh chocolate, it will become thicker in consistency. A bit of new chocolate should be added to the used batch each time it is worked.

Buying Chocolate

Chocolate should be covered by an opaque wrapper to prevent exposure to sunlight and foreign particles; its surface should be appealing and shiny. Chocolate should have a sharp, clean break. It should always be tasted before buying; it should taste and smell like chocolate and have a deep, rich flavor. It should not taste chalky, like cocoa powder. When tasted, the chocolate should melt evenly on the tongue and have a smooth texture, with a soft flavor that is not harsh.

Pralines

The term *praline* is the professional term for chocolate candies. It refers to a small, bite-sized, chocolate-based product. Chocolate is always involved in a praline. The name comes from the Duke of Plessi Praslin, a field marshal of the French armies under Louis XIII and Louis XIV who lived during the seventeenth century. His chef accidentally mixed toasted nuts with caramelized sugar and served the result as a candy, which he named *praline,* after the name of the Duke. The term *praline* also can refer to the flavor of praline, which is a mixture of toasted hazelnuts or almonds and caramelized sugar; in the southwestern United States and Mexico, pralines are candies made from a sugar and pecan mixture.

Types of Fillings

The filling of a praline refers to the filling that is not yet shaped. After the filling is shaped, it is then referred to as the center, or intèrieur. The number of fillings or pralines is endless due to the countless combinations that can be acquired by mixing together different fillings.

Chocolate-Based Fillings

Widely used fillings containing chocolate are ganache, butter ganache, and gianduja.

Ganache

The two main ingredients in ganache are chocolate and a water-based liquid: milk, cream, teas, or orange juice. Any other ingredients, such as fat, flavorings, or alcohol, are optional. Additional sugars, such as glucose, corn syrup, and granulated sugar, also can be added to improve the texture and shine of the ganache. Egg yolks are sometimes used to make a richer ganache.

Ganache is prepared by bringing the liquid to a boil. The liquid is removed from the heat and added to the finely chopped chocolate. The mixture is whisked until all of the ingredients are well blended, the chocolate has completely melted, and the mixture is smooth. A rubber spatula should be used to scrape the sides of the bowl to ensure that all of the chocolate is incorporated.

Any fats to be added to a ganache should be added with the chocolate or at a later point and not boiled with the liquid; this prevents overheating the chocolate. Additional sugars should be brought to a boil with the liquid to prevent graininess in the final product. Flavorings or liqueurs should be added after the mixture is completely smooth to avoid the evaporation of the alcohol and loss of flavor. The cold liquor can also interfere with the melting of the chocolate, if added too soon. Egg yolks, if used, are heated with the liquid until they are thickened, as in a crème anglaise.

Points to remember when making ganache for filling pralines:

- The boiling of the liquid not only raises the temperature high enough to melt the chocolate, but also prolongs the shelf life of the ganache by destroying the bacteria present in the liquid.
- Using cream or milk that is too old will result in the separation of fat(s).
- Overheating the ganache causes separation of the fat.
- Overwhipping or overmixing the ganache once it has set also will cause the fat to separate.
- If the fat content in the ganache is too high, the ganache will separate; most ganaches should have a fat content of approximately 30%.
- If the amount of liquid added to a ganache is too low, the ganache will separate. This can be corrected by adding more liquid to it.

- Ganache has a very short shelf life due to the high percentage of water and/or dairy products used. It should never be handled directly with unprotected hands.
- Ganache will stay fresh for approximately 2 weeks if handled properly. After this time, a flavor change will occur, diminishing the fine quality of the praline.
- When used in pralines, ganache should be completely covered with chocolate to prevent its drying out and spoiling. The ganache filling will spoil long before the chocolate.
- Ganache may have fat-based or water-based flavorings added to it. It also can have the addition of nuts, candied fruits, praline paste, crushed nougat, or dried fruit.

Butter Ganache

The two main ingredients in a butter ganache are butter and chocolate. Optional ingredients are sugar (the best sweetener to use is fondant), alcohol, and flavorings. To prepare butter ganache, the butter and sweetener are whipped to a light consistency; then the alcohol and/or flavorings are added. This mixture is whipped again for a short while and then folded into tempered chocolate by hand using a rubber spatula. This filling should be used quickly.

Points to remember when making butter ganache:

- The butter must be brought to room temperature (70° F) before whipping. Cold butter will not incorporate air well, and it will take a long time to become light and fluffy.
- The butter should be well whipped before adding any alcohol or flavorings, because butter with too small an amount of air incorporated will not emulsify well with a liquid.
- The amount of air incorporated into the butter can vary depending on the firmness of the praline: If the filling is to be cut, less air should be incorporated; if the filling is to be piped, more air should be incorporated.
- Tempered chocolate should be used in the filling to ensure a smooth, homogenous product that is consistent in texture. If an untempered chocolate is used,

the result may be a product that is not well emulsified, and it may become grainy once set.
- Tempered chocolate must be at the maximum temperature possible; this will allow enough time for the chocolate to be folded into the butter without solidifying. If the chocolate is untempered or too warm, the filling will separate, giving the filling too soft a consistency and a grainy, less smooth texture when set.
- Because the filling will firm up rapidly once it is made, it should be used immediately.
- A butter ganache should be dipped in chocolate quickly and completely, because it will absorb foreign odors and change taste, as well as dry out faster than most other fillings. The shelf-life of a butter ganache, however, is longer than that of a regular ganache. As with most fillings, the flavor of a butter ganache can change during storage; therefore, the finished praline should be consumed quickly.

Gianduja

Gianduja is a filling that is based on toasted hazelnuts or almonds and sugar, ground to a very fine consistency, and mixed together with chocolate and/or cocoa butter. One easy method of making gianduja is mixing together dark, milk, or white chocolate and praline paste. Praline paste is a mixture of sugar and toasted hazelnuts (almonds also are used) that have been refined to a peanut butter consistency. Gianduja can be purchased pre-made and used in a variety of ways as a filling. It also can be made with other nuts, such as peanuts, cocoa nuts, or pistachios. Gianduja is waterless and has a much longer shelf life than does ganache. It can keep well for several months.

Gianduja can be prepared by heating chocolate to 113° F, adding the praline paste, and then tempering the mixture in the same manner that chocolate is tempered; the cold-water bath method works particularly well for giandujas. The filling can than be shaped as desired. Another method for preparing a gianduja is to simply mix the praline paste with chocolate that already has been tempered; then the filling can be shaped as desired. Because it contains real chocolate, a handmade gianduja should always be tempered to ensure the proper setting of the cocoa butter in the filling. Using an untempered gianduja will result in a filling that does not set well, making it difficult to cut; in addition, the texture of the filling will not be as smooth as that of a tempered gianduja.

Nut Fillings

The main ingredient in nut fillings is plain or toasted nuts. The methods of using them may vary by using chopped, whole, or ground nuts. Marzipan and nougat are both considered nut fillings. The nuts can be used by themselves or with other fillings.

Marzipan Filling

Marzipan is a commonly used filling in a European praline. Marzipan is an almond dough of almond paste, fondant, confectioner's sugar, and glucose. For praline fillings, the marzipan is flavored and sometimes softened with liqueurs to obtain a range of different consistencies. It is important that the marzipan is not overmixed; this may cause its oil to separate, causing it to be crumbly. Because marzipan can be purchased rather than made, marzipan fillings are quick and easy to make.

Nougat Fillings

There are two types of nougat: brown and white. Both can be used as a filling for pralines.

Brown nougat is also called croquant (French) or krokant (German); it is a mixture of caramelized sugar and lightly toasted nuts, classically almonds. Soft nougats are used in pralines and are made by mixing the nougat with other ingredients, such as cream, corn syrup or glucose, honey, or fruit juices. Candied fruits, chocolate, almond paste, praline paste, or other flavorings also can be added.

White nougat is also called Torrone or Montelimar and is similar to what Americans would call divinity. It is a mixture of a type of Italian meringue and honey that is beaten over a bain marie until most of the water in the meringue has evaporated, giving the meringue a firm consistency when it is cold. Toasted nuts, flavorings, and sometimes candied fruits are folded into the meringue immediately before it is pressed between bars for shaping

and cutting. Once cut, the nougat is dipped in tempered chocolate.

Most nougat fillings are sensitive to moisture because of their high sugar content; if exposed to air for too long before dipping, they will become sticky, soften, and lose their shape. Because of their high sugar content, they have a longer shelf life than most other fillings and will keep for several months.

Fruit Fillings

Fresh fruit should never be used in fillings because the water content is too high and will cause spoilage and make the praline too difficult to dip for finishing. The acid content is also very high and will actually begin to dissolve the chocolate; the filling also may begin to leak out of the chocolate shell. Preserved fruits, therefore, must be used.

There are several different methods of preserving fruits for pralines:

- Liquor fruits are soaked in alcohol until the water in the fruit is actually exchanged for the alcohol and the fruit is completely saturated.
- For candied fruits, the water in the fruit is exchanged for sugar in a process that completely saturates the fruit with a sugar syrup.
- When using dried fruits, the drying of the fruit removes the moisture. The dried fruits are usually cut and cooked or soaked in alcohol or sugar syrup to ensure that they are not too tough to eat. They provide a particularly distinctive flavor.
- Fruits cooked in a high percentage of sugar also can be used. Preserves, jellies, and jam compounds are examples. The high sugar content and the cooking process preserve the fruit.

Sugar Fillings

Sugar fillings are very inexpensive to use and have an extremely long shelf life. They are also easy to produce by machine. For these reasons, sugar fillings are commonly used in the manufacture of cheaper chocolate candies. These fillings consist of a high amount of different types of sugar. Most sugar fillings are based on a concentrated cooked sugar solution. After cooking, this mixture is cooled, either with the formation of small, fine crystals (fondant, cream fillings, or fudge) or without the formation of crystals (caramel, taffy, brittle, or toffee).

Liquid Fillings

Liquid fillings are completely liquid, based on a sugar syrup that is usually flavored and that is completely covered with chocolate. There are five different ways to fill the chocolate with liquid fillings.

Starch Method

The starch method is one of the oldest methods and also one of the most difficult. Wheat or cornstarch is used. The starch used should be dried for several days in a low-temperature (140° F) oven. The starch is then placed in a 3-inch-high frame. Then the starch is packed down lightly using a ruler until it is level with the sides of the frame. A praline stamp is then pressed into the starch in at least 1-inch intervals.

A sugar syrup is then made for the filling. The density of the sugar syrup must be precise in the final liquid; a Baumé measure should be used. The syrup must have 32° Baumé after being flavored. The starch molds are then filled with the warm liquid using a funnel that can be controlled at its opening with a wooden spoon or stick to prevent leakage of the syrup.

At this point, a half-inch layer of starch is sifted over the filled molds so that they are completely covered; the molds are then allowed to rest for at least 24 hours. During this process, the sugar will begin to crystallize around the starch, but remain liquid in the center, forming a crust around the filling. Once a crusty layer has formed, the sugar shells are removed from the starch. The starch is then removed with a soft brush. The fillings can then be dipped carefully in tempered chocolate.

Prepared Shell Method
The most popular way to use liquids is to use already prepared chocolate shells. These shells are filled with a liquid center and then sealed and dipped into tempered chocolate.

Chocolate Molds
Regular candy molds can be used, but for this method, a sealing chocolate must first be sprayed, not spread, over the filled molds.

Fruit and Fondant I
If using a combination of liqueur, fruit, and fondant as a filling, after a few days the fruit will dissolve the fondant and turn it into a liquid.

Fondant and Invertase
Invertase can be used with fondant. Invertase is an enzyme that will break down the creamy texture of the fondant into a sugar syrup after the fillings have been surrounded by a shell of chocolate.

Items Not Used for Fillings

- Fresh fruit, for reasons discussed previously.
- Flour or starch in the filling, or products made with flour or starch. The use of these would make the praline a petít four.
- Compound chocolate, because the taste of compound chocolate is not of high quality and the consistency is different than that of chocolate; most fillings made with compound chocolate will not have the proper consistency or flavor.
- Fresh egg products. If eggs are used, they should be heated and/or pasteurized because of their high spoilage factor and the threat of contamination by salmonella. Egg products also will cause a filling to change its flavor after a shorter period and cause the praline to have a shorter shelf life.

Dipping Conditions for Pralines
Temperature

The process of dipping pralines is known as enrobing. The temperature of the room, the filling, and the chocolate are all very important when dipping pralines. These conditions will greatly determine the final appearance, quality, and shelf life of the finished product. The room temperature should be 68° F. The temperature of the filling should be the same as the room temperature, or a little higher, but no more than 74° F. The temperature of the filling should never be lower than the room temperature. The chocolate should be tempered to the highest temperature possible: 90° F for dark, 88° F for milk, and 86° F for white. Problems will arise if the temperatures are ignored.

If the filling is too warm when dipped, the chocolate around the warm filling will take too long to set, allowing enough time for some of the cocoa butter to separate. The cocoa butter will then float to the surface, resulting in a fat bloom.

If the filling temperature is colder than room temperature, condensation of water will collect around the filling. The wetness of the filling will make the filling difficult to dip. Consequently, the moisture from the filling will end up in the dipping chocolate and cause the chocolate to paste up. If the filling *can* be dipped, the chocolate layer will be too thick because of the coldness of the filling and because the chocolate will not run off as easily. The praline will be too large, the taste will be overpowered by the chocolate, and the food cost will rise due to the overuse of chocolate. In addition, the cocoa butter will set unevenly (from the inside out) and will result in a dull appearance. Also, when the chocolate cools to the temperature of the filling, condensation will collect on the chocolate due to the coldness of the filling in opposition to the warmth of the room. This condensation eventually will cause sugar bloom. Finally, the filling eventually will warm to the temperature of the room; as it warms, it will expand and cause the chocolate shell to crack, exposing the filling to air and causing it to spoil or dry out.

If the room temperature is too warm while dipping, the chocolate around the filling will take too long to set, and the same problems will occur as when the filling is too warm.

If the room temperature is too cold while dipping, the dipping chocolate will set too fast, making the dipping procedure difficult. In addition, the chocolate will have to be reheated constantly.

If the chocolate temperature is too warm while dipping,

the chocolate becomes untempered. The result will be a fat bloom. If the chocolate temperature is too cold while dipping, the set chocolate will be too thick and will have the tendency to incorporate a lot of air when stirred; this also will result in a dull appearance when set.

Storage of Pralines

The storage of pralines is basically the same as for chocolate; however, the shelf life of each type of praline is not the same due to the different fillings. The enemies of pralines are the same as the enemies of chocolate.

Molded Chocolates

Pralines that use a mold and are filled and then sealed are referred to as molded pralines. Molding chocolates is a time-efficient way of making pralines. There are molds designed specifically for use in molding chocolates. The molds can be made of different substances, including hard plastic, metal, silicone, and soft plastic. Hard plastic molds are the best to use, but they are the most expensive. Soft plastic molds are inexpensive, but do not last as long as the others and can be more difficult to handle.

Procedures for Molded Pralines

The same procedures are used for all molds. Tempered couverture chocolate should always be used:

1. The molds should be at room temperature. The cavity of the molds should be rubbed with cotton before use to remove impurities and foreign particles. The tempered couverture should always be at maximum temperature for maximum fluidity, and there should be no lumps in the chocolate.
2. A warmed ladle is used to ladle the chocolate into each of the mold's cavities. If the molds have a very detailed design, they should be brushed first with a thin layer of chocolate before they are filled.
3. Once filled, the molds should be tapped with the end of a spatula in two different directions to remove air bubbles.

4. The tapped molds should then be inverted over the source of chocolate (for drips) to release the excess; then the molds should be tapped again very lightly.

5. The molds then should be placed upside down over a dipping screen and left on the screen to set until the wet, melted appearance of the chocolate has disappeared, but the chocolate is still soft.

6. As soon as the wet, melted appearance of the chocolate has disappeared, the excess chocolate is scraped off with a bench scraper. If the chocolate sets completely, it will crack when scraped. If the chocolate is scraped too soon, all of the scraped chocolate will be pushed into the cavities of the molds.

7. At this point, the shells are ready to be filled. The filling is piped in, and it should have a somewhat fluid consistency to fill the shells evenly. A filling that is too stiff cannot be filled evenly and will leave too much head space; this will require too much chocolate to seal off this space. The temperature of the filling should be between 80° F and 85° F so as not to affect the chocolate. The filling will shrink a bit when cooling down. The shells can now be filled. A 1/10-inch space should be left between the top of the mold and the filling: A space is needed for the covering of the chocolate. The filling should be allowed to set a bit.

8. The remaining space is then covered with tempered couverture, using a spatula. The chocolate should be gently poured over the filling and spread with the spatula: Any excess chocolate should be scraped off, using the spatula, while the chocolate is still melted.

9. The chocolate should then be left to set completely; it can be put in a refrigerator for a few minutes, if necessary. The chocolate should have released from the molds before it is removed from the molds; this will be indicated by the appearance of a lighter-colored chocolate than that previously poured into the molds. The finished chocolates can be removed from their molds by twisting the molds, inverting them, and releasing the pralines. There are several reasons why pralines will not come out of the mold: The mold may be damaged or scratched, the choco-late was not tempered, the filling was too warm and melted the chocolate, the layer of chocolate on the mold was too thin, or the chocolate had not completely set and released itself. If the chocolate was not completely released, the unreleased section will be dull.

Points to Remember

- If the molds get too cold before the unmolding, allow the chocolate to warm to room temperature before unmolding them, to prevent condensation around the pralines.
- After using the molds, if they are going to be used again soon, they may be wiped with cotton. If they are to be stored, they should be washed with a very mild soap and warm water, and then dried for storage.
- Chocolate that is too cold and thick should not be used for molding; this will cause the chocolate shell to be too thick, and air bubbles present in the chocolate may cause holes to form in the shell. In addition, the base of the praline will not adhere to the shell, and the filling will leak or dry out.

Molded Pralines Used in Production

Ganache Cordials

Ganache cordials use a liqueur-flavored ganache that is softened and piped into shells using a no. 1 straight tip; then the molding procedure is followed.

Chocolate Fondant Liqueur

Chocolate fondant liqueur incorporates two fillings: a liqueur-flavored fondant and a fruit soaked in the liqueur; any flavor can be used. The fondant used should be heated to 105° F so that it will dry faster and create a skin. This gives it more structure, so that it is easier to cover with chocolate. Before using the fondant, the temperature should be reduced to 85° F. The fruit is placed on the bottom of the mold, and the fondant is piped on top of the fruit.

24

Dessert Presentations

Dessert Presentations

dessert *di-'zert***n**: a course of fruit, pastry, pudding, ice cream, or cheese served at the close of a meal.

What is a dessert? At its most basic, it is a food that satisfies a craving for something sweet. At its most elaborate, it is an elegant, sometimes complex presentation of a series of components—these components are all well-thought out and executed with critical timing behind the scenes by the chef. The diner is simply there to enjoy. In this way, plating desserts for presentation is like being on stage; the cue comes when the order is placed, and the ovation is seeing a satisfied customer enjoy a seemingly effortless task.

In reality, of course, dessert presentations require an extreme amount of mise en place and expertise from the pastry chef; most desserts also require crucial timing from the wait staff as well. Chefs use the plate as a sort of frame to display the food items in a visually artistic and creative way.

There are many considerations that must go into the design of a dessert plate. First, the menu must be designed according to the season (many pastry chefs change their menus weekly) and the style of the restaurant. As soon as the chef knows what product is available, a menu can be designed based on the freshest ingredients possible. Most dessert menus are comprised of at least six desserts; some have as many as 12.

By presenting the dessert in a visually pleasing light, the perceived value of the dessert is increased; in other words, even though the dessert components are basically the same as they would be if they were presented in another manner (such as on a dessert cart), the extra effort put into the dessert makes it so much more appealing to the customer that he or she is willing to pay more for it. The concept of plating in this manner has been popular in the United States for about 15 to 20 years; by the late 1980s and early 1990s, the idea of plating desserts for presentation had almost completely replaced the dessert cart as a means of presentation (the dessert cart is once again on the rise, as of this writing).

Restaurateurs and chefs have always known to use their dessert menu as a way to boost check averages and create signature items that arouse and keep customers' interest. In today's restaurant, the dessert may be the reason a customer initially steps through the door. Many pastry chefs use the idea of a menu standard, or filler, as some chefs refer to it, as a way to fill out the menu and create association between themselves and their customers. Fillers are signature items that both the chef and the restaurant become known for and that customers come to expect.

Simple presentations with the focus of the plate's components relying more on flavor than on architecture are an underlying theme in today's desserts. Chefs agree that unless a restaurant or hotel boasts a large staff that can accommodate the orchestration involved in a complicated dessert presentation, the best option is to stick to simple presentations that do not intimidate or confuse the customer.

Most restaurants are reducing their staffs to a minimum, and the rising popularity of bistros—great food for less money—makes a complicated plate presentation impossible for most restaurants. The presentation also should match that of the dining room and the abilities of the wait staff. A soufflé cake served à la minute could not be served without the pastry chef's reliance on the competence of the wait staff; this is why pastry chefs must build and maintain a constant connection with the front of the house.

Flavor is obviously the most important consideration when designing a dessert for presentation. Chocolate is a constant flavor consideration when creating a dessert menu, but just because it is popular does not mean it should be overused. Fruit, in almost any form, is extremely popular on dessert menus and, while some chefs order off-season fruits from South America and New Zealand, most chefs stress the importance of using locally grown produce to produce menu items that will always be fresh and available. Sorbets and ice creams are prevalent on dessert menus even in winter; many chefs are using sorbets and ice creams as a way of complementing other items in a presentation and developing a contrast between hot and cold. Chefs are also experimenting with the array of dried fruit available, particularly for use on winter menus; although the cost can sometimes be as expensive as shipped fresh fruits, the flavor is more reliable, and chefs are finding exciting ways to use these fruits in winter compotes and fruit chutneys.

The Four Components of a Plated Dessert

There are four basic components to work with when creating a dessert:

1. *The main item:* This is the main part of the dish, what is designated on the menu. The main item is usually between 3 and 5 ounces for plating.
2. *The sauce:* There can, of course, be more than one sauce, but the total weight of all sauces should be between 1 and 2 ounces. Sauces can complement or contrast with the flavor of the main item.
3. *The garnish:* One of the most interesting components, the garnishment is anything from powdered sugar dusted lightly over the plate to a sorbet or ice cream for a contrast in temperature and texture.
4. *The crunch component:* Used when the main item does not contain flour, it is a decorative cookie that gives textural contrast to the main item. It can be used for any dessert, if desired, but should always be used if the main item contains no flour.

Types of Plating

There are two methods of executing a plated dessert:

Banquet Style

In banquet plating, sometimes as many as several thousand plates may be needed for a function. This type of plating usually takes place at large hotels and banquet halls. With this type of plating, all the plates are prepped and plated ahead of time and for service. This limits the type of dessert designed for this type of service; ice cream, soufflés, and other items that must be served immediately cannot be considered for large banquets. Many banquets are prepped before the time of service, and then a line is created by the pastry chef and his staff during service to pass the plate from worker to worker, each one with a specific task that will complete the plate. This can only be done with small banquets, however; large banquets require the plates to be entirely set up ahead of time.

À la Minute

Literally, "by the minute," this type of plating is found more often in restaurants where the pastry chef puts together all the items as they are ordered. This type of plating demands a great deal of prep work; otherwise, the customer would have to wait too long to receive a dish. In addition, often the wait staff is instrumental in seeing that the final garnish is put on the plate, or that the dessert is carried to the table at just the right moment (as in a soufflé); this requires a great deal of teamwork between the pastry staff and the wait staff.

Plating Contrasts

Certain contrasts are available to the pastry chef when plating; although only one or two might be used on a given plate, all provide interest for the diner and should be considered when creating a plate design.

Texture

One of the most effective contrasts available is one of texture: Smooth, velvety-textured components, crunchy components, or chewy-textured items, when placed together, all make the dessert more interesting to eat. A crunch component is always used when the main item of the plate does not contain flour—or if the item does contain flour but is particularly smooth.

Temperature

Temperature contrasts are excellent ways to develop interest on the plate. Hot items should be served hot, and cold items should be served cold; this means an à la minute plating style and much coordination between the front and back of the house.

Shape

The plate will be more visually interesting if there are a number of visual contrasts. Overcomplexity should be avoided, however; the customer should never feel as if he or she needs to dismantle the food before it can be eaten.

Flavor

Just because desserts are sweet does not mean that everything on the plate has to be; a contrast of sweet versus sour, or dark, heavy flavors contrasted with light ones make the dessert more appealing.

Color

Color provides one of the easiest and most visually interesting ways to add contrast to a plate.

Tips for Plating

Plated desserts require a great deal of mise en place and time management skills. Every chef will develop her own philosophy regarding the design and execution of plated desserts according to her background and experience. The following tips are mentioned as guidelines and suggestions, not steadfast rules.

- Subtle flavors should never be completely overpowered by stronger, contrasting flavors.
- Too much complexity in a plate design confuses the eye and the palate; keep designs and contrasts interesting, but simple.
- Balance the plate: Everything about the plate—the flavors, the colors, the shapes—should balance with one another. Asymmetric or symmetric balance can be used, but it is important to create the type of balance that will allow the main item to be the focal point.
- All the elements on the plate should work together to harmoniously combine, rather than just use components to fill space. Items should work together as a single offering.
- A flow or movement should be created with the placement and shape of the components that leads the eye toward the main item.
- Piped items should be piped thinly and neatly. Chocolate, food gels, and thickened sauces are often used as barriers for the sauce—a way of holding the sauce within a certain design.
- Glazes should be used sparingly and only if they can enhance the natural shine or color of an item.
- All the items on the plate should be edible, with the exclusion of stems or other natural parts of the food.
- Unnatural colors, such as blue, black, or pink, should be avoided.
- The plate selection should be taken into consideration before designing the dessert.

Sauces

The consistency and appearance of the sauce is tantamount to the success of the plate design. Most sauces should be smooth in texture and thick enough to coat the back of a spoon. Multiple sauces that are to be married together for feathering into a design should be of the same consistency; a heavy sauce will sink into a thin sauce and ruin the design. Like consistencies in the sauces will also prevent one sauce from bleeding into another. Following are the 10 basic types of sauces that can be used for plating a dessert:

- *Coulis:* A coulis is a puréed fruit sauce. It is made by puréeing the fruit and adjusting the sauce's flavor and consistency with simple syrup. It can be made with fresh, canned, frozen, or dried fruits, but it is never cooked.
- *Cooked fruit sauce:* This is basically a coulis that is reduced to thicken or alter its color or flavor. Reduction of any sauce should be done in a wide, shallow pan over low heat. Some fruits should be sweetened after they are heated to avoid a candylike flavor.
- *Thickened sauce:* This is a sauce that is thickened with a thickening agent; cornstarch, arrowroot, or instant starches can be used. These sauces often use the cooked-juice method for making a pie as their method of procedure.

To thicken a sauce with instant ClearJel, use 1 ounce of starch for every pint of liquid used. Twenty percent of the weight of the starch is the weight for the amount of sugar needed.

- *Egg-yolk–based sauces:* These sauces are basically curds; they are made with egg yolks, sugar, and butter, and are usually flavored with citrus. They are tart, yet sweet and usually thicker than other sauces.
- *Crème Anglaise:* This is a classic custard sauce made from egg yolks, milk, cream, and sugar.
- *Sabayon:* This is a classic sauce of egg yolks, sugar, and Marsala wine. The mixture is whisked over a water bath until it has reached a light peak. It should be cooked at 145° F for 3 minutes to pasteurize the eggs. It is also known by its Italian name, *zabaglione.* Sabayon is classically served over fresh fruits that are lightly tossed with sugar and a liqueur.
- *Chocolate sauce:* There are three types: crème anglaise based, which is made with a crème anglaise that is flavored with chocolate; syrup or ganache based, which is made by using the method of procedure for a ganache—often, instead of heavy cream, a sugar syrup is used; and cocoa based, which is made by making a paste of cocoa and water and cooking with sugar over low heat until it boils.

- *Reductions:* Almost any sauce can be reduced to thicken it, but this category generally encompasses reductions of juices or sweet wines that are used for sauces.
- *Caramel sauce:* This sauce is the combination of caramelized sugar, heavy cream, and butter.
- *Preserve-based sauces:* These sauces are any sauce made with a preserve and sugar syrup. The most well-known preserve-based sauce is Melba sauce, which was invented to go with the classic ice-cream dessert *peach melba.*

Buffets and Buffet Catering

Buffet is a fairly loose term that applies to many different types of occasions. There may be no more than sandwiches and other finger foods served, or it may be an elaborate meal of many courses. A buffet may contain both hot and cold dishes, or just desserts, and the food might be picked up by the guests or served by waiters.

Planning Buffets

When planning any menu, gastronomics, economics, and practicalities should be taken into consideration. The same applies to a buffet. Some considerations in planning a buffet are

- Placement of the table and available space.
- Number of zones.
- Centerpieces.
- Theme of the buffet, if any. Decor should follow the theme.
- Space needed behind the buffet table for people to serve from platters.

Many times, the chef (usually a pastry cook) will attend a station or stations at a buffet. There are advantages and disadvantages to chefs serving at buffets, which must be taken into account when planning. The advantages to chefs serving at buffets include the following:

- The chef is on site to explain to guests accurately what is being served.
- The flow of guests moves more quickly.
- Platters are kept neater.
- Guests enjoy seeing professionals serve elegant and dramatic dessert presentations such as crêpes suzette or cherries jubilee.

The disadvantages to having chefs serve are that

- The cost of labor is higher than for a self-service buffet.
- More space is needed for service personnel.

Different Types of Buffets

Breakfast Buffets

Many hotels offer patrons a buffet breakfast with a wide selection of dishes organized for self-service. The selection varies widely from one region to another and from one continent to another. Included are breads and rolls with butter, cheeses, jams and marmalades, cold meats and fish, hot grilled items on hot plates, fresh and stewed fruit, fruit juices, and possibly breakfast cereals.

Full Buffets

A full buffet is a main meal, only distinguished from a dinner or luncheon because the food is displayed in the dining room. For a full buffet, tables and chairs are essential for all guests, and the tables should be fully laid with china, cutlery, and glassware. The food is displayed on the buffet table, which gives the chef an opportunity to demonstrate skill at decorating and garnishing dishes. It must be remembered, however, that if the guests are to choose their own food, the garnishing cannot be overly elaborate. Simple but effective garnishing is needed, which may either be

removed just prior to service or served to the guests without spoiling the appearance of the dish.

Fork Buffets

A *fork buffet* has been defined as a meal that can be eaten standing up, with a plate in one hand and a fork in the other. These events are ideally suited when space will not permit tables and chairs for everyone. Nevertheless, as many tables and chairs should be provided as possible. A fork-buffet table should look just as attractive as that for a full buffet, but the range of foodstuffs cannot be as varied. A menu at the buffet is required because dishes are not always easy for guests to identify. A fork buffet is obviously less formal than a sit-down buffet, but people tend to eat less, possibly because it is more difficult to eat standing up. It is important to provide plenty of table napkins of good quality and adequate size.

Finger Buffets

Finger buffets are the least formal type of buffet. Like fork buffets, they are particularly suitable when the host wishes guests to mingle with each other. This ability to circulate makes a finger buffet particularly appropriate for a modest wedding reception when distant relatives are attending. A finger buffet may take the place of a main meal, but it is generally only a snack meal, frequently served at a time of day when guests will not be anticipating a substantial amount of food.

Care must be taken that the food offered can be eaten without cutlery, and most foods should be in bite-size pieces. A slice from a large quiche, for example, cannot be eaten without a fork, whereas small, individual quiches are ideal finger foods. With a finger buffet, plenty of large napkins are essential, and finger bowls are in good taste. Although the food can readily be eaten standing up, it is still advisable to have as many chairs and tables available as possible at least for the convenience of elderly guests and others who may not be comfortable standing for long periods.

Basic differences between formal and informal buffets

are the type of service, the ingredients, and the layout of the buffet table.

Zones

A zone represents the design and plan of each buffet area for the smooth and speedy flow of patron traffic. A single-zone buffet may serve 75 to 125 people. Additional zones should be added accordingly to ensure rapid service and shorter lines. The size of the dining room must also be taken into consideration when determining zones. Each zone should contain the same menu items.

Centerpieces and other items should be presented to enhance the appearance of the buffet table. Many buffets are based on a theme, and their centerpieces and decor are chosen to enhance the theme. Suggestions include

- Ice carvings.
- Bread, pastillage, or sugar centerpieces.
- Flowers, bouquets, or heads.
- Ferns or vines arranged around the platters.
- Velvet or other colored fabrics to act as a socle.
- Napkin folds.
- Ornate silver platters, mirrors, or glass bowls.
- Baskets of fruit or bread.
- Candelabras.

Food Presentation on Buffet Platters

Most people eat with their eyes. The first impression, perceived through vision, will set the tone for the palate. The flowing harmony of ingredients on a plate or platter should arouse the appetite of the guest or customer. To achieve that harmony, the chef will need to use his or her imagination, talent, creativity, and skill. Some of the characteristics needed to make a harmonious presentation are color, texture, shape, height, and contrast.

Color

Color is the most important factor of presentation. The eyes will be attracted to a pleasing mixture of colors. If the color is uniform, then one item will not be differentiated from another. The color may be an indication of the pastry chef's skills. The vibrancy of the color should reflect the use of the proper cooking technique.

Texture

The foods on a plate or platter should be of varying consistencies. The palate should enjoy a mixture of textures. Not all foods should be crisp because this will have a tendency to hurt the mouth. Not all food products should be soft because the mouth will become bored. The diner should encounter food products with a variety of textures.

Shape

Foods should be of proper proportions. No food item should be so large that everything else becomes insignificant. Shapes can be natural or created. Do not try to change the pleasing curve created by nature. Use it as is.

Height

Height will give dimension and depth. The main items should have the most height because they are the focus of attraction. If a product is too flat, use a socle to raise it. Socles can be made of bread, fruits, or starches.

Contrast

Contrast encompasses all aspects of presentation. Different colors, shapes, sizes, textures, and heights help create the proper contrast. If one characteristic is more dominant, then the proper balance has not been achieved.

Appendix A
The Chef's Uniform

As the brigade system changed from classical to modern, out of necessity so too did the chef's uniform. According to Betty Wason, in *Cooks, Gluttons and Gourmets,* the white cap became a symbol of a good cook.

The 6th century was the zenith of the Byzantine Empire. Before another hundred years had passed, signs of decay were apparent. The loss of freedom of expression was one; philosophers and artists, persecuted for daring to question established dogma, fled to the monasteries for refuge. Most of the men of letters and the arts were also cooks in the ancient Hellenic tradition. So were the monks; the love of good food was a rapport between them. The Greek Orthodox priests wore crowned black caps; the "eggheads" within their walls were offered priests' caps for disguise, but they felt it was wrong to wear exactly the same headgear. So, instead, white caps were made for them. Eventually, the white cap became the symbol of a good cook; today we call it a *chef's cap*—only later the crowns of the chef's cap would tower higher and higher as a symbol of culinary status, the master chef demanding a higher crown than that of his assistants.[1]

In the 16th century, the standard uniform of a Turkish chef consisted of a cylindrical hat and a long tunic (see Figure A–1 on page 404). Today, chefs still wear cylindrical hats; white jackets are worn instead of tunics, although the similarity is apparent.

In the late 1800s, the chef's uniform was revolutionized. In 1878, a family by the name of Angelica lived in the port of St. Louis. Cherubino Angelica, a chef on one of the railroads, had his wife fashion for him a very special cook's outfit that was unlike anything then available. The hat had an impressive-looking high crown, to lend distinction to the wearer, and was close fitting about the head for the mutual protection of both hair and food. The coat was double-breasted, with two layers of cloth in front to protect the cook against direct heat

---

[1]Betty Wason, *Cooks, Gluttons and Gourmets: A History of Cooking,* Garden City, N.Y.: Doubleday, 1962, pp. 150–151.

Figure A–1

kitchen today and is worn by thousands of professional chefs throughout the world (see Figure A–2).

Apron   Styles of the white apron evolved through time. The main purpose of the apron was to protect the uniform from being soiled.

Double-breasted jacket   A crossover style, the buttons were designed for elegance and appearance as well as function. The chef's coat was developed to provide protection from the heat of the ovens or from the cold of the refrigerator. The long sleeves are to protect the chef from hot boiling liquid.

Kitchen footwear   The chef's shoes should be made of leather with a hard-bottom sole. The shoe is one of the

Figure A–2

and grease. Also, when one front became soiled, the fronts could be reversed to help the cook maintain a professional appearance on the job as well as to save on laundry. In addition, the cuffs of the coat were split, so when turned down they could serve as pot holders.

Mr. Angelica put considerable thought into the design of this coat. He was aware of the problem of lost buttons and the danger of them falling into food. He had his wife use cloth knot buttons and place them off to the sides a bit, rather than right down the front of the coat. Not surprisingly, this highly functional coat, offering such obvious advantages in terms of image, protection, and economy, caught the attention of other chefs and cooks. This simple outfit, born out of a functional necessity, is still the uniform found in virtually every commercial most important parts of the uniform. It protects the wearer from slippery kitchen floors and falling knives and tools.

Neckerchief   The neck cloths of today can be purchased in many colors for fashion or style. The most common color is white. Traditionally, the neck cloth was designed to protect the chef from the heat of open fires and to absorb perspiration.

Side towel   Side towels are tucked neatly into the apron for ease of use. The side towels were originally designed as protection when the chef carried hot pots and pans.

Side towels are not designed for cleaning and, because they are not thrown away after each use, it would be unsanitary to use them throughout the kitchen.

Toque   The toque is the chef's hat. The height designates status. Traditionally, the chef's hat was a cloth hat made from cotton and was laundered regularly. Today, the modern chef uses disposable paper hats.

Trousers   Chefs today wear black and white checked pants or just plain black slacks. Throughout history, chefs had many different styles. The styles depended on the country of origin and status.

Appendix B

Vitamin and Mineral Charts and RDA Chart

Water-Soluble Vitamins

Vitamin	Functions	Deficiency	Sources	Causes of Loss in Storage, Preparation, Cooking, and Holding
Thiamin-B_1	Coenzyme for energy utilization	Beriberi: nerve damage	Pork, milk, and whole grains	Water, baking soda, heat, and oxidation
Riboflavin-B_2	Coenzyme for energy utilization	Aeriboflavinosis: cracked and dry skin around mouth	Milk, fish, and green vegetables	Water, light, and baking soda
Niacin	Coenzyme for energy utilization	Pellagra (4 Ds): diarrhea, dermatitis, dementia, and death	Liver, peanuts, chicken, and fish	Water
Pyridoxine-B_6 (toxic at high intake)	Coenzyme for protein metabolism	Abnormal protein metabolism	Liver, fish, meat, and wheat	Water, baking soda, light, and oxidation
Biotin	Energy production, protein metabolism; helps convert tryptophan to niacin	Rare	Organ meats, meats, eggs, milk, and legumes	Water, baking soda, and oxidation

(continued)

Water-Soluble Vitamins (continued)

Vitamin	Functions	Deficiency	Sources	Causes of Loss in Storage, Preparation, Cooking, and Holding
Folic Acid (folacin)	Cell growth and reproduction	Megaloblastic anemia: large, amino-acid metabolism	Dark-green leafy vegetables; immature, Red blood cells	Water, heat, and oxidation
Cobalamin-B_{12} (requires intrinsic factor for absorption)	Red blood cell maturation	Pernicious anemia: megaloblastic anemia and nerve damage	Only in animal products; vegetarians have no natural source	Water and baking soda
Ascorbic acid-C	Collagen formation—connective tissue then holds cells together; may help protect against cancer	Scurvy: bleeding and swollen gums, poor wound healing, heart failure; rebound scurvy may occur; some people are sensitive to large doses	Citrus fruits, broccoli, and strawberries	Water, baking soda, heat, and oxidation

Fat-Soluble Vitamins

Vitamin	Functions	Deficiency	Sources	Causes of Loss in Storage, Preparation, Cooking, and Holding
Vitamin A Retinol: active form; Carotene: precursor	Enables eyes to adjust to changes in light; maintains cells of skin, eyes, intestines, and lungs; may help protect against cancer	Night blindness; keratinization: thick, dry layer of cells on skin and eyes	Liver, butterfat, egg yolk, carrot, and pumpkin	Sunlight, frying, and drip loss
Vitamin D Calciferol: Activated by kidneys; made in skin when exposed to sun	Bone formation: increases calcium absorption and regulates phosphorus in blood	Rickets: in children; osteomalacia: soft bones in adults	Fortified milk and sunlight	Stable, drip loss
Vitamin E Tocopherol	Antioxidant: protects substances that are damaged by exposure to oxygen, fats, and other vitamins	Very rare; may cause a type of anemia	Vegetable oils and products made from them	Some loss in baking soda and light; oxidation
Vitamin K	Blood clotting	Very rare; hemorrhaging	Dark-green leafy vegetables, liver, and egg yolks	Some loss with baking soda, acid, light, and oxidation

Minerals

Mineral	Functions	Deficiency	Sources	Causes of Loss in Storage, Preparation, Cooking, and Holding
Calcium	Forms bones and teeth	Osteoporosis: caused by long-term low calcium intake; calcium is taken from bones, which then become brittle and break easily; most likely to occur in older women	Milk, soybeans, and fish canned with bones	Water, some with baking soda. For some, such as calcium, adding an acid increases loss into the cooking liquid. Therefore, use the cooking liquid
Phosphorus	Combines with calcium to form bones and teeth	Unlikely	Meat, poultry, and carbonated drinks	
Potassium	Muscle contraction; regulates fluid balance	Disturbance in heart rhythm	Oranges, bananas, and winter squash	
Sodium	Regulates fluid balance	Very unlikely	Naturally occurring in milk, cheese, and salt; preservative uses in cured meat, pickles; added to canned foods; also in medications such as Alka Seltzer	
Iron	Part of hemoglobin: carries oxygen in blood	Hypochromic, microcytic anemia: small red blood cells, less hemoglobin; blood carries less oxygen to tissues; symptoms of fatigue	Meats, especially in liver, foods cooked in iron pots, nuts, and spinach; absorption increased in the presence of vitamin C, decreased by tea, milk, egg yolks	
Zinc	Involved in collagen formation; contributes to wound healing	Rare; causes impaired growth, wound healing, sexual and taste function	Meat, fish, milk, and whole grains	

Summary of the Recommended Dietary Allowances (RDA), 1989*

	Infants		Children			Males					Females					Pregnant	Lactating	
																	1st 6 mos	2nd 6 mos
	0.0–0.5	0.5–1.0	1–3	4–6	7–10	11–14	15–18	19–24	25–50	51+	11–14	15–18	19–24	25–50	51+			
Weight (kg)	6	9	13	20	28	45	66	72	79	77	46	55	58	63	65			
(lb)	13	20	29	44	62	99	145	160	174	170	101	120	128	138	143			
Height (cm)	60	71	90	112	132	157	176	177	176	173	157	163	164	163	160			
(inches)	24	28	35	44	52	62	69	70	70	68	62	64	65	64	63			
Protein (g)	13	14	16	24	28	45	59	58	63	63	46	44	46	50	50	60	65	62
(RE) Vitamin A	375	375	400	500	700	1,000	1,000	1,000	1,000	1,000	800	800	800	800	800	800	1,300	1,200
(mg) Vitamin D	7.5	10	10	10	10	10	10	10	5	5	10	10	10	5	5	10	10	10
(mg) Vitamin E	3	4	6	7	7	10	10	10	10	10	8	8	8	8	8	10	10	10
(mg) Vitamin K	5	10	15	20	30	45	65	70	80	80	45	55	60	65	65	65	65	65
(mg) Vitamin C	30	35	40	45	45	50	60	60	60	60	50	60	60	60	60	70	95	90
(mg) Thiamin	0.3	0.4	0.7	0.9	1.0	1.3	1.5	1.5	1.5	1.2	1.1	1.1	1.1	1.1	1.0	1.5	1.6	1.6
(mg) Riboflavin	0.4	0.5	0.8	1.1	1.2	1.5	1.8	1.7	1.7	1.4	1.3	1.3	1.3	1.3	1.2	1.6	1.8	1.7
Niacin (mg equivalent)	5	6	9	12	13	17	20	19	19	15	15	15	15	15	13	17	20	20
(mg) Vitamin B_6	0.3	0.6	1.0	1.1	1.4	1.7	2.0	2.0	2.0	2.0	1.4	1.5	1.6	1.6	1.6	2.2	2.1	2.1
(mg) Folate	25	35	50	75	100	150	200	200	200	200	150	180	180	180	180	400	280	260
(mg) Vitamin B_{12}	0.3	0.5	0.7	1.0	1.4	2.0	2.0	2.0	2.0	2.0	2.0	2.0	2.0	2.0	2.0	2.2	2.6	2.6
(mg) Calcium	400	600	800	800	800	1,200	1,200	1,200	800	800	1,200	1,200	1,200	800	800	1,200	1,200	1,200
(mg) Phosphorus	300	500	800	800	800	1,200	1,200	1,200	800	800	1,200	1,200	1,200	800	800	1,200	1,200	1,200
(mg) Magnesium	40	60	80	120	170	270	400	350	350	350	280	300	280	280	280	320	355	340
(mg) Iron	6	10	10	10	10	12	12	10	10	10	15	15	15	15	10	30	15	15
(mg) Zinc	5	5	10	10	10	15	15	15	15	15	12	12	12	12	12	15	19	16
(mg) Iodine	40	50	70	90	120	150	150	150	150	150	150	150	150	150	150	175	200	200
(mg) Selenium	10	15	20	20	30	40	50	70	70	70	45	50	55	55	55	65	75	75

Note: The Committee on Dietary Allowances has published a separate table showing energy allowances in ranges for each age-sex group and another table of estimated safe and adequate daily dietary intakes for selected vitamins and minerals. The FDA has published a special table of selected RDA values for use on food labels.
*The allowances are intended to provide for individual variations among most normal, healthy people in the United States under usual environmental stresses. They were designed for the maintenance of good nutrition. Diets should be based on a variety of common foods to provide other nutrients for which human requirements have been less well-defined.
Reprinted with permission from Recommended Dietary Allowances, 10th Edition, © 1989 by the National Academy of Sciences. Published by National Academy Press, Washington, D.C.

Appendix C

Chart for Converting Units of Measurement from Weight to Volume

Table for Identifying the Serving Utensils Required for a Specified Portion Size

Container Portion and Conversion Chart

Fluid Ounces	Cups	No. 8 Scoops	No. 12 Scoops	Containers	No. 16 Scoops	No. 24 Scoops	No. 30 Scoops	No. 40 Scoops
130	16	32	48	One gallon	64	96	120	160
					62	93		
120	15	30	45		60	90		150
					58	87		
110	14	28	42		56	84	105	140
					54	81		
	13	26	39		52	78		130
100				One #10 can	50	75		
	12	24	36	Three quarts	48	72	90	120
				Two #5 cans	46	69		
90	11	22	33		44	66		110
					42	63		
80	10	20	30	Three #2½ cans	40	60	75	100
					38	57		
70	9	18	27		36	54		90
					34	51		
	8	16	24	One-half gallon	32	48	60	80
60					30	45		
	7	14	21		28	42		70
50				Two #2½ cans	26	39		
	6	12	18	One #5 can	24	36	45	60
					22	33		
40	5	10	15		20	30		50
					18	27		
30	4	8	12	One quart	16	24	30	40
					14	21		
	3	6	9	One #2½ can	12	18		30
20					10	15		
	2	4	6	One #303 can	8	12	15	20
	1	2	3	One cup	4	6	7½	10

Source: Milton C. McDowell and Hollie W. Crawford, *Math Workbook for Foodservice Lodging*, 3rd edition (New York: Van Nostrand Reinhold, 1988), p. 235 © by Van Nostrand Reinhold. Reprinted with permission.

Table of Weights and Approximate Equivalents in Measure

Food	Weight	Volume
Allspice	1 ounce	5 tablespoons
Apples, peeled, sliced	1 pound	1 quart
Apples, peeled, diced	1 pound	3½ cups
Apricots, dried, stewed halves	1 pound	2¼ cups
Bacon fat	6 ounces	1 cup
Bacon, raw, sliced	1 pound	15–20 slices
Bacon, raw, diced	1 pound	1 pint
Baking powder	1 ounce	2⅔ tablespoons
Bananas, diced	1 pound	3 cups
Bananas, mashed	1 pound	2 cups
Bananas, whole	1 pound	3 medium
Barley	1 pound	2 cups
Beans, baked	1 pound	2 cups
Beans, dried, Lima, A.P.	1 pound	2½ cups
Beans, dried, Lima, lb. A.P. after cooking	2 pounds, 9 ounces	6 cups
Beans, dried, kidney, A.P.	1 pound	2⅔ cups
Beans, dried, kidney, lb. A.P. after cooking	2 pounds, 6 ounces	7 cups
Beans, dried, Navy, A.P.	1 pound	2½ cups
Beans, dried, Navy, lb. A.P. after cooking	2 pounds, 3 ounces	6 cups
Beef, cooked and diced	1 pound	3 cups
Beef, raw, ground	1 pound	2 cups
Beets, medium whole	1 pound	2–3 beets
Beets, cooked and diced	1 pound	2⅓ cups
Bread, soft, broken	1 pound	10 cups
Bread, dry, broken	1 pound	9 cups
Bread crumbs, dry ground	14 ounces	1 quart
Bread crumbs, soft	1 pound	8 cups
Butter	1 pound	2 cups
Cabbage, shredded, A.P.	1 pound	8 cups, lightly packed
Carrots, fresh, whole	1 pound	6 small
Carrots, diced, A.P., topped	1 pound	3¼ cups
Carrots, ground, raw	1 pound	3¼ cups
Carrots, diced, cooked	1 pound	3 cups
Carrots, raw, sliced	1 pound	3 cups
Catsup	1 pound	2 cups
Celery, diced	1 pound	1 quart
Celery salt	1 ounce	2 tablespoons
Celery seed	1 ounce	4 tablespoons
Cheese, cottage	1 pound	2 cups
Cheese, grated or ground	1 pound	1 quart
Cherries, Maraschino, whole or chopped	1 pound	2 cups
Chicken, diced, cooked	1 pound	3 cups
Chocolate, grated	4 ounces	1 cup

(continued)

Table of Weights and Approximate Equivalents in Measure (continued)

Food	Weight	Volume
Chocolate, melted	8 ounces	1 cup
Cinnamon, ground	1 ounce	4 tablespoons
Cloves, ground	1 ounce	5 tablespoons
Cloves, whole	3 ounces	1 cup
Cocoa	4 ounces	1 cup
Coconut, medium shredded	1 pound	6 cups
Coffee	1 pound	5 cups
Corn syrup	10 ounces	1 cup
Corn, whole kernel	1 pound	2 cups
Corned beef, canned	1 pound	2½ cups
Cornflakes	1 pound	4 quarts
Cornmeal	5½ ounces	1 cup
Cornstarch	5 ounces	1 cup
Cracker crumbs	1 pound	6 cups
Cranberries	1 pound	1 quart
Cranberry, pulp	1 pound	2 cups
Cream of tartar	1 ounce	3 tablespoons
Cucumbers, diced	1 pound	3½ cups
Cucumbers, 50–60 ⅛-inch slices	1 pound	2–3 large
Curry powder	1 ounce	4 tablespoons
Dates, chopped	1 pound	3 cups
Dates, pitted	1 pound	3 cups
Dates, whole	1 pound	2½ cups
Eggplant, diced	1 pound	3 cups
Eggs, hard-cooked, chopped	1 pound	3 cups
Eggs, uncooked, whole	1¾ ounces	1 egg
Eggs, uncooked, whole	1 pound	9 eggs
Eggs, uncooked, whole	1 pound	2 cups
Eggs, uncooked, whites	1 ounce	1 egg white
Eggs, uncooked, whites	1 pound	15 egg whites
Eggs, uncooked, whites	1 pound	2 cups
Eggs, uncooked, yolks	¾ ounce	1 yolk
Eggs, uncooked, yolks	1 pound	12 yolks
Eggs, uncooked, yolks	1 pound, 2 ounces	2 cups
Farina, raw	6 ounces	1 cup
Flour, sifted once before measuring		
Bread	1 pound	4–4½ cups
Cake, pastry, and rye	1 pound	4–5 cups
Whole wheat	1 pound	3–4 cups
Gelatin, flavored	1 pound	2 cups
Gelatin, granulated	4 ounces	1 cup
Gelatin, granulated	1 ounce	4 tablespoons
Ginger, ground	1 ounce	4 tablespoons

(continued)

Table of Weights and Approximate Equivalents in Measure (continued)

Food	Weight	Volume
Grapes, purple	1 pound	2¼ cups
Grapes, white, seedless	1 pound	3 cups
Green peppers	1 pound	6 medium
Green peppers, chopped	1 pound	1 quart
Ham, cooked, diced	1 pound	3 cups
Ham, ground	1 pound	2 cups
Honey	12 ounces	1 cup
Horseradish, prepared	8 ounces	1 cup
Ice cream	6 pounds	1 gallon
Jam	1 pound	1⅓ cups
Jelly	1 pound	1½ cups
Lard	8 ounces	1 cup
Lemon juice	8 ounces	1 cup (4–5 lemons)
Lemon rind, grated	1 ounce	3 tablespoons
Lemons, size 300	1 pound	4 lemons
Lettuce, shredded	8 ounces	1 quart
Lettuce, medium heads	1 pound	2 heads
Macaroni, cooked	1 pound	2½ cups
Macaroni, cut, A.P.	18 ounces	1 quart
Macaroni, 1 lb. before cooking, after cooking	5 pounds	2¼ quarts
Macaroni, cut, A.P.	4½ ounces	1 cup
Mayonnaise	1 pound	2 cups
Meat, cooked diced	1 pound	2½ cups
Milk, fresh	8 ounces	1 cup
Milk, evaporated	1 pound	2 cups
Milk, evaporated, No. 1 tall can	14½ ounces	1⅔ cups
Molasses	1 pound	1⅓ cups
Molasses	11 ounces	1 cup
Mushrooms, canned	1 pound	2 cups
Mushrooms, fresh, sliced	1 pound	1¾ quarts
Mustard, dry	1 ounce	4 tablespoons
Mustard seed	1 ounce	3 tablespoons
Mustard, prepared	½ ounce	1 tablespoon
Mustard, prepared	10 ounces	1 cup
Noodles, cooked	6 pounds	1 gallon
Noodles, cooked	1 pound	2¾ cups
Noodles, raw, dry	12 ounces	1 quart
Nutmeg, ground	1 ounce	4 tablespoons
Nuts, chopped	4 ounces	1 cup
Oatmeal, raw	1 pound	5 cups
Oil	1 pound	2⅓ cups
Olives, chopped	6 ounces	1 cup

(continued)

Table of Weights and Approximate Equivalents in Measure (continued)

Food	Weight	Volume
Onions, chopped	1 pound	3 cups
Onions, grated	1 ounce	1⅓ tablespoons
Onions, sliced	1 pound	4 cups
Onions, dehydrated	2 ounces	1 cup
Onions, dehydrated, reconstituted (1 quart water)	2 ounces	6 cups
Oranges, 150 size	1 pound	2 each
Oranges	8 medium	1 quart, sections
Oranges	3 medium	1 cup juice
Oranges, grated rind	3 counces	1 cup
Oysters	¾ ounce	1 large
Oysters	1 quart	60–100 small
Oysters	1 quart	24–40 large
Oysters	1 pound	2¼ cups
Paprika	1 ounce	4 tablespoons
Parsley, chopped	1 ounce	¾ cup
Vinegar	8 ounces	1 cup
Water	8 ounces	1 cup
Wheat cereal, granulated	1 pound	1½ pints
White sauce	9 ounces	1 cup
Worcestershire sauce	2⅓ ounces	1⅓ tablespoons
Yeast, compressed	½ ounce	1 cake

A.P. = as purchased
Source: Milton C. McDowell and Hollie W. Crawford, *Math Workbook for Foodservice Lodging*, 3rd edition (New York: Van Nostrand Reinhold, 1988), pp. 244–246. © by Van Nostrand Reinhold. Reprinted with permission.

Size Portions and Serving Utensils Required

Food	Size Portions	Serving Utensil
Beverages		
Cocoa	8 oz.	
Coffee	8 oz.	
Milk	8 oz.	
Tea	8 oz.	
Breads		
White, rye, whole wheat, French, or Italian	2 slices	Tongs
Biscuits	2 each	Tongs
Cornbread	1 piece: 2½ in. × 2½ in. × 2 in.	Spatula
Crackers	4 each	Tongs
French toast	1½ slices	Spatula
Wheat cakes	3 cakes	Spatula
Rolls	2 each	Tongs

(continued)

Size Portions and Serving Utensils Required (continued)

Food	Weight	Volume
Butter or margarine	1 pat	Tongs or fork
Cereals		
Cracked wheat	6 oz.	6-oz. ladle
Farina or cream of wheat	6 oz.	6-oz. ladle
Oatmeal	6 oz.	6-oz. ladle
Steamed rice	6 oz.	6-oz. ladle
Whole wheat	6 oz.	6-oz. ladle
Bran flakes	1 oz. or 1 pkg. (individual)	6-oz. ladle
Corn flakes	1 oz. or 1 pkg. (individual)	6-oz. ladle
Raisin Bran flakes	1 oz. or 1 pkg. (individual)	6-oz. ladle
Rice Krispies	1 oz. or 1 pkg. (individual)	6-oz. ladle
Special K cereal	1 oz. or 1 pkg. (individual)	6-oz. ladle
Sugar Pops	1 oz. or 1 pkg. (individual)	6-oz. ladle
Sugar Frosted Flakes	1 oz. or 1 pkg. (individual)	6-oz. ladle
Sugar Krisp	1 oz. or 1 pkg. (individual)	6-oz. ladle
Assorted individuals	1 pkg.	
Cheese		
Cottage cheese	3 oz.	#12 scoop
Sliced cheese	2 oz.	Tongs or spatula
Eggs		
Whole	6 servings per dozen, boiled; 8 servings per dozen, fried	Tongs Spatula
Scrambled	3 oz.	Serving spoon
Fruits and juices		
Apples, eating	1 each	
Apples, baked	1 each	Serving spoon
Banana	1 each	
Orange	1 each	
Grapefruit	½ grapefruit	
Applesauce	4 oz.	4-oz. ladle
Apricots	4 oz.	4-oz. ladle
Cherries	4 oz.	4-oz. ladle
Fruit cocktail	4 oz.	4-oz. ladle
Peach halves	4 oz.	4-oz. ladle
Peaches, sliced	4 oz.	4-oz. ladle
Pear halves	4 oz.	4-oz. ladle
Pineapple, sliced	4 oz.	4-oz. ladle
Pineapple, crushed	4 oz.	4-oz. ladle
Prune plums	4 oz.	4-oz. ladle
Strawberries	4 oz.	4-oz. ladle
Stewed apricots	4 oz.	4-oz. ladle
Stewed peaches	4 oz.	4-oz. ladle
Stewed prunes	4 oz.	4-oz. ladle

(continued)

Size Portions and Serving Utensils Required (continued)

Food	Weight	Volume
Stewed mixed fruit nuggets	4 oz.	4-oz. ladle
Grapefruit juice	4 oz.	4-oz. ladle
Orange juice	4 oz.	4-oz. ladle
Pineapple juice	4 oz.	4-oz. ladle
Tomato juice	4 oz.	4-oz. ladle
Jelly, jam, honeys, peanut butter	1 oz.	1-oz. ladle
Meat		
Baked beef loaf	One 3-oz. slice	Spatula
Beef à la mode	4 oz.	Serving Spoon
Beef barbecue, Swiss style	4 oz.	Serving spoon
Beef liver	2½ oz.	Tongs
Beef liver loaf	One 3-oz. slice	Spatula
Beef and noodles	8 oz.	8-oz. ladle
Beef stew	8 oz.	8-oz. ladle
Boiled beef (New England)	3 oz.	Tongs
Braised beef cubes and noodles	8 oz.	8-oz. ladle
Braised beef tenderloin tip	4 oz.	Serving spoon
Chili con carne	8 oz.	8-oz. ladle
Chop suey	6 oz.	6-oz. ladle
Corned beef hash	6 oz.	6-oz. ladle
Creamed chipped beef	6 oz.	6-oz. ladle
Hamburger patties	Two 2-oz. or one 4-oz.	Tongs or spatula
Italian spaghetti	8 oz.	8-oz. ladle
Pot roast of beef	3 oz.	Tongs or fork
Roast round of beef	3 oz.	Tongs or fork
Round steak, oven-fried	3 oz.	Tongs or fork
Salisbury steak	3 oz.	Tongs or spatula
Swiss steak	3 oz.-1 piece	Tongs or fork
Baked lamb loaf	3 oz.-1 slice	Spatula
Roast leg of lamb	3 oz.	Tongs or fork
Canadian bacon	2 slices (cut 14 per lb.)	Tongs or fork
Baked ham	3 oz.	Tongs or fork
Fried sausage links	2 each	Tongs
Smoked pork butts	Two 1½-oz. slices	Tongs or fork
Pork chops, baked	1 each (cut 3 per lb.)	Tongs or fork
Pork chops, breaded	2 each (cut 6 per lb.)	Tongs or fork
Pork roast	3 oz.	Tongs or fork
Pork steaks	1 steak-3½ oz.	Tongs or fork
Spareribs	8 oz.	Tongs or fork
Veal loaf	3 oz.-1 slice	Spatula
Roast leg of veal	3 oz.	Tongs or fork

(continued)

Size Portions and Serving Utensils Required (continued)

Food	Weight	Volume
Veal cutlets, breaded	1 cutlet (cut 5 per lb.)	Tongs or fork
Cold cuts	2 oz.	Tongs or fork
Poultry		
Baked chicken	3 oz.	Spatula or serving spoon
Chicken à la king	6 oz.	6-oz. ladle
Creamed chicken	6 oz.	6-oz. ladle
Fricassée of chicken and noodles	8 oz.	8-oz. ladle
Chicken pie	6 oz.	Serving spoon
Fried chicken	¼ or 6 oz.	Tongs
Fish		
Baked haddock	4 oz.	Tongs or spatula
Baked halibut	4 oz.	Tongs or spatula
Fried perch	4 oz.	Tongs or spatula
Creamed salmon	6 oz.	6-oz. ladle
Salmon loaf	3 oz.	Spatula
Salmon salad	4 oz.	No. 8 scoop (level)
Tunafish à la king	6 oz.	6-oz. ladle
Tunafish salad	4 oz.	No. 8 scoop (level)
Tunafish and macaroni casserole	6 oz.	Serving spoon
Tunafish and macaroni salad	4 oz.	No. 8 scoop (level)
Tunafish and noodle casserole	6 oz.	Serving spoon
Fish croquettes	2 each (#12 scoop)	Tongs or spatula
Potatoes		
Au gratin potatoes	4 oz.	Serving spoon
Baked potato	1 med. (6 oz. with skin)	Tongs
Creamed potatoes	4 oz.	Serving spoon
Escalloped potatoes	4 oz.	Serving spoon
Hot potato salad	4 oz.	Serving spoon
Mashed potatoes	4 oz.	No. 8 scoop (level)
Parsley potatoes	4 oz. (2 small)	Serving spoon
Potatoes in cheese sauce	4 oz.	Serving spoon
Sweet potatoes, candied	4 oz.	Serving spoon
Sweet potatoes, glazed	4 oz.	Serving spoon
Sweet potatoes, mashed	4 oz.	Serving spoon
Sweet potato, baked	1 each	Serving spoon
Potato substitutes		
Baked beans	4 oz.	Serving spoon

(continued)

Size Portions and Serving Utensils Required (continued)

Food	Weight	Volume
Boiled navy beans	4 oz.	Serving spoon
Spanish pinto beans	4 oz.	Serving spoon
Baked macaroni and cheese	4 oz.	Serving spoon
Buttered noodles	4 oz.	Serving spoon
Cornbread dressing	4 oz.	Serving spoon
Bread dressing	4 oz.	Spatula or serving spoon
Salads		
Beef and cabbage salad	3 oz.	Serving spoon
Cabbage-apple salad	3 oz.	Serving spoon
Carrot-apple-raisin salad	3 oz.	Serving spoon
Chef's salad	3 oz.	Serving spoon
Cole slaw	3 oz.	Serving spoon
Cranberry-orange relish	3 oz.	Serving spoon
Cucumber-onion salad	3 oz.	Serving spoon
Kidney-bean salad	4 oz.	No. 8 scoop (level)
Mixed-vegetable salad	3 oz.	Serving spoon
Molded cherry salad	4 oz.	Spatula
Pear-lime gelatin salad	4 oz.	Spatula
Perfection salad	4 oz.	Spatula
Tomato aspic	4 oz.	Spatula
Tossed salad	3 oz.	Serving spoon
Waldorf salad	3 oz.	Serving spoon
Sliced tomatoes	3 oz. (2 slices)	Tongs or fork
Salad dressings		
All dressings	1 oz.	1-oz. ladle
Sauces and gravies	One 2-oz.	1- or 2-oz. ladle
Soups		
All soups and oyster stew	8 oz.	8-oz. ladle
Vegetables		
All vegetables	4 oz.	Serving spoon
Desserts		
Cakes, cottage pudding	1 piece: 2½ in. × 2½ in. × 2 in.	Spatula
Pies	1 piece (cut 6 per 9-inch pie)	Spatula
Cobblers	1 piece: 2½ in. × 2½ in. × 2 in.	Spatula
Cookies	2 each	Tongs
Jello	4 oz.	Spatula
Custard	4 oz.	Spatula or 4-oz. ladle
Puddings	4 oz.	4-oz. ladle
Ice cream	24 servings per gallon	No. 12 scoop

Source: Milton C. McDowell and Hollie W. Crawford, *Math Workbook for Foodservice Lodging,* 3rd edition (New York: Van Nostrand Reinhold, 1988), pp. 247–250 © 1988 by Van Nostrand Reinhold. Reprinted with permission.

Appendix D

Classical Garnishes for Consommés

Ailerons Chicken consommé garnished with fowls' wings, boned, stuffed, and braised.

Albion Consommé garnished with foie gras quenelles, asparagus heads, julienne of truffles, and cocks' combs.

Alexandra Chicken consommé thickened with tapioca, garnished with julienne of chicken, quenelles, and shredded lettuces.

Allemande Consommé thickened with tapioca, flavored with genièvre, garnished with julienne of red cabbage, roundels of Frankfort sausages, and scraped horseradish.

Alsacienne Consommé garnished with nouillettes and profiteroles stuffed with foie gras purée.

Ambassadeurs Chicken consommé garnished with dice of royale with chopped truffles, mushrooms, and white of chicken in dice.

Ambassadrice Chicken consommé garnished with three royales, chopped truffles (black), tomato (red), green peas (green); julienne of chicken and mushrooms.

Ancienne Petite marmite consommé garnished with croûtes filled with vegetable purée and gratiné.

Andalouse Consommé blended with tomato purée, garnished with dice of royale and dice of tomato, julienne of ham, boiled rice and vermicelli, and threaded eggs.

Source: L. Saulnier, *Le Repertoire de la Cuisine,* distributed in the United States by Christian Classics, Westminster, Maryland.

Arenberg   Chicken consommé garnished with balls of carrots, turnips, truffles, peas, small round chicken quenelles, and roundels of asparagus royale.

Aurore   Consommé thickened with tapioca and tomato purée, garnished with julienne of chicken.

Béatrice   Consommé garnished with semolina, roundels of chicken farce blended with tomato and royale.

Belle fermière   Consommé garnished with julienne of cabbage, lozenges of French beans, and Italian paste.

Belle gabrielle   Consommé thickened with tapioca, garnished with rectangles of chicken, mousseline, and crayfish tails.

Berchoux   Game consommé garnished with dice of royale, blended with chestnut purée and quails' essence, julienne of truffles, and mushrooms.

Bergère   Oxtail consommé thickened with tapioca, garnished with asparagus tips, minced mushrooms or mousserons, tarragon leaves, and chervil shreds.

Berny   Consommé thickened with tapioca and garnished with small balls of dauphine potatoes, combined with chopped grilled almonds and chopped truffles, and chervil shreds.

Blanc-manger   Chicken consommé garnished with green peas and chervil shreds. Serve separately some small tartlets filled with minced chicken.

Bohéminenne   Chicken consommé thickened with tapioca and garnished with dice of royale blended with foie gras purée, profiteroles (separately).

Boieldieu   Consommé thickened with tapioca garnished with three sorts of quenelles, foie gras, chicken, and truffles.

Bouchère   Petite marmite consommé garnished with small squares of cooked cabbage; serve separately some marrow bones, cut thin and poached.

Bouquetière   Chicken consommé thickened with tapioca, garnished with French beans, asparagus heads, and green peas.

Bourbon   Consommé thickened with tapioca, garnished with sago and large quenelles, decorated with truffles representing fleurs-de-lis, chervil shreds.

Bourdaloue   Consommé garnished with four different royales, tomato (red), ordinary (white), asparagus purée (green), and carrot pure (red). Cut no. 1 into dice, no. 2 into lozenges, no. 3 into leaves, and no. 4 into stars.

Bretonne   Consommé garnished with julienne of leeks, celery, onion, mushrooms, and chervil shreds.

Brieux   Consommé thickened with tapioca, garnished with royale made with pistachio powder and cut into stars, dice of truffles, and Japon perles.

Britannia   Consommé thickened with tapioca, garnished with dice of royale, and blended with lobster cullis and julienne of truffles.

Brunoise   Consommé garnished with small cubes of carrots, turnips, leeks, celery, peas, and chervil. Can be done with the addition of rice, barley, and quenelles.

Cancalaise   Fish consommé thickened with tapioca, garnished with oysters, julienne of fillets of sole, and quenelles of whiting.

Carmélite   Fish consommé thickened with arrowroot, garnished with roundels of fish forcemeat and plain boiled rice.

Carmen   Consommé clarified with raw tomato purée and mild capsicums, garnished with lozenges of tomato, julienne of capsicum, rice, and chervil shreds.

Caroline   Chicken consommé garnished with lozenges of royale, rice, and chervil shreds.

Castellane   Game consommé flavored with woodcock fumet, garnished with roundels of royale made with woodcock purée and lentil purée, yolk of eggs chopped and thickened with the usual liaison, and julienne of woodcock fillets.

Célestine   Consommé thickened with tapioca and garnished with julienne of pannequets or pancakes, mixed with chopped truffles or fine herbs.

Chancelière Chicken consommé garnished with roundels of royale with purée of fresh peas, julienne of chicken, truffles, and mushrooms.

Charolaise Petite marmite consommé garnished with small glazed onions, carrot balls, roundels of braised cabbages, and small sections of oxtail.

Chartreuse Consommé thickened with tapioca, garnished with three differently stuffed ravioli: one foie gras, one spinach, and the other chopped mushrooms; chervil shreds.

Chasseur Game consommé, garnished with julienne of mushrooms and game quenelles, or (separately) profiteroles stuffed with game purée.

Châtelaine Chicken consommé thickened with tapioca, garnished with dice of royale made with three parts Soubise and one part artichoke purée; chicken quenelles stuffed with chestnut purée.

Cheveux d'anges Chicken consommé garnished with very small vermicelli, or (separately) grated parmesan.

Chevreuse Chicken consommé garnished with large quenelles of chicken, stuffed with asparagus purée and julienne of truffles.

Colbert Consommé garnished with printanier of vegetables and small poached eggs.

Colombine Chicken consommé garnished with vegetables, julienne of pigeons, and poached pigeons' eggs.

Comtesse Chicken consommé thickened with tapioca and garnished with lozenges of royale and asparagus purée, roundels of stuffed lettuces, and round quenelles decorated with truffles.

Crécy Chicken consommé thickened with tapioca, garnished with lozenges of royale, blended with purée of carrots, and brunoise of carrots and chervil shreds.

Croûtes-au-pot Petite marmite consommé garnished with dice of vegetables, or (separately) croûtes dried in the oven.

Cussy Game consommé flavored with partridges garnished with roundels of royale made with chestnut purée and partridges, quenelles, julienne of truffles, and a half-glass of Madeira and brandy when about to serve.

Cyrano Consommé with duck fumet garnished with large quenelles of duck, glazed and sprinkled with Parmesan, and gratinéd.

Dame blanche Chicken consommé thickened with tapioca, garnished with dice of royale made with almond milk, stars of chicken, and Japon perles.

Demidoff Chicken consommé garnished with printanier of vegetables, truffles, quenelles with fine herbs, and chervil shreds.

Deslignac Chicken consommé thickened with tapioca, garnished with dice of royale, roundels of stuffed lettuces, and chervil shreds.

Diablotins Chicken consommé garnished with slices of French bread cut ¼-inch thick, buttered, coated with cheese, and set to gratin.

Diane Game consommé garnished with julienne of game, dice of truffles, and a glass of Madeira when serving.

Diplomate Chicken consommé thickened with tapioca, garnished with roundels of chicken forcemeat blended with crayfish butter and julienne of truffles.

Doria Chicken consommé garnished with printanier and cucumber, large macaroni, filled with tomatoed chicken forcemeat, poached, and cut into short lengths; profiteroles.

Douglas Consommé garnished with roundels of sweetbreads, artichoke bottoms, and asparagus heads.

Dubarry Consommé thickened with tapioca, garnished with roundels of royale, small bouquets of cauliflower, and chervil shreds.

Duchesse Chicken consommé garnished with Japon perles, dice of royale, and julienne of lettuces.

Duse   Consommé with tomato fumet, garnished with tomatoed quenelles, poached tortellini, and small Gênes pastes.

Ephémères   Chicken consommé garnished with large julienne of carrots, asparagus heads, and peas.

Favorite   Consommé thickened with tapioca, garnished with potato balls, julienne of artichoke bottoms and mushrooms, and chervil shreds.

Flamande   Consommé garnished with dice of royale blended with brussels sprouts purée, green peas, and chervil shreds.

Floréal   Chicken consommé garnished with carrots, turnips, peas, asparagus heads, small quenelles with pistachio powder, and chervil shreds.

Francillon   Chicken consommé garnished with poached eggs and chicken quenelles.

Garibaldi   Chicken consommé garnished with Japon perles and spaghetti.

Gauloise   Chicken consommé thickened with yolk of eggs garnished with cocks' combs and kidneys, and roundels of ham royale.

George Sand   Fish consommé garnished with fish quenelles blended with crayfish butter and quarters of cooked morels, or (separately) serve slices of carp soft roe on roundels of French soup bread.

Germaine   Consommé garnished with chicken quenelles, roundels of royale blended with peas purée and mirepoix, and chervil shreds.

Germinal   Consommé with tarragon flavor garnished with peas, dice of French beans, asparagus heads, quenelles, and chervil shreds.

Girondine   Consommé garnished with lozenges of royale and chopped ham, and julienne of carrots.

Grande duchesse   Chicken consommé garnished with chicken quenelles, julienne of chicken suprême, tongue, and asparagus heads.

Grenade   Consommé with tomato flavor garnished with dice of royale and vegetable purée with tomato, dice of tomatoes, and chervil shreds.

Grimaldi   Consommé clarified with fresh tomato purée, garnished with dice of royale and julienne of celery.

Hongroise   Consommé flavored with tomato and paprika, garnished with roundels of chicken forcemeat and quenelles of calves' livers.

Impératrice   (a) Chicken consommé garnished with cocks' combs and kidneys, asparagus heads, and roundels of royale. (b) Chicken consommé garnished with roundels of chicken forcemeat made in the shape of a black pudding and inserted with French beans, and sticks of truffles and carrots.

Impérial   Chicken consommé thickened with tapioca, garnished with quenelles, cocks' combs and kidneys, green peas, and chervil shreds.

Indienne   Consommé flavored with curry, garnished with dice of royale made with coconut milk, or (separately) serve plain boiled rice.

Infante   (a) Chicken consommé thickened with tapioca, garnished with croutons coated with vegetable purée and gratinéd. (b) Same as above, with profiteroles stuffed with foie gras and served separately.

Italienne   Consommé garnished with dice of red royale (with tomato) and green royale (with spinach), or (separately) spaghetti and grated cheese.

Jacobine   Chicken consommé garnished with dice of potatoes, French beans, turnips, peas, and julienne of truffles.

Jockey club   Chicken consommé garnished with dice of royale of carrots, peas purée, and chicken purée.

Joinville   Chicken consommé garnished with quenelles of three different flavors and colors: green, red, and white.

Jouvencel   Consommé thickened with tapioca, garnished with stuffed lettuce leaves rolled cigarette shape and poached, or (separately) round croutons coated with carrot purée sprinkled with cheese and set to gratin.

Juanita   Chicken consommé, garnished with dice of tomatoed royale and hard yolks passed through the sieve.

Judic   Chicken consommé garnished with braised lettuces, chicken quenelles, and shreds of mushrooms.

Julienne   Consommé garnished with carrots, leeks, turnips, celery, cabbage, cut into fillets 2 inches long. Stew the vegetables with a little butter, salt, and a pinch of sugar; moisten with the consommé; and cook gently, removing the grease as the vegetables cook. Add green peas, sorrel chiffonade, and chervil shreds.

Léopold   Consommé with semolina and garnished with shreds of lettuce, sorrel, and chervil.

Lorette   Chicken consommé flavored with pimientos, garnished with julienne of truffles, asparagus heads, and chervil, or (separately) small balls of Lorette potatoes.

Macdonald   Consommé garnished with roundels of royale made with brain purée, dice of cucumber, and small ravioli.

Madrilène   Consommé with celery flavor, tomato, and pimientos (can be served cold), garnished with tomato julienne, sorrel shreds, and vermicelli (hot).

Marguerite   Chicken consommé garnished with marguerites made with chicken forcemeat, poached, and cut into thin roundels and stamped with fancy cutter to the shape of marguerite. Yolk of egg in the middle in imitation of the flower center, asparagus heads.

Maria   Chicken consommé thickened with tapioca, garnished with roundels of royale made with beans purée and printanier of vegetables.

Marquise   (a) Consommé with celery flavor, garnished with roundels of veal amourettes and quenelles of chicken mixed with chopped avelines. (b) Chicken consommé garnished with tomato chicken quenelles, julienne of lettuce, and truffles.

Martinière   Chicken consommé garnished with roundels of stuffed cabbage, peas, and chervil shreds.

Médicis   Consommé thickened with tapioca and garnished with cubes of green and red royale sorrel shreds.

Mégère   Consommé garnished with gnocchi made with potato, shredded lettuces, and large vermicelli.

Mercédès   Consommé with Xérès wine garnished with rings of red pimientos and stars of cocks' combs.

Messaline   Chicken consommé flavored with tomato, garnished with julienne of sweet pimientos, cocks' kidneys, and rice.

Metternich   Game consommé with pheasant fumet, garnished with dice of royale made with artichoke purée and julienne of pheasant.

Mikado   Chicken consommé with tomato flavor, garnished with dice of tomato and chicken.

Milanaise   Chicken in consommé with tomato flavor garnished with mushrooms, ham, and truffles in julienne spaghetti, or (separately) grated cheese.

Mimosa   (a) Chicken consommé garnished with pink, green, and yellow royale (carrots, green peas, and hard yolks). (b) Chicken consommé garnished with hard-boiled yolk of eggs pressed through a large sieve.

Mireille   Chicken consommé garnished with semolina and roundels of royale, and of tomato chicken forcemeat.

Mirette   Petite marmite consommé garnished with chicken quenelles, shredded lettuce, and chervil, or (separately) serve some cheese croutons.

Monaco   Chicken consommé, garnished with pea-shaped truffles, carrots, turnips, and profiteroles.

Monte-Carlo   Chicken consommé garnished with roundels of carrots and turnips, stuffed pancakes, and slices of truffles.

Montmorency   Chicken consommé thickened with tapioca, garnished with asparagus heads, white quenelles, rice, and chervil shreds.

Montmort   Consommé garnished with roundels of chicken forcemeat, mixed with chopped truffles and tongue, dice of green royale (peas purée), carrots, and turnips (crescent shaped), asparagus heads, and chervil shreds.

Mosaïque   Consommé garnished with various shapes of royale and chicken forcemeat of various flavors.

Moscovite   Consommé of sterlet or sturgeon and cucumber essence, garnished with julienne of salted mushrooms and dice of vesiga poached in consommé.

Mousseline   Chicken consommé garnished with small chicken mousseline poached in grooved molds.

Navarin   Consommé garnished with roundels of green royale (green peas), crayfish tails, and blanched concasséed parsley.

Neige de Florence   Consommé garnished with special Italian paste.

Nelson   Fish consommé thickened with arrowroot, garnished with rice, or (separately) serve small bouchées filled with dice of lobster Américaine.

Nemours   Chicken consommé thickened with tapioca, garnished with Crécy royale with dice of carrots, Japon perles, and julienne of truffles.

Nesselrode   Game consommé prepared with hazel hen fumet, garnished with roundels of royale made with chestnuts purée and game (cut with a grooved cutter), julienne of hazel hen fillets, and mushrooms.

Niçoise   Consommé with tomato flavor garnished with dice of tomatoes, French beans, potatoes, and chervil shreds.

Nids d'Hirondelles   Chicken consommé garnished with swallow nests, thoroughly cleaned and poached. *Note:* The nests must be soaked in cold water for 24 hours to swell the mucilaginous elements and make them transparent; then place them in the boiling consommé and cook gently for 30 minutes, until the gummy portions are melted in the consommé.

Nilson   Consommé thickened with tapioca, garnished with quenelles of chicken and ham, chopped truffles and chives, green peas, and chervil.

Ninon   Chicken consommé garnished with small balls of carrots, turnips, truffles, and chervil shreds, or (separately) serve tartlets filled with minced chicken and yolk of eggs; decorate with a star made of truffle.

Olga   Consommé with Port wine flavor, garnished with julienne of leeks, celeriac, salted gherkins, and carrots.

Orge perlé   Consommé garnished with pearl barley.

Orientale   Consommé garnished with crescents of carrots, turnips, and beetroots; rice with saffron.

Orléanaise   Consommé garnished with large cubes of royale made with purée of spinach, French beans, flageolets, and chervil.

Orléans   Consommé thickened with tapioca, garnished with quenelles made in three different colors (white with chicken, red with tomato, and green with spinach).

Orsay   Chicken consommé garnished with poached yolk of eggs, quenelles of pigeons, julienne of pigeons suprêmes, and asparagus heads.

Parisienne   Consommé with leek flavor, garnished with julienne of potatoes and leeks.

Parmesane   Consommé garnished with Parmesan biscuits.

Pâtés diverses   Consommé garnished with vermicelli, Gênes paste, Italie alphabet, and so on.

Petite mariée   Chicken consommé, very white, garnished with small roundels of royale made with chicken purée and almond milk, and chervil shreds.

Petite marmite   Strong consommé of beef and chicken garnished with carrots and turnips, leeks and cabbage, julienne of celery, roundels of marrow, and dice of beef and chicken. Served in special marmite, or (separately) dry thin toast.

Petite marmite béarnaise   Same as above with the addition of rice and julienne of potatoes.

Princesse   Chicken consommé garnished with dice of green peas royale, pearl barley, and thin slices of white chicken.

Printanier   Consommé garnished with balls of carrots, turnips, peas, and chervil shreds.

Quenelles   Consommé garnished with quenelles to taste.

Quenelles à la moelle   Consommé thickened with tapioca and garnished with quenelles made with marrow.

Quenelles à la Viennoise   Same as above with quenelles made with calf liver and fennel.

Queue de boeuf (oxtail soup)   Consommé made with oxtail cut into sections and browned with mirepoix in the oven. Moistened with stock and clarified in the usual manner. Garnish with carrots, turnips of the oxtail, and a glass of old Madeira when serving.

Rabelais   Consommé flavored with lark and truffles essence, garnished with julienne of celery, quenelles of truffled larks, and a glass of Seuilly wine when serving.

Rachel   Chicken consommé thickened with tapioca, garnished with julienne of artichoke bottoms, or (separately) croutons fried in butter and filled with slices of poached marrow.

Ravioli   Consommé garnished with small ravioli.

Reine   Chicken consommé thickened with tapioca, garnished with dice of royale made with chicken purée, and julienne of chicken.

Réjane   Chicken consommé with tapioca garnished with shredded eggs and small roundels of Crécy royale made with avelines milk.

Renaissance   Chicken consommé garnished with balls of vegetables and royale cut into shapes, and chervil shreds.

Richelieu   Consommé garnished with chicken quenelles stuffed with chicken jelly, stuffed lettuces rolled into paupiettes, julienne of carrots and turnips, and chervil shreds.

Riso a fegatini   Chicken or white consommé; when boiling, cook rice; drop in at the last minute small cubes of chicken liver just to be poached, or (separately) grated Parmesan cheese.

Rossini   Chicken consommé thickened with tapioca and flavored with truffles essence, garnished with profiteroles stuffed with foie gras purée and chopped truffles.

Rothschild   Game consommé garnished with roundels of royale made with purée of pheasant, chestnut purée, and salmis sauce. When about to serve, add a glass of Sauterne.

Royale   Chicken consommé garnished with cubes of royale, lozenges, and so on.

Rubens   Tomato chicken consommé garnished with hop shoots.

Saint-Hubert   Game consommé with white wine, garnished with royale of game purée and lentil purée, and julienne of game.

Sarah Bernhardt   Consommé thickened with tapioca, flavored with turtle herbs and Madeira wine, garnished with tomato quenelles and roundels of marrow.

Sévigné   Chicken consommé garnished with white quenelles, julienne of lettuces, and asparagus heads.

Solange   Consommé garnished with pearl barley, squares of lettuce, and chicken julienne.

Soubrette   Tomato chicken consommé seasoned with cayenne pepper; garnished with round, flat quenelles decorated in the middle with a roundel of truffle in imitation of a eyepink shrimp's tail.

Souveraine   Chicken consommé garnished with large quenelles stuffed with vegetable brunoise and chervil shreds.

Surprise   Same as above with quenelles stuffed with jelly mixed with beetroot juice.

Tapioca   Consommé with tapioca; boil 10 minutes.

Théodora   Chicken consommé garnished with chicken julienne and truffles, dice of royale, and asparagus heads.

Tosca Chicken consommé thickened with tapioca flavored with turtle herbs and Madeira, garnished with julienne of leeks, and profiteroles.

Trévise or trois filets Consommé garnished with chicken julienne, tongue, and truffles.

Tzarine Chicken consommé flavored with fennel, garnished with dice of vesiga.

Valois Consommé garnished with tomato quenelles, pearl barley, and asparagus heads.

Vatel Fish consommé with sole fumet, garnished with roundels of royale made with crayfish, and lozenges of fillets of sole.

Vénitienne Consommé flavored with chervil, tarragon, and thyme, garnished with rice, or (separately) serve small gratinéd gnocchi.

Vermicelli Consommé with vermicelli.

Véron Consommé flavored with truffles essence, garnished with dice of royale made with flageolets purée and julienne of capsicums, and a glass of Port when serving.

Vert-pré Consommé thickened with tapioca, garnished with asparagus heads, peas, French beans, shredded lettuce and sorrel, and chervil shreds.

Viennoise Consommé with pink paprika garnished with julienne of cheese pancakes and gnocchi, and seasoned with paprika.

Villeneuve Chicken consommé garnished with dice of royale and lozenges of lettuce coated with chicken forcemeat combined with chopped ham, poached in oven.

Viveurs Consommé duck flavor, celery, and beetroot juice, and cayenne pepper, garnished with julienne of celery, and diablotins with paprika.

Xavier (a) Consommé garnished with royale of chicken purée, peas, and chervil. (b) Consommé garnished with shredded eggs.

Windsor Consommé with calves foot and flavored with turtle herbs, garnished with julienne of calves foot-and-chicken quenelles with chopped yolk of eggs.

Bibliography

Fuller, John; John B. Knight; and Charles A. Salter, *The Professional Chef's Guide to Kitchen Management.* New York: Van Nostrand Reinhold, 1985.

Gisslen, Wayne, *Professional Cooking,* 2nd ed. New York: Wiley, 1989.

Glutamate Association, *Monosodium Glutamate: A look at the facts* (no date).

Gunst, Kathy, *Condiments.* New York: Putnam, 1984.

Hanni, Tim, "The Cause and Effect of Wine and Food," *Wine World Estates* 1991: 1–11.

Haines, Robert G., *Math Principles for Food Service Occupations,* 2nd ed. Albany, New York: Delmar Publishers, 1988.

Hamilton, Eva May; Frances Sizer; and Eleanor Whitnew, *Nutrition Concepts and Controversies,* 5th ed. St. Paul, Minnesota: West, 1991.

Hatchwell, Leora C., "Overcoming Flavor Challenges in Low-Fat Frozen Desserts," *Food Technology* February 1994: 98–102.

Heath, Henry B., *Source Book of Flavors.* Westport, Connecticut: AVI Publishing, 1981.

Herbst, Sharon Tyler, *Food Lover's Companion.* New York: Barron's Educational Series, 1990.

Hirsch, Alan R., "Smell and Taste: How the Culinary Experts Compare to the Rest of Us," *Food Technology* September 1990: 96–101.

IFIC Foundation, "Experiments in Good Taste," *Food Insight: Current Topics in Food Safety and Nutrition* March/April 1995: 1–8.

Kotshevar, Lendal H., *Standards, Principles and Techniques in Quantity Food Production,* 3rd ed., Boston: CBI, 1966.

Levenson, Thomas, "Accounting for Taste," *The Sciences* January/February 1995: 13–15.

Lewis, Ricki, "When Smell and Taste Go Awry," *FDA Consumer,* November 1991: 29–33.

Lingle, Ted, "Coffee Taster's Flavor Wheel," Specialty Coffee Association of America, no date.

Mader, Sylvia S., "Senses" in *Inquiry into Life,* 7th ed., Dubuque, Iowa: Wm. C. Brown, 1994, pp. 322–341.

Martland, Richard E., and Derek A. Welsby, *Basic Cookery—Fundamental Recipes and Variations,* London: Heinemann, 1980.

McVety, Paul J., and Bradley J. Ware, *Fundamentals of Menu Planning.* New York: Van Nostrand Reinhold, 1989.

Mela, David J., and Richard D. Mattes, "The Chemical Senses and Nutrition: Part I," *Nutrition Today,* March/April 1988: 4–9.

Montagné, Prosper, *Larousse Gastronomique,* Edited by Charlotte Turgeon. New York: Crown, 1977.

National Restaurant Association, *Attitudes Towards Nutrition in the Restaurant: Assessing the Market.* Washington, D.C.: National Restaurant Association, March 1990.

National Restaurant Association, *Current Issues Report, Nutrition Awareness and the Foodservice Industry.* Washington, D.C.: National Restaurant Association, 1990.

National Restaurant Association, Foodservice Industry 2000. Washington, D.C.: National Restaurant Association, 1988.

National Restaurant Trends, *Tableservice Restaurant Trends.* Washington, D.C.: National Restaurant Trends, January 1989.

O'Mahony, Michael A.P., "How We Perceive Flavor," *Nutrition Today* May/June 1984: 6–15.

Pauli, Eugene, *Classical Cooking the Modern Way,* Edited by Marjorie S. Arkwright, R.D. New York: Van Nostrand Reinhold, 1979.

Peddersen, Raymond B., *Foodservice and Hotel Purchasing,* Boston: CBI, 1981.

Pennisi, Elizabeth, "Valentine Bind," *Science News,* 141; 1992: 110–111.

Peterson, James, *Sauces: Classical and Contemporary Sauce Making*. New York: Van Nostrand Reinhold, 1991.

Saulnier, L., *Le Repertoire de la Cuisine,* Distributed in the United States by Christian Classics, Westminster, Maryland.

Schiffman, Susan S., "Taste and Smell Losses with Age," *Contemporary Nutrition,* 16(2) 1991: 1–2.

Stauffer, Clyde E., "Balance and Impact," *Baking & Snack* September 1995: 24–30.

Stobart, Tom, *Herbs, Spices and Flavorings,* Woodstock, New York: Overlook Press, 1982.

Stone, Judith, "Like Chips in the Night," *Discover* February 1994: 88–91.

The Surgeon General's Report on Nutrition and Health, Public Health Service Publication No. 88–50211, Public Health Service, U.S. Department of Health and Human Services, Washington, D.C., 1988.

U.S. Department of Health and Human Services, *Dietary Guidelines for Americans,* USDA Home and Garden Bulletin No. 232, U.S. Department of Health and Human Services, Washington, D.C., 1990.

Wason, Betty, *Cooks, Gluttons & Gourmets, A History of Cooking.* Garden City, New York: Doubleday, 1962.

Glossary

à la   In style, e.g., à la Francaise.

à la mode   In the fashion.

à la carte   A list of food items each priced separately.

A-B-C-D   Storage system of classification used to help ensure that perishable products do not deteriorate.

Abaisse   A piece of dough rolled to required size.

Abattis   Winglets, giblets of poultry (de Volaille).

Abricot   Apricot.

Accrual expense   Growth expense.

Agiter   To stir.

Agneau   Lamb.

Aigrefin   Haddock.

Aiguillettes   Meat or fish cut into fine strips.

Ail   Garlic.

Airelle Rouge   Cranberry.

al dente   To the bite.

Allumettes   Match size cut (usually potatoes), e.g., pommes de terre allumettes.

Almond paste   A preparation of finely ground, skinless almonds that have been blanched but not roasted, mixed with sugar.

Aloyau   Sirloin of beef (contre-filet).

Anchois   Anchovy.

Ancienne (à l')   Old fashioned.

Anglais (à l')   English style, plainly cooked food.

Anguille   Eel.

Anis   Aniseed.

Annoncer   To announce (to call out orders).

Antipasto   Italian cold appetizer.

A.P.   As purchased price. Price per unit paid to wholesalers.

Apricot glaze   A syrup that is brushed on pastries to seal and to improve appearance.

Arc   An electric discharge.

Argenteuil   District in France famous for its asparagus.

Aromates   Herbs, spices, and flavorings.

Arrowroot   Starch obtained from the roots of the arrowroot plant.

Artichaut   Artichoke.

Asperge   Asparagus.

Aspic   A clear jelly made from concentrated liquid in which meat, poultry, or fish was cooked.

Assiette   Plate or dish.

Assiette Anglaise   Dish of assorted cold meats.

au bleu   Term used to describe mode of cooking fish, carp, or trout when live, in court-bouillon.

au four   In the oven (e.g., pommes au four).

au jus   With natural juice.

Aubergine   Eggplant.

Baba   Small yeast-raised cake, soaked in rum-flavored syrup, and topped with whipped cream.

Bain-Marie   A double-boiler insert for slow cooking, when direct boiling is to be avoided. Also a steam table in which smaller pans and their contents are kept hot.

Baked Alaska   Modern version usually consists of vanilla, chocolate, and strawberry ice cream layered in a bombe and lined on the bottom with a thin layer of sponge. The bombe is decorated with an Italian meringue and is often served flambéed in a waiter's parade.

Baking soda   Bicarbonate of soda.

Baking powder   A chemical leavening agent containing bicarbonate of soda, an acid, and cornstarch.

Baklava   Very well-known, made by layering many layers of phyllo dough, each sprinkled heavily with melted butter and with a mixture of ground pistachios and walnuts.

Ballotine   Stuffed boneless game or domestic bird.

Bananas Foster   New Orleans classic consisting of flambéed bananas with sugar and spices traditionally served with vanilla ice cream.

Bar   Bass.

Bar-Raye   Rock salmon.

Barbeau   Barbel.

Barbue   Brill.

Barder   To cover meats with slices of salt pork.

Baron   Of mutton or lamb; the saddle with legs.

Barquette   A small boat-shaped piece of pastry or mold.

Basilic   Basil.

Baste   To moisten meat in the oven to prevent drying.

Baton or Batonnet   Stick (commonly denotes small stick garnish).

Batter   A liquid dough thin enough to pour.

Batterie de cuisine   Kitchen equipment.

Bear claw   Well-known Danish dessert, which gets its name from the characteristic cuts made after the bear claw has been filled with a frangipane or almond cream and shaped to resemble a bear's claw. Scandinavian name for them, *kamm*, means comb and refers to a cock's comb.

Becasse   Woodcock.

Becassine   Snipe.

Béchamel   Basic milk sauce (white); one of the foundation sauces.

Beignets   Fritters.

Bench rest   The period allowed dough between cutting and molding; sometimes referred to as intermediate proof.

Benzoate of soda   A preservative.

Betterave   Beetroot.

Beurre   Butter.

Beurre manié   Kneaded butter used for thickening sauces.

Bien cuit   Well or thoroughly cooked.

Biscuit cutter   A metal or plastic mold used to cut individual pieces of dough.

Bisque   A thick cream soup made from shellfish; e.g., Bisque d'homard (lobster soup).

Blanc d'oeuf   White of egg.

Blanc   Water with flour and lemon juice (used to cook vegetables to keep them white).

Blanchir   To blanch (meat, vegetables, etc.) by immersing in cold water, bringing to boil, draining, and refreshing by reimmersion in cold water.

Blanquette   Ragoût or stew made of veal or lamb in a rich velouté sauce.

Bleu   Blue, applied to very rare broiled meat.

Boeuf   Beef.

Bombes   Ice-cream dessert.

Bordure   Border, usually a bordure of rice (ring of rice).

Bouchées   Small puff pastry.

Boudin, noir   Blood sausage or black pudding.

Bouillabaisse   A fish stew, a speciality of southern France.

Bouillir, bouilli   To boil, boiled.

Bouillon   Reduced meat stock.

Boulanger   Baker.

Bouquet garni   Aromatics tied together in a sachet bag, consisting of thyme leaves, bay leaves, whole black peppercorns, and parsley stems. A combination of kitchen herbs such as bay leaf, thyme, and parsley tied in celery or leek, to flavor soups and sauces.

Bourgeoise   Dish prepared in "bourgeois" family style, meats served with vegetables.

Bourgogne   Burgundy (wine).

Boutons (de Buxelles)   Buttons (of Brussels), poetic menu term for Brussels sprouts.

Braiser   To braise.

Braisière   Braising pan or stewing pan with lid; wide, round pot, heavyweight, sides are shorter than base is wide, lateral handles.

Brème   Bream.

Brider   To truss, to tie poultry or meat.

Brigade system   System that identifies and uses the professional staff performing its duties in a kitchen operation.

Brine   Salt solution.

Brioche   Yeast-leavened sponge dough.

Brochette   Skewer or cubes of meat broiled on skewer.

Brunoise   Vegetables cut into fine dice.

Brut   Coarse.

Bruxelloise (à la)   In the Brussels style (with Brussels sprouts).

Buttermilk   The liquid left after butter has been churned from cream.

Cabillaud   Codfish.

Caille   Quail.

Cake   A sweet, baked mixture of flour, liquid, eggs, and other ingredients in loaf or layer form. There are basically three different types of cake: sponge, layer, and pound.

Calibrated   Adjusted to standard.

Calorie   One calorie is equal to the unit of heat needed to increase the temperature of 1 liter of water (0.26 gallon) 1° C, from 15° to 16° C (59° to 60.8° F).

Canapés   Pieces of toasted bread garnished and served as appetizers or snacks.

Canard   Duck.

Canard sauvage   Wild duck.

Candy stove   Round, low-sectioned stove used by confectioners.

Caneton   Duckling (male).

Cannoli   Means pipes, which is an accurate description of the shape of cannoli; it is a popular dessert from Sicily. The cylinders of sweet, crispy pastry are filled with a variety of fillings, from sweet ricotta cheese to pastry-cream fillings with dried fruit and nuts.

Cantaloupe   Melon.

Caramel   Melted sugar in a light-brown syrupy stage.

Caramelizer   To caramelize, to cook sugar until it reaches a brown color.

Carbohydrates   Compounds made up of sugar units; classified as simple or complex.

Carbon dioxide   Gas formed during periods of fermentation caused by the action of yeast or chemical leaveners, baking powder, or baking soda.

Carbonnade   Braised steak.

Carcasse   Carcass; the bone structure of meat or poultry without the meat on it.

Carpe   Carp.

Carre   Rack of veal, lamb, or pork.

Carrelet   Flounder.

Cartouche   A greased round of paper for covering meat dishes during cooking.

Casserole   Fireproof dish, or name of dishes cooked and served in a casserole.

Cassis   Blackcurrant (and blackcurrant liqueur).

Cassoulet   Earthenware dish featuring beans with pork, mutton, goose, or duck.

Caveat emptor   Let the buyer beware.

Cayenne   A very hot, red pepper.

Celeri   Celery.

Celeri-rave   Celeriac or celery root; a turniplike rooted celery.

Cepe   Edible fungus, a kind of yellowish flap mushroom.

Cerefeuil   Chervil.

Cerise   Cherry.

Cervelle   Brain.

Champignon   Mushroom.

Chanterelles   Mushrooms (Cantharellus variety).

Chantilly   Refers to dishes served with crème chantilly.

Chantilly cream   Whipped cream with the addition of sugar and flavorings; the name comes from the château of Chantilly where the famous French chef Vatel worked in the 1800s.

Chapelure   Bread crumbs.

Chapon   Capon (castrated cock).

Charcuterie   Butcher shop where sausages are made and sold.

Charcutier   Sausage maker.

Charlotte royal   Bavarian filling surrounded by ladyfingers, usually molded in a large brioche mold.

Charlotte Russe   Bavarian filling lined with a jelly-roll sponge cake filled with jam or preserves and rolled.

Châteaubriand   Double steak cut from the center of the beef fillet.

Chaud-froid   Food coated with cold white sauce.

Chef de Partie   Chef in charge of shift or section of the kitchen (e.g., Chef Garde-Manger).

Chef de Cuisine   Chef in charge or executive chef.

Cherries jubilee   Macerated bing cherries flambéed in Kirshwasser traditionally served with vanilla ice cream.

Chevreuil   Venison.

Chicoree   Endive.

Chiffonnade   Leaf vegetables shredded or cut into thin ribbons.

China cap   *See* Chinois.

Chinois   A cone-shaped fine strainer or sieve.

Chipolata   A type of small sausage.

Cholesterol A fatlike substance in the body cells of all animals, found only in foods of animal origin; needed by humans to produce hormones, cell membranes, bile, and vitamin D.

Chou de mer Sea kale.

Choux paste *See* Pâte à choux.

Chou Cabbage

Choux Type of pastry used for eclairs, profiteroles, etc.

Chou-fleur Cauliflower.

Chou-frise Curly kale.

Choucroute Sauerkraut, cabbage pickled with salt and fermented.

Choux de Bruxelles Brussels sprouts.

Clarifier To clarify or clear liquids (e.g., consommé, aspic) with ground beef, egg whites, and seasonings.

Clouter Oignon cloute—onion with cloves.

Cobbler A deep-dish dessert of the pie type. The top crust can be made with biscuit rather than pastry dough.

Cocotte A small ovenproof dish.

Coeur Heart (e.g., coeur de laitue—heart of lettuce).

Colin Coal fish.

Commis An apprentice in the kitchen or dining room.

Comparative buying Purchasing from two or more vendors to study the differences between them.

Competitive buying *See* Open-market buying.

Complex carbohydrates Made up of long chains of sugar units linked together.

Compote Stewed fruit.

Compound butter Butter with one or more ingredients added to change the color or flavor.

Concasser To chop roughly (commonly tomatoes that have been blanched, peeled, and seeded).

Concombre Cucumber.

Condensed milk Milk that has been evaporated and condensed, with sugar added as a preservative.

Condiments Accompaniments (to meat products); e.g., relishes, pickles, cold sauces on the dining room table, mustard, ketchup.

Conduction Direct exchange of heat.

Confectionery sugar Icing sugar; granulated sugar that has been pulverized to a powder state with the addition of cornstarch.

Confit Meats cooked and preserved in fat. Fruits preserved in sugar or liquor.

Confiture Jam.

Conformation The shape and form of an animal, and the proportion of meat to bone.

Congre Conger eel.

Consolidate To put together.

Contamination To make impure through contact or mixture.

Contre-filet Sirloin that faces the tenderloin.

Convection The direct exchange of heat through a liquid or gas.

Cooking line The equipment for the production of food normally included in most kitchen designs.

Coq au vin Chicken stewed in wine sauce.

Coquille St. Jacques A scallop.

Coquille (1) A shell-shaped dish; (2) cooked and served in a shell.

Coral The roe of lobster.

Corbeille Basket.

Corn syrup An invert sugar, not as sweet as cane sugar.

Cornstarch One of the most easily digested starch foods. Cooks transparent. Should always be dissolved in cold liquid before adding to a hot liquid.

Corser To flavor and enrich.

Côte A cut of meat; a piece of meat attached to the rib (Côte de boeuf).

Côtelette Cutlet.

Cottonseed oil A vegetable oil expressed from the seed of the cotton plant.

Coulibiac (de Saumon) Salmon in brioche paste with kasha (Russian dish).

Coulis Fruit or vegetable purée (e.g., tomato coulis).

Couper To cut.

Coupes Small bowls to serve cream or compote.

Courge Vegetable marrow.

Courgette Zucchini.

Court-Boullion An aromatic vegetable broth that usually includes vinegar or wine. Water, vinegar, or wine, herbs and seasoning for poaching fish, sweetbread, and so on.

Coustade Pastry crust.

Couverture Bulk chocolate that is used in the making of confections, pralines, and fine pastries. It is a finer, higher-grade product than in regular chocolate and is more expensive.

Crabe Crab.

Cream of tartar Made from tartar deposits from fermented grape juice. Used as an acid in the preparation of commercial baking powder.

Cream puff A light, delicate hollow puff made with choux paste usually served as a dessert with whipped cream or custard filling.

Credit voucher A form that is used by a receiver to report returned goods, incorrect prices, or product substitutions.

Crème Cream.

Crème Anglaise Base uses a basic custard of milk, heavy cream, sugar, and eggs or egg yolks that is cooked to nappé over a water bath.

Crème brûlée Means burnt cream, it has been a popular English dessert since the 1600s. It is a thicker custard than a flan or crème caramel, made with all heavy cream, eggs, and egg yolks rather than milk and whole eggs. It is very soft after baking.

Crème caramel Basic custard of milk, sugar, and eggs, crème caramel is the classic French version of a flan. After baking, some of the sugar, which is placed in the ramekin before it is filled with custard, melts to create a sugar-syrupy sauce.

Crème diplomat Composite cream consisting of a 1:1 ratio of pastry cream and whipped cream.

Crème fraîche Similar taste and consistency to that of sour cream; made commercially by adding an acid to culture and thicken the cream.

Crème patissiere Pastry cream.

Crêpes Thin pancakes.

Crêpes Jacques Crêpes filled with sautéed bananas, seasoned with butter and spices.

Crêpes Suzette Most famous of all flambéed desserts. It consists of crêpes served with oranges and sugar that have been flambéed with Grand Marnier and cognac.

Crêpine Pig's caul used as casing for sausage and forcemeat.

Crêpinettes Individual portions of meat, chicken, or pork enveloped in crêpine or breaded and sauteed or baked.

Crevette (Grise) Shrimp.

Crevette (Rose) Prawn.

Croissant A crescent-shaped roll made with a rich butter dough. Crescent-shaped French rolls.

Croquette   Foodstuff, molded, breaded, and deep-fried.

Croûte au pot   A beef broth, popular in France, garnished with vegetables and dried crusts.

Croûtons   Fried or toasted pieces of bread of various sizes and shapes served as accompaniments to soups or used as socle.

Cru   Raw.

Crustaceans   Shellfish with jointed exterior skeletons.

Cuire   To cook.

Cuisine brigade   (1) Tournant—Rounds cook, (2) Saucier—Sauce cook, (3) Rotisseur—Roast cook, (4) Entremetier—Vegetable cook, (5) Potager—Soup cook, (6) Buffetier—Pantry cook, (7) Poissonnier—Fish cook, (8) Garde-Manger—Cold cook, (9) Patissier—Pastry cook, (10) Boulanger—Baker, (11) Boucher—Butcher.

Cuisinier   Cook.

Cuisse, cuissot   The leg of veal, beef, and so on.

Cuit   Cooked.

Culotte   Rump of beef.

Currants   The dried fruit of a seedless grape, smaller than a raisin.

Custard   The basic is made up of a combination of eggs, sugar, milk, or cream; the coagulation of the egg protein from the heat in the oven to make them firm.

Cygnes, or swans   One of the most beautiful of the choux pastries, swans are made by cutting a shell-shaped puff in half horizontally and filling it with a decorative cream.

Dairy product   Usually associated with products that are derived from milk; this category has been extended to include eggs, cheese, and margarine.

Darioles   Small baba-mold shape.

Darne   A thick middle-cut slice of salmon steak.

Débarrasser   To clear away.

Debrider   To remove trussing string after cooking.

Decorer   To decorate platters, cakes, and so on.

Déglacer   To dilute roasting plaque (with wine, stock, etc.).

Dégraisser   To skim off grease from stews, sauces, and so on.

Demi-glace   Half glaze, brown sauce.

Demi-tasse   Literally a half cup; also a small cup of black coffee.

Denaturation   The breakdown of protein by acid.

Depositor   In bake-shop terms, a pastry bag without a metal tube.

Dépouiller   To remove scum from the surface of liquid during cooking.

Des   Dice.

Désosser   To bone out poultry or fish.

Dextrose   Another name for glucose. Used in yeast dough for its easy fermenting qualities. Also improves crust color.

Diabetes   A disorder of blood-sugar regulation.

Diablotins   Small gnocchi or croutons topped with grated cheese and browned; soup garnish.

Diet   The food and drink that a person usually consumes.

Dinde   Turkey.

Dindonneau   Young turkey.

Dough divider   An implement used in the bake shop to divide a piece of dough into 36 equal pieces.

Dough docker   A tool used in the bake shop to perforate many holes in dough.

Dough hook   Implement used on the baker's mixer to develop dough.

Dough wheel   A cutting wheel mounted on a handle used for cutting or stripping dough.

Dredge To coat lightly, usually with flour or sugar. To coat food with flour by rolling or sprinkling.

Dresser To dress, to decorate.

du Jour Of the day (soup du jour—soup of the day).

Duxelle Chopped shallots and mushrooms cooked in butter.

Echalote Shallot.

Éclair A rich, finger-shaped pastry made from choux paste, usually filled with pastry cream. Choux pastry baked in thick fingers, filled with cream or pastry cream and iced with fondant or chocolate.

Ecrevisse Crayfish.

Egg wash A mixture of egg or milk and water used for brushing on a pastry before baking to improve the finished appearance.

Egg shade A yellow food coloring that is in liquid, paste, or powder form.

Egoutter To drain, strain off liquid.

Emincer To mince, to chop as fine as possible.

Emulsifier A substance that allows the mixing of two or more liquids that usually do not mix to form a stable mixture or emulsion.

Emulsion Suspension of one insoluble liquid in another insoluble liquid.

en Tasse In a cup (consommé en tasse).

en In, served in.

En papillote Mode of cooking (particularly fish) in greased paper.

Entrecôte Steak cut from the sirloin of beef, literally "between the ribs."

Entrée In the United States, the main course.

Entremets Sweets, desserts.

Entremettier Cook who prepares vegetables and egg dishes.

Envelopper To wrap.

Enzymes Class of protein substances produced by living cells; act as catalysts in metabolism.

E.P. Edible-portion price is the cost of a usable portion of the product. This incorporates loss from trimming, shrinkage, and packaging.

Épaule Shoulder.

Éperlan Smelt.

Épinards Spinach.

Escalope A collop or slice.

Escargot Edible snail.

Espagnole Basic brown sauce.

Estouffade Brown meat stock.

Estragon Tarragon.

Esturgeon Sturgeon.

Étouffer, étuver To cook slowly under cover with minimum of added liquid (stock, etc.).

Fagot Faggot, bouquet garni.

Faisan Pheasant.

Farce Stuffing of forcemeat.

Farcir (farci) To stuff (stuffed).

Fat cap Layer of fat that surrounds the muscle tissue.

Fats Fats belong to a class of chemical compounds called lipids; fat is a lipid that is solid at room temperature. Fatty acids are the basic chemical units in fat.

Faux-filet Boned out sirloin.

FDA Food and Drug Administration.

Fecule Cornstarch or flour used for thickening soups, sauces, etc.

Fenouil   Fennel.

Fermentation   The chemical reaction in a yeast-raised dough or other mixture brought about by carbon dioxide gas.

Feuilletage   Puff pastry.

Fiber   The part of plants the human body cannot digest.

FIFO   First-in, first-out rotation of goods in storage.

Filet   Fillet; a thin cut of meat, poultry, and so on, or the skinless flesh of fish removed from bone.

Filet mignon   Small steak cut from tenderloin of beef, veal, lamb, and so on.

Fines herbes   A fine mixture of fresh herbs to season meats, fish, and sauces.

Finish   Quality and distribution of fat around and within the meat.

Flamber   To flame.

Flan   Open tart.

Flanchet   Flank.

Flat paddle   Implement used on the baker's mixer for creaming.

Flavorings   Substances commonly added to food to change and strengthen its flavor.

Flétan   Halibut.

Fleurons   Small crescent-shaped puff pastry.

Foie gras   Fat goose liver.

Foie   Liver.

Folded dough   Dough after a fat has been added and the dough folded numerous times, as in croissant dough.

Folding in   The use of the hand or a rubber spatula when combining two or more mixtures without the loss of air.

Foncer   To line the bottom dish with bacon or paste.

Fond brun   Brown stock.

Fond blanc   White stock.

Fondant   Thick liquid sugar icing.

Fonds de cuisine   Basic stocks or essences.

Fonds de artichaut   Artichoke bottoms.

Fondue   A cheese dish of melted cheese in which pieces of bread are dipped.

Fontaine   The well or hole made in the dry ingredients, before adding liquid to make pastry.

Food mill   Basically, a mechanical sieve, a hand-turned paddle forces cooked food through a strainer plate, removing skin, seeds, and fiber. Food mills may come with interchangeable plates ranging in size from small to large.

Fouetter   To whip or whisk.

Fraise   Strawberry.

Framboise   Raspberry.

Frangipane   An almond-flavored, custardlike pastry cream.

Frappé   Iced.

Frapper   To ice.

Friandises   Small candylike sweets, petits fours.

Fricandeau   Veal braised until very tender.

Fricassée   A white stew.

Frire   To fry.

Frit   Fried.

Friture   Deep-fat frying.

Fructose   Also called fruit sugar or levulose. This is a single sugar and the sweetest sugar.

Fumer (Fume)   To smoke (smoked).

Fumet   Concentrated stock or essence from fish or shellfish.

Galantines   Stuffed chicken or veal in the form of a large roll usually glazed with chaud-froid sauce and decorated for cold buffets.

Ganache   The two main ingredients are chocolate and a water-based liquid: milk, cream, teas, or orange juice; other ingredients, such as fat, flavorings, or alcohol, are optional. Mixture is used when firm as fillings for tortes and pralines or, when liquid, as a glaze for tortes and other desserts.

Gaping   The separation of fish flesh, which indicates that connective tissue between muscle has deteriorated; in bivalves, partial opening of the shell.

Garbure   A thick vegetable soup.

Garde-Manger   Literally translated, means "keeper of food to be eaten"; evolved into an important department in the classical brigade system, which artistically prepares cold food items such as appetizers, pâtés, mousses, and galantines. Cold kitchen; chef who is in charge of Garde-Manger.

Garnir (Garni)   To garnish, garnished, to decorate.

Garniture   The garnish: starches and/or vegetables served with the main course.

Gâteau   Cake.

Gelatin   Obtained from the cartilage in skin and bones of food animals, usually pig, veal, and fish.

Gelée   Jelly (aspic).

Gianduja   Filling that is based on toasted hazelnuts or almonds and sugar, ground to a very fine consistency, and mixed together with chocolate or cocoa butter.

Gibier   Game.

Giblets   Offal.

Gigot d'agneau   Leg of lamb.

Glace   Frozen, glazed, or iced.

Glace de poisson   Fish glaze or extract, made by reducing stock or fumet to the consistency of syrup.

Glace de viande   Meat glaze or extract, usually made by reducing meat stock to a dark, thick semiliquid.

Glacer   (1) To freeze or chill; (2) to cook in such a way as to acquire a shiny surface; (3) to color food under a salamander or in a hot oven.

Gliadin   Component that provides the dough with its elasticity.

Glucose   Also called dextrose. This is a single sugar that makes up half of sucrose (table sugar). *See* Dextrose.

Gluten   A tough, rubbery substance formed when flour is mixed with water. Gluten serves as the structure in yeast dough.

Glutenin   Component that gives the dough the strength and ability to retain the gases given off by the yeast.

Glycogen   The form in which animals store carbohydrates.

Gnocchi   Dumplings of semolina, flour, or potatoes.

Goujon   Gudgeon; meat or fish cut into small strips, roughly or gudgeon size, also small freshwater fish.

Granita   French *granite;* Italian ice made with puréed fruit, sugar syrup, and sometimes fruit juice or alcohol; the difference from a sorbet is the freezing process, sorbets are churned during freezing while granitas are still frozen then scraped after they are solid. Granita gets its name from the Italian *grana,* meaning grainy.

Granite   Water ice.

Gratin   Browned surface of foods cooked in a hot oven or under a salamander.

Gratiner   To brown a dish sprinkled with grated cheese under a salamander or in the oven.

Griller (grille)   To grill, to broil.

Groseille   Currant.

Hacher   To chop finely.

Hachis   Hachis de boeuf, minced meat.

Hand whisk   A tool used in the bake shop for dissolving, blending and mixing. Helps to aerate products.

Hareng   Herring.

Haricot blanc   Bean (white).

Haricot vert   French bean (green bean).

Hatelet   Decorative silver skewer used in decorating buffet pieces.

Heat transfer   Heat transfer can be accomplished by conduction, convection, and radiation. The greater the friction, the greater the heat produced.

Herbs   Fragrant leaves of various perennial or annual plants.

High-ratio shortening   Vegetable shortening with mono- and diglycerides added to improve emulsifying properties.

High-gluten flour   Hard wheat flour with additional gluten properties.

Homard   Lobster.

Homogenization   Most commercially sold milk is homogenized to prevent the separation of the fat; this separation is commonly referred to as *creaming*.

Honey   One of the oldest sweets known; stored in honeycombs by the honeybees that produce it.

Hors d'oeuvre   The first course of appetizer, canapés served hot or cold at the beginning of a meal.

Huitre   Oyster.

Hydrogenated fat   A shortening, processed from a vegetable oil by the addition of hydrogen to improve color, melting point, firmness, and emulsification.

Hydrogenation   Process that forces hydrogen into fat and oil.

Ice-cream bombes   Generally, bombes are made up of layers of ice cream; when the bombe is cut, it reveals the intricate layers. The outside layer is best if made with a custard or French-style ice cream; the last inside layer is usually made with a parfait mixture. A classic bombe is Baked Alaska.

Icing rack   Used for pouring icing or fondant in the bake shop. Sometimes used as a cooling rack.

Internal invoice   *See* Requisition.

Invoice   A listing of the products that are being delivered, including amount, description, weight or count per package, unit price, and extension, as well as terms of payment and total cost to the operation, including taxes and transportation costs.

Isinglass   Gelatin obtained from air bladder of certain fishes.

Issuing system   The removal of product from the storeroom.

Jambon   Ham.

Jardinière   Garnish of fresh vegetables cut into small dice or julienne.

Jarret (de veau)   Knuckle (of veal).

Jaune d'oeuf   Egg yolk.

Julienne   Meat or vegetables cut into fine strips.

Jus   The natural juice of meat, vegetable, or fruit.

Jus lie   Thickened juice.

Kitchen machinery   Equipment used in the preparation of food.

Kromeski   A type of meat croquette.

Laitue   Lettuce.

Lamproie   Lamprey.

Langouste   Spiny lobster.

Langue   Tongue.

Lapin   Rabbit.

Lard   Fat obtained from the hog. Graded by the part of the animal from which it was obtained or by the type of feed the animal was fed—bacon or salt pork.

Larder   To lard, that is, to insert strips of fat with a larding needle into lean meat.

Lardons   Strips of salt pork or bacon used for larding.

Laurier   Bay leaf.

Leavening agent   A substance used to lighten a dough or batter.

Lecithin   An emulsifier found in egg yolks.

Levulose   Another name for fructose.

Liaison   The thickening or binding agent used in the preparation of a sauce; commonly egg yolk and cream, to thicken soups and sauces.

Lie   Slightly thickened.

Lier   To thicken (usually with starch or egg).

Lievre   Hare.

Limande   Dab, lemon sole.

Lipid   An organic compound that is insoluble in water but can be used by the body.

Macedoine   Diced, mixed vegetables or fruits.

Maigre   Lean; lenten meal without meat.

Mais   Maize, sweet corn.

Maître d'hôtel   Restaurant manager.

Major minerals   *See* Minerals.

Malt   Obtained from barley, often referred to as malt barley; used to improve color, flavor, fermentation, and crumb in bread dough.

Maquereau   Mackerel.

Marbling   Fat that is contained within the muscle tissue.

Margarine   Often referred to as a butter substitute. Made from blending animal or vegetable fats with additives for color, flavor, and absorption.

Marinade   Blends of liquids and flavorings used in marinating.

Marmite   Stockpot; a heavy pot that is very large, sides are taller than base is wide, lateral handles.

Marmite, la petite   A type of broth with beef, chicken, vegetable, and rice cooked and served in a small earthenware pot.

Marron   Chestnut.

Masquer   To coat or mask with sauce, jelly, and so on.

Measurement   The amount of an ingredient that is included in the baker's formula or chef's recipe.

Medaillons   Round pieces of meat.

Melanger   To mix two or more ingredients together.

Menthe   Mint.

Meringue   A delicate, fluffy mixture of stiffly whipped egg whites plus sugar; used as an icing, ingredient, or dried pastry item.

Merlan   Whiting.

Merluche   Hake.

Mesolithic   Middle Stone Age.

Metric system   A simple system of measurement that is commonly used worldwide.

Meunière   A method of cooking in which the meat of fish is dredged in flour and shallow-fried in butter, served with sauce meunière.

Microbiology   The study of small physical life such as bacteria.

Mignonnette   Whole peppercorns roughly ground.

Minerals   Essential elements needed by the body in very small amounts; they are classified as major minerals and trace minerals.

Mirepoix   Diced vegetables and herbs sautéed in fat used in flavoring for soups and sauces.

Mise en place   Literally, put-in-place; the kitchen expression for being prepared for cooking or for service.

Moelle   Marrow from a beef bone.

Mollet   Soft-boiled egg.

Mollusks   Various types of unjointed shellfish, including bivalves, univalves, and cephalopods.

Monder   To blanch, peel, and seed (tomatoes).

Monter   The beating of cream, egg whites, and so on.

Monter au beurre   To enrich a sauce or reduction by dropping in small pieces of butter and tossing to blend.

Morue   Salt cod.

Moule   Mussel.

Moulin   Hand mill (pepper grinder).

Mousse   A sweet or savory dish prepared in molds made on a cream base.

Mouton   Mutton.

Mulet   Mullet, grey.

Mur   Ripe.

Mure   Blackberry (sometimes referred to as a *mure sauvage*).

Mustards   Condiments prepared from a combination of ground white, black, or brown seeds of the cabbage family.

Napoleons, or mille feuilles   One of the most well-known puff items in the United States; means "thousand leaves." Pastry is docked heavily before it is baked and cut into rectangles, which are filled with a pastry cream or chiboust, and the top is decorated with fondant.

Napper   To coat with sauce, aspic, sugar, and so on.

Navarin   A brown lamb or mutton stew.

Navet   Turnip.

Neolithic   New Stone Age.

Noisette   Nut or, in reference to meat, a round piece of veal or lamb tenderloin; also small potato balls.

Nonpareils   A garnish; colored sugar crystals.

Nonfat dry milk   Whole milk in dry form after the fat has been removed.

Nonperishable   Nonperishable food items are those with a long shelf life, whose quality is unaffected when stored for up to one year.

Noques   Flour dumplings.

Nouilles   Noodles.

Nulomoline   An invert sugar, used to retard drying of a baked good.

Nutrients   Compounds that make up food and perform one or more functions: supply energy, build and repair tissue, or regulate body processes.

Nutrition   The process by which an animal takes in and uses food.

Oie   Goose.

Oignon   Onion.

Oil   A lipid that is liquid at room temperature.

Old dough   A yeast-raised dough in which the gluten has overdeveloped or the dough has overfermented.

Opacity   Degree or quality of opaqueness.

Open-market buying   A common system of buying that requires a restaurateur to secure price quotes for identical items from several sources of supply.

Oseille   Sorrel.

Overhead   All expenses an organization incurs except food, labor, and profit.

Oxidative rancidity   To become rancid when exposed to oxygen.

Pailles   Straws (pommes pailles, straw potatoes).

Paillettes   Cheese straws.

Paleolithic   Old Stone Age.

Palmiers Commonly referred to in the United States as *elephant ears,* these pastries can be large or petits fours sized. Pastry is delicately rolled out with granulated sugar and folded in a fourfold to look like a palm leaf.

Pan liner A paper sheet, used to eliminate pan greasing.

Panade/panada A binding agent, usually for forcemeats or stuffing.

Paner, pane To coat with bread crumbs.

Pannequets Pancakes.

Panure As chapelure—fine crumbs from dried breads.

Papillotes Cooking in paper wrapping (en papillote).

Paprika Hungarian red pepper.

Par Inventory system that establishes the range of minimum to maximum desirable amount of product on hand.

Parer To trim meat, and so on.

Parfumer To impart bouquet by addition of aromatic herbs, and so on.

Paris-Brest The pâte à choux is piped in the form of a wreath and baked with almonds on top. The filling is traditionally praline flavored.

Parures Trimmings, cooked or raw.

Passer a l'etamine To pass through tammy cloth.

Pasteurization Processing milk and other liquids to kill bacteria.

Pastillage Sugar pastes used in modeling.

Pastry brush A brush used in the bake shop for applying egg wash or water on a pastry before baking or for applying syrup after baking.

Pâté Paste or pastry.

Pâte à bombe Mixture of whipped egg yolks and sugar syrup.

Pâte à choux Sometimes referred to as *choux paste.* Used to prepare many desserts, including éclairs and cream-puff shells.

Pathogens Disease-producing organisms.

Paupiettes Thin, flattened slices of meat, stuffed and rolled.

Paysanne Triangular-shaped slices of mixed vegetables.

Peach melba The modern version of this dessert consists of a slice of sponge cake, vanilla ice cream, peaches, and melba sauce.

Pears belle Hélène This simple, but classic dessert consists of a poached pear or pear half with a scoop of vanilla ice cream and is served with a rich, chocolate sauce.

Pecan smear A preparation for pecan-roll pans.

Pêche Peach.

Pectin Occurs naturally in many fruits, especially blueberries, cranberries, apples, and citrus fruits; it is also derived from plant cells. Substance most responsible for thickening and gelling jams and jellies and preserves. Made in either powdered or liquid form.

Pelamide Pilchard.

Perche Perch.

Perdreau Partridge.

Periodic ordering The periodic-ordering method establishes how much product will be used for a given period of time.

Perishable Perishable items are those food products that have a relatively short shelf life.

Perpetual inventory A sophisticated inventory system used to maintain constant records of expensive and highly perishable inventory items.

Persil hache Chopped parsley.

Persil Parsley.

Persillade   Minced garlic and chopped parsley for flavor and garnish; added to dish just before served.

Persille   Sprinkled with chopped parsley (parsley potatoes).

Petits pois   Peas.

Petits fours   Small, fancy cakes or biscuits, dipped in icing and decorated.

Piccata   Small veal cutlets.

Pièce montée   Centerpiece on a platter or buffet.

Pied   Foot.

Pieds de boeuf   Cow heels.

Pieds de porc   Pork feet.

Pilaw, pilaf   A rice dish with or without meat (usually lamb).

Pilferage   Theft in small quantities.

Piment   Capsicum.

Pintade   Guinea fowl.

Piquer   To insert small pieces of fat into lean meat with a special needle.

Plaque a rôtir   Roasting plaque.

Plat   Plate or dish.

Plat du jour   Dish of the day (specialty of the day).

Plie   Plaice. A flatfish similar to sole and flounder.

Plongeur   Pot washer.

Pluvier   Plover.

Pocher   To poach or cook young chickens or fish in liquid, on simmering temperature.

Poeler   A method of oven cooking that is similar to braising or pot roasting.

Pointe   Tip (of a knife or of asparagus).

Poire   Pear.

Poireau   Leek.

Poitrine   Breast (poitrine de volaille—chicken breast).

Poivrade   Flavored with pepper.

Poivre   Pepper.

Pojarski   A minced cutlet of veal in the shape of a cutlet.

Pomme   Apple; also used in menus and in kitchen as short for pomme de terre.

Pomme de terre   Potato.

Porc   Pork.

Portion   The amount of a menu item that is served to the customer.

Pot-au-feu   Rich soup with meats and vegetables.

Potage   Soup.

Potiron   Pumpkin.

Poularde, poulardine   Young, fat chicken.

Poule   Hen.

Poulet   Young chicken.

Poulet d'Inde   Young turkey.

Poussin   Young, immature chicken.

Praline   Toasted almonds and nuts in caramelized sugar.

Presale   Lamb or mutton raised on salty grass on the French seacoast. A high quality of meat.

Press out   To distribute using a pastry bag with a metal tube, such as for an éclair or butter cookie.

Printanière   Garnish of spring vegetables.

Processed eggs   Shell eggs that have been frozen or dried.

Profiteroles   Small or medium-sized balls made out of choux paste.

Proof box   Enclosed cabinet capable of producing heat and moisture for proofing of bread, rolls, and other yeast-raised items.

Protein   One of a class of complex compounds that are an essential part of living matter.

Prune   Plum.

Purchasing   The functions of planning, obtaining quotes, ordering, receiving, storage, and issuance of product for an establishment.

Purée   Mashed or sieved potatoes, vegetables, fruit, and so on.

Purveyor   Vendor.

Q factor   The price the cook must charge to recover the cost of all the ingredients that are too small to calculate.

Quartier   Quarter; to divide or cut into quarters.

Quenelles   Dumpling made of meat, poultry, fish, and so on.

Quiche lorraine   Savory flan of egg custard and Gruyere cheese in a thick pie dough.

Quick breads   Items that have breadlike texture but contain no yeast products.

Radiation   Energy (heat) transmitted through space by the propagation of a wave through any form of matter.

Radis   Radish.

Raft   Coagulated protein formation that floats on a stock and acts as a clarifying agent.

Ragoût   A rich brown stew of meat or poultry.

Raifort   Horseradish.

Ramekin   A savory tartlet or earthenware dish in which food is baked and served.

Ravioli   An Italian pasta dish.

Rechauffé   Reheated.

Rechauffer   To reheat.

Reduction   The result of reducing by boiling down sauces to increase the flavor and richness.

Relative humidity   The percentage of moisture or water vapor contained in air at any definite temperature.

Religieuses   Means nun, which is what the French think this pastry looks like. Two small, filled choux are decorated with fondant and stacked. The bottom choux has a decorated teardrop of buttercream piped around it where the two choux fit together.

Requisition   Form that allows management to track the physical movement of inventory items and costs.

Retard   To cool; used to slow down the movement of dough; usually achieved in the refrigerator.

Revenir   To fry quickly to color.

Ricer   Also called *potato ricer;* cooked foods such as potatoes, carrots or turnips may be mashed or riced with this apparatus.

Rigor mortis   A condition that sets into the body of a dead animal, stiffening muscles; it is caused by chemical changes in the flesh.

Rind   The skin or outer coat that may be peeled, grated, or taken off certain citrus fruits, such as the lemon or orange.

Ripe dough   A yeast-raised dough that has reached its highest volume and is ready to be made up.

Ris   Sweetbreads.

Rissole   Deep-fried small turnover.

Rissoler   To brown.

Rizotto   Italian rice dish.

Rognon   Kidney.

Rognonnade (de veau)   Saddle (of veal) complete with kidneys.

Rolling pin Implement used to flatten dough to a smooth, even sheet.

Romaine Cos lettuce.

Rondeau Heavy pan with straight sides that are less than the width of the base; lateral handles.

Roquefort A blue semisoft French cheese.

Rôtir, Rôti To roast, roasted.

Rôtisseur Roast cook.

Rôtissoire Also referred to as a *roasting plaque;* pan is heavyweight with a large surface area, relatively shallow sides, and lateral handles.

Rouget Red mullet.

Rounding up Term used for rounding out cut pieces of bread dough to seal after cutting.

Roux Thickening agent made of flour and melted butter or other fat used to thicken soups and sauces.

Royale Type of custard cut into various shapes and used as a garnish.

Russe Stew pan; heavy pan with straight sides of medium height, elongated handles.

Sabayon French name for *Zabaglione;* dessert made of whipped eggs, sugar, and wine.

Saignant Rare.

Saisir To sear meat surfaces in hot fat.

Saint Honore Named for the patron saint of pastry chefs (and the street in Paris that is home to so many *patisserie,* or pastry shops; this classic gateaux is made with a puff-pastry base that has a ring of pâte à choux piped around its edge. It is filled with a cream filling, usually a crème diplomat and decorated with a chantilly cream that is piped using a special tip that creates a woven pattern.

Salamandre Salamander (a top-fired grill) for glazing or browning of food.

Sale Salted.

Salpicon A mixture of finely diced meat of ham or tongue and mushrooms bound in sauce.

Sanitation Knowledge of healthy and clean conditions; application of methods to remove disease-causing bacteria.

Saucisses Sausages.

Sauerkraut Choucroute.

Sauge Sage.

Saumon Salmon.

Sauter Literally, to jump; cooking by tossing in a small amount of hot fat.

Sauteuse Round, shallow, heavy pan with sloping sides.

Sautoir Round, shallow, heavy pan with straight walls and a long handle.

Savarin Light yeast dough; usually baked in ring mold.

Scrod A descriptive term meaning a young fish under three pounds, usually applied to cod and haddock.

Seafood Any edible animal that lives in water.

Seasonings Blend of herbs, spices, or salts used to enhance the flavor of foods.

Selle Saddle (selle d'agneau—saddle of lamb).

Semiperishable Semiperishable products are food items with a longer shelf life than perishables.

Sherbets Made from a sugar-syrup base with the addition of fruit, fruit juice, and sometimes alcohol; basically made from the same type base, but a sherbet contains the addition of a milk product; it is not a solid.

Shrink dough To relax dough, to release air formed during rolling.

Sieve Implement used in the bake shop to sift, or make fine in texture.

Simple carbohydrates   Made up of single sugars and pairs of sugars linked together.

Single-source buying   The linking of a foodservice establishment with one purveyor for most of the products that will be bought. Single-source buying is typically used for nonperishable items.

Smallwares   Small, nonmechanical kitchen equipment.

Socles   Platform to elevate a product to improve presentation and appearance; for example, toasted bread used to raise an entrée item on a dinner plate.

Sorbet   A water ice served between meals to stimulate appetite.

Soubise   A thick sauce with puréed onions stewed in butter or puréed onions and rice.

Soufflé   A light sponge either sweet or savory, made to order.

Soufflé Glace   Frozen in a ramekin with a collar; when mixture is hard, the collar is removed to reveal a frozen parfait that resembles a baked soufflé. The parfaits are made from a pâte à bombe or crème anglaise base that has a lightly whipped cream folded into it.

Sous chef   Assistant to the chief cook.

Spätzle   Tiny noodles or dumplings made from flour, eggs, milk, and seasonings. Spätzle are usually boiled and tossed with butter.

Spätzle maker   Apparatus for making spätzle. It has small holes through which the plunger pushes spätzle batter into boiling water.

Spatula   An implement consisting of a flat, thin blade set in a handle.

Specification   A written description of each product to be procured; commonly referred to as a spec.

Spices   The fruits, flowers, bark, seeds, and roots of plants and trees.

Spooms   Made from a sugar-syrup base with the addition of fruit, fruit juice, and sometimes alcohol; made just like sorbet except an Italian meringue is folded into them during freezing; often they are made from wine or champagne; spooms are not a solid.

Staling   Process of firming starch particles after a product is baked.

Standard   Rules or measures used for making comparisons and judgments.

Standard of quantity   Measurement of weight, count, or volume.

Standard of quality   The degree of excellence of a raw or finished product.

Staples   Nonfood items, such as cleaning materials, paper goods, and smallwares.

Starch   The form in which plants store carbohydrates.

Stippling   Term used for the characteristic and decorative cuts made on the top of certain types of bread.

Stockpot   *See* Marmite.

Storage   A two-way function in which goods are received and issued from the storeroom.

Streusel   A crumb mixture of sugar, shortening, and flour with spices and flavors added; used as a topping.

Strudel   Most famous of all Austrian pastries; patience and dedication is needed to work with this dough; the dough, like baklava, is sprinkled with butter for added flavor and flakiness, then filled. Strudel should be served hot and traditionally sprinkled with confectionery sugar.

Suprême   The best part of meat, game, or poultry; for example, breast of chicken (suprême de poulet).

Surimi   Processed product manufactured with various fish and flavorings to mimic shellfish.

Swans   Meringue that is piped into the shape of a swan and filled with mousse or chantilly cream for an elegant dessert.

Table d'hôte   The set menu for the day at a fixed price.

Tasse   Cup, *en Tasse*—served in a cup.

TDZ Temperature danger zone; 40° to 140° F.

Terrine Earthenware casserole; also a term for pâté cooked in a terrine.

Tête (de veau) Head (calf's head).

Thermal death point (TDP) The temperature when yeast is no longer active (dies): 138° F.

Thon Tunny, tuna fish.

Timbale A straight-sided, 2-inch deep dish or mold.

Tiramisu Most well-known of these Italian spoon desserts; best when made with the traditional *savoiardi* (ladyfingers) that have been soaked in an espresso-flavored simple syrup laced with rum. Mascarpone and cream cheeses are usually creamed together to create the filling. Many chefs use their innovative variations to interpret the dish.

Tomate Flavored with tomato product.

Topinambour Jerusalem artichoke.

Tournedos A small steak from the center cut of tenderloin.

Tourner To turn, to shape vegetables or potatoes with a tourner knife; also to turn sour.

Toxin Poison produced in organic matter.

Trace minerals Minerals present in the body in amounts less than 5 grams.

Tranche A slice.

Trancher To carve or slice.

Trancheur Carver.

Travailler To work, to manipulate, or to knead.

Trifle Spoon dessert of English origin; originated in the 1600s; also known to the Victorians as *tipsy pudding* because they enjoyed the spirit-laden layers at a time when drinking openly was frowned upon and when they were often inebriated by it.

Truffe Truffle, a pungent black fungus that grows underground in northern Italy or France.

Truite saumonée Salmon trout.

Truite Trout.

Tube pan Cake pan with a center tube, usually used for angel-food cake.

Turban Dishes molded into turban shape.

Turbotière Turbot kettle.

Turnovers In French, *chaussons*, meaning slippers; fruit-filled pastries often look like slippers.

Turntable A stand used in cake decorating.

Vacherin Classic French term for a meringue that is piped into a basket shape to hold mousses, creams, fruits, and so on.

VCM Vertical cutter mixer.

Veau Veal.

Velouté Literally, velvet; a thick-textured white soup or sauce.

Venaison Venison.

Vendor Anyone who supplies food or nonfood products to a foodservice operation.

Viande Meat.

Viennoise (à la) In Viennese style (breaded).

Vinegars Flavorings made when bacteria attack alcohol contained in alcoholic liquids such as ale or wine.

Vitamins Essential nutrients needed by the body in very small amounts. There are two classes of vitamins: fat soluble and water soluble.

Vol-au-vent Puff-pastry shell in which ragoût or fricassée is served (vol-au-vent, financière).

Volaille Poultry.

Wholesalers Large companies that purchase from manufacturers and provide warehousing, delivery, and credit services to operations.

Yeast A microscopic plant used to aerate breads and pastries.

Young dough A yeast-raised dough in which the gluten has not properly developed; underfermented.

Zabaglione *See* Sabayon.

Zeste Zest, the outer rind of citrus fruit.

Zuppa Inglese Means English soup, this delicacy is usually rum- or liqueur-soaked cakes or cookies layered with a cream-type filling, often including ricotta or mascarpone cheese. They are traditionally served in clear, large bowls so the layers can be seen and they can be spooned out by the diner.

Index

Accidents, 37
Acesulfate K, 84
Achenes, 271
Acid ingredient, in clarification of consommé, 198
Actual food cost percentage, 46
ADA (azodicarbonamide), 241
Adaptation, tasting ability and, 153
Additional cost, 45
Adjustment, in recipe modification process, 21–22
Agar-agar, 228, 263
Age, tasting ability and, 153
Aging
    flour, 241
    meat, 119
Air
    in chocolate, 387
    as physical leavening agent, 260–261
Air cell, 70
A la minute dessert plating, 398
Albufera sauce, 195
Albumin, 188, 198
Alcohol, 17, 152
Al dente, 165
Allemande sauce, 195
All-purpose flour, 240
All-purpose shortening, 260, 320
Allspice, 85, 264
Almond butter, 194
Almond flavoring, for ice cream, 374
Almond lace cookies, 314
Almonds, 71, 269
Aluminum, 143, 167
America
    cookery in, 11–14
    history of baking in, 236–237
American buttercream, 337
American Cookery (Simmon), 11–12
American Danish, 302–303
Amino acids, 18
Ammonium carbonate, 261
Anchovy butter, 197
Anchovy paste/fillets, 82
Angelica, 264

Anise, star, 82, 266
Anise seed, 85, 264
Anthocyanins, 183
Antioxidants, 77
AP (as-purchased amount), 44
Apicius, Marcus, 5
Appearance, food, 147–148, 154
Appetizers
    canapés, 211
    forcemeats, 212–216
    hors d'oeuvre, 206–212
    salad as, 206
Apple butter, 82
Apple corer, 141
Apple pie spice, 90, 267
Apples, 64
Applesauce, 82
AP price, 53
Apricots, 65
Apron, chef's, 404
Aroma
    flavor and, 148–149
    of fresh fish, 102
    nutritive value and, 182–183
Arrowroot, 82, 192, 262
Artery pumping method, for brining, 217
Artichoke, 57
Art of Cookery Made Plain and Easy, The (Glass, Hannah), 7
Ascorbic acid, 241
Asparagus, 57
Aspartame, 84
Aspic, 227–229
Aspic powder, 82
As-purchased amount (AP), 44
Aurore sauce, 195
Automatic potato peeler, 139
Avocado, 65
Azodicarbonamide (ADA), 241

Babas, 285
Bacon-wrapped hors d'oeuvre, 207
Bacteria, 31–32
Bagels, 282–283
Baguette, 282

Bain-Marie spoon, 142
Baked Alaska, 376
Baker's cheese, 351
Baker's dozen, 236
Baker's margarine, 260
Baker's yeast, 244
Baking
    blind, 326
    of bread, 238
    of cakes, 335
    of cookies, 312–313
    crossover, 313
    defined, 170
    historical aspects, 234, 235–237
    ingredients in
        cream, 258
        eggs, 251–255
        fats/oils, 258–260
        gelling agents, 263
        herbs/spices, 264–268
        leavening agents, 260–262
        milk, 255–258
        nuts, 268–271
        sweeteners, 247–251
        thickening agents, 262–263
    meringue, 352–353
    pâte à choux, 364–365
    process, 171
    slow. See Slow baking
    of yeast-raised dough, 280
Baking powder, 82, 261, 332
Baking soda, 82, 261, 332
Baklava, 236, 367–368
Ballottine, 214
Balsamic vinegar, 89
Bananas
    banana bread, 308
    banana pudding, 367
    Bananas Foster, 363
    characteristics/use, 65
    as flavoring for ice cream, 374
Banquet dessert plating, 398
Barbecue sauce, 90
Barbecue spice, 90
Barding, 172

Barley, 73
Barquettes, 207
Bases
 canapé, 211
 soup, 82, 187
Basil, 85, 267
Batard, 282
Batter, 172
Baumé scale (hydrometer), 377
Baumkuchen, 336
Bavarian cream, 358–359
Bay leaves, 85
Bay scallops, 97
Bean paste, 82
Beans, 57, 72, 74
Bean sprouts, 57
Bear claws, 303
Béarnaise sauce, 195
Béchamel sauce, 190, 194, 195–196
Beef, 26, 119–120
Beets, 57
Beignets, 365
Belly burn, 101
Beluga, 210
Bench rest, for yeast-raised dough, 278
Benzoyl peroxide, 241
Bercy sauce, 195
Berries, 65
Beurre manié, 192
BHA (butylated hydroxyanisol), 77
BHT (butylated hydroxytoluine), 77
Bialys (bagels), 282–283
Bigarade sauce, 195
Binding agents, for ice cream, 374
Biscuit mixing method, 307–308, 320
Bivalves, 97, 112–114. *See also* Clams
Black Forest Torte, 336
Black peppercorns, 266
Black strap molasses, 84
Black vinegar, 89
Black walnut, 271
Blanchan, 88
Blanching, 162, 165, 182
Bleaching, 241
Blending methods, 307, 333
Blind baking, 326
Blinis, 208
Blitz method for, puff pastry dough,
 296–297
Block method for, puff pastry dough, 296
Bloom Gellometer, 263
Bocuse, Paul, 10
Boiled icing, 338
Boiling process
 description, 162, 165
 for rice, 184
 vs. simmering process, 165
Bolognaise sauce, 195
Bombes, ice-cream, 375
Bones, 117
Boning knife, 161
Bonnefoy sauce, 195

Bordelaise sauce, 195
Boston Cooking School, 12
Boston Cooking School Cookbook, The
 (Farmer), 12–13
Boston cream pie, 336
Bouchées, 207, 208, 298
Boucher (butcher), 203
Bouchette, 208
Bouillon cubes, 82
Bouillon strainer, 142
Bouquet arrangement, for vegetable
 carvings, 225
Bouquet garni, 187
 in clarification of consommé, 198
Bowls, for making meringue, 352
Braising, 179, 180, 182
Braising fork, 141
Bran, wheat, 241
Brazil nuts, 72, 74, 269
Bread
 historical aspects, 234, 235–237
 ingredients, basic, 237–238
  dough improvers, 247
  flour, 238–244
  salt, 238, 246–247
  water, 238, 244
  yeast, 238, 244–246
 for low-fat meals, 26
 making, ten steps of, 276–280
 sourdough, 286–288
 storage of, 280–281
Bread crumbs, 82
Breading, standard procedure, 172, 175
Bread pudding, 350
Breakfast buffet, 220
Breakfast buffets, 401
Breaking, 191
Brewer's yeast, 244
Brigade system, 9
Brining, 103, 217–218
Brioche dough, 284–285
Britain, historical aspects of baking in, 236
Broccoli, 57
Broilers, 127–128
Broiling, 179
Bronze Age, 3
Brownies, 314
Brown sugar, 81, 83, 250
Brunch buffet, 220
Brussel sprouts, 58
Buckwheat, 73
Buffalo chopper, 138
Buffets
 creating/planning, 221
 defined, 220, 400
 food display for, 225–227
 food presentation for, 402
 planning, 400–401
 preparation on day of event, 231
 preparation schedule, 222–227
 traffic flow zones, 221
 types of, 220–221, 401–402

 zones for, 402
Buffettier, 204
Butcher (boucher), 203
Butter
 in baking, 258
 compound, 194, 197
 grading, 71
 in pie dough, 319–320
 in puff pastry dough, 295–296
Butter buds, 79
Buttercreams, 337–338
Butter-flavored oil, 79
Butter ganache, for filling pralines, 389
Buttermilk, 257
Butternuts, 271
Butterscotch sundaes/coupes, 375
Butylated hydroxyanisol (BHA), 77
Butylated hydroxytoluine (BHT), 77
Buying
 of chocolate, 388
 vs. purchasing, 53

Cabbage, 58
Cake flour, 239
Cakes
 baking, 335
 formula conversions, 343–344
 historical aspects, 331
 ingredients for, 331–332
 mixing methods for, 332–335
 mousse, 360
 storage of, 335
 types, classic, 336–337
 vs. torte, 335
Calcium, 409, 410
Calico scallops, 97
Calories, 17
Canapés, 211
Candling, 254
Canelloni, 80
Cannoli, 368
Canola oil, 79
Caper butter, 197
Capers, 82, 88
Caramel sauce, 400
Caraway seed, 85, 264
Carbohydrates, 18
Carbon knives, 160
Carborundum, 159
Cardamom, 85, 264–265
Cardinal sauce, 195
Carême, Marie Antoine, 8
Caribbean sundaes/coupes, 375
Carotenoids, 183
Carrots, 58
Carryover cooking, 170–171
Casein, 256
Cashews, 74, 269
Cauldron, 5, 6
Cauliflower, 58
Caviar, 82, 209–210
Cayenne, 85

CCPs (Critical Control Points), 33–36
Celeriac (celery root), 58
Celery, 59
Celery seed, 85
Centerpieces, 222
Cereals, for low-fat meals, 26
Chalazae, 70, 253, 254
Champagne vinegar, 89
Chantilly cream, 357–358
Charcutier, 204
Charlotte aux pommes, 359
Charlotte royal, 359
Charlotte russe, 359
Chasseur sauce, 195
Chaud-Froid sauce, 229, 231
Cheese
    balls, 208
    for cheesecake, 351
    fondue, 208
    hard, 71
    for low-fat meals, 26
    pies, 319
    semihard, 71
    soft, 72
Cheesecakes, 351
Chef garde-manger
    brigade, 203–204
    duties, 203
    kitchen equipment for, 203
    tools for, 203
Chef's uniform, 403–405
Chemical leavening, for pâte à choux, 364
Cherries jubilee, 363
Cherry sundaes/coupes, 375
Chervil, 86
Chestnuts, 74, 88, 267, 269–270
Chicken, 122
Chiffon pies, 321, 325
Chiffons, 352
Child, Julia, 13
Chili powder, 90
Chili sauce, 82, 90
Chives, 86, 268
Chivry butter, 197
Chlorine, for flour bleaching, 241
Chlorophyll, 183
Chocolate
    in baking, 267
    buying, 388
    candies. *See* Pralines
    centerpieces, 222
    cleaning/roasting of cocoa bean,
        382–383
    compound, 386, 391
    conching, 381, 384
    description/uses, 88
    excessive heat and, 386–387
    in fillings, for pralines, 388–390
    historical aspects, 381–382
    as ice cream flavoring, 374
    ingredients, 383
    love of, 381

making of, 382
melted, texture changes in, 387
melting, 384
moisture and, 386, 387
molded, 392–393
molds, 391
nontempered, 386
producing, 382
storage of, 387
substitution, 345
syrup, 82
tempering, 384–386
Chocolate chip ice cream, 374
Chocolate fondant liqueur, 393
Chocolate fudge sundaes/coupes, 375
Chocolate liqueur, 383
Chocolate mousse, 360
Chocolate sauce, 400
Choice grade, of meat, 118
Cholesterol, 19–20, 26
Choron sauce, 195
Chrome griddle, 129
Chutney, 82, 362
Cider vinegar, 89
Cigarette paste, 313–314
Cigarette smoking, tasting ability and, 152
Cinnamon, 86, 265
Cinnamon sugar, 90, 267
Clafoutis, 366–367
Clam juice, 82
Clam opener, 141
Clams
    description/use, 82
    hard-shell, 97
    preparation/fabrication, 112, 113
    soft-shell, 97
Clarification, of consommé, 198
Cleaning, 36–37
Clear soup, 184
Clostridium perfringens gastroenteritis, 32
Cloves, 86, 265
Coagulation, 182
Coarse sugar, 248
Coat, chef's, 403–404
Cobblers, 327
Cocoa, 88, 267, 345, 382
Cocoa bean, 382–383
Cocoa butter, 383
Cocoa liqueor, 383
Cocoa powder, 381, 383
Cocoa tree, 382
Coconut, 74–75, 88, 267, 270
Coconut oil, 79
Coffee
    as ice cream flavoring, 374
    off-flavors in, 149
    sundaes/coupes, 375
Coffee cakes, 307–308
Cold emulsion sauces, 194
Cold meringue, 352
Cold-water bath method, for tempering
    chocolate, 385–386

Collagen, 117
Collards, 59
Color, food
    appearance and, 147–148
    cooking process and, 182
    in menu planning, 204
    perception of, factors affecting, 148
    in plate composition, 153–154
    in presentation, 399, 402
    of sauce, 193
Columbus, Christopher, 6
Commercial grade, of meat, 118
Commis, 204
Common chemical sense, 149
Common meringue, 352
Competitive buying, 55
Complementation, protein, 18, 19
Complex compound butters, 197
Compotes, 362
Compound butters, 194, 197
Compound chocolate, 386, 391
Compound sauces, 194
Conching, 381, 384
Condensed milk, 256–257
Condiments, 89
Confectioner's coating (compound
    chocolate), 386
Consommé, 198–200
Consommé garnishes, 421–427
Contrast, in food presentation, 398–399,
    402
Convection low-pressure steamers, 135
Convection ovens, 131, 132
Convenience-food products, 78, 82–83
Conventional ovens, 131
Conversion
    for cake formulas, 343–344
    of measurement to container portion, 412
    recipe, 46
    temperature, 47–49
Conversion measure, in costing, 45
Cookie flour, 240
Cookies
    baking, 312–313
    decorating, 313
    forming, 312
    ingredients, 311–312
    petits fours, 314–316
    preparation tips, 316
    texture, 311
    types, 313–314
Cooking
    aroma and, 182
    color changes and, 182
    defined, 162
    food texture changes and, 182
    guidelines
        for grains, 184
        for pasta, 184
        for rice, 183–184
        for vegetables, 183
    high-fat method, 25

internal temperatures for, 34, 35
low-fat method, 25
meeting nutritional principles and, 24–25
nutritive value and, 182–183
techniques, 162
combination, 162, 178–179, 180–182
dry, 162, 167–168, 170–178
moist, 162, 165–170
Cooking line, 127–128. *See also specific
equipment in cooking line*
Cooling times, 36
Copper, 143
Coriander leaves, 86
Coriander seeds, 86, 265
Corn, 59
Cornmeal, 73
Corn oil, 79
Cornstarch
description/purchasing information/uses,
73, 82
as thickening agent, 192, 262
Corn syrup, 251
Cortés, Hernando, 6
Costing
assigning responsibility for, 42
process of, 42–46
Cottonseed oil, 79
Coulis, 400
Country-style forcemeat, 213
Coupes, 375
Court-boullion, 113
Couverture, 384. *See also* Pralines
Crab oil spice, 90
Crabs, 97, 103
Cracked-wheat flour, 242
Crackers, 82
Cranberries, 65
Cranberry sauce, 82
Cream
Bavarian cream, 358–359
chantilly, 357–358
crème chiboust, 358
crème diplomat, 358
grades/types of, 70, 258
in ice cream, 373–374
pastry, 357
use of term, 357
whipped, 357–358
Cream cheese, 351
Creaming
in cake making, 332–333
in cookie making, 311
of milk, 256
in quick bread making, 307
Cream pies, 321, 324–325
Cream puffs, 365
Credit voucher, 56
Crème Anglaise, 359, 400
Crème brûlée, 349
Crème caramel, 349
Crème chiboust, 358
Crème diplomat, 358

Crème fraîche, 257–258
Crème sauce, 195
Creole sauce, 195
Crêpes, 360–361
Crêpes Empire, 361
Crêpes Jacques, 361
Crêpes Suzette, 361, 363
Crips, 327
Critical Control Points (CCPs), 33–36
Croissant miniatures, 208
Croissants, 298–302
Croquant, 390
Croquettes, 208–209
Crossover baking, 313
Croûtes, 208
Crudités, 209
Crustaceans, 96–97. *See also* Crab; Shrimp
Cucumber, 59
Cumin, 86, 265
Curdling, 332
Curing, 217
Currants, 66
Curry, 86
Curry butter, 197
Curry powder, 90
Curry sauce, 195
Custard pies, 321, 325
Custards, 349–350
Cygnes (swans), 353, 365

Dairy products
butter. *See* Butter
cheeses, 71
cream, 69, 258
eggs, 69–70
fermented, 257–258
for low-fat meals, 26
margarine, 71, 258–259
milk. *See* Milk
Danish pastry dough, 301–303
Dates, 66
DAY (dry active yeast), 245
DDT. *See* Desired dough temperature
De Béchamel, Marquis, 7
Deck ovens, 133, 134
Decorating, cookies, 313
Deep-fat fryers, 129–130
Deep fat skimmer, 142
Deep frying, 172, 175–176, 177
De Honesta Voluptate et Valetndine, 6
De la Varenne, François Pierre, 6, 7
Delmonico, John, 12
Delmonico's restaurant, 12
De Medici, Catherine, 6–7, 236
Demi-glace mix, 82
Demi-glace sauce, 190, 194, 195–196
Denaturation, protein, 182
Denaturization, 352
Deposit cookies, 312
Dépouillage, 188
Desired dough temperature (DDT)
calculating, 275–276

for lean dough, 284
for soft-roll dough, 284
water temperature for flour soaking and,
242
for yeast-raised dough, 275
Desired overall food cost percentage, 45
Dessert plate, design/creation of, 397, 398
Desserts
defined, 396, 397
frozen, 371. *See also* Ice cream
fruit-based, 361–363
for low-fat meals, 26
presentations, 397
plating, 398–399
sauces for, 399–400
spoon, 365–367
Development stage, of mixing process, 277
Dextrose (glucose), 248, 251
Diable sauce, 195
Diarrhea, epidemic, 32
Diatase, 245, 246
Diet, for healthy lifestyle, 20–24
Dill, 86, 268
Dill seed, 86
Disaccharides, 18, 248
Disease
food-borne, control of, 31–33
tasting ability and, 153
water-borne, control of, 31–33
Dishwashing, 36–37
Distilled white vinegar, 89
Distributors, 53, 55
Divinity, 390
DMS (dry milk solids), 238, 257, 320
Dobos Torte, 336
Domestic game, 123
Dough
conditioners, 278
croissant, 300–301
improvers, in bread making, 247
laminated. *See* Laminated dough
pie. *See* Pie/pies, dough
stretched, 367–368
tart, 326–327
yeast-raised. *See* Yeast-raised dough
Dredging, 172, 175
Dressings, salad, 82, 205, 206
Dried eggs, 70
Drum sieve, 141
Dry active yeast (DAY), 245
Dry aging, of meat, 119
Dry cooking techniques, 162, 170–179
Dry milk solids (DMS), 238, 257, 320
Dry slow baking, 351–353
Dry storage, 35
Duck sauce, 91
Durgin Park, Boston, 12
Durum wheat, 184
Dutch process, for chocolate making, 383
Duxelles, 7
Duxelles sauce, 195

Eclairs, 365
Edible product (EP), 44
Egg/eggs, 69–70
  air pocket, 253, 254
  in baked goods, 251–253, 312, 331
  components/parts, 69–70, 253–254
  dried, 252
  fresh, 252
  frozen, 252
  in ice cream, 373–374
  liquid, 252–253
  for low-fat meals, 26
  for meringue, 352
  for pâte à choux, 364
  products, alteration of, 25
  quality, 254
  sanitation, 254–255
  sizes, 70
  whites, 69, 253–254
    in clarification of consommé, 198
    whipping, 334
Eggnog flavoring, for ice cream, 374
Eggplant, 59
Egyptians, Ancient, 3–4
Elastin tissue, 1115
Elephant ears, 298
Ell-shaped cooking line, 127
Emotions, tasting ability and, 152
Emulsification, 192, 252
Emulsifiers, in bread making, 247
Emulsions, 192–193
Endive, 59–60
Endosperm, 241
English sauces, 194
English soup (Zuppa Inglese), 366
En papillote cookery, 169–170
Enrobing, 391–392
Enteritis, 32
Entrées, with less meat, 25
Enzymes, in bread making, 245, 246, 247
EP (edible product), 44
Epicurean, The, 12
EP price, 53
Equipment. *See also specific equipment*
  arrangement, 127–128
  for food display, 225–227
Escargots, 82
Escarole, 60
Escherichia coli enteritis, 32
Escoffier, Georges Auguste, 9–10
Espagnole sauce, 190, 194, 195–196
Essences, 88, 190, 267
European Danish, 303
Evaporated milk, 256–257
Experience, tasting ability and, 152
Extracts, 82, 190

Farfalle, 80
Farmer, Fannie Merritt, 12–13
Fast aging, of meat, 119
Fat. *See also specific fats*
  animal, 78

in baking, 258–260
for cake making, 331
caloric content of, 17
characteristics of, 19
content, in ice cream, 372–373
in cookies, 312
defined, 19, 76
economic aspects, 77
hidden, reduction of, 24
hydrogenation, 77, 260
low, food selection for, 26
for low-fat meals, 26
melting point of, 258
for pâte à choux, 364
for pie dough, 319–320
product selection, 77–78
reducing from recipe, 24
shortenings, 78
smoking point, 77
types of, 258–260
Fat cap, 117
Fat compounds, 78
Fat-free foods, special flavor challenges of, 155
Fat or hot smoking, 219
Fat-soluble vitamins, 20
Fat substitutes, 78, 79
Fatty acids, 19, 76–77
FCMA (Fishery Conservation and Management Act), 95
Feeling factors, in sensory perception, 149
Female chefs, 12
Fennel seeds, 86, 265
Fenugreek, 86
Fermentation
  in bread making, 237, 261
  bulk or floor, 277–278
  in yeast-raised doughs, 275
Fettuccine, 80
Fiber, dietary, 18, 25
Fiddlehead ferns, 82
FIFO (First In, First Out inventory system), 35, 56
Figs, 66
Filberts (hazelnuts), 75, 270
Filier knife, 161
Filled Danish twists, 303
Filligrees, 353
Fillings
  chiffon pie, 325
  cream pie, 324–325
  custard pie, 325
  fruit, 321–324
  for pralines, 388–391
  specialty pie, 325–326
Final proof, of yeast-raised dough, 279
Financière sauce, 195
Fine mesh sieve, 142
Finger buffets, 220–221, 401–402
Finger foods, 207
Finish, meat, 117
First-clear flour, 239, 242

First In, First Out inventory system (FIFO), 35, 56
Fish
  aspic, 227
  catching, 101, 102
  caviar production, 210
  classifications, 96
  cleaning/storing, 101
  cuts, 99, 100
  drawn, 99, 100
  dressed, 99, 100
  filleting procedure, 106–109
  fillets, 99, 100, 103
  fin, 98–99
    cooking of, 113
    fabrication of, 105–110
  flat, 106, 107–109
  found, 99, 100
  fresh
    feel of, 102–103
    smell of, 102
    storage of, 103–104
    vs. frozen, purchasing of, 100–101
  freshness, 102–103
  frozen, 100–101, 104
  gutting procedure, 105–106
  for low-fat meals, 26
  purchasing, quality assurance for, 101–102
  raw, 114
  round, 106–107
  scaling procedure, 106
  selling, 102
  skinning, 109
  sorting, 101
  steaks, 99, 100, 109–110
  supplier, 102
  trash, 95
  yield, 109
Fishery Conservation and Management Act (FCMA), 95
Fish server, 142
Five-spice powder, 86
Flambéed fruit, 363
Flan, 349
FlashBake oven, 131–132
Flat-top range, 128, 129
Flavones, 183
Flavor
  basic, 148
  in dessert plating, 397–398, 399
  of fat-free foods, 155
  perception, 150–152
  in plate composition, 154–155
  of sauce, 193
Flavored salt, 90
Flavor enhancers, 151
Flavorings, 88–89, 267, 374
Flour. *See also* Wheat flour
  bleaching, 241
  blends, 240
  for cake making, 331

components/make-up of, 240–241
in cookies, 312
description/purchasing information, 72, 73
hard-wheat, 238–239
for pâte à choux, 364
for pie dough, 319
protein in, 240–241
purposes, in baking, 240
rye, 242–243
starch in, 240
as thickening agent, 191–192, 262
Flour mill, 237
Focus, tasting ability and, 152–153
Folding over, of yeast-raised dough, 278
Fondant, 315, 338, 391
Fonds, 186
Food. *See also specific types of food*
definition of, 16
display, for buffet, 225–227
dollars, 25
enhancers, 85–92
expense/cost, 40, 41–42
factors affecting flavor perception, 150–152
low-fat, high-complex-carbohydrate, 17
potentially hazardous, 31
preservation, 216–218
sensory properties. *See Sensory properties, food*
Food chopper, 138
Food Guide Pyramid, 21
Food mill, 141
Food processor, 138
Food slicer, 138
Footwear, kitchen, 404–405
Forcemeats
assembling, 215, 216
derivatives, 213–215
elements of, 212–213
guidelines, 215
panadas, 215
types, 213
Fork buffets, 220, 401
Foyot sauce, 195
Frangipane, 315
Freezer storage, 35–36
French bread, 282
French knife, 161
French meringue, 352
French method, for puff pastry dough, 296
French Revolution, 8
French-style cheesecake, 351
Friandise, 315
Fricassée, 208
Fritters, 363
Frostings, buttercream, 337–338
Frozen desserts, 371. *See also* Ice cream
Frozen yogurt, 378
Fructose, 83, 248, 250
Fruit. *See also specific fruits*
canned, for fruit pies, 322

characteristics of, 64–68
chutneys, 362
desserts, flambéed/tableside, 363
dressings, 206
dried, for fruit pies, 323–324
fillings, 312–324, 390, 391
fresh, 323–324
fritters, 363
frozen, for fruit pies, 323
for low-fat meals, 26
poached, 361–362
salad, 205, 362
Fruit-based desserts, 361–363
Fruit flavored vinegar, 89
Fruit pies
cooked juice, 321–322
cooked juice and fruit, 322
fillings, 321–324
homestyle, 322
Fruit sauce, cooked, 400
Fruit tart, 328
Fryers, deep-fat, 129–130
Frying, 172, 175–176, 177
Fryolators, 130
Fudge icing, 338
Full buffets, 220, 401
Fumet, 190
Fusing, in advanced ice carvings, 224

Galactose, 248
Galantine, 214
Game, 122–123
Ganache, 359–360, 388–389
Ganache cordials, 393
Garde-manger
buffets/buffet catering and, 220–232
defined, 202
food preservation, 216–218
functions
forcemeats, 212–216
hors d'oeuvre, 206–212
menu planning for, 204–205
salads, 205–206
Garlic, 60, 82
Garnishes
canapé, 211–212
consommé, 421–427
sensory perception and, 155
Gastroenteritis, 32
Gastronomic Regenerator, The (Soyer), 9
Gelatin, 263
Gelatin salad, 205–206
Gelling agents, in baking, 263
Gels, 79
Gender, tasting ability and, 152
Genetics, tasting ability and, 152
Genoise, 335
German buttercream, 337
Gianduja, 389–390
Ginger, 86, 265
Gingerbread, 308
Gipfels, 299

Glazes (glaces), 189, 327
Glazing, 103
Gliadin, 238
Glucose, 248, 251
Glutamate, free, 151
Gluten, 238, 277
Glutenin, 238
Gluten-oxidizing agents, 241
Glycogen, 18
Godiveau, 213
Goma sauce, 91
Goose, description/cooking method, 122
Grading, poultry, 121
Graduated heat-top range, 128–129
Grains, 72, 73, 184. *See also specific grains*
Granita, 371, 378
Grapefruit, 66
Grapes, 66
Grapeseed oil, 79
Gratin, 366
Gratin forcemeat, 213
Gravymaster, 82
Gravy whisk, 142
Greeks, Ancient, 4–5, 235
Green butter, 197
Green flour, 241
Green peppercorns, 266
Grenadine syrup, 82
Griddle, 129
Griddling, 176
Grilling, 176, 179
Grills, 127–128
Grinder, meat, 139
Grits, 73
Guéridon cart, ravier dishes, 207
Guilds, 236
Guinea hens, 122
Gums, 79, 263

Handling, food, 36, 258
Hard water, 244
Harissa, 90
Hasty pudding, 350
Haute cuisine, 8
Hazard Analysis Critical Point System (HACCP), 33–35
Hazelnuts (filberts), 75, 270
Hearth breads, 282
Hearts of palm, 82
Heat, chocolate and, 386–387
Height
in food presentation, 402
in plate composition, 154
Hepatitis A, 32
Herb balls, 197
Herbs, 85–88, 267–268. *See also specific herbs*
Herb seasoning, 90
High-carbon knives, 160
High-gluten flour, 239
High-ratio shortening, 260

High Temperature, Short Time method of pasteurization (HTST), 70, 256
Hippen paste, 313
Hoisin sauce, 82, 90
Holder process, of pasteurization, 70, 256
Holding, 36
Holding ovens, 132
Hollandaise sauce, 190, 193–196
Homogenization, of milk, 256
Honey, 84, 251
Honey melon sundaes/coupes, 375
Hors d'oeuvre
    cold, 209–212
    finger foods, 207
    hot, 207–209
    single food, 206–207
    varies, 207
Hors d'oeuvre, 204
Horseradish, 86
Hot sauces, 90–91
House Servant's Directory, The (Roberts), 12
HTST (High Temperature, Short Time method of pasteurization), 71, 256
Hussarde sauce, 195
Hydrogenation, 77, 260
Hydrometer (Baumé scale), 377

Ice carvings, 222–224
Ice cream
    classic presentations of, 376
    eggs in, 373–374
    formula, 373–374
    freezing process for, 372
    hardening process for, 372
    ingredients in, 373–374
    overrun, 372
    products from, 374–376
    qualities of, 371–372
    types of, 371
Ice crystallization, in frozen desserts, 377
Ices, 376–378
Icings, 337–338
IMPS (Institutional Meat Purchase Specifications), 119
Indian hot sauce, 90
Induction cook tops, 129
Induction deep-fat fryers, 130
Infectious hepatitis, 32
Ingredients
    adjusting, 21–22
    alternative, for seasoning, 24–25
    cost of, 45
    function/purpose, determination of, 22–23
    substitution of, 23
Inspection
    meat, 117–118
    poultry, 121
Institutional Meat Purchase Specifications (IMPS), 119
Intermediate proof, for yeast-raised dough, 278

International soups, 198
Inventory-control procedures, 56
Invertase, 245, 246, 391
Invert sugars, 250
Invoice, 55
Iron, recommended daily requirements, 409, 410
Iron cookware, 143
Isinglass, 227
Issuing system, 56
Italian bread, 282
Italian buttercream, 337
Italian meringue, 352
Italian seasoning, 90
Italienne sauce, 196

Jacket, chef's, 403–404
Jelly, 82
Jerez, 349
Johhnycake, 237
Johnson & Wales University, 13
Joy of Cooking (Rombauer), 13
Juniper berries, 86

Kaiser rolls, 283
Kale, 60
Ketchup, 82, 90
Ketjap maniss (ketjap benteng), 91
Kettles, 136
Kitchen
    Critical Control Points, 34–37
    equipment, cleaning, 37
    fork, 142
    machinery, 136–139
    safety, 37
    utensils, 139–142
Kiwi, 66
Knives
    alloys, 160
    cuts, types of, 162, 163–165
    edge straightening, 160–161
    historical aspects, 7
    parts of, 160
    safety, 159
    sharpening, 159–160
    types, 160, 161
Krokant, 390

Labor expense, 41
Lactoglobulin, 256
Lacto-ovo-vegetarian, 21
Lactose, 248
Lactose intolerance, 255
Lacto-vegetarian, 21
La Cuisiniere Bourgeoise, Menon, 7
Ladle, 142
Ladyfingers, 314
Lamb, 26, 120
Laminated doughs
    defined, 295
    puff pastry, 295–298
    yeast, 298–303

Language/terminology, in menu planning, 204–205
Lard, 77, 78
    characteristics/uses, 258–259
    for pie dough, 320
Larding, 172
Larding tube, 141
L'Art du Cuisinier (Carême, Marie Antoine), 8
Lattice pie crust, 322
Layer cakes. See Cakes
Leading sauces (mother sauces), 190
Lean dough, 281–283, 284
Leavening agents
    for baking, 260–262
    for cake making, 332
    for cookies, 312
    eggs as, 252
Lecithin, 193, 252
Lecithin, in chocolate, 383
Le Cuisinier François, 6, 7
Leeks, 60
Le Guide Culinaire (Esoffier), 9–10
Legumes, 57, 72, 74
    dried, 71, 74
    for low-fat meals, 26
Lemon grass, 87
Lemons, 66
Lentils, 73
Lettuce, 60–61
Le Viander De Taillevent, 5–6
Levulose. See Fructose
Liaison, 191
Liason finale, 193
Licorice, 88, 267
Lifter, 142
Lighting, food color perception and, 148
Limes, 66
Liner, for canapé, 211
Linguine, 80
Linzer torte, 328
Lipids. See Fats
Liquid. See also specific liquids
    for cake making, 332
    measuring, 47, 48
    for pâte à choux, 364
    for pie dough, 320
    in stock, 188
    thickening of, 191–194
Liquid fillings
    for pralines, 391
Liquid shortening, 260
Liquid smoking, 219
Lobster
    cooking, 114
    live, 103–105
    preparation/fabrication, 111–112
Louisiana hot sauce, 91
Low-fat foods, 26, 256
Low-pressure steamers, convection or tabletop, 135
Lumping, 191
Luster, of sauce, 193

Macadamia nuts, 270
Mace, 87, 265
Machine method, for tempering chocolate, 385
McLaughlin, Lt. General John, 13
Madeleines, 314
Madère sauce, 196
Magnetic induction cook tops, 129
Maître d'hôtel, 197
Majoram, 87
Makeweight loaf, 236
Mallet, 141
Maltaise sauce, 196
Maltose, 248
Malt sugar, 245
Malt syrup, 251
Malt vinegar, 89
Mandarins, 67
Mangos, 67
Manicotti, 80
Manual searing, 170
Maple syrup, 83, 251
Marbling, 117
Margarine, 71, 258–259
Marinades, 218
Marjoram, 268
Marquise, 360
Marzipan, 82, 222, 390
Mastering the Art of French Cooking (Child), 13
Mayonnaise, 194
Mayonnaise collée, 231
Measurements, 46–47
    conversions, 412–416
Meat. *See also specific types of meat*
    aging, 118–119
    aspic, 227
    composition, 117
    cuts, 119–121
    fabrication/cooking chart, 119–120
    grading, 118
    handling, 119
    inspection, 117–118
    lean ground, in clarification of consommé, 198
    for low-fat meals, 26
    muscle fibers, 117
    storage, 119
    structure, 117
    variety, 121
Meatballs, 209
Meat grinder, 139
Meat Inspection Act, 117
Melanosis, 103
Melba sauce, 400
Melons, 67
Menon, 7
Menu planning, 24, 204–205
Meringue, 351–353
Mesopotamians, 3, 4
Metals
    alloys, for knives, 160

aluminum, 143
    copper, 143
    heat efficiency of, 143
    iron, 143
    stainless steel, 143
    steel, for knives, 160–161
Metric system, 47–49
Meurette sauce, 196
Mexican salsa, 90
Microbiology, 31
Microorganisms, pathogenic, 31, 32
Microparticulated protein, 79
Microwave method, for tempering chocolate, 385
Microwave ovens, 132, 133
Middle Ages, 5–6
Mignardise, 315
Milk
    in baking, 255–258
    components, 69, 255
    composition, 256
    handling/storage, 258
    homogenization, 256
    in ice cream, 373–374
    pasteurization, 255–256
    for pie dough, 320
    raw, 255
    types of, 256–257
Milk products, 71
Mille feuilles, 295, 298
Millet, 184
Minerals, 20, 409, 410
Minor, Dr. Lewis, 13
Minority chefs, 12
Mint, 87, 268
Mirepoix, 162, 187, 198
Mixed pickling spices, 90, 267
Mixer
    sizes, 136–137
    standard/universal, 136–137
    vertical cutter, 137–138
Mixing
    cleanup, 277
    development, 277
    final clear, 277
    methods
        for layer cakes, 332–335
        for quick breads, 307–308
    overmixing, 277
    pickup, 277
    of yeast-raised dough, 276
Mocha flavoring, for ice cream, 374
Modern cooking, 6–10
Modified food starches, 263
Moist cooking techniques, 162, 165–170
Moisture
    bacterial growth and, 31
    chocolate and, 386, 387
Molasses, 84, 250
Molds, for aspic, 230
Mollusks
    freshness, 103

live, storage of, 105
    types of, 96, 97–98
Monder, 165
Monosaccharides, 18
Monosaturated fats, 76–77
Monosodium glutamate (MSG), 88, 151
Monounsaturated fats, 19
Montelimar, 390
Monter au beurre, 193
Mornay sauce, 196
Mostaccioli, 80
Mostaccioli rigati, 80
Mother sauces (leading sauces), 190, 194, 195–196
Mousse, 214–215
Mousse cakes, 360
Mousseline, 213
Mousseline sauce, 196
Mousses, 360
MSG (monosodium glutamate), 88, 151
Mushroom butter, 197
Mushrooms, 61
Mussels, 98, 105
Mustards, 92
Mustard seed, 87

Nam prik, 90
NAMPS (National Association of Meat Purveyor Specifications), 119
Nantua sauce, 196
Napoleons, 298
National Association of Meat Purveyor Specifications (NAMPS), 119
National Marine Fisheries Service (NMFS), 95
National Restaurant Association, current food industry trends and, 24
Natural clarification, 188
Neckerchief, chef's, 405
Nectarines, 68
Neolithic revolution, 3–4
Neufchâtel cheese, 351
New York-style cheesecake, 351
NMFS (National Marine Fisheries Service), 95
Noisette sauce, 196
Non-B hepatitis, 32
Nonperishables, 54, 72–76. *See also specific nonperishable items*
Noodles, 78
Normande sauce, 196
Norwalk virus, 32
Notching, in advanced ice carvings, 224
Nougat, 82, 374, 390
Nourishing element
    in canapé, 211
    in forcemeats, 212–213
    in stock, 187
Nouvelle cuisine, 10–11
Nulomoline, 84, 250–251
Nutmeg, 87, 265
Nutrients
    caloric content of, 17
    classes of, 17

energy-yielding, 17–19
function/purpose in recipe, 17, 22, 23
managing in food preparation, 25, 27
Nutrition
    definition of, 16
    educational policy for, 17
    in foodservice industry, 24–27
    principles, for food service professionals, 24–25
    value, cooking process and, 182–183
Nuts. *See also specific types of nuts*
    in baking recipes, 268–271
    characteristics/uses of, 72–76
    fillings for pralines, 390

Oats, 73
Odor. *See* Aroma
Offset metal spatula, 141
Oils
    for baking, 258–260
    economic aspects, 77
    flavor perception and, 151–152
    for low-fat meals, 26
    smoking point, 77
    vegetable, 79
Okra, 61
Olive oil, 77, 79
Olives, 82
1–2–3 dough, 326
Onions, 61
Opacity, of sauce, 193
Open-burner range, 128, 129
Open-market buying, 55
Open-spit roasting, 172
Opera Torte, 336
Orange butter, 197
Oranges, 68
Oregano, 87, 268
Oriental sauces, 91
Orzo, 80
Ossetra, 210
Ovens
    searing method, 170
    temperature, for puff pastry doughs, 297
    types of, 131–134, 235
Overhead expense, 41
Overheating, of chocolate, 387
Overrun, 372, 378
Overuse, of chocolate, 387
Oxidants, 247
Oxidative rancidity, 77
Oxygen, bacterial growth and, 31
Oyster opener, 141
Oysters, 97, 112–113
Oyster sauce, 91

Palmiers, 298
Paloise sauce, 196
Panadas, 215
Pancake syrup, 83
Panning, of yeast-raised dough, 279
Pans, 140–141

Pan smoking, 219
Papayas, 68
Paprika, 87
Paprika butter, 197
Parallel cooking line, 127, 128
Paralytic shellfish poisoning (PSP), 96
Parfait glace, 375
Paring knife, 161
Paris-Brest, 365
Parisienne/noisette scoop, 141
Parsley, 87, 268
Parsnips, 62
Parties, menu planning for, 204–205
Pasta, 78, 80, 184
Pasta machine, 141
Pasteurization, 70, 255–256
Pastry cream, 357
Pastry flour, 239–240
Pâté, 213
Pâte à bombe, 359
Pâte à choux, 363–365
Pâté en croûte, 213
Patent flour, 239
Pavlovas, 353
PC (portion cost), 45
Peaches, 68
Peach melba, 376
Peanut oil, 79
Peanuts, 75, 270–271
Pears, 68
Pears Belle Hélène, 376
Pearson square, 373
Peas, 62, 74
Pecans, 75, 271
Pectin, 263
Peeler, automatic potato, 139
Pepper, 87, 265–266
Pepper butter, 197
Peppercorns, 265–266
Peppers, 62
Perciatelli, 80
Perforated lifter, 142
Periodic-ordering method, for quantity purchasing, 54
Perishable items, 54
Permanent emulsion, 192
Perpetual-inventory method, for quantity purchasing, 54
Persimmons, 68
Petits fours, 314–316
Pfannkuchen, 360
pH, bacterial growth and, 31
Pheasant, 122
Phosphorus, 409, 410
Phyllo dough, 82, 367
Physical leavening, 295
Piano whisk, 142
Pickle injector, for brining, 217–218
Pickles, 82
Pies
    dough, 319–321
    fillings. *See under* Fillings

historical aspects, 319
    open, 325
    types, 321
Pigeon, 122
Pigments, 182, 183
Pignoli (pine nuts), 75, 271
Pilaf, 184
Pimentoes, 82
Pineapples, 69
Pine nuts (pignoli), 75, 271
Pink peppercorns, 266
Piquante sauce, 196
Pistachios, 75–76, 271
Pithiviers, 298
Plankton, 96
Plate composition, sensory perception and, 153–155
Plated desserts, 397, 398–399
Platters, for food display, 225–227
Plums, 69
Plum sauce, 91
Plunder, 299
Poached fruit, 361–362
Poaching, 166–167
Point, Fernand B., 10
Poissonnier, 203
Poivrade sauce, 196
Polysaccharides, 18
Polyunsaturated fats, 19, 76–77
Pomegranates, 69
Popcorn, 82
Poppy seeds, 76, 266
Pork, 26, 120
Portion
    cost, 45
    measurement conversions, 412
    number of, 43
    scale, 47
    size, 43
        reduction of, 25
        serving utensils for, 416–420
        standard, 41
Porto sauce, 196
Portugaise sauce, 196
Potassium, 409, 410
Potassium bromate, 241
Potato chips, 82
Potatoes
    characteristics of, 62–63
    cuts/shapes, 163–164
Potato flour, 192
Potato masher, 142
Potato nest fryer, 142
Potato starch, 262–263
Pots, 140–141
Pots de crème, 349–350
Poullette sauce, 196
Poultry
    defined, 121
    description/cooking method, 122
    grading, 121
    handling/storage, 122

inspection, 121
  for low-fat meals, 26
  market forms, 122
Poultry seasoning, 90
Pound cake, 308
Pouring ladle, 142
Powdered dry milk, 257
Praline flavoring, for ice cream, 374
Pralines, 388
  dipping conditions for, 391–392
  fillings for, 388–391
  molded, 392–393
  storage, 392
Praline sundaes/coupes, 375
Predough method, 275
Pregelatinized starches, 263
Preparation, 36
Prepared shell method, for filling pralines with
    liquid, 391
Preserve-based sauces, 400
Pressed caviar, 210
Pressureless steamer, 135
Prime grade, of meat, 118
Prime steam lard, 258
Printainer butter, 197
Processed eggs, 70
Products. *See also specific food products*
  identification of, 56
    dairy, 69–72
    fruits, 64–69
    nonperishables, 72–76
    vegetables, 57–64
  types, for purchasing, 54
Professional cooking, recognition of, 13
Profiteroles, 365
Profit expense, 41
Protein
  caloric content of, 17
  coagulation, 182
  complementation, 18, 19
  complete *vs.* incomplete, 18
  composition of, 18
  denaturation, 182
  in flour, 238, 240–241
  functions of, 18
  sources of, 19
Provençale sauce, 196
Puff pastry
  doughs, 295–298
    historical aspects, 295
    ingredients in, 295–296
    oven temperatures for, 297
    roll-in methods, 296–297
    troubleshooting, 297
  scraps, 298
  storage, 298
Puff-pastry shortening, 259, 260
Puff pastry-type margarine, 260
Pumpkin pie spice, 90, 267
Pumpkin seeds, 76
Punchdown, of yeast-raised dough,
    278

Purchasing
  of fish, 100–102
  methods, 55
  objectives, 52
  pricing and, 53
  procedure, 53
  products for. *See* Products
  in quantity, 54–55
  specifications, 54
  vs. buying, 53
Purchasing agent, 54, 55
Puréed soups, 200
Puréeing, 200

Q factor, 45
Quail eggs, 82
Quality
  assurance, in fish purchasing, 101–102
  of eggs, 254
  recipe standardization and, 41
  of sauces, 193–194
Quantity, 41
Quenelle, 214
Quick breads, 307–308

Radicchio, 63
Radishes, 63
Rafraichir, 165
Ragôut, 208
Raisins, 83
Ranges, 128–129
Ranhofer, Charles, 12
Ravier dishes, for Guéridon cart, 207
Ravigote sauce, 196
RDAs (recommended dietary allowances),
    20, 407–410
Receiving, 34, 55–56
Recipe
  conversion, 46
  format, 41–42
  identification number, 42–43
  modification process for, 21–24
  standardized, 41
Recipe-costing form, 42
Recommended dietary allowances (RDAs),
    20, 407–410
Record-keeping systems, for HACCP, 34
Recovery time, 130, 175
Reduction, for thickening, 193, 400
Red vinegar, 89
Reel ovens, 132–133
Refrigerated cookies, 312
Refrigerated storage, 35
Reheating, 36
Religieuses, 365
Relish, 83
Remouillage, 188
Requisition, 56
Resting method, for tempering chocolate,
    385
Rhubarb, 69
Ribs (cocoa), 382–383

Rice, 73, 183–184
Ricer, 141
Rice vinegar, 89
Rich sweet yeast dough, 284–285
Rigatoni, 80
Risotto, 184
Ritz, Cesar, 9
Roasting, 170–172
Roast smoking, 219
Roberts, Robert, 12
Rolled cookies, 312
Rolls, 284
Romans, Ancient, 4–5, 235–236
Rombauer, Irma, 13
Rosemary, 87, 268
Rotary ovens, 133–134
Rotini, 80
Rouennaise sauce, 196
Rounding, of yeast-raised dough, 278
Roux, 7, 191–192
Royal icing, 338
Rubbing method, 307–308, 320
Rum and raisin flavorin, for ice cream, 374
Rustic-wheat flakes, 242
Rutabaga, 64
Rye, description/purchasing information, 73
Rye bread
  ingredients in, 243
  sourdough, 286–288
  yeast-raised dough for, 286–288
Rye flour
  characteristics, 242–243
  dough, 244
  types, 243, 286

Sabayon, 400
Saccharin, 84
Sacher Torte, 336–337
Sacristains, 298
Safety, 37, 159
Safflower oil, 79
Saffron, 87, 266
Sage, 88, 268
St. Clement of the Misery of Bakers,
    Fraternity of, 236
Saint Honore, 365
Salad, 205–206
Salad oil, 79
Salaisons, 218
Salamanders, 127–128
Salmis sauce, 196
Salmon and dill butter, 197
Salmon butter, 197
Salmonellosis, 32
Salpicons, 208
Salsa, 83, 362
Salt
  for baking, 267
  for bread making, 246–247
  description/uses, 89
  for pie dough, 320
  for preserving, 217

Salt-dough centerpieces, 222
Salting, 218
Sambals, 91
Sandwich cookies, 314
Sandwiches, 210–211
Sanitation
    definition of, 30
    eggs and, 254–255
Sanitizing, cleaning and, 36–37
Sardines, 83
Sashimi, 114
Satay sauce, 91
Saturated fats, 19, 25, 76
Sauces. *See also specific sauces*
    cold emulsion, 194
    compound, 194
    defined, 190
    for dessert presentations, 399–400
    independent, nonderivative, 194
    mother or leading, 190
    quality of, 193–194
    thickening of, 400
Sauce sieve, 142
Sauerkraut, 83
Sausage, 215
Sautéing process, 172, 173–174
Savarins, 285
Savory, 88, 268
Scaling of ingredients, for yeast-raised
        dough breads, 276
Scallops, 97
Scandinavian Danish, 303
Scappi, Bartolomeo, 6, 7
Scones, 308
Seafood. *See also specific types of seafood*
    breaded, 98
    cooking, 113–114
    defined, 94
    fabrication, 105–113
    freshness, 102–103
    frozen, 103
    historical aspects, 95
    manufactured products, 98
    market forms, 98–99
    nutritional benefits, 95–96
    regulations, 95
    shellfish, 26, 103
Seafood purveyor, 102
Seafood seasoning, 90
Searing, 170
Sea scallops, 97
Seasonings
    alternative ingredients for, 24–25
    for baking, 267
    in clarification of consommé, 198
    description/uses, 89
Seaweed, 228
Second-clear flour, 239
Seeds, 76
Select grade, of meat, 118
Selling price, preliminary *vs.* actual, 46
Semifreddo, 360, 376

Semiperishable items, 54
Semipermanent emulsion, 192–193
Semolina flour, 184
Sensory properties, food
    appeal of, 22–24
    evaluation of, 150–155
    perception of, 147
    types of, 147–150
Serving utensils, for portion size, 416–420
Sesame oil, 79
Sesame paste, 83
Sesame seeds, 76, 266
Seven Minute Icing, 338
Sevruga, 210
Sewage poisoning, 32
Shallots, 63
Shallow frying, 176, 178
Shape
    in food presentation, 399, 402
    in plate composition, 154
Shaping, of yeast-raised dough, 278
Sharbat, 371
Sharpening stone, 159
Shell eggs, 70
Shellfish, 26, 103
Shells, pasta, 80
Sherbets, 376–378
Sherry vinegar, 89
Short dough, 326–327
Shortening
    for baking, 259, 260
    for bread baking, 238
    characteristics, 78
    for pie dough, 320
    types of, 260
Shoyu sauce, 91
Shrimp, 96–97
    cooking, 113–114
    cost per pound, 97
    fabrication, 110–111
    market forms, 97
Shrimp spice, 90
Side towel, 405
Sieves, 142
Simmering process, 165–166
Simmon, Amelia, 11–12
Singer, 191, 200
Single-source buying, 55
Single straight-cooking line, 127
Skim milk, 256
Skimming, 188–189
Skimming ladle, 142
Slicer, food, 138
Slow baking, 348
    dry, 351–353
    wet, 349–351
Slow or cold smoking, 219
Slushing, in advanced ice carvings, 224
Smallwares, 139–142
Smoking, for food preservation, 218–219
Smoking point, 77
Snecken, 303

Sodium, 409, 410
Sodium bicarbonate. *See* Baking soda
Soft-roll dough, 283–284
Sorbet, 376–378
Sorbetti, 371
Sorrel, 88
Soubise sauce, 196
Soufflées, 350–351
Soufflé glace, 375
Soup
    classification of, 197–198
    making, general methods for, 198–200
    puréed, 200
    terminology, 197
    thin, 200
Sour cream, 257
Sourdough bread
    rye, 286–288
    starters, 287–288
    wheat, 288
Sous prik, 91
Soy, 73
Soybean oil, 79
Soyer, Alexis Benoit, 8–9
Soy sauce, 83, 90
Spaetzle maker, 141
Spanakopita, 208
Spatula, 141
Specialty pies, 321, 325–326
Specialty soups, 198
Specification (spec), 54
Spices. *See also specific spices*
    in baking, 264–267
    characteristics/uses of, 85–88
Spinach, 63
Sponge cakes, 334
Sponge cookies, 314
Sponge dough conversions, 290–292
Sponge-dough method, 275
Spooms, 376–378
Spoon deserts, 365–367
Spray pumping method, for brining, 217
Spreads, for canapé, 211
Spring wheat, 240
Squash, 63
Squid, 98
Stabilizers, for sherbets/ices, 378
Stack ovens, 133, 134
Stainless steel, 143
Stainless steel knives, 160
Staling, 280–281
Standard grade, of meat, 118
Standardization, food costs and, 41
Staphylococcal food poisoning, 32
Staple items, 54
Star anise, 82, 266
Starch
    defined, 18, 191
    in flour, 240
    as thickening agent, 191, 262, 263
    types of, 191–192

Starch method, for filling pralines with liquid, 391
Steak sauce, 90
Steam, as physical leavening agent, 261
Steamers, for cooking, 135
Steamers (clams), 97
Steaming
  nutritive value and, 183
  process, 167–170
    en papillote, 169–170
    with pressure, 168–169
    pressureless, 167–169
  of rice, 183–184
Steam-jacketed kettle, 136
Steam pressure cooker, 134–135
Steam table, 131
Steel, for knife edge straightening, 160–161
Steward, 56
Stewing
  process, 179, 181, 182
  vs. braising, 182
Stippling, 279
Stir-frying, 172, 175–176
Stocks
  classification of, 188
  cold, flavorful, in clarification of consommé, 198
  composition of, 187–188
  defined, 186
  production of, 188–189
  types of, 188
Stone Age, 3
Storage. See also under specific foods
  of chocolate, 387
  facilities, 56
  of food, 35–36
  of meringue, 353
  of pâte à choux, 365
  of pralines, 392
Storeroom clerk, 56
Straight-dough method, 275
Straight-method forcemeat, 213
Strawberry
  as ice cream flavoring, 374
  sundaes/coupes, 375
Stretched doughs, 367–368
Strudel, 236, 368
Sturgeon species, producing caviar, 210
Substitution of ingredients, 23
Sucrose, 248
Suet, 78
Sugar
  in baking, 267
  for bread baking, 238
  for bread making, 247
  brown, 250
  for cake making, 331
  characteristics/uses, 81, 83
  complex or double, 248
  confectionary or powdered, 248, 250
  in cookies, 311
  crystallization, in frozen desserts, 377

fine and superfine, 248
forms, common, 83
granulated, 248, 250
historical aspects, 248
invert, 250
in meringue, 352
for pie dough, 320
raw, 250
refinement process, 245, 246, 248, 249
in sherbets/ices, 378
simple, 248
Sugar fillings, for pralines, 390–391
Sugar pastillage, 222
Sugar production, 249
Sugar substitutes, 84
Sugar syrups, 81, 84, 377
Summer coating (compound chocolate), 386
Sundaes, 375
Sunflower oil, 79
Sunflower seeds, 76, 271
Super stainless steel knives, 160
Supertasters, 152
Suprême sauce, 196
Surimi, 98
Sushi, 114
Swans (cygnes), 353, 365
Sweating, 172
Sweet and sour sauce, 91
Sweetened condensed milk, 256–257
Sweeteners. See also Sugar
  in baked goods, 247–248
  characteristics/uses, 81
  for ice cream, 374
  liquid, 250–251
  molasses, 250
Sweet marjoram, 88
Sweet potatoes, 63
Sweet taste, 148
Swiss apple flan, 328
Swiss buttercream, 337
Swiss chard, 59
Swiss meringue, 352
Syrup, 83
Szathmary, Chef Louis, 13, 14

Tabasco sauce, 91
Table method, for tempering chocolate, 385
Tableside desserts, 363
Table sugar, 248, 250
Tabletop low-pressure steamers, 135
Taco sauce, 83
Tamarind, 89
Tamari sauce, 91
Tangerines/tangelos, 67
Tapioca, 83, 192, 263
Tarragon, 88, 268
Tarragon butter, 197
Tarte Tatin, 328
Tartlets, 207
Tarts, 326–328
Taste. See Flavor
Taste buds, 148, 149

Taste cells, 148
Tasting ability, factors affecting, 152–153
Tea cakes, 307–308
Temperature
  bacterial growth and, 31
  chocolate and, 386–387
  conversion, 47–49
  in dessert plating, 399
  for dipping pralines, 391–392
  flavor perception and, 151
  internal cooking, 34
  oven, for puff pastry doughs, 297
  in plate composition, 155
  simmering, 189
  of yeast-raised doughs, 275–276
Tempering, 191
Tempering chocolate, 384–386
Template, for ice carvings, 223
Temporary emulsion, 193
Tentsuju sauce, 91
Teriyaki sauce, 91
Terms, glossaries of, 421–428, 433–452
Terrine, 213–214
Texture
  changes, cooking and, 182
  changes, in melted chocolate, 387
  of cookies, 311
  in food presentation, 398–399, 402
  of frozen desserts, 377
  of ice cream, 371–372
  in menu planning, 204
  perception, time and, 150
  in plate composition, 154
  of sauce, 193
  sensory perception and, 149–150
Thickening
  of dessert sauces, 400
  of liquids
    emulsions for, 192–193
    liasons for, 191–192
    reduction for, 193
    sauce quality and, 193–194
Thickening agents, in baking, 262–263
Thickness/consistence, flavor perception and, 151
Thick soup, 197
Thin soups, 197, 200
Thyme, 88, 268
Tilting skillet, 135–136
Time, importance in flavor and texture perception, 150
Tiramisu, 366
Tomato butter, 197
Tomatoes, 64, 83
Tomato products, in clarification of consommé, 198
Tomato purée, 89
Tomato sauce, 190, 194, 195–196
Tonkatsu sauce, 91
Tools
  for ice carvings, 223
  for vegetable carvings, 224–225